Lebanon

General Editors
Bernard Lewis
Itamar Rabinovich
Roger Savory

The Turban for the Crown
The Islamic Revolution in Iran
Said Amir Arjomand

The Arab Press in the Middle East
A History
Ami Ayalon

Language and Change in the Arab
Middle East
The Evolution of Modern Arabic
Political Discourse
Ami Ayalon

Iran's First Revolution
Shi'ism and the Constitutional
Revolution of 1905–1909
Mangol Bayat

Saddam's Word
Political Discourse in Iraq
Ofra Bengio

Islamic Reform
Politics and Social Change in Late
Ottoman Syria
David Dean Commins

King Hussein and the Challenge of
Arab Radicalism
Jordan, 1955–1967
Uriel Dann

Pan-Arabism before Nasser
Egyptian Power Politics and the
Palestine Question

Michael Doran

Egypt, Islam, and the Arabs
The Search for Egyptian Nationhood,
1900–1930
Israel Gershoni and James P.
Jankowski

East Encounters West
France and the Ottoman Empire in
the Eighteenth Century
Fatma Müge Göçek

Nasser's "Blessed Movement"
Egypt's Free Officers and the July
Revolution
Joel Gordon

The Young Turks in Opposition
M. Şükrü Hanioğlu

Preparation for a Revolution
The Young Turks, 1902–1908
M. Şükrü Hanioğlu

Lebanon
A History, 600–2011
William Harris

Cross-Cultural Encounters and
Conflicts
Charles Issawi

The Fertile Crescent, 1800–1914
A Documentary Economic History
Edited by Charles Issawi

Lebanon

A History, 600–2011

WILLIAM HARRIS

OXFORD
UNIVERSITY PRESS

OXFORD
UNIVERSITY PRESS

Oxford University Press is a department of the University of Oxford.
It furthers the University's objective of excellence in research, scholarship,
and education by publishing worldwide.

Oxford   New York

Auckland   Cape Town   Dar es Salaam   Hong Kong   Karachi
Kuala Lumpur   Madrid   Melbourne   Mexico City   Nairobi
New Delhi   Shanghai   Taipei   Toronto

With offices in

Argentina   Austria   Brazil   Chile   Czech Republic   France   Greece
Guatemala   Hungary   Italy   Japan   Poland   Portugal   Singapore
South Korea   Switzerland   Thailand   Turkey   Ukraine   Vietnam

Published in the United States of America by
Oxford University Press
198 Madison Avenue, New York, NY 10016

© Oxford University Press 2012

First issued as an Oxford University Press paperback, 2015.

Library of Congress Cataloging-in-Publication Data
Harris, William W.
Lebanon : a history, 600-2011 / William Harris.
p.   cm. — (Studies in Middle Eastern history)
Includes bibliographical references and index.
ISBN 978-0-19-518111-1 (hardcover : alk. paper); 978-0-19-021783-9 (paperback : alk. paper)
1. Lebanon—History. I. Title.
DS80.9.H29   2012
956.92—dc23   2011042934

To my wife, Afife Skafi Harris
To my father, Douglas Harris
And to the memory of Didem Yaman, who perished in the February 22, 2011,
Christchurch earthquake, three months short of completing her PhD.

TABLE OF CONTENTS

ACKNOWLEDGMENTS

I have received support from many people in my work on this book. I am most grateful to Bernard Lewis for getting me moving on this project and for his kind encouragement along the way. I am indebted to several libraries for access to vital resources. The University of Otago library has been wonderfully efficient in providing primary materials on interloan from near and far. The Firestone library of Princeton University and the libraries of the American University of Beirut and L'Université Saint-Esprit at Kaslik have been most helpful and hospitable. Special thanks are due to Luke Trainor of the University of Canterbury who gave me access to his private collection of nineteenth-century primary materials relevant to Lebanon.

During writing and publication, I have been the beneficiary of invaluable support and advice. Susan Ferber, executive editor at Oxford University Press in New York, stands out for her insightful comments and patient critical probing of the text. This book owes a great deal to Susan. I am much in the debt of two anonymous referees for their constructive reviews and sensible suggestions. I am most grateful to Cassie Tuttle for superb attention to detail in her incisive copyediting, to OUP production editor Marc Schneider and Marian John Paul for their highly effective oversight of the publication and their sorely tested patience with my corrections, and to OUP design and marketing for their great presentation work. I thank Latif Abul-Husn and Nadim Shehadi for sound reactions to my ideas, and Michel Aoun, Walid Junblat, Abd al-Halim Khaddam, and Detlev Mehlis for giving their time to talk with me.

Tracy Connolly converted my sketches into an excellent series of maps and diagrams, Iona Mylek saved me much time with the index and bibliography, and Leon Goldsmith diligently helped proofread the text. For the photographs, I acknowledge the generosity of Børre Ludvigsen, Cyril Mango, and Paul Zhgeib. I thank the American University of Beirut, Arch Net, the Associated Press, the British Library,

Dumbarton Oaks, Princeton University Library, the Harvard Fine Arts Library, and the Hocken Library of the University of Otago for assistance with artwork. I am obligated to Diane Lowther, who at short notice constructed a magnificent index out of a collection of headers.

I am grateful to the University of Otago for providing a grant for my research travel to Lebanon and the United States, and a sabbatical leave year in 2009. I thank Philip Nel and Marian Simms for their support, Geraldine Barrett, Donna Jackson, and Sharon Pine for help with computer concerns, and Andrew and staff at Dunedin's Everyday Gourmet café where I wrote a substantial part of the text in longhand in relaxing surrounds. In Lebanon and the United States a number of people have helped with their thoughts and hospitality during my trips connected with this project: Georges and Muna Assaf, Rima and Bassam Atiyeh, Tony Badran, Diana and John Conway, Fadia Geha, Hani Hammoud, Nasser Kalawoun, Farid el-Khazen, Wa'il Kheir, Habib Malik, Amal Mudalalli, Greg Marchese, Bulos Na'aman, Babette Neuberger, Lina Osseiran, Bernard and Madeline Reich, Michael Rubin, Elie Salem, David Schenker, Joseph and Françoise Sfeir, Lee Smith, Markus Wiener and Shelley Frisch, Michael Young, and the Payan and Skafi families.

My books for Markus Wiener Publishers—*Faces of Lebanon* (1996) and *The Levant* (2003)—provided a platform for work on this history, and I thank Markus Wiener for giving me the opportunity. I am grateful to Barry Rubin for enabling me to trial ideas in his edited book, *Lebanon: Liberation, Conflict, and Crisis* (Palgrave Macmillan, 2009). Otherwise I am obligated to the collected historians of Lebanon, whose writings are the base for my work and whom I acknowledge in detail in the notes. I would particularly like to mention Kamal Salibi, the leading modern historian of Lebanon, who sadly passed away in 2011. Finally, I thank my wife Afife and Adam, Chris, and Hadi for being unbelievably tolerant and seeing me through this project.

William Harris, Dunedin, New Zealand,
February 2012

A NOTE ON TRANSLITERATION

This book renders Arabic words into Latin script according to a substantially simplified version of the system used in the *International Journal of Middle East Studies*. All diacritical marks have been dropped, except apostrophes representing ayn and hamza in the middle of words. At the ends of nouns and associated adjectives, "yy" has been reduced to a single "y." Some modern Lebanese family names have been spelled in forms common in the Western media (for example, Berri, Chamoun, and Gemayel). The same applies for major Arab personalities (for example, Nasser of Egypt and King Hussein of Jordan). Otherwise, the definite article "al-," which features in many Arab family names, has been dropped whenever "the" is used ("al-Khazen" therefore becomes "the Khazens"), as well as in the case of stand-alone surnames for the most widely known politicians (for example, Hariri and Asad). The collective "Shia" is used for this community in almost all circumstances, as both noun and adjective. The overall purpose is to have the most simplified transliteration consistent with intelligibility and compatibility with other works.

GLOSSARY

Unless otherwise specified, non-English and non-French terms are Arabic. The Lebanese communities (Christian sects, Sunni and Shia Muslims, and Druze and Alawites), modern Lebanese political parties, and most Eastern Christian terms are defined in the main text and are therefore not included here.

Abbasids   The caliphs from the Abbasid branch of the Prophet Muhammad's family, who ruled much of the Islamic world from Iraq after displacing the Umayyads in 749. They lost control of areas beyond Iraq by the early ninth century.

Ahd   The period of a president's tenure in modern Lebanon

Ahl al-Asiya   A medieval term for the people of the Kisrawan hills north of Beirut

Ajnad   See jund

Alim (pl. ulema)   Muslim religious scholar

Amir tablkhana   The second officer rank in the Mamluk forces. It carried the entitlement to have forty horsemen in the officer's service and to have a musical band (tablkhana) perform at the officer's residence.

Ammiya   Commoner uprising in nineteenth-century Mount Lebanon

Aqdiya   See qada

Arabism   ideology of (political) unity among Arabs

Assassins Isma'ili Shia, who maintained a small mountain principality in the coastal hills of Syria in the twelfth century, immediately north of the Frankish County of Tripoli. Assassin agents undertook political killings, chiefly of Sunni Muslim leaders but occasionally also of Franks. Termed Hashishiyun (corrupted to Assassin) because they allegedly smoked hashish.

Ashura Shia holy day commemorating the martyrdom in 680 of the Imam Husayn, grandson of the Prophet Muhammad

Bahri Mamluks Bahri signifies "from the sea," meaning the island in the Nile where these Mamluks were originally stationed. Kipchak Turkish slave soldiers who ruled Egypt, 1250–1382.

Burji Mamluks Burji signifies "from the tower," meaning the citadel in Cairo that was the initial base of these Mamluk sultans. Circassian Mamluks who ruled Egypt, 1382–1516.

Caliph Originally meant "successor" of the Prophet Muhammad as spiritual and temporal leader of the Islamic community. Late Abbasid caliphs lost temporal authority to warlords; eventually they granted Seljuk Turkish leaders the title sultan, or "ruler." The office of caliph, however, continued to imply Sunni Islamic spiritual authority.

Comité Central Syrien Syrian central committee, a Lebanese Christian lobby in Paris, 1917–1918

Confessional democracy Lebanon's system of proportional distribution of political power among religious communities within a democratic framework

Dar al-Ifta Office of [Sunni Islamic] legal opinions

Emir General term for a prince; also the top level of the chiefly hierarchy of the informal principality of Mount Lebanon

Emir of Twenty A third ranking officer in the Mamluk forces. The position entitled the officer to have twenty horsemen.

Fatimids Tenth century Isma'ili Shia rulers of Tunisia who claimed descent from the Prophet Muhammad's daughter Fatima and the Caliph Ali. The Fatimids had strong Berber military support and in 979 took Cairo, where they established an Isma'ili caliphate that lasted until it was abolished in 1171 by Salah al-Din.

Fatwa Islamic legal opinion

Al-gharbiya West Beirut (from 1976)

Grand Liban Greater Lebanon

Hadith Record of a saying or action of the Prophet Muhammad. The corpus of such records assembled in the first two centuries of Islam is one of the foundations of Shari'a, or Islamic law.

Hakim The paramount Shihab emir and head of the informal principality of Mount Lebanon, 1697–1842

Halqa Mamluk elite regular forces

Hanafi The oldest Sunni Muslim law school and predominant among Lebanese Sunnis since middle Ottoman times. It allows use of reason in deriving legal rulings and has a reputation for flexibility. Follows the teaching of Abu Hanifa (700–767).

Hanbali The most conservative law school of Sunni Islam. Established by Ahmad Ibn Hanbal (780–855)

Iftar Evening fast breaking during Ramadan

Imam Saintly personalities descended from the Prophet Muhammad in the early Islamic world; also honorific for respected Islamic religious leaders.

Ilkhan Leader of the Mongol state founded by Hülegü in Iran, Iraq, and the Jazira in the 1250s. Literally "provincial Khan" subordinate to the supreme Khan (leader) in China (Turkic/Mongolian)

Imara Principality, here mainly the informal principality of Mount Lebanon

Iqta Grants of lordship over land in return for taxes and/or military service

Ja'afari Shia school of Islamic law. Differs from the Sunni schools in detail rather than essentials. Established by the sixth Imam, Ja'afar al-Sadiq (702–765)

Janissaries Ottoman infantry corps, originally Balkan Christians converted to Islam and enslaved in the sultan's service

Jizya Islamic head or poll tax on adult Christian and Jewish males. Payment theoretically compensated for exemption from military conscription and indicated acceptance of Islamic rule. Introduced by the Umayyads and abolished by the Ottomans as part of the Tanzimat reforms in the mid-nineteenth century.

Juhhal Druze not of the religious class; literally "ignorant people"

Jumhuriya Republic

Jund (pl. ajnad) Umayyad/Abbasid province; literally the territory of an army regiment

Ka'ba The most sacred Islamic shrine, located in Mecca

Khan Building for merchant accommodation and for exchange of goods

Khatt al-tamass The "contact line" between East and West Beirut, 1976–1990

Kishlak The quartering of Ottoman troops (Turkish)

Kızılbaş Shia rebels; literally "red head," after their headgear (Turkish)

Lebanism Ideology of a distinctive, pluralist Lebanon, in practice dominated by Maronites/Christians

Maliki Sunni Islamic law school based on the teaching of Malik Ibn Anas (711–795). Follows the practice of early Muslims of Medina in applying hadith.

Mamluks	Literally, "owned." Slave soldiers who seized power in Egypt in 1250 and who continued to maintain slave soldier households, regularly replenished from the Caucasus and what is now southern Russia. Leading Mamluk families continued to hold authority in Ottoman Egypt after 1517.
Mashyakha	Druze spiritual leadership
Mudabbir	Steward/manager for a senior lord in early modern Lebanon
Mufti	Islamic religious official who can issue an Islamic legal opinion (fatwa)
Mukhabarat	Intelligence services
Muqaddam	Maronite (and sometimes other) clan chief in medieval/early modern period; also the second rank of the chiefly hierarchy of the informal principality of Mount Lebanon
Muqata'ji	Chief holding territorial tax collection rights (Iqta) for the Ottoman authorities
Muqata'a	Tax collection area held by a muqata'ji
Murabitun	Muslim troops holding the land or sea frontier, originally against Byzantium; literally "stationed"
Mutasallim	An Ottoman deputy provincial governor
Mutasarrif	Governor of a mutasarrifiya
Mutasarrifiya	Special Ottoman province
Mutawali	A Mamluk district governor (for example, of Beirut)
Mutawila	A local term for Twelver Shia in Lebanon; literally "successors" (of the Caliph Ali)
Muwahhidun	The Druze name for themselves; literally, "witnesses to God's oneness"
Na'ib (pl. nuwwab)	A "deputy" of the Mamluk sultan as a provincial governor; also a Lebanese parliamentary deputy
Najjada	Sunni youth movement founded in the 1930s; literally "scouts"

Niyaba Mamluk province, literally "deputyship"; also termed mamlaka

Ottomans A Turkish Sunni Muslim clan that migrated from eastern Iran to Anatolia after 1220. Given land by the Seljuks on the Byzantine frontier, where they carved out an expanding state. Name from Osman, their initial ruler in northwest Anatolia, 1280–1326

Qabaday Street leader

Qada (pl. aqdiya) An administrative district in modern Lebanon

Qaim-maqam Sub-governor responsible for a qaim-maqamate

Qaim-maqamate Administrative unit in Mount Lebanon, 1843–1861

Qirsh Main Ottoman currency unit from 1688 to 1844, originally established at parity to the Spanish dollar but much debased through the eighteenth century

Ra'aya The "flock" or ordinary subjects of the Ottoman sultan

Rawafid "Refusers," a Mamluk and Ottoman term for Shia

Rawk Mamluk survey of lands for reassignment of tax and service obligations

Règlement organique Organic statute

Saj bread Flat bread, with dough spread thinly over a domed metal piece ("saj") for baking

Salname Ottoman yearbook of populations and socioeconomic data, begun in the provinces in 1867 (Persian)

Sancakbey Ruler of a "sanjak" (Turkish)

Sanjak Sub-province (Turkish)

Sayyid An Arabic title of respect, generally for a male accepted as descended from the Prophet Muhammad through his grandsons Husayn and Hasan

Seljuks Turkish clan south of the Aral Sea that became Muslim in the early eleventh century. Invaded Iran in 1040 and captured Baghdad in 1055.

Sephardic Jews Jews expelled from the Iberian Peninsula in the late fifteenth century; Sefard is the Hebrew for Spain

Shafi'i The Sunni Islamic law school of Muhammad Ibn Idris al-Shafi'i (767–819). Considered middle of the road.

Al-Sham Greater Syria or a popular name for Damascus; literally "the north"

Shari'a The law of Islam, the divine framework for the lives of Muslims. For Sunni Muslims, sources of Islamic law comprise the Quran, hadith, consensus of the early Islamic community (ijma), and analogy from precedent (qiyas). The four Sunni law schools differ in detailed emphasis. For Shia, who reject three of the four "right-guided" caliphs after Muhammad, consensus of the Imams replaces that of the early Muslim community.

Al-sharqiya East Beirut (from 1976)

Shaykh al-aql Chief of wisdom (Druze spiritual leader)

Shaykh al-Islam Chief Islamic jurist in the Ottoman state; also a senior jurist in Safavid Iran

Shaykh al-shabab Chief of the lads

Shaykh al-shuyukh Chief of chiefs

Sheikh Tribal leader or a respected Islamic religious personality; also the third rank of the chiefly hierarchy of the informal principality of Mount Lebanon

Al-shu'bat al-thaniya Lebanese Military Intelligence (also referred to as "deuxième bureau")

Sijill Record

Sirdar Commander of the Ottoman army (Persian)

Sultan Literally, "ruler" (also see caliph)

Tanzimat Westernizing reforms implemented in the Ottoman Empire between 1839 and 1876, encompassing religious equality, new legal codes, tax and land reform, and constitutional change; Arabic term in Ottoman Turkish literally meaning "reorderings"

Taqammus	Transmigration of souls
Taqiya	The practice of non-Sunnis pretending to be Sunni Muslim
Tawtin	Naturalization (Palestinians becoming Lebanese)
Tax farm	In its ultimate form, a contract to collect land or other taxes for the Ottoman regime. Holder would deliver a specified sum for a specified period and seek a profit. Some contracts involved bids.
Templars	A monastic order of knights installed in the Temple area of Jerusalem in 1118. Put under direct papal authority in 1139.
Thughur (sing. thaghr)	Break-out points on the Islamic land or sea frontier with Byzantium
Troupes Spéciales	Locally recruited troops under the French mandatory regime
Ulema	See alim
Umayyads	Prominent Mecca merchants at the time of the Prophet Muhammad. They were the family of the Caliph Uthman and his governor in Syria, Mu'awiya. They ruled the caliphate, 661–749, after Mu'awiya displaced the family of the Caliph Ali.
Uniate church	A Christian community in union with the Roman Catholic Church
Uqqal	Druze religious class; literally "wise men"
Wakil (pl. wukala)	Agent or representative for a tax farmer, or for one of the qaim-maqams in mid-nineteenth-century Mount Lebanon
Waqf	Islamic religious endowment; term also used for Maronite church endowments
Wilaya	Normal Ottoman province
Wukala	See Wakil
Za'im (pl. zu'ama)	Communal boss in twentieth-century Lebanon

TIMELINE FOR LEBANON
AND ITS COMMUNITIES

634–644	Arab Islamic conquest of the Levant
Late 650s	Probable arrival of Maronite monks and followers in Mount Lebanon from the Orontes Valley during the first Arab civil war.
677	Byzantine military auxiliaries known as Mardaites infiltrate Mount Lebanon.
758	Abbasid Caliph Mansur commissions Arab Tanukhs to guard Beirut hills.
845	Clash between Tanukhs and Kisrawan Christians.
980s	Isma'ili Shia Fatimids of Cairo assert lordship over Mount Lebanon.
1021	Tanukh chiefs accept "call" to acknowledge Fatimid Caliph al-Hakim as divine, thereby founding Druze sect in Mount Lebanon.
1099	First Crusade inaugurates Frankish Christian rule of Levant coast.
1110	Franks devastate Tanukhs in Beirut hills; Buhturs thereafter emerge to lead Druze.
1190s	Twelver Shia chief Husam al-Din Bishara controls Jabal Amil.
1215	Maronite patriarch Irmia accepts papal investiture.
1289	Mamluk Sultan Qalawun takes Tripoli from Franks; Buhtur chiefs submit to Mamluk service.
1305	Mamluks purge Kisrawan Alawites and Shia and introduce Sunni Turcoman settlers.
1348–1349	"Black Death" cuts population by one third in a few months.
1422–1438	Druze Buhtur peak under Mamluk Sultan al-Ashraf Barsbay, with Iz al-Din Sidqa made governor of Beirut.
1505	Biqa Shia scholar Ali al-Karki backs Safavid conversion of Iran to Twelver Shi'ism.

1516–1517	Ottoman Sultan Selim I conquers the Levant from the Mamluks; Druze Buhturs offend Selim for not submitting.
1540s	Maronite al-Khazens and Gemayels migrate into Kisrawan and Matn districts.
1585	Ottoman punitive expedition against Druze.
1593	Fakhr al-Din Ma'n made sub-governor of Sidon.
1606–1607	Fakhr al-Din joins Ali Janbulad of Aleppo to defeat Sayfas of Tripoli.
1633	Ottomans overthrow Fakhr al-Din.
1660	Ottomans send expedition against the Ma'n, Shihab, and Hamade chiefs.
1697	Ahmad Ma'n dies without heir; Druze chiefs select his Sunni nephew Bashir Shihab as their paramount lord.
1711	Haydar Shihab with al-Khazens and Junblats destroys Ottoman-backed Yamani faction at Ayn Dara.
1736	Maronite church reforms under papal oversight.
1764	Yusuf Shihab and his Maronite manager backed by Ottomans to destroy Shia Hamade hold on northern Mount Lebanon.
1780	Ottoman governor al-Jazzar represses Jabal Amil Shia.
1789–1790	Al-Jazzar awards Bashir II Shihab Mount Lebanon tax contracts.
1820–1821	Maronite peasants rise against tax demands.
1831	Egyptians seize the Levant in alliance with Bashir II and Maronites.
1838	Bashir II mobilizes Maronites to repress Druze.
1840–1841	Maronites rebel against Bashir II; British expel Egyptians from Levant; Bashir II exiled; first Druze/Maronite sectarian war.
1845	Ottomans introduce first sectarian representation in administration of Mount Lebanon.
1860	Druze/Maronite sectarian war brings European intervention.
1861–1864	Ottoman/European agreement for new special province of Mount Lebanon with Christian governor and elected sectarian administrative council.
1915	Ottomans abolish special province in midst of war with Britain and France; famine in Mount Lebanon.
1918	Ottoman defeat and loss of the Arab provinces.
1920	France follows Maronite wishes in setting extended boundaries for new Lebanese state with bare Christian majority.
1926	France gives Shia legal separation from Sunnis.
1926–1929	French/Lebanese establishment of Lebanese constitution.
1943	Maronite/Sunni agreement on National Pact for independent Lebanon, with Maronite president and Sunni prime minister.
1948	120,000 Palestinian Arab refugees arrive in Lebanon.

1958	Disagreements on Lebanese relations with the West and with external Arab nationalists feed into brief civil war.
1967	Israeli defeat of Arabs sparks Palestinian militarization in Lebanon.
1975	Lebanese state breaks down as Maronites fight Palestinians and Leftist/Muslim National Front.
1976	Mutual massacres, Syria intervenes to hold line between sides.
1978–1982	Mobilization of Shia in response to disappearance of their leader Musa al-Sadr.
1982	Israeli invasion; Arafat's PLO forced to depart; Syria humiliated; Bashir Gemayel elected president and assassinated; Israel retreats after massacre of Palestinians at the hands of its militia allies.
1983–1984	Syria recovers leading role with surge of its Shia and Druze allies.
1984–1990	Lebanon fragments among and within communal territories.
1989	Ta'if agreement of Lebanese parliamentarians for modest constitutional revision in favor of Muslims.
1990–2004	Lebanese state reemerges under U.S.-approved Syrian hegemony; Sunni Premier Rafiq al-Hariri promotes economic revival; Shia Hezbollah resists Israeli occupation of far south, with Israeli departure in 2000.
2004–2005	Sunnis, Christians, and Druze backed by United States and France repudiate Syrian hegemony; Syrian army departs amid outcry after assassination of Rafiq al-Hariri; pro-Western "March 14" camp faces Hezbollah-led "March 8" camp.
2006	Hezbollah hostilities with Israel in July/August.
2007	UN Security Council establishes Special Tribunal for Lebanon (STL) to deal with political murder.
2011	STL indicts Hezbollah members for Hariri assassination; Lebanon's future tied to outcome of uprising in Syria.

Lebanon

Introduction

In the short story "Register: I'm not an Arab Woman," Syrian Lebanese novelist Ghada Samman's protagonist proclaims from a dream:

> I see a cat giving birth to a mouse, a tiger, a squirrel, a snake, and a kitten—all from the same womb.
> I wake up terrified: How are they going to live together? But, then, why should they live together?[1]

Such has been the dilemma of cohesion in the country of Lebanon that has existed in its current boundaries since 1920. On the one hand, Lebanon is a conglomerate of Christian, Muslim, and Muslim-derived communal minorities, with distinctive identities, legal personalities, and political representation. At the same time, the country has overall features of Arabic ethnicity and dialect, acceptance of religious diversity, common family traditions, and shared pride in one of the world's finest cuisines. Issues of social justice and political allegiance have cut across sectarian affiliation. The commonalities enabled substantial national coalescence by the 1960s, while shares in sectarian political pluralism made Lebanon's politicians increasingly comfortable together. Cohesion devolved into warfare and crisis in the late twentieth and early twenty-first centuries. Political, communal, and clan divisions became inflamed in hothouse conditions of state breakdown and external interference. Today the Lebanese people are left with their shared fate and the certainty that most will not have a decent life if they do not restore a measure of unity.

A major purpose of this book is to explore problems of cohesion in modern Lebanon since its creation in 1920. Above and beyond family networks and political ideologies, sectarian communities have been central to these problems. The book reaches back to the late Roman period to interpret the origins of the communities. How did the neighborhood of Mount Lebanon, an area about the size of Connecticut or Northern Ireland, come to host almost the entire religious diversity of the Arab world? Origins extend from establishment of Christianity as the official religion of the Roman Empire in 380, through the Islamic conquest of the Levant in 636–644, to the breakaway of the Druze sect from Isma'ili Shia Islam in the 1020s.

The book considers the evolution of the Druze, Maronite Christians, and Twelver Shia of Mount Lebanon through Frankish, Mamluk, and Ottoman rule. This leads from the origins of the mountain communities to politicization of communal identity and the origins of modern Lebanon after 1800. Notwithstanding the significance of Shia and Sunni Muslim chiefs, the Druze lords, who commanded critical terrain above the towns of Beirut and Sidon, had a pivotal role under the Mamluk and Ottoman regimes. From about 1750, the increasingly fraught interplay of Druze lords, rising Maronite chiefs, Sunni Shihab "princes," and a dynamic Christian population led to Maronite/Druze estrangement. This book analyzes how the modern multicommunal polity—the Ottoman special province of 1861 and its later enlargement—variously contained, softened, and inflamed the new political sectarianism.

From their inception, the communities had identities derived from their religious orientations. The communities became leading cultural features of the neighborhood of Mount Lebanon from the medieval period, recognized by contemporary Arabic and Frankish sources. The understanding of being Maronite or Twelver Shia was of course not the same in the tenth or eleventh centuries as today; there were no institutions resembling the Maronite church or Ja'afari courts of recent times, nor today's public proceedings for saints' days or Ashura. Nonetheless, if such chroniclers as the geographer Muqaddasi and the geographer/historian al-Mas'udi could recognize Shia and Maronites respectively as distinctive populations, then they undoubtedly recognized themselves.[2]

The communities were not primordial. They represented cultural constructs that grew out of disputation in early Christianity and Islam. Concentration in compact hilly areas for Maronites, Druze, and Twelver Shia and the sense of being the community of state under the Mamluks and Ottomans for Sunni Muslims facilitated several distinctive collective identities in and around Mount Lebanon. These identities bore no relation to the modern concept of nation and displayed no political dimension through most of their history. Nonetheless, their existence carried the potential for political expression, and from the seventeenth century on, the demography, economy, and politics of Ottoman Mount Lebanon gradually increased the possibility of the Maronite Christian community assuming such expression. It only required one community to become "politicized" for prickliness about group political roles, status, and shares to start spreading among the others.

For the peasant majority in and around Mount Lebanon, life until the mid-nineteenth century was focused on clan, village, and agricultural existence. People married within their clan and village and, apart from intermittent major resettlement, enforced or voluntary, rarely traveled more than a few kilometers. Festivals, religious ceremonies for major family events (baptisms, circumcisions, marriages, and funerals), religious law for dividing property, and local religious personalities gave people communal markers above clan and village. Otherwise, there was sub-servience to a leading clan that supplied the district lord (muqaddam or sheikh), who collected taxes, dispensed basic justice, and mobilized armed followers on behalf of the distant political authority and himself. The lord was often from a different community, but peasants could compartmentalize loyalties.

Following the Islamic conquest, the evolution of military and tax delivery awards to chiefs and other regime agents into proprietary claims on lands and villages varied across Mount Lebanon. It probably went furthest with the Tanukhs, Abbasid-sponsored settler leaders who later become the first Druze lords. The Franks intensified feudal-style subordination of peasantry on the coastal side of the mountain. Thereafter, commoner deference and obligations to local lords, native or immigrant, prevailed under the Mamluks and Ottomans. Maronites preserved smallholding in the far north, but their expansion southward in the sixteenth and seventeenth centuries was as tenants under leading families, with subsequent partial conversion to smallholding. Peasant ownership and property fragmentation with inheritance, purchase, and exchange of land for planting developed across Mount Lebanon after the Ottomans inaugurated full private land registration in 1856 and ended the rural elite's tax farming and other prerogatives in 1864.

On top of land taxes, which were applied regardless of religion from the Abbasids onward, Christians and Jews owed Islamic regimes the *jizya*, or poll tax. Collection of the latter from mountain Christians can only have been patchy up to the First Crusade, when it ceased under Latin rule. It returned under the Mamluks, finally being abolished by Ottoman edict in 1856.

Many Christians, especially Maronites and other Catholics, broke out of the peasant mold with revenue from the late nineteenth-century silk boom, emigration to the Americas, and return migration in the early twentieth century.[3] They retained their basic communal markers but mixed them with Western values. Most Muslims and Druze continued in the old mold decades longer, with a long lag in access to modern education. Below elite level, a broad new cultural gap therefore opened between the Christians of the Ottoman special province of Mount Lebanon and most neighboring non-Christians from the 1880s.

No notion of a Lebanese political entity existed before late Ottoman Maronite interest in such an entity. This book does, however, argue that early Ottoman delegation of authority to collect taxes in the central districts of Mount Lebanon to emirs or "princes" of the Ma'n and Shihab families gradually evolved into the nucleus of a political entity: a loosely integrated multisectarian elite across much of the mountain. From the Islamic conquest to the sixteenth century, Mount Lebanon was highly compartmentalized at elite as well as peasant levels, with little interaction among the communal zones apart from that between coastal towns and their hinterlands. Under the Mamluks, the Druze Buhtur chiefs had political and social dealings with Mamluk officials in Cairo and Damascus and

their Druze and Sunni neighbors, for example the Turcoman Assafs. They had
no serious contact with Maronites or Jabal Amil Shia.

A first step toward sustained multicommunal elite interaction only came
when the ambitious Druze lord Fakhr al-Din Ma'n presided over an assemblage
of Ottoman district headships encompassing Druze, Maronite, Shia, and Sunni
areas in the early seventeenth century. This became a common social arena of
mountain lords under Haydar Shihab after 1711, which in turn provided the
context for the double district (qa'im-maqamate) and special province of Mount
Lebanon from the 1840s. The brutal internecine conflicts of the chiefs within,
across, and regardless of their communities through the seventeenth and eighteenth centuries—an increasing intimacy through violence—in a strange way
defined and affirmed the common arena. In a further curious twist, the Druze
Ma'ns of the seventeenth century and their Sunni Muslim Shihab relatives after
1697 evolved an informal "principality" that Maronites appropriated in the nineteenth century as their heritage for a Maronite-dominated Lebanese homeland.

Reviewing antecedents of today's Lebanon is not intended to give an impression of preordained historical outcomes. The medieval consolidation of sectarian
identities and territories around Mount Lebanon could have contributed to any
number of political situations five or six centuries later. Many counterfactual histories may be contemplated that would not have led to a country of Lebanon in
the twentieth century. If thirteenth-century Europe had given more support to the
Frankish principalities or the Mongol invasion of 1260 had not been weakened by
the departure of Hülegü Khan, there may well have been different political land-
scapes later, with less room for Maronites, Druze, and local Muslims. The survey
of medieval and early modern conditions in and around Mount Lebanon in this
book attempts to present political and social phenomena in terms of what seems
to have been important at the time rather than to modern Lebanon. Thus the
emergence of Maronites, Shia, and Druze in Mount Lebanon between the Islamic
and crusader conquests is treated as a salient social development for that time.

Political history provides the central thread of the book because the exercise
of power by local elites and external authorities, stabilizing or destabilizing the
course of local life, conditioned economic and demographic trends and influenced social relations and educational and cultural horizons. Of course there
were reverse influences, and local elites were the products of their social and cultural settings, but this author believes the exercise of political power to be the
most powerful dynamic. Also, the lives of the people of modern Lebanon are
much constrained by its peculiar sectarian political framework. Lebanon's communities began as cultural expressions but ended up being politicized. Illustration of the potency of political affairs is readily available. The economic and
demographic surge of Catholic Christians through the eighteenth and early nineteenth centuries owed much to sheltered political circumstances for Christians

relative to others. Similarly, modern Lebanon's peak of cultural creativity, particularly as regards prose literary output, reflected the country's political breakdown and savage warfare of the late twentieth century.

The book offers a sustained political narrative and analysis through fourteen centuries of the affairs of Mount Lebanon and its vicinity. Economic and cultural developments feature where they are particularly significant, for example the silk trade that kept Ottoman Mount Lebanon afloat and the educational advances from the eighteenth century that advantaged Catholic Christians. From time to time, the physical environment and epidemic disease have intruded: bubonic plague and an earthquake in the sixth century, the climatic fluctuations of medieval times, the Black Death in 1348–1349, and landscape degradation in the twentieth century. For a tiny area only equivalent to large national parks in some Western countries, it is a mark of a rich past that the narrative proceeds in several settings simultaneously: the Maronite north, the Druze Shuf, Shia Jabal Amil, and Sunni Tripoli.

From 1920 onward, rapid population growth was unbalanced among the communities; a political economy fostering inequality and turmoil in the surrounding Middle East together ensured difficulties for modern Lebanon. From the last Ottoman decades, Beirut became hegemonic in both politics and commerce, and the narrative of the modern state therefore centers on Beirut. The book attempts fair consideration of this state's predicaments and achievements. On the one hand, Lebanese leaders established pluralist politics accommodating the sectarian communities. By the 1960s, the system provided individual and public freedoms, electoral competition, commercial dynamism, and some reduction of communal disparities in education and income. On the other hand, France established the new country after the Ottoman defeat in World War I primarily for the Maronites, who had disproportionate influence, especially after the non-Christian communities became more than half the population by the 1940s. The system lacked mechanisms to respond to change, though Lebanon's domestic capacity to maintain stability was never really tested. The disruptive overflow from the 1967 Arab-Israeli War overwhelmed the country and its politicians by the mid-1970s. Early twenty-first century Lebanon still lives in the shadow of its collapse into violence between 1975 and 1990.

Within what sort of physical setting did the crystallization and evolution of the Lebanese collection of communities proceed? The word Lebanon derives from the name of the coastal mountains—*Jabal Lubnan* or Mount Lebanon—originally the heights north of Beirut. It is a slight adaptation of an old Semitic word for whiteness. The Arabic *laban* refers to sour milk and the Hebrew *lavan* means white. The name could reflect either the whiteness of the mountain's limestone cliffs or the "snow of Lebanon" noted in Jeremiah 18:14.

Today's Lebanon (see figure 0.1) comprises Mount Lebanon as defined by the Ottoman autonomous province of 1861 and the crescent of districts around

Mount Lebanon added by France in September 1920. It has natural coherence: the coastal and interior Lebanon mountain ranges and between them the trench of the Biqa, an elevated plain almost entirely above 3,000 feet (914 meters), represent the topographic climax of the Levant. Lebanon is a compact country of 4,015 square miles (10,400 square kilometers)—135 miles (217 km) long and an average of 35 miles (56 km) wide.

Mount Lebanon, the coastal mountain range, is the historical and geographical core of the country, the main stage for its distinctive social development. For the purposes of this book, Mount Lebanon means the whole mountain bloc from

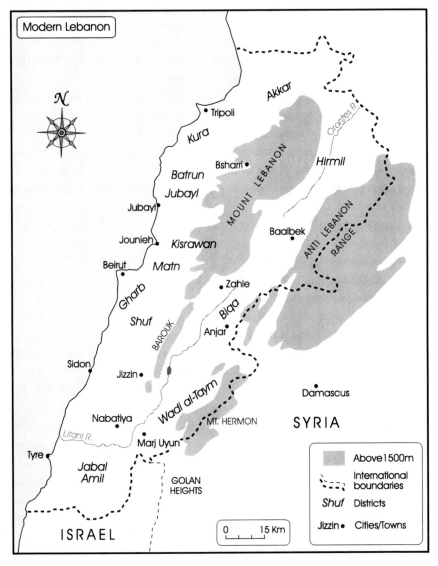

Figure 0.1 Modern Lebanon.

the Akkar north of Tripoli to the Barouk ridge inland from Sidon, reaching south to the Litani River. It is a continuous limestone massif, with peaks varying in height from 10,130 feet (3,088 meters) in the far north to 6,235 feet (1,900 meters) on the Barouk crest. On the western side a jumble of hills, deeply dissected by mountain streams flowing into the Mediterranean, rises steadily from the coast to the main divide. To the east, the divide presents a wall to the Biqa. Below the subalpine heights, Mount Lebanon's natural vegetation mixes evergreen oak and coniferous forest, the latter including the famous cedars with juniper and pine, and dense hard-leaved scrub. Cultivation and timber cutting made significant inroads into the forest from Phoenician times, reducing the cedars to isolated patches, but much of the rest remained into the Ottoman period to make the rough terrain more forbidding. In the late twentieth century, however, uncontrolled development brought widespread degradation of remaining tree cover.

Other parts of Lebanon may be conceived as outliers of Mount Lebanon. Intermittent coastal flats, broadening from Tripoli north, have historically provided space for town and port development and associated intensive agriculture, including at Beirut, Sidon, and Tyre. South of the Litani, the hills of Jabal Amil grade into the Upper Galilee of present-day Israel. To the east of the coastal mountains, the Biqa floor is up to ten miles (fifteen kilometers) wide and is the modern country's major expanse for grains, horticulture, and hardier crops like potatoes. Historically it has been a granary and a north/south corridor. It is flanked by the Anti-Lebanon Range, only a little less imposing than Mount Lebanon, but much drier and sparsely vegetated. The present Lebanese/Syrian border mostly follows the high points of the Anti-Lebanon, but deviates here and there and has never been properly demarcated. In the south, the Anti-Lebanon ends in the limestone mass of Mount Hermon, 9,232 feet (2,900 meters) high. The western flank of Hermon shelters a valley known as Wadi al-Taym. This was an important location of Arab settlement after the Islamic conquest, and a medieval hideout for Isma'ili Shia and Druze.

Lebanon's climate is the classic Mediterranean type, with cool, wet winters and hot, dry summers, though with steamy summer humidity on the coast. Annual rainfall varies from 80 inches (2,000 millimeters) on the coastal heights to less than 12 inches (300 millimeters) in the northeast of the Biqa. Because Lebanon is a high-altitude country by Arab and European standards, with 70 percent of its surface above 2,000 feet (500 meters), it is subject to fierce blizzards in January and February. Snow can close the main route from Beirut to Damascus, and winter military activity in Mount Lebanon has always been a chancy affair.

Climate change has affected Lebanon's history. The Medieval Warm Period, from about 800 to the late thirteenth century, assisted the initial consolidation of the mountain communities. The rise of a couple of degrees Celsius in average northern hemisphere temperatures meant milder winters and facilitated mountain farming.[4] This spurred both Maronite population growth and Shia movement into Mount Lebanon from the Biqa. In contrast, Mamluk persecution of the Shia in the hills north of Beirut in the early fourteenth century coincided with cooling toward the Little Ice Age. The increased precariousness of settlement above approximately one thousand meters dictated that Shia recovery predominantly meant oscillation of tribes back and forth from the Biqa, while mountain residents of whatever community probably undertook more seasonal shifting between lower and higher altitudes. Maronite expansion south into the Kisrawan, taking over from the Shia, occurred in the depth of the Little Ice Age in the early Ottoman period.[5] A more adverse climate probably intensified both Shia demoralization and Maronite need for more land. The impacts of the Medieval Warm Period and the Little Ice Age deserve closer investigation.

Through most of its history since the Islamic conquest, Mount Lebanon and its coast has been the strategic key to the Levant. For the Umayyad, Abbasid, Mamluk, and Ottoman Sunni Muslim imperial authorities, it hosted religiously suspect people who linked or could link to external powers. It was open to penetration from the sea and flanked Damascus, the Levant's chief provincial center. Mount Lebanon was also sufficiently difficult terrain to make direct rule problematic; imperial armies could reach and punish anywhere, but this required substantial mobilization. For local governors with limited manpower, the narrow trails of the mountain were forbidding, with the pine forest and rocky defiles inviting ambush. Hence the Ottomans tolerated the autonomy of the Ma'ns and Shihabs in the hills above Sidon and Beirut, provided they remitted taxes and respected imperial sovereignty. The paramount "prince" of the mountain kept his small court in Deir al-Qamar, while his overlord, the governor, exerted direct authority along the coast from the nearby port of Sidon.

Mount Lebanon and its coast have also been alternating poles of their joint economic affairs. From the Roman collapse to late Ottoman times, the port towns experienced sharply fluctuating fortunes; and for long periods, mountain life and activities overshadowed them. In contrast, from the 1880s on, Beirut boomed as a great commercial hub, dominating the mountain.

In the century before the Islamic conquest, the plague, a great earthquake, and Persian occupation laid the ports low. After the conquest, Mediterranean trade remained in abeyance for three centuries because of maritime warfare between the caliphate and the Byzantines. The half-ruined ports were vital to the caliphate, but principally as naval strongholds. Even with troops and the planting of new settlers, the populations of Tyre, Sidon, Beirut, and Tripoli would not have exceeded a few thousand apiece through the Umayyad and Abbasid periods. They had the stone debris of a more prosperous past available for defense works, mosques, markets, and limited residential clusters. Between them there were no roads in the modern understanding from the conquest until the mid-nineteenth century—only dirt trails for camels and horses along the coast and into the interior, with bridges and lodgings the main investments.[6] Carts largely went out of use from late Roman to late Ottoman times; camels were more efficient.[7]

A larger population than on the coast, though probably not greater than 100,000 in the seventh and eighth centuries, subsisted in the hills and in the high valley of the Biqa. The mountaineers had grains for survival and would have been able to conduct a limited trade in fruit, olive oil, timber, and pastoral products with the ports, Baalbek, and Damascus. The Tanukh chiefs provided rudimentary organization above Beirut, while little is known of the role of village and district leaders among the Christians of the north and the proto-Shia of Jabal Amil. Winter, even at lower altitudes, dictated spartan little dwellings with roughly assembled stonewalls and flat timber and dirt roofs in scattered, tightly knit hamlets. Peasants moved up and down the mountain with the seasons, especially in the north. Regardless of social standing, most members of chiefly families would have had little substantive advantage in accommodation. From the ninth century, the Medieval Warm Period fostered modestly better living conditions.

Revival of Mediterranean commerce in the late tenth century with the takeover of Egypt and the Levant by the Isma'ili Shia Fatimids of North Africa brought real economic life back to the Lebanese coast. The Fatimids were Mediterranean-oriented and developed relaxed trading relations with Byzantium and Italy. Tripoli and Tyre boomed into the eleventh century, mainly exporting local products—cotton and silk textiles, sugar, and glassware. Long-distance trade in spices and fine silks from Iran, India, and eastern Asia through the Levant to the Christian West also resurfaced. The crusader conquest in the early twelfth century accentuated the trend. Tripoli and Tyre remained the leading towns, with Franks displacing Muslims as the urban majority. Italian merchant colonies became established, local textile and sugar production expanded, and the long-distance spice and silk trade flourished under Frankish/Muslim collaboration. Inland from Tripoli, Maronite Christians benefited materially during Frankish rule and built new churches.[8] Inland from Tyre, a Shia population inflated by refugees from Palestine intensified settled agriculture under Frankish lords.

Egyptian Mamluk expulsion of the Franks in the late thirteenth century reasserted Sunni Islamic hegemony. The Mamluks sacked the Frankish towns and punished infidel and heretic mountaineers, but soon became more discriminating. They razed less defensible ports south of Sidon, but reconstructed Sidon, Beirut, and Tripoli and invested in Baalbek as an inland center. Tyre disappeared while Tripoli became the leading port town of the Levant—a provincial capital, a center of Sunni religious learning, and the leading Syrian outlet of the long-distance trade. In Tripoli the Mamluks rehabilitated the Frankish citadel, while a collection of their own stone buildings survives to this day, including seven mosques.[9] Both the port inhabitants and the mountaineers suffered a savage blow from the Black Death of 1348–1349, which cut the population by a third in a few months and truncated economic activity for more than two centuries.

Sustained recovery began only in the early seventeenth century, well after Ottoman displacement of the Mamluks in 1516. Fakhr al-Din Ma'n energetically enticed European traders and French and Italian cultural and political interest to underpin his autonomy from his Ottoman suzerain. He participated in contraband grain trade, promoted mulberry tree cultivation to feed silk worms in Christian and Druze districts, and encouraged cotton growing in the Shia south. Sidon, base for the Ottoman customs and the French official presence, served as his cover for smuggling elsewhere; otherwise, the coastal towns were sideshows to economic and political developments in the mountain until Beirut gained strength in the mid-nineteenth century.

Money from the intensified commodities trade increased the tax base but made Maronite peasants, of whom many in the Christian north were freeholders, not tenants, more resentful of taxes. It also buttressed church revenues, expressed after 1700 in imposing monasteries. By 1800, the mountain also acquired its first towns—Deir al-Qamar and Zahle. Around 1900, returning emigrants imported the resources and Westernized outlooks to begin transforming many villages, establishing the larger red-tiled "traditional" homes of today's tourist propaganda.

The English painter Edward Lear vividly described the mid-nineteenth-century landscape of northern Mount Lebanon in a May 1858 letter:

> The interior of Lebanon is . . . wonderfully fine:—a kind of Orientalized Swiss scenery:—innumerable villages dot the plateaus & edge the rocks which are spread on each side of & rise above dark ravines, winding downward to the plains of Tripoli and the blue sea.[10]

Lear portrayed an already well-peopled terrain on the verge of further Maronite population growth with the silk boom of the late nineteenth century. Mulberry trees, their leaves fodder for silkworms, even crowded out food provision. Around 1900, silk monoculture reached its peak, generating half the income of Mount Lebanon.[11] By this stage, returns per capita were sliding and men who had resources but narrowing prospects migrated to the Americas by the thousands. After the trade suspension and catastrophic famine of World War I, silk production flattened and the Greater Lebanon of 1920 went forward on a new commercial basis, boosted by returning Christian migrants.

Through the nineteenth century, Beirut established itself as the Levant's center of services, finance, and import/export business. By 1900, it eclipsed Tripoli and Sidon and rivaled Damascus and Aleppo. At first, a few Orthodox Christian and Greek Catholic families commanded Beirut's new commercial enterprises, which helped maintain the old rural elite, the new Maronite bourgeoisie of the mountain, and the Sunni bourgeoisie of the coast. Beirut's ascent was of limited utility to poorer Muslims and Christians; nonetheless, Lebanese of all varieties flocked to the capital. The population of Beirut and its suburbs climbed in 1930 from 150,000, or one-quarter of Lebanon's people, to well over one million, or around half, by the early 1970s. Greater Lebanon became a city-state, with its diverse sectarian and social elements pressed into close and eventually explosive proximity within Greater Beirut.

Modern Lebanon's five-fold population increase, from around 800,000 in the flawed 1921 census to over four million resident Lebanese citizens by 2011, reflected the global population explosion of the twentieth century. In Lebanon, however, it involved changing communal proportions, while the inflow of Maronites and Shia into separate segments of Greater Beirut heightened consciousness of difference. In a reversal of Ottoman trends, Shia Muslims grew fastest, recovering from a low of 17 percent in 1921 to around 30 percent by 2011, while Christians fell from above 50 percent to about 36 percent. Among Muslims, the Sunni advantage gave way to a Shia edge. The three biggest communities all remain above 20 percent; and while Shia and Sunnis have overtaken Maronites, Christians as a whole are still ahead of either of the big Muslim communities. Age distributions vary considerably among communities in the early twenty-first century, with a youth and young middle-aged bulge for Shia and Sunnis. Thwarted expectations within this bulge have contributed to a surge of Islamist organizations, for example Shia Hezbollah and Sunni Salafists. The next generation will be relatively smaller and may assert different perspectives.

How do we estimate early twenty-first-century proportions, when sectarian sensitivity has precluded a census since 1932? Specialists have drawn an outline of today's communal demography from post-1932 fertility records and population surveys.[12] The latter include the 1970 Lebanese government survey of 30,000 households; a population count from the 1988 Hariri Foundation food distribution program; and national family surveys in 1996 and 2004. Lebanon remains a country with no majority, and it has no prospect of acquiring one. With decline in the Shia natural increase rate since the 1980s, the demographic configuration may stabilize by the 2020s.

Lebanon's communities color its politics and society. Senior Shia religious scholar Muhammad Husayn Fadlallah summarized this reality when he remarked at a 1998 Ramadan *Iftar*, or fast breaking:

> We are several sects, but we feel that we are several states. . . . Is it
> believable that the country is occupied by an enemy [he meant Israel]
> and we spend our time debating whether the Shia sect or the Sunni sect
> or the Maronite sect has the biggest numbers?[13]

Officially recognized Lebanese sects, 2011				
Non-Christians	**Conjectured Population**	**%**	**Parliamentary Seats**	**%**
Twelver Shia Muslims	1,160,00	29	27	21
Sunni Muslims	1,120,000	28	27	21
Druze	200,000	5	8	6
Alawites	80,000	2	2	1.5
Isma'ili Shia Muslims	negligible	-	-	
Jews	negligible	-	-	
Total	2,560,000	64	64	
Christians				
Maronite Catholics	880,000	22	34	26.5
Orthodox	240,000	6	14	11
Greek Catholics	120,000	3	8	6
Armenian Orthodox* Armenian Catholics	120,000	3	5 1	5
Syrian Orthodox (Jacobites)* Syrian Catholics Assyrians Chaldeans (Assyrian Catholics) Latin Catholics Evangelical Protestants Copts*	80,000	2	2 (1 for Protestants, 1 for "minorities")	1.5
Total	1,440,000	36	64	

Total resident population		* Monophysite Christian sects
Lebanese citizens	4,000,000	
Palestinians (about 90% Sunni Muslims)	c.300,000	

Given the impact of communal identities in modern Lebanon, it is worth defining the communities. There are eighteen officially recognized Christian, Muslim, and Islamic derived sects (see table, "Officially recognized Lebanese sects, 2011"). In Lebanon, religious law continues from Ottoman times as the law of the land for personal status—marriage, divorce, and inheritance. The communities operate their own courts for personal status issues: the Christian sects have their various versions of canon law; Twelver Shia, Druze, Alawites, and

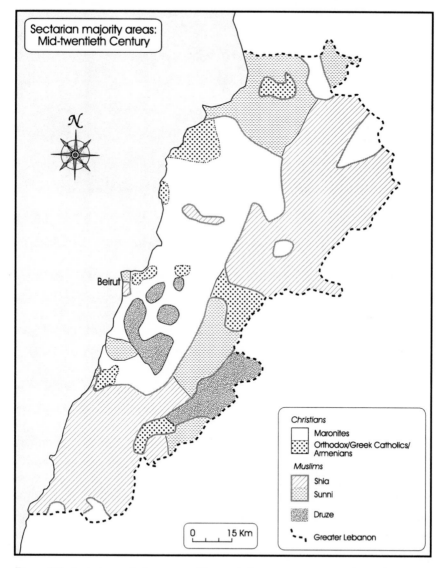

Figure 0.2 Sectarian majority areas: mid-twentieth century. *Source:* Data from *Tübinger Atlas des Vorderen Orients* (TAVO), Sheets A VIII 7 (Lebanon: Religions) and A VIII 9 (Lebanon: Christianity), Tübingen, 1979.

Figure 0.3 Religious leaders of the three largest communities, February 1984: Maronite Patriarch Butros Khreish (left), Shia Sheikh Muhammad Mehdi Shams al-Din (center), and Sunni Grand Mufti Hasan Khalid (right). Associated Press/Mell.

even the few Isma'ilis have escaped their late Ottoman subjection to Hanafi Sunni Islamic law into their own jurisdictions; and Jews have separate standing, as under the Ottomans. Figure 0.2 depicts sectarian majority areas as of the mid-twentieth century, and figure 0.3 shows the spiritual heads of the three largest communities together at the Maronite patriarchate in 1984.

This overview begins with the Maronite Catholics because creation of the modern country expressed their will for insulation from their Islamic sur-rounds, though Maronite leaders insisted on boundaries making the popula-tion almost half Muslim. Maronites today comprise about 60 percent of Lebanese Christians. They originally professed the doctrine of two natures (divine and human) but one will in Christ, suggested by the Emperor Heraclius in the 630s to reconcile Orthodox (two natures) and Monophysite (single nature) Christians. Part of the community entered communion with Rome in 1215, but not until the seventeenth century did the Vatican manage to impose sufficient conformity to establish the Maronites as the prototype Uniate church. Rome, for example, shares the Orthodox position on two natures and two wills in Christ. As a Uniate church, the Maronites accept Roman doctrine and the pope but keep their Syriac ritual and religious hierarchy, headed by the Maronite patriarch who since 1830 has been based at Bkirki above Jounieh. Maronites are extensively represented among less well-off Lebanese as well as having a powerful elite. They remain the bulk of the population in northern Mount Lebanon, with outliers southward and in the Biqa.

Half non-Maronite Christians adhere to the Orthodox Church, the heir of Byzantine tradition. Their leading families have historically been commercial partners with Sunni Muslims. They are under the religious jurisdiction of the Orthodox patriarch of Antioch, who resides in Damascus—unlike other heads of major Lebanese Christian sects, who live in the vicinity of Beirut. Orthodox played a prominent role in formulating the Arab nationalist and Greater Syrian ideologies. Away from Beirut and Tripoli, Orthodox Christians inhabit the Kura district, the Matn above Beirut, and Marj Uyun and Wadi al-Taym in the south.

In the 1720s, after decades of French-instigated Catholic infiltration of the Orthodox of northern Syria, Catholic converts in Aleppo asserted a separate church in communion with Rome. During the eighteenth century, many migrated to Mount Lebanon. These Greek Catholics retained Orthodox ritual and set up their own patriarchate, on the Maronite model. Today about 120,000 remain in the country, and they disproportionately feature in the upper bourgeoisie. They live in Beirut, Zahle, and scattered villages, notably east of Sidon.

Armenians, today also numbering around 120,000, mainly arrived in Lebanon in 1918–1920 as refugees from the massacres in eastern Anatolia at the hands of Turks and Kurds during and after World War I, although they have a much longer history of coming and going. The refugees settled in shanties in marshland east of Beirut that became the suburb of Burj Hammoud. A smaller group, fleeing the Turkish annexation of Alexandretta (Hatay) in 1939, set up the Biqa town of Anjar. Armenians have tried to balance being Lebanese with continued membership of their own nation, and have kept a distance from Lebanon's sectarian factions. In Burj Hammoud and the coastal Matn northeast of Beirut, they have sustained Armenian language media and political parties. Most belong to the Armenian Gregorian Orthodox Church, but there are also Armenian Protestants and Catholics.

Seven small Christian denominations have individual legal status, headed by the Syrian Orthodox, remnant of the Jacobite Monophysites who rivaled the Maronites in medieval times. These sects are together less in number than the Greek Catholics or Armenians.

Lebanon's non-Christians comprise five Muslim and Islamic-derived communities, but 90 percent are Sunni or Twelver Shia Muslims. Lebanese Sunnis are part of the majority religious orientation of the Arab world, though a minority around Mount Lebanon. In their view, they represent Islamic orthodoxy, following the Quran and the *sunna* (custom) of Muhammad, the first four caliphs, and the early Islamic community. Sunnis have no place for the Shia veneration of Imams, saintly personalities of the family of the Prophet Muhammad.

Since the late Ottoman period, Lebanese Sunnis have followed the Hanafi legal tradition for personal status and *waqf* (religious endowments), currently administered by the *Dar al-Ifta* (office of legal opinions) under the Chief Mufti of the Lebanese Republic. The Shafi'i, Maliki, and Hanbali law schools have also historically operated in Beirut and Tripoli. In the fourteenth century, Sunnis recovered their domination of the coastal towns, established in the Islamic conquest but lost to the Isma'ili Fatimids and the Franks. In Beirut they ceased to be the majority in the 1840s, but Tripoli and Sidon remain their domain. They have a rural presence in the north, the Biqa, and the Shuf.

Shia means the faction of the Caliph Ali, cousin and son-in-law of Muhammad, who confronted the "Sunni" elite of the early Islamic world. Partisans of Ali settled in the Lebanese hills from the mid-seventh century. They may be termed proto-Shia, because Shia belief only crystallized in the ninth and tenth centuries. The Shia acquired a tradition of martyrdom and resistance when Ali's son Husayn rebelled and was killed at Kerbala in 680. Ali and his sons Hasan and Husayn began the line of Imams, cosmic poles of their times. In the tenth century, most proto-Shia around Mount Lebanon adopted the line of twelve Imams accepted by most of their counterparts in Iraq, as opposed to the seven of the Isma'ili Shia. The deviation occurred after the sixth Imam, Ja'afar al-Sadiq, who founded the Shia Ja'afari school of religious law. For Twelvers, the last Imam went into hiding and will reappear before the Final Judgment. By crusader times, Twelver Shia were the main population in the hills south of Mount Lebanon, in much of the Biqa, and in parts of central Mount Lebanon later taken over by Maronites. When they came under the modern Lebanese state they were the poorest community and geographically peripheral.

Lebanon's Druze acknowledge the Isma'ili Shia Fatimid Caliph al-Hakim, who disappeared near Cairo in 1021, as a manifestation of God.[14] Their name comes from an early follower of al-Hakim, al-Darazi. The gate to converts closed in 1043, by which time mountain clans of the Shuf district and Wadi al-Taym adhered. As a faith, Druzism conceives God as an impersonal source of being and does not ascribe literal significance to "pillars" of Islam such as prayer and pilgrimage to Mecca. *Uqqal* (wise men) have guarded religious knowledge. After 1450, the position of *shaykh al-aql* (chief of wisdom) emerged in the Buhtur family as the Druze spiritual head. In 1825, the position split between the Junblati and Yazbaki factions.[15] In 1962, the *shaykh al-aql* became a government official responsible for Druze legal affairs and religious property, and in 1970, Kamal Junblat and Majid Arslan agreed on reunification—only one *shaykh al-aql* at any one time.

Alawites derive from Twelver Shi'ism; they regard the Caliph Ali as divine. Alawites became established in Mount Lebanon under the crusaders, but the Mamluks removed them. Today they have a presence in Tripoli and the Akkar as an extension of the community of coastal Syria. In 1973, Lebanese Shia leader Musa al-Sadr gratified Syria's Alawite president, Hafiz al-Asad, by confirming the community as Shia, and therefore as Muslims.[16]

Finally, though few remain, Jews have a deep history in Lebanon. The Umayyads and Abbasids encouraged Jewish settlement in the coastal towns in the early Islamic centuries, notably Tripoli (644) and Sidon (922). When Benjamin of Tudela visited the Lebanese coast in 1161, at the height of the Crusader Kingdom of Jerusalem, he recorded two hundred Jews in Jubayl, fifty in Beirut, twenty in Sidon, and five hundred in Tyre.[17] Many came from Europe, and the Mamluks did not distinguish between Franks and Jews when eliminating the crusader presence. In Beirut, Jews only reappeared after the expulsions from Spain in 1492. A Jew ran customs in the first Ottoman years.[18] A visitor reported five hundred Sephardic Jews in Beirut in 1856, and migrants from interior Syria raised those numbers to five thousand by 1914, about 3 percent of the city's population.[19] The Beirut community thrived through the French mandate, with schools and a prominent synagogue. Jewish numbers increased toward 10,000 in the 1950s, with Syrian and Iraqi Jews arriving after the creation of Israel. The community collapsed in the charged atmosphere after the 1967 Arab-Israeli War, and almost all Jews departed Lebanon by the early 1980s.

In political terms, the religious communities (or "confessions") structure the peculiar Lebanese pluralism termed "confessional democracy." The idea of a sectarian community as a political platform for its members arose among Maronites and Druze by the mid-nineteenth century. Political sectarianism conditioned the formal communal representation within the Ottoman institutions that replaced the informal principality of Mount Lebanon: the double *qaim-maqam*ate of 1845 and the special province of 1861. Such representation was the precedent for the communal carve-up of parliament, administration, and government in modern Lebanon after 1920.[20] Communal political shares reflected late Ottoman circumstances, and their entrenchment under the French mandate had positive and negative dimensions. On the one hand, communal shares guaranteed representation of different groups in decision making, even if their elites made the decisions. Nowhere else in the Arab world was there such a vested interest in preserving bourgeois parliamentarianism. On the other hand, communal shares reinforced sectarian identity at the expense of commitment to the country. Further, they privileged loose coalitions among communal bosses over national parties with proper programs. The control of segments of the bureaucracy by communal bosses, termed *zu'ama* (sing. *za'im*), invited distribution of jobs and contracts as favors to clients. Given family and social obligations, patronage would have disfigured any system, but political sectarianism was fertile soil.

What has been the reality of "confessional democracy"? Pluralism in power, popular representation through communal quotas, free electoral competition, and orderly changes of government following elections justified the label in the 1960s and early 1970s. The 1926 constitution, the 1943 National Pact among politicians advantaging Christians in line with the 1932 census, and mild recalibration in the 1989 Ta'if agreement set the parameters. The three biggest communities each have a leading office of state—Maronite president, Sunni prime minister, and Shia speaker of parliament. Four other communities—Orthodox Christians, Druze, Greek Catholics, and Armenians—have guaranteed cabinet seats alongside the big three.

Since independence in 1943, the single-chamber legislature has had four-year terms, though general elections were suspended through the war period from 1975 to 1990, and the 1972 chamber voted itself four extensions. Parliament elects the Maronite president for a six-year term by a two-thirds majority. Between 1943 and 1989, the president selected the Sunni prime minister. The August 1990 constitutional amendments, however, required him (or, theoretically, her) to coordinate with the Shia parliamentary speaker and accept the candidate for prime minister most favored in consultations with parliamentary deputies. The president had primary executive authority between 1943 and the 1989 Ta'if agreement. After 1989, this authority passed to the council of ministers, split evenly between Christians and non-Christians and chaired by the prime minister. In practice, even before 1989, for the regime to function the president needed a cooperative prime minister who was respected by Sunnis. Sectarian rationing has extended beyond elected officials to the public service, including permanent heads of ministries, diplomatic posts, and security positions. For example, convention since 1943 requires that the army commander be a Maronite and his chief of staff a Druze.

Allocation of seats in parliament has drifted out of alignment with demography, even with Christian/non-Christian equality since 1989. Today, non-Christians should have 80 out of the 128 seats rather than 64. However, the Christian advantage means little; their deputies are split among factions, and Shia votes, for example, determine their representatives in the south. The electoral system, in which all voters elect all deputies in multimember constituencies, encourages competing multisectarian lists of candidates. The Shuf electorate, in 2009 taken by the partners in the March 14 movement, returned three Maronites, two Druze, two Sunnis, and one Greek Catholic. Further, despite Shia underrepresentation, the "winner takes all" constituency results in 2005 and 2009 gave the Shia alliance of Hezbollah and Amal, with its dependent Christians, a fair reflection of its popular base.

Eighty years after modern Lebanon's last census, the lack of a solid numerical foundation for shares in a communal federation has become intractable. Christians are sensitive about their relative decline, while Shia and Sunnis are not enthusiastic to have their respective proportions defined. The fact that no one is desperate to have a head count and probable stabilization of proportions as natural increase and migration rates converge in the early twenty-first century means that the status quo is still tolerable.

For all its frailties, the pluralism of political sectarianism enabled a twentieth-century flowering of civil society in Lebanon unmatched in the Arab world. Universities, print and audio-visual media, chambers of commerce, professional associations, and trade unions all created their own arenas of competition and debate—and in many cases sectarian jostling. Sami Baroudi's account of the Shia bid for fair representation in the Beirut Traders' Association and the Beirut Chamber of Commerce in the 1990s, and the Sunni resistance, is a reminder of the conversion of almost anything into sectarian stakes.[21] Nonetheless, disputation over shares in "confessional democracy" did not cause Lebanon's disintegration in 1975.

Sectarian politics have, of course, been almost exclusively male politics. Historically Mount Lebanon's communities and competing clans nourished a rigid patriarchy that left little space for female involvement other than backstage influence on husbands or sons. The female half of the population was obviously essential in providing labor, reproduction, and marriage alliances that kept society and politics functioning, but otherwise recorded history was by men, for men, and about men until the late nineteenth century. Figure 0.4 provides a nineteenth-century scene of village women making flat bread.

From Roman times to the French mandate, only four women—all from the Druze aristocracy—featured in the sources as persons of political significance, all through being mother or wife to leading males. Fakhr al-Din Ma'n's chronicler al-Khalidi al-Safadi refers to the role of Fakhr al-Din's mother *al-Sitt al-Kabira* (the grand lady).[22] In February 1613, Fakhr al-Din's brother Yunis sent her to pacify the Ottoman commander of a punitive expedition. Al-Safadi notes that in winter conditions the *Sirdar* was amenable to being paid off. Two centuries later, in 1807, the wife of Abbas Arslan caused problems for Bashir II Shihab. Otherwise, Sa'id Junblat's widow headed his Druze faction after his death in 1861, and Sitt Nazira Junblat, widow of Fuad Junblat, fulfilled this role through the French mandate until her son Kamal could take over.

Change came to gender relations among Mount Lebanon's Christians with the destabilization of peasant society in the silk boom and mass emigration of the late nineteenth century.[23] Women provided labor for the silk-spinning factories that multiplied in the central mountain districts. It was poorly paid work in foul conditions but gave thousands of women independent resources and a new outlook. When many males emigrated, women either stayed behind as household heads or themselves left for the New World. With a significant return of migrants before World War I, Christian women had accumulated experiences of peasant labor, factory work, household headship, and life in the Americas to

Figure 0.4 Peasant women making *saj* bread, late nineteenth century. American University of Beirut/Library Archives. Photographer: Bonfils.

make them less comfortable with assigned female roles. From the 1890s on, Christian women established female associations and wrote in the print media about female roles.[24] Most accepted continued male supremacy, but gender discrimination in the new Lebanese state rankled.

Muslim and Druze women did not go through this late nineteenth-century experience, and their questioning of tradition came more gradually. In Beirut, ferment among Christian women affected the non-Christian bourgeoisie, but in general, divergent female circumstances became another illustration of communal differences, even as the whole female population stayed disadvantaged. For Twelver Shia, emigration to West Africa in the early and mid-twentieth century did not have the same effect on gender relations as the Maronite experience in the West. Returning migrants created a new middle class in Jabal Amil, but, as Hanan al-Shaykh's novel *The Story of Zahra* illustrates, for a young woman in the 1970s moving back and forth from West Africa made little difference to gender situations.[25]

Bourgeois Sunni women of Beirut began to unveil themselves in public in the late 1920s. Samir Kassir discusses the case of the daughter of Salim Salam, a leading Beirut personality, who gave a lecture without a veil in 1926.[26] Ordinary Shia women took advantage of the French institution of Ja'afari courts for personal status issues to make legal challenges to men in divorce and inheritance disputes.[27] Nonetheless, women working outside of the home, entering higher education, and joining public activities remained overwhelmingly Christian until the 1960s. Thereafter, secularized Muslim women became more prominent.

From the 1980s, a new style of Islamic social activism emerged among Shia women, reflecting self-help in Beirut's southern suburbs and religious dynamism propelled by resistance to Israel. Lara Deeb, a Lebanese Christian researcher, has studied female involvement in Shia welfare and religious associations, whether independent, under Hezbollah, or under the *marja* (source of religious emulation) Muhammad Husayn Fadlallah.[28] Female Shia religious activists have their own view of what it means to be "modern," combining spiritual sophistication with assisting the advancement of their community.[29] Today's Shia gender scene is intricate, including secular women unsympathetic to Islamists and general female failure to break through the glass ceiling above a few middle-management positions.

Indeed, Lebanon's performance regarding women's legal status, employment conditions, and political participation since the creation of the modern country has been uneven in detail and mediocre in general. For inheritance, religious personal status law means that Sunni and Shia women receive consideration inferior to men and Christian and Druze women.[30] For divorce, Orthodox Christians join Sunnis and Shia in having more difficult conditions for women than men, whereas Druze law is egalitarian. State law on adultery discriminates against women, and men receive light penalties for murdering female relatives suspected of besmirching family "honor." Citizenship law is unfair; men who marry foreigners can transfer citizenship to their spouses and children, whereas women cannot.

Many women from poorer Christian families went to work in textile factories and the tobacco industry after World War I. Female tobacco workers led a 1946 strike in a Beirut Christian neighborhood, but the regime, the media, and the union tried to ignore the female voice.[31] The regime forcibly broke the strike; female militants did nonetheless succeed in getting maternity leave written into the 1946 labor law, and subsequent labor law was modestly more attentive to female circumstances.

In the political arena, women received the right to vote in 1952, three years after Syria, but their initial participation in elections was low and manipulated by male relatives. There were no female deputies until Myrna Bustani succeeded to her deceased father's seat in 1963, and no more until 1991; they peaked at 6 out of 128 members in 2005, and declined to 4 in 2009. Of the latter, three are Christian and one a Sunni; there has never been an elected female Shia deputy. The Lebanese parliament refused a 10 percent female quota for Lebanon's 2010 municipal elections. While the Lebanese blame "sectarianism" for male political hegemony, in fact there is no reason women should not play a larger part in "confessional democracy." Noncommunal organizations like Lebanon's Communist party have never promoted women.

Despite modern Lebanon's poor showing on gender equity, women have advanced in education, the professions, and literary expression. They still trail men in literacy levels, but since the 1990s they have comprised half of university graduates. In 1992, the army permitted women to serve as officers, and in 1994 women gained full rights to undertake commercial activity.[32] In the late twentieth century, women broke into media jobs, and in the legal profession they have achieved top positions. In 2009, Amal Haddad became president of the Beirut Bar Association, and Joyce Thabet was appointed Lebanese deputy prosecutor for the international tribunal pursuing the Hariri murder. There was also the uneasy duality of Jibran Tuwayni's second wife and daughter at the head of *al-Nahar*, the family's newspaper, after Jibran's assassination in December 2005.

Women have enriched Lebanese literature since the 1960s. Writers such as Hanan al-Shaykh (Shia) and Emily Nasrallah (Christian) explored the impact of Lebanon's 1975–1990 war period on women and the whole tormented society. They touched on themes of the breakdown of paternal domination, the implosion of families, and the ambiguities of escape into the Lebanese Diaspora. For example, in Emily Nasrallah's novel *Flight Against Time*, the elderly Radwan Abu Yusef, visiting his children in Canada in late 1975, rejects the opportunity to sit out Lebanon's war abroad.

> Which was better: remain in one's homeland and be subjected to all kinds of humiliation . . . or emigrate to another country where one suffers from the cold and the constant yearning for one's homeland.[33]

Radwan returned to his village in Wadi al-Taym only to be murdered.

Like gender, the Diaspora is a critical dimension, but not easy to incorporate in a history of Lebanon. Overseas Lebanese remain the most numerous of any Arab country. The financial remittances to families inside Lebanon, the foreign cultural influences, and the return migration have had substantial effects on Lebanon. However, in contrast to the Christian emigration to the Americas and Australia from the late 1880s onward, Muslims did not migrate on a large scale until the late twentieth century. There were exceptions—Shia fled agricultural depression in southern Lebanon and set up as small traders in West Africa, a few arriving in the Ivory Coast before 1900, while Druze reached South Australia. In the 1950s, Shia began returning with their profits, given that Lebanese could not integrate into West African societies.[34] Through the first half century of modern Lebanon, from 1920 to the 1970s, and particularly after the 1950s, returning migrants and remittance income buttressed the middle class and supplied "social security" to many poorer Christian and Shia Lebanese.

Rising from peddling and poverty, Lebanon's children prospered abroad, some joining the commercial elite in Anglo and Latin America. Inter-marriage makes estimates problematic, but the Diaspora probably exceeded six million by the 1970s, with Brazilian Lebanese approaching Lebanon's home population. While the Christian population may have been slipping within Lebanon, the overseas Christian majority represented the largest Arab presence in the West. The wealth, political influence, and continued connection of the Diaspora with the homeland made it an important factor in modern Lebanon's affairs.

A new wave of Lebanese emigration accompanied the warfare starting in 1975. Perhaps 800,000 departed during wartime up to 1990, and the outflow continued as skilled and professional people experienced discouraging conditions under Syrian hegemony. Although Christians were initially the largest element, a Sunni and Shia wave soon joined them. The Sunni bourgeois of Beirut headed for Europe and the Americas from the late 1970s, and hostilities in Tripoli in the 1980s propelled many other Sunnis to Australia. The Shia already had footholds in West Africa and North America; their new migration encompassed Latin America and Australia. Particularly for Maronites and Shia, money flowed from the Diaspora into militia war chests. After 1990, the principal beneficiary was the Shia Hezbollah, which pulled in contributions from Shia across the world. It also used its community to generate funds by smuggling and other illicit activities, such as contraband trade in the tristate border area of Argentina, Paraguay, and Brazil.[35]

Within the Arab world and the eastern Mediterranean, after chaos overtook Beirut, expatriate Lebanese of all communities assisted the rise of new commercial centers. This benefited Greek Cyprus and the oil principalities of the Persian Gulf. One question is whether a return of Lebanese from near and far, if the Levant can ever be stabilized, might bring a real renaissance of Beirut that would build on the cosmopolitan qualities of this fractured yet globalized people. Much also depends on the transcending of sectarian proclivities.

Tracing the history of the people of Mount Lebanon and its surrounds from the Roman twilight to the twenty-first century, the chapters of this book form a chronological progression, each with a key theme for its period.

The three chapters of Part I present the evolution of the communities, up to the creation of a political entity in late Ottoman Mount Lebanon. Chapter 1, "Emerging Communities," examines the establishment of Orthodox, Jacobite, and Maronite Christians, Sunni and Shia Muslims, and Druze and Alawites, with consolidation of the mountain sects in the crusader period. Chapter 2, "Druze Ascent," explores the role of the Druze chiefs who dominated central Mount Lebanon under renewed Sunni Islamic supremacy from the 1290s to the early 1600s, when Fakhr al-Din Ma'n reopened Mount Lebanon to Europe. Chapter 3, "Mountain Lords," considers the transition from Ottoman-patronized Druze and Shia lordships in the seventeenth century to Maronite Catholic supremacy in Mount Lebanon after 1800.

The three chapters of Part II present the evolution of the modern country of Lebanon out of mid-nineteenth century attempts to dampen Druze/Maronite tension. Chapter 4, "Emerging Lebanon," traces the production of the pluralist but Maronite-inspired modern state through two stages between 1842 and 1942: the Ottoman special province of Mount Lebanon and the Greater Lebanon of the French mandate. Chapter 5, "Independent Lebanon," portrays the vibrant but divided state and society that escaped France in 1943 to become overwhelmed in the 1970s by Middle Eastern turbulence. Chapter 6, "Broken Lebanon," records multiple stresses since 1975: the collapse and flawed resuscitation of the state amid various wars, the impact of Syrian Ba'thist hegemony, and the kaleidoscopic interrelations of the Lebanese.

Lebanon's history combines the story of the sectarian communities with that of the modern country. The two parts of this book express two aspects of Lebanon's past, the former reaching back to Roman and early Islamic times and the latter spanning the past two centuries. In a small but highly compartmentalized mountain territory, there is inevitable tension between a multiplicity of identities and building a common home.

PART ONE

FOUNDATIONS

1

Emerging Communities, 600–1291

Progenitors of Lebanon's mountain communities occasionally feature in early medieval sources. In June 659, Mu'awiya bin Abi Sufyan, Muslim governor of Syria and soon to become the first Umayyad caliph, summoned followers of "the House of Lord Maron" to debate in his presence Christian doctrine with their Jacobite opponents. The reference, from a Syriac chronicle written in about 664, is the first documentary trace of Maronite monks.[1] The Maronites apparently had the better argument; the chronicle relates: "When the Jacobites were defeated, Mu'awiya ordered them to pay 20,000 denarii and commanded them to be silent."[2]

In December 758, an Islamic judge in Ma'arrat al-Nu'man recorded:

> The emir Mundhir and his brother Arslan came to me and asked me to make a written record of the deaths of their fathers on parchment so that they could keep it safe from the ravages of events . . . because they had determined to go forth [to live] in the mountains of Beirut on the orders of the commander of the faithful [the Abbasid caliph] Mansur.[3]

This opens the chronicle of the Arslan family, a branch of the Arab Tanukh clan who settled in Mount Lebanon to help hold the coast for the caliphate against the Byzantines, and who 250 years later spearheaded the establishment of the Druze sect in the hills above Beirut.

In 842, economic distress drove the peasants of Jabal Amil, the hills of modern southern Lebanon inhabited from the early days of Islam by partisans of the Caliph Ali and the Shia Imams, to insurrection against Abbasid authority. The Arab historian al-Ya'qubi wrote in the 870s:

> A man in Palestine called Tamim al-Lakhmi, known as Abi Harb and also named al-Mubarqa'a, incited the Lakhm, Judham, Amila, and Balqin tribes to rebellion. . . . [The Abbasid caliph] al-Wathiq dispatched

Rija bin Ayyub al-Hadariy . . . who came to Palestine and overthrew
Tamim al-Lakhmi and took him prisoner.[4]

The incident gives rare exposure to the Shia-minded population on the fringes of
Mount Lebanon a century before Twelver Shi'ism fully crystallized in Iraq.

Over half a millennium—from the stand-off of Christian orthodoxy and
Monophysite dissent in Mount Lebanon in the late sixth century through "Maronite" adoption of a Christian compromise and the Islamic conquest in the seventh century to appearance of the Twelver Shia and Druze in the tenth and
eleventh centuries—the area of Lebanon acquired most of its modern communal patchwork. Under the Arab Muslim caliphate from about 640, Mount
Lebanon also became a maritime frontier in the caliphate's holy war against Byzantium, but otherwise was peripheral in a new empire oriented inland and
toward the east. The coastal towns only rebounded with the takeover of much of
the Levant in the 980s by the Isma'ili Shia Fatimids, based in Egypt, who revived
Mediterranean trade in cooperation with the Byzantines. Tripoli and Tyre flourished under the Fatimids, and together with the mild climate of the Medieval
Warm Period, this favored population increases in Mount Lebanon, including
Maronite growth inland from Tripoli and probable immigration of Shia from the
Biqa and Alawites from the north.

This chapter identifies a mix of Christians, Sunni Muslims, Shia Muslims, and
Shia-derived groups in and around Mount Lebanon through the early Islamic
centuries. Such a mix characterized the whole Levant at that time given it was
about three centuries before Christians became an overall minority. The pecu-
liarity of Mount Lebanon was the longer-term endurance of a collection of rural
sectarian heartlands.

Notwithstanding the geopolitical shock, creation of the Frankish principalities on the Levant coast from 1099 and their conflict and coexistence with the
Muslim interior facilitated consolidation of the mountain communities and
long-distance trade. The Egyptian Mamluks reimposed Islamic rule in the late
thirteenth century, in the process disciplining the mountaineers and disrupting
commerce, but they soon found it expedient to tolerate the former and patronize
the latter.

Only fragmentary contemporary references exist for the medieval Mount
Lebanon of the seventh and eighth centuries. Thereafter, Abbasid Iraq provided
a flood of Arabic chronicles, but these gave only modest attention to Mount Lebanon and were a century or more removed from developments following the
Islamic conquest. The situation changed in crusader times. Whatever else the
Franks did, they certainly elevated the Levant in the Muslim mind. An array of
contemporary Arabic chroniclers and Franks, such as the famed William of Tyre,
closely followed developments along the Levant coast. The main problem was

that while Mount Lebanon was no longer peripheral, its native inhabitants still were; most chronicles offer only glimpses of them.

No comprehensive survey of medieval Mount Lebanon and its vicinity exists in English. This chapter synthesizes the treatments in the modern Arabic literature, incorporating additional material from the Arabic, Syriac, and Byzantine chronicles, in order to flesh out the origins and entrenchment of the Lebanese communities and the factors that influenced this evolution.[5] The latter involved intrusion of a succession of external authorities—prominently the Umayyads, Abbasids, Byzantines, Fatimids, and Franks—and accompanying shifts in strategic and commercial circumstances. Developments depended on events that could have had different timing or not happened at all. For example, the Islamic conquest triggered the whole evolution, the Druze would not exist without Fatimid extension north of Palestine, and Maronite and Shia consolidation owed much to the crusaders. Conversely, Sunni Muslim recovery was contingent on recession of the Shia and crusader ascendancies of the tenth to twelfth centuries.

The Twilight of Roman Phoenicia

Despite the financial strain of Emperor Justinian's campaigns to reconquer the western Mediterranean between 533 and 554 and the substantial population losses in the unprecedented bubonic plague of 542, the East Roman empire remained viable in the late sixth century. Trade continued and wars could still be fought, but urban and commercial life lost some vigor, and there was diminishing margin for strategic errors.[6]

In 600, Mount Lebanon and its surrounds comprised the province of Phoenice Maritima, created in the administrative reform of Emperor Theodosius II in the early fifth century. Phoenice Maritima looked back to ancient Phoenicia and approximated the territory of modern Lebanon more closely than any other political division up to 1920, though of course without modern boundary precision. It included much of the Biqa and the Anti-Lebanon massif, but not Baalbek (Heliopolis). To the south it extended into the Galilee, and to the north it incorporated Baniyas on the Syrian coast.

Phoenice Maritima centered on the old Phoenician ports of Tyre, Sidon, Byblos (Jubayl), and Tripoli, as well as Beirut, in antiquity a lesser town reinvented in 14 BCE. as the Roman veterans' colony of Berytus, the only Latin settlement in the Roman Levant. Tyre was the main seat of the governor and metropolis of a Christian ecclesiastical province. Beirut acquired special prominence because of its renowned law school, the source for much of Emperor Justinian's codification of Roman law. Whatever the general picture in the eastern Mediterranean, all of these towns were at least partially ruined in the late sixth century, and their populations were substantially depleted. Along the coast, the catastrophic earthquake of 551, about 7.5 on today's Richter scale, compounded the impact of plague.[7] A tsunami accompanied the earthquake, destroying Beirut and its law school. The Byzantine historian Theophanes, using contemporary sources, observed: "The following cities suffered: Tyre, Sidon, Berytos, Tripolis, and Byblos, and a great many people perished therein."[8]

In cultural terms, the coastal population of Phoenice Maritima in the early 600s was Christianized and partly Hellenized, with the Aramaic and Greek languages in roughly equal use. As a belief system, the Orthodox Christianity laid down at the church council of Chalcedon in 451 predominated. Chalcedon defined Christ as having separate and equal divine and human natures. Even on the coast, however, the perspective that Christ had only one nature, in which the divine subsumed the human, had many adherents. This was the Monophysite (single nature) doctrine, declared a heresy at Chalcedon. After 542, the renegade bishop of Edessa, Jacob Baradaeus, propagated the Monophysite outlook across the Levant. The bishop's name stuck to the Monophysite "Jacobite" community, which became the majority in the Levant by the early seventh century. Jacobites paralleled the Monophysite Copts of Egypt.

Little information exists regarding the interior of Phoenice Maritima around 600. Rural people overwhelmingly spoke Aramaic, with Greek and Arabic influences, and seem to have favored Monophysite Christianity. The Iturean Arabs of Mount Lebanon had rebelled against Roman authority six centuries earlier, causing the Romans to establish military veteran colonies at Beirut and Baalbek. The highlands behind Beirut, Byblos, and Tripoli featured orchards, grain cropping, and pagan sanctuaries. The latter were presumably disused, though Baalbek had a pagan majority even after 550.[9] The cedar, pine, and juniper forest of northern Mount Lebanon remained imperial reserve, which applied to the timber rather than the land.[10]

Phoenice Maritima away from the coast was sparsely populated, facilitating Bedouin infiltration from the desert. Mount Lebanon has (and had) the most reliable rainfall in the Levant, while its blocking effect on rain-bearing winds from the Mediterranean means an abrupt transition to semi-arid conditions inland. Mount Lebanon and the well-watered hills behind Tyre were both desirable and accessible to Arab tribes. From 502 until 580, the Monophysite Christian Ghassanid confederation, a Roman ally, dominated the steppe beyond Damascus and the Anti-Lebanon. Ghassanids settled in Mount Lebanon; the present-day Orthodox Atiyah family of Baynu in the Akkar, for example, sources its family tree with "Ghassan." In the 580s, the Ghassanid/Roman alliance dissolved in internecine violence. The Ghassanids were weakened and embittered, while Rome lost its eyes and ears in the desert. Thereafter, nothing constrained Arab clans moving from the Hawran south of Damascus into the Galilee and southern Lebanese hills. One such clan was the Amila who, according to the great tenth-century Muslim chronicler al-Tabari, were an affiliate of the Ghassanids who later supplied troops for the Emperor Heraclius.[11] The Amila became the progenitor of Shia Islam in Lebanon.

For Phoenice Maritima, the beginning of the end came in 613, when the Sassanid Persians seized the Roman Levant in the course of the last and most devastating Roman-Persian war. The Persian occupation lasted fifteen years, until Heraclius smashed the Persian army in a thrust from Anatolia into Iraq in 628. Persian rule ended Mediterranean commerce for the ports of Phoenice Maritima, and living standards in the Levant descended to subsistence levels. The Persians initially persecuted the Orthodox Christian hierarchy as an enemy institution, but the occupation was no comfort to the Monophysites. Many Greek-speaking inhabitants of the Lebanese coast presumably left for unoccupied Roman territory, and when Rome returned in 628, the ports were barely functioning. Inland, one can surmise Arab movement into the Biqa Valley and parts of Mount Lebanon. Otherwise, the ninth century Arab historian al-Baladhuri records a significant Persian settler presence in Baalbek at the time of the Islamic conquest soon after.[12]

Persian occupation highlighted the need to find a doctrinal compromise between Orthodox Christianity and the Jacobite Monophysites, for the cohesion of the Roman Levant. On his triumphal visit to Jerusalem and the Levant provinces in 630, Heraclius promoted the concept of two natures but a single will in Christ. The monks of the monastery of Maron, north of Mount Lebanon in the Orontes Valley near modern Hama, adopted the compromise, bringing with them a local following. The monks were Monophysite, previously hounded by the authorities.[13] Their adherence to the new Monothelite doctrine put them on the right side of the emperor. These monks and their monastery were the origin of the Maronite community, distinguished by its association with the Monothelite compromise of Heraclius.[14] Apart from the monks of Maron, the new doctrine elicited only grudging acquiescence; both Orthodox and Jacobites increasingly scorned it.

The attempt at a Christian accommodation proved superfluous. Within six years, the Levant faced the powerful challenge of the new religion of Islam surging out of Arabia. Given the pathetic condition of the local provinces in the 630s, the Roman military orientation toward Persia, and the lack of defense or intelligence toward the southeast, the Roman Levant was highly vulnerable. Arabic sources record the soaring morale, energy, and initiative of the Muslim Arab armies.[15] The Muslim impetus also drew on a demographic and commercial upswing in the Arabian Peninsula. In 634–636, Muslim raids overwhelmed Palestine and reached Baalbek and Emessa (Homs). In July 636, two years after a stunning surprise thrust across the desert from Iraq by Khalid Ibn al-Walid, the

Arabs came together above the Yarmouk River south of Damascus, to destroy
the army sent by Heraclius to counter them.

The battle of the Yarmouk sealed the fate of Phoenice Maritima. It fell to the
Muslims virtually without resistance, apart from a Roman holdout in Tripoli
until 644. Monophysite hostility to Orthodox Christianity, whether in Phoenice
Maritima or other Levant provinces, was not a factor in the Roman collapse.
Some Jacobites opposed the Muslims, some welcomed them—it made no difference. Considering the speed of the Arab advance across Iraq and the Iranian
plateau between 633 and 652, which annihilated Sassanid Persia, it was astonishing that East Rome survived, grimly hanging on in Anatolia. After 636, developments in Mount Lebanon and its surrounds hinged on the struggle between
the new Arab Muslim caliphate and East Rome—medieval Byzantium—and on
the internal dynamics of the caliphate.

Muslims and Christians in Mount Lebanon, 636–940

Three centuries of domination of the Middle East by the Arab Muslim caliphate,
ending with Muslim fragmentation and the Iranian Buyid capture of Abbasid
Baghdad, saw Muslim and Maronite establishment in Mount Lebanon. On the
coast, the ports became mainly Sunni Muslim and bulwarks of the Umayyad and
Abbasid states against Byzantine sea power. Meanwhile, Arabs already living in
the southern Lebanese hills included clans whose leaders disapproved of
Umayyad and Abbasid rule and instead favored the Islamic leadership of the
family of the Prophet Muhammad through his son-in-law the Caliph Ali. The
principal political divide in Islam, which became the Sunni/Shia divide, appeared
early in Mount Lebanon. Simultaneously, from the mid-seventh century through
the eighth century, Christian partisans of the monastery of Maron—the first
Maronites—moved south from the Orontes Valley into the heights inland from
Tripoli. In the tenth century, Maronites were probably the majority of the predominantly Christian population of the Tripoli and Jubayl hills, with Shia Muslim
penetration of the Kisrawan district north of Beirut.

For the Caliphs Umar and Uthman, who presided over Muslim dispositions
in the Levant up to 656 through Uthman's lieutenant Mu'awiya bin Abi Sufyan,
the ports had to be secured. Al-Baladhuri refers to expulsion of residents from
Sidon, Beirut, and Byblos, and to Tyre as "having fallen into ruins."[16] He notes
resettlement of these towns up to the 660s with Arab Muslim troops, Persians
from Baalbek and Homs, who were enemies of the Romans and converts to
Islam, and others from as far away as Basra and Kufa in Iraq.[17] Such efforts indicate that there was only a modest movement of Arab tribes into Lebanon with
the conquest.[18] In the case of Tripoli after its fall in 644, Mu'awiya brought in

Jewish settlers, which indicates both the degree of depopulation and Muslim concern to have functioning cities quickly. Al-Baladhuri observes that "many Greeks," meaning Orthodox Christians, stayed, perhaps a factor in a brief Byzantine seizure of Tripoli in the days of the Caliph Abd al-Malik.[19] The caliph thereafter awarded one-fifth of the town to loyal Persians.[20]

Developments away from the coast through the mid- and late seventh century are largely conjecture. Southern Lebanese tradition, according to the respected early twentieth-century local historian Muhammad Jabir Al Safa, holds that Arabs in the hills behind Tyre gave their loyalty to the "shi'ah" (faction) of the Caliph Ali from the 650s on.[21] The most notable of these proto-Shia were the Arabian Amila tribe.[22] The Amila came before the conquest, and their name remains applied to the hills south of the Litani River—Jabal Amil. In the Biqa, one can surmise that the mixed population of Arabs, "Greeks," and Persians identified by al-Baladhuri for the 630s persisted.[23]

As for Maronite movement to Mount Lebanon, al-Mas'udi's tenth-century report of the destruction of the monastery of Maron and dispersal of its residents from the Orontes likely relates to the 656–661 Arab civil war.[24] It may also refer to inter-Arab fighting in the 680s. As already observed, "Maronites" first appear in the contemporary Syriac chronicle that has Mu'awiya sponsoring the 659 debate in Damascus between the monks of Maron and their Jacobite opponents.[25] It seems logical to suppose that Mu'awiya's interest meant that the House of Maron had wide influence, including among "Greeks" in Mount Lebanon, not far from the new Muslim capital. It should be remembered that up to 680, the Monothelite position was Orthodox Chalcedonian doctrine, which probably assisted "Maronite" co-opting of Orthodox Christians through the mid-seventh century.

Maronite history in its early decades is controversial not just because of the paucity of sources, but also because of an extraordinary mythology generated by the fifteenth-century Maronite writer Jibra'il Ibn al-Qila'i and the seventeenth-century patriarch Istifan Duwayhi.[26] According to Ibn al-Qila'i and Duwayhi, the Maronites derive from an ascetic fifth-century monk named Marun, have never wavered from Orthodox belief, had early connections with Rome, and began an unbroken line of patriarchs of Antioch with John Maron of the monastery of Maron in the late seventh century. Ibn al-Qila'i even has the pope invest John Maron in Rome. Duwayhi conflates the Maronites with the Mardaites, Christian confederates of the Byzantines who attacked the caliphate between 677 and 690 from the coastal hills between the Amanus Range of Cilicia and Mount Lebanon. These same Maronites/Mardaites then defeated a Byzantine army allegedly sent to northern Lebanon in 694 to capture a renegade John Maron.

While mythology has been important since the fifteenth century in constructing Maronite identity, modern historians dismiss it in terms of provable fact. First, there is scant evidence of any line of Maronite patriarchs before the Crusades, the claimed early link with the West cannot be substantiated, and the monastery of Maron was demonstrably Monothelite with Jacobite antecedents.[27] Second, the notion of a Byzantine army attacking a Byzantine client inside Arab territory commanded in 694 by the redoubtable Caliph Abd al-Malik is absurd.[28] Neither the Byzantine historian Theophanes nor any other medieval sources mention such an event.

What, then, was the most plausible reality? Theophanes, writing in Constantinople around 800 and using Syriac sources, provides the earliest surviving reference to the Mardaites. He has them "entering the Lebanon range" in 677 while capturing hill country from the Amanus south to Palestine. He observes: "Many slaves, captives, and natives took refuge with them, so that in a short time they grew to many thousands."[29] The implication is that they came from outside the Levant and hence cannot be conflated with the Maronites. The Syriac author Dionysius of Tel Mahri, writing slightly after Theophanes and possibly using the same source(s), identifies the Mardaites as "certain Romans [Byzantines]" who in 677 "launched an invasion of Mount Lebanon from the sea, landing on the coasts of Tyre and Sidon." Again, "they controlled the heights from Galilee to the Black Mountain (the Amanus), sallying out all the time into Arab territory to plunder and destroy."[30]

It seems that the initial Mardaites were Byzantine troops, perhaps supplemented by Christian tribesmen from Cilicia, dispatched by the Byzantine authorities to exploit defeats of the Arabs in Anatolia in 677. This would correlate with the interpretation that the name Mridoye (Mardaites) may represent the Syriac rumoye, or "soldiers."[31] "Natives" of Mount Lebanon, meaning local Christians, flocked to join the Mardaites. Many of these "natives" would have been followers of Monothelite monks from the monastery of Maron. John Maron, mentioned by al-Mas'udi simply as the man from Hama who started the Maronite community, may have moved independently to Mount Lebanon from the Orontes Valley during the Arab civil war between the Caliph Ali and Mu'awiya.[32] Such speculation is as far as we can go in linking Maronites with Mardaites.

Mardaite pressure on the caliphate, particularly toward Damascus from Mount Lebanon, reaped dividends for the Byzantines. According to Theophanes, the Caliph Mu'awiya almost immediately agreed to negotiations for a truce and payment of tribute to the emperor.[33] The upper hand temporarily passed to Byzantium. In 685, the Byzantines launched naval attacks along the Levant coast as far south as Ascalon. The Caliph Abd al-Malik, harassed by Mardaite raids in "the regions of the Lebanon," and facing plague, famine, and the challenge of the anti-caliph Ibn Zubayr, sought peace, renewed the tribute, and asked that "the emperor should remove the host of the Mardaites from the Lebanon."[34] Justinian II, perhaps anticipating future imperial overreach, consented.

In the late 680s, the Byzantines evacuated 12,000 Mardaites with families, principally from Mount Lebanon, acknowledging Arab primacy in the Levant. Theophanes was not impressed, condemning Justinian for "injuring the Roman state."[35]

Nonetheless, many Mardaites remained, probably with Byzantine sanction. Al-Baladhuri observes that Abd al-Malik had to make further terms with Justinian ("the Greek tyrant") around 689–690 after "certain Greek [Byzantine] horsemen went forth to Mt. al-Lukam [the Amanus] under a Greek leader and started for the Lebanon, after having been joined by a large body of al-Jarajimah [inhabitants of a town in the Amanus], Nabateans, and runaway slaves once possessed by the Muslims."[36] The Byzantines evidently still had a friendly outpost in Mount Lebanon. After 690, as Abd al-Malik consolidated his grip on the caliphate, Justinian withdrew more Mardaites from Mount Lebanon to assist the Anatolian defenses. A residual group must have persisted as military leaders among the Christian population, because the family record of the Arslans refers to fights against the "Marada" (Mardaites) through the eighth and ninth centuries, up to 915.[37] In any event, they ceased to be a significant issue between the empire and caliphate.

As for Maronites, the Orthodox reassertion of two natures and wills in Christ at the sixth church council in Constantinople in 680–681 heralded an end to the period in which followers of the House of Maron could also be Orthodox Christians. The sixth council formally declared Monothelites heretics. However, it took decades for the decision to filter into caliphal territory, so it had no negative impact on the relations of local Christians with the Mardaites. There were strong incentives even for Jacobites to assist the Mardaites: the opportunity for plunder, discord among the Arabs, and the brief prospect of East Roman resurgence. Citing Dionysius of Tel Mahri, Moosa suggests that the council edict did not affect the Levant until the 720s.[38] News of it came from Anatolia with war captives in 727, and among Orthodox Christians, only the House of Maron rejected it.[39]

After about 720, three Christian orientations coexisted in Mount Lebanon. First, there was the Orthodox community of the coast, particularly around Tripoli, which adjusted to the sixth council. Second, Monothelites on the slopes of northern Mount Lebanon went their own way as the incipient Maronite community. Third, Jacobite Monophysites persevered alongside the Maronites. Mardaites remaining in Mount Lebanon after Byzantine disengagement in the 690s would have integrated with native mountaineers when the orthodoxy of Maronites was not yet an issue.

Through the early eighth century, the Umayyad regime continued to be tolerant of Christians, its principal tax base, and was relaxed about Mount Lebanon after neutralization of the Mardaites. Arabic quickly became the predominant language of Christians as well as Muslims, with brief persistence of Greek in administration and longer-term survival of Syriac, the written form of Aramaic, for Maronites and Jacobites. In strategic terms, the caliphate had the initiative from the 690s to about 740, before and after the abortive Arab siege of Constantinople in 717–718.

From the establishment of Arab rule in the 640s, Mu'awiya organized the Levant into four military districts (*ajnad* [sing. *jund*]), which became five after division of the unwieldy *jund* of Homs in 680.[40] These lasted until the tenth century and bore no relation to the Roman provinces, though they may have reflected Roman military arrangements.[41] Mu'awiya split Roman Phoenice Maritima between the new districts of al-Urdun (Jordan) and Dimashq (Damascus), both extending from the coast to the desert. Al-Urdun, which had its center at Tiberias, included Jabal Amil and Tyre, which inaugurated a persistent administrative separation of modern Shia southern Lebanon from Mount Lebanon. Almost all of the rest of modern Lebanon came under Damascus, with military authority exercised from Baalbek. The far northern foothills of Mount Lebanon—the Akkar—were assigned to Homs.

Umayyad strategic interest in the vicinity of Mount Lebanon remained focused on the ports. By 700, these were entrenched garrison towns purposed for defense against Byzantine coastal raids and for participation in naval offensives against Byzantium. They represented the naval equivalent of the citadels of the Arab/Byzantine land frontier in the Taurus Mountains. Tripoli weathered a Byzantine assault in 708, and around the same time, Tyre replaced Acre as the chief military supply and shipbuilding center of the Levant coast.[42] The male Muslim population of the ports tended to be zealous and ascetic, proud of the designation *murabitun* (front-line troops). Sarafand, north of Tyre, briefly hosted Abu Dhar al-Ghafari, a companion of the Prophet Muhammad and prominent in the party of Ali bin Abi Talib, another marker of the early Shia predisposition of many Muslims in that area. [43]

Around 710, the Caliph al-Walid established an impressive palace and market complex at Anjar in the Biqa (figure 1.1). The two main streets accommodated several hundred shops. Use of the facility, however, depended on nearby Damascus remaining the Islamic political center; it was abandoned when that situation changed under the Abbasids only four decades later. The complex may have been partially destroyed by the Caliph Marwan II in 744.[44]

Geopolitical shifts affected Mount Lebanon between 740 and 760. The Umayyad regime weakened with a declining tax base in the Levant and internal warfare in 743–744 with the takeover of the caliphate by Marwan II. He defeated his Umayyad cousins in a battle near Anjar and shifted the capital from Damascus to Harran in the Jazira.[45] Marwan in turn fell victim to the Abbasid revolution in 749, and Iraq replaced the Levant as center of the caliphate. As the Muslim proportion of the population in the Levant and Iraq increased, the Abbasid caliphs depended less on Christians. They enforced religious restrictions through the 750s.[46] Concurrent with dynastic change in the caliphate, the formidable Emperor

Figure 1.1 Ruins of Umayyad palace and market, Anjar. Cyril Mango.

Constantine V made the first deep Byzantine thrusts across the land frontier in half a century from 742, sacking the major Arab garrison town of Malatya in 751.

A truce with Byzantium in 757 enabled the Caliph Mansur to take stock of the situation in the eastern Mediterranean. The distance from Abbasid Iraq, compared with Umayyad Damascus, and the heightened danger of Byzantine aggression likely made Mansur nervous about Mount Lebanon, with its coastal exposure and poorly supervised Christian population. In 758, he commissioned two leaders of the Tanukh clan of northern Syria, the brothers Mundhir and Arslan, to take charge of the hills above Beirut.[47] On the way to Lebanon, the Tanukh emirs asked a religious sheikh to record their family affairs, an exercise repeated by their descendants every few decades and collated as *al-Sijill al-Arslani* (the Arslan record). Tanukhs led by the brothers settled in Wadi al-Taym on the slopes of Mount Hermon, as well as in the designated area of the Gharb, the Shuf, and the Matn.[48] Near the coast, the caliph identified the line between Muslim and Christian settlements and gave Beirut buttressing against the Byzantines. The Tanukhs already had a fine record in Islamic military history, though there were still Christian Tanukhs in northern Syria.

Only a year later, in 759–760, the Abbasids faced a severe test in northern Mount Lebanon. Tax impositions fueled a Christian rebellion in the Biqa and the neighboring Munaytara district of Mount Lebanon, led by a Munaytara agitator named Theodore (Baydar in Arabic).[49] The Byzantines simultaneously attacked Tripoli. Given that Theodore fled to the Byzantine landing force, the naval raid was probably synchronized. Were the Maronites involved?[50] The background of tax grievances and sharper Abbasid attitudes toward Christians meant that

Orthodox, Maronites, and Jacobites probably came together. The Orthodox alone could not have sustained the uprising. Ibrahim Beydoun notes that there is no evidence of Maronite problems with the caliphate,[51] but there is also no evidence of estrangement from the Byzantines. Indeed, there may not yet have been a proper distinction of Maronites in Mount Lebanon. Whatever the case, the Abbasid commanders in Baalbek and Damascus responded vigorously, crushing the rebels with heavy casualties. The Abbasid regime deported many Christians from the Munaytara and the vicinity of the Beirut-Damascus road, which provided more space for the Tanukhs. Some were later permitted to return, after the great Muslim legal scholar of Beirut al-Awza'i censured the regime for injustice.[52]

By 800, a long-term sectarian geography was crystallizing (see figure 1.2). Mount Lebanon north of the Beirut River retained a Christian majority, with the new Maronite community comprising a large element. The ports of Sidon, Beirut, and Tripoli had Sunni Muslim populations, with Christian and Jewish minorities. Mount Lebanon between Beirut and Sidon as well as Wadi al-Taym alongside Mount Hermon represented the domain of incoming Tanukh settlers, at this time upholders of Sunni Islamic authority. The Biqa became a patchwork of Christians and Muslims, both Sunnis and partisans of Ali, with Baalbek continuing its Roman function as a significant military base. In the coastal hills south of Sidon, the partisans of Ali were the majority, and proto-Shia presumably were important in Tyre. Proto-Shia also had a strong presence in northern Palestine and Jordan, as later confirmed by the Arab geographer al-Muqaddasi.[53]

The old Phoenician ports rebounded from their late Roman degradation, but from the seventh century, they were eclipsed by Damascus and Baghdad in a continental caliphate. The Mediterranean was a war front. Nonetheless, the Islamic fervor of the ports as "breakout points" (thughur [sing. thaghr]) had intellectual spillover, illustrated in the career of Abd al-Rahman al-Awza'i (707–774).[54] This renowned interpreter of Islamic law was born in the Biqa to Arab immigrants. He began his training at Kark in the Biqa, traveled to Basra and Kufa in Iraq for further study, and settled in Beirut.[55] Al-Awza'i gave 70,000 religious rulings, and founded a school that lasted two centuries. In the mid-eighth century, he had moral sway in the Levant exceeding that of the Abbasid state, and the Caliph Mansur made sure to consult with him on a visit to Beirut.[56] He was buried near Beirut in an area that still bears his name. Al-Tabari records that twelve years after his death, in 786, when in one night the Caliph Musa al-Hadi died, the Caliph Harun al-Rashid succeeded him, and the Caliph al-Ma'mun was born, al-Hadi's mother al-Khayzuran reported that al-Awza'i had predicted the conjunction to her.[57] No other native of Mount Lebanon approached such eminence in the early Islamic centuries.

Al-Awza'i aside, the coastal towns and the mountain population both left traces of scholarly activities in the sources. Specialists studied traditions of the prophet (hadith) in Tripoli and Jubayl (Byblos) from the late seventh century,

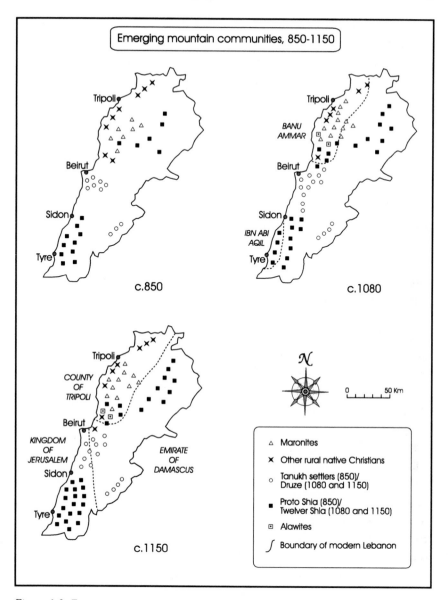

Figure 1.2 Emerging mountain communities, 850–1150.

and a Mu'tazilite group formed around al-Awza'i in Beirut.[58] The Mu'tazilites emphasized reason in religious discourse. A poet from Jabal Amil, Uday bin al-Riqa al-Amili, joined the court of the Umayyad Caliph al-Walid I in Damascus,[59] and an astrologer of Maronite origin, Tawfil bin Tuma al-Rahawiy, appeared in the circle of the Abbasid Caliph al-Mahdi in Baghdad.[60]

Learned Muslim ascetics from the central Islamic lands migrated to Mount Lebanon in Abbasid times and interacted with Christian monks.[61] These included

Ibrahim bin-Adham, reportedly killed in a Byzantine sea raid around 778, Thubar Dhu al-Nun from Upper Egypt (died 859), and Ahmad bin Abi al-Hawari al-Ghatfani from Kufa in Iraq (died 860). The ascetics frequented Jubayl, Beirut, and Tyre as well as the hills, and may have been fleeing religious disputes in the main Islamic centers.

For scientific endeavor, one personality from the environs of Mount Lebanon stands out. Qusta Ibn Luqa (820–913), an Orthodox Christian from Baalbek, translated Greek texts for various court patrons in Baghdad in the mid-ninth century.[62] He contributed about sixty original works in medicine, philosophy, mathematics, and astronomy; in medicine he ranked as one of the top scholars of Abbasid times. His treatise on the causes and treatment of sleeplessness includes entertaining comments on "bodily humours" and the effects of overeating.[63]

Otherwise, between the late eighth and mid-tenth centuries, the region of modern Lebanon hardly registers in the historical record. Intermittent disturbances and steady entrenchment of Shia sympathies indicated discontent with marginalization of the Levant under the Abbasids. There were also Byzantine raids and scrapping between the Tanukhs and the Christians. In the late 770s, according to the nineteenth-century Maronite historian Tannus al-Shidyaq, relying on unspecified family sources, the Tanukhs defeated Christians, still termed "Marada," at Nahr al-Mawt and Antelias.[64] Nahr al-Mawt (River of Death) acquired its name from the high number of casualties. In 791 at Sinn al-Fil, the Tanukhs again pushed back Christians. In 801, a Byzantine landing party kidnapped a Tanukh emir near Beirut.[65] In 813, during the fighting for the caliphate between Harun al-Rashid's sons al-Amin and al-Ma'mun, an Umayyad pretender briefly seized Sidon and the southern Biqa. Al-Shidyaq claims that around 820, more Tanukh settlers came from northern Syria.[66]

In 842, in a parallel to the 759 Christian uprising, Shia-minded peasants in the Upper Jordan and Jabal Amil rebelled under a local tribal chief, Mubarqa'a.[67] The Abbasid authorities waited until the harvest—when Mubarqa'a lost much of his following—and repressed the rebels.[68] In 845, the *Sijill al-Arslani* registers further Tanukh success against the Christians. The Christian force included fighters from *ahl al-Asiya* (the people of the *Asiya*, an old name for the Kisrawan hills north of Beirut).[69] Apart from the Munaytara rebellion, this is the only mention in the sources of Kisrawan Christians between the Islamic conquest and the crusader arrival. These people clearly had some organizational coherence, presumably under village headmen, and were probably mostly Maronite by the late ninth century.

The repetition of Christian insurrections in Mount Lebanon through the eighth and ninth centuries may reflect external inspiration. It is worth noting that the 759, 791, and 845 episodes all followed strong Byzantine military performance on the Anatolian land frontier.

After 860, when the Abbasid caliphs fell under the sway of Turkish slave soldiers in their new Iraqi capital of Samarra, Mount Lebanon slipped out of Abbasid
command, apart from a brief revival in the early tenth century. First, the governor
of the *junds* of Urdun and Filistin, Ibn Shaykh, repudiated the Caliph Mu'tazz in
866.[70] He controlled southern Lebanon until the governors of Egypt and Damascus, with the assistance of the Mount Lebanon Tanukhs, subdued him in the early
870s. He was compelled to leave Tyre for Armenia in about 873. Thereafter, the
Levant came under Ahmad Ibn Tulun, a Turkish warlord whom the Abbasid
regime commissioned to govern Egypt. The Tulunids failed to remit taxes and ran
an independent principality, while the Caliph al-Mu'tamid made the loyal Tanukh
emir Na'aman governor of Beirut.

In 902–903, the Qaramita (Carmathians), fierce Ismai'li Shia who scorned
Islamic authority, led Bedouin tribesmen into central Syria from Salimiya, on
the edge of the Syrian Desert. They overran the Homs area and the Biqa,
where Muslims resented the Abbasids and Tulunids. They seized Baalbek but
failed to take Damascus.[71] This began a long Shia assertion and, more immediately, triggered an Abbasid expedition to curb the Qaramita and displace the
Tulunids. The Abbasid restoration after 904 marked the peak of Tanukh power
in Mount Lebanon, with the son of the long-lived Emir Na'aman marrying the
daughter of an Abbasid prince in 924.[72] It also coincided with the colorful
career of Leo of Tripoli, a renegade Byzantine sailor and convert to Islam who
coordinated Abbasid naval activity out of Tripoli.[73] In 904, Leo commanded a
fleet that sacked Thessalonica, Byzantium's second city. Leo's exploits puffed
up Abbasid prestige, until the Byzantines defeated and killed him in the
Aegean in 923.

A new provincial coterie in Cairo, the Ikhshidids, emulated Tulunid usurpation of caliphal authority in the Levant from the late 930s. However, the major
developments of the mid-tenth century were the Shia ascendancy over the
Abbasids in the central Islamic lands and the onset of a Byzantine challenge in
the northern Levant unprecedented since the Islamic conquest.

Twelver Shia, Isma'ilis, and Druze, 940–1099

Shia Islam took full shape in the early tenth century.[74] Followers of Isma'il, seventh in the line of the prophet Muhammad's family through the Caliph Ali, went
their own way after about 850. Isma'ilis developed an esoteric Islam, interpreting
hidden meanings behind the literal text of the Quran, and looked to leaders who
claimed descent from Isma'il. In the early 900s, their spearheads were the
Qaramita of northeast Arabia and the Syrian steppe, and the Fatimid dynasty
that emerged in North Africa, centered on modern Tunisia.

For most of the partisans of Ali, Isma'il's brother Musa al-Kazim was the real Imam, or rightful leader of Muslims. A crisis came after 874, when the eleventh Imam in the line of descent from Ali through Musa al-Kazim died in Samarra in Iraq. He was said to have a young son, Muhammad, designated as twelfth Imam, who disappeared. The belief gradually crystallized that Muhammad was in a timeless, deathless suspension and would only reappear at the end of the human age to set the world right before the Final Judgment. At first, Muhammad's followers accepted that "ambassadors" were maintaining contact with the Hidden Imam, but by 941 he was assumed to be in full withdrawal. Between 874 and 941, Shia religious scholars in Iraq produced foundational writings and elaborated the legal apparatus of the Imami, or Twelver, Shia. They built on the legal output of the sixth Imam Ja'afar al-Sadiq, father of Isma'il and Musa al-Kazim. Ja'afar's name persists to the present in the Ja'afari legal tradition of the Twelver Shia, which parallels the four great Sunni law schools, differing from them in detail rather than in fundamentals.

Partisans of Ali in southern Lebanon kept in close touch with Imami affairs in Iraq. It is therefore appropriate to refer to these people in Jabal Amil and Tyre as Twelver Shia from about 940. Meanwhile the Qaramita brought Isma'ili influence to the Biqa and the adjoining Wadi al-Taym. Through the mid-tenth century, Isma'ili and Twelver Shia advanced in all the lands around Mount Lebanon—the Arabian peninsula, interior Syria, Iraq, and Egypt. In 930, the Qaramita briefly occupied Mecca; in 944, the Twelver Shia Hamdanids took control of Aleppo and the Jazira; and in 945, the Buyids of northern Iran, Zaydi Shia who became Twelvers, captured Baghdad and subordinated the Abbasid caliph. Finally, in 969 the Isma'ili Fatimids overran Egypt from the west and quickly extended themselves into Palestine. The Sunni-minded went into demographic decline and political eclipse in the central Islamic lands from the early 900s until the Seljuk Turkish conquest of Baghdad in 1055.

Shia ascendancy and Abbasid disintegration coincided with resurgent Byzantine power. The empire profited from expansion in the Balkans and capable management by the Macedonian dynasty. In the late tenth century, Byzantium had the initiative in the eastern Mediterranean, and Roman armies led by Roman emperors came to Mount Lebanon for the first time since Heraclius.

Byzantine dynamism buttressed Shia and Christians around Mount Lebanon. Shia regimes, the Twelver Hamdanids on the frontline and the Isma'ili Fatimids to the rear, defended the Islamic world. Shia prestige therefore rose among Mount Lebanon's Muslims. In the late tenth century, the Tanukhs shifted allegiance from the Abbasids to the Fatimids. Further, the Muslim collapse in the Jazira, then the sight of the Emperors Nicephorus Phocas, John Tzimisces, and Basil II on the Lebanese coast, must have boosted Maronite and Orthodox Christian self-confidence. Problematic security in the Orontes Valley, now a border zone, presumably precipitated new Maronite migration to Mount Lebanon.[75] A Byzantine military treatise of the 990s refers to northern Syria as "emptied of foodstuffs by frequent devastations," another good reason for relocation.[76] There is no evidence that the Byzantines harassed Maronites as heretics. Indeed, Nicephorus Phocas brought Monophysite Armenians from eastern Anatolia to expand Christian settlement in Cilicia.

Hostilities between the Ikhshidids in Cairo and the Qaramita from Arabia for control of Palestine enabled the Tanukh emir Mundhir, with his Abbasid wife, to assert autonomy in Mount Lebanon from the 940s to the 960s. It was perhaps around this time that Twelver Shia became established in the Kisrawan and Jubayl districts north of the Tanukh emirate, moving back and forth across the mountains from the Biqa. The origins of the Shia presence in the Kisrawan in crusader times are shrouded in mystery, with no clues in Arabic chronicles. It is possible that proto-Shia tribespeople were present from the Umayyad period or arrived with the uprooting of Christians after the 759 Munaytara uprising. The reference in the *Sijill al-Arslani* to the Kisrawan in 845 implies a surviving Christian population,[77] though this does not exclude proto-Shia.

In 968–969, events around Mount Lebanon led to the eventual production of a new Lebanese community—the Druze, an offshoot of the Isma'ilis. That winter, Nicephorus Phocas took the Byzantine field army on a great raid down the Orontes Valley and through the Homs gap to Tripoli before returning to the siege of Antioch, which fell in October 969. The twelfth-century historian Ibn al-Athir relates: "The King of the Romans entered Syria [al-Sham], and no-one stood in his way. . . . He came to Tripoli, and pillaged its countryside. He laid siege to the Arqa fortress, seized it, despoiled it, and took those in it as prisoners."[78] In a single year, the Byzantines moved their frontier two hundred kilometers down the Levant coast to the modern boundary between Lebanon and Syria. Mount Lebanon was suddenly near the frontier. In 969, the Twelver Shia Hamdanids in Aleppo accepted defeat, went under Byzantine protection, and paid tribute. In the same year, the Fatimid conversion of Egypt into the base for an Isma'ili Shia great power offered Mount Lebanon's Muslims their only protection from Byzantium.

Confusion followed. The Tanukhs submitted to the Fatimids when the latter briefly took Damascus in 970. Almost immediately, the Turkish adventurer Alptakin usurped Damascus, defying the Fatimids in collusion with the Qaramita. The Tanukh emir Tamim, son of Mundhir, refused to join Alptakin in attacking the Fatimid governor of Baalbek, and Alptakin took revenge by installing another Tanukh in Beirut.[79] The Isma'ili Qaramita sustained Alptakin against the Fatimids. The Tanukhs were thus caught between contesting Isma'ilis when in 975 the Byzantine Emperor John Tzimiskes probed south. Tzimiskes swept past Baalbek and Damascus, received Alptakin in his camp, and extracted the submission of all the Lebanese ports except Tripoli as he proceeded up the coast on return to Antioch. The Fatimids were not yet ready to face Byzantium, and the Qaramita avoided the emperor. The Tanukhs, faced with a show of power rather than occupation, did not oppose Tzimiskes.[80] In crisis they closed ranks.[81] In 978, Tamim recovered his lordship when the Fatimids smashed the Qaramita and subordinated Alptakin. The Fatimids consolidated their command of Mount Lebanon, Damascus, and Palestine in the early 980s.

As emir of Beirut and the Gharb hills, Tamim maintained good relations not just with his Fatimid overlords, but also with the Aleppo Hamdanids—and therefore Byzantium. This came unstuck in 993 when the governor of Damascus ordered him to join a Fatimid force to subject the Hamdanids. Tamim fled to Aleppo, returning when al-Hakim became Fatimid caliph in 996.[82] Al-Hakim made Tamim's son Mutawwi emir of Beirut and one of Tamim's Arslan relatives commander of Sidon. In 995 and 999, the Byzantine Emperor Basil II conducted punitive expeditions against the Lebanese coast, reprisals for Fatimid maneuvers against Aleppo. Like Nicephorus Phocus and John Tzimiskes, Basil had to abort operations against the fortifications of Tripoli, but plundered the coastal plain. For al-Hakim, Basil's raids increased the value of the Tanukhs as Fatimid agents. The Emir Mutawwi was in a good position when the Fatimids negotiated a long truce with Byzantium in 1001, inaugurating détente between the great powers.

Mount Lebanon was quiet through al-Hakim's remaining two decades. The Fatimid caliph was eccentric, demolishing the church of the Holy Sepulcher in Jerusalem and allowing propagandists to spread the idea of his own divinity. Al-Hakim was careful, however, not to endorse such notions. After 1017, an extremist Persian Isma'ili, Hamza al-Labbad, evolved the doctrine that the incarnation of God in the Fatimid caliphs, culminating in al-Hakim, superseded the Quran and Isma'ili Islam.[83] Religious rituals became superfluous, and the believer simply needed to acknowledge God's "oneness," manifested in al-Hakim. A group of missionaries propagated Hamza's concepts in Cairo, Mount Lebanon, and the Summaq hills of northern Syria. The most active was al-Darazi, whose name stuck to adherents of the resulting community—the Druze. Adherents prefer the title *muwahhidun* (witnesses to God's "oneness"). The sixteenth-century Lebanese historian Ibn al-Hariri claims that al-Hakim sent "the author" of the extremist writings, meaning Hamza, to Wadi al-Taym in Lebanon, where "he spread money . . . and deluded many people."[84] Certainly al-Hakim conversed with Hamza and tolerated the movement, which infuriated Isma'ilis.

A majority of the Tanukhs accepted the "unification call" of Hamza and his associates, inaugurating Lebanon's Druze community.[85] The Emir Mutawwi, who died in 1019, evidently fostered a close relationship between his clan and al-Hakim's devotees. Al-Hakim disappeared in February 1021, and his body was never found. One interpretation is that he was murdered on the orders of his sister.[86] The Tanukh emirate passed to another lineage within the clan. Sami Makarim speculates about a clan agreement to support a personality likely to be acceptable to the new Fatimid Caliph al-Zahir, who frowned on his father's heretical inclinations.[87] The Druze Tanukhs temporarily became a secret group, and the Druze call was suspended between 1021 and 1026. The Emir Fawarasi kept Beirut and the Gharb insulated from disorders resulting from tribal challenges to al-Zahir backed by the new Mirdasid rulers of Aleppo. The wisdom of not provoking the caliph was underlined when al-Zahir defeated his opponents near Tiberias in 1029. After 1036, the Druze of the Beirut hills and Wadi al-Taym could operate more openly as Fatimid control loosened under the boy Caliph al-Mustansir.

In 1043, Druze religious leaders terminated the "call," which technically meant that there could be no more converts. By 1050, the Tanukh emirate returned to the lineage of Mutawwi. From the earliest days, a class of sheikhs took charge of Druze religious knowledge, meaning the writings of Hamza and his associate Baha al-Din al-Muqtana. The detail of these writings was to be kept away from other members of the community, whether Tanukh lords or peasant followers. From Hamza, Druzism inherited a belief in transmigration of souls (*taqammus*) from Druze to Druze, an idea alien to Sunni and Shia Islam. This helped foster Druze solidarity and military prowess. For survival, Druze, like all Shia, could also practice dissimulation (*taqiya*), pretending to be Sunni Muslims. Hamza favored both neo-platonic ideas of God as an aloof universal intellect and the incarnation of God in humans.

Apart from the appearance of the Druze, the most notable development in Fatimid Lebanon was the resurgence of the coastal ports as mediators of commerce, after three centuries of military emphasis. Later, Tripoli and Tyre asserted political autonomy under Islamic jurist families.

Mediterranean trade resurfaced through the late tenth century with convergence of favorable developments. Paradoxically, the ascent of Byzantium boded well for the Sunni Muslim garrison towns of coastal Lebanon. Greater Byzantine power, population, and economic capacity meant expanded markets and improved security in much of the eastern Mediterranean.[88] Byzantine vitality also eased the path of Italian traders, who reappeared in eastern waters. In turn, the Fatimid takeover of Cairo strengthened Egyptian interest in Indian Ocean trade already apparent under the Ikhshidids. The Isma'ili Fatimids linked with Isma'ilis in Yemen to control the whole Red Sea trade route. The increased flow of spices and other high-value goods to Egypt boosted Mediterranean commerce. By happy coincidence, explosive growth in population and demand in western Europe, particularly northern Italy, meant that the West was eager for reconnection. As for the Lebanese ports, the Fatimid interest in trade meant interest in naval power and in the revival of these ports as political and commercial nodes under Fatimid command.

Tripoli, as the northern bastion of the Fatimid maritime domain, facing Byzantium by land and sea, had to be held in force from the 980s. With Alexandria, it was one of the two main Fatimid naval bases, and it became an administrative center rivaling Damascus. Trade expansion began with the plentiful products of the Levant itself; al-Muqaddasi, describing the commerce of "al-Sham" for around 985, does not feature long-distance caravans from the east. For Tyre, which he describes as "a beautiful and delightful city," he mentions sugar and glass items among specialties.[89] Al-Muqaddasi gives an upbeat impression, concluding: "the trade of Syria is profitable."[90] Thereafter, unprecedented truces with Byzantium, from 1001 to about 1030 and from 1038 to 1054, which included trade exchange provisions, contributed to a fruitful commercial environment.[91]

Both Tripoli and Tyre could be politically unreliable, which emphasized the strategic salience of the Tanukhs who were located between them (see figure 1.2). In 997, Tyre rebelled against Fatimid impositions and appealed to Byzantium.[92] The Fatimids recovered the town after a rigorous siege. The rebel chief was sent to Egypt where he was skinned alive and crucified. In 1032, the governor of Tripoli rejected a Fatimid tax demand and put himself under Byzantine protection. He had to be expelled twice after being returned once by a Byzantine fleet.[93] In contrast to Tyre, the Tripoli population staunchly backed the Fatimids.

One visitor to Tripoli in 1047 estimated the population to be 20,000, no doubt a big increase since the tenth century.[94] Apparently, the majority had become Isma'ili Shia through seven decades of Fatimid rule, expressing erosion of Sunni Islam on the Lebanese coast.[95] The built-up extent of Tripoli was similar to Tyre, which may indicate that Tyre also had around 20,000 people.[96] Muqaddasi rated Sidon and Beirut as much smaller than Tripoli in the 980s, meaning that they probably had only a few thousand residents in the 1040s.[97] Tripoli and Tyre drifted out of Fatimid control during al-Mustansir's minority, paralleling Druze entrenchment in the Tanukh areas. The emergence of jurist families as town leaders was novel but not surprising. Chief judges had greater legal authority than governors and, under the Fatimids, headed military forces. In particular, an Isma'ili Shia chief judge wielded the religious "call" of the Imam-Caliph within his jurisdiction.

The Abi Aqil family appears in the record as judges in Tyre in the 1030s.[98] They seem to have been Sunni, but initially loyal to the Fatimids. In 1057, Ibn Abu Aqil helped repel a Byzantine assault on Tripoli and participated in a Fatimid takeover of Aleppo.[99] He repudiated the Fatimids in 1063, at a time when the Sunni Seljuk Turks challenged the Fatimids from Baghdad and Tripoli headed for autonomy. He quickly extended Abi Aqil authority to Sidon. The family's hold later weakened. In 1089, the Fatimids took advantage of dissent among the Seljuk Turks who had overrun much of the Levant after 1070 to recover Tyre and the coast up to Jubayl.

Tripoli's independence under the Banu Ammar Isma'ili Shia judges proved more solid.[100] The Banu Ammar derived from the Katama clan of Fatimid North Africa, which provided high officials for the Fatimids in Cairo. It is not known how they became established in Tripoli, but Amin al-Dawla of the Banu Ammar, who ceased to acknowledge Cairo's suzerainty in about 1065, was chief judge and governor by Fatimid appointment. Amin al-Dawla rounded out a territory that included Jubayl to the south and the Akkar to the north. He also founded Dar al-Ilm (The House of Knowledge), which hosted poets and religious scholars. It encompassed a library that reputedly grew to 100,000 volumes, massive for its time and famous throughout the Islamic lands.[101]

In 1071, Mount Lebanon's Middle Eastern environment altered dramatically when the Seljuk Sultan Alp-Arslan, only sixteen years after Seljuk displacement of the Shia Buyids in Baghdad, defeated the Byzantines at Manzikert. Turcoman troops and tribes rapidly overran central Anatolia. Simultaneously, the Turkish warlord Atsiz seized much of Fatimid Palestine and besieged Damascus, which he took in 1075. Tripoli, the Tanukhs, and Tyre all had to adjust to the Seljuk Turks, only persisting as autonomous actors courtesy of Seljuk divisions. Amin al-Dawla accepted Turcoman settlers in Tripoli.[102] Otherwise, his regime had to balance various Turks as well as the humiliated, vengeful Fatimids.

Amin al-Dawla's nephew Jalal al-Malik, who succeeded him in 1072, did his best to keep Tripoli afloat in trying conditions, With the Byzantine duchy of Antioch cut from the rest of the empire by the Turkish advance in Anatolia, Jalal al-Malik profited from its weakness to seize Jabala. Substantial productive lands gave the city-state a good economy, and commerce was largely unaffected by political turbulence. Indeed, long-distance land trade from the east to the Levant ports and the Mediterranean surged in the late eleventh century. Jalal al-Malik was even more of a patron to scholars than his uncle, developing Dar al-Ilm and earning a panegyric from the poet Ibn al-Khayyat.[103]

Tripoli's political situation, however, deteriorated. In 1085, the Seljuks finally laid their hands on the Byzantine coast to the north. The city became caught between Tutush, brother of the new Seljuk Sultan Malikshah, who had expelled Atsiz from Damascus in 1078, and a Fatimid reassertion along the coast to the south in 1089. Jalal al-Malik lost Jubayl to the Fatimids and most land north of Tripoli to Tutush before he died in 1098. When the First Crusade passed by in early 1099, on its way from Antioch to Jerusalem via the Lebanese coast, Tripoli was still independent but had been reduced to its immediate orchards and market gardens.

The Crusaders in Lebanon, 1099–1291

From 1099, for almost two centuries, the Lebanese coast was a beachhead for a west European presence of fluctuating power and extent. The crusaders, or Franks, who came to restore long defunct Christian mastery of Jerusalem, manifested a surge of Western piety, energy, and cupidity surprising and shocking to Muslims and Byzantines alike. They thrust through Byzantium and Turkish Anatolia to a splintered Muslim Levant where they quickly carved out a collection of principalities from Cilicia to the Red Sea. Mount Lebanon represented the tight waist of their north-south distribution. The Lebanese mountain communities, the Maronites, Druze, and Twelver Shia, therefore occupied terrain significant to both the Franks of the coast and the Muslims of Damascus. Their consolidation in no-man's land or under Frankish rule through the twelfth and thirteenth centuries was crucial to their viability and to the character of today's Lebanon.

It took the Franks more than two decades to secure the Lebanese coast, much longer than to establish themselves in Palestine or northern Syria. Tripoli, Beirut, and Tyre proved particularly obstinate, falling in 1109, 1110, and 1124, respectively. Any of these in Muslim hands meant a base that the emir of Damascus or the Fatimids could deploy against crusader communications on land and water. Inland from Tyre, the Franks built the fortress of Tibnin in Jabal Amil in 1106–1107 to cut the town from Damascus, to protect their forces on the coastal plain, and to deter the Twelver Shia rural population from aiding the besieged.[104] Inland from Beirut, the Tanukh association with the emir of Damascus brought a brutal Frankish reaction in 1110. Shortly before the attack, the writer of the 1110 entry in the *Sijill al-Arslani* recounts in a dramatic passage that the Tanukh emir entrusted him with the family papers "so that I might keep them with other records, in case of the coming of the Frankish infidels . . . and he commanded me that if, God forbid, he did not succeed in fighting the infidels or was killed, I should deliver all these documents to his children or family."[105]

Thereafter, from 1124 until 1187, the Franks maintained a precarious hegemony on the seaward side of Mount Lebanon. The Kingdom of Jerusalem included the south and Beirut, with the County of Tripoli as the crusader successor of the extinguished city-state of the Banu Ammar (see figure 1.2). The Druze in the Beirut hills recovered from the devastation of 1110, and their new Buhtur emirs represented continuing Muslim influence in central Mount Lebanon. Baalbek and much of the Biqa remained with the emirate of Damascus, though revenues in the northern Biqa were shared between Damascus and Frankish Tripoli. Around Mount Hermon, territorial jurisdiction fluctuated, with Wadi al-Taym under Damascus but the fortified town of Baniyas changing hands twice. Away from the walled ports, the Franks established only a few strong points. In the south, the castles of Hunin, Tibnin, and Beaufort (Shaqif Arnun) projected powerfully across Jabal Amil toward Mount Hermon. Apart from the small cave fortress of Tyron inland from Sidon and minor positions above Beirut and Jubayl, there was no fortification on Mount Lebanon. In the far north, the castle of Gibalcar (Jabal Akkar) looked across the Homs gap to the mighty crusader pile of Krak des Chevaliers, the eastern bastion of the County of Tripoli.

In social terms, the coastal towns experienced a drastic upheaval with the crusader conquest. Many Muslims were killed or departed for the interior with the crusader sieges and capture of Tripoli, Beirut, and Tyre (figure 1.3). Through several decades, they were replaced by tens of thousands of Franks. Beyond the agricultural surrounds of the ports, however, Frankish settlement was limited in Mount Lebanon, restricted to the strong points. Overall, the native population, Muslim and Christian, always remained a majority of at least four to one in Frankish Lebanon and vital for revenues. The population for the whole Kingdom of Jerusalem around 1180 has been estimated at 480,000 to 650,000, including 120,000 to 140,000 Franks.[106] This would imply there were at least 100,000 people in the Lebanese portion of the kingdom, including perhaps 20,000 Franks. No estimates exist for the County of Tripoli, but similar figures seem reasonable. Assuming around 20,000 people lived in the Muslim-ruled Biqa, including Baalbek and Wadi al-Taym, the overall population of the territory of modern Lebanon in the 1180s would have been around 200,000 to 250,000. Given a modern scientific finding that the Crusades left a significant western European genetic imprint in the Lebanese population, especially among Christians, the Franks were a substantial minority of the total. [107]

Among the ports, Tripoli and Tyre had Frankish majorities, though with a continuing indigenous presence. The Arab courtier Usama Ibn Munqidh relates that one of his "mamluks" received help from a native Christian neighborhood chief in Tripoli around 1139.[108] Evidently his "mamluk" had no compunction about traveling through Frankish territory to avoid unfriendly Muslims. William of Tyre reports a pogrom against natives in Tripoli after the killing of Count Raymond II at the hands of the Isma'ili Shia Assassins in 1151: "The people flew to arms and without discrimination put to the sword all those who were found to differ either in language or dress from the Latins."[109] Ibn Jubayr compared Tyre with Acre for 1184: "Its people are by disposition less stubborn in their unbelief, and by nature and habit they are kinder to the Muslim stranger. . . . The state of the Muslims in this city is easier and more peaceful."[110] Salah al-Din's secretary Imad al-Din observed in 1187 that the smaller towns of Sidon, Beirut, and Jubayl had Muslim majorities.[111] Probably Sidon's Muslims were Sunni, a legacy of the peaceful surrender of the town in 1110. Beirut included Druze, and Jubayl Muslims were presumably Twelver Shia, reflecting the Shia population in the nearby hills.

Figure 1.3 Crusader assault on Tyre, 1124, from Old French manuscript of William of Tyre's *Histoire d'Outremer* (dated to 1232–1261)—severed head is that of Balak, ruler of Aleppo. © The British Library Board (Yates Thompson 12 175).

Establishing town sizes for Frankish Lebanon is difficult, though the native population was mostly in villages of a couple hundred people each. It seems reasonable to assume that Frankish Tripoli and Tyre grew to populations equivalent to the Fatimid peak, certainly through the decades of calm up to 1187 and again after 1210. There were four thousand weavers of cotton and silk in and around Tripoli in the mid-twelfth century, and there must have been a similar number of people involved in administration, religion, and trade.[112] This would point to well over 20,000 inhabitants in the main Frankish walled town a little inland and its port, considered together. For Tyre, Joshua Prawer proposes 25,000 residents, assuming relatively dense settlement with multifloor apartments.[113] In 1161, the Jewish traveler, Benjamin of Tudela, reported five hundred Jews at Tyre, including scholars, shipowners, and glassmakers.[114]

Italians from Venice, Genoa, and Pisa who were engaged in the Levant trade represented a large component of the Frankish population. For their role in the siege, the Venetians received one-third of Tyre as an autonomous commune, and the Genoese Embracio family controlled Jubayl under the Count of Tripoli. Long-distance trade redeveloped relatively slowly after the shock of conquest and depended on local production, most prominently textiles and sugar, for western European markets. The Italians otherwise profited from the large pilgrim traffic, military demands, and interaction with Byzantium. By the late twelfth century, however, the land caravans from the east were again coming to Acre, Tripoli, and Tyre, regardless of the political or religious division.[115]

Decimation of Muslim townsfolk and alien Christian rule interrupted Islamic culture on the Levant coast through the crusader period. On the other hand, the Frankish rulers and their ecclesiastical hierarchy encouraged learning. The Ottoman survey of Mount Lebanon published in Arabic under the supervision of the Shia governor of the territory, Isma'il Haqqi, just before the Ottoman collapse in 1918, observes:

> The Frankish princes ruling the coast of Syria and Lebanon loved the sciences and encouraged both peoples [Franks and Arabs] to study them. And what has come through the historical record is the interest of the Franks in the study of oriental languages and absorption of eastern science and their respect for Arab scholars.[116]

For example, Jacobites founded a school of philosophy and medicine in Frankish Tripoli.[117] The great Spanish Muslim botanist Ibn al-Baytar received Frankish hospitality and collected plants in Mount Lebanon in the early thirteenth century. Istifan Duwayhi in *Tarikh al-Azmina* recorded a cultural surge among Maronites in his entry for 1112, marking the early days of the County of Tripoli:

> And in that time our people in Mount Lebanon began to beat bells of brass rather than wood for prayers and mass, and those whose hands overflowed with the grace of God established churches and monasteries and schools.[118]

An outstanding Frankish scholar was William, Latin Archbishop of Tyre—among the greatest medieval historians and a contemporary of such luminaries as Ibn Asakir and Ibn al-Qalanisi in Damascus. William was born in Jerusalem of

humble origins around 1130 and died in Tyre in 1185. He almost certainly had
a decent command of Arabic, and much of our picture of the Latin states comes
through his often surprisingly modern eyes.

Coastal Lebanon was less affected than Palestine by the crusader military debacle at the hands of Salah al-Din Yusuf Ibn Ayyub [Saladin] at Hattin in July
1187. The Kingdom of Jerusalem south of Tyre collapsed in 1187–1188, being
revived—minus Jerusalem and with Acre as capital—only because of the campaigns of Richard the Lionheart (Richard I, King of England) in 1189–1191. In
Lebanon, the Franks held out in Tyre and Tripoli, reinforced by refugees from
elsewhere. Stiff crusader resistance at the Beaufort castle on the border of Jabal
Amil delayed Salah al-Din for months. He took the Shia rural hinterland of Tyre
as well as Sidon, Beirut, and the Jubayl and Batrun districts of the County of
Tripoli, but Frankish persistence paid off after his death in 1193 in a steady
recovery of territory up to 1240.

For a while, the Muslim challenge receded, as the Ayyubid successors of Salah
al-Din squabbled. Damascus and Egypt, unified under Salah al-Din, again separated. Ayyubid princes sought alliances with the temporarily resurgent Franks.
The crusaders recaptured Beirut and Jubayl in 1197, which together with a condominium in Sidon restored the Frankish coastal strip between Tyre and Tripoli.
In 1240, a deal with the Ayyubid ruler of Damascus brought back Tibnin and
Beaufort in Jabal Amil, as well as suzerainty of the hills of Sidon and Beirut.[119]
After half a century of Shia and Druze autonomy, however, the Frankish hold
inland could only be tenuous. This was emphasized in 1244, when the Franks
lost the majority of their indigenous knighthood in the battle of La Forbie, near
Gaza. Here the sultan of Egypt and the Khawarizmian nomads defeated the cru-
saders and their Syrian Ayyubid allies.

In 1250, displacement of the Egyptian Ayyubids by the militantly Sunni
Mamluks, a caste of Turkic slave soldiers, heralded the final Frankish slide
toward oblivion. The slide took four decades, but the outcome was inevitable.
Europe lost interest in sustaining the Franks, and the Italian communes in the
Levant ports were divisive and subversive. On the Muslim side, the Mamluk victory over the Mongols at Ayn Jalut in the Jordan Valley in 1261 led to reunification of Damascus and Egypt under a Mamluk state more potent than the
Fatimids. Aside from their religious impetus, the Mamluks could not tolerate
perpetuation of the Frankish coastal strip—a second front—while they conducted deadly warfare with the Mongol Ilkhanate to the north and east.

Between 1265 and 1271, Sultan Baybars cut away at the southern and northern flanks of Mount Lebanon. In 1268, he took Beaufort and Jabal Amil and demonstrated Mamluk field superiority by marching past Sidon, Beirut, and Tripoli
on his way to storm Antioch. The Mamluk parade echoed John Tzimiskes and the
First Crusade. In 1271, the sultan seized Krak des Chevaliers and Gibalcar. With

the northern slopes of Mount Lebanon in Mamluk hands, Baybars recounted in a letter to Bohemond VI, Count of Tripoli and titular Prince of Antioch, "how we moved the mangonels [ballistic siege engines] through mountains where the birds have difficulty in making their aeries.... Our yellow banner has taken the place of your red one, and the sound of the church bell has given way to *Allahu akbar*." He informed the prince-count: "The remnants of your men [at Gibalcar] have been released" to warn "the people of Tripoli . . . that only a little time remains in your lives."[120]

Nonetheless, Baybars awarded truces, including to Tripoli in 1271–1272, and campaigns against the Ilkhanate and the Armenian Kingdom of Cilicia preoccupied him until his death in 1277. Mamluk succession disputes and an abortive Mongol offensive in 1281 then intervened. Only in the mid-1280s could the forceful Sultan Qalawun return the sultanate's attention to the Franks, reducing their possessions on the coast north of Tripoli. Tripoli's own affairs were troubled in these last years, with civil warfare between the prince-count and the Templar order of knights. At the same time, a leadership struggle in Acre disturbed Tyre and Beirut. Eventually, some Italians went to Qalawun to request him to stop Tripoli from being turned into a Genoese naval base, which might threaten Alexandria.[121] The sultan duly appeared before the walls of Tripoli in March 1289. The siege was ferocious, and the city was captured and sacked, with Frankish refugees pursued to a small island where they were massacred or enslaved.[122] Qalawun then reestablished Tripoli closer to the port. In 1291, the Sultan al-Ashraf Khalil stormed Acre with similar ruthlessness, and the Franks evacuated Tyre, Sidon, and Beirut.

Mount Lebanon thus came under Mamluk hegemony. The Mamluks thereafter faced the task of subordinating the mountain communities. To appreciate the resilience of these communities, it is worthwhile to review their distinctive affairs through the Crusades period. Figure 1.2 depicts their approximate geographical distributions in the twelfth century.

Maronites

William of Tyre refers to "Syrian Christians" who lived "high up in the lofty range of Lebanon" and who came down to meet the First Crusade when it paused north of Tripoli in early 1099, offering "their congratulations to the pilgrims."[123] Given William's subsequent discussion of the community by name,[124] these were plainly Maronites. Their "experienced men" gathered with the Frankish leaders to advise the coastal route as the "safest and easiest road to Jerusalem."[125] Maronite chiefs thus showed readiness to take initiatives and discontent with the turbulent affairs of the Seljuks and Fatimids. They were also indifferent toward the Banu Ammar of Tripoli; Ibn al-Athir mentioned local

Christian assistance to the Franks during the intermittent siege of Tripoli up to its capture in 1109.[126]

Duwayhi in *Tarikh al-Azmina* commented on the distribution of the Maronites at the outset of crusader rule in describing the wanderings of Tuma al-Kafrtabi, who allegedly sowed heresy in the districts of Jubayl, Batrun, and Jibbat Bsharri after 1103.[127] Duwayhi singles out the preaching of "one will," the Monothelite concept common to Maronites and Jacobites, perhaps to highlight his claim that Maronites rejected the idea. Away from Maronite core districts, stories in Ibn al-Qila'i's *Madihat ala Jabal Lubnan* [A Eulogy on Mount Lebanon] would extend the community south into the Kisrawan heights.[128] In particular, Ibn al-Qila'i mentioned two chiefs of Biskinta. The *Sijill al-Arslani* has already been cited as indicating a Christian presence in the Kisrawan in the ninth century. By the twelfth century, the Kisrawan between Beirut and Nahr Ibrahim, just south of Jubayl, had a mixed population: Twelver Shia, Druze of the Abi Lama clan, Maronites on the heights, and Jacobites in Jounieh, the last reported by the great Muslim geographer al-Idrisi.[129] There were also Alawites, or Nusayris.[130]

Sourcing Ibn al-Qila'i, Duwayhi refers to submission by Maronites to a papal envoy in Tripoli in the 1130s.[131] Maronites seem to have been reticent about integration with the Roman church, which would be expected if one accepts their Monothelitism. This should not be taken as implying deteriorating relations with the Franks. William of Tyre's blaming of "Syrians who lived on the heights of Lebanon" for the betrayal and killing of Count Pons in 1139 does not specify Christians, still less Maronites.[132] Jacobites, Twelver Shia, and Alawites were all conceivable suspects.

Not until about 1182 is there clear evidence of doctrinal convergence of some Maronites with Rome. William of Tyre has a famous passage:

> At this time . . . a race of Syrians in the province of Phoenicia . . . underwent a wonderful change of heart. These people had followed the heretical doctrines of a certain Maro, from whom they took the name of Maronites. . . . They repaired to Aimery, the patriarch of Antioch . . . [and] renounced the error by which they had been so long enslaved.[133]

William is absolute on the Monothelitism of the Maronites. Further, he gives us a valuable population estimate for the Maronites of the County of Tripoli—about 40,000. The figure would make the Maronites around one-third of the population of the county, its largest community. William's testimony is that of a learned Arabic-speaking Frank residing in Lebanon.

Even at this point, the Maronite church did not officially surrender independence. Only in the early thirteenth century did a Maronite patriarch, the first patriarch for whom we have clear historical documentation, take the plunge.[134]

In about 1203, a papal legate visited northern Lebanon, received Maronite allegiance, and investigated the Maronite church. In 1213, Pope Innocent III invited Patriarch Irmia of Amshit to the 1215 Lateran council. In Rome, Irmia accepted investiture as a primate under the Latin patriarch of Antioch—a grade below patriarchal status. The pope gave him a letter outlining Maronite beliefs and practices considered objectionable, including Monothelitism, procession of the Holy Spirit from the Father alone, and other items Maronites shared with Jacobites. Patriarch Irmia returned from Italy in 1216, accompanied by a second papal legate. For a few years the Maronite church conformed, at least superficially.

Trouble bubbled up when Patriarch Irmia died in 1230 and Maronites in the Munaytara and Lihfid areas above Jubayl turned to "heresy."[135] Thereafter, the church split and the new patriarch had to move downhill, toward the coast. By 1280, an anti-patriarch in the heights of Bsharri openly espoused Monophysite beliefs. The patriarch still loyal to Rome visited the Vatican in 1282 at the urging of the Embriaco lord of Jubayl to reaffirm Maronite allegiance. Ironically, the Mamluk Sultan Qalawun disposed of the Jacobite-inclined party in 1283 when he sent a force to devastate the surrounds of Bsharri.

Mamluk attacks on the Maronites in 1266, 1268, and 1283 demonstrated that Maronite doctrinal dissension did not seriously upset Maronite alignment with the Frankish secular authorities of Tripoli. Certainly Baybars and Qalawun saw no reason to discriminate. The Mamluk historian Taqi al-Din Ahmad Ibn Ali al-Maqrizi recorded Baybars' 1268 activities around Tripoli:

> The sultan came to Tripoli, and made camp there. He skirmished with its people and seized a tower. . . . The army attacked the people in those mountains. The soldiers seized much booty and took several caves by the sword. They presented the plunder and prisoners to the sultan, beat the prisoners, cut down the trees, and destroyed the churches.[136]

Maronite irregulars continued to serve in Frankish forces, particularly the highly respected archers. Religious disputation triggered by the submission of church authorities to Rome forced the community to rely more on the secular leadership of its muqaddams, or clan chiefs, some of whom the Franks endorsed in their feudal hierarchy.[137] Diversified leadership was a positive feature for the longer term.

Otherwise, the Franks brought the Maronites into a wider world, and the linkage with Rome would later prove a powerful reinforcement for the community. Although most Maronites regretted the Frankish collapse, after painful lessons dealt to them and the heterodox Muslims, their leaders were sensible enough to adjust to Mamluk supremacy.

Druze

Frankish seizure of Beirut and devastation of the Gharb hills in 1110 dramatically affected the new Druze community. The killing of the Tanukh Emir Adud
al-Dawla and most of his family ended the line of Arslan bin Malik, one of the
Tanukh settler brothers of 758, as emirs of the Gharb and Beirut.[138] Integrating
the Arslani *Sijill*, the fifteenth-century *Tarikh Beirut* of Salih bin Yahya, Tannus
al-Shidyaq's mid-nineteenth century family histories in his *Kitab Akhbar al-
Ayan*, and the modern interpretations of Sami Makarim and Kamal Salibi,
analysis of developments becomes viable.

Adud al-Dawla's kinsman Majd al-Dawla, who appeased the Franks, followed
in 1137 by the former's surviving son Nahid al-Din Abu Asha'ir Buhtur, took
over clan lands in the Gharb.[139] However, the decimation of the family opened
space for one Sharaf al-Dawla Ali, of the distantly related Tanukh lineage of
Jumayhar. Sharaf al-Dawla's paternal grandfather had been an emir in al-Bira, on
the Euphrates, in the 1020s.[140] His male ancestral line included a Tanukh who
probably came to Mount Lebanon around 820.[141] There is no proof of Salibi's
assumption that Sharaf al-Dawla entered the Gharb after 1110 on orders from
the warlords of Damascus.[142] He may have been in Mount Lebanon already.
What is clear is that Sharaf al-Dawla and his son, Nahid al-Dawla Abu Asha'ir
Buhtur, presented themselves to Damascus as the most capable leaders for the
Gharb.[143]

In 1147, the Jumayhar Buhtur received investiture from Damascus as commander of the Gharb; in 1148, he may have sent archers to assist Damascus
against the crusader siege; and in 1151, he was probably the Buhtur who skirmished with the Franks near Beirut. In 1162, Nur al-Din of Damascus granted
Buhtur's son Karama most of the Gharb, as well as villages in the Biqa and Wadi
al-Taym. So began a new line of emirs of the Beirut hills, the Buhturids. In the
fifteenth century, Salih bin Yahya, their historian, promoted the identification of
their rivals, the original Arslani Tanukhs, termed "Bani Abi al-Jaysh" by 1300,
with Bedouin from the Hummayra tribe of the Biqa.[144]

Bin Yahya and the 1179 entry in the Arslani *Sijill* disagree on Buhturid origins. Whereas Bin Yahya, citing the 1147 land award, puts Buhtur in the Jumayhar line of Sharaf al-Dawla Ali, the *Sijill* makes him the heir of Adud al-Dawla of
the original Arslani line. Neither admits two Buhturs, which for Makarim was
the only answer.[145] Also, Salibi's claim of a leadership change in the Beirut hills to
Damascus-sponsored newcomers seems debatable. A combination of Buhturids
with a local Tanukh connection, remnant Arslani Tanukhs, and new arrivals—
including Druze from northern Syria—is more likely.

Beyond the Gharb, toward Sidon and Mount Hermon, al-Shidyaq's genealogical
explorations suggest new immigrants in the early twelfth century. In al-Shidyaq's

account, only the Ma'n family, arriving in the Shuf above Sidon in 1120, illustrates Salibi's hypothesis of settlement in response to orders from Damascus to fight the Franks.[146] The Ma'n emir may have married a Tanukh and may have been commissioned to buttress the Tanukhs.[147] He came fresh from clashes with the crusaders near Antioch and found the high Shuf deserted. The Jumayhar Buhtur helped him to construct permanent dwellings.[148] Members of the Abi Nakad and Talhuq clans accompanied the Ma'ns from northern Syria.[149] The Talhuqs joined the Shihabs in the Hawran and shifted to Beirut in 1144.

Through the early twelfth century, the southern Shuf and Wadi al-Taym beneath Mount Hermon was the haunt of Druze of the longer settled Jandal clan. Their chief, Dahhaq bin Jandal, made friends with the Franks, feuded with the Isma'ilis of Baniyas, and in 1133 provoked the Atabeg of Damascus into expelling him from the fortified cave of Tyron inland from Sidon.[150] In 1173, the Sunni Shihabs, stalwarts of Salah al-Din, took over Wadi al-Taym.[151] According to al-Shidyaq, they developed family ties with the Ma'ns of the Shuf.[152] Apart from the Shihabs, all of the immigrants to the Shuf and Wadi al-Taym were or became Druze, despite Druzism having supposedly closed its doors.

Druzism was preeminent in southern Mount Lebanon from the Gharb to Wadi al-Taym in the mid-twelfth century. Benjamin of Tudela, who visited Sidon in 1161, describes the Shuf Druze:

> Ten miles [from Sidon] a people dwell who are at war with the men of Sidon; they are called Druses and are pagans of a lawless character. They inhabit the mountains and the clefts of the rocks; they have no king or ruler, but dwell independent in those high places, and their border extends to Mount Hermon. . . . They say that at the time when the soul leaves the body it passes, in the case of a good man, into the body of a newborn child; and in the case of a bad man, into the body of a dog or an ass. . . . They roam over the mountains and hills, and no man can do battle with them.[153]

William of Tyre conflates the Druze with the Isma'ili Assassins:

> In the province of Tyre in Phoenicia and in the diocese of Tortosa [Tartus] there lives a tribe of people who possess ten fortresses with the villages attached to them. Their numbers, as we have often heard, is about sixty thousand or possibly more.[154]

Certainly, both Druze and Assassins were Isma'ili-derived, and both held highlands of strategic significance.

The Franks of Beirut and Sidon were sensitive about Druze interactions with Damascus. In 1125 they built a small fort (Mont Glavien) above Beirut; they supervised the Awali valley near Sidon from Belhacem; and in 1139 they acquired the Tyron cave. In the twelfth century, the lords of Sidon maintained better relations with the Ma'ns than Beirut had with the Buhturids.[155] In 1166–1167, Nur al-Din of Damascus dealt the Franks blows that tilted the balance in Mount Lebanon. He captured the Munaytara fort north of Beirut, Tyron above Sidon, and Baniyas below Mount Hermon. Beirut became exposed. Bin Yahya reports that around 1170, the Frankish governor invited the adult heirs of the Buhturid Emir Karama to a wedding and had them murdered.[156] The Franks sacked the Buhturid citadel, and Karama's youngest son Hajji and his mother fled into the hills. Nonetheless Beirut remained vulnerable, as Salah al-Din demonstrated in 1182 when he thrust across from the Biqa.[157]

Buhtur's grandson Hajji resurfaced when Salah al-Din took Beirut in 1187 and met Hajji, confirming his lordship over the villages of his father and grandfather. Makarim claims Salah al-Din and his Ayyubid heirs preferred to recognize several chiefs, not a paramount emir.[158] Hajji had poor relations with the Franks after they retook Beirut in 1197, and they harassed him so much that the Ayyubid sultan in Damascus requested them to leave him alone as part of truce arrangements.[159] Competing Ayyubids offered favors to Hajji and his son Najm al-Din Muhammad, indicating the value of the mountain. Apart from Hajji, there was no trouble in the Druze country through the Frankish resurgence up to 1240. The Ma'ns of the Shuf pragmatically consolidated.

A new phase began with the Ayyubid concession of the Gharb and the Shuf to the Franks in 1240, followed by the Frankish defeat near Gaza in 1244. In 1241, either Franks or Kisrawani villagers killed Najm al-Din Muhammad and another Buhturid while they were riding in the Kisrawan.[160] In 1245, the Ma'ns attacked Sidon.[161] Thereafter, the Mamluk coup in Egypt in 1250, hostility between Mamluk Cairo and Ayyubid Damascus, and the Mongol approach disturbed the Druze. The Mamluks offered the Buhturids Cairo's favor, and in 1256 the Buhturids defeated a challenge from the Biqa, involving Baalbek tribesmen and al-Nasir Yusuf of Damascus. Under pressure, the Buhturids repaired relations with the Franks. Bin Yahya reported that the Buhturid Sa'ad al-Din loved falcons, and "the [Frankish] ruler of Cyprus gave him birds, or perhaps it was the lord of Beirut because this is closer to reason."[162] Later, Sa'ad al-Din's brother Jamal al-Din and cousin Zayn al-Din played sides when the Mongols occupied Damascus in 1260 and the Mamluks marched against them. Jamal al-Din went to Damascus to propitiate the non-Muslim invader. Zayn al-Din joined the Mamluks and fought for Islam at Ayn Jalut. One of them was sure to back the winner, and Zayn al-Din interceded for his cousin with the victorious Mamluks.[163] The Franks behaved similarly, receiving the Mongols at Safed and supplying the Mamluks from Acre.

Zayn al-Din illustrates contradictions in the sources.[164] The Arslani *Sijill*, in its entry for 1271, named him as Abu al-Jaysh, the supposed enemies of the Buhturids. It deployed Abu al-Jaysh (literally "father of the troops") as an informal title, reflecting Zayn al-Din's martial reputation. Bin Yahya, in contrast, portrayed him as a target of Abi al-Jaysh. The *Sijill* lauded Zayn al-Din's defense of Islam, claiming that in 1258 he "rebuilt a mosque, baths, and two quarters of Aramoun burned by the infidel Franks."[165] As noted, Bin Yahya had Zayn al-Din's cousin receiving presents from the same infidels. All that is clear is that there were Druze factions and that the Franks and others exploited them.

Under Mamluk Damascus in the early 1260s, the Gharb stabilized with Sultan Baybars favoring the Buhturids and satisfied with their monitoring of Frankish Beirut.[166] The situation deteriorated around 1268 with accusations of Buhturid contacts with the Franks. Despite previous Buhturid duplicity with the Mongols, Baybars was uncertain.[167] He imprisoned the three Buhturid lords, but refrained from seizing their lands. In their absence, the Beirut hills became anarchic. The murder of a Mamluk commander in the Gharb shortly after the death of Baybars in 1277 provoked a punitive expedition, beefed up with Biqa tribesmen anxious to avenge 1256. The Mamluk force sacked the Gharb, reprising the Frankish attack of 1110. According to Makarim the Sultan Baraka Khan and his deputy in Damascus probably looked to demonstrate state power.[168] In 1278, the Mamluks released the imprisoned Buhturids.

Throughout the 1280s, Sultan Qalawun continued the policy of Baybars. He dismissed accusations of Buhturid correspondence with the Franks as forgeries. However, he must have been suspicious. On the eve of his 1289 assault on Tripoli, he transferred authority over the Beirut hills to Mamluk officers, dispossessing the chiefs.[169] Qalawun wanted closer control along the coast during the final campaign to expel the Franks. The measure was not effective, and Qalawun's son Al-Ashraf Khalil reversed it. The price was truncation of autonomy; the Mamluks expected the Gharb lords to become Mamluk officers.

For the rest of the Druze country, only al-Shidyaq's *Akhbar al-Ayan* provides data for the late thirteenth century.[170] From 1253 to 1287, Emir Qurqmas Shihab dominated the neighborhood of Mount Hermon. In 1281 he earned the gratitude of Qalawun for participation in defeating the Mongols near Homs. Al-Shidyaq has his son Sa'ad facing a Mongol incursion into Wadi al-Taym in 1287, which only made sense as a raid accompanying Ghazan's capture of Damascus in 1300. The main significance is the refuge provided by the Ma'ns in the Shuf, confirming an alliance of the Shihabs and Ma'ns, four centuries later pivotal to Mount Lebanon.

Shia

On the eve of the First Crusade, Twelver Shia in Jabal Amil and parts of the Biqa represented an outlier of Shia northern Palestine, as described by Muqaddasi.[171] We may assume a Twelver presence alongside Sunnis in Tyre, though Fatimid rule implied Isma'ili infusion, as in Tripoli. In the hills north and east of Jabal Amil, the neighbors were Druze, Isma'ilis, and Sunnis. The Twelvers of the Kisrawan were geographically separate.

Given its marginal location for Twelver Shia in the late eleventh century and insecurity because of Fatimid/Seljuk conflict, Jabal Amil likely became thinly populated.[172] This would fit with al-Shidyaq's reference to settlement desertion in the nearby Shuf hills. As with the Druze country, Jabal Amil probably received a population influx as a result of the First Crusade. Rather than clan chiefs on the make, however, the influx comprised Shia refugees from the swift crusader advance in interior Palestine. The Franks took the Jordan Valley, Tiberias, Nablus, and much of the Galilee in a thrust northward from Jerusalem in late 1099. Many Shia would have fled into southern Lebanon, where the Franks only extended their rule with the fortification of Tibnin in 1106. Frankish military vulnerability would have been an incentive to treat an inflated population carefully. For their part, as modern Lebanese Shia historian Ja'afar al-Muhajir suggests, incoming Shia would have been demoralized and preoccupied with settlement— in short, not interested in disturbing the Franks.[173] When the Franks were at their peak in the mid-twelfth century, a reconfigured Shia community would still have been crystallizing. Admittedly, such a picture of Jabal Amil is speculative.

Anyway, there is no trace of Shia resistance to the Franks up to the first collapse of the Kingdom of Jerusalem in 1187. Contemporary sources indicate cooperation within the framework of feudal subjection. Unlike the Maronites and Druze, who enjoyed some autonomy, the Shia of Jabal Amil lived under direct Frankish rule, exercised through rent and tax gathering stewards on behalf of lords in Tyre and fortresses such as Tibnin.[174] Like other Muslims and the eastern Christians and Jews within the Latin states, the Twelver Shia were at the bottom of the Frankish social heap, but were left alone in the exercise of their religion and application of personal status law. They had no impetus to adopt Frankish ways, but that does not mean they hated the Franks. William of Tyre undoubtedly referred to Shia in reporting that when the funeral procession of King Baldwin III passed southward from Beirut in February 1163, "there came down from the mountains a multitude of infidels who followed the cortege with wailing."[175] The Damascus historian Ibn al-Qalanisi, writing in the late 1150s, refers to "Muslims of the Jabal Amila" as military auxiliaries of the Franks.[176] Shia may have joined Frankish forces in response to the emphatic Sunni orientation of the Nur al-Din regime in Damascus.

Over the decades, fugitives from the Galilee quietly integrated with local Shia to create the well-developed countryside that impressed the Spanish Muslim traveler Ibn Jubayr in 1184 when he accompanied a caravan from Damascus (see Tibnin castle in figure 1.4).

> We came to one of the biggest fortresses of the Franks called Tibnin. At this place, customs' dues are levied on the caravans. . . . We moved from Tibnin at daybreak. Our way lay through continuous farms and ordered settlements, whose inhabitants were all Muslims, living comfortably with the Franks. God protect us from such temptations. . . . The Muslim community bewails the injustice of a landlord of its own faith, and applauds the conduct of its enemy and opponent, the Frankish landlord, and is accustomed to justice from him.[177]

Ibn Jubayr's well-known passage has aroused the ire of modern Lebanese Shia. Al-Muhajir, who condemns Ibn Jubayr as a naïve visitor, maintains that he missed antipathies that must have existed.[178] It is dangerous, however, to dismiss an eyewitness, particularly when he accords with other sources. The riposte is colored by modern Shia hostility to the West, projecting the present into the past.

Salah al-Din's seizure of Jabal Amil in July 1187 gave most Shia autonomy similar to that of the Druze and the Maronites, after eighty years of incubation of a new Shia society under the Kingdom of Jerusalem. The sultan endorsed the authority of Husam al-Din Bishara, an officer of local Shia origin.[179] Husam al-Din inaugurated the semi-feudal order of rural bosses of Jabal Amil who patronized religious scholars. His command of the Tibnin castle enabled him both to resist the Franks and to hold off his Ayyubid overlords in Damascus. Husam al-Din's leadership from 1187 until 1200 fed into a new Twelver Shia self-confidence.

Figure 1.4 Crusader redoubt of Tibnin, southern Lebanon, 1859. Paul Zgheib Collection. Photographer: Louis le Clercq.

Between 1187 and the surrender of Tyre to the Mamluks in 1291, Jabal Amil Shia divided between the newly autonomous hills and a coast still subject to the Franks. In 1217, a Hungarian contingent from the Fifth Crusade attacked Jizzin, then a Shia locality north of Jabal Amil.[180] Ibn al-Hariri relates:

> Five hundred Franks came to take Jizzin. They descended into Marj al-Awamid, a valley beneath Jizzin, and chased off its inhabitants. The Muslims of the surrounds then gathered together and routed the Franks. They killed most of them, took their commander prisoner, scattered them, and finished off the remnant. When the lord of Acre heard he was angry and launched attacks on Jizzin and the villages around it, then King al-Mu'azzam Isa mobilized the army of Damascus and the Franks retired.[181]

Presumably, much of Jabal Amil participated in blocking such a large Frankish force. In contrast, Ibn al-Athir observed that in 1228, Shia around Tyre joined the army of the Emperor Frederick II.[182] We may surmise that they were from territory under Frankish control or were dissidents from Jabal Amil.

Division between Jabal Amil and its coastland continued into the Mamluk period, scarcely affected by the brief Frankish recovery of Tibnin from 1240 until their removal by Sultan Baybars in 1266. The thirteenth century saw the emergence of strong landed clans like the Wa'ils, who came from Arabia to join Salah al-Din, and the Shukrs.[183] These clans balanced frontier freedom with services to the Ayyubids, the Mamluks, and probably the Franks as their interests required.

Beyond southern Lebanon, Twelver Shia inhabited the Kisrawan district between Beirut and Jubayl at the time of the First Crusade, but whether they were a majority is unknown. The infiltration of Alawite (Nusayri) missionaries from the hills north of Mount Lebanon complicated the issue.[184] The Alawite faith was an extreme development of Twelver Shi'ism, asserting the divinity of the Caliph Ali and the Imams. Its appearance paralleled the emergence of Druzism out of Isma'ili Shi'ism. After around 1030, when its promoter al-Tabarani moved from Aleppo to Byzantine Latakia, the Alawite perspective won over the Muslim peasantry of the mountains behind Latakia and Tartus, then Byzantine territory.[185] The Alawite faith probably seeped into Mount Lebanon through the Akkar and Dinniya districts during the political turmoil after 1070.[186] Shia in the Kisrawan and around Mount Hermon may have been susceptible. The Muslim historian Abu al-Fida, who witnessed the final crusader recession in the late thirteenth century, refers to Alawites in the Kisrawan, and the village of Ghajjar, at the foot of Mount Hermon, remains an isolated Alawite relic to this day.[187] There was probably an Alawite population in the Kisrawan and scattered elsewhere in

Mount Lebanon through the Frankish period.[188] However, the Mamluks devastated Alawites and Twelvers in the Kisrawan in the early fourteenth century. Unlike the Twelver Shia, still present near Jubayl, the Alawites vanished. Survivors presumably fled north or rejoined Twelver Shi'ism. It seems unlikely that Alawites ever outnumbered local Twelver Shia.

Another Shia population that became virtually extinct by the fourteenth century was the Isma'ili presence that flourished under the Fatimids in the Lebanese coastal towns, to some degree displacing Sunni Islam. The Franks did the main damage in their initial takeover of the ports, clearing the way for the Mamluks to restore full Sunni preeminence in Tripoli, Beirut, and Sidon. Isma'ilis also died out in the southern Biqa and Wadi al-Taym, being absorbed into the more dynamic Druze community. Only the Druze offshoot of Isma'ili Shi'ism continued to express the Isma'ili imprint in Lebanon into the Mamluk and Ottoman centuries.

2

Druze Ascent, 1291–1633

Unlike the Maronites and Twelver Shia who cemented external relationships during the sixteenth century, the former with the Vatican and the latter with Safavid Iran, the Druze had only Mount Lebanon. A very early use of the term "Lebanese" may be found in the 1381 entry in the family record of the Druze Arslans, which refers to a prominent Druze chief as "the Lebanese emir of the Gharb" (*al-Amir Sayf al-Din Mufarrij al-Arslani al-Gharbi al-Lubnani*).[1] This chapter elucidates the interplay between renewed Sunni Islamic supremacy, represented by the Mamluks of Egypt and after 1516 by the Ottoman Turks, and the communities of Mount Lebanon. The Druze chiefs above Beirut had pride of place in the interaction. The Buhturids avoided submission to the Franks and served as the most valued Mamluk agents, even above imported Turcomans, because they were people of the mountain. The Ma'ns, in contrast, presented the Ottomans with their most serious problem in the Levant in the sixteenth century, compelling the new authorities eventually to accept Druze salience.

At the same time, as the Maronites and Twelver Shia developed connections beyond the Ottoman realm, the distinctiveness of the communities sharpened. In this context, because Druze held the core of Mount Lebanon, a Druze leader had the best chance to give the mountain the beginnings of interplay among its communities, starting with their chiefs. My argument is that Fakhr al-Din Ma'n did this, which is different from claims that he created a "principality" or that he founded "Lebanon."

By the late thirteenth century, Lebanon's mountain communities were sufficiently established to cope with Sunni Islamic imperial authority, back after an absence of almost four centuries. The practical flexibility of the Mamluk and Ottoman regimes, and their need to manipulate local power structures to maintain their authority, diluted the impact of the Sunni resurgence. Ironically, the Ottomans, despite being the more formidable regime, depended more on local chiefs because of their far-flung preoccupations. The history of Mount Lebanon and its surrounds between the fourteenth and seventeenth centuries is a bewildering interaction of regime agents, petty lords, clans, and sectarian communities. Clan chiefs played within and across communities, but communities were the focus of cultural identity, as indicated by the Maronite activist and writer, Ibn al-Qila'i or the Shia "first martyr" Ibn Makki al-Amili.

Mamluk sultans integrated Druze and Muslim chiefs around Beirut, Tripoli, and Baalbek into the *halqa*, or Mamluk elite forces. The Mamluks also imposed a hierarchy of administrative districts within the division of Mount Lebanon and its surrounds among the provinces of Damascus, Tripoli, and Safad. A *na'ib* (pl. *nuwwab*), or deputy of the sultan, headed each of the provinces. At the next level, Beirut, Baalbek, and Sidon, for example, had governors and garrisons under the *na'ib* of Damascus. The Ottomans applied a similar structure, with Damascus and Tripoli each a provincial capital in the late sixteenth century.

In 1291, the Mamluks aimed to solidify their acquisition of Beirut and its hinterland and to secure the mountains between Beirut and Tripoli. These areas comprised the coastal flank of Damascus, lynchpin of Mamluk domination of the Levant. Beirut was the maritime outlet of Damascus, including for communication with Egypt. The Kisrawan district north of Beirut was lawless terrain separating the Mamluk provincial capitals of Damascus and Tripoli. After 1291, the Mamluks were apprehensive of a western European reappearance on the Levant coast, using Cyprus as a base of operations. Any substantial landing at Beirut would menace Damascus, and it might coincide with a Mongol thrust from the north. The Mamluks had little comprehension of European politics, particularly the struggle for power in Italy, which virtually ruled out further crusading expeditions.

South of Mount Lebanon, the Mamluk regime had all coastal fortifications demolished because the coastal plain might invite Frankish re-entrenchment in any strongpoint.[2] Hence Tyre became desolate. From Sidon north, however, the Mamluks believed command of the hills that come down to the sea would make port facilities defensible, whether against crusaders or pirates. Here the prospects of revenues outweighed the risk of incursions.

Mount Lebanon's Druze lords—the Buhturids, Arslans, and Ma'ns—inhabited territory vital to Beirut and Damascus. With some hiccups, they had indicated their readiness to be useful since the time of Baybars. The Mamluks could overlook their heterodoxy because of a uniquely sharp segregation of sacred from profane in the Druze community. Religious specialists guarded spiritual knowledge, including from their own community, while secular lords adopted whatever outward religious appearance served their interests. Hence Buhturid and Arslani Tanukhs built Sunni Muslim mosques and paraded themselves as Sunni to hold office in the Mamluk *halqa* and government service. For the Mamluks, they were Sunni.

Through their Druze allies, the Mamluks could be sure of the Gharb and the Shuf. The Mamluks had already disciplined the Maronite heights above Tripoli, and Twelver Shia Jabal Amil, peripheral to the Beirut-Damascus-Tripoli triangle, presented no problem. For the Mamluk regime, the Kisrawan remained an anomaly after victory over the Franks. First, unlike the other mountain areas, even the Maronite heights, the mixed Shia, Alawite, Christian, and Druze population of the Kisrawan never caused trouble for the Franks. Hence the loyalty of the district appeared suspect in 1291. Second, the Kisrawan represented the heart of the Beirut-Damascus-Tripoli triangle. It was these elements, not the heterodox population, that predisposed the Mamluks to military action. Neither the Shia hinterland of Tyre nor the Alawite hills north of Mount Lebanon attracted such attention—only the Kisrawan.

Reestablishment of Sunni Islam in Beirut, Tripoli, and Sidon—buttressed by Sunni Turcoman settlers—proved a crucial Mamluk legacy for Lebanon. Readiness of the Druze lords to assist Sunni restoration was the basis of their local ascendancy in the fourteenth and fifteenth centuries. Druze entrenchment spearheaded by the Buhturids, however, made the Druze country a problem for the Ottomans after 1516. Ottoman pragmatism and Druze recalcitrance under the new authorities opened the way for the rise of the Ma'n family of the Shuf hills through the sixteenth century. Fakhr al-Din Ma'n, a leading member of the family, exploited Ottoman difficulties to accumulate a large territory in the central Levant under his control in the early seventeenth century.

Away from the Druze hills and the resuscitated Sunni presence on the coast, the Maronite districts of northern Mount Lebanon and Shia Jabal Amil also witnessed seminal developments between the fourteenth and seventeenth centuries. These developments were of long-term rather than instant significance. First, in the late fifteenth and sixteenth centuries, the Maronite church came under Roman Catholic hegemony, involving diversifying Maronite relations with Italy. Second, Jabal Amil became a serious contributor to Twelver Shia religious scholarship. Even if Lebanese scholars initially suspected the eccentric imposition of Shi'ism in Safavid Iran in the early sixteenth century, Jabal Amil later reinforced the Iranian religious institution.

Local primary sources for the Mamluk period indicate communal compartments in Mount Lebanon. Salih bin Yahya and Ibn Sibat, chroniclers of the Druze lords, concentrated on Beirut and what might be termed the Druze/Sunni arena, paying little attention to Christians and Shia. Similarly, Ibn al-Qila'i and Istifan Duwayhi focused on Maronite affairs in the north, though in *Tarikh al-Azmina*, Duwayhi gives attention to wider developments. Overall, the sources portray distinctive evolutions in the mountain.

In the sixteenth and seventeenth centuries, the picture changed, as can be traced in Duwayhi's narrative and al-Khalidi al-Safadi's *Lubnan fi Ahd al-Amir*

Fakhr al-Din al-Ma'ni al-Thani.[3] Maronites moved into the Kisrawan and collaborated with Turcoman and Druze lords near Beirut, while rising Shia clans in the northern Biqa interacted with them all. Fakhr al-Din's domain and his European outreach depended heavily on the Maronites. Early Ottoman hegemony, from removing the Mamluks in 1516 to overthrowing Fakhr al-Din in 1633, thus saw a new mixing of the communal strands of Lebanon's history.

Mamluk Assaults on the Kisrawan, 1292–1305

According to the Mamluk chronicler Badr al-Din al-Ayni, who gives the best account of the disastrous Mamluk expedition into the Kisrawan in July 1292, closure of the coastal road between Beirut and Tripoli to travelers forced the hand of the Sultan al-Ashraf Khalil.[4] Mamluk officers in Damascus were unenthusiastic: "The emirs of Damascus were deterred by what they knew of the numbers and resolution [of the mountain people] and the narrowness of the tracks to them, which a horseman cannot negotiate."[5] The sultan had to compel his deputy, Badr al-Din Baydara, to take three thousand cavalry up the Levant coast from Egypt, entering the Kisrawan from the south. Al-Ayni names the target as *kafarat rawafid* ("refusing infidels"), contemporary Sunni terminology for Shia.[6] He relates that the mountaineers mobilized 10,000 defenders, who lured Mamluk contingents into ambushes. According to the Maronite historian Ibn al-Qila'i, the Mamluk column also penetrated the Jubayl district, where Christian inhabitants attacked it.[7] Al-Ayni does not mention the Maronites, and Ibn al-Qila'i does not mention the Shia. The overall picture is of a Mamluk force stretched along the coastal road through the Kisrawan and Jubayl, with units cut off in mountain valleys and harassed by the sectarian groups.

Apparently, Baydara was only able to extricate his troops when the mountaineers realized that they were engaging the sultan's army headed by the sultan's chief lieutenant—not simply a provincial force from Damascus.[8] He had to offer gifts and release prisoners, and his commanders condemned him to al-Ashraf Khalil for bribery and incompetence. He gave his excuses to his overlord in Damascus, and the sultan treated him leniently.

Through the 1290s, Mamluk preoccupation with the Franks, Mongols, and Cilician Armenians, intrigues in Cairo, and circumspect Kisrawani behavior ensured that there was no further attempt to discipline the Kisrawan. Otherwise, however, the Mamluks shored up their position in Mount Lebanon. In 1294 Kitbugha, minder of the new sultan, al-Ashraf Khalil's nine-year-old half-brother al-Nasir Muhammad, confirmed the incorporation of the Druze Buhturid emirs into the sultanate's regular army and assigned them rotating guard duty in Beirut.[9] To the north, the Mamluks rebuilt Tripoli on a new site with stout fortifications.

From 1290, it was the seat of a *niyaba*, or deputyship, like Damascus, with a territory larger than the Frankish county, extending from the Kisrawan almost to
Latakia, and inland almost to Homs. The Tripoli garrison grew to four thousand
regulars, mainly Turks.[10]

In late December 1299, in a surprise winter offensive, the Mongol Ilkhan
Ghazan swept across the Euphrates to defeat a hastily assembled Mamluk army
at Khazindar near Homs and briefly occupied Damascus. Mamluk troops fled
south along the Lebanese coast and through the Biqa Valley, and reactions in
Mount Lebanon returned the Kisrawan to the Mamluk priority list. Kisrawan
mountaineers sensed Mamluk collapse and plundered the retreating forces. In
contrast, the leading Buhturid lord, Nahid al-Din, and the Biqa chief, Ala al-Din,
offered Mamluk soldiers sanctuary, for which they were later rewarded.[11] Unfor-
tunately for the Kisrawanis, Ghazan could not sustain his victory and the sultanate swiftly recovered. In the summer of 1300, the Mamluks implemented
retribution, with troops mobilized from most of the Levant. The Mamluk historian al-Maqrizi commented:

> Emir Aqush al-Afram [*na'ib* of Damascus] advanced from Damascus, to
> attack the Druze of the Kisrawan hills, because of their outrages . . . and
> the governors of Safad, Hamah, Homs, and Tripoli accompanied him
> with their forces. [The Kisrawanis] prepared to fight, fortifying them-
> selves in their mountain, which is difficult to invade. . . . The [sultan's]
> army attacked them from several directions, and battled them intensely
> for six days. The mountain people could not hold out, and were routed.
> The [sultan's] army ascended the mountain after killing and capturing
> many of them. . . . Their chiefs were summoned and compelled to return
> everything stolen from the army at the time of its defeat. . . . Aqush
> al-Afram imposed a fine of 100,000 dirhems, took some of their chiefs
> and elders hostage, and returned to Damascus.[12]

Whereas al-Maqrizi refers to "Druze," al-Ayni defines the rebels more broadly as
"the most extreme turncoats and free-thinkers."[13]

It was plain that the punishment did not suffice, and the standoff of the
1290s continued. Reduction of the Kisrawan required the main Mamluk field
army, and up until 1304, the menace of Ghazan tied up regular forces. Ghazan's
death in 1304 changed the situation, and the Mamluks determined to administer a lasting lesson in Mount Lebanon. The sultanate dispatched several religious personalities, including the Hanbali scholar Taqi al-Din Ibn Taymiyya,
to demand that the Kisrawani sectarians, including Twelver Shia, "return to
obedience" to Sunni Islam.[14] Their refusal supplied the legal justification for an
assault.

Al-Maqrizi, al-Ayni, and Salih bin Yahya all refer to 50,000 troops marching from Damascus in July 1305 to meet another army under the *na'ib* of Tripoli coming south by "the most difficult paths.[15] The numbers are surely an exaggeration but indicate the scale of the operation. The Mamluks also summoned their Druze Buhturid allies from the Beirut hills to join the expedition. The Mamluk pincer movement converged on the rebels in the heart of the mountain, where fierce battles resulted in the crushing of the Kisrawanis. Many hundreds were killed, and six hundred were taken prisoner.[16] The dead included senior Mamluks and two Buhturid lords.[17] The Mamluks then devastated villages and cultivation through August 1305 and expelled much of the population. Local Christians were not spared, with destruction of most churches, while the Kisrawani Druze Abi Lama family featured among the rebel leaders.[18] The latter supports al-Maqrizi's reference to Druze activity against the Mamluks in 1300. However, the main targets were the Twelver Shia and the Alawites. The best summary comes from the Ayyubid emir of Hama, Abu al-Fida, who, unlike other Mamluk chroniclers, participated in early fourteenth-century events:

> Jamal al-Din Aqush al-Afram led the army of Damascus, and other forces from the Levant [*al-Sham*] into the hills of the disloyal people, who were recalcitrant deviants from true religion. The Islamic armies encircled these . . . hills. The troops dismounted and climbed on foot into the mountains from all directions. They killed and seized all the Nusayris [Alawites] and renegades they encountered, and other heretics, and cleared them out of the hills. These lofty mountains stand between Damascus and Tripoli. The roads became secure thereafter, because [the rebels] had cut traffic and kidnapped Muslims, selling them to the infidels.[19]

After 1305, there is no trace of Alawites in the Kisrawan. The Shia may have been confused with Alawites, but were less subjected to "clearance," to use Abu al-Fida's term. The *na'ib* of Tripoli removed a large group to his town, which was still undergoing re-population.[20] Even a Mamluk ally like the Druze Nasir al-Din evidently tried to stem the exodus, which may have included his confederates north of the Gharb.[21] The Mamluks at first gave land in the Kisrawan to some officers, including Ala al-Din of the Biqa, but cancelled the awards in favor of settling Sunni Turcoman immigrants on the Kisrawan coast. The settlers, who had already entered the Kura and Akkar districts with the collapse of Frankish Tripoli, would provide more direct security.[22] The sultanate required the Turcomans, most notably the Assaf clan, to maintain three hundred mounted troops to supervise the coast between Beirut and Jubayl, and to control entry to the Kisrawan from Beirut.[23]

After the "clearance" of the Kisrawan, the Mamluk regime inaugurated military arrangements that persisted through the fourteenth century. The Sunni Turcomans and the Druze Buhturids staffed the front line against Frankish Cyprus and Italian pirates. Nasir al-Din, son of Nahid al-Din, became the leading Buhturid when the sultan retired Sa'ad al-Din, last of the Buhturid triumvirate of the late thirteenth century, in 1305. Nasir al-Din assumed responsibility for Beirut, with a rotation of Mamluk regulars from Baalbek. He held the rank of "emir" in the Mamluk army, though at the modest level of "emir of ten" (meaning ten knights, or cavalrymen). For the Mamluks, the value of incorporating the Buhturids in the *iqta*—grants of lordship over land in return for military service—was that they were defending their ancestral domain. The *na'ib* of Damascus also had fire beacons built between Beirut and Damascus, to warn of trouble.[24] Given Turcoman ambitions and jealousy toward the Buhturids in the Druze hills, there were risks of instability in the Mamluk dispensation that became more visible later.

Mamluk reduction of the Kisrawan had important consequences. The population remained largely Twelver Shia tribal groups coming in and out from the Biqa. The Hamade family that dominated the north in the seventeenth century may have had its origins among them.[25] However, they were pushed back from the coast and the numbers probably never recovered. Through the fourteenth and fifteenth centuries, local Shia are virtually absent from the sources. In addition, the Alawites were written out of Mount Lebanon's affairs. The Kisrawan became more thinly settled and this situation persisted. The district was therefore vulnerable to non-Shia settler penetration, especially if encouraged by the Sunni Assafs. Eventually Maronite clans moved south from Jubayl, which jumpstarted their relations with the Druze lords. The Maronite-Druze interaction of Ottoman times would have been inconceivable had these communities been separated by Twelver Shia/Alawite domination of the Kisrawan.

Mamluks in Charge, 1306–1516

Reduction of the Kisrawan in 1305–1306, which coincided with recession of the Mongol challenge from Iraq and Anatolia, confirmed Mamluk hegemony over Mount Lebanon and the wider Levant. The Mongols became Muslim in the early fourteenth century, and their Ilkhanate in Anatolia, Iraq, and Iran decomposed. Their last eruption under Timurlane at the close of the century was within a Sunni Muslim framework. It represented a brief destructive episode that actually rescued the Mamluks in their new contest with the Ottoman Turks, whom Timurlane hit harder. As for western Europe, the impetus was toward profitable trade between the Mamluks and the Italians, especially the Venetians. Frankish

Cyprus and the Genoese and Catalan rivals of Venice bothered the coast and ports from time to time, but they were never an existential threat. In 1426, al-Ashraf Barsbay, the last great Mamluk sultan, invaded Cyprus and forced the Franks into a tributary relationship. Through two centuries, the Lebanese chiefs and communities had to operate within Mamluk parameters.

Mamluk attention after 1305 concentrated on the port towns of Beirut, Tripoli, and Sidon; on the coastal route connecting the ports; and on the vital Beirut-Damascus track, through the Druze country and the Biqa. This comprised the political, military, and commercial arena of Mamluk Lebanon, with only a subdued extension to the Maronite mountain or Shia Jabal Amil (see figure 2.1). Cultural developments in Mount Lebanon, however, were more diffuse, with the Sunni recrudescence on the coast paralleled by Maronite and Shia ferment in the north and south of the coastal mountains.

A. N. Poliak's population estimate for Lebanese districts in 1343, just before the Black Death, is similar to that suggested earlier for the Frankish apogee.[26] Poliak proposes about 150,000 people for Lebanon, except Tripoli, on the basis of a Mamluk levy of 500 cavalrymen for Beirut, Sidon, and the Biqa, and an official calculation of 250 civilians to support each "knight." Adding Tripoli and the north would raise the total to perhaps 220,000. In 1348–1349, the Black Death killed up to one-third of the population of the Levant.[27] Not merely was there no recovery up to the Ottoman conquest, but repeated epidemics of bubonic plague imply prolonged reduction. In the late fifteenth century, the population of the territory of modern Lebanon may have been static at around 150,000 to 200,000.

What were the implications? The grip of the state weakened as its tax base declined, allowing local actors more mobility. With less revenue from land and towns, the sultanate increasingly valued long-distance trade, which advantaged Italian merchants and made the Mamluks more tolerant of Western Christians. Druze lords, Biqa Sunni clans, the Maronite church, and Shia scholars all benefited in one way or another from the constraints on the sultanate, especially in the fifteenth century. Of course, episodic plague and a smaller population did not preclude periods of prosperity—Tripoli and its hinterland did well in late Mamluk times. And al-Ashraf Barsbay demonstrated that a capable ruler could still coax great power performance out of the sultanate.

Druze and Sunnis at Center Stage

Mount Lebanon's politics in the fourteenth and fifteenth centuries centered on Mamluks stationed in Damascus, Tripoli, and Beirut; Druze leaders (principally the Buhturids); and Sunni chiefs in the Biqa and Beirut, including Turcomans. These politics involved struggles for power, land, and income from trade. Sami

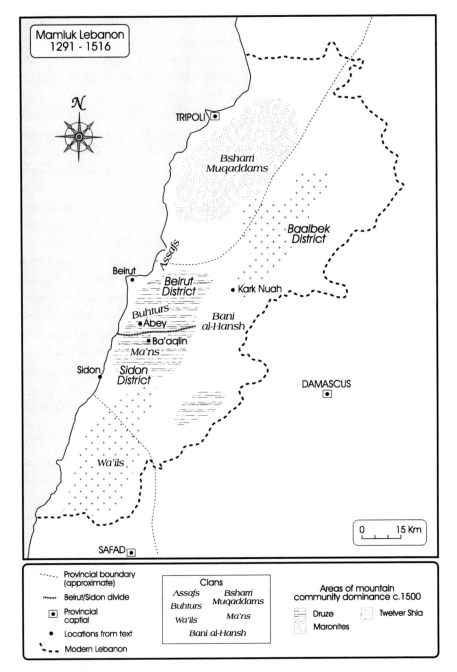

Figure 2.1 Mamluk Lebanon, 1291–1516.

Makarim provides the indispensable modern Arabic account of the activities of the Buhturid lords, the core of Mount Lebanon's affairs through the Mamluk period. Umar Tadmuri does the same for Mamluk Tripoli, the sultanate's provincial capital in Lebanon.

After 1305, the Druze lord Nasir al-Din al-Husayn built on service in the Kisrawan and seniority among Buhturids to consolidate his position as the Mamluks' favored agent in Beirut. His breakthrough came in 1313 with the sultanate's reallocation of *iqta* land-holdings in the province of Damascus. The Sultan al-Nasir Muhammad wished to extend the state domain, reward the loyal, and streamline taxes.[28] The revision increased al-Nasir Muhammad's command of resources and restricted the autonomy of his vassals. The Damascus survey, or *rawk*, gave army officers land distant from existing holdings, which were reassigned. In Mount Lebanon, the process threatened to uproot the Buhturids and other Tanukh chiefs from inherited lands, which contradicted the idea of the Tanukhs defending the sultanate by defending their ancestral soil. Nasir al-Din personally protested in Damascus claiming that deprivation of inherited property violated Islamic law.[29] He achieved acceptance of the Beirut hills as a special case, including renewed designation of the Gharb as an *imara*, or "principality." The *rawk* raised Nasir al-Din's rank to "emir of twenty [horsemen]," then revised to *amir tablkhana* (forty), far above any other Druze lord.[30] His intercession with the sultanate of course inflated his prestige.

Following the *rawk*, stability prevailed in Mount Lebanon for three decades, until the death of the Sultan al-Nasir Muhammad in 1341. The ascendancy of Nasir al-Din in the hinterland of Beirut paralleled the tenure of Sayf al-Din Tankiz (1312–1340) as *na'ib* of Damascus. For much of the period, Tankiz was a super-governor of the Levant, through whom resentful *nuwwab* of Tripoli, Aleppo, and Safad had to conduct their relations with Cairo. Tankiz, like his master in Cairo, left his mark as sponsor of building projects, including mosques and an aqueduct for Damascus. Nasir al-Din did the same, endowing a mosque and bathhouse in his beloved home village of Abey and supervising construction of a new seaside quarter in Beirut.[31] In the military sphere, the Genoese made a destructive raid on Beirut in 1334, targeting Catalan traders and the town. Tankiz, unhappy with Nasir al-Din, ordered him to move to Beirut from the mountain. In local politics, Nasir al-Din reached out to other Tanukhs and to the Ma'ns of the Shuf. He prevented the advancement of various opponents: the Kisrawan Turcomans, who coveted the Gharb; the Bani Hamra clan of Beirut, originally of the Biqa; and the "Abi al-Jaysh" Arslans. The only documented trace of Druzism from the leading Druze was advice to his son to look to the "seven pillars of *tawhid*" (oneness with God).[32]

From 1341 to 1382, twelve descendants of al-Nasir Muhammad acceded to the sultanate, generally minors manipulated by Mamluk grandees. Up to 1354, eight sons of al-Nasir Muhammad succeeded one another in a maelstrom of violence. The Buhturids struggled to retain supremacy in Beirut in this turbulent environment.

In 1342, the Druze lords joined an army from Egypt to besiege the sultan's deposed half-brother, holed up in the Transjordan fortress of Kerak. Nasir al-Din left after only five weeks because of a Frankish threat to the Lebanese coast. One of the rival Abi al-Jaysh Arslans stayed and was made an "emir of ten."[33] Nasir al-Din's son Zayn al-Din Salih succeeded him in 1348 and had to face down challenges through three decades as paramount chief. In 1361, the Abi al-Jaysh plotted to have the na'ib of Damascus hand them military control of Beirut, which the Buhturids managed to reverse.[34]

In 1365, Peter of Cyprus went to war with the sultanate and sacked Alexandria. The Mamluks poured resources into a fatuous project to build a fleet at Beirut to invade Cyprus. The Kisrawan Turcomans offered a thousand men if Cairo would give them command of the Gharb, displacing the Buhturids. Cairo consented, and a shocked Zayn al-Din sent his son to Egypt, salvaging the family inheritance with the support of the sultan's chief secretary.[35] Thereafter, both the Turcomans and the Buhturids were required to finance Mamluk troops in Beirut. Zayn al-Din died in 1377, having preserved his father's legacy.

By picking the right side, the Buhturids survived the late fourteenth-century transition from the Turkish (*Bahri*) Mamluk dynasty to the Circassian (*Burji*) Mamluks. Their Abi al-Jaysh and Turcoman rivals fell by the wayside. In 1382, the leading Buhturid, Sayf al-Din Yahya, father of the historian Salih bin Yahya, sparred with the na'ib of Damascus. Sayf al-Din repelled a Genoese attack on Beirut, but the na'ib accused him of dereliction.[36] Around the same time, Sayf al-Din suppressed a clash between Sunnis and Twelver Shia in Beirut, and the na'ib slated him for Shia sympathies. In fact, the Mamluks brought the Shia to Beirut.[37] The seizure of the sultanate in 1382 by the *Burji* Mamluk Al-Zahir Barquq thus gratified the Buhturids.

When a rebellion briefly restored the last *Bahri* sultan in 1389, the Buhturids maintained allegiance to Barquq. They joined him in besieging Damascus after he escaped detention in Kerak. The Turcoman Assafs of the Kisrawan, on the other hand, opposed Barquq and attacked the Druze Tanukhs in Beirut and the hills.[38] They killed four Abi al-Jaysh emirs and captured four others, all of whom the Arslani *Sijill* reports as suffering execution by being cut in half.[39] One emir escaped; though the Arslan line survived, it was the end of the Abi al-Jaysh. When Barquq emerged victorious in 1390 and the Buhturid emirs rushed to Cairo, the Turcomans again assaulted the Beirut hills.[40] However, they failed to take the strongholds of Aynab and Aramoun. Barquq mobilized Mamluk regulars, Biqa tribesmen, and Druze. These forces crushed the Kisrawan Turcomans. Barquq did not award the Buhturids the Kisrawan; instead he left the chastened

Assafs in place—the sultan may not have wanted the Buhturids too strong, or he may not have wanted them overextended.[41]

By the early fifteenth century the Buhturid chiefs dominated central Mount Lebanon. Along with their *Burji* Mamluk masters, they absorbed humiliations in defeats of the sultan's forces by rebels in 1391 and by Timurlane in 1400. Their leaders attended to peasant concerns, earning widespread respect. For example, in the late 1370s, the Emir Shihab al-Din Ahmad deflected Mamluk interest in cutting down plum trees in the Shuf hills to make arrows, sparing the peasants agricultural losses and forced labor.[42] The son of the surviving Abi al-Jaysh Arslan emir married the daughter of the paramount Buhturid, bringing the Tanukhs back together. In 1413, this emir received supervisory rights for the coast south of Beirut.[43] The Buhturids also had expanding commercial interests; Salih bin Yahya's father traded silk, olive oil, and soap from Beirut, imported grain from Egypt, and developed business relations with Egyptian Mamluks.

Buhturid fortune peaked under the Sultan al-Ashraf Barsbay (1422–1438). Early in his reign, Barsbay made the Emir Iz al-Din Sidqa governor (*mutawali*) of Beirut, the first time a Buhturid held this position. Salih bin Yahya, historian and cousin of Iz al-Din, was a Mamluk officer, possibly an "emir of twenty," and handled rural affairs.[44] Bin Yahya commanded a ship in the sultan's 1425 attack on Cyprus, and the Mamluks invited him to Cairo. This sparked a showdown between the Buhturids and their remaining Beirut rivals, the Bani Hamra clan. A Bani Hamra emir also participated in the 1425 expedition and went to Cairo afterward. Barsbay awarded this emir property in Beirut, another officer assassinated him, the property award went to Salih bin Yahya, and the Bani Hamra blamed the Buhturids.[45] The murdered emir's brother assaulted the governor's house in Beirut and laid an ambush in the Biqa for Salih bin Yahya. At the command of the *na'ib* of Damascus, the Bani al-Hansh chief in the Biqa arrested and beheaded the miscreant. The Bani Hamra fell out of the historical record, but the major street of West Beirut still bears their name. They encouraged Sunnis to come to Beirut from the Biqa and Wadi al-Taym.[46]

After 1450, Druze spirituality and religious teachings, stagnant since the eleventh century "call," received energetic input from the Buhturid Jamal al-Din Abdullah, better known as *al-Amir al-Sayyid*. Jamal al-Din had a formidable reputation for piety and moral rectitude, finessed Druze writings—the collected epistles of the early "call"—into their modern form, and exemplified the ideal of spiritual unity with God.[47] His learning encompassed Islam in general; he acquired his honorific of *sayyid* from Sunni Muslims in Damascus. Jamal al-Din, however, split the Buhturids and Druze society even as he revitalized the Druze faith. His branch of the Buhturids had no property, and his command of peasant loyalty throughout the Druze Levant, with disciples organizing village councils, threatened the legitimacy of the lords.[48] Between 1454 and 1466, their hostility forced him into exile in Damascus. In his last years up until 1479, he disposed of considerable wealth, donated by admirers like the Buhturid poet Emir Sayf al-Din Yahya, which further angered the lords.[49]

Jamal al-Din's successor as holder of the *mashyakhat* (spiritual leadership) of the Druze, Sayf al-Din Abu Bakr, was a grandson of Emir Iz al-Din, former governor of Beirut. He bridged the rift between religious and secular leaders while entrenching religious reforms. Sayf al-Din died of the plague in 1492, and the religious institution again lost momentum. The Buhturid lords prevailed, but the long challenge of *al-Amir al-Sayyid* sapped their popularity.

The last Buhturid paramount emir of Mamluk times, Jamal al-Din Hajji, was an abrasive wheeler and dealer who exploited Mamluk factionalism as the *Burji* sultanate decayed.[50] In the late 1490s, he became only the second Buhturid to achieve the governorship of Beirut, but he drifted into conflict with old friends, the Bani al-Hansh. This Sunni clan profited from the eclipse of the Bani Hamra, and by the 1490s they controlled much of the Biqa. After 1496, Nasr al-Din Muhammad Ibn al-Hansh succeeded his kinsman Emir Assaf Ibn al-Hansh as governor of Sidon. He defied the *na'ib* of Damascus, and Jamal al-Din Hajji engineered his dismissal.[51] In 1505 he rebelled and also raided Beirut, pillaging Jamal al-Din Hajji's soap stocks. By 1512 the Mamluks restored him as governor of Sidon, a blow to Buhturid prestige.[52]

In the hinterland of Sidon, the Druze Ma'n clan maintained their Shuf lordship based on Ba'aqlin, founded in 1120. Through Mamluk times they also continued their close relations with the Buhturids and the Sunni Shihabs of Wadi al-Taym.[53] In the 1490s, however, an energetic Ma'n chief, Fakhr al-Din Uthman, allied with the Bani al-Hansh against the Buhturid Jamal al-Din Hajji. The Mamluks imprisoned him in 1505 but quickly released him "covered with honor."[54] They clearly thought highly of him. Al-Shidyaq described Fakhr al-Din Uthman's appearance as "the sun setting on the Tanukh emirate and rising on the Ma'n emirate."[55]

If Beirut and Sidon and access to them were the concerns in Mount Lebanon of the *na'ib* of Damascus, usually the senior Mamluk in the Levant, Tripoli represented the major Mamluk presence in Mount Lebanon. It was the seat of a *na'ib*, a garrison town, and by the fifteenth century the leading port. It was thus the focus in Mount Lebanon of intrigue among senior Mamluks and the center of Sunni cultural revival. The *na'ib* of Tripoli also handled Mamluk interactions with Mount Lebanon's Christians.

Occasionally Tripoli became the eye of the storm in the sultanate's restless politics. In 1349, a young Mamluk emir from Egypt, humiliated by the *na'ib* of Damascus during his posting there, pulled strings in Cairo to become *na'ib* of Tripoli at the age of nineteen.[56] Together with another emir, he used his new position to murder the *na'ib* of Damascus in 1350, forging an order from the sultan. The two emirs took refuge in Tripoli and fled south into the Kisrawan when the Sultan al-Nasir Hasan ordered their arrest. Troops from Tripoli and Baalbek captured them after a major mobilization. In late 1399, the *na'ib* of Tripoli, Yunis Balta, joined Tanam, *na'ib* of Damascus, in rebellion against the child Sultan al-Nasir Faraj. The elite of Tripoli repudiated Balta, and he and Tanam then sacked part of the city in December 1399.[57] They killed three of the four chief judges of the Sunni law schools, the Mufti, twenty other leading personalities, and up to one thousand local residents in an appalling massacre. The sultan's forces captured them both north of Gaza in April 1400, and they were executed in Damascus. Given such diversions, the shambolic Mamluk reaction to Timurlane's invasion of the Levant a few months later becomes intelligible. In 1405, another senior Mamluk, Jakam, seized Tripoli in an abortive revolt against al-Nasir Faraj.[58] Al-Muayyad Shaykh found the city more useful. He was *na'ib* four times after 1400 before taking the sultanate in 1412.[59]

Tripoli represented a natural coastal outlet for the Eurasian land trade crossing the Jazira into northern Syria. It also exported local produce and manufactures from the coastal plain stretching north from Mount Lebanon, whether grain, fruit, and other foodstuffs for Egypt or silk textiles and sugar for Europe. Tripoli had excellent access to the land trade through the Homs gap, midway between Aleppo and Damascus, and as a provincial capital it had better security than Beirut or Latakia. The new Tripoli of the *Bahri* Mamluks after 1289 (figure 2.2 gives an approximate impression) depended substantially on commerce between Syria and Egypt. In both Fatimid and Mamluk times, Tripoli dispatched ice from Mount Lebanon for the sultan's palaces in Cairo.[60]

Recovery of Tripoli's trade to Europe after the collapse of the Frankish states was unstable. A papal embargo, Cypriot raids, the Black Death, and the precedence of Egypt's trade with Italy all deterred recovery. Nonetheless, long-distance trade picked up with the ending of hostilities between the Mamluks and the Mongols and the eagerness of the Venetians and Mamluks. Venetian convoys came with treaties in 1355 and 1361, but initially to Beirut.[61] Under the *Burji* Mamluks, commerce improved and the advantage swung to Tripoli, where several thousand artisans manufactured silk fabrics prized in the West. Under Sultan Qa'itbay after 1468, the commercial ascendancy of Tripoli over Beirut caused friction with Damascus. In 1473, the Venetian consul infuriated the *na'ib* of Damascus by bringing a shipment of European woolens to Tripoli rather than Beirut.[62] In 1499, when Venetian ships unloaded goods worth customs dues of ten thousand ducats at Tripoli instead of Beirut, the *na'ib* of Damascus confiscated Venetian wares to extort compensation.[63] Given the opportunities to load goods at Tripoli, it made sense to unload there as well and risk the wrath of officialdom in Beirut and Damascus.

As for cultural activities, Mamluk Tripoli ranked with Damascus and Aleppo in producing and hosting scholars, mainly Sunni Muslim religious specialists, poets,

Figure 2.2 Tripoli with Mamluk mosque in the background, 1859. Paul Zgheib Collection.

historians, and copyists. A number of scholars born in Tripoli rose high in the Mamluk judicial and religious hierarchies, for example Shams al-Din Abu Abdullah who became Hanafi "judge of judges" (*qadi al-quda*) in Egypt in the late fourteenth century.[64] For the fourteenth and fifteenth centuries, Umar Tadmuri in his *Tarikh Tarabulus* lists fifteen authors, mostly on religious matters but including two on horsemanship; seven calligraphers, copyists, and interpreters of texts; eight poets, including senior officials in the provincial chancery and treasury; twelve visiting scholars from all parts of the sultanate; and thirty-one other prominent religious specialists, judges, and artists.[65] Tadmuri's seventy-three names include two women with religious expertise and a musician. The story of Mamluk Tripoli is the story of Sunni Islamic revival on the Lebanese coast after the Sunni eclipse under the Isma'ili Fatimids and the Western Christians.

Maronite and Shia Peripheries

Little concrete material exists on the Maronites of the province of Tripoli under the *Bahri* Mamluks after 1305, until the 1380s. According to Duwayhi, Mamluk troops camped in the Bsharri area in 1309, demonstrating that the *na'ib* of Tripoli could exert authority there.[66] Otherwise, the Maronites seem to have been left to their own affairs. They presumably practiced a limited seasonal trans-humance, some people shifting to villages on the lower slopes or the outskirts of Tripoli in winter.[67] However, for security reasons, Bsharri and other high villages would have remained partly occupied through winter.

Maronite patriarchs resided at Mayfuq above Batrun through the fourteenth century, about twenty kilometers from Bsharri, where a senior chief, or muqad-dam, held sway. There is little doubt that the community was splintered among various mountain districts—Dinniya, Bsharri, Batrun, Jubayl, and Munaytara—all technically Mamluk administrative divisions. Further, the church lost com-munications with its recently acquired Roman patron for many decades. The Monothelite doctrine persisted, and Jacobites probably made inroads. On the other hand, patriarchs and much of the priesthood asserted loyalty to Rome, even if isolation meant that they deviated from Roman procedure and doctrine. There is no evidence that the Maronites dwindled or became overshadowed by the Jacobites.[68]

A first sign of revived Vatican influence came with the return of the Fran-ciscans to Beirut in 1345. This reflected increasing Mamluk interest in trade with the Italians, but it was a small outpost with no initial impact in the moun-tains. Apparently no blame attached to Christians in Mount Lebanon for what al-Maqrizi describes as a Christian plot to burn markets and the Umayyad mosque in Damascus in 1340, with two participating monks escaping through Beirut to Cyprus.[69] However, the assaults of Peter of Cyprus on Tripoli in 1366 and 1367, after his attack on Alexandria, were a different matter. The Mamluks suspected Christians on the coast of espionage and burned Maro-nite Patriarch Jibra'il of Hajula at the stake.[70] They also harassed Maronites in Ihdin and other villages. There is no evidence that the Mamluk crackdown lasted beyond the military emergency.

Maronites reemerged from the shadows under the *Burji* Mamluk sultans, beginning with Barquq. Duwayhi reports that Barquq visited Bsharri when tem-porarily deposed in 1389–1390, receiving hospitality from the monks of the Qannubin monastery.[71] In return, he conferred favors on the monastery.[72] Barquq may also have confirmed the young local muqaddam, Ya'qub Ibn Ayyub, as the Mamluk tax gatherer for the district. Whatever the case, the Ayyubs dom-inated Bsharri through the *Burji* period. Ya'qub provided stable lordship from 1382 until 1444, and his good relations with the Tripoli Mamluks assisted Maronites within and beyond Bsharri to prosper, particularly taking advantage of the relaxed, expansive sultanate of al-Ashraf Barsbay.[73]

In Barsbay's time, Rome reinforced the Franciscan mission in Beirut and rees-tablished its link with the Maronite patriarchate. In 1438, the year of Barsbay's death, Patriarch Yuhanna al-Jaji asked Father Juan, head of the mission, to repre-sent him at the 1438–1439 Church Council, meeting in Ferrara and Florence.[74]

At Florence, Father Juan transferred the patriarch's profession of obedience and orthodoxy and returned to Tripoli in October 1439 with papal confirmation of Yuhanna al-Jaji as head of the Maronite church. A crowd sufficiently large to unnerve the Mamluk authorities greeted him—a good indicator of Maronite vitality and the popularity of the link with Rome.[75]

The late fifteenth century proved decisive for the religious and cultural orientation of the Maronites. There were conflicting pressures. First, after the Council of Florence, the Vatican sent Franciscan envoys to the Maronite church to compel coordination with Roman doctrines and traditions. In the early 1440s, a papal envoy discovered that Maronites in Cyprus, under the authority of Patriarch al-Jaji, professed that there was "one will in the Lord," meaning they were Monolethites.[76] A Father Gryphon frequented Maronite Mount Lebanon in the 1450s and 1460s. He condemned customs shared with Jacobites such as administering Communion to baptized infants, but advised Rome to be flexible about ritual.[77] Acceptance of papal supremacy was not an issue after 1439. Overall, Roman orthodoxy had a solid beachhead, but Monothelite tendencies persisted into the Ottoman period.[78]

Monophysite Jacobites certainly intervened. Jacobites were still entrenched in the Syrian interior under the Mamluks and were relatively numerous on the coast. Maronites were vulnerable to Jacobite preaching because their old Monothelite doctrine was halfway to Monophysite belief. Jacobite missionaries gained converts around Bsharri through the fifteenth century. They seized the upper hand in 1472 when Abd al-Mun'im Ayyub, an enthusiastic convert, became muqaddam of Bsharri. This alarmed the patriarchate, which had shifted from Mayfuq to Qanubin near Bsharri in 1440.[79] The crisis came in 1488, when a muqaddam from Dinniya district led a horde of Maronites to expel Jacobites from Ihdin, west of Bsharri.[80]

Thereafter, Jacobite influence receded. The Maronites recaptured the headship of Bsharri when Abd al-Mun'im died in 1495, in the midst of a Roman reaction spearheaded by the zealous Jibra'il Ibn al-Qila'i, priest and historian. Ibn al-Qila'i returned to his native land in 1493 after more than two decades of study in Italy, sponsored by Father Gryphon.[81] The ephemeral Jacobite coup in Bsharri did not affect the Maronite majority, who lived in other districts under other muqaddams. Through the sixteenth century, the Maronites reabsorbed the Jacobite converts, and the Jacobite community in Mount Lebanon entered its final decline.

The Mamluk period closed on a high note for the Maronite church. In 1515, after an exchange of letters, Pope Leo X confirmed the sitting patriarch, memorably commending the Maronites as "roses among thorns." Nonetheless, the pope also expressed lingering doubts about Maronite commitment to Roman orthodoxy.[82]

At the other end of the Lebanese coastal mountains, south of Sidon, the Twelver Shia refuge of Jabal Amil paralleled the Maronite redoubt in the Tripoli hills. Restored Sunni supremacy in the Levant was more intimidating for the Shia, devastated in the Kisrawan and dominated in the Biqa in the early four-teenth century. Further, through the fourteenth and fifteenth centuries they had to adapt to Mamluk rule without any prospect of external aid. They had no equiv-alent of the buttressing that the Roman church represented for the Maronites. Fortunately, Jabal Amil, strategically significant to the Franks, was a backwater for the Mamluks. Modern southern Lebanon was split between the Mamluk prov-inces of Damascus and Safad and peripheral for both. In contrast to the situation under the Franks, the port of Tyre meant nothing to the Mamluks; the political and economic core of the Mamluk Levant was farther north. Provided Twelver Shia chiefs respected the authorities and religious personalities avoided attract-ing outside attention, there was no reason for the Mamluks to bother Jabal Amil.

After the collapse of the Franks, as after their arrival, Twelver Shia migrated to Jabal Amil. There was, however, a significant difference. In the early twelfth cen-tury, Jabal Amil received refugees as an area marginal to what was probably a Shia majority in the Levant, since the takeover of the region by Twelver or Isma'ili regimes in the mid-tenth century. From about 1070, the Shia faced a Sunni revival headed by the incoming Seljuk Turks and, after 1099, the Frankish invasion, which stampeded Shia out of Palestine and intensified Sunni fervor in interior Syria. Jabal Amil, especially before the Franks took Tyre in 1124 and after 1187, provided refuge, at the outset from the Franks and later from Sunni rigor.

By the early fourteenth century, Jabal Amil, beyond Sunni authority through most of the crusader period, was becoming the Twelver Shia center of the Levant. Salih bin Yahya observed that Jizzin, the northern entrance to Jabal Amil, received many fleeing the Kisrawan in late 1305.[83] Otherwise, Shi'ism in Damascus and Aleppo lost ground as the prestige of Salah al-Din boosted Sunni Islam from the 1170s, and especially after the Mamluk takeover in 1260. A stream of scholarly families probably shifted to Jabal Amil.[84] Shia religious training became localized, with certificates to interpret religious law (*ijazat*) issued at small places of learning within Jabal Amil or nearby, including Mash-ghara, Nabatiya, Mays al-Jabal, Juba, and Jizzin.[85] Scholarly interaction with Sunnis at Kark Nuah in the Biqa, Damascus, and elsewhere was normal. The bulk of Shia jurisprudence was shared with the Sunni law schools, the Mamluks rarely forced definition of Islamic affiliation after smashing the Kisrawanis, and Shia could adopt a Sunni appearance.

Two Jabal Amil scholars made particular impacts under the Mamluks. Shams al-Din Ibn Makki al-Amili, known as "the first martyr" (*al-shahid al-awwal*) fell afoul of the Sunni authorities and was executed in 1384. Much later, in 1505, Ali al-Karki of Kark Nuah visited Isfahan to meet the Safavid Shah Isma'il, who had just imposed Shi'ism on Iran. Al-Karki became the propagandist of a radicalized Shi'ism, authorizing Isma'il and himself to pronounce for the Twelfth Imam.[86] The singularity of each personality demonstrated, first, the rarity of Sunni persecution of Shia once the Mamluks felt secure in the Levant and, second, initial indifference in Jabal Amil toward Shah Isma'il. It was only in early Ottoman times, after Isma'il's death in 1524, that Jabal Amil scholars became more engaged with Safavid Iran.

Ibn Makki al-Amili, born in Jabal Amil in 1333, received religious training in Al-Hilla in Iraq and returned home in 1354. He advocated developing Shia religious law through debate with Sunni scholars.[87] He became too forthright for his own good, exciting jealousy in Jabal Amil and suspicion among Sunni officials in Sidon and Damascus. Shia enemies condemned him to the Mamluks. He was accused of promoting heresy, cursing the first two caliphs, and even of being an Alawite. "The first martyr" suffered a gruesome death in Damascus.[88]

Generally, Shia scholars and learning had protection from Shia chiefs, beginning with Husam al-Din Bishara after the Frankish retreat from Jabal Amil in 1187. The Wa'il clan, ancestors of the modern Asa'ad family, who entered Jabal Amil with Salah al-Din, took over local leadership in the early thirteenth century.[89] Presumably they were Shia, or swiftly became so. Under the Mamluks, they competed with the Shukr chiefs of Bint Jubayl.[90] Another family called Sudun appeared in southern Jabal Amil by the early sixteenth century. Al Safa notes that a Sudun was *na'ib* of Damascus in 1478 and speculates that he established his relatives in the area.[91] If so, they were of Mamluk origin.

As for Bishara, the sixteenth-century Damascus chronicler Ibn Tulun reports that an Ibn Bishara sponsored rebuilding in the ruins of Tyre in 1425.[92] The modern Shia writer Muhsin al-Amin suggests a coming together of the Bishara and Wa'il lines.[93] Ibn Sibat's reference to an Abd al-Satir bin Bishara around 1500 also indicates that the Bisharas continued after Husam al-Din.[94] Abd al-Satir, clearly a leading chief, could mobilize enough fighters to crush an attempt in the winter of 1504–1505 by the Biqa lord Nasr al-Din Ibn al-Hansh to subject Jabal Amil.[95] In a fierce encounter in driving rain, Abd al-Satir's force killed two hundred invaders.[96]

Away from Jabal Amil, Twelver Shia represented much of the population of the Biqa, especially around Kark Nuah.[97] However, Sunni chiefs were dominant, and little was heard of the Shia. In the fifteenth century, Biqa Shia may have reinforced Munaytara Shia in the Kisrawan. In 1482, the local Maronite bishop fled.[98] Also around this time the Shia Harfush family entered the record. In 1498, an Ibn al-Harfush was governor of Baalbek.[99] A Harfush chief may have led a raid across the mountains into Bsharri, reported by Ibn al-Qila'i.[100] Disputes over summer grazing were a regular irritant. From end to end of Mount Lebanon, clan feuds, personal ambitions, land conflict, and communal friction served "divide and rule" by regimes that still lacked the capability and ideology to underpin direct rule.

Ottoman Entry, 1516–1602

In a single campaign from August 1516 to January 1517, the Ottoman Sultan Selim the Grim (*Yavuz Selim*) reached out of Anatolia to destroy the Mamluk army north of Aleppo, occupy Damascus, and march to Cairo to liquidate the Mamluk state. A dynamic, rising Sunni Islamic authority replaced a faction-ridden and loosening one in the Levant. The Lebanese lords and communities faced a more vigorous sovereign, but one that still had to indulge local power play. In sixteenth-century Mount Lebanon, the Ottomans, more than the Mamluks, used local chiefs with local capability to collect taxes and administer districts of the sub-provinces (sanjaks) of Tripoli and Sidon/Beirut, and often the sanjaks themselves. It was an amalgam of change and continuity.

As for the communities, the Ottomans were prepared to be pragmatic to assure their sovereignty, but individual senior officials varied in their attitudes. There was certainly prejudice against heterodox Muslims, and Sunni religious leaders and chroniclers in Damascus incited the new regime against Shia and Druze. The historian Ibn Tulun (died 1546), for example, condemned the heterodox and blamed the Isma'ili Fatimids for the crusader conquest:

> In their [the Fatimids'] day the refusers multiplied. And their rule strengthened. . . . And they corrupted the beliefs of communities of mountain people on the sea frontier of al-Sham, like the Nusayris and the Druze and the Hashish smokers. And their proselytizing weakened their minds. . . . And the Franks took most of al-Sham, and even took Jerusalem.[101]

At the outset, Druze were exposed because the preceding regime had favored their chiefs, and the Buhturids had failed to submit to Sultan Selim while he was in Damascus. In the 1520s, the Damascus religious scholar Taqi al-Din al-Balatinsi recommended in a fatwa the killing of Druze and the seizure of Druze property.[102] Whether influenced by the propaganda or not, the Ottoman regime took a hard line on taxes, and Druze chiefs refused to pay. This inaugurated a spiral of rebellion and repression through the sixteenth century, unprecedented in the history of the Lebanese communities. In the end, it mainly proved that the Ottomans had to bow to communal reality, and it took the Druze to lows and a subsequent high never experienced under the Mamluks.

Twelver Shia had to cope with suspicion arising from the Ottoman conflict with Shia Safavid Iran. Partly because of this, a number of Lebanese Shia scholars migrated to Iran through the sixteenth century. The Shia, however, did not defy the Ottomans as did the Druze, at least not until later. As a consequence, they were not disciplined with massacres as were the Druze, and in early Ottoman times, their chiefs were generally in good standing with the authorities.

Compared to the Druze and even the Shia, Mount Lebanon's Christians did not perturb the Ottomans in their first century in the Levant. The Vatican's embrace of the Maronites rated as a mere curiosity. At their height, the Ottomans had a solid awareness of the diversity of Christian Europe. Italy meant trade—and friction with Venice—while Valois France and Elizabethan England were allies. Most pertinently, Lebanese Christians had no contact with the actual enemy—the Habsburgs of Austria and Spain.

As for individual chiefs, the Ottomans altered the playing field. They favored Sunni Turcomans and Kurds and some Biqa Shia. Hence they brought the eclipsed Assafs of the Kisrawan back into prominence. In the north, the Turcoman Sayfas planted themselves in the Akkar and later took charge of Tripoli. Similarly the Hamades, minor chiefs of Shia moving between the Biqa and the Jubayl heights, emerged under Assaf patronage as candidates for appointments.[103] As for the Druze country, the Ottomans did not want one dominant clan like the Buhturids under the Mamluks. The Ottomans preferred to have several district chiefs responsible for order and taxes in the hills of Beirut and Sidon; this opened space for the Ma'n and Alam al-Din families. In the Biqa, the Sunni Ibn al-Hansh went down in rebellion. The Shia Harfush clan took their opportunity to advance.

Through the sixteenth century, between 1519 and 1570, the Ottomans conducted surveys of adult males for tax purposes in one or another of the sanjaks covering the territory of modern Lebanon. Isam Khalife has analyzed the survey records to map Lebanon's population and sectarian makeup in an atlas of Lebanese districts for the first Ottoman decades.[104] It involves an arbitrary multiplier of six to get from adult males to overall numbers and imperfect devices to establish communal identity, including individual names, known village affiliations, and separation of Christians and Muslims in the Ottoman lists. Nonetheless, Khalife's results enable a demographic description of early Ottoman Lebanon for comparison with Mamluk and Frankish Lebanon and with the late Ottoman situation.

Khalife estimates a Lebanese population of 257,000 for the mid-sixteenth century,[105] almost identical to the late twelfth century and Poliak's estimate for the mid-fourteenth century, just before the Black Death. In other words, a modest increase occurred during the late fifteenth century, bringing the population back to pre-Black Death levels. The distribution was more rural than under the Franks. Khalife proposes 9,400 people in early Ottoman Tripoli, 5,200 in Beirut, and 6,000 in Sidon.[106] Tyre was a ruin. Baalbek, with 12,000 residents, ranked as the largest town, a position it held from Mamluk times until it suffered considerable damage and casualties in the November 1759 earthquake. Around 1550, it was 90 percent Sunni and 10 percent Christian (with twenty-nine Jewish households) in the otherwise mostly Shia central Biqa.[107] Across the valley, 4,500 Shia lived in Kark Nuah and Zahle—the latter did not become Christian until after 1750.[108] Highest rural population densities were in the Orthodox Christian Kura, the Druze Shuf, Shia Jabal Amil, and the Biqa Valley. Larger villages included Druze Deir al-Qamar in the Shuf with 1,200 people, and Shia Bint Jbayl in Jabal Amil with 1,500 people.[109] Much of the Christian north and Kisrawan were thinly settled.

An early Ottoman communal breakdown represents Khalife's most interesting contribution. He assesses the Shia at 38 percent, the Sunnis at 29 percent, the Christians at 17 percent, and the Druze at 13 percent.[110] The high Shia fraction supports the idea of a Shia influx from other parts of the Levant in the Frankish period, as Sunni Islam reasserted its primacy. Similarly, the strong Sunni showing demonstrates the Sunni recovery in the Levant under the Ayyubids and the Mamluks. Christians maintained a majority in northern Lebanon. Their relative slippage across the wider territory of Lebanon reflected Muslim immigration from interior Syria and farther afield into the Biqa, the south, and the towns, rather than actual Christian decline.

Looking forward, the sectarian geography of neighborhoods of Mount Lebanon added to the modern Lebanese state in 1920 was already established in the sixteenth century, indeed from the aftermath of the Frankish collapse. Tripoli, its coastal plain to the north, the lower hills of the Akkar, and Sidon were largely Sunni. The Shia dominated Jabal Amil north and south of the Litani River, with Druze and Sunnis on the slopes of Mount Hermon. Shia, Sunnis, and Christians shared the Biqa—in that order in terms of numbers, but all significant.

Mount Lebanon and Beirut, the core of the modern state, were a different matter. Beginning in the sixteenth century, Maronites moved south into the Kisrawan. By 1569, they were already almost the same number as the local Shia (38 percent of 892 households compared with 43 percent).[111] At this point, Christians had not yet established themselves in the Matn (96 percent Druze).[112] Between the seventeenth and nineteenth centuries, Maronites surged, and by the nineteenth century they and other Christians were a substantial peasant presence throughout the Druze country, where they had never been before. They even replaced the Shia in Jizzin.

The Druze lords achieved their political peak in the seventeenth and eighteenth centuries, but otherwise the Ottoman centuries were the time of the Christians, who gradually swamped Mount Lebanon. Beirut remained predominantly Sunni

Muslim into the nineteenth century, but after about 1750, when it was briefly part
of the Shihab domain, more Christians with commercial ambitions began arriving
in the town from the mountain and elsewhere in the Ottoman eastern Mediterranean. The trickle from the hinterland became a flow after 1800 and a refugee
flood in the disturbed times after 1840.

Consult figure 2.3 for the conjectured evolution of Lebanon's communal
composition from the mid-sixteenth century to the present.

Irrepressible Druze

Despite the emphatic Sunni face of the Ottomans, the Lebanese Shia convergence with Safavid Iran, and the first stirrings of the Maronite surge, the Druze
were the pivot of Mount Lebanon's affairs through the sixteenth century. Repression only produced an ascendancy of their new leading clan, the Ma'ns of
the Shuf, which the Ottomans eventually recognized. This was remarkable given
the swing of the pendulum against the Druze at the outset of Ottoman rule.

While in Damascus in late 1517, Sultan Selim made clear that he favored the
Turcoman Assafs, old foes of the Druze Buhturids, as his chief agents between
Beirut and Tripoli. The regime awarded them the Kisrawan and taxing rights in

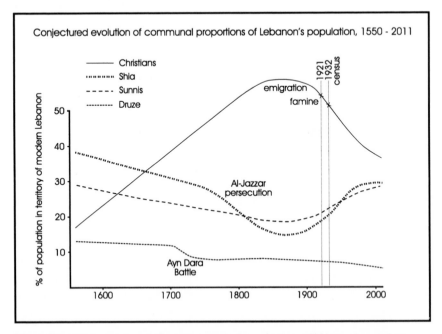

Figure 2.3 Conjectured evolution of communal proportions of Lebanon's population,
1550–2011. *Source:* Sixteenth century data from Isam Khalife, *Nawahi Lubnan fi al-Qarn al-Sadis
Ashr*, 224.

Figure 2.4 Druze girl in traditional dress including a tantour (conical hat made of silver), 1883. American University of Beirut/Library Archives. Photographer: Dumas.

Beirut and Jubayl. Its agent in Tripoli, Muhammad Shu'ayb, subcontracted revenue collection in hill districts of the Tripoli sanjak, as far as the Akkar, to the Assafs.[113] In the meantime, the leading Buhturid, Jamal al-Din Hajji, failed to give allegiance to Sultan Selim, failed to appear on time for a military expedition in 1518, and was imprisoned until his death three years later.[114] Three Ma'n chiefs did give allegiance, but were also detained before being confirmed in their Shuf districts. In contrast, even Qa'itbay Assaf's flirtation in 1521 with the rebellion of the governor of Damascus, Janbirdi al-Jazali, did his family no lasting

damage. In 1523, his astute nephew, Mansur Assaf, took over. Mansur patronized the Turcoman Sayfas, immigrants from Anatolia, in the Akkar, which provoked a fierce reaction from Muhammad Shu'ayb. In 1528, Mansur had Shu'ayb
murdered, and the young Yusuf Sayfa then supervised Tripoli as an Assaf client.
Between 1528 and 1541, Mansur sponsored the killing of Sunni and Shia rivals
to consolidate his power.[115] These included the Kurdish official in charge of
Batrun, two Kisrawan Shia chiefs, and a dissident group of Kisrawan Turcomans
and Ibn al-Hansh clansmen. In the style of the Frankish blow against the Buhturids in 1170, Mansur had the last butchered at a banquet in his headquarters in
Ghazir, above the Bay of Jounieh.

Emir Mansur favored Maronite Christians from northern Lebanon. They
were less threatening than his Muslim subordinates and were the majority of his
tax farm. He drew his chief lieutenants from the Hubaysh family of the Munaytara district, who settled in Ghazir.[116] Yusuf Hubaysh was Mansur's right hand
and was keen to remove Shia competitors. By the 1540s, low taxes and land
availability in the Kisrawan attracted additional Maronite settlers. According
to Duwayhi, several families came from the village of Jaj near Jubayl. A Sarkis
al-Khazen established himself at Balluna, near Ajaltun, and the Gemayels arrived
in Bikfaya.[117] The Khazens and Gemayels became leading families of the Kisrawan
and are still in the same locations. At about the same time, Orthodox Christians
of the Ma'luf clan moved from the Hawran south of Damascus into the Jubayl
and Kisrawan hills, founding, for example, the village of Duma.[118]

Mansur also extended his influence over the Maronite muqaddams of the
Tripoli hills. In the early sixteenth century, these chieftains still buffered residents from external authority. In particular, the Ayyubs persevered in Bsharri
until the 1547 killing of Abd al-Mun'im III and his children in a conspiracy
involving the widow of a murdered rival and a Shia Hamade chief from Jubayl.[119]
A family from the Anti-Lebanon hills who were descended from Ya'qub Ibn
Ayyub assumed the Bsharri chieftainship. By the 1560s, these held their position
at the gift of Mansur Assaf.[120] In the 1560s and 1570s, Emir Mansur, through the
Maronite Yusuf Hubaysh, ran a de facto principality from Beirut to Homs. He
built small palaces in Ghazir, Beirut, and Jubayl. It was a precursor of the Druze
lordship of Fakhr al-Din Ma'n. Mansur delivered taxes, but the Ottomans
repented of their permissiveness.[121] In 1579, Sultan Murad III created a full province based on Tripoli and made Yusuf Sayfa governor, ending his subjection to
Emir Mansur. Tax farming in all districts north of the Kisrawan passed to Yusuf
Sayfa, who became master of the Maronite chiefs.

On the one hand, the resurrection of the Assafs for a time diminished the
Druze country. On the other hand, Mansur Assaf did so well because the Ottomans were diverted by Druze recalcitrance. From the beginning, punitive taxes and
religious abuse met Druze refusal to pay or even to receive Ottoman officials.

In 1523, Khurram Pasha in Damascus sent an expedition against "the Shuf of Sulayman Ibn Ma'n" to compel obedience and extract tax arrears. It burned forty-three villages, and cartloads of heads and incriminating religious writings went back to Damascus. In 1524, the Druze killed several Ottoman officials, and another punitive force proceeded against the Shuf, burning more villages and filling more carts with heads.[122] Such brutality entrenched resistance.

Ottoman hostility brought the Druze clans together, with Qurqmaz Ma'n as their leader.[123] After Jamal al-Din Hajji, the Buhturids accepted Ma'n precedence. The last substantial Buhturid personality was that political rarity—a woman— the redoubtable Sitt Nassab, mother and advisor of Fakhr al-Din Ma'n. The Alam al-Dins, who also had family links with the Buhturids, resented the Ma'n/ Buhturid alliance, but they refrained from making trouble through the decades of insurrection.

In 1545, the governor of Damascus had Yunis Ma'n, son and successor of Qurqmaz, murdered.[124] The Druze imported firearms, forbidden by the Ottomans. They acquired muskets superior in range and caliber to Ottoman issue from European merchants and Venetian Cyprus.[125] They rejected tax demands. In 1565, they defeated an Ottoman column at Ayn Dara, near the Dahr al-Baydar pass between the Biqa and Beirut. The Ottoman regime, preoccupied with the Habsburgs and the death of Sultan Suleyman, did not respond.

Through the next twenty years, Ottoman writ did not apply to the Shuf and Gharb, and Ottoman officials did not enter. Abdul Rahim Abu-Husayn's translations of Ottoman documents in *The View from Istanbul* indicates the desperation of governors of Damascus from 1546 onward about loss of control and repeated exhortations from Istanbul to attack the Druze country.[126] Only for 1581 is there evidence of actual Ottoman military activity, after Druze and Shia in the sanjak of Safad, south of the Shuf (presumably Wadi al-Taym and Jabal Amil), joined the rebellion.[127] The janissary operation had no impact on the Druze ringleader, Qurqmaz Ma'n, probably the grandson of the earlier Qurqmaz. In his 1581 order, Sultan Murad III commanded the governors of Damascus and Tripoli "to get rid of Ibn Ma'n, whose trouble and evil deeds exceed all others."[128] Nothing happened. In 1583, the sultan noted the challenge of "rebellious Druzes ... in the provinces of Aleppo, Damascus, and Tripoli," in the midst of war against Safavid Iran in the Caucasus.[129]

When Ibrahim Pasha, governor of Egypt, came to Damascus in June 1585, escorting the Egyptian tribute to Istanbul with a large body of troops, Sultan Murad instructed him to divert to Mount Lebanon to subdue the Druze. Duwayhi later promoted a story that the tribute was plundered in the Akkar, but it arrived intact in Istanbul; certainly the sultan's orders only mentioned generalized Druze defiance.[130] Ibrahim boosted his army to 20,000 from all the garrisons in the Levant and marched into the Shuf from the Biqa.[131] The Druze chiefs apart from Qurqmaz Ma'n submitted, as well as Muhammad Assaf of the Kisrawan, and they were taken to Istanbul. Druze attacked Ibrahim Pasha's rearguard, and he conducted massacres and plundering. It is uncertain whether Qurqmaz Ma'n died during the campaign or escaped Ibrahim and died later.[132] Ibrahim confiscated thousands of rifles, extracted taxes, and imposed Ottoman authority. After his departure, the Druze chiefs, disobedient and fractious, again became ungovernable.

Securing Ottoman authority in the Druze country and the sanjak of Sidon/ Beirut went together with stabilizing the administration of Tripoli after downsizing Mansur Assaf in 1579. Yusuf Sayfa proved an indolent governor of the new province. In 1585, the Ottomans replaced him with a tough outsider, but the latter was soon needed on the Iranian front.[133] They then returned the hinterland to Muhammad Assaf, son of Emir Mansur, leaving Tripoli town to Sayfa. Muhammad made a positive impression in Istanbul, but the regime disliked his Maronite associates. In 1591, the Assaf realm suddenly collapsed when Muhammad marched north to squeeze taxes for the Akkar out of Yusuf Sayfa, and the latter had him shot dead short of Tripoli.[134] He had no heirs, and the Ottomans wanted the arrears on his tax farms. As titular governor, Sayfa recovered the Tripoli districts and paid the regime out of Muhammad's possessions. He chased out the Maronite Hubayshes and promoted the Shia Hamades of Jubayl. In 1593, Sayfa married Muhammad Assaf's widow and took over the Kisrawan and Assaf possessions in Beirut. As tax farmer for the Kisrawan, the governor of Tripoli exercised power within the province of Damascus and directly abutted the Druze.

By this time, a Druze strongman was emerging out of the wreckage left by Ibrahim Pasha. The older son of Qurqmaz, Fakhr al-Din Ma'n, came of age in the late 1580s, guarded by his Buhturid mother Sitt Nassab. By the early 1590s, the young Fakhr al-Din was operating as muqaddam of his father's district in the Shuf, delivering taxes on time, giving presents to Damascus officials, and developing relations with Maronites in Sayfa's domains and Shia Harfush chiefs in the Biqa.[135] His hospitality to the new governor of Damascus, Murat Pasha, when the latter arrived in Sidon in 1592 paid dividends. The governor had the opportunity to see Fakhr al-Din's influence in the Shuf and believed him to be the anchor the regime required. In 1593, he promoted Fakhr al-Din, barely into his twenties, to sub-governor for the sanjak of Sidon/ Beirut.

In 1594/1595, Fakhr al-Din combined with Musa al-Harfush to hunt down the head of the Bedouin Furaykh in the Biqa. The Furaykhs had joined Ibrahim Pasha against the Ma'ns in 1585. The alignment of Fakhr al-Din, Musa al-Harfush, and the governor of Damascus then swung against Yusuf Sayfa of Tripoli. Sayfa's aspiration to incorporate the sanjak of Sidon/Beirut into his province was intolerable both to governors of Damascus and to Fakhr al-Din. Sayfa also worked to detach Druze chiefs from Fakhr al-Din and to split the Harfush family. In 1598, Murat Pasha's successor in Damascus instigated Fakhr al-Din and Musa al-Harfush to attack the governor of Tripoli.[136] Fakhr al-Din led a force that defeated Sayfa at Nahr al-Kalb north of Beirut, driving him out of the southern Kisrawan. The Harfush contingent killed a close relative of Sayfa.

The vengeful governor of Tripoli soon rebounded. In 1600, his Hamade friends overpowered Fakhr al-Din's Maronite allies in Jaj, above Jubayl.[137] In 1601, he conspired with the Damascus janissaries to capture Baalbek and kill relatives of Musa al-Harfush. Fakhr al-Din, however, had an enhanced military reputation with the Ottoman authorities and his Druze power base. In 1602, the governor of Damascus appointed him sub-governor of Safad, concurrent with his position in Sidon/Beirut. He now administered the Druze country, Jabal Amil, and northern Palestine. Fakhr al-Din could only hold these posts by dissimulating Sunni Islam. Nonetheless, no Druze had ever before risen to such eminence.

Maronite and Shia Foreign Connections

While the Druze chiefs and Emir Mansur Assaf vexed the Ottomans with their imported weaponry and autonomist inclinations in the 1570s, the Maronite church and Shia scholars pushed ahead with their interests beyond the empire. The Maronites moved from formal submission to the Vatican to partial Latinization of their doctrine and ritual. The Lebanese Shia moved from diffidence toward the Shia pretensions of the new Iranian dynasty to intensifying participation in the Safavid state. These trends accompanied Vatican and Italian buoyancy in the High Renaissance and rising Iranian Shia self-confidence under Shah Abbas in the 1590s.

By Ottoman times, the Maronites were well cemented to the Roman church. Unsurprisingly, religious manuscripts in mountain monasteries exhibited Jacobite influence. Also, the Maronite church had not explicitly rejected Monophysite concepts.[138] However, patriarchs craved papal confirmation and would have their church approve whatever doctrinal formulations papal legates required. Through his long patriarchate, from 1525 to 1567, Patriarch Musa al-Akkari regarded the exchange of documents with successive popes as the Maronite lifeline. He repeatedly stressed "the submission of his community" via traveling bishops (one who was kidnapped en route by pirates), Franciscan monks, and Italian merchants.[139] In 1543, the patriarch asked Pope Paul III to authorize six Franciscans to open a school in Mount Lebanon to teach children Latin "so they may understand holy books."[140] The Vatican sent back greetings and communion vessels, but the patriarch only got his confirmation in 1561. Evidently there were reservations.

In 1567, Maronites in Cyprus accused the new patriarch, Mikhail al-Ruzzi, of Jacobite tendencies. The patriarch protested his orthodoxy. The Vatican also took up the "heresy" of Maronites attributing the birth and crucifixion of Christ to the whole Trinity.[141] In 1578, Pope Gregory XIII sent the Jesuit Giovanni Eliano, a converted Jew fluent in Arabic, to examine Maronite religious books. Eliano noted many "errors." He authorized the burning of texts, chaired a Maronite council at Qanubin in 1580 that specifically endorsed two natures and two wills in Christ, and recommended a school for young Maronites in Rome.[142] In 1584, with a substantial number of Maronite students arriving in Rome, the pope established the special Maronite college.[143]

Pope Clement VIII sent another envoy, Jerome Dandini, in 1596 to check Maronite implementation of reforms. Dandini extracted another protestation of Roman doctrine at a Maronite church council and expressed satisfaction with religious texts.[144] During Dandini's visit, Mikhail al-Ruzzi died and "the people" elected his brother Yusuf as patriarch.[145] Yusuf was a committed Latinizer, pruning Syriac language and ritual. He changed fasting periods and introduced the Gregorian calendar. As for the general Maronite condition around Bsharri at the end of the sixteenth century, Dandini offered a survey in his travel diary. He described rigidly enforced Ottoman taxation, with tough "receivers" coming up from Tripoli, but gave an impression of a productive mountain landscape.

> [It] abounds in corn, excellent wines, oil, cotton, silk, honey, wax, wood, savage and tame animals, and especially in goats: as for small animals there are but a few, because the winter there is very sharp, and they have snow continually. They have a great number of sheep, big and fat as those in Cyprus.[146]

Dandini further observed: "the Maronites will not suffer the Turks [meaning Muslims] to live amongst them . . . so that you cannot see one there."[147]

For the Shia religious class of Jabal Amil and Kark Nuah and Baalbek in the Biqa, the Ottoman arrival had uncertain, potentially difficult implications, especially considering the confrontational relationship between the Ottomans and the Shia Safavids of Iran. The Ottoman authorities mostly refrained from indulging the prejudices of the Sunni religious class. The episode of Zayn al-Din Ibn Nur al-Din Ali, "the second martyr" (al-shahid al-thani), illustrated the complexity of Sunni-Shia affairs under the new regime.[148] In the 1530s and 1540s, Zayn al-Din, from a family of scholars in Juba, had to conceal his methods of interpreting Islamic law and, without access to Ottoman employment, lived in poverty. His learning eventually enabled him to get an official teaching position in Baalbek, where he had Sunni and Shia students. His legal opinions soon aroused the suspicions of Sunni judges in Sidon and Damascus. He fled to Mecca, but was arrested and taken to Istanbul, where he was killed in 1558. On the one hand, a contemporary source asserts that he was "in a state of fear" and "continually in hiding and seclusion."[149] On the other hand, his fate seems to have reflected the anger of a Damascus judge about his dissimulation rather than Ottoman policy.[150]

In the mid-sixteenth century, regardless of fluctuations in Ottoman attitudes toward Shia, the pull on Jabal Amil scholars of the new Iranian regime became consolidated. Before 1516, the unstable character of the Shia revolution in Iran made it an ambiguous attraction. By mid-century, Safavid Iran was a fixture. It seemed committed to mainline Twelver Shi'ism, and Shah Tahmasp welcomed Jabal Amil Shia expertise. The relationship between Jabal Amil and Iran was the reverse of that between the Maronites and the Vatican. Southern Lebanon played the Vatican role of provider of experts and teachers. Such a role represented a tremendous morale boost for a Shia island in an Ottoman Sunni sea. Yet Iran would prove a mixed blessing. As receivers, the Maronites drew strength from western Europe without themselves aiding the Habsburg foe. As senders, Jabal Amil Shia aided the Middle Eastern enemy of the Ottomans. Also, the brain drain to Iran serviced a new center of Shi'ism and would diminish Jabal Amil at the same time it provided a channel to a Twelver Shia great power.

After the pioneering role of al-Karki under Shah Isma'il, Jabal Amil scholars were vital, from at least the 1550s, in anchoring Shi'ism and Shia institutions in Safavid territories. They were particularly prominent as teachers and held the position of *shaykh al-Islam* (chief jurist) of major towns, for example Husayn Ibn Abd al-Samad from Juba in the eastern city of Herat in the 1570s.[151] Jabal Amil influence peaked under Shah Abbas the Great (1587–1629), when Ibn Abd al-Samad's son Baha'i became supreme *shaykh al-Islam*, Lutfallah al-Maysi's daughter married the shah, and Lebanese specialists regularized Shia Islamic law.[152] Through the sixteenth century, Jabal Amil scholars exhibited several orientations toward the Safavid enterprise.[153] Al-Karki and his grandson Husayn, Shah Tahmasp's top judicial expert, favored wide latitude for scholars as interpreters of religious law and purging of Sunni tendencies. Ibn Abd al-Samad and his son favored a more cautious approach, but were committed to consolidating Shi'ism in Iran. Ironically, Zayn al-Din, "the second martyr," and his son never went to Iran, and they shunned the Safavids. A Shia regime in the absence of the Twelfth Imam was apparently not to their taste.

Fakhr al-Din Ma'n's Mount Lebanon, 1602–1633

From 1602 until 1633, Fakhr al-Din Ma'n, whether present or in exile, overshadowed the affairs of Mount Lebanon. Through most of these decades, the Ottoman state faced rebellions, principally in Anatolia and northern Syria, or was at war with the Austrian Habsburgs and/or the Iranian Safavids. When the Ottomans could focus on the Levant, as in 1613 and 1633, they moved against Fakhr al-Din. Between 1613 and 1618, the Ma'n emir lived in exile in Tuscany and elsewhere in Italy. His brother Yunus and young son Ali maintained Ma'n interests against considerable challenges until circumstances in Istanbul allowed the emir's return. After 1618, Fakhr al-Din expanded his domain to include all modern Lebanon and more. He acknowledged Ottoman sovereignty, operated as an appointed official, presented himself as a Sunni Muslim, and remitted taxes, but his collaboration with European Christians could only be intolerable. His armed forces—by 1630 including many Maronite Christians and overshadowing Damascus—compromised Ottoman prestige in the Arab provinces. In 1633, when the Ottomans felt some relief within the empire and in their contest with Iran, they deposed Fakhr al-Din.

A local lord cobbling together the districts of Mount Lebanon, however briefly, represented something new. From one perspective, Fakhr al-Din could simply be seen as an Ottoman tax farmer who exploited imperial laxity to indulge ambitions beyond his station. He was an emir, or "prince," only by virtue of his social standing in the Druze Shuf, and his fluctuating collection of Ottoman sub-provinces was never an actual "principality" (see figure 2.5). He exemplified a category of super-chief in the late sixteenth- and early seventeenth-century Levant, serviceable for the Ottoman pursuit of "divide and rule." The Kurdish Janbulads of Aleppo, the Turcoman Assafs and Sayfas in Mount Lebanon, and the Bedouin Turabeys of northern Palestine were other players. They could war among themselves and even with the governor of Damascus, but any of them, including Fakhr al-Din, were in deep trouble if the Ottomans became agitated about revenue or loyalty.

None of this detracts from the significance of Fakhr al-Din. For the first time in a thousand years, a local leader, the paramount Druze chief, brought the communal elites of Mount Lebanon into sustained mutual interaction. As overlord of the sanjak of Safad, Fakhr al-Din supervised the Shia of Jabal Amil; the emir's Maronite Christian advisors thus became acquainted with Jabal Amil. During his long conflict with Yusuf Sayfa of Tripoli, Fakhr al-Din penetrated the Maronite and Sunni Muslim north, taking command of Tripoli in 1627. Fakhr al-Din asserted himself in the Biqa, alternately cooperating and clashing with the Shia Harfush clan. In the circle of friends and family that passed for administration under Fakhr al-Din, the Maronite Khazen family of the Kisrawan became salient. In parallel, Maronite and Orthodox Christian peasants began to enter the Druze districts south of the Kisrawan. Ottoman devastation of the Druze country in the 1520s and 1585 probably meant that Druze peasants could not satisfy the labor requirements of Druze lords. Certainly the inauguration of a Druze-Maronite collaboration was central, but the Ma'n emir gave a broader boost to interchange among Druze, Christians, Shia, and Sunnis.[154]

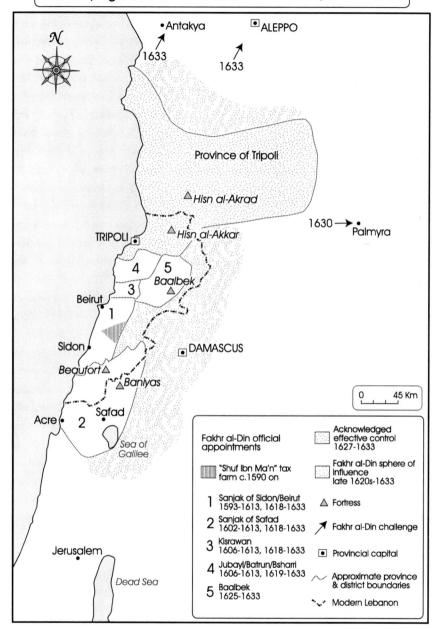

Figure 2.5 Druze Apogee: Domain of Fakhr al-Din Ma'n, 1590–1633.

Fakhr al-Din also brought western Europe back to Mount Lebanon. Since the collapse of the Frankish Levant, there had been Mamluk-Venetian trade, a restored Franciscan monastic presence in Beirut, and revived Vatican discourse with the Maronites. Fakhr al-Din, however, encouraged Western political and economic penetration of Sidon and Beirut. From the outset in the early 1600s, he had ready partners in the Grand Duke Ferdinand II of Tuscany and Pope Clement VIII. Both drew hope for a Western reassertion in the Levant from the 1601 Iranian mission to Europe and from uprisings in Anatolia and Syria.[155] The Grand Duke oversaw contacts with Fakhr al-Din in 1605, when he was also negotiating with the Janbulads in Aleppo. After Ali Janbulad's demise in 1607, Ferdinand's envoys traveled to Sidon and agreed on a comprehensive treaty with the Ma'nid emir. It included the pope mobilizing Christians in Mount Lebanon to back Fahkr al-Din, weaponry, and guarantees of exile for the emir in Tuscany.[156]

Fakhr al-Din promoted cotton, silk, and grain for commerce with the West. Mount Lebanon's prosperity kept Fakhr al-Din afloat. The revenues from traffic through Sidon, Beirut, and Acre enabled him to pay off Ottoman governors and grand viziers, to dispatch magnificent gifts when required, and to remit taxes on time. He thereby kept the Ottomans off his back until 1612, despite his collusion with Ali Janbulad and Tuscany. Later, he appeased Istanbul until 1633. Fakhr al-Din reactivated the port of Tyre, convenient for clandestine exchanges "with the Florentine."[157] The emir was open to all Europeans; and the French, who enjoyed the advantage over Tuscany of a formal treaty with the Ottoman state, made Sidon a major base. According to the French traveler Laurent d'Arvieux, the French maintained impressive commercial buildings, or khans, in Sidon by the mid-seventeenth century, including an inn, cabarets, and galleries of shops.[158] D'Arvieux observed a bustling intermingling of Muslims, Maronites, Orthodox Christians, and Jews in the town. Such was the legacy of Fakhr al-Din's long command of Sidon, his political center, down the hill from his home in the Shuf mountain redoubt of Deir al-Qamar.

What do we know of Fakhr al-Din as a personality? The English traveler George Sandys, who visited Sidon in April 1611, gives the best description:

> As for this emir, he was never known to pray, nor ever seen in a mosque. His name is Faccardine; small of stature, but great in courage and achievements: about the age of forty [see figure 2.6, portrait of Fakhr al-Din Ma'n]; subtle as a fox, and not a little inclining to the Tyrant. He never commenceth battle, nor executeth any notable design, without the consent of his mother.[159]

Sandys portrays a ruthless realist and, in the early Ottoman world, a rare proponent of economic development. Fakhr al-Din could flatter, cajole, and corrupt, but could also be a grim taskmaster:

Figure 2.6 Portrait of Fakhr al-Din Ma'n from Giovanni Mariti's *Istoria de Faccardino* (Livorno, 1787). Princeton University Library.

When Murat Pasha . . . came first to his government of Damascus, [Fakhr al-Din] made him his, by his free entertainment and bounty. . . . The opinion is that he hath a mass of treasure, gathered by wiles and extortions, as well from the subject as from the foreigner. He hath coined of late a number of counterfeit Dutch dollars, which he thrusteth away in payments . . . so that no new Dutch dollars, though never so good, will now go current in Sidon. . . . A severe Justice: re-edifies ruinous, and replants depopulated places; too strong for his neighbors,

and able to maintain a defensive war with the Turk, but it is to be suspected that his people would fall from him in regard of his tyranny.[160]

On events in early seventeenth-century Mount Lebanon, Abdul-Rahim Abu-
Husayn provides the authoritative account in his *Provincial Leaderships in Syria,
1575–1650.*[161] Abu-Husayn has mined the sources, most notably al-Khalidi
al-Safadi's *Lubnan fi Ahd al-Amir Fakhr al-Din al-Ma'ni al-Thani.* It is most useful
here to offer a summary and to consider implications for the subsequent character of Ottoman Mount Lebanon, with its hierarchy of lords conditioned by
Druze-Maronite cohabitation. Which major clans gained under Fakhr al-Din?
Significant names include the Maronite Khazens, the Druze Junblats, and the
Sunni Shihabs. In particular, the swift rise of the Khazens and the abrupt appearance of the Junblats remain little explored in the literature. Otherwise, it is worth
assessing the impact of Fakhr al-Din on his various districts, and his interaction
with the Ottomans.

After 1602, Fakhr al-Din needed to prove himself in his management of Safad,
encompassing Jabal Amil and northern Palestine. He was proactive, stabilizing
security and encouraging agriculture. In 1605, he received congratulations from
Istanbul.[162] The emir brought balance among the Shia Ali al-Saghirs (the Wa'ils
renamed after a revered chief) and Shukrs of Jabal Amil, and presumably consulted his confederates in the neighborhood, the Shihabs and Druze of Wadi
al-Taym. Fakhr al-Din also had the Maronite Khazens at his side. Regardless of
the story that the Khazens protected Fakhr al-Din as a teenager in the late 1580s,
Fakhr al-Din certainly acquired the family as an ally against Yusuf Sayfa in the
Kisrawan in the 1590s.[163] Al-Shidyaq indicates that Abu Nadir al-Khazen succeeded his father Ibrahim as the emir's steward (*mudabbir*) in 1600.[164] The relationship resembled that between the Maronite Hubayshes and the Kisrawan
Assafs and like the Hubayshes, the Khazens took the title of sheikh, entering the
predominantly Druze hierarchy of chiefs.

Developments in 1605–1606 offered Fakhr al-Din the chance to cripple his
rival Yusuf Sayfa of Tripoli. In 1605, the Ottomans executed Husayn Janbulad,
governor of Aleppo, after he refused to join a campaign against Iran.[165] The Janbulads were Kurdish chiefs from Kilis in Anatolia. Husayn's nephew Ali seized
Aleppo, and in 1606 he routed Ottoman troops under Yusuf Sayfa near Hama.
Fakhr al-Din promptly allied with Ali Janbulad. The Janbulads expelled Sayfa
from Tripoli, while Fakhr al-Din absorbed the Kisrawan. In October 1606, Ali
Janbulad and Fakhr al-Din, joined by Ali Shihab and Yunus al-Harfush, defeated
Sayfa's troops outside Damascus, and the humiliated Sayfa submitted to Janbu-
lad. Ali Janbulad's exploits and his collusion with Tuscany were too much for
Istanbul. Grand Vizier Murat Pasha patched up problems in Anatolia and led an
army to Aleppo, where he crushed Ali Janbulad and executed all the Janbulads

he could capture. On this occasion, Fakhr al-Din wisely stayed at home. He had bought Murat Pasha's goodwill when the latter was governor of Damascus, and he now sent his son Ali to Aleppo with gifts to propitiate the grand vizier.[166] Murat Pasha readily forgave Fakhr al-Din's complicity with the rebellion and let him retain the Kisrawan. Yusuf Sayfa was relieved of Tripoli and was under a cloud until 1613, though the Ottomans preserved him as an option.

Fakhr al-Din gave sanctuary in the Druze country to members of the Janbulad family, perhaps immediately as well as later. Ali Janbulad himself escaped to Anatolia, obtained forgiveness, and did not reappear in the Levant. According to al-Shidyaq, Fakhr al-Din welcomed a "Janbulad," possibly a grandson of Ali Janbulad, to the Shuf in 1630.[167] This Janbulad, with his son, settled in Mazra'at al-Shuf and became an associate of Fakhr al-Din and the Khazens in the emir's last years. In the Shidyaq version, these Janbulads married locally and became accepted as Druze. The name was changed to Junblat. However, al-Khalidi al-Safadi records a "Shaykh Junblat" in the Druze country as early as 1614.[168] There is no information on the origin of "Shaykh Junblat," or of any link to the Janbulads. It is only clear that the name Junblat did not feature before the Janbulad affair.

Guile and presents notwithstanding, Fakhr al-Din's consolidation of autonomy pointed to trouble with Istanbul. Murat Pasha died in 1611, and a less sympathetic grand vizier took office. Fakhr al-Din disregarded orders to dismantle his fortifications at Baniyas and the old Frankish castle of Beaufort.[169] In 1612, the governor of Damascus dismissed Fakhr al-Din's protégés as subgovernors of the Hawran south of Damascus and Ajlun in Transjordan. Fakhr al-Din sent a small army to restore his friends, and in May 1613 defeated the governor's forces. The grand vizier then authorized the governor to head an expedition against Fakhr al-Din, who in September 1613 fled into exile in Tuscany. Cosimo II de' Medici welcomed the emir and provided comfortable quarters for him until he moved to Sicily in July 1615.[170]

Back in Mount Lebanon, all Fakhr al-Din's Muslim allies, including the Shihabs and Yunus al-Harfush, appeased the Ottoman authorities. The following year marked a low point for the Ma'ns. Yusuf Sayfa made common cause with hostile Druze, most notably Muzaffar al-Andari, who was probably an Alam al-Din.[171] The Shia Ali al-Saghirs, whom Fakhr al-Din raided before his exile, also turned against the Ma'ns.[172] The Ottomans cancelled Ma'n control of Sidon-Beirut and Safad, reducing Fakhr al-Din's brother Yunus and son Ali to their Shuf fiefdoms.

Recovery began in 1615 with changes of grand vizier in Istanbul and governor in Damascus. The Ma'ns had to suffer demolition of their fortresses, but in late 1615, Yunus and Ali regained Sidon/Beirut and Safad. In August 1616, they smashed a Druze uprising incited by the Sayfas and once more evicted the latter from the Kisrawan. The Ma'ns retained Maronite support, thanks to Abu Nadir al-Khazen. Yusuf Sayfa literally burned the Khazens out of Ajaltun in the Kisrawan in 1614, but they returned after the 1616 Ma'n victory.[173] In June 1617, a disloyal Ma'n agent secretly outbid Ali Ma'n for control of Safad. The Shia favored this Husayn Yaziji, but he was killed while being hunted by Ali Ma'n's men.[174] Yunus al-Harfush also interfered in Jabal Amil from the Biqa. The position of the Ma'ns was solidified when the pardoned Fakhr al-Din returned from Italy in December 1617.[175]

From 1618 to 1627, Fakhr al-Din engineered advances never before or after achieved by a Druze lord. Druze and Shia opposition in his heartland evaporated the moment he set foot again in Mount Lebanon. Muzaffar al-Andari agreed to be his official for the Jurd district, Ali al-Saghir and Shukr chiefs fled to the Biqa, and Shia enlisted in his forces.[176] That left the Sayfas of the north and Yunus al-Harfush of Baalbek. Against the Sayfas, Fakhr al-Din had the satisfactions of Ottoman support—because Yusuf Sayfa could not deliver revenues—and defections from the Sayfa family.[177] Yusuf, who was around a hundred years old, was on the defensive. In 1619, Fakhr al-Din attacked the family seats in the Frankish castles of Gibalcar (Hisn al-Akkar) and Krak des Chevaliers (Hisn al-Akrad). The intrepid Abu Nadir al-Khazen starred at the Krak in an attempt to pull down its bridge.[178] The Sayfas only persevered because the Ottomans hesitated about removing a check on Fakhr al-Din. Nonetheless, Fakhr al-Din gathered the tax farms for Jubayl and Batrun in 1619 and expelled Sayfa agents from Bsharri in 1622. He installed an al-Khazen chief in Bsharri. Yusuf Sayfa died in 1625, and the splintered Sayfas became useless for Ottoman purposes. Fakhr al-Din shrewdly assisted Ottoman appointees to Tripoli in their security and revenue functions, and from about 1627, he had effective mastery of the province.[179]

Conflict with the Shia chief Yunus al-Harfush pulled Fakhr al-Din into the Biqa. The ambition of Harfush to move into the Ma'n realm during Fakhr al-Din's exile was especially galling because he had been an ally. Harfush also denied Shuf grazing and property rights in the Biqa. Matters climaxed in 1623 when Harfush colluded with Mustafa Pasha, governor of Damascus, and Damascus janissaries to take the sanjak of Safad from Fakhr al-Din.[180] Harfush paid the governor an impressive bribe. The outraged Fakhr al-Din had the good fortune of a change of sultan in Istanbul to get the decision reversed. In November 1623, he marched across the Biqa, with the Shihabs as vanguard, against Mustafa Pasha and Harfush. The two forces met at Anjar, and Fakhr al-Din carried the day in his supreme military triumph. He captured the governor, sacked Baalbek, and broke the Harfush clan. In 1625, the Ottomans awarded him the district of Baalbek. Developments again illustrated Ottoman pecuniary interests in violent competition between local chiefs and the impact of shifts in senior Ottoman personnel—whether sultans, grand viziers, or Damascus governors.

After 1627, Fakhr al-Din enjoyed six years of command of the central Levant. He had mulberry trees planted near Tripoli and brought European commerce back to the port.[181] Yusuf Sayfa had demonstrated no interest in either cash crops or trade.[182] In Beirut, Fakhr al-Din built a tower, a small zoo, and gardens.[183] The Maronites certainly did well, though to be fair, those near Tripoli did not do so badly under the Sayfas. Duwayhi details extensive work on churches and monasteries in the Kisrawan around 1630.[184] Foreign monks from various orders settled in the Bsharri area "because of the surfeit of security and tranquility."[185]

On the other hand, at his peak, Fakhr al-Din behaved with a high hand and stored up trouble. In 1630, he reached east from Baalbek to seize a fort at Palmyra, which must have alarmed the governor of Damascus.[186] In 1631, he encouraged European merchants to buy up grain from a poor harvest, inflating prices.[187] Fakhr al-Din doubtless pocketed a healthy margin. Duwayhi reports 120 vessels in the port of Acre alone. One can only imagine the strain on the emir's standing among Druze and Shia. The Ottoman admiralty sent warships to patrol the coast from Tripoli to Acre and discourage the trade. Also in 1631, Fakhr al-Din faced demands for the quartering of Ottoman troops from the Iranian front among the population, the dreaded kishlak. On a visit to Tripoli, a protesting crowd met him at the city gate.[188] The emir apparently refused the kishlak, throwing the burden onto Damascus.[189] This must have multiplied his enemies in Istanbul.

The last straw in 1633 was a complaint from Aleppo that Fakhr al-Din was building forts near Aleppo and Antakya, to the north of his bloated domain.[190] With forces freed from the Iranian front in the improved military circumstances since the death of Shah Abbas in 1629, Sultan Murad IV ordered the usurpation of the central Levant to be terminated. Küçük Ahmet Pasha, fresh in Damascus from crushing rebels in Anatolia, gathered troops "from the borders of Anatolia to the borders of Egypt" and marched against Fakhr al-Din.[191] Despite the emir's military capacity, there was no hope of prolonged resistance. After his son Ali was killed during fighting in Wadi al-Taym, Fakhr al-Din fled to a cave near Jizzin. Küçük Ahmet Pasha smoked him out and shipped him to Istanbul. As in 1613, the emir's allies paraded their loyalty to the empire, as indeed did the emir himself. Pent-up hostility to the Ma'ns bubbled up in the Druze community. The Alam al-Dins took the opportunity to massacre the Buhturid allies of the emir, extinguishing an illustrious name in Lebanon's medieval history. Fakhr al-Din's "principality" instantly collapsed back into its individual Ottoman provinces, sanjaks, and districts. In 1635, the recalcitrance of his nephew in the Shuf led to Fakhr al-Din's execution.

3

Mountain Lords, 1633–1842

Fakhr al-Din Ma'n's intensification of interaction among chiefs and communities of Mount Lebanon and its surrounds outlasted him, as did the new European commercial and cultural intrusion. The Ottomans continued to balance among petty lords of whatever sect for revenue extraction and anchoring imperial sovereignty, but in the eighteenth century, they preferred the most visibly potent agents. The Druze/Maronite combination inaugurated by the Ma'n and Khazen families in the 1580s was well positioned to take advantage of evolving Ottoman requirements because of the Druze hold on the core of the mountain between Beirut and Damascus and developing Maronite relations with France and Italy. In this respect, the succession of the Ma'ns as paramount lords of the Druze country by their Sunni Muslim Shihab relatives when Ahmad Ma'n died childless in 1697, giving clear religious compatibility with the Ottomans, was perfectly timed. Increasingly advantaged in both political and economic terms, the Shihab sway advanced from part to most of Mount Lebanon through the eighteenth century until it bequeathed a real Lebanese entity under Bashir II Shihab between 1790 and 1840. Along the way, however, the Druze lost their primacy to the more numerous and economically dynamic Maronites, while the Shihab rulers recognized the trend by adopting Maronite Catholicism.

This chapter explores the evolution from the political advantage held by the Druze lords in the early seventeenth century, with the Ottomans also favoring Sunni Kurds and Turcomans and Shia and Sunni Arab tribal chiefs in the north and Biqa, to powerful Maronite assertion and a Maronite-defined Mount Lebanon by the early nineteenth century. Through these two centuries, the Christian proportion of the population of the territory of the modern country of Lebanon probably doubled to a slight majority. This overwhelmingly reflected Maronite growth and the immigration of Orthodox-turned-Catholics from interior Syria, the latter creating the Greek Catholic community in Mount Lebanon. The new Catholics may be regarded as auxiliary to the Maronites. The population of the area later to become the Ottoman special province of Mount Lebanon increased from around 80,000 in the mid-sixteenth century to 235,000 as estimated by the French traveler Constantin-François de Chasseboeuf (comte de Volney) in 1783, an impressive rise in pre-modern conditions.[1]

In contrast, Twelver Shia, Druze, and Sunnis all lost ground in relative terms, though the Sunnis slipped the least. The Shia, in the sixteenth century the largest community within the territory of today's Lebanon, slid from around 38 percent to not much above 20 percent by the 1840s, being overtaken in numbers by Maronites and Sunnis. Given the Ottoman-endorsed hold of Shia chiefs on northern Mount Lebanon and the Biqa in the seventeenth century and the cotton boom in Shia Jabal Amil in the early eighteenth century, the Shia decline requires consideration. The Druze demographic position was more obviously precarious. Even at their political peak under Fakhr al-Din Ma'n, attrition of their modest one-eighth of the people of the mountain and its surrounds was already underway, inaugurated in the warfare against the Ottomans in the sixteenth century.

The Shia demographic decline to some extent reflected the political eclipse of their chiefs in the mid- and late eighteenth century, leaving Shia exposed and demoralized under weak leaders after 1800. Shia became prey to Ottoman governors and to the Shihab emirs, and sidelined by Christian dynamism. It did not start that way under the Ottomans. Through the seventeenth century, the Shia Hamade and Harfush families of northern Mount Lebanon and the Biqa equaled the Ma'ns of the Druze country.[2] The authorities made tax delivery appointments on assessment of likely returns to the treasury, experimenting with "marginal tribal factors" as agents—hence the procession in northern Mount Lebanon from the Turcoman Assafs to the Turcoman Sayfas to the Shia Hamades and various Kurds between 1516 and the 1680s.[3] In the Biqa and the Druze country, they adjusted to entrenched Shia Harfushes, Sunni Shihabs, and Druze Ma'ns. Before the eighteenth century, the authorities did not appoint Christians, and the Maronite Hubayshes and Khazens rose as protégés of the Assafs and Ma'ns.

For the Shia chiefs, the tide began to turn in the late seventeenth century when the Ottomans concluded that the Hamades were too unruly and tried without success to get the Ma'ns to help contain them.[4] After 1700, the Shihabs proved more serviceable in this function, also presenting themselves as effective deliverers of tax from the expanding Maronite economy.[5] Between Haydar Shihab's victory over Druze rivals at Ayn Dara in 1711 and about 1780, the Shihabs displaced the Hamades in the Maronite north by the 1760s, exploited Harfush quarrels in the Biqa, and encroached on Jabal Amil. The Druze Junblat lords and Christian peasants backed by the Maronite church bought or pushed Shia out of Jizzin and the hills above Sidon.[6] The significant Shia minority in the Tripoli hills largely departed for the Biqa while Jabal Amil became a war zone between the

Ottoman authorities and rebels in northern Palestine even before the depredations of the Ottoman governor Ahmad al-Jazzar in the 1780s.

With Shia chiefs reduced and al-Jazzar's punishment of Jabal Amil after Shia
collaboration with rebels and Russians during the Ottoman/Russian war of
1768–1774, the Druze/Maronite arena and Shihab interaction with Ottoman
governors came to dominate the Lebanese narrative. The modern Lebanon in
which the Maronites took center stage came into view in the last decades of the
250-year informal principality of the Ma'ns and Shihabs, after 1800. In earlier
Ottoman times, such an outcome would have seemed far-fetched, though signs
of a Christian upthrust were evident under Fakhr al-Din.

Maronite undercutting of Druze ascendancy in the center of the mountain,
paralleling the Shia decline, is a major theme of this chapter. Politically, the Maronites were the subjected community at the outset of Ottoman rule, which
spared them much of the attrition of the infighting of Druze and Shia lords. The
infighting climaxed in the late eighteenth century, with constant mobilization
for rivalries among Shihab princes and Ottoman governors. The Jabal Amil Shia
chief Nasif al-Nassaar, for example, fought Yusuf Shihab and his Druze troops in
1771 and joined them against the governor of Damascus in 1773.

Through the turmoil, Maronite and Greek Catholic commercial, cultural, and
population advances promised eventual political dividends. Druze lords needed
Christian labor for silk and other farming, and Christian settlers, including
Orthodox, thus moved into the Matn and the Shuf. By the early nineteenth century, parts of the Druze country had Christian majorities, and the Maronite
church was stirring peasants against landlords. Reorganized after its 1736 council, the church became an instigator of social leveling and communal hegemony,
mobilizing the peasantry. Maronite and Greek Catholic skills also made the old
Druze center Deir al-Qamar a Christian emporium, with the new rich living in
fine houses. Druze and Maronite chiefs had warm relations, but the Druze "principality" of the seventeenth century mutated into a Maronite vehicle. The
Maronite-Druze sectarian troubles of 1840–1860 reflected a long drift toward
change in communal balances, exacerbated by nineteenth-century European
interference.[7] If what Salibi terms a Maronite-Druze symbiosis came out of
Fakhr al-Din Ma'n's exertions, it was symbiosis with seeds of self-destruction.[8]

After 1798, when Bonaparte seized Egypt, French and British military incursions in the eastern Mediterranean during the Napoleonic Wars certainly
spurred European influence. Ideas of liberty and equality from the French Revolution penetrated the Maronite peasantry, reinforced in the 1820s by the Greek
War of Independence. Under the restored monarchy, France upgraded its special
association with the Maronites and their church, articulated in Louis XIV's
declaration of protection in 1649. Up to the Egyptian occupation of Mount
Lebanon in the 1830s, however, European ideological, cultural, and economic

intrusion had only a limited impact on already destabilized Druze-Maronite and landlord-peasant affairs.

Egypt's separation from Istanbul under the Albanian adventurer Muhammad Ali following the French occupation decisively affected Mount Lebanon. In the 1820s, France armed and encouraged Muhammad Ali while the British began to worry about the integrity of the Ottoman state and the implications of its disruption for the European power balance. Tensions between Istanbul and Muhammad Ali, who coveted Syria and Palestine as a reward for services to the sultan, his suzerain, put Shihab command of Mount Lebanon under terminal stress. Bashir II Shihab, together with the Maronite Church and France, preferred Muhammad Ali to the sultan. After an Egyptian army—under Muhammad Ali's son Ibrahim Pasha—seized the Levant and parts of Anatolia in 1832, the emir found himself trapped by his Egyptian alliance. First, Ibrahim Pasha wanted to deploy Maronite fighters against Druze and Muslim rebels. Second, Egyptian occupation through the 1830s privileged Christians, to Muslim frustration, but its taxation and conscription also alienated the Maronites. British naval intervention and Ottoman restoration in 1840, in circumstances of a Maronite insurrection that evolved into Maronite/Druze fighting, brought the downfall of Bashir II in October 1840 and the disbandment of the mountain principality in January 1842.

Whatever the status of the Shihabs as underlings of the governor of Sidon, the political vacuum after the principality's collapse spoke volumes for its actual significance. The Ottomans aspired to direct rule but could not manage local complexity. Druze resentment of Maronite advances, Maronite peasant hostility against mountain lords, and Druze and Sunni jealousy of Christian wealth resulted in a dangerous coalescence of sectarian and social grievances.

Changing of the Guard, 1633–1711

After Fakhr al-Din, the Ottomans attempted closer supervision by provincial governors. In the mid-seventeenth century, annual renewal of tax-gathering rights prevailed through much of Mount Lebanon, particularly in the Druze country and the hinterland of Tripoli. Ottoman requirements remained rudimentary: tax delivery; protection of the pilgrimage caravan from Damascus to Mecca; obedience to military demands; and respect for imperial sovereignty.

Closer supervision involved transferring Tripoli from a local dynasty, the Sayfas, to imperial officials after 1640 and the creation of a new province of Sidon in 1660. Otherwise, the Ottomans found it convenient to operate through the Druze Ma'ns and the Shia Hamades in the mountain, even as they abused them as "Druze villains" and "heretic (or accursed) *kızılbaş*."[9] The *kızılbaş* [literally "red head," after their headgear] were Shia rebels in eastern Anatolia in the sixteenth century who were sympathetic with the Iranian Safavids.

Removal of Fakhr al-Din and reversion of his domain to its constituent Ottoman districts destabilized Mount Lebanon. At first, the authorities preferred the Alam al-Dins as tax gatherers in the Druze country, but they could not displace Fakhr al-Din's nephew Mulhim in the Ma'n home territory of the Shuf. In Tripoli, they returned the governorship to the Sayfa clan, but the Sayfas feuded viciously.[10] The top Maronite Khazen sheikhs of the Kisrawan, Fakhr al-Din's assistants, went into exile in Tuscany when the Ottomans executed the emir in 1635. In 1636, the governor of Damascus sent troops against Ali Alam al-Din for failing to deliver taxes. Ali Alam al-Din was aligned with Ali Sayfa, estranged nephew of the senior Sayfa in Tripoli. The first Ali fled north, plundering the Kisrawan en route. The second Ali competed with his uncle in extorting money out of the residents of the Tripoli hinterland. The Ottomans needed Mulhim Ma'n to bring Ali Alam al-Din to heel and to stabilize Tripoli. In 1637, Mulhim Ma'n defeated Ali Alam al-Din near Beirut and regained taxing rights for the Shuf.[11] The Khazens then returned from Tuscany to the Kisrawan.

Henceforth, Mulhim Ma'n and his Druze and Maronite confederates had the upper hand over Druze rivals. In 1638, however, there was a brief interruption. According to Istifan Duwayhi, "Ibn Alam al-Din . . . had recourse to the Shia of the Bishara country [Jabal Amil]. Emir Mulhim took them by surprise at the village of Ansar and killed a great number."[12] Modern Shia historian Muhammad Al Safa claims up to sixteen hundred Shia died in "the massacre."[13] As a result, the Ottoman deputy governor [mutasallim] of Damascus, instigated by the Alam al-Dins, advanced against Mulhim Ma'n. The latter "fled before them," as did "the people of the Shuf, the Gharb, the Matn, and the Jurd, and the Druze country emptied."[14] Emir Mulhim plainly had the preponderant Druze following. In 1642, he defeated the Ottoman governor of Damascus in an armed clash.[15] Because he was otherwise loyal, the Ottomans let him have preeminent tax farmer status in the Druze country by the early 1640s. With the grip of his subordinate Abu Nadir al-Khazen in the Kisrawan, this reasserted the heartland of Fakhr al-Din. In the meantime, the Ottomans tired of the Sayfas in Tripoli and in 1640 deposed them.

Duwayhi's *Tarikh al-Azmina* is valuable for developments in mid- and late seventeenth-century Mount Lebanon. Here Duwayhi provides a contemporary Lebanese narrative. For example, for the 1690s when he was Maronite patriarch (1670–1704), he gives unique information on the Ma'n/Shihab transition. Abu-Husayn plays up Duwayhi's friendship with Mulhim Ma'n's son Ahmad to devalue his reports.[16] It is, however, problematic to discount the patriarch's credibility in his own days.

Between the 1640s and 1680s, two developments prefigured late Ottoman Mount Lebanon: Maronite consolidation in the Kisrawan under the Khazens and the rise of the Junblats in the Druze elite. Both families owed their opportunities to the Ma'ns. Mulhim Ma'n stabilized al-Khazen control of tax gathering in the Kisrawan. The Khazens invested their profits in land purchases, silk cultivation, and commerce with France and Tuscany.[17] They already commanded Maronite church appointments. Abu Nawfal al-Khazen, who succeeded his father Abu Nadir as head of the clan when the latter died in 1647, developed this base. Abu Nawfal patronized Maronite settlement from the north, producing a Maronite majority in the Kisrawan. He intensified al-Khazen intervention in the church through founding monasteries on family lands, including Dayr Ayn Tura for French Jesuits in 1652.[18] The family monopolized silk exports from the Kisrawan through control of the local silk press. In 1656, the Vatican decorated Abu Nawfal; in 1658, the French appointed him their vice-consul in Beirut; and in 1671, Sultan Mehmet IV confirmed al-Khazen tax farmer status in the Kisrawan.[19]

Data for the Junblats after Fakhr al-Din patronized their settlement in the Druze country are scanty, but the trajectory is clear. According to al-Shidyaq, the original Janbulad from Aleppo died in 1640, after guarding the Beaufort castle for Fakhr al-Din between 1631 and 1633 and establishing his son in Mazra'at al-Shuf.[20] At some unspecified time, his grandson Ali Junblat married the daughter of Qabalan al-Qadi al-Tanukhi, the paramount sheikh of the Shuf. He thereby gave his descendants Tanukh lineage—the most illustrious Druze name. In 1712, when Qabalan died without issue, the chiefs of the Shuf agreed that Ali Junblat should be their leader.

Mulhim Ma'n and his son Ahmad could rely for military support on the Sunni Shihabs of Wadi al-Taym, allies for five centuries. Al-Shidyaq reports that in 1629, Emir Mulhim's daughter married Husayn Shihab, and in 1674, Emir Ahmad's daughter married Musa Shihab.[21] In 1650, the Shihabs helped Mulhim Ma'n smash a force that Ali Alam al-Din had persuaded the governor of Damascus to loan him.[22] To illustrate the vagaries of Ottoman behavior, in the same year that Mulhim confronted Damascus, the governor of Tripoli awarded him the tax farm for Batrun.[23] In 1654, when Ali Alam al-Din tried to rouse the sultan's new grand vizier against him, Mulhim bought off the vizier, also acquiring the tax farm for Safad.[24]

In 1660, after Mulhim's death in 1658, his sons Ahmad and Qurqmaz faced another Ottoman expedition, initially sent against the Shihabs and the Shia Hamades.[25] The expedition followed the creation, also in 1660, of the new Ottoman province of Sidon—Duwayhi refers to involvement of its governor. The expedition and the administrative change aimed to stiffen imperial authority and to increase revenue. Reformer grand vizier Köprülü Mehmet Pasha sent his son and successor Ahmet. The Shihabs fled to the Hamades in the high Kisrawan, while Ottoman troops pillaged Wadi al-Taym. Claiming the Shihab chiefs were with the Ma'ns, the Ottomans demanded the latter deliver both them and money for the army. Ahmad and Qurqmaz Ma'n refused and in turn fled to the Kisrawan. Ottoman troops scoured the area in vain for the Ma'n, Shihab, and Hamade lords, causing misery to the peasants. Sirhal Imad, sheikh of the Barouk, and the Alam al-Dins were briefly entrusted with the Druze country. The Shihab emirs hid in the Jabal Ala near Aleppo for six years, and the Ma'n brothers spent two years with the Hamades.

Duwayhi reports that in 1662, the governor of Sidon enticed the two Ma'ns to a meeting with his steward, offering their restoration.[26] He had Qurqmaz murdered, but Ahmad escaped. Thereafter, Ahmad Ma'n prepared his Druze faction for a showdown. In 1667, Emir Ahmad and his supporters, termed Qaysis in Duwayhi's rendition, defeated the Alam al-Dins, al-Sawafs and others, termed Yamanis, near Beirut. The latter went into exile in Damascus, and Emir Ahmad resumed Ma'n command of "the Shuf, the Gharb, the Jurd, the Matn, and the Kisrawan."[27] The labels Qaysi and Yamani derived from pre-Islamic tribal divisions in Arabia and were applied to Druze division in seventeenth-century Mount Lebanon; there was no historical connection. For the next thirty years, Ahmad Ma'n had a firm hold on the Druze country. The 1662 murder attempt doubtless soured the emir's view of Ottoman authority; Abu-Husayn notes that Emir Ahmad resumed Ma'n correspondence with the Tuscans after 1667.[28]

In the mid- and late seventeenth century, Twelver Shia experience was not much different from that of the Druze. The Ottomans worked through the Shia chiefs, who were put in charge of Christian and Sunni taxpayers. Ottoman relations with Shia leaders were in constant flux, depending on individual Ottoman officials and the availability of alternative agents. Ahmad Ma'n and the Shia Hamades and Harfushes were in the same predicament, and their collusion was hardly surprising. In parallel, ordinary Shia were highly vulnerable to the shifts in Ottoman favors toward their chiefs. A downturn might mean extra tax extraction or even expulsion for Shia villagers. Outside walled Beirut, Duwayhi identified a local Shia community (*mutawila burj bayrut*), plainly humble.[29] He noted that in 1661 these Shia excavated a sarcophagus. According to Isam Khalife's research, the *burj* housed about one thousand people.[30] For the Twelver heartland of Jabal Amil, the association of the Wa'ils and other chiefs with the Druze Alam al-Din faction meant more trouble with the Ma'ns after the Shia debacle of 1638. Muhammad Al Safa claims there was substantial settlement desertion through the period.[31] Ma'n recovery of Fakhr al-Din's Safad tax farm in 1654 would not have been good news for Jabal Amil Shia, squeezed between the hostile Ma'ns and Ottoman officials. According to Al Safa, in 1666 local Shia repulsed the governor of Sidon and a Ma'n force near Nabatiya.[32]

As for the Biqa Shia, the Ottomans continued to give leaders of the powerful Harfush clan district commands, sometimes Homs as well as Baalbek. They suffered vicious family feuds while the Ottomans had more day-to-day interest and a stronger hand in the Biqa than in Mount Lebanon. The Biqa provisioned Damascus with grain and other foodstuffs and hosted important Islamic endowments. Governors of Damascus would play among the Harfushes or bring the Sunni Shihabs of Wadi al-Taym, the southern extension of the Biqa, into Biqa district commands. The Harfushes had Biqa tax contracts in the mid-1630s, but evidently lost Baalbek—the Ottomans thwarted their attempt to retake the town in 1636.[33] Duwayhi records Harfush control of Baalbek in 1671, but against the backdrop of a violent struggle within the family.[34] Faris Shihab displaced them in 1680, but was killed in a face-off with the Harfushes and Hamades. When the Shihabs mobilized for revenge, the Harfushes successfully appealed to Ahmad Ma'n to mediate.[35]

In Mount Lebanon, even as the Khazens bought Shia property in the Kisrawan to accommodate more Maronites, the Shia Hamade clan turned their sixteenth-century penetration of the Maronite districts farther north into full domination. Their bloody contests with governors of Tripoli accelerated Maronite migration southward. They acquired productive properties near Tripoli and in the Batrun and Jubayl districts, which gave them independent resources.[36] They also had a refuge in the Jubayl heights—Wadi Almaat.

Ottoman governors of Tripoli respected Hamade capabilities; well into the eighteenth century they had no compunction and often not much choice about appointing them as tax agents. The Hamades had the tax farm for Jubayl and Batrun from 1636 to 1641, until an altercation with the governor.[37] Through the mid-seventeenth century, the Ottomans denied them contracts. In 1659, when they heard that the governor of Tripoli was coming for them "because of their depredations," the Hamades fled into the Kisrawan.[38] This proved significant, because in 1660 they were fugitives there together with the Ma'ns and Shihabs, and became friends with Emir Ahmad Ma'n.

In 1674, because of difficulties with tax collection, the Ottomans brought the Hamades back into the fiscal system, again awarding them contracts for Jubayl and Batrun.[39] However, the clan interfered in other districts and withheld revenue. In 1675, the governor sent troops against them and forced the cousins of two detained Hamade sheikhs to execute their kinsmen. The clan took its revenge in a rampage through the Jubayl, Batrun, and Bsharri districts. They repeated the exercise against villages above Jubayl in 1676, after the governor razed their properties in Wadi Almaat and Munaytara. In 1677, the governor restored quiet at the price of handing the Hamades the tax farms for Jubayl, Batrun, and Bsharri.

For the next seven years, the Hamades remained quiescent, but the balance changed after 1683. The Ottomans went to war with Austria and were distracted from their Arab provinces. In 1684, the Hamades took advantage of the absence of the governor to raid Tripoli and free hostages from the citadel.[40] Short of military resources, the Ottomans offered Ahmad Ma'n the Hamade tax contracts if he would discipline them. Emir Ahmad obeyed, but with reluctance. He advanced into the Kisrawan and burned some Hamade property, but returned to the Shuf at the earliest chance, declining the tax farms. In 1686, the governor of Tripoli faced troubles from Bedouin, the Hamades, and the Harfushes of Baalbek.[41] The Hamades took the opportunity to kill Ottoman-backed rivals. The governor was preoccupied with restoring order around Baalbek on behalf of his colleague in Damascus. The Harfush rebels fled the Biqa, taking refuge with the Hamades above Jubayl. The governor pursued them, but lost dozens of men in an ambush. When he retired to Tripoli, the Hamades raided the town of Jubayl. Figure 3.1 indicates these events did not deter tourists.

Despite such impudence, the Ottomans felt compelled to offer the Hamades an enlarged tax farm in 1691, including the Orthodox Christian Kura district near Tripoli.[42] Meanwhile, the imperial government in 1689 summoned Ahmad Ma'n to serve against Austria.[43] The Druze emir ignored the order. There was no

Figure 3.1 Page from a 1694 handwritten copy of Abd al-Ghani al-Nabulusi's 1689 *Rihlat Ba'albak wa al-Biqa* ("Journey to Baalbek and the Biqa"). Princeton University Library.

sanction because in 1692 the Ottomans decided again to repress the Hamades, after the latter murdered an opponent in the Kura.[44] For this, the regime needed Emir Ahmad. For the last time he answered the call. His al-Khazen allies contributed one thousand fighters but agreed with Emir Ahmad that they would not pursue the Hamades into the Biqa. When the Hamades fled over the mountain, losing many men in a blizzard, the Khazens declined to follow, and the governor then had to persevere alone.

A breaking point came in 1693 when Emir Ahmad rejected a final Ottoman appeal to assume the Hamade tax farms and "stop [Hamade] havoc in the province of Tripoli."[45] This coincided with another Hamade ambush of an Ottoman force. Forty men died, including the Jubayl commander and Emir Ahmad Qalawun, a descendant of the great Mamluk sultan. The infuriated Ottomans stripped Ahmad Ma'n of his tax farms, from the Kisrawan to Jizzin, handing them to Musa Alam al-Din. According to Duwayhi, the Ottomans mustered 18,500 troops in the Biqa and scoured Wadi al-Taym for Emir Ahmad, now a fugitive. The army installed Musa Alam al-Din in the Ma'n palace in Deir al-Qamar. In 1694, Musa sought refuge with the governor of Sidon when Ahmad Ma'n resurfaced in Wadi al-Taym and marched with the Shihabs into the Shuf.[46]

Abu-Husayn's work in the Ottoman archives has uncovered imperial orders fulminating against Ahmad Ma'n and the Shihabs in 1694 and 1695.[47] The orders to the governors demanded heads in vituperative language. Nonetheless, Emir Ahmad moved back into Deir al-Qamar and nothing happened. Duwayhi claimed that after Sultan Mustafa II took power in 1695, Ahmad Ma'n recovered his tax farms.[48] Abu-Husayn is skeptical, but it is possible that Emir Ahmad made a deal to deliver revenue and restrain the Hamades. There were no more Hamade provocations while the emir was alive.

Sultan Mustafa was absorbed with the Balkan campaigns in the last years of the long war. Mustafa personally led Ottoman forces to Belgrade in July 1695.[49] In 1697, Prince Eugene of Savoy destroyed most of the sultan's army at Zenta on the Tisza River. Thereafter, the empire had to submit to the Treaty of Karlovitz in 1699, by which it lost Hungary and Transylvania to the Habsburgs. In the late 1690s, the Ottomans were threadbare in Mount Lebanon.

Ahmad Ma'n died in his bed in September 1697, the month of the Ottoman catastrophe in Hungary. He was the last Ma'n and had no surviving sons. To deter Yamani resurgence, Druze lords of his dominant Qaysi faction wanted a credible successor; the Shihabs were militarily potent, relatives of the Ma'ns, Sunni Muslim, and, coming from Wadi al-Taym, removed from Shuf jealousies.[50] For their part, there was no question that various Shihabs coveted the Ma'n inheritance. The Qaysi lords invited Emir Ahmad's maternal nephew, Bashir Shihab, to come to Deir al-Qamar to be their paramount chief and to assume Ahmad's financial obligations.[51] Abu-Husayn's Ottoman documents make plain that Emir Ahmad held his old tax farms at his death.[52] The Ottoman governor of Sidon confirmed the Shihab succession, authorized from Istanbul. Nonetheless, the tax farms remained annual contracts; the Ottomans might award them to different Shihabs, and the resentful Alam al-Dins—Yamani chiefs in exile in Damascus—were available as an Ottoman instrument.

Bashir I Shihab had a busy year in 1698.[53] The governor of Tripoli sent troops against the Hamades for withholding revenue. Their chiefs fled to Deir al-Qamar; Emir Bashir guaranteed their obligations, and in return, the governor released Hamade hostages. In the same year, the governor of Sidon appealed to Bashir Shihab for help against Mushrif Ibn Ali al-Saghir of the Wa'ils, chief of the Bishara region of Jabal Amil, who had killed officials. According to Duwayhi, Emir Bashir mobilized eight thousand men. The emir delivered the rebels to the governor and received "the safekeeping of the province of Sidon from the environs of Safad to the Ma'amaltayn bridge [in the Kisrawan]."[54]

Into the new century, Emir Bashir I enjoyed the confidence of Arslan Pasha, Ottoman governor of Sidon. He delegated tax gathering in Safad to a Bedouin Qaysi Sunni, Umar Ibn Ali Zaydan, father of the subsequent strongman of northern Palestine, Zahir al-Umar. Emir Bashir dominated Shia Jabal Amil, where the Munkir and Sa'b clans gave allegiance to the Qaysis.[55] He also worked with the French consul in Sidon to calm a dispute among the Khazens about revenues from fees on French ships accruing to the Khazen vice-consul in Beirut.[56] The consul confirmed that Husn al-Khazen had exclusive rights as French vice-consul, warning the office might be cancelled if it gave no benefit to France. Husn al-Khazen offered to forgo the fees, indicating that he only wanted to facilitate French cultural influence. The incident illustrated Shihabi reach into the Kisrawan and French reach into Mount Lebanon.

In 1705, the fortunes of the Shihabs and Qaysis changed when Emir Bashir died of poisoning. Family historian Haydar Ahmad al-Shihabi, whose chronicle *Lubnan fi Ahd al-Umara al-Shihabiyin* is a leading source for eighteenth-century Mount Lebanon, indicated that Bashir's nephew Haydar was responsible.[57] Emir Haydar, a grandson of Ahmad Ma'n and in his twenties in 1705, had a stronger claim on the Ma'n inheritance than Bashir himself. The Ottomans approved Haydar's succession to Bashir, but a new governor of Sidon determined to constrain the Shihabs. Zahir al-Umar received responsibility for the Safad taxes, and the governor deprived Haydar of Jabal Amil, putting the Ali al-Saghir, Munkir, and Sa'b chiefs in charge of tax collection.[58] The Munkirs and Sa'bs deserted the Shihabs to join the Ali al-Saghirs in a Yamani-inclined Shia front. These Ottoman maneuvers reflected resurgent imperial capability.

Ottoman documents indicate impatience with Haydar's tax arrears.[59] At first, there was little reaction when Haydar invaded Jabal Amil, defeated the Shia chiefs, and put a Shuf crony, Mahmud Abi Harmush, in charge.[60] Abi

Harmush, however, became estranged from Haydar and in 1709 fled to Sidon. The governor granted Abi Harmush the tax contract for the Shuf, deposing Haydar Shihab.[61] The latter fled to Ghazir in the Kisrawan, where he and other Qaysi lords received sanctuary from the Maronite Hubayshes. Abi Harmush pursued Haydar with Ottoman troops, sacked Ghazir, and forced Haydar north to Hirmil in the Biqa. In the Shuf, Abi Harmush welcomed the Alam al-Din chiefs back from Damascus. The Yamani coup was complete, but its local support was shallow.

In early 1711, Qaysi appeals stimulated Haydar Shihab to return to the Druze country where he took up residence with the Abi Lama clan, who commanded the Matn district.[62] The leading Qaysis, prominently the Maronite sheikh Khazen al-Khazen and the Druze chiefs Qabalan al-Qadi al-Tanukhi, Ali Junblat, Ali Abi Nakd, Sayyid Ahmad Imad, Janbulat Abd al-Malik, and Muhammad Talhuq, joined them in Ra's al-Matn to march on the Shuf. In response, Abi Harmush assembled the Alam al-Dins and their allies, including Arslans from the Gharb, at Ayn Dara above the Matn. Help also came from the Harfushes of the Biqa.[63] The governors of Damascus and Sidon led troops to the Biqa and Beirut, respectively, to join Abi Harmush in a pincer attack on Ra's al-Matn. Emir Haydar preempted them, throwing his forces into Ayn Dara before dawn on March 20, 1711 (1710 according to al-Shihabi).[64] The Qaysis routed the Yamanis, killing seven Alam al-Din chiefs and capturing Abi Harmush. Haydar sent soothing messages to the governors, who accepted the fait accompli and returned home.

Ayn Dara had clear consequences. The triumphant emir forced most Yamanis and their followers to leave for the eastern Hawran (Jabal Druze) in Syria, where they joined a Yamani group who had shifted in 1685.[65] Their migration cut Druze numbers and led to Druze chiefs acquiring more Maronite, Greek Catholic, and Orthodox tenants (in that order of magnitude), although the Christian, principally Maronite, demographic ascent was a long-term trend, not dependent on single events.[66] Haydar Shihab also significantly reengineered the elite of Mount Lebanon. Ayn Dara determined leadership in the core of the mountain, which was no trivial outcome.[67]

Emir Haydar elevated the Abi Lama sheikhs to the courtesy title of emir, joining the Shihabs and Arslans. The Arslans, a branch of the original Tanukhs, paid for their Yamani sympathies by having their lands in their Gharb district reduced in favor of the Talhuqs, but Haydar tolerated their continuation. Otherwise, Haydar distributed *muqata'as* (tax collection districts) in Mount Lebanon to reward his party. The Junblats, Imads, and Abi Nakads consolidated as the leading Druze families, with the social rank of sheikh. Haydar also designated the Abd al-Maliks and Talhuqs as sheikhs. Designation involved a letter from the paramount Shihab addressed "dear brother."[68] Their status assisted these clans to mobilize Druze tribal retinues and extend land holdings. The sheikhs later produced new political divides. One family, the Muzhirs of Hamana, held the rank of muqaddam, between emir and sheikh, but they had no serious resource base.

Among Maronites, Haydar confirmed the supremacy of the Khazen and Hubaysh sheikhs in the Kisrawan. To the north, however, Haydar's victory advantaged the Shia Hamade allies of the Shihabs over the Maronites of Jubayl, Batrun, and Bsharri.[69] In Haydar's hierarchy, the paramount Hamade was a muqaddam. Ayn Dara was so clear-cut and Haydar's exploitation of it so ruthless that the governors of Sidon and Tripoli had little room for maneuver up to the emir's death in 1732. As long as Emir Haydar and the Hamades delivered taxes, there was no point in disturbing them. Hamade control inland from Tripoli coincided with relaxation for the Shia of Jabal Amil, for whom the rising star of Zahir al-Umar in Acre balanced the Shihabs.

After Ayn Dara, Emir Haydar's prolonged hegemony cemented the informal principality of the Shihabs until the 1840s. The Alam al-Dins and their Yamani party vanished; Kamal Salibi suggests that they may have had Ma'n ancestry and felt usurped, but there is no evidence.[70] Otherwise, the Alam al-Dins were of Buhturid and, probably, Tanukh descent and had no need of a Ma'n connection to assert rights. We may never be sure of the underlying cause of this seventeenth-century feud.

The Mountain Principality, 1711–1842

Between 1711 and 1842, the Shihab family represented a center of gravity in the affairs of Mount Lebanon and its neighborhood. The family provided the paramount lords and chief Ottoman agents in the mountain, an arrangement accepted by Ottoman governors of Sidon, Tripoli, and Damascus.[71] The Shihabs were the summit of a distinctive social and political hierarchy in their domain and interacted intensively with its surrounds—Shia Jabal Amil, the Biqa Valley, the port towns, and the Maronite hinterland of Tripoli. Shihab interactions with Druze, Shia, and Sunni strongmen crisscrossed a Mount Lebanon that increasingly became Christian, predominantly Maronite Catholic. At the same time, west European resurgence in the Levant developed from cultural and commercial infiltration of Ottoman territory to full-fledged political and military intrusion by 1800. Russian naval sieges of Beirut and Sidon in the early 1770s and Bonaparte's conquest of Egypt and advance into Palestine in 1798–1799 signaled a transformed international context. The mountain principality achieved its apogee in the early nineteenth century under Bashir II Shihab, just as the Ottoman system became critically destabilized.

Shihab Politics, 1711–1790

For the Ottoman governors of Sidon who annually invested a Shihab as tax gatherer of the mountain and for the Druze lords who periodically selected a Shihab as anchor of a turbulent elite, the "prince of the Druze," who was initially a Sunni Muslim and in the end a Maronite Christian, was simply a convenience. For these parties, there was a leader prince, in Arabic termed Hakim, but only a shadowy "principality," or *imara*.[72] The Maronites evolved a different perspective.

Within his super tax farm of the Shuf, the Gharb, the Matn, and the Kisrawan, the paramount Shihab had fiscal, political, social, judicial, and military precedence (see figure 3.2). The other emirs, muqaddams, and sheikhs had subsidiary tax farms and paid through the paramount Shihab. There was rigid social protocol by rank, evident at the emir's receptions in Deir al-Qamar, and the Hakim had judicial authority on behalf of the governor.[73] He could not, however, violate the local jurisdictions of lesser tax farmers (*muqata'ji*s). The governor also expected the emir to mobilize military force in the mountain. In these respects, a "principality" existed, even if only Christians defined it as such.

With regard to the majority of the population, in much of the mountain and especially the Druze country, peasants were tenants of *muqata'ji* families and paid rents as well as taxes. *Muqata'ji*s could demand labor, receive customary gifts from peasants, dispense first instance justice, and issue marriage licenses. Whatever the Ottoman theory of ultimate state ownership of land, the *muqata'ji*s of Mount Lebanon were hereditary land barons at the apex of a patron/client system supposedly dispensing protection in exchange for fees and services.[74] However, in the Maronite north in the seventeenth century, peasants increasingly established private smallholder status out of silk production arrangements with *muqata'ji*s and other landholders.

Geographical centrality in Mount Lebanon, command of the Beirut/Damascus road, domination of the hills above Sidon and Beirut, and allegiance of the Maronite community made the paramount Shihab the pivotal personality of Mount Lebanon and its surrounds. This was the case despite the prosperity of Shia Jabal Amil in the mid-eighteenth century and the power of the strongman Ahmad al-Jazzar as governor of Acre/Sidon a little later. Beyond his core domain, the Hakim had entanglements in the old Shihab home district of Wadi al-Taym, with the Maronites and Shia Hamades of northern Lebanon, and in the port of Beirut. He intervened in Jabal Amil, which separated the Shuf from Wadi al-Taym and where Shihab ambition and the governor of Sidon embroiled him with the Shia. Shihabs also sometimes had tax farmer status in the Biqa.

Haydar Shihab and his son Mulhim after 1732 benefited from a long afterglow of Ayn Dara, when they had supremacy in their own family and rare quiescence among Druze. Haydar clashed with the Shia chiefs of Jabal Amil in 1718,

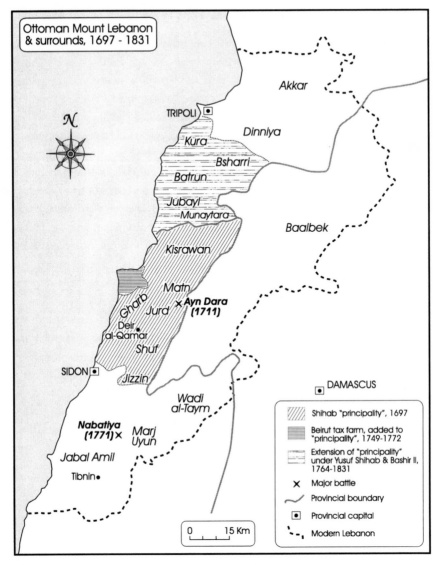

Figure 3.2 Ottoman Mount Lebanon and surrounds, 1697–1831.

and the Ali al-Saghirs dyed their horses' tails green in celebration when he died.[75] When Mulhim heard, he marched against them, capturing their leader Nasif al-Nassaar. At the time, governors of Sidon were cooperative, and the Shia had poor relations with Zahir al-Umar, the strongman of Safad. Mulhim was contemptuous of the Ottoman state, but careful. In the early 1730s, it was said that the governor of Sidon detested Mulhim so much that he covered his name with his hand when letters arrived from Deir al-Qamar.[76] However, he backed Mulhim's foray into Jabal Amil. Mulhim acquired the tax farm for Beirut in 1749 after he sent the Talhuqs to raid its outskirts to demonstrate the sub-governor's impotence.[77] Beirut remained in the Shihab domain until Ahmad al-Jazzar removed the concession in 1776.

From the late 1740s, the Shihabs operated in a more difficult environment. Rivalry to be Hakim among descendants of Haydar Shihab coincided with resurgent Druze factionalism. Sheikh Abd al-Salam, head of the Imad clan, resented Sheikh Ali Junblat, paramount chief of the Shuf after 1712. Sometime in the 1740s, Abd al-Salam gathered around himself the Imads, Talhuqs, and Abd al-Maliks against the Junblats. He adopted an ancestral Imad name, Yazbak, for his party.[78] The Yazbaki faction first appears in the record in Haydar al-Shihabi's reference to it sheltering opponents of the governor of Damascus in 1748.[79] The governor compelled Emir Mulhim Shihab to burn Talhuq and Abd al-Malik properties and expel the miscreants and their protectors from the Druze country. Mulhim later compensated the Talhuqs. After 1759, Abd al-Salam Imad and Ali Junblat backed competing Shihab brothers, consecrating the Yazbaki/Junblati estrangement. The Maronite Khazen sheikhs of the Kisrawan gravitated to the Junblati camp, while the Maronite Hubaysh sheikhs tended to the Yazbakis. Of the remaining Druze lords, the Abi Nakads, Arslans, and Abi Lamas stood apart.[80] Shihab emirs were above the factions, but were their principal target.

Problems among the Shihabs came into the open in 1753 when Emir Mulhim fell ill and his brothers Mansur and Ahmad, backed by the Druze chiefs, forced him to resign.[81] Mulhim retired to Beirut, where he died in 1759. He and his nephew Qasim had tried to overturn Mansur and Ahmad but failed when their patron, a former governor of Sidon, lost office as a vizier. In 1760, this patron returned to favor and the governor of Sidon received an order to hand Qasim the Shuf tax contract.[82] Mansur and Ahmad paid the governor 50,000 qirsh (about $600,000 in modern purchasing power) to restore them.[83] The brothers fell apart in 1763. Ahmad mobilized the Yazbakis against Mansur, who turned to the Junblats and the governor. Mansur's hand was stronger and Ahmad accepted his supremacy.

One conflict precipitated another. Emir Mulhim's son Yusuf, brought up a Maronite Christian, supported Ahmad and fled to Ali Junblat in Mukhtara in fear of Mansur.[84] His uncle seized his property and spurned Junblat's mediation. Incited by Yusuf's Maronite manager, or *mudabbir*, Sa'ad al-Khuri, Ali Junblat broke with Mansur while Yusuf appealed to the governor of Damascus. In 1764, the latter arranged with his son, the governor of Tripoli, for Yusuf to assume the tax farms of Jubayl and Batrun. Yusuf Shihab and Sa'ad al-Khuri entered a scene ripe for exploitation. Rising Maronite leaders, the Dahdahs, Karams, and Dahirs, together with Maronite and Sunni peasants had been in rebellion against Shia Hamade tax farmers in the north since 1759.[85] Guided by al-Khuri and allies from the Shuf, the sixteen year old Yusuf headed assaults that broke the Hamades.[86]

Yusuf Shihab thus collected part of the hinterland of Tripoli, which gave him a power base against Mansur in the Shuf but more significantly a major opportunity for Shihab patronage, particularly of the Maronite church. The Hamades, regardless of being Shia, supported Maronite bishops and monks resentful of the interference in church affairs of the Khazen sheikhs of the Kisrawan.[87] For example, the Hamades had excellent relations with the *baladi* or "country" wing of the Lebanese Order of monks, who favored Vatican reduction of Maronite secular interventions in the church.[88] On the one hand, Yusuf Shihab had al-Khazen backing in bringing down the Hamades. On the other hand, the Shihabs could themselves appropriate the Hamade role in the north, distribute Hamade lands, and ingratiate themselves with both Rome and the Maronite church. For the Shihabs, displacement of their old Hamade friends was all gain.

To the south of the Shihab domain, Shia Jabal Amil greatly benefited from foreign demand for dyed cotton cloth by the 1750s. In the mid-eighteenth century, Jabal Amil paid more tax than Mount Lebanon.[89] In 1750, however, a cloud came over this relative prosperity when Shia leader Nasif al-Nassaar entered hostilities with Zahir al-Umar, who dominated northern Palestine and coveted Jabal Amil. In one incident, after recapturing a village and sending back Zahir's horse, al-Nassaar made the remark: "It doesn't matter that we returned al-baraysa [the horse] after we recovered al-basaysa [the village]."[90] These hostilities only ended in 1768, when al-Nassaar and Zahir reconciled and assaulted Ottoman authority together with Ali Bey of Egypt. The opportunity was Ottoman entry into war with Russia. Ali Bey liaised with Catherine the Great, who dispatched a fleet to the eastern Mediterranean in 1770.

Among the Shihabs, Emir Yusuf stayed loyal to the Ottomans while Emir Mansur tended to Zahir al-Umar and was delighted when the Egyptians advanced against Damascus in 1770.[91] The Ottomans bought off the Egyptian commander, Muhammad Abu al-Dhahab, and the Druze lords withdrew confidence from Mansur.[92] The governor of Damascus recommended he be replaced by Yusuf. In 1770, in the midst of a regional crisis, Mount Lebanon acquired its first Maronite Hakim, though Yusuf publicly pretended to be Sunni.

Yusuf Shihab and the governors of Damascus and Sidon took the offensive in 1771 against Zahir al-Umar and the Jabal Amil Shia. Reverses drained Emir Yusuf's prestige. First, when the governor of Damascus led troops into the Hula Valley below Jabal Amil, Zahir and the Shia ambushed them.[93] Second, when Yusuf led a large force from the Shuf and Wadi al-Taym against Nabatiya, the outnumbered Shia, rallied by al-Nassaar, broke up their disorganized assailants.[94] Haydar al-Shihabi reports 1,500 Druze killed, a loss probably matching Ayn Dara.[95] Jabal Amil Shia took revenge for Ma'n and Shihab depredations. Third, after the governor and Ali Junblat's contingent abandoned Sidon, Zahir and the Shia occupied the town (see figure 3.3 for a nineteenth-century Sidon street

Figure 3.3 Street in Sidon, late nineteenth century. American University of Beirut/ Library Archives.

scene). Emir Yusuf and the governor of Damascus scraped together troops and artillery for a siege.[96] The artillery came with one Ahmad al-Jazzar, a Bosnian soldier of fortune, previously Ali Bey's executioner in Egypt, where he earned his nickname "Jazzar" [butcher]. However, Russian warships bombarded the besiegers, who were routed by Zahir's army assisted by the Shia. The Russian flotilla then attacked Beirut; Emir Yusuf had to pay the Russian admiral to desist.

Alignments became fluid through 1772. The governor of Damascus asked Ahmad al-Jazzar to garrison Beirut; Yusuf consented, declining 200,000 Spanish reales (about $700,000 in modern purchasing power) for al-Jazzar's head from Muhammad Bey Abu al-Dhahab of Egypt.[97] The Hakim immediately had cause for regret. Al-Jazzar fortified Beirut and flaunted independence. Yusuf applied through his uncle Mansur to Zahir al-Umar to bring back Russian warships to expel al-Jazzar, thereby provoking the governor of Damascus. After a four-month siege, al-Jazzar agreed to leave to join Zahir in Acre. The Russian admiral charged Yusuf 300,000 qirsh (over $3 million in modern purchasing power), part of which the latter extracted from the Yazbakis Abd al-Salam Imad and Husayn Talhuq as a penalty for conspiring with al-Jazzar.[98] In 1773, Yusuf's refractory brother, Sayyid-Ahmad, occupied Qabb Elias in the Biqa and robbed Damascus merchants.[99] Yusuf repudiated Sayyid-Ahmad, evicted him from Qabb Elias, and acquired the Biqa tax contract in reconciliation with Damascus.

The balance of forces in the Ottoman Levant shifted after the sultanate made peace with Russia in 1774 in the treaty of Küçük Kaynarca. The departure of the Russian warships finished Zahir al-Umar, who was killed in the 1775 Ottoman siege of Acre. More broadly, however, the Russian incursion of the early 1770s devastated Ottoman standing. It compelled the Ottomans to look for a new strongman to uphold their basic interests, and the candidate was at hand. After fleeing Acre with stolen tax money, in two years Ahmad al-Jazzar ingratiated himself with the governor of Damascus, moved to Istanbul where his charisma won the affections of two sultans, and was appointed governor of Afyon.[100] In 1775, he succeeded Zahir al-Umar as governor of Sidon, resident in Acre.

Al-Jazzar aimed to make himself indispensable, while respecting Ottoman sovereignty. He intended to discipline the Jabal Amil Shia on the Ottoman account; he had a score to settle with Yusuf Shihab and looked to bring the Shihab domain to heel; and he sought to become governor of Damascus as well as Sidon.

As regards the Shia, after a few forays, al-Jazzar led an army north from Acre in 1780. He killed Nasif al-Nassaar, and his forces looted religious buildings, carting their books to bonfires in Acre.[101] Al-Jazzar terminated the autonomy of local chiefs and persecuted the religious class. Many of the Shia ulama fled to Iraq, Iran, Afghanistan, and India. In 1783, a group under Ali al-Saghir chief Hamza Ibn Muhammad al-Nassaar launched resistance against al-Jazzar's Albanian and Kurdish garrison.[102] They killed al-Jazzar's local commander, who had appropriated the crusader fort in Tibnin, seat of Nasif al-Nassaar. Government forces pursued and executed Hamza Ibn Muhammad. An insurgency ensued, which outlasted al-Jazzar, who died in 1804. It was a miserable time for the population, caught between the governor and the rebels and suffering from a terminal slide in demand for their cotton fabrics through the Napoleonic Wars.[103] The Shia surge of the mid-eighteenth century thus collapsed.

Al-Jazzar's long campaign to subordinate Mount Lebanon began with forcing Emir Yusuf out of Beirut in 1776. Thereafter, he exploited challenges to Emir Yusuf from within the Shihab family, at first from his brothers Sayyid-Ahmad and Efendi and in the 1780s from his relatives Isma'il and Bashir. Sayyid Ahmad and Efendi gained support from the Abi Nakads and Junblats and purchased the Shuf tax contract from al-Jazzar in 1778.[104] In the same year, Sheikh Ali Junblat died, removing a stabilizing influence. Yusuf withdrew north to Ghazir, mobilized his friends the Ra'ads and the Sunni Kurdish Mir'ibis from beyond Tripoli, and skirmished with his brothers. He won by buying the Shuf concession back from al-Jazzar, setting a pattern in which the wily governor extracted competing Shihab tax bids. The brothers conspired again in 1780, when Yusuf levied a new tax on silk.[105] They intended to depose him and murder his *mudabbir* Sa'ad al-Khuri, but the plot failed and Efendi was killed instead. Sayyid-Ahmad rallied both Junblatis and Yazbakis against Yusuf. The latter offered al-Jazzar 300,000 qirsh for troops, the Yazbakis deserted Sayyid-Ahmad, and Yusuf again prevailed. Yusuf and al-Khuri struggled to keep the Shihab patrimony intact in their hands while al-Jazzar looked to break up the *imara* and make money.

Haydar al-Shihabi's record of Isma'il Shihab's bid to overthrow Yusuf further illustrates al-Jazzar's methods.[106] Isma'il was the lord of Hasbaya in Wadi al-Taym and Yusuf's uncle on his mother's side. In 1783, al-Jazzar ordered Yusuf to take over Marj Uyun, part of Isma'il's territory within the province of Sidon. Al-Jazzar suspected Isma'il in the killing of a Jewish merchant. Isma'il faced ruin without the Marj Uyun revenues and Yusuf refused relief. Isma'il then offered al-Jazzar increased taxes from the Shuf if the governor dispossessed Yusuf. Al-Jazzar saw his chance to split Mount Lebanon; Isma'il united with Yusuf's brother Sayyid-Ahmad, and al-Jazzar awarded them the tax contract. The Junblats joined Isma'il, and Yusuf had to flee north to the Alawite hills. Suddenly, however, al-Jazzar's *mudabbir* contacted Yusuf's *mudabbir*, offering safe conduct for Yusuf to return. Al-Jazzar sensed new avenues for extortion; he took Yusuf from Beirut to Acre as a prisoner. Isma'il and Sayyid-Ahmad offered half a million qirsh for his murder, and Yusuf countered with one million for his release and restoration. Al-Jazzar thereupon restored Emir Yusuf, who took revenge on his enemies. He heavily fined the Junblats and arrested Isma'il Shihab, who soon died. Yusuf, however, lost his *mudabbir*. Sa'ad al-Khuri was a hostage with al-Jazzar for Yusuf's ransom, and fell mortally ill while in captivity.

Meanwhile, al-Jazzar's talents in mobilizing revenues and building military capability secured him his first appointment as governor of Damascus, from 1783 to 1785. When holding Damascus jointly with Sidon, he had Mount Lebanon in a vice. When Damascus was separate, the Shihabs had depth in the Biqa, and al-Jazzar could be rebuked if he sent troops into another governor's domain. In the early 1780s, Emir Yusuf sheltered dissident Jabal Amil Shia chiefs at

Mashghara, outside al-Jazzar's jurisdiction. In 1783, as governor of Damascus, al-Jazzar demanded Yusuf deliver the dissidents. Yusuf bowed, and al-Jazzar executed the Shia chiefs, another blow to Yusuf's standing.[107]

In the mid-1780s, a distant cousin of Yusuf, Bashir Shihab, emerged in politics. Bashir sympathized with Isma'il and Sayyid-Ahmad against Yusuf in 1783, but made up with the Hakim. His chance came in 1788, in the climactic clash between Yusuf and al-Jazzar.[108] Yusuf refused to pay off the enormous 1783 ransom, and al-Jazzar assisted Isma'il Shihab's son Ali in attacking Yusuf and avenging his father. In response, the Hakim took advantage of rancor against al-Jazzar among his officers and backed a rebellion in Acre. Al-Jazzar beat the rebels and determined to depose Yusuf. At first, Yusuf's brother Haydar repulsed Ali Shihab's thrust into the Biqa, but Ali and al-Jazzar returned with al-Jazzar's main force. The Harfushes of Baalbek deserted Haydar, leaving about seven hundred horsemen—loyal Shihabs, Abi Lamas, and former mercenaries of al-Jazzar—to face perhaps two thousand. Al-Jazzar carried the field in a fierce fight near Jubb Jannin in the southern Biqa. The Hakim had no option but to ask the Druze lords to select a successor. Bashir Shihab, with Junblati lobbying, won their assent. Bashir received the tax contracts for Mount Lebanon from al-Jazzar in Acre in September 1789.

Al-Jazzar gave Bashir a thousand Albanians and Moroccans to remove Yusuf, who rallied supporters in Jubayl and Bsharri. Bashir crushed Yusuf's band in the Munaytara hills, but the governors of Tripoli and Damascus gave the deposed Hakim cover. A short time later, al-Jazzar enticed Yusuf and his new *mudabbir* Ghandur al-Khuri to Acre and even considered more blackmail, now between Yusuf and Bashir. The new Hakim was vulnerable, with the Junblats as his only loyalists, but he convinced al-Jazzar that Yusuf was stirring unrest among the Druze. In 1790, al-Jazzar executed both Emir Yusuf and Sheikh Ghandur.[109]

Communal and Social Transformation

In 1700, the Druze lords and their peasants still commanded the central part of Mount Lebanon, and the Shia of Jabal Amil were about to enter a political and economic upswing. The Maronites had absorbed the Kisrawan and they and other Christians were penetrating the Druze country. However, in the Kisrawan they remained firmly under the thumb of the Khazen clan, subordinate members of the Druze dominated elite, while the Shia Hamades consolidated their grip on the Maronite north. There was no autonomous Christian leadership to compare with the Druze and Shia chiefs and the Sunni Shihab emirs. On the coast, European traders had a firm foothold in the port towns since the time of Fakhr al-Din, especially the French in Sidon. The export of local silk and the circulation of European coinage had become the commercial mainstay of the Ma'n/Shihab domain. However, European cultural and political influence had stalled since Fakhr al-Din. It was limited to the ruling emirs, top Maronite families, and the Maronite church, which in 1700 was still a small, disorganized entity pushed around by rural chiefs and Ottoman officials.

A different communal and social landscape presented itself by the early nineteenth century. The Druze, with lords and peasants reduced in war and factional conflict under the Shihabs, retained shaky supremacy in the south of the old Druze country. Their political capacity had become dangerously narrow, depending on the Junblat clan. The Shia reeled after Ahmad al-Jazzar's devastation of Jabal Amil and the overthrow of Hamades in the Tripoli hinterland. The Hamades retreated to the Biqa, where many from Jabal Amil also took refuge. Both Druze and Shia may have suffered population decline through the eighteenth century. Some remaining Kisrawan Shia probably became Maronite at this time.

In contrast, Maronites and other Christians advanced. They migrated into the Druze districts, welcomed by local lords who were anxious for taxpayers. These new residents were tenants, in contrast to those in the Tripoli hills and Kisrawan, where many Maronite commoners owned their plots. The latter had fewer obligations. Such a landholding peasantry was unusual in the Ottoman east, and the distinction between the Maronite situations in the north and south of Mount Lebanon would feed into trouble later.

As for the Maronite church, its expansion in the Kisrawan through the seventeenth century, at first under al-Khazen tutelage, gave it momentum in the eighteenth century to begin challenging *muqa'taji* constraints. After 1800, the church became an autonomous power with assertive patriarchs, cohesive organization, and landowning monastic orders supporting the peasantry. North of Beirut clerical land acquisition, whether through pious endowment on the Hanafi Sunni model, private title, or encroachment on state domain, increasingly curtailed the sway of *muqata'jis* like the Khazens.[110] In parallel, church educational activity made Maronites the reservoir of literate administrators for the Shihabs. This produced another new power—the Maronite *mudabbirs*, advisors of the emirs whom the latter made sheikhs, extending Maronite membership of the elite. In the late eighteenth century, through the influence of monks, Shihab and Abi Lama emirs themselves became Maronites.

The Maronites received reinforcement from the Syrian interior in the form of the Greek Catholics. These were Orthodox Christians who entered communion with Rome, starting in Aleppo in 1683. Hounded by their former coreligionists, some thousands shifted to Mount Lebanon. They included merchants and artisans, and together with enterprising Maronites rising out of the peasantry, they inaugurated a Catholic Christian commercial bourgeoisie. This new class emerged in two booming mountain towns in the late eighteenth century—Zahle and Deir al-Qamar.[111] Greek Catholics from a variety of Syrian urban and rural backgrounds flocked into Zahle, strategically placed on the eastern flank of Mount Lebanon alongside the main route from the coast to Damascus. They created a trading entrepot, supplying grain and meat to Mount Lebanon and exchanging goods with Damascus. In the process, they established mutual interests with local chiefs, but otherwise sidelined Druze and Shia. By 1800, Zahle had more than one thousand inhabitants.[112] Similarly, Maronite and Greek Catholic traders set up in the Shihab "capital" Deir al-Qamar, making it the center of silk exchange and turning it from a Druze village in 1700 to a bustling small city of four thousand by 1800, almost as populous as the port towns.

After 1800, Bashir II Shihab fostered this emerging Catholic Christian bourgeoisie, educated in the new church schools, because it supplied him with revenue and administrative staff. It helped him to free himself from the *muqata'ji* lords, especially the Druze. It made his regime viable after he got rid of Bashir Junblat in 1825. It acquired Druze land when *muqata'ji*s were forced into exile. The urban Christian population it attracted to Zahle and Deir al-Qamar provided him with hundreds of soldiers.[113] There can be no doubt that Druze and Muslims, who had almost no access to education equivalent to Maronite schools and were disadvantaged in the Greek Catholic trading network, felt threatened. Even many Maronites resented the cultured Greek Catholic Butros Karameh, Bashir II's subservient *mudabbir* after 1828.[114]

The impact of the European great powers deserves careful definition. On the one hand, European dynamism, mediated through command of Mediterranean shipping and cultural influence on Catholic Christians, reinforced Maronite clerical and secular self-confidence. In psychological terms, the Russian, French, and English military interventions between 1770 and the early 1800s sent the message that Europeans were back as arbiters for the first time since the Crusades. On the other hand, the military interventions were as disruptive for Mount Lebanon's Christians as for other communities. Also, the Maronite ascent through the eighteenth century was an indigenous process. Druze and Shia slippage through local conflict and the depredations of Ottoman governors opened space for Maronites and Greek Catholics. Their religious institutions and traders took advantage of the opportunity.

Between the Druze and Shia recession and the Maronite and Greek Catholic advance, the Sunni Muslims and Orthodox Christians of the coast shared mixed fortunes. Compared to the reestablishment of Sunni populations in the ports under the Ayyubids and Mamluks, after the humiliation of crusader hegemony, Tripoli, Beirut, and Sidon stagnated through the first three Ottoman centuries. Merchants made money from Mediterranean commerce, but frequent strife, unruly soldiers, and extortion by Ottoman governors meant most people saw little benefit up to the nineteenth century. The Ottomans often failed to fulfill their Islamic obligation to secure order and justice for the *ra'aya*—the bedrock of their minimalist concept of the state. In 1783, Volney estimated the populations of Tripoli, Beirut, and Sidon as five thousand, six thousand, and five thousand respectively—numbers had hardly changed since the sixteenth century.[115]

According to Volney's account, Tripoli was dilapidated. Compared with Khalife's estimate of 9,400 people in the sixteenth century, it had shrunk. Volney described the environs as derelict and disease prone. Landowners would not replant mulberry trees for fear of new taxes.[116] Nonetheless, the town's fortunes fluctuated through the period. By the 1640s, after Fakhr al-Din's investments had boosted it in the 1620s, the depredations of the Sayfas and Ottoman garrisons left Tripoli destitute.[117] In contrast, when the young Venetian Ambrosio Bembo visited in 1671, the town had evidently recovered. Bembo noted that "commerce in silks and ashes to make glass" attracted "vice-consuls from every country . . . appointed by the consuls in Aleppo."[118] He listed various resident foreign clergy—Franciscans, Jesuits, Capuchins, and Carmelites—some serving the mountain "where there are many Christians without clergy." Bembo described a bizarre use of what was presumably an Islamic endowment, or *waqf*:

> Not far from the marina there were some rather good fig orchards that had been left to the city by a Turk [i.e. local Muslim] to benefit cats. The proceeds of the orchards were to go to feed the cats of the city.[119]

Into the eighteenth century, leading Sunni families implemented robust survival strategies. Traders put their savings into Islamic endowments, which would protect against confiscation while providing income for administering families. Traders, religious families, and local military leaders intermarried, reinforcing their social prestige. From 1666, Islamic court records track individuals and transactions, while reports from travelers like Abd al-Ghani al-Nabulusi and Ramadan al-Utayfi give supplementary data.[120] In these sources, religious specialists like Ibrahim Mikati and Ali bin Karama, forebears of leading families of modern Tripoli, emerge in the late seventeenth century.[121] After 1700, Tripoli's artisans and neighborhood bosses formed militias. Religious specialists in the mosques, *waqf*s, and courts also actively coordinated townsfolk.[122]

Tripoli's leaders proved their mettle in 1730–1731 when they overthrew the oppressive governor Ibrahim Pasha al-Azm and his successor in a double coup.[123] Ibrahim al-Azm provoked the town with monopolies that ramped up commodity prices. The townsfolk waited until 1730, when rebels in Istanbul deposed Sultan Ahmad III and the Azm family temporarily lost clout. Local janissaries and militia led thousands against the governor's house in a near total turnout of the town and its environs.[124] A new governor came with a large force; his soldiers provoked the militia, who drove them out. The next governor promoted improvements, notably a canal from Nahr al-Barid to irrigate orchards. Through the eighteenth century, Tripoli's religious class adopted the Ottoman-favored Hanafi rite while maintaining their firm Sunni orthodoxy.

Prospects for Sunni and Orthodox Christian chiefs in nearby rural districts slowly improved. In 1686, the Sunni Ra'ad clan wrested largely Sunni al-Dinniya, the district immediately inland from Tripoli, from the Shia Hamades.[125] In 1714, the Mir'ibis did the same in the Sunni and Christian Akkar, in the far north of modern Lebanon.[126] In the 1760s, the Orthodox Azars gained the tax contract for the mainly Orthodox Kura south of Tripoli, which secured the community's position in its principal rural pocket. The Ra'ads and Mir'ibis became allies of Yusuf Shihab, and the former offered Yusuf sanctuary in 1789.[127] The two clans stabilized the Sunni rural north into the nineteenth century, and their chiefs sometimes served as deputies of the governor of Tripoli. Through the eighteenth century, the Ra'ads annually paid 9,799 qirsh for the Dinniya tax concession, one-third being a gift to the governor.[128]

Beirut and Sidon drew level with Tripoli in the eighteenth century, the former as gateway to relatively well-populated Mount Lebanon and the latter as "the emporium for Damascus."[129] Both received a modest infusion of Sunnis from across the Ottoman Mediterranean, including North Africa. Volney observed the health and freshness of the mulberries near Beirut because of less arbitrary taxing than in Tripoli.[130] The governor of Sidon resided in Acre after the 1770s, but Tripoli's experience showed that a governor's presence was not necessarily an asset. Sidon was at the center of the war zone in southern Lebanon in the early 1770s, which paralyzed its trade for four years and exposed its people to abuse.[131] With the Maronite ascent in its hinterland, Beirut surpassed Sidon by the early 1800s.

Small populations in the ports highlighted economic activity in the hills. From Fakhr al-Din, the Maronites rose with silk cultivation, combined with fruit orchards, olives, and viticulture. The traveler Jean de la Roque estimated there were around 50,000 Maronites in the north and the Kisrawan around 1690.[132] Volney's comparable number for 1783 was 115,000. He also assessed the population of the Druze country, possibly half of which would have been Christian after a century of in-migration, at 120,000.[133]

Together with a productive diversified rural economy, elaboration of the Maronite church through the eighteenth century underpinned Maronite settlement expansion. Interest among Aleppo Maronites in Mount Lebanon led in the 1690s to Aleppo monks founding a monastic association in Bsharri, the Lebanese Order. Between 1696 and 1764, the Lebanese Order, most dynamic of several emerging monastic movements, established eighteen estates.[134] These were mostly in the north but included a major outpost in the Druze Shuf, Dayr Mashmusha, on invitation from the Junblats. Aleppo Maronites provided seed money, and in the 1760s, Yusuf Shihab transferred Hamade land in Jubayl and Batrun.[135] Monasteries also received land as Christian *waqfs* from Shihabs, al-Khazens, and other *muqata'jis*. Through the eighteenth century, Greek Catholics were active in the Matn, where the Shwayr monastery bought Abi Lama properties and became the largest landholder around the villages of Shwayr, Khanshara, and Bolonya.[136] Maronite and Greek Catholic monks were frugal farmers and artisans. Their foundations accumulated impressive stocks of land and capital by 1800. In the Druze country as far south as Jizzin, they furnished services, investment, and guidance for Christian villagers.

Rapid expansion of Maronite church personnel and properties after 1700 exposed poor organization. Lay interference in appointments of patriarchs and bishops ramified because al-Khazen patrons squabbled.[137] The election of Yusuf Dargham al-Khazen as patriarch in 1736, first of his family to hold the position and an enemy of change, impelled the Vatican to seek reform. At a crucial Maronite church council at Lawayza in the Kisrawan in 1736, the papal envoy pushed through strong definitions of the authority of the patriarch and the bishops and rejection of lay interventions.

Ferment characterized church affairs through the late 1700s, involving obstinate patriarchs, factions of bishops and monks, the Shihab Hakim, and the Vatican. The Lebanese Order split openly in 1768, with the *baladi* wing asserting the autonomy of mountain monks.[138] The Hindiya Order of female mystics, backed by Patriarch Yusuf Istifan and al-Khazen sheikhs against the Jesuits and leading bishops, came and went between 1750 and 1780.[139] The Vatican stood against the *muqata'jis*; al-Khazens continued to hold clerical posts, but their influence declined. In 1795, Emir Bashir II's *mudabbir* Jirjis Baz helped Filibus Gemayel, descendant of Maronite settlers in Bikfaya, become patriarch.[140] In 1808, the reformist Yuhanna al-Hilu ascended to the patriarchate against al-Khazen opposition, and in 1818, backed by Rome, he chaired a church council that loosened the hold of founding families on monasteries.

Part of the energy of the Maronite and Greek Catholic churches went into sapping Christian peasant acceptance of *muqa'taji* supremacy. From the establishment of the Maronite college in Rome in 1584 and the patriarchal founding of a small Maronite school in Bsharri in 1624, the first such school since the Frankish period, the church introduced young Maronites to a wider world free of charge.[141] Literacy and numeracy—even among a small fraction of commoners—was socially subversive, and the concentration on religious texts fostered sectarian sensibility. It is ironic that Catholic schools in Mount Lebanon promoted Arabic literacy in a manner unprecedented in the Ottoman east, while mediating Western cultural infiltration. The church also commanded the first printing presses in the Levant. The Maronites had a press as early as 1610, and in 1733 the Greek Catholics set up a sophisticated operation at the Shwayr monastery.[142] With the backup of the Vatican presses, the Uniate churches could sustain a substantial flow of materials to parishes and schools. In 1751, the Orthodox followed the Catholics with a first printery in Beirut.[143]

The Maronite church founded at least ten schools in the eighteenth century.[144] Schools at Ayntura (1724) and Zgharta (1735) led the way, with vigorous endorsement from the Luwayza church council.[145] The most prominent was Ayn Waraqa, a miniature college established in the Kisrawan in 1789 teaching literature, philosophy, and foreign languages as well as basics. By the 1840s, the Maronite church had five schools teaching advanced subjects, twenty-seven smaller schools, and eight monasteries conducting classes for villagers.[146] The Jesuits ran four additional schools. In the late eighteenth century, most had a dozen or so students, while Ayn Waraqa produced fifty graduates between 1789 and 1818.[147] Perhaps one thousand males passed through the network in the late eighteenth and early nineteenth centuries, enough to unsettle the existing order. The best educated went into the clergy, which gave the Maronite church intellectual resources to supplement its power after 1800. An army of monks and parish priests stimulated a sharp-edged Maronite self-consciousness.

At the same time the church equipped commoners to question lordly authority, the political balance in Mount Lebanon shifted. Incorporation of the Maronite north into the Shihab domain in the 1760s made the Maronites a decisive majority of the people of the *imara*, even without Orthodox Christians or Greek Catholics. It brought the lesser Maronite sheikhs of Jubayl, Batrun, and Bsharri—the Dahdahs, Karams, Dahirs, and al-Khuris—as well as the Orthodox Azars into the elite. Conversions of Shihab and Abi Lama emirs to Maronite Catholicism, decimation of Druze elite families in factional conflicts, and the pretensions of Maronite *mudabbir*s could only make Druze lords feel besieged.

The crisis precipitated by Bonaparte's 1799 advance from Egypt to Acre illustrated sectarian dissonance. Maronites rejoiced, Druze prepared to flee, and Shia offered the French control of Jabal Amil. Haydar al-Shihabi commented:

> When [the French] came to Acre the sheikhs of the Mutawila [Shia] went to them and offered them the mastery of the Bishara country. . . . And the people of the mountain [Christians] rejoiced at their advance because of the tyranny of al-Jazzar. And representatives of the mountain went to them with wine and other goods. . . . And the Druze of the mountain and their *uqqal* [spiritual sheikhs] were afraid of French control of Arabistan.[148]

Bashir II Shihab and the Fall of the Principality, 1791–1842

Bashir II Shihab, who achieved the longest tenure as paramount emir of any Ma'n or Shihab and took the "principality" to its height, also turned Maronite/Druze divergence into conflict, dooming the Shihab *imara*. Not belonging to the main Shihab line through Mulhim and Yusuf, Bashir had to maneuver frantically through the 1790s against the nephews and sons of Yusuf. He took advantage of the talents of the Maronite *mudabbir* Jirjis Baz to outlast his dangerous Ottoman overseer, Ahmad al-Jazzar, and then had Baz murdered in 1807, decapitating Maronite secular leadership. He whittled down Druze *muqata'jis*, culminating in the disposal of his long-time ally, Bashir Junblat, in 1825. Thereafter he depended on the Maronite church and its authority in its community, leaving it wide latitude to consolidate communal exclusivity. His exactions helped transform the Maronite peasant self-awareness established through the eighteenth century into organized sectarian mobilization, which fed into friction with the marginalized Druze after 1825. Along the way, Bashir II transmuted from a closet Maronite who paraded Sunni Islam into the proud Christian patron of an *imara* that the Maronites and Greek Catholics came to consider their own property.

It might be said that only an unscrupulous opportunist like Bashir II could have kept the *imara* intact through the early nineteenth century. Bashir had to cope with strong-willed and mercenary Ottoman governors of Sidon from al-Jazzar to Sulayman Pasha to Abdullah Pasha and an Ottoman state that reacted to the Wahhabi rebellion in Arabia with its own Sunni Islamic assertion. After 1830, he had to survive an Egyptian incursion that the Ottomans could not stop. His alliance with Muhammad Ali of Egypt preserved Mount Lebanon at the price of disaster later. For good or bad, and whatever his personal responsibility, Bashir II's half-century bequeathed the beginnings of modern Lebanon. These included the idea of an autonomous Lebanese entity, popular identification with sectarian community above loyalty to local lords, popular communal political representation, and sectarian tensions.

Mount Lebanon proved a match for al-Jazzar in the 1790s. Almost immediately, most Shuf lords repudiated Bashir II, and in 1791 they persuaded al-Jazzar to transfer tax rights to Yusuf Shihab's nephews Qa'dan and Haydar.[149] Thereupon Jirjis Baz, ambitious *mudabbir* for Yusuf's two young sons, Husayn and Sa'ad al-Din, got Qa'dan and Haydar to grant his wards Jubayl.[150] Baz, a nephew of Yusuf's *mudabbir* Sa'ad al-Khuri, distributed gifts to the Druze lords. Meanwhile, Bashir Shihab and Bashir Junblat thwarted tax collection and Qa'dan and Haydar gave up. The two Bashirs, backed by al-Jazzar, now faced Jirjis Baz and the sons of Yusuf, who were backed by the Abi Nakads and Imads. Bashir Shihab briefly returned as Hakim by force, but in 1794 al-Jazzar swung to Yusuf's sons after Bashir cheated him of revenue.[151] Al-Jazzar again changed his mind because of complaints against Baz, and in 1795 Bashir was back. Baz and Yusuf's sons found sanctuary in Tripoli and Damascus, after al-Jazzar lost the latter in 1795. Baz moved ahead in 1797 when he took Husayn and Sa'ad al-Din to al-Jazzar, who welcomed them and thereby extracted more taxes from a shaken Bashir Shihab.[152] Also in 1797, Emir Bashir II plotted with Bashir Junblat and the Imads to destroy the Abi Nakads, Druze allies of Yusuf's sons. The Hakim invited the Abi Nakad sheikhs to his council chamber in Deir al-Qamar, where Junblat and the Imad sheikhs killed them by the sword "one by one."[153]

Overall, these confused events involved armed deployments, pillaging of property, and tax hikes in competitive bidding with the governor of Sidon. Against the backdrop of the French revolutionary decade and Maronite monastic activism, peasant recalcitrance appears in the sources. For example, in 1794 "when oppression increased in the country the people determined on an uprising, and Emir Qa'dan and Jirjis Baz went to Hamana and calmed this movement."[154] The awakening was probably of both Christians and Druze, but while Maronites looked to their church, Druze looked to co-religionist *muqata'ji*s.

During the French siege of Acre in 1799, Bashir Shihab angered al-Jazzar when Bashir ignored demands for troops. After British naval intervention forced Bonaparte to retreat, al-Jazzar lent Baz a military column to depose the Hakim.[155] Bashir left Deir al-Qamar, but made friends with the English naval commander, who pleaded his case with Ottoman authorities.[156] He also sent gifts to the Ottoman grand vizier, then in Aleppo. The grand vizier granted him authority over Mount Lebanon, Wadi al-Taym, the Biqa, and "the Shia country"; he would be independent from any governor and would submit taxes directly to Istanbul.[157] In reality, Yusuf's sons had Mount Lebanon, and Bashir could not capitalize on this fleeting offer. Al-Jazzar thereafter increased his demands for revenue from Husayn and Sa'ad al-Din, the "Matn people" expelled the tax collectors, the *muqata'ji*s swung to Bashir, and al-Jazzar bolstered Jirjis Baz with Albanian mercenaries.[158] In late 1800, however, Baz and Bashir Shihab compromised to stop al-Jazzar playing them off: without informing the latter, they agreed that Bashir would control the Druze country and the Kisrawan, and Yusuf's sons would command the north. Presented with a fait accompli, the governor of Sidon "flew into a rage."[159]

Thereafter, al-Jazzar incited the Yazbaki Druze, who felt sidelined in the coming-together of Jirjis Baz, Bashir Shihab, and Bashir Junblat. Each year until al-Jazzar died in 1804, the Yazbaki leaders, the Imads, vainly promoted a disgruntled Shihab to replace Bashir.[160] The persistent conflict cemented the alignment of Bashir with Baz, who took over a Shihab mansion in Deir al-Qamar and displaced the Maronite Dahdah sheikhs as *mudabbir* for Bashir. In 1803, the Druze lords repudiated the Imads, informing al-Jazzar that they backed Bashir. The governor feebly pretended he still had an advantage when he asked Bashir's

Dahdah envoy what had happened to Bashir's former props—the French, the English navy, and the Ottoman grand vizier.[161] Soon al-Jazzar was also gone, and Bashir Shihab had new horizons.

From 1804, Bashir had less need for Jirjis Baz, while Baz behaved as his overlord. This was the first Maronite political surge, with the cocky *mudabbir* in cahoots with an assertive Maronite patriarch, Yusuf al-Tiyyan. It deeply offended the Druze lords because it represented upstart power, delegated from the Shihabs.[162] The airs of the *mudabbir*, who ran relations with Ottoman governors, grated on Bashir. Baz would have done well to reflect on the fate of the Abi Nakads and take more care. According to Tannus al-Shidyaq, the breaking point came in Baz's humiliation of Bashir's brother Hasan.[163] When the wife of Emir Abbas Arslan, Sitt Habous, provoked an assault on Hasan, Baz pushed Bashir into reconciliation. And when Hasan attempted a land survey in the Kisrawan to revise al-Khazen taxes, Baz had it cancelled.

Bashir plotted a coup. Ibrahim al-Awra, contemporary chronicler of Sulayman Pasha, governor of Sidon from 1804 to 1819, relates that the emir was so deterred by Baz that he took care to preserve normal relations and "not to show the least sign that anything was amiss."[164] He enrolled Bashir Junblat, who also feared Baz, and the Yazbaki Imads, Talhuqs, and Abd al-Maliks, who were desperate for tax relief.[165] On May 15, 1807, Emir Bashir had Druze retainers strangle Baz on a visit to his chamber. Simultaneously, Bashir's agents descended on Jubayl, where they killed Baz's brother and seized and blinded Haydar and Sa'ad al-Din, the sons of Yusuf Shihab. Bashir reassured the governors of Tripoli and Sidon of his loyalty. In 1810, Sulayman Pasha granted him lifelong rights for the Shuf and Kisrawan. In the meantime, he compelled Patriarch al-Tiyyan to resign.[166]

Bashir also stabilized the Shia country to his south. After al-Jazzar's death in 1804, he helped Sulayman Pasha settle with the Jabal Amil rebels, which included the return of Shia chiefs exiled in the Akkar.[167] The Ali al-Saghirs, Sa'abs, and others took up tax-free land west of Nabatiya, but they could not interfere in Jabal Amil south of the Litani River. The Ottoman state kept confiscated property and strategic points near the coast south of Sidon. The governor appointed Faris Ibn Nasif al-Nassaar, head of the Ali al-Saghirs, as *shaykh al-mashayikh* (chief of chiefs), based in al-Zarariya north of the Litani. However, Sulayman Pasha refused full restoration of the Jabal Amil sheikhs and became irritated when Bashir Shihab pressed the matter.[168] Only in 1821 did a new governor, Abdullah Pasha, agree to the full return of Ali al-Saghir lands and rights.[169] He added Marj Uyun to Jabal Amil and forgave taxes on the condition that the Shia sheikhs supply two thousand armed men when required. Abdullah Pasha then immediately enrolled them in his warfare against the governor of Damascus, during which one of the Ali al-Saghir chiefs was killed.

From 1807, Emir Bashir II had supremacy in Mount Lebanon, albeit constrained by Sulayman Pasha's revenue demands and Bashir Junblat's lock on
Druze. The buoyancy of agricultural and silk production generally meant that
the governor's appetite could be satisfied. However, extra tax impositions riled
the northern Maronite peasantry, who already paid heavily. Behind the shield of
Bashir Junblat, the Druze *muqata'jis* would not pay supplements. Junblat's pivotal position reflected the reduction of opposition to the two Bashirs within the
secular elite, from the killing of the Abi Nakads to the subordination of the Yazbakis to the murder of Baz. It also reflected a general decline of the *muqata'ji*
class; both Maronite al-Khazens and Druze elite families lost leadership capability as lands and authority splintered among clan branches. Only the Junblats
preserved unified leadership and assets, leading to an unhealthy elite imbalance.

Mount Lebanon's economy remained afloat through the disruption of European trade during the Napoleonic Wars because Egypt became the main market
for silk. This occurred with a decline in French demand from the 1770s and promotion of silk processing and trade within the eastern Mediterranean by Greek
Catholic and other Christians.[170] Dislocation of the European market in the
early nineteenth century thus proved less significant for silk producers than
cotton farmers. The takeover of Egypt by Muhammad Ali in 1805 had further
implications for Mount Lebanon. Deploying French experts who came either
after Bonaparte's invasion in 1798 or after the French defeat in Europe in 1815,
Muhammad Ali developed agriculture and industry and a European style state
and military. Coincident with Bashir Shihab's supremacy in Mount Lebanon,
the expanding Egyptian market pushed up silk production and prices, and Egypt
emerged as an autonomous power. Bashir II Shihab's *imara* came under substantial Egyptian influence by the early 1820s.

In the early nineteenth century, Mount Lebanon's politics entered a new
phase of outright sectarian sensitivity. The Maronite majority and its spearhead,
the Maronite church, lost elite representation with the elimination of Baz and
the decline of the Khazens. Patriarch Yuhanna al-Hilu hardly had contact with
Bashir, and the church lost patience with the latter's secrecy about being a
Maronite. At the same time, the Ottomans, embarrassed by the puritanical
Wahhabis, who seized Mecca between 1806 and 1813, emphasized public Sunni
piety. In 1818, coincident with Ottoman destruction of the Wahhabi/Sa'udi
revolt, Bashir infuriated the church when he advised the Shihab family publicly
to observe Ramadan. Here, Bashir Junblat's display of Sunni Islam undercut the
Hakim, who had no choice but to offend the Maronites when his Druze ally
dissembled his own religion.

Maronite anger flared in 1820 when Bashir II tried to unload the governor's
latest financial imposition in a special tax hike on Maronite peasants in the Matn,
the Kisrawan, and the north.[171] Bashir spared the Druze *muqata'jis*. The church,

particularly Bishop Yusuf Istfan, organized the Maronite response. About six thousand Christians met by the Antelias stream near Beirut and agreed to appoint representatives (*wukala*, [sing. *wakil*]) from each village and to refuse anything beyond basic taxes. The movement acquired the name *ammiya*, meaning popular rising. Two Shihabs, the Druze Yazbaki leader Ali Imad, and Shia sheikhs backed the *ammiya*, and the governor of Sidon wavered, but Bashir overrode opposition.

In 1821, peasants and clergy held a second assembly at Lihfid, above Jubayl. According to Haydar al-Shihabi:

> News came to the emir from his son Emir Qasim who was in Lihfid that all the people of that area were rebellious and would not pay the land tax. . . . The emir was furious with their insolence but showed forbearance and sent messengers to threaten and warn them against such insolence, promising mercy and that he was simply asking for what he was also taking from the [Druze] Shuf and the Matn. . . . Then the people of Batrun and Jubayl districts met. And some of people of the Kisrawan went to Haqil village. And the people of Jibbat Bsharri met in Ihmij, and the Shia met in Ram Mishmish. They all agreed on rebellion, and they appointed representatives for each district.[172]

The assembly demanded equality with the Druze in taxation and that the Hakim not be appointed by the Ottomans. Bashir mobilized armed assistance from Bashir Junblat and repressed the Maronite north.

The *ammiya*, which expressed discordance between Bashir II's ambition and the interests of an increasingly coherent majority community, was a major step toward modern Lebanon. It represented the first peasant articulation of identity and the first demand for autonomy for Mount Lebanon. Indeed, one of its movers was Abu Khattar al-Aynturini, a Maronite *muqata'ji* and historian who propagated the notion of the Shihab *imara* as a Maronite communal vehicle.[173] The *ammiya* also represented class and church defiance of the *muqata'ji* elite, including Maronite chiefs like the Khazens and Abi Lamas. From 1820 onward, the rift widened between Maronites who conceived their superiority in the mountain and Druze lords and peasants who felt affronted. Both sectarian breakdown and sectarian political pluralism now figured on the horizon.

Later in 1821, Bashir II aligned with Abdullah Pasha, governor of Sidon, in his confrontation with the governor of Damascus. Their military exploits angered Istanbul, which deposed them both.[174] This had fateful implications, because Emir Bashir departed for a year's exile in Egypt where he coordinated with Muhammad Ali, and Bashir Junblat exploited his absence to manipulate a puppet Shihab. Bashir Junblat had also opposed the campaign against Damascus.

When Bashir II and Abdullah Pasha recovered Ottoman favor and their positions in late 1822, the former broke with Bashir Junblat and forced him to leave
Mount Lebanon for exile in the province of Tripoli. The falling out of the two
Bashirs and estrangement between Bashir II and the Shuf Druze facilitated a
rapprochement between the Hakim—now more relaxed about appearing as a
Maronite—and the Maronite church. The new patriarch, Yusuf Hubaysh, was
enthusiastic, and Bashir Shihab had nowhere else to go.

In 1825, Bashir Junblat moved back to Mukhtara and mobilized the Druze for
a showdown. He tried to capitalize on coolness toward Bashir II in the Maronite
north, but few Maronites joined him.[175] His role in suppressing the *ammiya* and
the enmity of the patriarch counted against him. The Hakim had most Maronites, soldiers from Abdullah Pasha, and some Yazbaki sheikhs—enough to defeat
Bashir Junblat. The latter fled but was captured and sent to Abdullah Pasha in
Acre, who had him strangled. In the aftermath, Emir Bashir confiscated Druze
muqata'ji properties and turned to the Maronite church as his main support.
Patriarch Hubaysh wielded great personal influence in the *imara*, connecting
with the Hakim and the foreign consuls through his bishops.[176]

Over decades, the maneuverings of the two Bashirs had emasculated the
Druze elite, politicized Maronite commoners, and opened space for the Maronite church. The church and peasants were on the rise anyway, but the two
Bashirs had personal responsibility for the blow-by-blow disruption of the
Shihab *imara*'s multicommunal ruling class. The Druze tax farm with a Sunni
frontman and subordinate Maronites that constituted the Shihab inheritance
from the Ma'ns in 1697 became in the late 1820s an actual Maronite principality.
The Ottomans tolerated the situation, mistakenly conceiving of Bashir Shihab as
a reliable agent. The Druze, however, did not disappear. Junblats and other
sheikhs were exiled after 1825, but the *muqata'ji* lords remained the focus for a
marginalized, resentful Druze population that had seen its universe inverted.

Bashir II enjoyed his highest point after 1825, ruling through Christian aides
from his spacious new palace at Beit al-Din outside Deir al-Qamar, to which he
moved in mid-1832 (see figure 3.4).[177] This high point ended in the early 1830s,
when the emir became trapped on the wrong side between Muhammad Ali of
Egypt and the Ottoman central government, which ultimately cost him the
imara. Muhammad Ali wanted compensation for his role in defeating the Wahhabis and supporting the sultan in Greece. He demanded a super-governorship
of the Syrian provinces. Istanbul refused, and in 1832 Ibrahim Pasha took the
Levant by force, also advancing deep into Anatolia. Bashir Shihab and the
Maronite church and *muqata'jis* backed the Egyptians, whereas Abdullah
Pasha of Acre/Sidon and the Druze *muqata'jis* opposed them. Bashir II had personal relations with Muhammad Ali and felt he was betting on the stronger,
more progressive side. Besides, resistance would have endangered the *imara*. For

Figure 3.4 Bashir II Shihab's palace at Beit al-Din, 1838 (Deir al-Qamar in the background). W. H. Bartlett engraving from Bartlett sketch.

the Maronites and Greek Catholics, Egypt represented the commercial center of the eastern Mediterranean, and its ruler promised legal equality for Christians with Muslims.

Egyptian occupation boosted the economic upswing already underway in Mount Lebanon in the 1820s. Silk production expanded in the Maronite north, as far as Bsharri, and Beirut benefited as an outlet for the whole mountain.[178] The Egyptians based themselves in the town, together with European consuls, marking a shift of the political center on the coast from Acre, seat of Ottoman governors of Sidon since 1773. In population, Beirut was still similar to Tripoli in the 1830s, at 10,000 to 15,000 each, but Tripoli and Sidon were peripheral to the mountain economy by the mid-nineteenth century.[179] Demand for silk from Egyptian factories in Damietta and Alexandria was so high that Egyptian officials attempted unsuccessfully in 1832 to impose a monopoly in Mount Lebanon.[180]

Both Catholic and Orthodox Christians did well in Beirut through the 1830s. The Egyptians tolerated a considerable expansion of already numerous European consular grants of European privileges, immunities, and tax exemptions to local Christian agents.[181] This was an elaboration of the "capitulations" the Ottomans had granted to European powers to encourage trade. Egyptian occupation thus widened an incipient rift between Christians and Sunni Muslims in the ports. The latter resented what they saw as unfair advantages acquired on the basis of religion.

As for Mount Lebanon, Bashir Shihab's loyalty to Muhammad Ali for a few years held off the Egyptian bureaucracy that vexed the rest of the Levant. Nonetheless, unpromising developments proceeded. In 1832, the Egyptians abolished the autonomy of the Shia chiefs in Jabal Amil and put the district under Bashir Shihab.[182] The latter delegated it to his son Majid, who behaved in a high-handed manner that recalled the bad old days of Ma'n and Shihab aggression. At one time, he had more than a thousand detainees in his prison in Tyre.[183] In 1836, Shia rebellions led by Husayn Ibn Shabib of the Sa'b family and Jawad al-Harfush broke out in Jabal Amil and Baalbek against the Shihabs and Egyptians.[184] Meanwhile, throughout Mount Lebanon, the Maronite church took advantage of Egyptian permissiveness and suspicion of the Druze to cultivate Maronite solidarity and reduce Maronite social ties with Druze. This potentially endangered the revenues and standing of Druze *muqata'jis*.[185] Bashir II tolerated such social engineering because the church promised Maronite troops to him.

Egyptian rule moved into heavy weather in 1838, with the outbreak of a Druze insurrection in the Hawran that spread to Wadi al-Taym.[186] This was one of several disturbances in Palestine and Syria, which included continuing Shia rebel activity in Jabal Amil. The overstretched Egyptians called on Bashir II to mobilize four thousand Maronites to subdue the Druze in Wadi al-Taym, a provocative new departure that could only inflame sectarianism.[187] Bashir futilely tried to square the circle. He did not oppose Hasan Junblat and Nasir al-Din Imad leading Druze volunteers to Wadi al-Taym; to do so would have violated custom on the rights of *muqata'jis*. He prevaricated, but in the end provided Ibrahim Pasha with two thousand Maronites. These proved critical in subduing the Druze, but at a high cost in inter-communal relations.

Bashir II received no thanks. Nervous about great power action after a European declaration to stiffen the Ottomans in July 1839, Ibrahim Pasha moved to buttress the Egyptian position in Mount Lebanon, vital to the Egyptian deployment in Syria. In early 1840, Muhammad Ali conscripted Maronite students in Egypt, which provoked the belief that the Egyptians would do the same in Mount Lebanon.[188] The Egyptians levied a steeply increased tax and, according to rumor, intended to terminate the *imara*.[189] Ibrahim Pasha also ordered collection of weapons from Christian civilians. Prospective disarmament, conscription, and abolition of the principality were enough to turn already disillusioned Maronites against the Egyptians.

In late May 1840, Maronites, Greek Catholics, and Druze in Deir al-Qamar refused to surrender their weapons.[190] Druze Abi Nakad sheikhs were in the vanguard. Maronites in the Matn and Kisrawan joined the revolt, including *muqata'jis* headed by an Abi Lama emir. Commoners played a significant role; a Maronite Abi Samra and a Shia Ahmad Daghir organized a new *ammiya* in the

Beirut woods.[191] They set up an al-Khazen as "general of the Christians" and interrupted the grain supply to the Beirut military camp. Bashir II sent "the leaders of the *ammiya*" a warning to disperse. They replied:

> We shall not go home unless the emir accepts these conditions. First, we shall only pay tax once. Second, he must get rid of Butros Karameh from his administration. Third, he should have in his administration two representatives from each sect. Fourth, he must give up forced labor, including in the mines. Fifth he must leave them [i.e. us] their [our] weapons.[192]

The most important item was the demand for representation and the association of representation with sectarian communities. The list clearly articulated the concerns of commoners—labor drafted into the Matn iron mine, personal weapons, and oppressive taxation—ahead of the affairs of the church and elite. Indeed, unlike in 1820, the church held back, reluctant to break with the Hakim. Over a few weeks, the mainly Maronite movement attracted Shia and Sunni participation from northern Mount Lebanon, but beyond Deir al-Qamar, Druze stood aloof. By July, Bashir II gained the upper hand with Egyptian troops. Despite British subversion of Druze and Maronites in the late 1830s through their able agent Richard Wood, including bribes to Maronite *muqata'ji*s to rebel, the insurrection was a domestic affair.[193]

Direct European intervention affected events from July 1840 on. The British, worried about Ottoman weakness vis-à-vis Russia, had been looking for an opportunity to roll Muhammad Ali back to Egypt. This became urgent after another Ottoman defeat at the hands of Ibrahim Pasha in June 1839. The European powers, including the Russians—who themselves opposed Egyptian ascendancy—united in July 1839 to forbid Ottoman capitulation. The French, however, were reluctant to abandon Muhammad Ali who was their friend and favored their role. For Britain, the peasant rebellion in Mount Lebanon was critical in again assembling the European powers, minus France, for the Convention of London of July 15, 1840. This required Muhammad Ali to retire from Syria except Palestine. The powers threatened use of force.

The convention, which Richard Wood propagandized in Beirut, galvanized the Maronite church, hitherto suspended between the peasantry and Bashir II, their ally since the 1820s.[194] Patriarch Hubaysh came out against the Egyptians, ordering Maronites to resist, but it was too late for Bashir II to follow suit. The rebellion rekindled in September as British and Austrian warships bombarded the Egyptians in Beirut, and British, Austrian, and Ottoman troops landed north of the town. Austria fancied that it might displace France among local Catholics, unlikely given the impressive dexterity of the French consul in backing the patriarch's adoption of the rebels.[195] In October 1840, the Egyptian army fell apart, Bashir II Shihab departed for exile in Malta, and Ibrahim Pasha abandoned Syria and Palestine.

Restored by European military power, the Ottomans had little choice but to accept European partnership in establishing a reformed administration in Mount Lebanon and its neighborhood. There is no question that the senior local British and French representatives, Richard Wood and Prosper Bourée, influenced subsequent developments. In the process of failing to pry Bashir II away from the Egyptians, Wood discovered an amenable cousin in the line of the Hakim Mulhim Shihab—Bashir Qasim Shihab.[196] In late 1840, Wood had the Ottomans accept his protégé as Bashir II's replacement as paramount emir of the mountain. Bashir III Shihab, gratuitously hostile toward the Druze elite, proved a disastrous choice.[197] For his part, Bourée tried to reconcile Maronites and Druze under French patronage, but his activism simply encouraged Maronite expectation of foreign cover.

Nonetheless, the main issue was not European meddling. There was a basic internal incompatibility. On the one hand, the Maronite patriarch and clergy, who resumed Maronite leadership, wanted continuation of the Shihab *imara* as a Maronite polity. On the other hand, the Druze *muqata'jis*—the most prominent of whom, the sons of Bashir Junblat and Imads, returned from exile in early 1841—wanted an end to the Shihabs and a Muslim governor. Complicating the situation was the fact that in the absence of Druze lords, their Maronite and Greek Catholic tenants in the Shuf and Jizzin had become accustomed to running their own affairs. These Catholics had come to regard the lands as effectively their own, equivalent to peasant holdings in the Maronite north, and refused the return of *muqata'ji* exactions on top of the basic tax. In short, intercommunal relations in the Druze country were delicate even without the dispute over the *imara*.

Maronite/Druze convergence against Ibrahim Pasha did not outlast Egypt's departure. Through 1841, the Druze lords, both those returning and those who had avoided expulsion by Bashir II but whose prerogatives and estates had been truncated, faced frustration. Maronites and Greek Catholics prospered on Druze land.[198] There had been confiscation in favor of the Shihabs. The lords had lost judicial authority in the *muqata'as* to Bashir II's administration. Patriarch Hubaysh and the new Hakim blocked restitution. The fact that the Maronite church disdained the elderly Bashir III and wanted Bashir II back only made matters worse. Grievance and humiliation united Druze *muqata'jis* and peasants. The Ottomans approved the first multicommunal administrative advisory council for the *imara* in May 1841, in line with provincial reform in the spirit of the 1839 Ottoman Tanzimat decrees. In Mount Lebanon, it became merely another focus of dispute.[199] Druze leaders demanded equal seating with Maronites, refused by the latter. Both Druze and Maronite *muqata'ji*s also suspected that the council would end their judicial authority. No council eventuated.

In September 1841, fourteen Druze and five Maronites died in a clash after a Maronite shot a partridge on Druze land near Deir al-Qamar.[200] On October 13, 1841, when Bashir III went to meet Druze chiefs to discuss the frozen collection of land taxes, the Abi Nakads tried to assassinate him. He escaped and hid in the old Shihab mansion in Deir al-Qamar while Druze surrounded the town. Maronites dispatched militia to a gathering of about six thousand armed men at Ba'abda, below the Shuf. Maronite *muqata'ji*s, however, distrusted the church and peasant activists; their social status was at risk with that of their Druze colleagues. The Ba'abda force therefore only attempted a half-hearted raid on Shwayfat, home of the Arslans and many Orthodox Christians. The inhabitants resisted and the result was a Maronite rout. On November 4, the Druze completed the capture of Deir al-Qamar and seized Bashir III, also descending on Ba'abda from which the Maronites fled. Between November 6 and 13, Druze from Wadi al-Taym attacked Greek Catholic Zahle, where Biqa Shia joined the Christians to repel them. Fighting thereafter subsided, with Na'aman Junblat preventing any Druze incursion into the Kisrawan.[201] In January 1842, the Ottomans extracted Bashir III, and shipped him into exile. Istanbul appointed a governor for Mount Lebanon, implementing direct rule in accord with the Tanzimat reforms. The Shihab *imara* would not return.

On the Brink of Modern Lebanon

The developments of 1840–1841 represented a watershed in the long evolution of the sectarian communities in and around Mount Lebanon. For the first time, two local communities came to blows over political claims and identification as communities. In the Abbasid period, Christians and Muslims clashed as an expression of the Islamic/Byzantine confrontation. Under the Franks, each of the mountain communities interacted separately with Latin and Muslim rulers. Under the Mamluks and Ottomans, Alawites, Twelver Shia, and Druze were targeted as challenges to imperial Sunni Islam. In and around the Ma'n/Shihab *imara*, people knew very well that they belonged to distinctive communities with distinctive traditions, but social ties between peasants and local chiefs were cross-communal. Even as demographic and social change fed into Maronite/Druze sensitivity from the late 1700s, sporadic armed collisions did not come as avowedly sectarian incidents, though they contributed to sectarian feeling. The Egyptians and Bashir II in 1838 precipitated the worst fighting; it did not come from within the two communities. However, the 1838 clashes exacerbated communal friction to a point at which internally driven confrontation could thereafter be expected.

Political sectarianism should not be seen simply as some alien manifestation parachuted on the hapless inhabitants of Mount Lebanon by scheming European imperialists. It was a natural outcome, though not the only possible outcome, for several religious communities crammed together in a small space and developing in different ways at different rates. The Maronite/Druze breakdown of 1841 happened quickly because it was bound to do so as soon as divergent development, focus on sectarian interests, and manipulation by local rulers reached a critical point. If there were personal responsibilities, more blame should be heaped on Bashir II Shihab, Bashir Junblat, Ibrahim Pasha, and Maronite clerics over decades than on European consuls in the last couple of years when a nasty denouement was already almost inevitable. The basic causation involved demography, different economic fortunes, cultural separation, and chronic instability among *muqata'jis*, emirs, *mudabbirs*, and Ottoman officials.

Concepts of communal representation on advisory councils accompanied concepts of communal political loyalty. The combination pointed toward modern Lebanon's "confessional democracy," institutional political pluralism arising out of representation of religious communities in proportion to population. The contrast between a majority community demanding political supremacy and a minority community demanding equal shares persists to the present. The Druze idea of equal council seating in 1841 has become the Druze interest in a parliamentary upper house or senate, with equal communal seating as if communities are equivalent to states in a federation. The assumption of all these notions has been that, beyond family, religious community represents the leading marker of individual identity in and around Mount Lebanon. This assumption came out of the sectarian turmoil of the mid-nineteenth century, beginning in 1841.

Apart from politics, the Mount Lebanon of 1840–1841 exhibited other features that pointed the way toward the state and country that emerged in 1920. The geographical spread of the communities, apart from the Armenians, took on its modern character by 1840 and proved resistant to adjustment through violence. The Maronites reached their maximum distribution in the mountain, from the Akkar to Jizzin, in the early 1800s. The Druze proved able to hold their own in the Shuf and the Matn, even in places where they were no longer a majority. Despite ups and downs, the Shia were stabilized in Jabal Amil and the Biqa and as a presence in Jubayl since the Ottoman conquest. The same applied to the Sunnis and Orthodox Christians in the coastal towns and various rural pockets. Through the 1700s, the Greek Catholics moved into Zahle and southern Mount Lebanon, preliminary to the descent of a new Christian mountain bourgeoisie on Beirut.

The year 1840 proved a critical one for Beirut. The returning Ottomans confirmed Beirut's new political role under the Egyptians by making it the governor's seat in their restored province of Sidon. This coincided with heightened

European interest in Mount Lebanon's Christians and potential returns from investment in Syria after the military intervention of 1840. Beirut was central to both the mountain and the whole Levant. In technological terms, its harbor had the advantage over Sidon and Tripoli in accommodating the larger steam-driven vessels of the mid-nineteenth century. Through the 1840s, it began to grow explosively, and it thrived on political instability in the mountain. The apprehensive Christian new rich flocked to the relative security of the new port city, meeting the influx of Western merchants, missionaries, and consular agents. The Ottoman restoration, with its emphasis on a more interventionist state whether in partnership with the Europeans or independent of them, also helped Beirut's rise. It represented a different Ottoman vision from the minimalist state tolerant of free-wheeling governors that preceded the Egyptian seizure of Syria. Western, Ottoman, and Arab bourgeois ambitions intermingled and fed off one another in the ferment of mid-nineteenth century Beirut, throwing up the hybrid culture that was to characterize modern Lebanon.

As for the *muqata'ji*s of the mountain, they were only partway to social reinvention. The old cross-communal landed elite was irreparably damaged. The Shihab summit that gave cover to the elite hierarchy was gone, and many lordly families were splintered and economically reduced. The peasantry, formerly not worthy of notice except as a source of revenue and militiamen, had been split since around 1820. The Maronite majority of peasants looked to their community, meaning themselves and their clergy. They no longer slavishly respected chiefs—of whatever sect. The Druze minority also looked to their community, but this still meant their *muqata'ji*s. The emirs and sheikhs of the old landed families—Abi Lamas, Arslans, Shihabs, Junblats, al-Khazens, and the rest—plugged into business with bourgeois partners to keep social pretensions afloat. They wielded their pedigrees and followings to continue a political role. They were on the way to becoming members of a more diverse multicommunal upper class based on a new combination of property, commercial wealth, urban professions, and social ascription. In the 1840s, however, the mountain lords had not yet accepted their shrunken position. They wanted to salvage their hegemony, and—like the peasants, Maronite clergy, Ottoman officialdom, and European consuls—they had considerable capacity to wreak havoc.

PART TWO

MODERN LEBANON

4

Emerging Lebanon, 1842–1942

Breakdown between Maronites and Druze in the early 1840s and ensuing multi-communal administrative experiments set the course that resulted a century later in the Republic of Lebanon. This chapter explores the trajectory through the autonomous little Lebanon of the Ottoman special province to the Greater Lebanon of the French mandate and the independent state that emerged in 1943, each step involving an increasingly elaborate and eccentric sectarian pluralism. Bashir II Shihab initiated the trajectory. Subsequent developments and the outcome in the mid-twentieth century involved special contingencies of communal collision, European intervention, and Ottoman collapse, though with strong momentum toward something like today's Lebanon. Three crises channeled the momentum: the Maronite-Druze mountain war of 1860, which produced the autonomous province; World War I, which ended Ottoman sovereignty and enabled the French-sponsored conversion of Mount Lebanon into Greater Lebanon; and World War II, by which Greater Lebanon gained independence from France.

This chapter considers Christian, particularly Maronite, social and demographic dynamism up to World War I. The vitality reflected the final silk boom, emigration and return migration, and Christian domination of Beirut. Only a small proportion of the Muslim and Druze population participated in the economic and social vibrancy, mainly their bourgeoisie. In the last Ottoman decades, the life experiences of most Christians in Mount Lebanon and Beirut diverged to an unprecedented extent from those of most Muslims and Druze in the mountain and its surrounds. Boundary setting for France's *Grand Liban* (Greater Lebanon) of 1920 incorporated this divergence into the new country.

Maronites were the focus of political instability and transformation. At the outset, Maronite pressure on the Druze between 1841 and 1860 fed into sectarian friction in and around Mount Lebanon. In parallel, Maronite peasant awakening nurtured by clerics turned against the Maronite and Druze landed elite. Sectarian and social conflict developed together in the mountain. A succession of upheavals after 1840, climaxing in massacres of Christians in 1860 (including in Damascus), brought waves of Christian refugees to Beirut. This facilitated the rapid growth that by the late 1880s made Beirut a political center rivaling Damascus.

Mount Lebanon's tortured Maronite/Druze symbiosis shaped production of a new political entity out of the turmoil of the mid-nineteenth century. The Ottomans did not want a successor to the Shihab *imara*, preferring direct rule. However, they lacked capability, and the sectarian explosion of 1860 brought another European military intervention and a negotiated new order. The autonomous province of Mount Lebanon (the *mutasarrifiya*) had boundaries equivalent to the *imara* of Bashir II Shihab, a Catholic Christian governor (*mutasarrif*) from elsewhere in the empire, and an elected multicommunal advisory council. The Ottomans achieved a step toward direct rule, with a governor who was an imperial official. The Maronites came out of defeat with a political entity in which they were a majority of 58 percent within a Christian majority of 80 percent.[1] Yet they fell short of command of the *mutasarrifiya*, which could not have been created simply for them.

Around Mount Lebanon, the peripheral Lebanese hills, the central valley, and the Mediterranean ports continued as parts of regular Ottoman provinces. The new "little Lebanon" interacted intimately with these surrounds. The Shia of Jabal Amil and the Biqa represented a community historically integral to mountain society. Tripoli was the long-standing center for the population of the north, of all communities. The leading families of the *mutasarrifiya* had properties and interests in the Biqa while Zahle, the commercial center of the Biqa, was inside the autonomous province. Above all, Beirut represented both a new Ottoman provincial capital disconnected from Mount Lebanon and the economic, social, and cultural capital of Mount Lebanon.

For both Maronites and Ottomans, the *mutasarrifiya* was unsatisfactory. The Maronite church wanted an indigenous governor, and secular Maronites were interested in better representation and territorial enlargement. The Ottomans looked toward proper integration into the empire. Nonetheless, "little Lebanon" promised tranquility for a population fed up with violence by the 1860s. It persisted in good order for more than half a century: the European powers guaranteed it, and the Ottoman regime reluctantly maintained it.

Various outlooks on identity, the empire, and the future evolved in the hothouse intellectual atmosphere of Beirut after 1860.[2] The city came to host a unique amalgam of Ottoman, French, Anglo-Protestant, and locally developed educational institutions. Together with diverse Christian schools in the mountain, these produced a commercial, professional, and intellectual class that asserted a local personality. The indigenous bourgeois of Beirut absorbed European ideas, but avoided being swamped.

Curiously, up to the early 1900s, the various outlooks did not involve any real impetus to escape the Ottomans. The Maronite church, initially nostalgic for the Shihab *imara*, came to embrace the *mutasarrifiya* as the only option for Maronite self-determination, but within the empire. The Maronite-turned-Protestant Butrus al-Bustani favored a Syrian Arab identity, encompassing Christians and Muslims from Gaza to Aleppo, but avoided political agitation. In the meantime, creation of modern literary Arabic, jump-started in Beirut in the 1840s by Western Protestant missionaries, went ahead as a mainly Lebanese Christian enterprise.[3] Greek Catholic Nasif al-Yaziji wrestled with a more flexible Arabic to carry learned writings, and the Maronite-turned-Protestant-turned-Muslim Faris al-Shidyaq developed Arabic journalistic discourse. The enterprise suggested a broad Arab identity, distinct from religion. In a famous poem in 1878, Nasif al-Yaziji's son Ibrahim called for Arabs to "awake." Such outbursts, however, had no concrete political agenda.

The mainly Christian ferment to a degree propelled the Muslims of Beirut and the coast. The Sunni bourgeois thirsted for modern education, and by the 1880s they had their own and Ottoman facilities.[4] These widened horizons, but pointed to reform within Ottoman parameters. The sultan was their co-religionist, and the Ottoman state represented the bulwark of Sunni Islam against Western Christians. After 1876, Sultan Abdülhamid II, who suspended the new Ottoman constitution and parliament in 1878 but demonstrated commitment to Sunni Islam and technical modernization, retained Beirut Sunni loyalty to the empire.

For Sunni Muslims, change only began with the Young Turk coup against Abdülhamid in 1908. The Young Turks believed in citizen equality, but also in a centralized Turkified administration. Apprehension in the Arab provinces led to an Arab decentralization movement in the restored Ottoman parliament and activist local committees in Syria and Iraq, including Beirut. By 1911, there were separatist demands and an appeal of thirty-five parliamentary deputies to the Sharif Husayn of Mecca to rise against the false Ottoman caliph.[5] The gravitation to Sharif Husayn gave the new Arabism an Islamic coloration. In response, after 1908, Maronites promoted entrenching the *mutasarrifiya* as a potentially detached "Lebanon." A Maronite lawyer in Paris, Bulus Nujaym, was the pioneer publicist of expanding "little Lebanon."[6] As long as the Ottoman state persisted, partisans of "Lebanon," "Syria," and Arabism could collaborate.

In October 1914, the Ottoman Empire entered World War I. Its defeat in October 1918 led to dismemberment at the hands of the British and French, who manufactured new entities in the Levant and Iraq. Britain and France had a 1916 understanding in which France would take Mount Lebanon and the Syrian coast and exert predominant influence in the Syrian interior. France regarded itself as the patron of Mount Lebanon's Catholics and had the largest foreign investment in local infrastructure.

What if the Ottoman regime had stayed out of the war? The empire was not in terminal crisis in 1914, and without the war it may have kept its hold on the Arab east for decades longer. The war brought other possibilities to center stage. In late 1914, the Ottomans abolished the Capitulations, in the French case dating back to the mid-sixteenth century, which had legalized European interests. This terminated the European guarantee for the *mutasarrifiya*. In 1915, Mount Lebanon became subject to military rule, and a Muslim replaced the Christian governor, with the administrative council disbanded. Also in 1915–1916, the Ottomans executed agitators whose promotion of Arabism or "Lebanon" had taken a subversive turn. By late 1916, repressive military rule and the Arab revolt of Sharif Husayn made either an Arab state or an independent Mount Lebanon the leading options of the local educated class.

Two years later, the Ottoman Levant came under British occupation. The new Arab nationalist movement briefly administered Damascus under Sharif Husayn's son Faysal, while in Beirut the British deferred to a French military contingent. In April 1920, France extracted a "mandate" from its allies to control Mount Lebanon and interior Syria. A French army then expelled Faysal from Damascus. In a new era, the mandate gave cover for colonialism, but France still had to report to the new League of Nations.

France molded modern Lebanon with initial input from Maronite Patriarch Ilyas al-Huwayyik. In September 1920, the French set boundaries for a Greater Lebanon, adding Beirut, Tripoli, Sidon, Jabal Amil, the Biqa, and the Akkar to late Ottoman little Lebanon. The boundaries reflected Maronite ambition but gave Greater Lebanon only a bare Christian majority, soon to vanish, and no dominant community. For Sunni Muslims, submission to local Christians within French hegemony represented double humiliation. France's other product, the new Syrian state, also contested the bigger Lebanon. In 1926–1927, the French High Commission oversaw Lebanese drafting of the first modern Arab constitution, modified in 1927 and 1929. French officials knew that they had to placate Sunni, Shia, Druze, and Orthodox leaders. They backed elaboration of the multicommunal council of the *mutasarrifiya* into a broadly fair "confessional democracy."

By the 1930s, courtesy of France, Twelver Shia had their own judicial institution, while Beirut Sunnis drifted toward accepting a large role in Lebanon as opposed to a small role in a Greater Syria. In contrast, by the 1930s, senior Maronites, including the patriarch, were cooling toward France. A top Maronite, Bishara al-Khuri, and a top Sunni, Riyadh al-Sulh, thereby came together and in the early 1940s designed a communal compromise for an independent Lebanon. By this time, France had surrendered to Germany in World War II, Britain had seized Lebanon and Syria, and the intransigent "Free French" of Charles de Gaulle could only goad the Lebanese to defy them.

Communal Crucible, 1842–1861

Just as indigenous developments, principally under Bashir II Shihab, produced conflict out of sectarian identities, indigenous characteristics of Mount Lebanon ensured that the Maronite/Druze breakdown would be prolonged and nasty. The belligerence of the Maronite clergy, the boldness of Maronite commoners, defense of privilege by Druze and Maronite *muqata'jis*, sectarian cohabitation in the Druze districts, and the sensitivity of the demographic imbalance coalesced with explosive effect. Anglo-French competition for influence and the Ottoman will for direct rule complicated the crisis, but they were responses to it more than causes of it. The crucible of conflict, an autonomous Mount Lebanon, came through the fire hardened; the informal principality of 1840 became the formal, European-guaranteed autonomous province of 1861.

Most immediately, the first round of Maronite/Druze fighting in the Shuf, Matn, and Gharb in late 1841 permitted the Ottomans to try direct rule. The Croat Muslim Ömer Pasha arrived in Deir al-Qamar in January 1842 as Ottoman administrator.[7] Ömer placated Druze and Maronite *muqata'jis*, restoring the tax farms of Druze exiles and confirming the tax exemptions of emirs and sheikhs. His presence in place of a Maronite Shihab alienated Patriarch Hubaysh; he had little chance with Maronite clergy. Ömer also discovered that Druze preference for an Ottoman official instead of the Shihabs did not extend to him exercising authority. Ömer owed his position to the Druze lords' defeat of the Maronites, and he depended on their grace and favor. When he employed suspect Maronites in his security force, the lords became obstructive.[8]

In April 1842, Ömer invited top Druze chiefs to dinner and imprisoned them. The Druze mobilized, calling for Maronite support. The latter, however, feared being double-crossed.[9] They stood aside, as Druze had in 1840. In October 1842, Shibli al-Aryan, leader of the 1838 Druze uprising, brought militia from Wadi al-Taym and blockaded Ömer in Beit al-Din. He demanded a three-year tax holiday, as granted to the Kisrawan Maronites in 1840. The Ottomans dispersed the Druze force in December, but direct rule could not be sustained. The Maronites, the French, and the British opposed it, while Druze sympathized in theory but sabotaged in practice.

Austrian Chancellor Klemens von Metternich suggested a compromise between direct rule and a new *imara* that the Ottomans implemented in January 1843, after removing Ömer.[10] It involved two sub-governors, or *qaim-maqams*, for Mount Lebanon—one Maronite and one Druze—responsible to the governor of Sidon. It has been termed the double *qaim-maqam*ate, and it invited conflict (see figure 4.1). Metternich soon disowned the idea in favor of reestablishing the *imara*.[11] The Ottomans would not allow the Maronite *qaim-maqam* to have

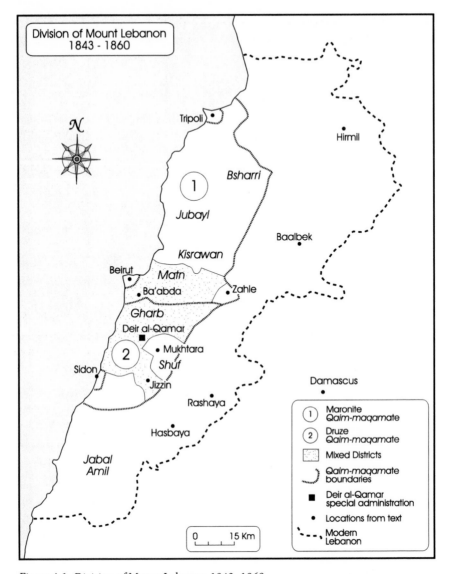

Figure 4.1 Division of Mount Lebanon, 1843–1860.

jurisdiction over Maronites or other Christians south of the Beirut-Damascus road, where Druze *muqata'ji*s wielded traditional authority in the so-called mixed districts. Yet Druze supremacy in the mixed districts promised trouble with the insubordinate Maronite peasantry. British consul Hugh Rose tended to the Druze outlook, backing geographical rather than sectarian division of the mountain.[12] The French lined up with the Maronite clergy in opposition.

Western entanglement certainly soured the atmosphere. British and American Protestant missionaries and schools infuriated the Maronite, Greek Catholic, and Orthodox churches in the 1840s, one of the only things Catholics and Orthodox could agree upon. In contrast, the Druze, impervious to Protestant proselytizing, protected the missionaries and welcomed the schools, ingratiating Britain. In any case, the social influence of Druze warlords, particularly the young Sa'id Junblat, impressed the British.[13] On the Maronite side, the French smuggled weapons, provided funds that were turned into weapons, and backed a Shihab restoration.[14] European consular patronage, however informal, encouraged Druze and Maronite intransigence over the mixed districts.

Otherwise, the internal situation in Mount Lebanon advantaged the Druze. The Ottomans let the jailed lords nominate the Druze *qaim-maqam* to bypass British-backed Sa'id Junblat.[15] The lords selected Emir Ahmad Arslan, a neutral figure who promised to uphold *muqata'ji* privileges and to operate through consensus. This enabled a solid Druze front. In contrast, Christians splintered. Because he was an emir but not a Shihab, Emir Haydar Abi Lama was a logical choice as northern *qaim-maqam*, but his selection aroused opposition from the Khazens and other sheikhs.[16] These chiefs lined up with Druze colleagues in defense of financial and judicial privileges. They had no interest in the clerical and commoner campaign for Maronite tenant rights in the mixed districts and a new Shihab *imara*. Further, Orthodox Christians refused Haydar Abi Lama's claim to represent non-Maronites. The Ottomans therefore designated him "Maronite" *qaim-maqam*.[17] Aside from their top merchant families, the Orthodox trailed Catholics in wealth and education; they detested the Maronite religious hierarchy and often identified with the Druze. They represented a significant minority of the Christians in the Druze country, originating from the rural north and interior Syria from the late sixteenth to the early nineteenth centuries.

Through the summer of 1844, an Ottoman mission under the fleet commander, Halil Pasha, considered refinements to the double *qaim-maqam*ate.[18] Halil recommended Maronite and Druze *wakils* (agents) for each of the mixed districts, with each *wakil* being responsible to his co-religionist *qaim-maqam*. A Maronite *wakil*, for example, would collect taxes from Maronites for the local Druze *muqata'ji*, and would exercise *muqata'ji* judicial functions among Maronites. Halil also addressed the thorny special case of the Christian majority town of Deir al-Qamar, deep in Druze territory, again proposing Christian and Druze *wakils*. The Maronite *qaim-maqam* demanded protection of Maronites living in the Druze areas. The Druze lords, released from detention in April 1844 after British intervention, reluctantly accepted dilution of their prerogatives. However, the powerful Maronite party—headed by Shihab emirs, clerics like Bishop Tubiya Aoun of Beirut, and militant commoners—rejected any continued authority of Druze *muqata'ji*s over Catholics. They prepared for battle and by early 1845 mobilized 11,000 Maronites and Greek Catholics.[19]

Starting in January 1845, Junblati and Yazbaki Druze lords closed ranks in meetings at Sa'id Junblat's mansion at Mukhtara, mobilizing their followers. In early May, Maronite forces attacked the Druze heartland of the Shuf from the north, the coast, and Jizzin in the south,[20] but they lacked coordination and were defeated. The Druze suffered a setback on May 9, 1845, when five thousand Christians invading from the Matn overcame eight hundred of their fighters. In response, they attacked the Shihab emirs in the Gharb and Ba'abda, sweeping down the coastal hills toward Beirut and driving thousands of Christians before them. By mid-May, the Maronite war party was smashed and prostrate. The Druze overran Jizzin, had Deir al-Qamar at their mercy, and threatened to besiege Zahle. The Maronite *muqata'jis* of the Kisrawan and the north spurned the Shihabs, and the foreign consuls blamed the latter for launching the affray. As in 1841, the Ottomans lacked the military resources to control the situation, but they arranged a cease-fire between Druze and Maronites in early June.

An overhaul of Mount Lebanon's administration followed. The Ottomans sought to pacify the communities and still aspired to direct rule. Ottoman Foreign Minister Şekip Effendi came to Beirut to devise the reforms, indicating the priority Istanbul assigned to Mount Lebanon. Under Şekip's "règlement" of October 1845, the double *qaim-maqam*ate would continue, with *wakils* for the mixed districts and a special sub-governor for Deir al-Qamar.[21] However, each *qaim-maqam* would have a tribunal representative of the communities to manage tax gathering and administer justice, compromising *muqata'ji* prerogatives. Each sect would have two tribunal members (an advisor and a judge), except the Shia, who would only have an advisor. The Ottomans still refused Shia legal distinction from Sunnis, though they conceded it to Druze. Religious institutions of the communities would recommend tribunal members, but the governor of Sidon would appoint them. Indeed, from *qaim-maqam*s down, all officials were salaried subordinates of the governor in Beirut. The tribunals inaugurated multicommunal representative institutions for Mount Lebanon, paralleling the governor's advisory council in Beirut.

But little changed on the ground. In light of the suspension of imperial authority through the 1830s, the tribunals could only implement their tax function on the basis of an updated property survey. The *muqata'jis* frustrated surveys in the late 1840s with the sympathy of the British, who defended mountain autonomy, meaning *muqata'ji* autonomy.[22] The activist Maronite Patriarch Hubaysh died in 1845, and his successor, Yusuf al-Khazen, supported the *muqata'jis* until his death in 1854. In the Maronite *qaim-maqam*ate, the clerics and chiefs preserved their tax exemptions. Commoner discontent continued. To the south, the new Druze *qaim-maqam*, Ahmad Arslan's brother Amin, sought to cut away from *muqata'ji* patronage, noting he owed his position solely to the Ottoman governor.[23] This only succeeded in bringing both Junblatis and Yazbakis together against him, under the British backed Sa'id Junblat. The Druze *muqata'ji*s did as they pleased, ignoring the tribunal, sidelining the *wakil*s, and themselves pocketing the taxes.

The Ottomans faced more general difficulties in resuming collection of land and other taxes through the 1840s.[24] Officials and soldiers endured pay reduction; fighting destroyed silk crops and hit customs revenues; contractors stole takings from the tobacco monopoly; and European consulates extended tax exemptions to hundreds more of their protégés.

Around Mount Lebanon, developments varied markedly between Beirut on the one hand and the other coastal towns and the Shia rural areas on the other. Beirut became more tied to the mountain. Its population doubled through the 1840s to around 25,000, and it became more than half Christian because of inflows of Catholics and Orthodox from Mount Lebanon.[25] The intense focus of Ottoman and European governments on the sectarian troubles also inflated Beirut because it was the natural base for all the diplomacy and missions. With intermittent interruption, commerce grew in parallel as Beirut became the preferred port on the Levant coast. Larger steam vessels patronized fewer ports, and from 1834, Egyptian establishment of Syria's only quarantine station in Beirut compelled every ship to call there.[26]

Closer Western engagement fed into expanded foreign Protestant and Catholic educational activity. By about 1850, from a start with a tiny girls' school in Beirut in 1834, American Protestants were catering for up to four hundred pupils in Beirut and the mountain, mainly local Christian boys.[27] Through the 1850s, British and local Protestant activity added nine "Lebanon Schools," to which Druze *muqata'ji*s sent their children.[28] French Jesuits opened eight schools for local Catholics in Beirut, the mountain, and the Biqa between 1839 and the 1850s. In 1847, Jesuits also established the Catholic Press, which became Beirut's principal publishing outlet.[29]

By the 1840s, the activities of a group of Orthodox, Greek Catholic, and Sunni Muslim merchant families based in Beirut clearly eclipsed Sidon and Tripoli.[30] These included the Orthodox Bustros, Sursuk, and Tuwayni families, the Catholic Abilas and Mudawwars, and the Sunni Itanis, Bayhums, and Barbirs, who together connected the trade of the mountain and the Syrian interior with that of Europe. Some were longstanding in Beirut; some appeared from the late 1700s. Their wider Mediterranean origins are interesting. The Itanis and Bayhums derived from Muslim Spain; the Bustroses from Cyprus in 1600; the Sursuks from Anatolia to Jubayl as rural tax farmers, moving to Beirut in the eighteenth century; and the Abilas from a Maltese doctor.[31]

By comparison, Shia in Jabal Amil and the Biqa became more marginalized through the mid-nineteenth century. Hamad al-Hamoud of the Ali al-Saghirs repudiated the Shihabs and Egyptians in 1840, giving the Ottomans military aid in northern Palestine.[32] The Ottomans made him *shaykh al-shuyukh* of Jabal Amil and tax agent there for the governor of Sidon. He was the inaugurator of the modern al-Asa'ad family and commanded a stagnant order in southern Lebanon until the Ottomans abolished the *iqta* arrangements in 1864. In the Biqa, tax agents from outside challenged the Harfush clan, which was debilitated by feuding.[33] Baalbek declined as Zahle rose and the Greek Catholics consolidated their commercial supremacy. In 1850, Harfush chiefs resisted conscription, while the Ottomans favored another family, the Haydars.[34] The Hamades survived in Hirmil north of Baalbek after expulsion from Mount Lebanon. They influenced the Shia remaining in Jubayl but otherwise had no sway beyond the northern Biqa, an area of pasturage and forest.

The year 1854 marked a turning toward renewed instability in Mount Lebanon. With the deaths of Patriarch Yusuf al-Khazen and *qaim-maqam* Haydar Abi Lama, more abrasive personalities assumed the top Maronite offices. The new patriarch, Bulus Mas'ad, came from peasant stock and detested the *muqata'jis*. He returned the Maronite church to social activism. Meanwhile, two of Haydar Abi Lama's nephews, Bashir Assaf and Bashir Ahmad, disputed the Maronite *qaim-maqam*ate.[35] The more pushy Bashir Ahmad Abi Lama won and sought to make *muqata'jis* bow to his authority. The new patriarch and *qaim-maqam* distrusted each other, but converged in their hostility toward Maronite chiefs and Orthodox Christians. British and French stirring exacerbated friction among Maronites; the British consul sympathized with the Khazens and other *muqata'jis* while his French counterpart backed Bashir Ahmad and the populist clerics. A freelance English gentleman, Charles Henry Churchill, whose daughter had married a Shihab emir, incited the *muqata'jis* to defiance.[36]

Over several years, Bashir Ahmad challenged the financial and judicial privileges of the chiefs and encouraged commoners to protest impositions. On their side, the Khazens bitterly resented Abi Lama precedence in the *qaim-maqam*ate. By 1857, the Khazen, Hubaysh, and other sheikhs, as well as the Greek Catholics of Zahle, were demanding Bashir Ahmad's removal.[37] Al-Khazen sheikhs took punitive action against peasants they thought were colluding with the *qaim-maqam*. The situation deteriorated in 1858 as the agitation against Bashir Ahmad created an atmosphere of disturbance that also stimulated peasant assemblies against his *muqata'ji* opponents. A meeting in Ajaltun in the Kisrawan advanced grievances against the Khazens.[38] Consumed with their dispute with Bashir Ahmad, the latter did not respond. As a result, Kisrawan peasants organized committees, each headed by a *shaykh al-shabab* (chief of the male youth). In January 1859, village delegates met the Khazens again, demanding equality in taxes between lords and commoners, an end to special levies, for example on holidays, and the right to represent themselves to officials.[39]

Not receiving satisfaction, the Kisrawan villages elevated a demagogic semi-literate artisan, Tanyus Shahin, as their leader and declared a *jumhuriya* [republic]. The peasants forcibly evicted six hundred members of the Khazen clan, who fled to Beirut destitute.[40] The Ottoman authorities were reluctant to become embroiled, and stalemate prevailed through 1859. However, humbling their own *muqata'jis* in the Kisrawan emboldened Maronite activists to look further afield—to the Maronites in the Druze *qaim-maqam*ate. The hard-line clerical faction headed by Bishop Tubiya Aoun of Beirut conceived of the Khazen affair as a prelude to tipping over Druze *muqata'jis*. In August 1859, a fracas in the Matn, the mixed district in the Maronite *qaim-maqam*ate, gave Aoun's well-prepared Maronite central committee in Beirut the excuse to mobilize. A clash between Maronite and Druze youths near Beit Miri led to an incursion by the Yazbaki Druze *muqata'ji* Yusuf Abd al-Malik and more than twenty deaths.[41] This reignited sectarian rancor.

Maronites and Druze steeled themselves for hostilities in late 1859.[42] Christians were buoyed by their local numerical superiority, yet despondent because of the hostile Muslim mood in Syria after Ottoman reforms. Druze leaders hesitated, apparently pessimistic about the military balance.[43] Tubiya Aoun organized Maronite arming while the Druze reportedly coordinated their preparations with Ottoman officials in Beirut through the winter of 1859–1860.[44] Druze *muqata'jis* finally decided on war at a meeting in Mukhtara in late May 1860, when Maronites were already attacking in the Matn and Kisrawan populist Tanyus Shahin was menacing the Gharb.[45] The Junblatis and the more militant Yazbakis elected Sa'id Junblat as their commander. Lesser sheikhs featured prominently, particularly Sa'id's assistant Ali Hamade.

Whatever the responsibility for events, in May 1860, Maronite militants rushed into a new military disaster.[46] As before, the Maronites could not maintain cohesion among their fighters. The Kisrawan and the north, still reverberating with the crisis of *muqata'jis* and commoners, made no effective contribution. The Druze had the advantage of compact internal lines, communal solidarity, and reinforcement from the Hawran in interior Syria. Tanyus Shahin, out of his depth in a real battle, retired in disorder. By mid-June, after only two weeks of fighting, the Druze controlled the mountain everywhere south of the Kisrawan.[47] The fall of Zahle on June 17, 1860, epitomized Maronite and Greek Catholic failings. Their disdain for Biqa Shia alienated earlier allies.[48] Inflated confidence collapsed into despair and flight after a stiff fight against superior Druze forces. The townsfolk vainly expected the Bsharri *muqata'ji* Yusuf Karam to relieve them from across the mountain.

In this third sectarian collision, Druze fury turned to massacre. Because of Protestant missionary activity, the Orthodox Christians of Wadi al-Taym identified with Maronites, unlike Orthodox elsewhere.[49] They clung to their Sunni

Shihab lords, whom Druze wanted removed because of their behavior in 1838. With the outbreak of hostilities in Mount Lebanon, the Wadi al-Taym Druze moved against the Shihabs and Christians, culminating in the mass killing of about one thousand males in Hasbaya and Rashaya on June 10–13, 1860 (view of Rashaya in figure 4.2).[50] Thereafter, a large Druze force converged on Deir al-Qamar, where Druze from the Abi Nakad sheikhs downward felt humiliated by the steady Christian takeover. The rank and file, incited by *uqqal* and lesser sheikhs, had autonomous momentum. On June 19–20, they massacred about 1,200 Maronites and Greek Catholics, mainly adult males, while women and children fled.[51]

In late June 1860, Beirut overflowed with refugees, and local Muslim feeling against Christians spiked.[52] The Ottoman governor hastened to arrange a settlement, fearing European intervention. Tubiya Aoun's sights had lowered to salvage, and in early July, a meeting of the tribunals of the two *qaim-maqam*ates declared peace on the basis of no punishment for excesses. Media outrage in Europe, particularly France, ran high, but the truce undercut justification for military action. Then, on July 9–12, Muslim mobs in Damascus, excited by the Druze sweep in Mount Lebanon, killed upwards of three thousand Orthodox and Catholic Christians.[53] Muslim leaders strove to save Christians, but there

Figure 4.2 Rashaya with citadel, Wadi al-Taym, late nineteenth century. Børre Ludvigsen Collection. Photographer: Bonfils.

was no stopping French Emperor Napoleon III. The Ottoman foreign minister, Fuad Pasha, rushed to Damascus and supervised draconian punishment of Muslims and Ottoman officials, which spared the city a European occupation. However, the sultan had no choice but to approve a French military landing at Beirut and a review of the status of Mount Lebanon, including assigning responsibility for the massacres. Six thousand French troops arrived in August 1860, camping in the Beirut pine forest.

Proto-state and New Society, 1861–1916

Along with pacifying the mountain and aiding refugees, the Ottomans and the five European powers (Britain, France, Russia, Austria, and Prussia) negotiated a new political system for Mount Lebanon in a commission chaired by Fuad Pasha. In June 1861, the commission agreed on an autonomous province of Mount Lebanon, and foreign troops departed. British representative Lord Dufferin originated the idea of a special province under an imported Christian governor to replace the discredited double *qaim-maqam*ate.[54] France and the Maronite church still looked to revive the Shihab principality, but the Ottomans and Britain refused. In September 1864, the Ottomans and Europeans signed the *règlement organique* defining the new entity, including French recommendation of an elected multicommunal council to advise the governor.[55]

For the Ottomans, the special province (the *mutasarrifiya*) combined unwelcome European supervision with a step toward normal provincial rule in line with the imperial reform drive (the Tanzimat). Maronite peasant humiliation of the Khazens and international commission punishment of Druze lords for war crimes diminished a major obstacle to reform—the *muqata'ji* elite.[56] Simultaneously with the new political dispensation, the Ottomans abolished the legal and financial privileges of the landed tax farmers of the Shihab *imara*. This was part of the general dismantling in 1864 of the *iqta* taxing and social order of the Arab provinces, in favor of direct tax collection and social equality, again in line with the Tanzimat. *Muqata'ji*s retained advantages in accumulated property and social prestige. Many moved into district headships and other senior positions in the new administration that replaced farming out local government to clan chiefs.[57] However, they had no guarantees and competed with a class of lesser sheikhs, wealthy peasants, merchants, and town professionals emerging in the mountain and Beirut. By the late nineteenth century, legal equality, commerce, and the educational boom produced a new social elite.

The *mutasarrifiya* built on multicommunal representation in the *qaim-maqam*ate, compelling collaboration to operate a structure in which sects had defined shares.[58] From the outset, the administrative council had the right to veto tax increases and oversee appointments, a far-reaching advance on the advisory function of the tribunals of the *qaim-maqams*. Electoral representation and rough demographic weighting of communal membership were also innovations. Governors' councils in regular Ottoman provinces did not have the rights of the Mount Lebanon council and were appointed, not elected.

Of twelve councilors, four were Maronite, three Druze, and two Orthodox, with one each for Greek Catholics, Shia, and Sunnis. This made a Christian majority of seven, but in formal terms a Maronite minority despite the Maronite population majority. A two-stage electoral process became refined over several decades, with secret balloting introduced in 1907. Adult male village and town residents elected headmen who met in six districts and the town of Zahle to elect one or more council members assigned to each of these seven constituencies (see figure 4.3 for the districts). For example, the Shuf contributed one Druze member while the Matn had four seats—Maronite, Druze, Orthodox, and Shia. All headmen voted for all district members, regardless of sect. Maronite votes could thereby influence non-Maronite outcomes, mitigating Maronite underrepresentation. Elections for one-third of council seats took place every two years. The *mutasarrifiya* introduced a core element of modern confessional democracy—multimember, multisectarian constituencies.

Apart from the administrative council, Mount Lebanon acquired a range of government institutions in place of the paramount prince and the *muqata'jis*. The governor, a non-Maronite Catholic from outside, was of Ottoman ministerial rank with the title of Pasha, though a step below a full provincial governor. A gendarmerie of 1,200 troops headed by a Maronite officer replaced the armed retainers of *muqata'jis*. The small salaried staff of the *qaim-maqams*, which had already taken over from the private staff of the Shihabs, expanded into the governor's new bureaucracy, which collected land and poll taxes. Three judicial levels filled the old judicial functions of *muqata'jis* and princes: village headmen as justices of the peace, district courts, and a central court with criminal and civil branches.[59] Staffing of all institutions observed sectarian balancing. For example, presiding judges of district courts were from the same sect as the largest religious group in the district, with the two deputy judges reflecting the next two largest groups. Court decisions had to involve the president and at least one other judge. The whole idea of such balancing was to erode the confessional sensitivity of the 1840s and 1850s.

The *mutasarrifiya* covered a little over one-third of modern Lebanon, comprising the old Shihab *imara* plus Zahle in the Biqa and the Orthodox Kura district near Tripoli. Between 1865—when the Ottomans incorporated the province of Sidon based on Beirut into a new province of "Syria"—and 1888, the rest was subject to the governor of Damascus. This included the coastal ports, Jabal Amil, Wadi al-Taym, the Biqa, and the far north. The governor of Damascus

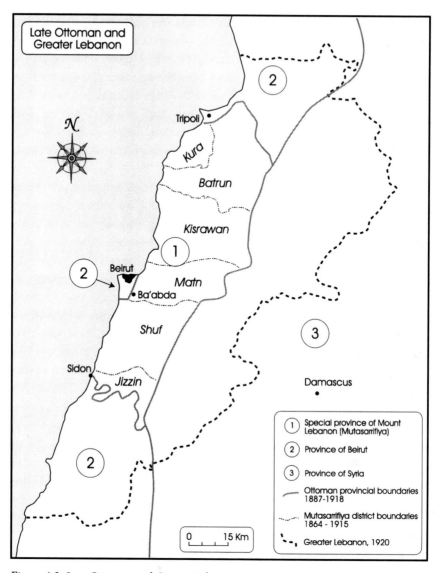

Figure 4.3 Late Ottoman and Greater Lebanon. *Source:* District and Mutasarrifiya boundaries from folded map in Isma'il Haqqi, *Lubnan.*

thus commanded the customs, quarantine, and commercial court for the *mutas-arrifiya*, all run by the old province of Sidon from Beirut. Apparently, the Ottomans wished to neutralize Mount Lebanon by surrounding it with an interior-based province and to counteract European influence in Beirut by shackling the city to Damascus. This prefigured abolishing the *mutasarrifiya* once good treatment tranquilized the Maronites.

Beirut's Christian and Sunni merchants, however, fiercely resented trekking to Damascus.[60] Beirut's cosmopolitanism elaborated regardless of "Syria." In 1888, the Ottomans relented and created a province of Beirut, restoring the city as a political center. Henceforth, modern Lebanese territory came under three Ottoman jurisdictions. The new province of Beirut included three coastal areas divided by the *mutasarrifiya*: Beirut and its immediate suburbs; Sidon and Jabal Amil as part of the sanjak of Beirut; and the sanjak of Tripoli. The truncated province of Damascus kept the Biqa and Wadi al-Taym. The change reinforced Beirut vis-à-vis the Syrian interior.

In the 1860s and 1870s, the *mutasarrifiya* secured Maronite acquiescence, Druze reintegration, and sectarian reconciliation. Unlike in surrounding areas, the tax base did not change after it was fixed at a generously low level in the 1860s, wartime conscription was excluded, and superior freedoms and security prevailed.[61] Communal pluralism came to characterize the *mutasarrifiya*, unfolding together with cultural and intellectual ferment in Beirut. Many participants in Mount Lebanon's affairs lived in Beirut much of the time, and it was the base for their activities. Starting in the 1880s, the governors relocated their administrations from Bashir II's palace of Beit al-Din to Ba'abda, within the *mutasarrifiya* but close to the city.

For the first three *mutasarrifs*—Davud (1861–1868), Franku Qusa (1868–1873), and Rustem (1873–1883)—the priority was to contain the Maronite church. The temporary eclipse of old elite families in the 1860s left the church as the leading mountain player, regardless of the Christian military defeat. Significantly, under Napoleon III and the subsequent republican regime, France became committed to the new multisectarian mountain entity as securing both Catholic Christian prosperity and Ottoman integrity.[62] After 1860, France and Britain converged in protecting their stakes in the empire against Russian encroachment. French defeat by Prussia in 1870 made France more risk averse.[63] French interest in Maronite clerical turf struggles with governors waned; indeed, France was the chief architect of the eventual competitor of the church—the elected administrative council. France was schizophrenic in upholding both the Ottomans and its own influence in Mount Lebanon and Syria.

Davud Pasha, an Armenian Catholic, developed fruitful relations with foreign consuls and strong local commitment. These were assets in resuscitating the local secular elite. In the Kisrawan, Davud reconciled the Khazen sheikhs and the peasants, the former retrieving much of their property and the latter mollified with tax and land concessions.[64] In the southern districts, Davud initially kept some Druze lords in exile, to Maronite approval, but soon relented for the sake of long-term harmony.[65] Christians gained land, but the Junblats, Arslans, and other Druze chiefs kept core estates and entered the system. The British protected Junblat property while Sa'id's widow was trustee for the heirs.

A Junblati/Yazbaki split reemerged, but with the Arslans taking the Yazbaki leadership in place of the defunct Imads.

Davud reacted with delicacy when the disgruntled Maronite chief Yusuf Karam (see figure 4.4 for an image of Yusuf Karam) rebelled in Bsharri in 1861, 1864, and 1866.[66] Karam had anticipated that his cooperation as last Maronite *qaim-maqam* would lead to stewardship of the mountain. Davud found Patriarch Bulos Mas'ad unhelpful, but had European backing. He isolated Karam and in 1866 detained and exiled him. Davud failed in 1868 when he demanded that the

Figure 4.4 Maronite *muqata'ji* Yusuf Karam, September 1860. Paul Zgheib Collection. Photographer: Gustave Le Gray.

mutasarrifiya incorporate Beirut, "the key to Lebanon," and much of the Biqa.[67] There was no chance of such truncation of the province of Syria, and the Ottomans brought in a Greek Catholic from Aleppo, Franku Qusa, as new *mutasarrif*. Franku set a pattern of loyalty to the Ottoman regime and horrified the consuls when he suggested that the governor of Syria might stand in for him when he went on leave.[68]

Rustem Pasha, a Latin Catholic Italian Ottoman, succeeded Franku in 1873. He felt that the *mutasarrifiya* was well grounded enough to be less deferential to the Maronite church. He preferred secular candidates for administrative appointments, sidelining church favorites.[69] In 1876, he appointed Mustafa Arslan as head of the Shuf district, buttressing Druze participation. Rustem preserved the new institutions in Mount Lebanon through the Ottoman crisis of 1878–1881. Defeat by Russia, territorial dismemberment in the Balkans, and central government bankruptcy left the empire reeling. In these trying conditions, Rustem responded to church hostility by exiling Bishop Bulos Bustani in 1878 for stirring up Maronite-Druze tension in the Shuf.[70] He only allowed Bustani's return after extracting a loyalty declaration from Patriarch Mas'ad. Rustem had the sympathy of both the French consul and ambassador, but the French government backed the church. Paris still envisaged its clients in the mountain as the bedrock from which to assert influence in Syria.[71]

Under the Albanian Catholic Vasa Pasha (1883–1892), Franku's nephew Na'um Pasha (1892–1902), and the Hungarian Muzaffar (1902–1907), the *mutasarrifiya* reached its peak. Administrative council elections became genuine cross-sectarian competitions under Vasa as the governor's candidates opposed those favored by the Maronite church and the French. Muzaffar encouraged progressive lesser sheikhs and bourgeois who had risen through the new bureaucracy—Habib Sa'ad, Jirjus Zuayn, and Kana'an Dahir—against conservatives from the Khazen and Hubaysh families.[72] Muzaffar also introduced a secret ballot in elections of councilors by village headmen. Among Druze, Nasib Junblat alternated with Mustafa Arslan as *qaim-maqam* of the Shuf. In the 1880s, Vasa managed to split the church, while the highly political Bishop Yusuf Dibs aligned with the Druze Mustafa Arslan. In 1890, Patriarch Mas'ad died, and his successor proved more amenable to the governors and the Ottomans. There was a new flexibility from the clergy. Under Na'um, the church began officially to inform governors of the elections of bishops.[73] Previously, as a mark of independence, it had guarded its unofficial status in the empire, in contrast to the Orthodox and Armenian millets. The church took care, however, to limit its formal links with the Ottoman state to the *mutasarrifiya*.

The most notable technological advance in the mountain during this period was the building of modern roads in place of tracks, reflecting the return of the wheel. By 1915, proper roading in the special province expanded from only forty kilometers in 1860, entirely the portion of the new Beirut/Damascus highway within the *mutasarrifiya*, to 1,144 kilometers.[74] It mainly comprised unpaved roads connecting mountain villages to each other and the coast. The administrative council had charge of the special taxes that financed the endeavor, collection of which was farmed out.[75] More than one-third of construction occurred between 1892 and 1902, and the Matn and Shuf districts accounted for almost 60 percent of road length, meaning a relative deficit in the north.[76] Beyond the special province, road building lagged badly. Proper roads focused the *mutasarrifiya* on Beirut and became one of the features distinguishing both from their surrounds in the last Ottoman years.

As for the livelihoods of the local population, silk production and earnings of the mountain Christians between the 1860s and 1880s boomed as never before. Before 1840, silk was a commercial mainstay but not a dominant land use or product, but lowered shipping costs, the French market, and surging rural factory production of silk thread after 1860 substantially turned mountain agriculture into silk monoculture. Between the 1840s and 1914, the proportion of usable land taken up by mulberry trees increased from about 10 percent to 40 percent.[77] Haqqi's 1917 survey of Mount Lebanon concluded that silk cultivation and processing accounted for 60 percent of the annual GDP of the mountain in the final decade of the *mutasarrifiya*.[78]

There were three main consequences. First, the factory operations—halls with hot water basins to break down silk cocoons into filaments and spinning wheels for the reeling—spread through the mountain districts near water supplies and mainly employed village girls. From a single French-owned factory in 1838, they multiplied to over 150 in the 1890s, mainly Lebanese owned.[79] In the late nineteenth century, almost one-quarter of the female population labored at one time or another in the factories.[80] For the first time Christian peasant women had independent incomes. The poor working conditions and male and church cleavage to the patriarchal order while benefiting from female earnings stirred recalcitrance among women, including strikes and wage demands.[81] Ordinary women thus began to register in Mount Lebanon's public arena.

Second, the high prices for silk in the 1860s and 1870s meant higher and more widely distributed disposable income, particularly among Maronite peasantry. There was more demand for education, and people began to improve their rudimentary residences. In lower social strata, the widening horizons were almost exclusively for Christians—not Muslims and Druze—and for the *mutasarrifiya*, not its rural surrounds in the north, the Biqa, and Jabal Amil.

Third, peace, medical advances, and relative prosperity allowed a renewal of Christian population growth, already vigorous through the seventeenth and eighteenth centuries but slowed by instability between 1830 and 1860. An Ottoman census of the *mutasarrifiya*, completed in 1867, reported 99,834 males over the age of fifteen.[82] On the assumption that this represented about two-thirds of total males, Mount Lebanon would have had a male population of 150,000 and a total of around 300,000 in the mid-1860s, about 80 percent of whom were Christian.[83] This total may be compared with the roughly 80,000 people that Ottoman district tax surveys (aggregated to match the territory of the *mutasar-rifiya*) indicate for the mid-sixteenth century and Volney's estimate of 235,000 (combining his estimates for northern and southern parts of the mountain) for the 1780s.[84] The population of the special province rose from 300,000 in the 1860s to 414,000 in a 1911 census.[85] Given that between the 1870s and 1911 about 300,000 people left Mount Lebanon, mainly for the Americas, and the 414,000 residents of 1911 included only 124,000 returned migrants, there was obviously a boom in natural increase and child survival in the late nineteenth century.[86] This should be treated not in isolation but as part of a Christian increase throughout the Ottoman period, with almost a quadrupling of the mainly Christian population of Mount Lebanon before 1860.

Mount Lebanon entered a more turbulent economic environment in 1875 when silk prices halved and never really recovered.[87] East Asian competition strengthened after the Suez Canal opened, and low-quality imported silkworm eggs depressed productivity.[88] An inflated population faced tougher times, and young men used savings to leave the country. Some women stayed as household heads; many joined their husbands in the Americas. The great Christian emigra-tion was an upheaval for both sexes, with a mixing of cultures and gender roles in the New World brought back to Mount Lebanon with the return of 40 percent of migrants by 1914.[89] Remittance revenue from relatives abroad rivaled silk as a source of personal income in the mountain after 1900.[90]

Even if many returnees were disenchanted with Western society and nostal-gic for their past lives, from 1900 on they brought back money and attitudes that transformed the affairs of Christian villages. They constructed spacious new family homes with tiled roofs and pushed their children of both sexes into schools and boys into clerical jobs. Their children often married outside the vil-lage and the clan; this had been almost unheard of before and was rare among rural Muslims for another half century.[91] Women joined social groups, though politics remained beyond them. Thousands of returned migrants across Mount Lebanon combined with the homegrown bourgeoisie of the provincial adminis-tration, the new professions (law, medicine, and teaching), and Beirut com-merce to make a heavily Christian middle class. Here the old elite families had to compete on bourgeois terms, but elsewhere in society, top clan exclusivity and ascribed standing still meant something. The Sunni north, the Maronite hinter-land of Tripoli, and the Shia and Druze communities as yet saw far less bourgeois development; the Shia did not go through their own version of the process until the mid- and late twentieth century.

More immediately, a political break loomed. The Young Turk overthrow of the long-standing regime of Sultan Abdülhamid in July 1908 unsettled Mount Lebanon. A new conservative *mutasarrif*, Yusuf Pasha (1907–1912), found himself under siege from Maronite and Druze reformers on the administrative council, including the Junblats and Arslans. The mountaineers declined a seat in the revived Ottoman parliament, guarding their eccentric status in the empire. Otherwise, debate among the mountain bourgeoisie favored the elite sentiment in the Arab provinces for decentralized government.

France found its interests awkwardly situated in new crosscurrents. Its Maronite friends wanted a coastal port within the *mutasarrifiya* for goods and emigrants, their own customs revenues, and inclusion of part of the Biqa. However, this would compromise French investments and concessions in Beirut. Decentralist Arab agitation from urban committees and provincial councils also potentially faced France with problems reconciling its stake in Ottoman Syria with its deep involvement in the Ottoman center. The mountain, Beirut, and Istanbul pulled France different ways.

In 1912, Maronite personalities like the young Beirut lawyer Bishara al-Khuri, Daud Ammun in Cairo, Shukri Ghanim, and the former *mutasarrifiya* official Khayrallah Khayrallah in Paris combined to propose the administrative council be converted into a nineteen-member elected Grand Council.[92] When the Armenian Ohanis Pasha became governor in late 1912, after six months of government by the administrative council, the European powers backed strengthening the council: its involvement in budget formulation; trial of councilors only by themselves; widening of the village franchise; and an extra Maronite member, from Deir al-Qamar.[93] In January 1913, Bishara al-Khuri coordinated demands for an elected native governor and more financial capability for an enlarged autonomous province.

On the eve of World War I, Christian elite opinion oscillated between developing the autonomous province and merging it into new decentralized Arab provinces. The defects of the *mutasarrifiya* included Maronite clerical interference and claustrophobic geography. Its attractions encompassed light taxes, multisectarian collaboration, security under international guarantees, and potential for self-determination. Centralizing and Turkifying impulses within the Committee for Union and Progress (CUP), which took full power in Istanbul in January 1913, sharpened discontent among Christians, Muslims, and Druze in Mount Lebanon, Beirut, and Damascus. Nonetheless, political options remained within the Ottoman framework. The outlook of the elite and middle class of Beirut, gateway for European influence, was decisive.

From 1860, Beirut cemented its place with Damascus and Aleppo as one of the three major cities of Ottoman Syria. After establishment of the province of Beirut in 1888, each was a provincial capital. Beirut was certainly the most dynamic, doubling its population from about 70,000 in the early 1860s, with an input of 20,000 war refugees in 1860, to 150,000 by 1914 (see figure 4.5).[94] In the 1860s, Beirut's population was one-quarter that of Mount Lebanon; by 1914, this increased to 36 percent. Maronites shifted down from the mountain, though they oscillated back and forth and most presumably retained their residence in the *mutasarrifiya* because of the tax advantages. The Christian majority in the city attained in the 1850s increased modestly. Sunni Muslims stayed the largest community within the municipal boundaries, but declined from 40 percent in 1860 to around 30 percent in 1914.[95] Orthodox Christians were steady at 25 to 30 percent from the 1830s, as were Greek Catholics at about 8 percent. The Maronites doubled their share from 10 percent in 1845 to 20 percent in 1860 through refugee flows, and then stayed a little above 20 percent. Druze and Shia numbers were negligible. Ottoman data in the *Salname* of 1900/1901 roughly confirm the Christian advantage, with "Islam" at 45 percent and Orthodox at 30 percent.[96]

Unlike in other big eastern Mediterranean port towns, such as Alexandria or Smyrna (Izmir), Beirut's local merchant and professional class kept a firm grip on the city's economy, restricting Europeans.[97] Christians dominated long-distance trade, banking, insurance, and silk processing. Sunni Muslims continued to specialize in eastern Mediterranean commerce. Sectarian incidents between Christians and Muslims increased on the streets with Christian in-migration. Christian and Muslim street leaders, or *qabadays*, emerged among

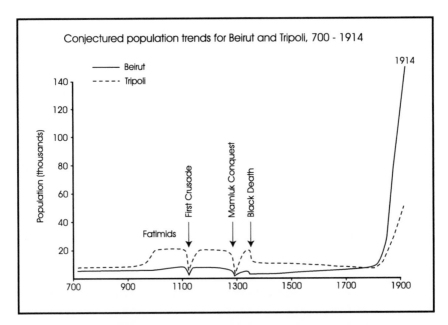

Figure 4.5 Conjectured population trends for Beirut and Tripoli, 700–1914.

shopkeepers, artisans, and laborers in response to confessional friction, but they had an interest in being useful to authority and containing conflict.[98]

Overall, the prosperous expanding elite and middle class cohered reasonably. They drew in *muqata'ji* families of the mountain, Maronite and Druze, who found alignment with urban merchants essential to maintaining their lifestyles. The Khazens took loans from the Lahouds and Thabits, the Abi Lamas from the Asfars, and the Arslans from the Baz family.[99] The Sunni Bayhums established a variety of cross-sectarian connections: financial partnerships with the Junblats and other Druze, marriage with Maronite Shihabs, and joint land purchases with the Orthodox Bustroses.[100]

Beirut's urban infrastructure improved in bursts in the 1860s and after 1890. The first years of peace after 1860 saw the opening of the new main road to Damascus, reducing travel time from two days to twelve hours, the establishment of telegraph communication with Istanbul, and widening of city streets.[101] The 1864 provincial law brought a more ordered urban bureaucracy. The second phase involved French private investment, beginning with the creation of a new port and associated facilities, the railway to Damascus, and gas lighting through the 1890s[102] and continued with the tramways after 1905. In commercial terms Beirut now dominated the Syrian interior, but change was not all positive. French investors demolished old monuments, including the crusader citadel, and exploitative labor arrangements provoked violent protests.

The period from the 1860s to the 1890s witnessed surging educational development, involving local, Ottoman and foreign sources.[103] Secondary and tertiary institutions rested on the older elementary schools of Beirut and Mount Lebanon, unique in the Ottoman Middle East in their number and variety. The Maronite and Greek Catholic churches and several French missions, especially Jesuits and Lazarists, provided the main elementary structure, followed by Anglo-American Protestant missions, most notably in Druze and mixed districts. Italy, Russia, and the Orthodox also contributed. The Ottoman state only entered elementary education in mid-century, meaning Muslim access greatly lagged. In the 1890s, the elementary schools of the Christian denominations catered to tens of thousands of students throughout modern Lebanon. For example, in Mount Lebanon in 1896 there were three thousand pupils in fifty-five Protestant schools for boys and nineteen for girls.[104]

Beyond the elementary level, Butrus al-Bustani founded his "national" secondary school in Beirut in 1863, which accommodated Christian and Muslim students from leading families and supported associations like the Syrian Scientific Society, founded in 1867.[105] In 1866, the American Daniel Bliss initiated the Syrian Protestant College in Ra's Beirut as an embryo tertiary institution. This prompted French Jesuits to establish a rival college in 1875, which became L'Université Saint-Joseph in 1881 and acquired a medical faculty by 1888.[106]

Both the Protestant and Jesuit institutions held land as *waqf*, avoiding property taxes.[107]

In 1878, the journalist Abd al-Qadir al-Qabbani mobilized Sunni personalities to form an umbrella charity, the Maqasid, for educating Muslims.[108] Within two years, the Maqasid sponsored elementary schools for several thousand pupils. In 1880, the Ottomans imposed state control, suspecting Muslim private education. On the secondary level, in 1883 the Ottomans sponsored the *sultaniya* (the Sultan's school) as an elite provider. In 1895, Abdülhamid's regime added the *uthmaniya* (the Ottoman College), which emphasized Arabic and fostered Arab nationalist sentiment among Muslim students, hardly its original purpose.[109]

Late Ottoman political consecration of the economic, demographic, and cultural weight of Beirut and Mount Lebanon had enduring consequences. Damascus lost its old superiority, though not its aspirations, as the political center of geographical Syria. On the coast, the old provincial capitals of Sidon and Tripoli, members of the historical trio headed by Damascus, became marginal to the new core of the Levant—Beirut as gateway provincial capital with its Maronite-dominated mountain hinterland (for a contemporary panorama of Beirut and the mountain, see figure 4.6).

Figure 4.6 Beirut and Mount Lebanon, late nineteenth century. Børre Ludvigsen Collection. Photographer: Bonfils.

Sunni Sidon and Shia Jabal Amil were backwaters in the late nineteenth century. Their eclipse came with social change, including decline of the Ali al-Saghir (al-Asa'ad) and Sa'b (Fadl) clans after abolition of the *iqta* system in 1864. The Asa'ads had maintained a strong presence through their lands and clients south of the Litani River, but their prestige had slipped and they were on the defensive. Peasant fortunes also had declined with substantial exclusion from the lucrative tobacco trade because of regulations imposed by an Ottoman monopoly. Peasant debt and dispossession had increased.[110]

It became possible for families trading with Beirut in the early nineteenth century to acquire land and enter politics. These included the Sunni Sulh and Shia Usayran clans of Sidon, the Shia Zayns of Nabatiya, and the Shia Khalils of Tyre. They particularly profited from the grain trade to Beirut and Mount Lebanon. Rural Shia religious families also emerged on the political stage, for example the Amins of Shaqra. From 1877, when Muhammad al-Amin, Nabil Usayran, and Ahmad al-Sulh participated in a secret separatist conference in Damascus called because the empire seemed about to collapse, new names entered politics.[111] After 1908, disillusion with the CUP and decentralist agitation pulled southern leaders, notably the Sulhs and Asa'ads, into Beirut (see figure 4.7 for an image of Kamil al-Asa'ad). Al-Sulh ascendancy in Nabatiya, the main Shia

Figure 4.7 Shia chief Kamil al-Asa'ad on horseback, southern Lebanon, late nineteenth century. American University of Beirut/Library Archives.

market town, and the opening there of an Ottoman school in the 1880s oriented Shia intellectuals to Beirut and to Sunni Arab priorities.[112]

Tripoli fared better than Sidon in the last Ottoman decades, but it still operated in the shadow of Beirut. It had insulation as a sanjak center even after it lost its provincial status in 1840. The population tripled from 15,000 to 50,000 between 1840 and 1914, trailing Beirut but leaving Sidon well behind (see figure 4.5).[113] The town also had a modern school sector, both foreign and Ottoman, by 1900. Nonetheless, Tripoli lost out to Beirut in port and railway development. Some members of leading families moved to Beirut. Christian Nawfals left early, before 1860, and the Sunni Husayn al-Jisr shifted in 1883 to be director of the *sultaniya*.[114] Most of the elite stayed. One Sunni family, the Karamis, took precedence on the basis of religious eminence since the late eighteenth century and accumulated properties. Other prominent names included the Sunni Muqaddims, Awaydas, and Mikatis, and Orthodox traders like the Burts and Khlats.[115]

A delicate political situation prevailed in Beirut and Mount Lebanon during and after the Ottoman crisis of 1911–1913 when the empire finally lost the Balkans and North Africa and the CUP unionists seized power in Istanbul. Through half a century of commercial florescence and deepening local political participation, Beirut and Mount Lebanon loomed as the dynamo of the Ottoman Arab provinces. In the tussle between proponents of a more centralized empire, mainly the Turkish-speaking unionists, and the Arab decentralists, few on either side wished to go over the brink. When exasperated Arab activists held their Arab congress in Paris in June 1913, the unionists retreated on imposing the Turkish language in the courts and administration of the provinces. Nonetheless, the clash brought decentralists to the brink of separatism.

Beirut and Mount Lebanon had a unique place in this affair. First, Beirut led decentralist activity, illustrated in the widely representative Reform Committee for the Province of Beirut, formed in January 1913 and dissolved in April by the governor amid protest. The province-wide and multicommunal nature of the committee had no parallel in any other Arab province.[116] Second, with their Christian majorities and Maronite autonomist sentiment, Beirut and Mount Lebanon had the potential either to lead Arab separation from the Ottomans or to separate from the Arabs. Alternatively, if the Ottoman unionists opted for a Turkish-Arab bargain, Beirut and Mount Lebanon could become the equivalent of Istanbul in the Arab part of a "dual monarchy." Of the possibilities, France and Britain, with their dispersed investments in the empire, would likely have preferred the last.

Rather than being a discontinuity, World War I and the Ottoman entry to it on the side of Germany and Austria-Hungary in October 1914 determined which of several already discernible scenarios would become real. The ruling CUP officers in Istanbul sent Cemal Pasha to be military overlord of the Syrian provinces. Cemal believed that confronting the British in Egypt required flattening both Arabist and mountain activism. He began with Jabal Amil and Sidon when Kamil al-Asa'ad and the mayor of Sidon, Misbah al-Bizri, jealous of local rivals, reported Arabist associations in Sidon and Nabatiya. Cemal ordered the arrest of Rida al-Sulh, his son Riyadh, leaders of the Shia Usayran, Zayn, Khalil, and Dhahir families, and Muhammad Jabir Al Safa, who later recorded events in his *Tarikh Jabal Amil*.[117] Through 1915 and into 1916, Cemal oversaw further arrests, trials, and sentencings. In May 1915, the government abolished the autonomous province of Mount Lebanon, putting the Maronites and other mountaineers under emergency military rule.

The repression culminated on May 6, 1916, with the hanging in Beirut of fourteen activists, including proponents of both Arab and mountain independence, Christians and Muslims, clerics and secularists. Among them were Sa'id Aql, Philippe and Farid al-Khazen, Abd al-Karim al-Khalil, Sheikh Ahmad Tabbara, and Muhammad and Ahmad Mahmassani. The location became Martyrs' Square, and respect for Ottoman sovereignty collapsed.

France's Lebanon, 1916–1942

Making Greater Lebanon

Facing the prospect of British seizure of the Levant after October 1914, France quickly staked its claim. For the allies, the war changed everything; for them the Ottomans were finished. Between December 1915 and May 1916, French and British negotiators François Georges-Picot and Mark Sykes hammered out an arrangement for the Ottoman Arab provinces. Picot had been France's consul-general in Beirut and envisaged French hegemony in the Levant while the British took Iraq. This was too much for the British given that they bore the military burden in the Middle East and needed to encourage their Arab ally, Sharif Husayn of Mecca and the Hijaz, into rebellion against the Ottomans. In a compromise, Picot obtained agreement to French command of a Mediterranean coastal strip north of Palestine to be ruled from Beirut, notably an expanded Mount Lebanon. The interior beyond the Biqa and the Orontes River would be an Arab state, with the areas from Damascus north under French "influence." For the British, nothing here contradicted their correspondence with Sharif Husayn, whom they had told from the outset that France would have preeminence on the northern Mediterranean coast of Syria.

For the people of the effectively defunct provinces of Beirut and Mount Lebanon, 1916 was the year in which decentralism flashed into concepts of Arab independence, mountain independence, and Maronite assertion under French protection. Ottoman repression, including insensitivity to a horrific famine that reduced the population on a medieval scale, discounted any Ottoman future. The allied blockade, Ottoman confiscation of grain, speculation by Beirut and Aleppo merchants, and a locust plague "sealed the fate" of Mount Lebanon.[118] Almost half the population of the grain-deficient mountain died between 1915 and 1918, compared with one-quarter in the wider Levant.[119] The penultimate Ottoman military governor of Mount Lebanon in 1917–1918, the Shia Isma'il Haqqi, devoted himself to an inventory of the territory, but the damage was done.[120]

Regardless of the Arabist excitement in Beirut and Damascus when Sharif Husayn launched his revolt to establish an "Arab kingdom" in mid-1916, local reality favored France. Catholics cowered before an Arab state coming out of the Arabian Peninsula that would be above all else a Muslim state. The intensifying famine hit the Maronites worst and raised existential issues.[121] It predisposed both church and secular leaders to demand a Lebanon that could better provision its people. It certainly did not favor putting the fate of the largest community of Beirut and the mountain in the hands of Arabian Hashemites. Ironically, the Maronite church acquired important freedom of maneuver when Patriarch al-Huwayyik, fearful of military pursuit for disloyalty, finally sought and received the protection of the sultan.[122] From early 1916, the church, France's client, could organize under less Ottoman attention than could either Arab or Lebanese nationalists.

In May 1917, the French government emphasized its intentions by appointing Georges-Picot high commissioner for the northern Levant. In June, Lebanese Christian emigrants established a *Comité Central Syrien* in Paris to coordinate with French church, commercial, and colonial interests. Into 1918, French intelligence officers operating through the island of Arwad off the Syrian coast liaised with Maronites in Mount Lebanon.[123]

Levantine affairs became fluid when British General Edmund Allenby broke the Ottoman front at Megiddo in northern Palestine in September 1918. Agents of Prince Faysal, Sharif Husayn's son who commanded the Arab contingents on the British eastern flank, arranged declarations of allegiance to their master on the Lebanese coast ahead of British occupation. Faysal himself arrived in Damascus with the British vanguard in October 1918, while French troops accompanied the British to Beirut, and also landed by sea. The British expelled Faysal's representative from Beirut and hauled down Sharifian flags. France declared its suzerainty on the coast and reactivated the administrative council of the *mutasarrifiya*.

In early 1919, France toyed with the idea of Mount Lebanon as a component of a Syrian Arab kingdom, provided Faysal accepted French tutelage.[124] Alarmed Maronites in both the church and the administrative council campaigned strenuously through 1919 for French commitment to an enlarged Mount Lebanon, and Patriarch al-Huwayyik lobbied for French rule. The administrative council, including the patriarch's brother, wavered between French protection and an arrangement with Faysal, though the objective of a Greater Lebanon was the same.

By late 1919, Maronite activism, support from French lobbies, and the hostility of Faysal's Syrian Arab nationalist colleagues in Damascus brought France and its Maronite friends into concordance. The American King-Crane fact-finding mission of July 1919 had a galvanizing effect. It highlighted Arab nationalism and rejection of France among the Sunni Muslims of Beirut, Tripoli, and Sidon, as well as a large part of the Shia, Druze, and Orthodox Christian communities of any Greater Lebanon. Conversely, Patriarch al-Huwayyik's personal mission to Paris and the Versailles peace conference between August and October 1919 raised Maronite stocks.[125] The patriarch also enlisted Vatican support. Meanwhile, British evacuation from the northern Levant in September 1919 left the French in Beirut facing Faysal in Damascus.

In November 1919, Premier Clemenceau gave written French endorsement for a Lebanon separate from the Syrian interior. He appointed the energetic General Henri Gouraud to succeed Georges-Picot as high commissioner in Beirut. In December, Clemenceau extracted Faysal's agreement to a Lebanon adding Sidon, Jabal Amil, Wadi al-Taym, and the western side of the Biqa to the mountain and Beirut.[126] This, however, fell short of Maronite aspirations in the Biqa and the north.

Maronite submissions to France and the Versailles conference reached back to a French map of a potential Greater Lebanon drawn under the auspices of General Charles de Beaufort d'Hautpoul in 1861.[127] Beaufort was the commander of the French expeditionary force sent after the 1860 disturbances and a proponent of France's mission to Lebanon's Catholics. Maronite leaders, especially Patriarch al-Huwayyik, shrewdly conflated a new Lebanon with ancient Phoenicia to highlight a unique personality. The Phoenician allusion derived from a European fashion for romanticizing antiquity, for example the 1864 book *Mission de Phénicie* of Ernest Renan.[128]

Among Maronite publicists, the demand for an enlarged Lebanon as a Catholic Christian homeland began with the tracts of Philippe and Farid al-Khazen and Bulos Nujaym between 1900 and 1908. Like Arabism, it gained ground after the 1908 Istanbul coup and developed through World War I into a Lebanese Christian nationalism fervently endorsed by exiles and emigrants from Egypt to Paris to Latin America. Its leading thinker after 1918 was the young Latin Catholic banker and journalist Michel Chiha, through his mother, a member of the influential Greek Catholic Far'un family. Chiha gave "Lebanism" a pluralist veneer appropriate for inclusion of non-Catholics and non-Christians.[129] There was no doubt, however, that Maronites and other Catholics would dominate.

Among a wider public, the resurrection of Phoenicia and the concept of a distinctive Lebanon received stimulus from the literary output of Jibran Khalil Jibran, who fashioned a dreamy image of Mount Lebanon. Jibran, from a humble Maronite family in Bsharri, lived continuously in the United States from 1902, but his Arabic evocation of a spiritualized mountain people and landscape had growing popular impact in the last Ottoman years. He also drew out feelings of oppression, conflict with established religion, and interpersonal tensions.[130] These had resonance for a multi-sectarian Lebanon. Jibran's combination of Christian ambience with outreach to Muslims reinforced Chiha, even if his appeal to Muslims was patchy. Incorporation of Jibran in school curricula after the 1920s helped make him by far Lebanon's most influential writer, apart from his international reputation for his post-1920 output in English.

"Lebanist" Greater Lebanon comprised the Lebanon and Anti-Lebanon mountains, with the Biqa Valley between them and the associated coast and ports. This was a clear unit on any map—as reflected in the political cartography of General Beaufort. Patriarch al-Huwayyik had most of it from Clemenceau and Faysal at the end of 1919. The wartime famine and Maronite outposts determined him to complete acquisition of the Biqa, the principal food-producing area. Military activity against the French in the first months of 1920 on the Biqa front between General Gouraud's forces and the Damascus-based Arab nationalists ensured Gouraud's backing. Gouraud favored a boundary well into the Anti-Lebanon Range.

To the north, it was unthinkable not to incorporate all of Mount Lebanon, bringing in the Christians of the Akkar. Tripoli proved more controversial. Gouraud's secretary and advisor Robert de Caix wanted a Greater Lebanon with a secure Christian majority and opposed inclusion of Tripoli's hostile Arab nationalists and Sunni Muslims.[131] For the Maronite church, however, Tripoli was their historical outlet to the Mediterranean. Gouraud went with the church.

To the south, the interaction between France and Britain took precedence. British commitment to a "national home" for the Jewish people in Palestine in the Balfour declaration of November 1917 determined the French to keep Britain and the Zionists distant from Beirut. The French agreed to British control of the Upper Jordan Valley, reflecting Jewish colonization near Lake Hula, but otherwise took their stand at Ra's Naqura, the natural barrier where a finger of the Galilee hills meets the sea in an impressive headland halfway between Acre and Tyre.

No one, apart from the French, paid much heed to the Shia of Jabal Amil, an indication of the community's marginality since the depredations of Ahmad al-Jazzar. The Shia had no coherent voice. Arab nationalism entranced the small intellectual class, camp followers of the Sunni Sulh family and the Damascus activists. The Asa'ads and leading religious families vacillated between the

French and Faysal. They also toyed with the Shia gangs that arose out of wartime chaos. The gangs proceeded from brigandage to confronting France and its Christian friends in the south. In April 1920, they bullied Shia leaders into Arabist declarations at a communal gathering in Wadi Hujayr.[132]

In early May 1920, a large gang from Bint Jubayl massacred fifty residents of the neighboring Catholic village of Ayn Ibl. In June, thousands of French troops marched through Jabal Amil in a punitive expedition. According to contemporary Shia writer Muhammad Al Safa: "The occupiers saw that the time had come to demonstrate their protection of the Christians, after they had deliberately neglected doing that."[133] The French also conducted aerial bombardment and imposed a collective fine. Maronite opinion hardened in favor of including the area in Greater Lebanon, to reassure local Catholics. Faysal had already signed Jabal Amil away, and the Damascus nationalists showed no interest.

Greater Lebanon from Ra's Naqura to Nahr al-Kabir north of Tripoli, and from the coast to the Anti-Lebanon, was thus already sketched out when France acquired a provisional "mandate" to command the northern Levant at an allied conference at San Remo in Italy in April 1920. The command would be exercised under the auspices of a new international organization, the League of Nations. The French "mandate" would be to guide the population to self-determination with progress reports to the League. To consolidate its command, however, France targeted proponents of self-determination. By early 1920, the majority on the mainly Christian administrative council of Mount Lebanon favored obtaining Greater Lebanon through their own deal with Faysal and the Arab nationalists.[134] The French arrested seven councilors who visited Damascus in June 1920. Added to armed provocations in the Biqa, this gave Gouraud an excuse to expel Faysal from Syria. In July, a well-prepared French army brought down the Arab nationalists at Maysalun outside Damascus. Faysal fled to the British, exchanging his three-month-old throne in Damascus for a kingdom in Iraq.

Through the summer of 1920, the French considered the character of a new Lebanon. De Caix raised the possibility of a Lebanese federation with a Shia "state" in the south and Tripoli and Beirut as autonomous districts.[135] Administrative complexity counted against this scheme, and Maronites did not want to hear about it. On September 1, 1920, the high commissioner proclaimed a unitary Greater Lebanon with an appointed administrative council of ten Christians and seven Muslims and Druze to oversee its domestic affairs. The proclamation detached the districts, or *aqdiya* (sing. *qada*), of Baalbek, Biqa, Rashaya, and Hasbaya from the Ottoman province of Syria, adding them to Mount Lebanon. However, it left the relationship between Lebanon and the new Syrian state unsettled. Customs, currency, posts and telegraph, and security became common functions under the High Commission, based in Beirut. On the other hand, the new Lebanese administrative council rejected a joint budget.[136] Gouraud conceded a Lebanese budget in April 1921. Senior Maronites were determined to have a distinctive political entity, equal to anything in the interior.

Maronite Overreach

France accepted that Greater Lebanon would elaborate the communal political allocations of the *mutasarrifiya*, assuming the supremacy of confessional identity. Such a system required data on communal proportions among the population, particularly after World War I disruption. The French therefore conducted a census in 1921 that demonstrated the Maronite overreach in demanding the Lebanon of the French mandate.

Maronites and Druze were the only communities to register both proportionate and absolute decline in the transition from Mount Lebanon to Greater Lebanon. Famine degraded the Maronites from 242,308 in Mount Lebanon, according to the last Ottoman count for the *mutasarrifiya* in 1911, to 199,181 in the bigger Lebanon ten years later.[137] In contrast, 65 percent of the population of the annexed areas was non-Christian. The overall Christian majority changed from 80 percent in Mount Lebanon to 55 percent in the new Lebanon. Maronites remained the largest community but with their proportion almost halved, from 58 percent to 33 percent. Courtesy of the annexed areas, Sunni Muslims were up from 3.5 percent to 20.5 percent, even with some boycotting the French census, and Shia increased from 5.6 percent to 17.2 percent. The rising Maronite tide of the Ottoman centuries, slowed by emigration after 1890, went into recession with the World War I famine and the creation of Greater Lebanon.

Through the initial years of the mandate, the French wavered about maintaining Lebanon's extended boundaries.[138] Certainly the Maronites had opportunities, up to and beyond establishment of a constitution in 1926, to reconsider. In early 1921, Robert de Caix briefly persuaded Gouraud that Tripoli might be detached, and in 1925 both High Commissioner de Jouvenel and Premier Briand favored reduction of Lebanon. In 1925, the staunch Syrian Arab nationalist Abd al-Rahman Shahbandar entertained letting Lebanon retain the Biqa if it gave up Tripoli.[139]

Nothing would budge Patriarch al-Huwayyik, the church, and most Maronite politicians. They persuaded themselves, especially with the 1925–1926 Druze and nationalist rebellion in Syria, that any retreat would unravel Lebanon. On demography, they looked to a continued return of emigrants and the influx of Armenian refugees from Anatolia. Anyway, new agricultural lands, "natural" boundaries, and myths of glory under Fakhr al-Din Ma'n and Bashir II Shihab trumped demography. The Maronite politician Emile Edde backed revision because he was clearest in wanting a proper Christian Lebanon rather than a multicommunal mélange, but he was almost alone. Nor did political instability in France and deadlock between left and right favor revision in the Levant. Briand's loss of the French premiership to the conservative Poincaré in the run-up to the 1926 Lebanese constitution entrenched Greater Lebanon.

On the basis of the 1921 census, Christians would have the majority in representative institutions, and the Maronites would have the leading role. Otherwise, the sensible approach for France was to make the state viable by persuading non-Christians, at Maronite insistence almost half of the population, that there was something in it for them. With the addition of Beirut, Tripoli, and Sidon to the mountain, Sunnis replaced Druze as the second community. Above all others, they repudiated the new entity and pressed reversal of the annexations. Senior figures from leading families such as Riyadh al-Sulh of Sidon and Beirut, Umar Bayhum and Salim Salam of Beirut, and Abd al-Hamid Karami of Tripoli organized regular petitions and protests. They chose occasions like the installment of Maxime Weygand as high commissioner in 1923 and the Syrian revolt of 1925–1926 for agitation.[140] Sunni leaders liaised with Druze and Shia such as Sabri Hamade of the Biqa. The French tried to entice the Sunnis, for example reserving them the vice-presidency of the early Representative Councils. This was not entirely a waste. Muhammad al-Jisr of Tripoli cooperated from the early days, and several significant Sunnis participated in drafting the constitution.

From the outset, Shia were less enamored of the Sunni-dominated Syrian interior. French destruction of the gangs left a bad taste, but French officials courted the Asa'ads and thereby quieted Jabal Amil. At first, they had less success with the Hamades and Haydars of the Biqa, who were closer to Damascus, and Baalbek proved troublesome during the Syrian revolt. France's masterstroke in January 1926 was to award the Shia official recognition of the Ja'afari law school for personal status matters. The Shia could now operate their religious law under the state umbrella: the Ottomans had denied them this privilege, forcing them to use Hanafi Sunni courts for anything requiring official affirmation.

Provision of a Shia institutional focus was a crucial development for both the Shia and the new Lebanon. Previously, the Shia had communal self-awareness but no coherence. In Jabal Amil, they intermittently came together under strong leaders like Husam al-Din Bishara in the 1190s or Nassif al-Nassaar in the mid-eighteenth century, and they had a common memory of grievance from the oppression of al-Jazzar. However, Jabal Amil had little interchange with the Biqa Shia, and there was nothing resembling the center of gravity the Maronite church or the Druze lords provided for their communities through the Ottoman period.

From the late 1920s, the Ja'afari courts in Beirut, Sidon, Nabatiya, Tyre, Marj Uyun, Baalbek, and Hirmil gave Shia a common instrument to work out family and clan affairs and to defend property like mosques and cemeteries from encroachment by Sunnis or Christians.[141] The courts joined ordinary Shia together in a sectarian framework and bound them and their new sectarian outlook into France's new Lebanon. In the 1930s and 1940s, several thousand Shia moved to Beirut, expanding the small Shia presence in Naba'a, Shiyyah, and Burj al-Barajneh.[142] These suburbs would later be the pivot of the Lebanese Shia, a conglomerate of Jabal Amil and the Biqa. In vital respects, the mandate supplied the base for Musa al-Sadr's Shia activism in the 1960s and the Shia sectarian radicalization of the 1980s.[143]

Druze split in facing the French. In the Shuf, the Junblats accepted Greater Lebanon, possibly a reason for the murder of Fuad Junblat in 1921. His capable widow, Nazira, took over family affairs through the mandate. Her signature remark was: "You British have told us that the country would be handed over to the French, so it is with them that we have to make arrangements."[144] Some leading Arslans, in contrast, were Arab nationalists. Shakib, an exile in Geneva through the mandatory period, had marked Sunni Islamic sympathies and strong influence within the Syrian National Bloc. In Lebanon, Adil opposed the mandate and linked with Riyadh al-Sulh, but Fuad entered Lebanon's French sponsored Representative Council.[145]

The Druze history of struggle in the mountain meant that Druze of the Shuf, the Gharb, and the Matn appreciated a distinctive Lebanon as much as Maronites. After 1860, they had accepted the Christian advantage. However, Maronite parading of Greater Lebanon as a Christian triumph was hard to bear. In particular, the Druze of Wadi al-Taym looked more to interior Syria. In November 1925, at the height of the Syrian revolt, Sultan al-Atrash's Druze forces from southern Syria crossed the Lebanese/Syrian boundary into Wadi al-Taym. Local Druze received them enthusiastically, and a contingent of the invaders killed thirty Christians. The Junblats and even most Arslans saw danger in provoking France and the Maronites; the Druze of Mount Lebanon stood aloof from the revolt. In the meantime, French troops in Rashaya repulsed Syrian Druze trying to enter the Biqa, and the crisis passed.

France confirmed the electoral system of the *mutasarrifiya* in setting up a Representative Council for Greater Lebanon in 1922.[146] Two-stage elections, universal adult male suffrage, and multimember multicommunal constituencies repeated the situation prevailing in Mount Lebanon in 1914. The new element was bringing distribution of the thirty seats in the six constituencies fully into line with communal proportions of the population indicated in an official census. Overall, Christians received seventeen seats and Muslims, including Druze, received thirteen, an exact reflection of the 1921 census. This was a major advance on the distorted allocation of the *mutasarrifiya*. "Confessional democracy" lurched forward.

Representative politics required an educated public. Private and Ottoman schools from the late nineteenth century provided a base ahead of anything else in the Arab east, but were biased toward servicing Christians and the Muslim elite, especially Sunnis. The mandatory authorities sponsored a limited extension of public elementary and secondary education. However by 1931, there were only 134 state schools including 1 secondary school, compared with 1,335 private schools including 69 at secondary level. State schools enrolled 14,435 students, more than 70 percent Muslims and Druze, whereas private schools enrolled 103,795, more than 70 percent Christians.[147] Plainly the public sector was not reaching most Sunnis and Shia. For Sunnis, the reinvigoration of the Maqasid as a communal enterprise from 1918 partially compensated. The Beirut merchant Salim Ali Salam retained his prewar supremacy in Maqasid affairs.[148] The Maqasid branched from subsidized education into other charities and became the preeminent private platform for patronage among Beirut Sunnis. Overall, the presence of a growing lower bourgeousie and working class in schools expanded literacy and grassroots political activity.

Jesuit, Maronite, Protestant, and other church schools, together with some minor input from the Maqasid and the incipient public system, fed students into the two private fee-paying universities. The Jesuit Université Saint-Joseph, based in the Christian suburb of Ashrafiya, headed French language education. From establishment of the Law Faculty in 1913, it produced lawyers, by far the leading profession among Greater Lebanon's politicians. These included upper-class Sunni Arab nationalists like Riyadh al-Sulh. The Syrian Protestant College, which had a coastal site west of the city, renamed itself the American University of Beirut in November 1920. It headed the Protestant system and catered to Christian, Muslim, and Jewish students from Lebanon and across the Middle East. By the 1930s, it was a hotbed of radical politics.

As for informing the literate, the print media had to start afresh in the 1920s. Liberal tracts sprang up in Beirut and the mountain beginning in the 1890s, but only *Zahle al-Fatat*, founded in 1910 in the Biqa town of Zahle, survived censorship through World War I. Thereafter, several Arabic and French newspapers emerged. In 1923, George Naqqash established *L'Orient*, which backed Emile Edde and his doubts about Greater Lebanon. When premier in 1928, Edde's rival Bishara al-Khuri suspended *L'Orient* in reply to allegations of misuse of public money.[149] In 1934, Michel Chiha sponsored *Le Jour* as a mouthpiece for al-Khuri. The major press event of the mandatory period was Jibran Tuwayni's establishment of the Arabic daily *al-Nahar* in 1933. The independent foundation of a prominent Orthodox family, *al-Nahar* took a liberal, centrist line and became the anchor of Lebanon's print media.

Given the dominance of French and English in education and promotion of French in official business, Arabic came under siege as an official language. Sunni

Muslims were particularly sensitive to this because of the prewar challenge of Turkish. Christian interest in the Lebanese vernacular as an alternative to standard Arabic only rubbed salt in the wound. In the competition between Maronites al-Khuri and Edde, al-Khuri flaunted his superior command of literary Arabic for the Muslim gallery.

Through the first years of French hegemony, a French governor, as deputy of the high commissioner for Lebanon and Syria, was chief executive of Lebanon. He and the high commissioner ruled through a council of directors, French-appointed Lebanese who functioned as a cabinet. The Representative Council was little more than advisory. As for the judiciary, the secular and religious courts (the latter for personal status issues) of the *mutasarrifiya* and Ottoman Beirut continued with revision of procedure and new higher courts for appeals, cassation, and supervision of the public service.[150] The French established mixed courts with French presiding judges for cases involving foreigners; after 1925, French judges became involved alongside Lebanese judges in all courts above first instance. The infusion of French law heavily colored the system and practices of independent Lebanon.

In June 1922, the League of Nations rubber-stamped the French mandate, and it came into full legal effect in September 1923. Unlike the original San Remo grant, the official League mandate to France distinguished Lebanon from Syria. France had three years to formulate a proper constitution (organic law) for self-government under the mandate. At first, the French intended to impose it. However, the behavior of anti-clerical High Commissioner Maurice Sarrail, who overrode the Lebanese Representative Council and personally provoked the Syrian Druze into rebellion, embarrassed France and made local participation imperative. Turmoil in Syria delayed progress there, but Lebanon was able to honor the 1926 target.

The brief term (November 1925–August 1926) of the first civilian high commissioner, French senator and journalist Henri de Jouvenel, proved decisive. De Jouvenel wanted to be remembered for sponsoring the constitution. A newly elected Representative Council became the clearinghouse for Lebanese input, and de Jouvenel endorsed it as the de facto constituent assembly. The Representative Council delegated drafting the constitution to a twelve-member committee.

Michel Chiha's concept of Greater Lebanon as a Christian/Muslim partnership distinct from its Arab hinterland underpinned the project. The leading lights of the committee were non-Maronite Christians—Chiha, Orthodox chairman Shibli Dammus, and the Orthodox Petro Trad. They adapted the 1875 French constitution, and De Jouvenel hastened the Representative Council to enact the draft in May 1926.[151] It included a republic, executive power shared between president and premier, a two-chamber legislature, equitable multicommunal representation, and Greater Lebanon as the final homeland of its inhabitants. The committee avoided defining communal allocations, apart from enshrining the principle. De Jouvenel and the Representative Council chose the Orthodox Charles Debbas to be president, replacing the governor. The premier and his cabinet, appointed by the president and dependent on the confidence of parliament, replaced the council of directors. As for France, the organic law entrenched the authority of the high commissioner and the mandatory power in the country's affairs. A liaison officer termed the delegate linked the high commissioner to the Lebanese government.

De Jouvenel and Chiha opened the door to modern Lebanon's politics. It was not pretty. The Lebanese elite took advantage of a two-chamber legislature and access to state resources to scramble for power and patronage. Politicians who were disappointed in the 1925 elections for the Council of Representatives became appointed senators and confronted the Chamber of Deputies, the continuation of the council as a lower house. For the new high commissioner, Henri Ponsot, the Lebanese constitution was too elaborate, and the parliament was both difficult to manage and a dangerous example for interior Syria.[152] In 1927 and 1929, Ponsot and President Debbas pressed the legislature to change the constitution. In 1927, they forced a strengthening of the presidency in relation to the premier and cabinet, and abolition of the senate. The senators moved into the lower house, one-third of which became appointed. In 1929, Ponsot and Debbas had the presidential term extended from three to six years and the president's prerogative to dissolve the single house of parliament reinforced.

Competition in the new framework after May 1926 illustrated poisonous double gaming. Individual ambitions produced shifting factions across communities. Nonetheless, intermingling was superficial. It was perilous for a politician to ignore communal parameters: for example, security and supremacy for Maronites, or Arabism for Sunnis. Communal loyalties discouraged formation of stable countrywide parties with serious policy programs. A Maronite might cooperate with Muslims to humble another Maronite, as Bishara al-Khuri and Emile Edde did from the late 1920s, but both intended a Maronite ascendancy that promised trouble with Muslims. Here Bishara al-Khuri's commitment to Christian supremacy in Greater Lebanon, tarted up in Chiha's pluralism, was more dangerous than Edde's preference for jettisoning the annexed areas except Beirut. As for Sunnis, virtually the whole leadership—from Arab nationalists to the pro-Greater Lebanon Muhammad al-Jisr—came together in early 1932 to advocate maximal Sunni and Muslim registration in the 1932 census and to oppose counting of second-generation Christian emigrants.[153]

Politicians who populated Lebanon's legislature in the late 1920s had a background in the most freewheeling arenas of the late Ottoman state, whether the *mutasarrifiya*, Beirut, or—in the case of the Sulhs and Kamil al-Asa'ad—in the revived imperial parliament. Their background was either direct or through the experience of their parents; Lebanon's political class of the mandate mixed old leading clans with the late Ottoman bourgeoisie of Beirut and the mountain. This class had no problem adapting to French high commissioners.

In the transition from the Maronite majority of the *mutasarrifiya* to a bare Christian advantage in Greater Lebanon, leading influence in politics passed from the Maronite church to the Christian merchant elite of Beirut. Through its clerical hierarchy—from the patriarch and bishops to monks and parish priests— the church of course continued to have a powerful role. If any single person had a claim to be founder of Greater Lebanon, it was Patriarch al-Huwayyik. By the late 1920s, however, money power was ahead of clerical power. It was not an improvement.[154]

The great Christian commercial families of Beirut channeled resources to political front men, helping them to win elections. They guarded Greater Lebanon and promoted Chiha's pluralist propaganda. Their interest was transparent; Beirut's commercial future required a larger Lebanon under its sway and preventing Tripoli or Sidon from being outlets for the interior.[155] They also fostered minimal state economic intervention but maximum public employment of clients of their political agents—meaning a free-for-all under a venal government machine disregarding the interests of the bulk of the population. The merchant elite were heavily Orthodox and Greek Catholic, epitomized by the Sursuk and Far'un families and operated through Maronite political bosses. Leading Sunni families of Beirut, including Arab nationalists like the Sulhs and Bayhums, shared their outlook. The Maronite church had to accept its reduction; it had committed itself to Greater Lebanon.

For Maronites, the presidency of the new state was their right not just because they comprised its largest community, but because they were the community without which the state would not have existed. For more than seven years after inauguration of the constitution in 1926, they had to bide their time; the French preferred to play it safe with a non-Maronite Christian on the model of the non-Maronite governor of the *mutasarrifiya*.

During the long tenure of the Orthodox Charles Debbas as president, Maronite politicians scrapped over the premiership and positioned themselves. The leading contenders, the lawyer politicians Emile Edde and Bishara al-Khuri, had indistinguishable backgrounds and ideologies.[156] The Eddes were an off-shoot of the Hubaysh clan, old Maronite *muqata'jis*, and al-Khuri belonged to the family of Sa'ad al-Khuri, *mudabbir* of Yusuf Shihab.[157] Both were Christian supremacists but were prepared to work with Muslim politicians; both adopted the mythology of Lebanon's Phoenician roots; and both featured prominently in the French mandatory apparatus from the early 1920s. Between 1927 and 1929, they came into conflict when Edde joined the opposition to al-Khuri's premierships. Edde regarded the government as financially ill-disciplined. He failed in turn as premier in 1930 when he tried to shut state schools teaching mainly Muslims.[158] Al-Khuri exploited the Sunni reaction to help bring him down, which made a bitter personal enmity irreversible.

The death of Patriarch al-Huwayyik led to a falling-out of the Maronite bishops over election of his successor Antoine Arida in January 1932,[159] which proved to be the pivotal year of the mandate. Rival bishops supported different Maronite candidates for the scheduled 1932 presidential election. The intrigues of Edde and the inability of Bishara al-Khuri to secure enough votes allowed Sunni speaker of parliament Muhammad al-Jisr to put himself forward.[160] Muslim deputies rallied to support him despite his collaboration with France. For the French, a Sunni of whatever provenance heading Greater Lebanon was too great a risk. Ponsot suspended the constitution and extended the term of President Debbas. The high commission thereby rebuffed both Maronite and Sunni hopefuls. Sunni participation in parliament, common economic interests, and shared impatience with France all favored an eventual convergence of senior Sunnis and Maronites.

Meanwhile, at Sunni prodding, the mandatory authorities conducted the new Lebanon's second and last census in March 1932.[161] On the one hand, the results showed a bare Christian majority courtesy of post-August 1924 emigrants who were still taxpayers, some of whom returned to Lebanon, as well as naturalized Armenians.[162] The Maronites remained the largest community, though their numbers were down from one-third to 29 percent. This enabled Christians in general and Maronites in particular to claim a political edge for the rest of the mandatory period and for Lebanese independence. On the other hand, the Muslim proportion had risen almost 5 percent in a decade, in part because of undercounting in 1921. Both Sunnis and Shia were up 2 percent each, to 23 percent and 20 percent respectively. Druze shared the Christian decline, slipping below 7 percent.

The trend toward a Muslim majority was unmistakable, and by the early years of independence, Sunnis claimed it, assuming a natural right to speak for Shia. More pertinently, given the fact that Sunni and Shia identities rendered the "Muslim" category artificial, it was plain that Greater Lebanon was fated not to have a majority community. There would eventually be triangular jostling of three "great" communities with several lesser sectarian identities. The second census made 1932 a landmark not just for the mandate, but also for twentieth-century Lebanon.

France's Unsteady Grip

Economic malaise afflicted Greater Lebanon and the bulk of its population through the 1920s, with an accentuation during the Great Depression in the early 1930s. The collapse of trade and privation of World War I suspended Beirut's dynamism and devastated Mount Lebanon's silk industry. The commercial elite of the coast survived the war in reasonable repair on the basis of their accumulated assets and war profiteering.[163] However, the French otherwise assumed responsibility for an impoverished people.

Through the 1920s, France was not well placed to offer more than modest relief. The immense sacrifices of the war had exhausted France, and the weakness and instability of the French currency disadvantaged Lebanon and Syria in world trade.[164] The silk industry struggled and agriculture received little investment. The new Lebanon became economically divided between Beirut and Mount Lebanon, which had the infrastructure for renewed development, and the surrounding annexed areas, which stagnated. This was also the geographical divide between Christian and Muslim majorities.

French investment concentrated on Beirut, seat of the high commission and showpiece of the mandatory regime. Beirut also tightened its grip on the trade and service requirements of the Arab interior, as far as Iraq and Arabia. The Ottoman collapse, the city's expertise, French promotion, and command of new sea and air transport connections all fed into Beirut's regional dominance. Mount Lebanon recovered from the war with the renewed flow of remittance income from emigrants and continuation of the privileged tax status of the *mutasarrifiya*. These offset the virtual extinction of silk production by the 1930s. The fact that residents of Mount Lebanon paid low taxes compared with the annexed areas became a persistent grievance of Sunnis and Shia.

Notwithstanding their tax advantage, there was class differentiation among the Maronites of the mountain. On the one hand, the large bourgeois component, reinforced by returning migrants, participated in the rebound of Beirut. In contrast, continuing departures of whatever duration, between 1924 and 1932 equivalent to 40 percent of the 1932 Maronite population, indicated that only remittances kept many Maronites better off than most Sunnis and Shia.[165] The price was the community's demographic erosion; aside from Shia migration to West Africa, Muslims did not have comparable opportunities to depart the country.

In all the communities, France relied on dividing and ruling among a small elite. Communal allocations after 1926 encouraged politicians to grandstand over sectarian shares in the administration and the country. The French enticed most rural Shia chiefs and several Sunnis (for example Abbud Abd al-Razzaq of the Akkar and Khalid Shihab of Hasbaya) into the game through the mid-1920s, forcing Sunni Arabists to consider the consequences of spurning chances to place clients and deploy state largesse.[166] Hence the Bayhums, Da'uqs, and Ahdabs entered the system, while protesting their rejection of it. Among the Shia, the Asa'ads, Fadls, Zayns, Khalils, and Usayrans of Jabal Amil, and Haydars and Hamades of the Biqa, participated in the parliament and regime. Some, for example Subhi Haydar of Baalbek, would blow the Syrian trumpet to get French attention.[167] The Druze, who had meager representation, went into eclipse for a decade when Fuad and Tawfiq Arslan split over a Shuf seat in the 1929 parliamentary elections.[168] By the early 1930s, France had the Sunni Arabists of Beirut and Tripoli—Riyadh al-Sulh, Salim Salam, and Abd al-Hamid Karami—on the defensive, even while it had problems managing Maronite factionalism.

French difficulties increased after 1932 when the Great Depression hit hardest, Maronite disgruntlement supplemented Arabist hostility, and French negotiations for a treaty with interior Syria agitated the Lebanese. Through the trough of the Depression in 1933–1934, remittance income slid, trade and tourism dwindled, and the bureaucracy contracted. Much of the new middle and working classes of Beirut, where population grew from about 80,000 in 1921 (after falling off from 150,000 just before World War I) to over 160,000 in 1932, was thrown out of work.[169] The merchant and political elite betrayed little concern; the vocal trade union movement that had burgeoned through the 1920s turned to protests and strikes, and students, intellectuals, and the unemployed became more open to radical politics. In 1933, the Communist Party first came to notice, and an Orthodox student at the American University of Beirut, Antun Sa'adeh, established the Syrian Social Nationalist Party (SSNP), which promoted a Greater Syrian identity with romantic and European fascist tinges.[170]

A new high commissioner, Damien de Martel, arrived in late 1933 committed to a more effective regime. He restored parliament and introduced direct voting for deputies in the 1934 elections. Bishara al-Khuri organized his supporters into a party framework termed the Constitutional Bloc. As usual, the high commission interfered with candidate lists and played favorites, in addition to the vote buying of the Lebanese political bosses. The young Camille Chamoun, one of al-Khuri's stalwarts and a future president, observed that:

> Electoral lists were cooked up [*un véritable cuisine*] between the French and Lebanese authorities on the one hand, and the candidates on the other. Generally, apart from vetoes dictated by higher politics—or personal antipathies—the authorities supported the candidates most preferred by public opinion, because their success required the least effort.[171]

Evidently de Martel was not yet overly concerned whether he had to deal with Edde or al-Khuri. The Constitutional Bloc had the advantage, and al-Khuri looked ahead to becoming president in a revived constitutional order.

In early 1935, de Martel brought a storm down on the French when he decided to revive the monopoly over production and marketing of tobacco that had prevailed between 1883 and 1929, this time without exempting Mount Lebanon.[172] The high commission believed that a streamlined monopoly would

assist economic development. Maronite Patriarch Antoine Arida reacted furi-
ously on behalf of the previously favored Maronite tobacco producers. Arida's
concern was his community and the church finances. He was careful, however,
to couch his position in terms of all tobacco producers. Arida thus received the
backing of the Arab nationalists in Damascus, and the Maronite collision with
France delighted the Arabist Riyadh al-Sulh.

Al-Sulh emphasized the priority of achieving Greater Lebanon's independence from France via Christian/Muslim collaboration, postponing union with
Syria to a later stage.[173] He parted company with Salam and Karami, who still
demanded transfer of the annexed districts from Lebanon to Syria. For al-Sulh,
this would leave a rump Christian state lost to the Arab World, fulfilling the
dream of Emile Edde. For Karami, however, Tripoli's commercial imperative for
linkage with the interior was paramount, and Arabism meant Sunni Islam—
signing away Mount Lebanon and its Christians did not bother him.[174] A largely
Sunni "conference of the coast" in Beirut in October 1933, under the patronage
of Salam and the Bayhums, featuring equality for Muslims within Lebanon as
well as union with Syria, indicated Sunni uncertainty.

Bishara al-Khuri swung his bloc behind Arida over the tobacco issue, also
coordinating with al-Sulh and the Syrians. He and al-Sulh manipulated each
other; al-Khuri wanted to force presidential elections and restoration of the constitution, whereas al-Sulh hoped to split the Maronites from France. De Martel
retreated, lowering taxes and customs, and announced a parliamentary vote for
president. However, the high commissioner punished al-Khuri for his subversion. French support went to Edde, which helped the latter to carry Muslim deputies.[175] In January 1936, Emile Edde became Lebanon's first elected Maronite
president. Al-Khuri was determined to ruin Edde's presidency.

Tumultuous events occurred through 1936 because of the success of the Syrian National Bloc in compelling France to agree to a Franco-Syrian treaty uniting
the Alawite and Druze areas with Damascus and paving the way to Syrian independence. With the initial Syrian disturbances in early 1936, al-Khuri's Constitutional
Bloc wrote to the French delegate to Lebanon requiring a Franco-Lebanese
treaty. Al-Khuri now backed Maronite loosening with France to maintain Greater
Lebanon as a stomping ground for himself and the Christian merchant elite.
However, concessions to the Syrians from the leftist Popular Front government
in Paris encouraged Syria's National Bloc to demand Lebanon's dismemberment. Riyadh al-Sulh failed to head off the Sunni clamor for union with Syria
at another "conference of the coast" in March 1936. Instead, his cousin Kazim
al-Sulh wrote a newspaper article advising Muslims to join Christians in seeking
independence for an unreduced Lebanon.[176]

Al-Khuri had little choice but to fall in line with Christian rejection of Arab
nationalist and Muslim demands, while the French made it plain that Greater

Lebanon was not under the auction hammer. Already, Maronite bishops seethed against Patriarch Arida for his enrollment of Damascus in the protest against the tobacco monopoly, and the patriarch himself promptly turned against the Syrians when they threatened Lebanon. When the Syrians finally signed treaty terms in September 1936, they avoided recognizing Lebanon's boundaries, but dropped their insistence on territorial revision.

Thereafter, al-Khuri juggled his needs for freedom from the French, Muslim acceptance of Greater Lebanon, and keeping France as a backstop. The Franco-Lebanese treaty of November 1936 reflected his calculations, President Edde's own clinging to France, and Muslim requirements for fairer treatment. The treaty and associated commitments promised independence and membership in the League of Nations within three years, fair sectarian shares, and equal taxes. In contrast to the limited French military bases permitted in Syria, it gave French forces freedom of movement in Greater Lebanon.[177] Although neither treaty came into effect, they set the parameters of the Levant of the late 1930s. A conservative comeback frustrated ratification in the French National Assembly, while the approach of war in Europe made France reluctant to implement change in the mandates.

In the spirit of the treaty with Lebanon, the high commissioner restored the Lebanese constitution in January 1937. The constitution stipulated a government responsible to parliament. President Edde proposed a Sunni Muslim prime minister to head such a government (see figure 4.8 for an image of Edde).[178] Al-Khuri feared Edde was outflanking him among Muslims. Edde brought in the pragmatic Arabist Khayr al-Din al-Ahdab of Tripoli, inaugurating the custom of Maronite president paired with Sunni prime minister. He also now accepted Greater Lebanon.

For his part, al-Khuri tightened relations with Sunni Arabists hostile to al-Ahdab, principally Riyadh al-Sulh and Umar Bayhum. He flaunted the Constitutional Bloc's grip on Mount Lebanon to de Martel, convincing de Martel that he should bring the Constitutional Bloc into a unity government with al-Ahdab.[179] The high commissioner manipulated the October 1937 elections for a new sixty-three seat Chamber of Deputies accordingly, and the Constitutional Bloc took twenty-seven seats. Thereafter, de Martel treated the government rather than the president as the predominant executive organ. On the eve of World War II, al-Khuri turned the tables on Edde.

Aside from managing the political class, France faced discontent from the urban middle and lower orders, many still unemployed into the mid-1930s. Sunni Muslim demonstrations in favor of union with Syria peaked in late 1936 after the signing of the Franco-Lebanese treaty. Rioting in Beirut and Tripoli caused many casualties, forcing the French to arrest Karami and other Sunni personalities.[180] In response, encouraged by both Edde and al-Khuri's Constitutional

Figure 4.8 President Emile Edde (left) with former French High Commissioner
Maxime Weygand, Beirut, February 1939. Associated Press.

Bloc, young Maronites in Beirut joined paramilitary organizations. In November 1936, a pharmacist from an old family of sheikhs in Bikfaya, Pierre Gemayel, helped found the Kata'ib (battalions) party on the model of European fascist youth movements. In April 1937, Gemayel took personal command of the Kata'ib, or Phalange. Sunni Arab nationalists, also impressed with European fascism, dragooned their youth into the less disciplined Najjada (scouts). Into 1937, the French authorities had the prospect of right-wing groups sparking violence. French troops clashed with Kata'ib supporters at the party's first anniversary parade in November 1937. The injured included Pierre Gemayel.

In the aftermath of the treaties, the Sunni elite tipped toward accepting Greater Lebanon. The Franco-Syrian treaty prompted Turkey to annex the disputed sanjak of Alexandretta (Hatay) in 1938; Syrian protests over French surrender of Alexandretta and nonfulfillment of the Franco-Syrian treaty led to France suspending the Syrian constitution and resuscitating Alawite and Druze autonomy in July 1939.[181] This truncated Syrian input into Lebanese affairs. Lebanese Arabists still favored union but felt deserted by the Syrian National Bloc after it acknowledged Greater Lebanon in the Franco-Syrian treaty.[182] In practice, Sunni leaders immersed themselves in the carving up of the Lebanese regime. Their inability to control the 1936 riots and Lebanon's utility for overseas trading made them see their Christian counterparts in a new light.[183] Even Abd al-Hamid Karami became quiescent as Tripoli's fortunes improved after the oil pipeline from Mosul reached the city's port in 1935.

More committed Sunni political engagement, especially a Sunni prime minister, disturbed the Shia elite of Jabal Amil and the Biqa. Shia proved prickly about their rights and shares in Greater Lebanon in the late 1930s.[184] In April 1936, the restrictions the French tobacco monopoly imposed on poor Shia growers sparked a violent disturbance in Bint Jubayl, one of the very few such outbursts from Shia during the mandate.[185] The young deputies Rashid Baydun, from a rising merchant family in Bint Jubayl, and Kazim al-Khalil of Tyre complained vigorously about comprehensive neglect of Shia regions. Ja'afari chief judge Munir Usayran pointed to the "lack of equality with similar Sunni jurisdictions."[186] The high commission's chief officer in the south, Zinovi Pechkoff, pleaded in vain for investment in schools and roads and warned of Shia bitterness about being sidelined.[187] Shia already felt they were second only to Maronites in population and deserving of one-quarter of official posts.[188]

The most positive feature in Lebanon after 1935 was the swift economic recovery from the Depression based partly on unprecedented industrial expansion. Capital became available because of poor income from the import trade; disastrous conditions overseas led to the return of Lebanese emigrants who had industrial experience; and the French mandate provided coastal Lebanon with superior infrastructure, boosted by additional strategic investment in Beirut port in the late 1930s.[189] Lebanon developed a solid foundation of factory production for the domestic and regional markets in consumer goods, cotton spinning, and food processing, as well as the Chekaa cement works.[190] The pioneering factory establishment of the 1930s indicated Lebanon had the option of a Singapore-style mixed economy for the mid- and late twentieth century, better suited to raising incomes across sects and classes than the narrow commercial impetus of the elite.[191] Whether or not this path would have worked, it was not taken, and probably realities of elite power in Lebanon meant it could not have been taken.

From early 1939, the European crisis leading up to World War II overshadowed all else. A new high commissioner, Gabriel Puaux, arrived in January, the Franco-Lebanese treaty became defunct, and political activity beyond the routine ceased. At the outbreak of war in September 1939, Puaux suspended the Lebanese constitution. He retained Edde as a figurehead president and put the executive in the hands of the Sunni Abdullah Bayhum as secretary of state and France's top Lebanese agent.

Nazi Germany demolished France in June 1940, and the Allies imposed a blockade on Lebanon and Syria when the Nazi-aligned Vichy French took authority. Food shortages brought Christians and Muslims together in the face of the Vichy regime. In the surreal atmosphere of a mandate that no longer had legitimacy after the demise of the League of Nations, the Druze, principally the Arslans, reemerged in early 1941 to demand a serious role.[192]

Increasingly worried about Nazi agents and sympathizers in the French mandatory territories, the British prepared to invade Lebanon and Syria.[193] On June 8, 1941, British Commonwealth troops, Free French, and local auxiliaries struck north from Palestine. This came after Britain crushed a pro-Nazi coup in Iraq. Given their poor situation in the war, the British could not waste time. They broke Vichy resistance in no-nonsense fashion, bombarded French positions in Sidon and Beirut, and compelled surrender on July 12, 1941.

Effectively, the British conquest ended France's Lebanon. It brought an Anglo-French condominium over the Lebanese and Syrian administrations. Britain allowed Free French General Georges Catroux to function as high commissioner. In the midst of war, however, the British wanted progress through elections to independence, to entrench Arab support for the allies. They were therefore proactive in contacts with local politicians. Free French leader Charles de Gaulle, on the other hand, was more concerned with entrenching French interests through new treaties. The British extracted a pledge of independence for Lebanon from Catroux in November 1941; Catroux insisted on confirming the boundaries of Greater Lebanon, questioned by the British.

Prime Minister Winston Churchill appointed General Edward Spears as British representative in Lebanon and Syria, where the British kept military preponderance. In Lebanon, Spears met politicians distrusted by Catroux, including Bishara al-Khuri (Maronite), Najib Usayran (Shia), and Majid Arslan (Druze). Through 1942 and 1943, the Lebanese sideshow featured factional jostling, Anglo-French disputation, and Free French obstruction. Its leading Christian and non-Christian politicians produced a brittle understanding for living together in an independent state.

5

Independent Lebanon, 1943–1975

For a few decades, after it escaped the French in 1943, France's Greater Lebanon almost worked as an independent country. Communities and communal elites were compelled to interact within the common framework that had been gradually built up between 1860 and 1943. The interaction gave a glimpse of cohesion that might have made a real nation. This chapter considers the political frailties and social gaps, but also portrays the Lebanese communal conglomerate at its historical apogee. From the 1940s to the early 1970s, Lebanon was a beacon of freedom and tolerance in an Arab world that descended into demagogy and dictatorship. Thereafter, however, the strains were too much. The coalescence of a hostile Middle Eastern environment with the country's contradictions overwhelmed its state and society.

Given the sectarian regime of the *mutasarrifiya* and the mandate, Lebanon had a preprogrammed basis for independence. When a majority of the urban and rural bosses of the non-Christian half of its population accepted that Greater Lebanon fitted better with their interests than Greater Syria, an independent Lebanon became viable. Such acceptance preceded the fall of France to Hitler in June 1940, which shattered French credibility. Between 1941 and 1943, the British oversaw convergence between Maronite and Sunni leaders about sectarian shares in an independent state, a deal known to the Lebanese as the National Pact. Non-Christians had to accept a leading Maronite role in a Lebanon open to the West; Christians had to accept that the new state was a partnership and that Lebanon was part of the Arab world.

Lebanon's National Pact of sectarian shares served the business interests of the Christian and Sunni Muslim elite of Beirut. Top Sunnis could contemplate a deregulated postwar Lebanese economy, perfect for moneymaking when taking into account the global reach of their Christian partners. The fee for being on board this "Merchant Republic" was to shelve Arab union schemes.[1] Given Maronite rejection and British, French, and conservative Arab preferences for the status quo, Syrian or Arab union was not practical. Lebanese Sunni leaders like

Riyadh and Sami al-Sulh in any case conceived Greater Lebanon's independence from France as a vital first step to reconciling the Maronites to Arabism. It was only sensible to make Lebanon work, and there was a commercial killing to be made while waiting for better conditions for Arab federations.

Securing adherence of Maronite, Shia, and Druze rural chiefs to the high bourgeois consensus raised no problem. The landed elite benefited from Allied wartime contracts for supplies, and Beirut's postwar boom in a deregulated Greater Lebanon offered investment opportunities for their surplus liquidity. The politics of patron and client in a perpetuated system of sectarian shares also promised continued prominence for the rural bosses. None of them had a serious interest in submergence in the Sunni Syrian Arab interior.

On the one hand, Lebanon's National Pact and Merchant Republic gave Lebanese independence political and economic underpinning into the 1950s and beyond. On the other hand, both were time bombs. The Christian advantage in the executive branch and the legislature with Maronite possession of the presidency and a six to five Christian/non-Christian distribution of parliamentary seats involved fictional demography. The National Pact rested on 1932 census results, whereas differential growth meant that Christians had parity at best by the 1940s. Sunni bosses rumbled about a new census for the 1943 parliamentary elections. They did not press the matter in the midst of the world war, but made it plain they wanted allocations revisited. Nonetheless, the National Pact did not include any understanding about a periodic census or adjustment mechanisms to cater for demographic shifts. The Maronite side feared political suicide.

As for the Merchant Republic, after 1945, Lebanon's government dismantled Anglo-French wartime control of trade, finance, and commodities. Into the 1950s, Lebanon's free market, minimalist state, and strong currency made Beirut the Middle Eastern hub of banking and financial services. Lebanon stood out against the global trend toward restricted markets and state intervention. Public freedoms and an attractive physical environment also assisted Beirut to cement its position as publishing, educational, and tourist capital of the Arab world. In the 1960s, non-Lebanese rose to 60 percent of university student numbers.[2] With surging oil revenues for the Arabs of the Persian Gulf and capital flight to Beirut as Egypt, Syria, and Iraq shifted to dirigisme from the late 1950s, Lebanon's financial sector thrived. Between 1949 and 1957, the Lebanese economy grew at more than 7 percent per annum, on constant 1950 prices.[3]

Such success, however, proved a mixed blessing. Income from services went overwhelmingly to the already well-off, whose conspicuous consumption dramatized income disparities. Industry—for which Lebanon had a decent skills base compared with other Arab countries and a head start from the late 1930s and Allied war contracts—languished because of unfettered free trade. Agriculture, which supported half the population, stagnated. Services, the focus of dynamism, had the least capacity for absorbing entrants to the labor force. In sum, much of the Sunni community, most Druze and Shia, and many rural Maronites shared only the crumbs of the Merchant Republic. These crumbs nourished resentment, dangerous for a service-oriented economy vulnerable to slips in confidence resulting from political trouble.

Independent Lebanon's story proceeded in several phases. Between 1942 and 1947, Lebanon came out of World War II and the French mandate with its new regime and commercial outlook. This transition closed with the first parliamentary elections of the era of independence in May 1947 and the November 1947 United Nations General Assembly resolution recommending partition of the neighboring British mandate of Palestine between Jewish and Arab states. The elections were an exercise of elite manipulation, with President Bishara al-Khuri packing parliament to override the constitution and obtain a second term. Partition of Palestine led to the emergence of the state of Israel, the discrediting of conservative Arab regimes in the first Arab-Israeli War, and the arrival of 120,000 Palestinian Arab refugees in Lebanon. Already events indicated turbulence to come.

The years 1947 to 1958 were the high noon of both the National Pact and the Merchant Republic. President al-Khuri besmirched his reputation as a hero of independence in trying to retain power against an unwilling political class and wider public, but his forced resignation in 1952 indicated some health in "confessional democracy." President Camille Chamoun was politically disadvantaged, lacking the parliamentary base al-Khuri had commanded. While Beirut soared as entrepot of the Middle East, Chamoun drifted into trouble as he confronted opponents and backed the West against Soviet-supported Arab nationalists—Egypt's Gamal Abdel Nasser and the Syrian Ba'thists. Nasser gained Muslim street sympathy in Lebanon, which forced Sunni Muslim bosses to adopt more radical postures. They and Chamoun accused each other of breaking the National Pact, and in May 1958, the political system briefly collapsed into civil war. On this occasion, fortuitous American intervention and the social grip of the political class enabled everyone to pull back from sectarian conflict.

Maronite army commander Fuad Shihab, a descendant of the paramount family of the *imara* and a respected neutral personality, succeeded Chamoun at the scheduled end of his term. President Shihab had decent relations with Nasser and sought to spread the benefits of Lebanon's commercial boom, resurgent after a 1958 downturn. Shihab promoted a modestly interventionist state, with public investment in the peripheries, particularly the Shia south and the Biqa. Again a president faced resistance from the political class, now against loading the Merchant Republic with social responsibility. At the end of his term in 1964, Shihab had stimulated expectations without time to answer them. The migration of Shia poor to Beirut, which accompanied the city's Middle Eastern ascendancy, accelerated without hope of jobs. Christian and Sunni elite obstruction hobbled the second Shihabist president, Charles Helou, after 1964.

Israel's trouncing of front-line Arab states in the June 1967 war inaugurated a chain reaction that was disastrous for Lebanon. Nascent Palestinian guerilla movements seized the initiative against Israel, using Palestinian refugee camps in Lebanon as bases for cross-border attacks. The rising Lebanese militant Left drew Palestinian paramilitaries into its parallel campaign against "Maronite hegemony." Both the Lebanese Left and the Palestinians mobilized youths in the Shia and Palestinian "belt of misery" fringing Beirut. Maronite party leaders in turn roused their frightened followers. After 1970, the anti-Shihabist president, Sulayman Faranjiya, dismantled Shihab's military intelligence. The Left and Palestinians then commandeered Beirut Sunni gangs previously under Shihabist steerage, putting Sunni bosses under the gun to demand the regime back the Palestinians against Israel and reform its communal allocations. Most Christians rejected Lebanon exposing itself to Israeli attacks, being at Palestinian disposal, or being reformed at gunpoint. The mainline Palestinian Fatah movement of Yasir Arafat and senior Lebanese politicians tried to stay above the fray, but the tides on the streets were stronger than in 1958 and the writ of *zu'ama* much weaker. In April 1975, a spark ignited hostilities that plunged Lebanon into fifteen years of warfare and political chaos.

National Pact and New Regime, 1943–1947

As early as June 1942, the British facilitated a meeting in Cairo of Bishara al-Khuri with Egyptian Prime minister Nahhas Pasha and Syrian Prime Minister Jamil Mardam.[4] The three established an understanding on Lebanon's Arab orientation, and the two premiers agreed to support al-Khuri, who had gravitas as leader of Lebanon's largest political faction. Through al-Khuri, the Christian commercial class looked for an understanding with local Sunnis and assured access to the depth of the Arab world. British interests were more immediate—a comfortable rear for the decisive battle against the German Afrika Korps in the Egyptian desert.

Little changed in Lebanon into early 1943. For Britain, the climax of the war in North Africa, from the defeat of Rommel at Al-Alamein in November 1942 to the final battles in Tunisia in spring 1943, was all-consuming. Free French leader Charles de Gaulle suspected that Britain intended to displace France in the Levant and indicated obduracy to Churchill in a September 28, 1942, meeting. According to de Gaulle: "The Prime Minister proceeded to the usual airing of our respective grievances in the Middle East. The British government, he said, insisted that elections be held this very year in Syria and in Lebanon; I replied that this would not be the case."[5] The French-appointed Lebanese president, Alfred Naqqash, also stalled; he wanted to keep his job.

Lebanon finally moved toward elections and renewed representative government in March 1943. High Commissioner Georges Catroux replaced Naqqash with the Protestant Ayyub Thabit and reinstated the Lebanese and Syrian constitutions. Meanwhile, Emile Edde organized his followers into a "National Bloc," which preferred a continued organic link with France.[6] Already in 1942, al-Khuri's Constitutional Bloc accepted that Lebanon would become independent as a country open to the Arab world, the Christian version of Kazim al-Sulh's 1936 call to Sunnis to accept that Greater Lebanon would become an independent Arab state. This created a Maronite bridge to Sunnis, though even al-Khuri's faction would never countenance the Sunni notion of Lebanon's independence being conditional on later absorption into a larger Arab state.

Thabit provoked Sunnis when he proposed in June 1943 to widen the Christian advantage in parliamentary seating from 22/20 to 32/22 using Lebanese emigrants.[7] British envoy Edward Spears suggested a six to five ratio (30/25), which enabled both Christians and Muslims to save face. The elections of August 28, 1943, favored al-Khuri by producing a pro-independence parliament, but Edde's list won in Mount Lebanon. Camille Chamoun, who was closest to the British and whose wife was half-English, personally outpolled al-Khuri and Edde. The French were buoyed by Edde's performance but alarmed by that of Chamoun. Eyes now shifted to the parliamentary session scheduled for September 21 to elect a president—only the second such election since 1920. The British opposed Edde and the French opposed Chamoun. Al-Khuri gained the support of both powers, and the Syrians recommended him to the Sunnis.

On September 19, 1943, al-Khuri as leading presidential candidate met Riyadh al-Sulh as senior Sunni politician. They confirmed understandings for operating the Lebanese constitution into independence. The president would be a Maronite and the prime minister a Sunni Muslim, as in the late 1930s. Spears' six to five ratio of Christians to non-Christians would continue for the Chamber of Deputies. With regard to foreign policy, Lebanon would not enter Western-led alignments, nor would it compromise its sovereignty in relations with Arab states. Shia and Druze leaders acquiesced on condition of spoils in the carve-up of the regime. The double compromise for sectarian shares and external neutralism assured al-Khuri the non-Christian votes he needed.

After becoming president, al-Khuri appointed Riyadh al-Sulh prime minister, and on October 8, the latter stressed confessional consensus on Lebanon's identity and regime in the government's policy statement. Shia, however, were aggrieved that they did not receive a reserved top office, which could only mean a Shia speaker of parliament. Al-Khuri and al-Sulh did not answer this in 1943; a

Greek Catholic ran for speaker in 1944, and an Orthodox took the position in 1946. Furious Shia protest ensured that the post became their communal preserve from June 1947.[8]

Unlike the Syrians, who acquired a nationalist government in parallel elections, the Lebanese needed to affirm their multicommunal cohesion in swift assertion of independence. Syria did not have such an imperative and, for once, the Lebanese led the way. As soon as he took office, Prime Minister al-Sulh required that all official business be in Arabic.[9] He and al-Khuri asked the new French delegate-general, Jean Helleu, to hand over the common interests of the mandate, from customs to ports and railways to local security forces. They also proposed to delete the authority of the mandatory power from the 1926 constitution. Helleu and the Free French committee in Algiers refused. On November 8, the Lebanese parliament unilaterally amended the constitution. Three days later the prickly Helleu ordered the arrest of al-Khuri, al-Sulh, and all government ministers. This covered leaders of all major sects, guaranteeing Lebanese unity against France. Six top politicians—al-Khuri, al-Sulh, Camille Chamoun, Adil Usayran, Salim Taqla, and Abd al-Hamid Karami—found themselves in the Rashaya prison. See figure 5.1 for a photograph of Prime Minister Riyadh al-Sulh after release from French detention.

Helleu appointed Edde to replace al-Khuri. He thereby misread the Maronites, for whom France no longer had credibility and who were focused on independence. He gambled further by detaining Kata'ib leader Pierre Gemayel, whose followers promptly joined the Sunni Najjada on the streets. Indeed, the Lebanese solidified their National Pact with uniform hostility under ministers who escaped arrest, for example Majid Arslan of the Druze. The British let the French flounder for a week, during which time the more realistic Georges Catroux returned. On November 19, they threatened to take charge unless the French revoked their measures. Catroux bowed on November 21, releasing the politicians and restoring Lebanon's constitutional order.

Al-Khuri and al-Sulh henceforth had the advantage in relations with France. Spears buttressed them until his recall in December 1944, while Soviet and American recognition of Lebanon and Syria in mid-1944 offset any French gain from de Gaulle's installment in Paris from August 1944. Through 1944, the Lebanese also used the kudos of defying France to dictate Arab respect for their independence in negotiations to establish a league of Arab states.[10] The initial conservative, pro-Western tilt of Arab regimes after the world war gave al-Khuri and al-Sulh a comfortable regional environment in the mid-1940s. In March 1945, Lebanon pocketed the prestige of being a founder member of the Arab League, the charter of which endorsed its freedom of maneuver.[11]

The French handed over the nonmilitary common interests of the mandate in early 1944 to joint Lebanese-Syrian management. However, as prime minister of the provisional government of France, de Gaulle remained insistent on treaties

Figure 5.1 Prime Minister Riyadh al-Sulh after release from French detention, December 1943. Associated Press.

with Lebanon and Syria giving France military bases and economic privileges. In April 1945, with the end of the war in Europe approaching, he approved sending additional troops to bolster French claims in the Levant. In early May, he made a forthright declaration to Churchill, a few days before French reinforcements, mostly the hated Senegalese, landed in Beirut.

> We have recognized the independence of the Levant states, as you have done in Egypt and Iraq, and we seek only to reconcile this independent

regime with our interests in the region. These interests are of an economic and cultural order. They are also of a strategic order.[12]

Decisive events followed in interior Syria while the Lebanese watched. Dama-
scenes responded to the French reassertion with fierce riots. Pushed back into
the streets, French troops escalated with artillery on May 29–30, killing about
eight hundred people. The British then demanded that the French cease fire and
retire to their barracks. France was on the wrong side of both its allies and the
recently established United Nations, while the mood in Syria and Lebanon after
the shelling precluded any treaties.

France had no option but to transfer the locally recruited *Troupes Spéciales* to
Lebanese and Syrian command and to leave the Levant empty-handed. On
August 1, 1945, Lebanon thus acquired 3,300 French-trained Lebanese soldiers,
almost 60 percent of whom were Christians, as the nucleus of a Lebanese army.[13]
Their commander was Colonel Fuad Shihab. The French refused to evacuate
their own forces while a British military presence continued, but British withdrawal in early 1946 removed all excuses. Even so, the last French soldiers only
departed, to Lebanese relief, in December 1946.

It was a sorry termination for a French intervention that created the modern
Lebanese territorial state and gave the Lebanese their constitution, administration, and military. Nonetheless, three centuries of French cultural and commercial interaction with Mount Lebanon guaranteed continued Lebanese fascination
with France, even as Britain, the Arab world, and soon the United States dominated the political horizon of independent Lebanon.

Within Lebanon, President al-Khuri invested his November 1943 success
against France in consolidating power. He depended on Prime Minister al-
Sulh to smooth Lebanon's Arab affairs and the fabulously wealthy Henri Far'un
to look after his electoral base.[14] Al-Khuri was a quiet manipulator, not a
strongman or showman—in other words an ideal front for an elite that simply
wanted a free economy. He was, however, vindictive toward his old rival Emile
Edde, the French promoted usurper. Here al-Sulh, a long-standing friend of
Edde, shielded the latter from punishment.[15] Edde merely suffered expulsion
from parliament, though his career was finished. In June 1944, al-Khuri and
al-Sulh removed the truculent Camille Chamoun from the government and
shunted him off to London as ambassador. Chamoun resented being cancelled
out by al-Khuri in the 1943 presidential election. Only in late 1944 did al-
Khuri move to prevent al-Sulh from entrenching himself as premier. Al-Sulh
had done the critical work with the Arabs and was frustrating al-Khuri's placement of clients. The president worked with Far'un and Abd al-Hamid Karami
to destroy al-Sulh's parliamentary support.[16] Al-Sulh resigned and Karami
became prime minister.

Al-Khuri's machinations represented a pattern of modern Lebanese political behavior, encouraged by the jockeying for sectarian shares. It reached back into the French mandate and forward to the 1990s, when it facilitated Syrian hegemony. Al-Khuri was a master of communal maneuver, and in 1945, this and his lust for power led him toward breaking the internal balance of the National Pact and abusing the constitution. He degraded the post of prime minister, managing top Sunni politicians through 1945–1946 by rotating them in the job.[17] He also aspired to a crushing victory in the 1947 parliamentary polls so that he could override the constitution and serve a second presidential term.

Governments headed by Karami, Sami al-Sulh, and Sa'adi al-Munla, a Tripoli protégé of Karami, came and went from 1945 to 1946. Sami al-Sulh was Riyadh's cousin and built a formidable patronage machine in Beirut while Riyadh preferred to float above such grubbiness. These governments had no policies beyond administering the status quo while the French mandate was wound up. Having little to do, their members busied themselves with placing their friends and relatives. Al-Khuri persuaded Riyadh al-Sulh to return as prime minister in December 1946 to supervise the coming elections.

In May 1947, political bosses aligned with the president swept Lebanon's first parliamentary poll after independence.[18] Sami al-Sulh and other friendly Sunnis won Beirut, containing Salim Salam's son Sa'ib. Al-Khuri's Shia allies Ahmad al-Asa'ad and Sabri Hamade delivered the south and the Biqa, including a seat for Riyadh al-Sulh. The Constitutional Bloc routed Edde's supporters in Mount Lebanon. The ailing Karami, estranged from the regime, gave way in the north to the Muqaddims, Jisrs, and the Maronite Hamid Faranjiya. Al-Khuri and al-Sulh could count forty-nine sympathetic deputies out of fifty-five. However, all was not what it seemed. Most deputies owed their seats to al-Khuri's allies, not to al-Khuri, and allies could shift. The president had to tolerate Chamoun and Kamal Junblat as heads of his bloc in Mount Lebanon. Chamoun returned from London in March aggrieved, while the young Junblat had a grudge against a system that had no top Druze post. The president's brother Salim surfaced as a crude vote manager and had to be sidelined. Generally, vote buyers could see ballots before they were cast because there were no official forms; voters wrote their choices on their own slips of paper.[19]

The result reflected popular satisfaction with al-Khuri, despite manipulation and irregularities. It made viable a two-thirds parliamentary majority to set aside the constitutional ban on consecutive presidential terms. Al-Khuri kept Riyadh al-Sulh as prime minister so that his second presidential election would proceed under respectable Sunni auspices. Yet al-Khuri still had to choose the moment.

Countdown to war in Palestine after Arab rejection of the November 1947 United Nations partition resolution provided perfect cover. Like the whole Arab world, al-Khuri assumed Arab armies would prevail over Jewish forces when they entered Palestine with the end of the British mandate on May 14, 1948. He planned for Lebanese participation in the fighting. Prime Minister al-Sulh toured Arab capitals to buttress military coordination. The atmosphere of crisis enabled al-Khuri to get parliament to allow an exceptional presidential extension on April 9, 1948. He already had British and American backing. In late April, thousands of Palestinian Arab refugees from Haifa "flooded the Lebanese coast especially Tyre and Sidon between night and morning," and al-Khuri "rushed to visit them."[20] The president thus projected himself as Lebanon's man of the hour. On May 27, at the height of Arab delirium in the initial Arab clashes with the new Jewish state of Israel, the Chamber of Deputies formally elected him for his second term, sixteen months ahead of time.

High Noon and First Cracks, 1948–1958

From 1948 onward, elaboration of Lebanon's service economy proceeded together with Middle Eastern turbulence (figure 5.2 depicts contemporary downtown Beirut). Confrontation between Israel and the surrounding Arab world was ultimately ominous for Lebanon, considering the large Palestinian Arab refugee presence in the coastal cities. More immediately, the new geopolitics implied a commercial windfall. The Arab boycott of Israel removed Haifa as a competitor for Beirut, made Lebanon a terminus for piped Saudi oil, and forced the Iraq Petroleum Company to shift from Haifa to Tripoli.[21] Middle-class refugees brought their expertise, and for almost two decades the ghetto-like refugee camps remained quiescent despite Lebanese treatment of their residents as unwelcome transients. In Iraq, the flight of the Jews of Baghdad to Israel allowed Lebanese traders and financiers to appropriate much of the country's commerce.[22] The emergence of radical republican regimes after the old Arab elite suffered defeat and disgrace in Palestine brought a flight of capital to Beirut as new Arab rulers confiscated property and hounded the upper class. Lebanon profited from the overthrow of the monarchies in Egypt and Iraq in 1952 and 1958.

By October 1948, the first Arab-Israeli War turned decisively against the Arab states. Thereafter, al-Khuri and al-Sulh promoted an armistice with the same enthusiasm they had earlier promoted war.[23] Lebanese troops did not cross the border, leaving the risks to Fawzi al-Qa'uqji and his Lebanese and Palestinian irregulars. Al-Qa'uqji was a Lebanese Sunni from Tripoli, a fervent Arab nationalist who became a Palestinian Arab hero. In fighting Qa'uqji, the new Israeli army occupied Lebanese villages and thereby brought reality home to the Lebanese government. The interest of the commercial class in its self-preservation took precedence; there was no stomach for the humiliation and chaos certain in further hostilities. Al-Khuri and al-Sulh, however, quaked at being in the

Figure 5.2 Downtown Beirut, January 1947. Associated Press.

vanguard of Arabs signing terms with Israel. Egypt resolved their dilemma by going first, in February 1949. The Lebanese then concluded their own armistice in March, with Israel withdrawing from their territory.

Lebanon's armistice with Israel came only days before change in Syria. On March 31, 1949, Colonel Husni al-Za'im deposed Syrian President Shukri al-Quwatli and Prime Minister Jamil Mardam in Syria's first military coup. Thus began the fallout from disgrace in the Arab-Israeli War. It was a body blow to al-Khuri and al-Sulh; both had close relations with al-Quwatli and Mardam.[24] Intimacy ended between the two states and has never been properly restored, certainly not at the level of the easy equality of the first years of their independence. Their economies headed in divergent directions, with pressures for state protection of agriculture and promotion of industry in Syria as opposed to Lebanon's determination on free trade. Nonetheless, high bourgeois civilian regimes in the two countries could have made amicable arrangements for customs and tariffs into the 1950s.

Lebanon hosted Syria's fugitive politicians, and tension rose; al-Sulh felt affronted at the overthrow of his old National Bloc friends. In May 1949, the Lebanese detained Syrian troops who crossed the border, and al-Za'im suspended

trade. Al-Khuri and al-Sulh felt insecure because defeat by Israel had destroyed
the popular credit al-Khuri had used to justify his presidential extension. They
faced a rising opposition headed by Chamoun and Junblat, who encouraged the
militant voice of Antun Sa'adeh of the Syrian Social Nationalists (SSNP). The
latter had returned from wartime exile, saw al-Za'im's coup as a chance to pro-
mote Greater Syria, and derided al-Sulh.[25] The government took the opportunity of June 1949 clashes between the SSNP and the Kata'ib, its street rival, to
crack down on the SSNP.[26] Sa'adeh escaped arrest and fled to Syria.

Al-Za'im initially allowed Sa'adeh to foment SSNP raids in Lebanon. However, when he felt that al-Khuri and al-Sulh were backing off from needling him,
he did a deal and handed Sa'adeh to the Lebanese on July 6. A military court
sentenced the SSNP leader to death within twenty-four hours. President al-
Khuri refused clemency, and Sa'adeh was executed on July 8, 1949. The Lebanese
regime thus made Sa'adeh pay for the bad turn in its fortunes. It was vindictive;
the SSNP did not have the capability to threaten the system. It could, however,
threaten persons, particularly al-Sulh, for persecuting it. The SSNP took revenge
in July 1951, when party gunmen killed al-Sulh while he was visiting Jordan.
This deeply embarrassed al-Khuri, coming soon after he pushed al-Sulh out of
the premiership in the run-up to the 1951 parliamentary elections.

In Syria, officers sympathetic to the SSNP disposed of al-Za'im in August
1949, and Colonel Adib Shishakli emerged as strongman of Syria in December.
He and Premier Khalid al-Azm despised the Lebanese leadership. They also
intensified state intervention in the Syrian economy, incompatible with the Leb-
anese/Syrian customs union. In March 1950, Khalid al-Azm demanded that
Lebanon accept economic union with Syria, meaning submission to Syrian
controls on trade and finance. Lebanon refused, and the Syrians abrogated the
customs union, closing the Syrian market to Lebanese manufactures and agriculture.[27] Lebanese industries faced a 60 percent cut in demand while Tripoli
traders lost their import/export business in Syria.[28] The economy briefly contracted, with a 10 percent cut in national income in 1951 and stagnation through
1952.[29] Thereafter, tertiary sector growth surged. Lebanon was free to liberalize
its economy as it pleased; the Merchant Republic leapfrogged Syria to take
advantage of the rising oil revenues of the Persian Gulf.

For Bishara al-Khuri, the economic downturn in 1951/1952 soured the
public mood just as the elite turned against him. The president's brother Salim
acquired influence over appointments, contracts, and internal security that
angered even old friends like Henri Far'un.[30] Salim did not shrink from thuggery
against opposition newspapers and rallies. Bishara al-Khuri's vote-mobilizing
machine in Mount Lebanon and Beirut and his alliances, especially with the
Shia, carried the April 1951 parliamentary elections, but there was no enthusiasm, and the president's enforcer brother was overly prominent. Al-Khuri's

ditching of Riyadh al-Sulh as prime minister in a return to rotating chairs inflamed Sunni resentment given that Salim organized it; al-Sulh became a martyr. In late 1951, Prime Minister Abdullah Yafi complained of presidential interference in appointments and targeted gambling involving the Khuris.[31] The president replaced him with Riyadh's cousin Sami al-Sulh in February 1952.

Into 1952, opposition leaders Chamoun and Junblat capitalized on al-Khuri's inability to curb his brother. They were determined to force the president's resignation. Chamoun, with his eye on the presidency since 1943, took care to present himself as a reformer out to drain the swamp of corruption. This enhanced his local standing and made him the darling of the Western embassies. The British and American envoys were cool toward the president; in October 1951 al-Khuri had rejected participation in an Anglo-American scheme for a Middle East defense command.[32] For his part, Kamal Junblat became head of his family after the death of his mother Nazira in 1949, when he also founded the Progressive Socialist Party (PSP) as his vehicle. Junblat moved toward the leftist and Arabist camp. Chamoun and Junblat aligned with Pierre and Raymond Edde, the sons of Michel, who had died in 1949, and with Hamid Faranjiya of the north, who blamed the Khuris for loss of his parliamentary seat in 1951.

Junblat forced the pace in May 1952 when he excoriated the Khuris in the PSP tract *al-Anba*.[33] The government suspended newspapers that printed Junblat's piece. The incident illustrated the new weight of the media. In the first years of independence, newspapers and news magazines multiplied to an unprecedented extent, with at least a dozen new titles in Beirut. Only *L'Orient* and Salim al-Khuri's *al-Wujdan* backed the president; the rest, including *al-Nahar*, endorsed the opposition. There is no doubt that the press campaign condemning corruption sapped respect for al-Khuri. Even Michel Chiha, the president's brother-in-law and ideological prop, wrote against him in *Le Jour*.[34]

The conclusive blow came from the Sunni elite in September 1952. Fed up with attempts by the Khuris to make him a fall guy for the regime, Prime Minister Sami al-Sulh repudiated the president in parliament on September 8 and resigned. Abdullah Yafi and Rashid Karami, son of Abd al-Hamid, also condemned the regime.[35] Only Sa'ib Salam, heir of Salim and Sami al-Sulh's ascending rival in Beirut, felt tempted to try his hand as premier. Chamoun and Junblat mobilized a general strike that closed the country and scared him off. No other Sunni would consent to form a government. Army commander Fuad Shihab, apprehensive about army unity, refused to intervene against the strikers. On September 18, 1952, Bishara al-Khuri gave up office to Shihab until the Chamber of Deputies could elect a new president.

Camille Chamoun became independent Lebanon's second president five days later (see figure 5.3 for an image of Chamoun). He had the credentials for both Muslim and Christian elites. He promoted administrative reform and

championed the Arab cause in Palestine as Lebanon's representative at the
United Nations in 1948. He also believed in the free economy and openness to
the West. However, his allies against al-Khuri—the "socialist front" of communal
lords—swiftly repudiated him. Hamid Faranjiya, foreign minister under al-Khuri,
tried for the presidency and disappointment rankled. Kamal Junblat expected
the new president to treat him as an equal partner, even though as a Druze he
could not be prime minister. Chamoun was simply unwilling. A decisive break
between the two men came at a meeting in the Beit al-Din palace the night of
Chamoun's election.

> [Junblat] said to President Chamoun: "We came to government today.
> The time has come to consider implementing the program of the
> Socialist Front that we prepared as a guideline for the operation of
> the regime. And we hope that we shall form the first government as the
> victorious front. . . ." Silence reigned. Everyone looked at Camille
> Chamoun. He stubbed out his cigar on the edge of the ashtray, blew
> smoke slowly, and said as if he was referring to trivialities of no conse-
> quence: "We want to go to see what's happening with Dani [Chamoun's
> son]. It's true we arrived, but you have to give me a little time." Kamal
> Junblat felt as if he had a brain seizure.[36]

Collapse of Chamoun's partnership with Junblat made it difficult to find a
Sunni prime minister to carry through with Chamoun's administrative reforms.
Chamoun appointed a second rank figure, Khalid Shihab, to head a cabinet of
technocrats. Under threat of dissolution, parliament granted decree powers,
including for revising the electoral law.[37] Chamoun demonstrated the potency of
presidential authority, and his government proceeded to address deficiencies in
the Lebanese system. Chamoun deserves credit for giving the vote to women,
thereby doubling the electorate, and for establishing the Higher Judicial Council
to appoint judges and shield the judiciary from interference. Previously, judges
were effectively political appointees. The government also liberalized newspaper
licensing, removing constraints on press freedom. About six hundred bureau-
crats were sacked from sinecures.[38]

In the November 1952 electoral law, Chamoun challenged political bosses;
he reduced the number of members of parliament from seventy-seven to forty-
four and increased the number of constituencies from nine to thirty-three.
Instead of making a single list of candidates in one large multimember constituency, a rural chief now had to cobble together a set of lists for several constituencies. For example, in the south one contest became seven for Ahmad
al-Asa'ad.[39] New regime-favored candidates had improved chances. The big men
clung to reduced stakes in parliament in the July 1953 elections.[40] Al-Asa'ad and

Figure 5.3 President Camille Chamoun with his wife Zalfa, Beirut, May 1953.
Associated Press/Pringle.

his son Kamil took seats and preserved their bloc, but lost three constituencies.
Junblat barely kept his seat. Sabri Hamade of Baalbek, Rashid Karami of Tripoli,
and Hamid Faranjiya of Zgharta all remained in parliament. Sa'ib Salam, Abdullah Yafi, and Sami al-Sulh were returned in Beirut. Happily, the rough balance
between Chamoun affirming his dignity and survival of Sunni chiefs made

Salam, Yafi, and al-Sulh amenable to forming governments based in parliament
from May 1953, after eight months of rule by decree.

Sectarian compartments and personality-dependent factions in independent
Lebanon meant presidents lacked the stable backing provided by political parties
in the West. Chamoun's problem was most acute because he did not have
al-Khuri's networks, nor did he stem from the elite. The Chamouns were an off-
shoot of the Saqr clan of Jubayl, which entered the written record with Father
Istifan Saqr, a leading Maronite monk.[41] Through the eighteenth and nineteenth
century they spread to the Biqa and Deir al-Qamar in the Shuf. Chamoun's
father, Nimr Efendi, was a senior official in the finance department of the *mutasarrifiya*. Camille, born in 1900, earned a law degree at L'Université Saint-Joseph
and worked in Emile Edde's office before moving into al-Khuri's camp from the
late 1920s to the early 1940s. The family exemplified the new middle class of late
Ottoman Mount Lebanon and became prominent in Deir al-Qamar, but this did
not provide the base of a Junblat, an al-Asa'ad, or even a Faranjiya. Nor did
Chamoun acquire institutional support such as Fuad Shihab wielded as army
chief, which also buttressed his presidency.

Chamoun relied more nakedly on presidential prestige and prerogatives.
Inevitably, because the position was a Maronite preserve, such reliance came
across as sectarian assertion, whereas al-Khuri and Shihab could use elite net-
working or the army to project a better "national" image. Of the three, Chamoun's disadvantages in the political system made him the most confrontational
head of state.[42]

From 1953 to 1956, Lebanon prospered in a stable local and Arab environment. In 1953 and 1954, the annual growth rate of the economy touched 15
percent, overwhelmingly in the service sector.[43] Limited government investment concentrated on transport and communications. Beirut's new airport terminal was the major innovation. Tourist numbers quadrupled in only three
years, with a substantial inflow from the Arab oil states.[44] Under Chamoun, the
Lebanese currency became almost entirely covered by gold reserves, and in September 1956, the government sponsored a law guaranteeing the secrecy of bank
deposits. Thereafter, total deposits doubled by 1961.[45]

Beyond Beirut, mountain resorts, and service activities, conditions were less
buoyant. Agricultural trade expanded, but benefits mainly accrued to big landowners who had privileged access to credits for investment in irrigation and horticulture.[46] Government spending was on a tight leash in a low tax environment,
kept at 11 to 14 percent of national product, and health, education, and peripheral
regions were not priorities.[47] Under free trade, commodity imports greatly exceeded
exports, covered by income from service sector "invisibles." The scale of economic
growth lifted the population in general, but the returns were skewed toward the
Christian bourgeoisie.

Even in Chamoun's good years, warning signs multiplied. In November 1953, an influential Sunni Muslim association circulated a tract that denounced Christian domination, demanded a new census, and asserted a Muslim majority.[48] More seriously, Gamal Abdel Nasser's seizure of power in Egypt in 1954 and his strident Arab nationalism through Radio Cairo stirred the Sunni Muslims in Lebanon. Under Chamoun's liberal media regime, it also fed into explosive elaboration of the opposition press in Beirut.[49] Nasser particularly objected to the pro-British Iraqi monarchy joining the Western-backed alignment of Turkey, Iran, and Pakistan in the February 1955 Baghdad Pact. This coincided with Nasser's campaign to remove the British from the Suez Canal zone. Given the West's support for Israel and Egypt's conservative Arab rivals, Nasser drifted toward the Soviet Bloc for arms and aid. When Chamoun and Prime Minister Sami al-Sulh visited Turkey in April 1955 and were rumored to endorse the Baghdad Pact, they had to give reassurances to counter opposition media.[50] Among top Sunni politicians, Sami al-Sulh was the most locally oriented and had the least Arab nationalist sensibility. Chamoun appointed the more Arabist Rashid Karami and Abdullah Yafi as prime ministers from mid-1955 and held back from commitment between Iraq and Egypt.

The Suez crisis of October/November 1956, when Britain, France, and Israel invaded Egypt after Nasser nationalized the Suez Canal in July, triggered the deterioration of Chamoun's final years. Whatever his contribution to the Arab cause in the late 1940s, Chamoun's pro-British orientation and his fear of Nasserite demolition of Lebanon guaranteed that he would tilt toward the West when cornered. He declined to cut diplomatic relations with Britain and France. Yafi resigned as prime minister, and the president faced a torrent of abuse from Radio Cairo and the local Nasserites. Chamoun was able to form a sympathetic government under Sami al-Sulh, with the pro-American academic Charles Malik as foreign minister, because the United States opposed the Anglo-French operation, and much of the non-Christian elite, including Yafi and Junblat, were uneasy about Nasser's influence on Lebanese Muslims.

In January 1957, worried about Soviet penetration of the Middle East and the security of oil supplies, the United States took the lead for the West. President Eisenhower offered American military support for any Middle Eastern country facing "armed aggression" from a state controlled by "international communism."[51] Egypt and Syria interpreted the Eisenhower doctrine as a bid to isolate and intimidate them. In contrast, in April 1957, Lebanon became the only Arab country to accord Eisenhower's proposal official endorsement. Malik had a substantial role, and opposition invective only stiffened Chamoun. The Nasserite sympathies of the *qabaday* enforcers of Sunni leaders gave most of the latter little choice but to follow Cairo. For Chamoun, Sunni adherence to Nasser broke the National Pact commitment not to take Lebanon into Arab alignments. For the opposition, Chamoun's adherence to the Eisenhower doctrine broke the under-standing not to align with a Western power.

Added to the confrontation with Nasser, Chamoun's ambition to command parliament, cutting back representation of unfriendly politicians, risked Leba-non's viability. Elections were due in mid-1957, and Chamoun again laid down the gauntlet in the April 1957 election law. The president supervised a gerry-mander of constituency boundaries to splinter supporters of leading opponents, which Sami al-Sulh's government forced through.[52] Chamoun's enemies accused him of seeking a two-thirds majority to sideline the constitution for a second presidential term, repeating the Khuri model. Chamoun's term was due to end in September 1958. Chamoun refused comment, but expressed interest in exten-sion to the British and American ambassadors.[53] He felt that he had not had a chance to make his mark since 1952 and that the country needed his firm man-agement. In the June 1957 elections, the regime had the gerrymander and Amer-ican money to counter Egyptian and Syrian financing of the opposition.[54] It was adequate for Chamoun, but barely so. Junblat and Sa'ib Salam lost their seats while the president's ally Kazim al-Khalil defeated Ahmad al-Asa'ad's list in the south. Nonetheless, the opposition won the Biqa, while Karami and Faranjiya clung to their seats in the north. Overall, Chamoun's intervention and the con-viction that he intended another term pushed Junblat, al-Asa'ad, and the Faran-jiyas toward rebellion.[55]

The Eisenhower administration unwittingly ignited the chain reaction that took Lebanon over the brink. In August 1957, the Americans promoted an abor-tive attempt to overthrow the weak regime in Damascus because they feared its drift toward Moscow. Syrian military intelligence uncovered the plot, the Egyp-tians landed troops in Syria, the Syrian Ba'thists appealed to Nasser for union, and in February 1958, Syria and Egypt came together in the United Arab Repub-lic (UAR) under Egyptian control. In Lebanon, the majority of Sunnis and Shia favored submergence in the Arabist tide. Their leaders were far less enthusiastic, but suspicion of Chamoun's domestic agenda eased submission to what seemed the march of history. Chamoun and the bulk of Christians, on the other hand, felt vindicated in their obdurate Westernism. The Egyptians fed weaponry across the Syrian/Lebanese border to buttress the opposition.

On May 8, 1958, unknown assailants killed the Maronite editor of the opposi-tion *al-Tayar* in Tripoli. Rioting in Tripoli and mainly Muslim West Beirut precip-itated military mobilization of radical parties—Nasserites, the Ba'th, and the Communists—and the *qabadays* of opposition leaders. The National Front, an association of opposition personalities and factions that Kamal Junblat organized for the 1957 elections, coordinated the insurrection (figure 5.4 shows Junblat in his mountain headquarters). The Kata'ib and the SSNP rallied in defense of Chamoun: Pan-Arabism was the common enemy of Christian Lebanon and

Greater Syria. General Fuad Shihab kept the army out of the conflict, except to block regime collapse. A few weeks of street battles and rural skirmishes reduced government authority to central Mount Lebanon and the eastern part of Beirut— the Christian heartland. All districts added to Mount Lebanon in 1920 came under rebel control, and for a time, the flow of arms and volunteers from the Syrian province of the UAR gave the opposition the advantage. Chamoun led the defense of the presidential residence in Beirut, rifle in hand.[56]

The 1958 violence was substantially a sectarian breakdown between Christians and non-Christians, involving challenges to the internal and external balances of the National Pact. Fortunately, cross-sectarian extensions of the two sides blurred the schism. Among Druze, Majid Arslan remained with Chamoun and guarded the airport, an echo of the old Yazbaki/Junblati split. In June, Druze shaykhs arranged a Druze truce. Among Sunnis, Sami al-Sulh stood by Chamoun, but this finished his career. Among Shia, Kazim al-Khalil also stayed loyal, but fled the south. Among Maronites, the Faranjiyas were steadfast with the opposition. Maronite patriarch Bulos Meouche, skeptical of the constancy of the West toward Lebanon's Christians, stayed aloof from Chamoun.[57] A number of Christians and Muslims attempted mediation between the sides, for example the deputies Raymond Edde, Charles Helou, Adil Usayran, and Fawzi al-Huss.

Figure 5.4 Druze leader Kamal Junblat with armed followers at his home in Mukhtara, July 1958. Associated Press/STR.

President Chamoun requested U.S. intervention under Eisenhower's doctrine. The United States feared entanglement in sectarianism, noted there was no invasion, and required Chamoun to abjure reelection.[58] Nasser too soon decided that he did not want a Lebanese headache to add to his Syrian one. By mid-June he backed away, ending assistance to the rebels. Fighting subsided and contacts among Lebanese and between the United States and Egypt indicated outlines of a settlement.[59] Chamoun would finish his term, to be succeeded by army commander Fuad Shihab. On June 30, Chamoun renounced interest in a second term. With tempers inflamed it remained for everyone to calm down. By summer 1958, there was serious economic damage— capital flight, paralysis of services, and suspension of tourism.

An exit for Lebanon appeared with the July 14, 1958, coup in Baghdad, which liquidated Iraq's Hashemite monarchy, the West's major Arab ally. Equipped with a renewed request from Chamoun, the United States landed 14,000 troops on the coast south of Beirut around the airport. Lebanon was the most accessible location to demonstrate U.S. resolve to its Middle Eastern friends. Although the intervention had little to do with Lebanon's domestic strife, the United States had to deal with Lebanon's crisis to extricate itself quickly and creditably. American envoy Robert Murphy mediated among the parties, providing a face-saving mechanism for all to agree to a normal presidential transfer.[60] On July 31, the Chamber of Deputies endorsed Shihab to replace Chamoun at the formal end of the *ahd* (presidential term) on September 24, 1958.

Upon assuming office, Shihab asked Rashid Karami of Tripoli to form a government. Karami did so, but excluded Chamounists, which enraged Maronites. The kidnapping of the deputy editor of the Kata'ib newspaper *al-Amal* triggered a final round of warfare between September 17 and October 19. The Kata'ib and SSNP dueled with Muslim groups across Beirut. The flare-up, however, did not derail the settlement, because its instigators did not aim to displace the new president. U.S. troops departed in stages between August and October, after an August 21 UN General Assembly resolution called on Arab states not to interfere in one another's affairs. A conclusive cease-fire came when Shihab and Karami shelved the proposed government. Instead, Karami headed a four-member emergency cabinet— two Muslims and two Christians, including Kata'ib leader Pierre Gemayel. After 2,500 deaths, the formula of "no victor and no vanquished" prevailed.

Shihabist Interlude, 1958–1967

As president, Fuad Shihab set precedents. He had the most illustrious family background of any Lebanese head of state, yet grew up in the most humble circumstances. His great-grandfather, Hasan Shihab, was the older brother of

Bashir II Shihab, and Fuad was thus an heir of the princely houses of Shihab and Ma'n, Sunni and Druze. His mother's ancestry combined the old Maronite leading families of Hubaysh and al-Khazen, and his Shihab line had of course been Maronite for several generations. Fuad Shihab's father Abdullah, however, possessed little apart from his title of emir and had disappeared in 1907 en route to America, where he had hoped to make money to support his almost destitute family.[61] Fuad Shihab spent his adolescence in the coastal town of Jounieh with his mother and Hubaysh relatives, who had nice residences but nothing else. In 1919, he escaped poverty by joining the French army. The mandatory power capitalized on his family name and facility for leadership, useful for legitimizing the local special troops. Through the 1920s and 1930s, he rose steadily in the officer corps and attended staff college in France. He married the daughter of a French officer stationed in Lebanon. In 1945, he became a general as Lebanon's first army commander. Fuad Shihab was Lebanon's first officer president, and his profession undoubtedly contributed to his aloof, austere, and technocratic inclinations as president.

Shihab's pride in his family history, especially Bashir II and Fakhr al-Din Ma'n, gave him a deep sense of responsibility for rehabilitating Lebanon during his "watch." He derived lessons from the overreach that had brought down the mountain overlords.[62] His constrained childhood helped him identify with ordinary people, even as decades in the military caste made the popular touch difficult for him. Further, the president was a devout Maronite Catholic, also acutely conscious of his father's Islamic antecedents. On the one hand, Shihab strove for a just Lebanon above and beyond its sects. Yet he had a fallback if the project faltered. He quietly promoted new roads to link Maronite mountain districts together.[63] He also favored investment in port facilities at Jounieh, justified as a Lebanese navy requirement, to give Maronites independent access to the outside world.

To secure Lebanon from a repetition of 1958, the new president intended moderate social welfare to incorporate deprived people and regions, principally Muslims, more adequately into a Lebanese nation. This implied a stronger state, with real communal equity in appointments and personnel more autonomous from the political elite, which Shihab regarded as corrupt, self-absorbed, and incapable of producing national integration. Shihab's outlook was that "the state must assure the basic rights of Lebanese, and they should come as rights . . . not gifts," and "we don't have politicians in Lebanon, we have traders in politics."[64] The president planned to move gradually from administrative reform to development investment to equalization in the Christian/non-Christian political balance, hoping for erosion of sectarianism along the way. To implement his policy, Shihab relied on trusted military associates and a new bureaucratic cadre of technocrats drawn from socially progressive members of the elite and the middle class. The combination of social intervention, mild étatism, and security service influences within a civilian regime was the core of "Shihabism," a term coined by *L'Orient* editor George Naqqash in an October 1960 lecture to the prominent intellectual forum, the Cénacle Libanais.[65]

Shihab learned from Chamoun's experience to avoid frontal confrontation with political bosses, despite his dismissive attitude toward them. He expanded the size of parliament from sixty-six to ninety-nine members for the 1960 elections to facilitate insertion of his own loyalists and the return of senior politicians Chamoun had displaced in 1957. The 1960 election law implemented voter seclusion in booths, though voters still brought ballot papers from outside.[66] Shihab favored enlarged governments in which several elite factions could enjoy perks of office and jostle in a contained environment. Meanwhile, he shifted authority to his planning and development agencies.

For a while, the chastening effect of the 1958 events on the high bourgeoisie and its desire for undisturbed economic recovery gave Shihab an easy ride. The president had excellent relations with his first prime minister, Rashid Karami, who did not allow his Arab nationalism to get in the way of commitment to Lebanese sovereignty.[67] Shihab established a solid alliance with the Biqa Shia overlord Sabri Hamade as parliamentary speaker and cultivated Pierre Gemayel and Kamal Junblat as close minister-advisors. Making the opposed warlords of 1958 pillars of Shihabism represented a masterstroke. As leaders of populist movements, the two sheikhs backed Shihab's social and development policies and shielded these from free market purists. Gemayel's Kata'ib, for example, helped create Lebanon's first social security scheme, funded by employer, employee, and government contributions. As minister of public works, Gemayel made sure the Christian mountain got its share of rural road building, serving Shihab's "Plan B." At first, the Chamounists and the SSNP were Shihab's only opponents. In September 1959, Raymond Edde joined Chamoun, resigning from the initial emergency cabinet. Edde was infuriated by military harassment of his associates and resented Shihab's favoring of Bishara al-Khuri's Constitutional Bloc, a significant source of converts to Shihabism.[68]

Compared with Chamoun, Shihab enjoyed relaxation in Lebanon's Arab affairs. 1958 proved the high tide of Nasserism—thereafter the new Iraqi republican regime opposed Egypt, and Nasser was diverted by Saudi hostility. Shihab moved swiftly to consolidate a modus vivendi with the Egyptian leader. In March 1959, he met Nasser in a carefully choreographed summit, asserting equality by sitting on the Lebanese side of a table bisected by the border with the Syrian region of the UAR.[69] Shihab guaranteed that Lebanon would not cause Nasser trouble, while Nasser disavowed any designs on Lebanon and offered political support. This upgraded Shihab's relations with Lebanese

Muslim bosses and street Nasserites. Thereafter, Syrian secession from the UAR in 1961 and Syria's subsequent hostility to Nasser, especially when the rival Arab nationalist Ba'th movement took power in Damascus in March 1963, dampened Arabist enthusiasm among Lebanese Muslims.[70] Lebanon's integrity was never again challenged by Arab nationalism and, more immediately, Shihab's apparatus could snap up Beirut Nasserite *qabadays* cut adrift, like Ibrahim Qlaylat who had originally been in the retinue of Sa'ib Salam.[71] Indeed, after 1961, Nasser needed Shihab more than Shihab needed Nasser. The two men never met again, and Shihab never left Lebanon during his presidency. He showed no interest in Arab summit gatherings. As for Syria's Ba'thists, in mid-1964, Shihab insisted that armed provocateurs caught infiltrating from Syria be tried and jailed, spurning demands from Damascus for their immediate release. He commented: "So that Lebanese can sleep in their beds, the Ba'thists must sleep in prison.... We must prove to Syria the dignity of the [Lebanese] state."[72]

Shihab's civil service reform revisited Chamoun's attempt. Shihab took reform further, introducing the Public Service Council to handle recruitment. Examination and merit would determine appointment and promotion, mediated by the requirement for Christian/non-Christian equalization—effectively positive discrimination in favor of Muslims. Into the 1960s, Christians maintained an advantage in filling front rank administrative and diplomatic posts, but in sectarian terms, Sunnis and Druze held their own with Maronites. The real deficit was for Shia, who had only 4 of 115 senior posts in the late 1950s.[73] The Shia deficit reflected the similarly low proportion of Shia university graduates in the mid-twentieth century.[74] Overall, from a stronger political position, Shihab had more success than Chamoun in restraining patronage in the bureaucracy, though as Shihabism weakened after 1967, it crept back.

Away from the main state machinery, Shihab backed creation of separate quasi-state authorities. His legal advisor Ilyas Sarkis headed an expanded presidential office, which oversaw the agencies. The new French *Institut de Recherche et de Formation en vue de Développement* (IRFED) sent a team to help with planning and data gathering, hitherto rudimentary in the Lebanese apparatus. Retired French colonel Jean Lay advised on legal and financial restructuring of the administration. In April 1964, Lebanon acquired a central bank to control money supply and regulate private banks.[75] The fact that two decades into independence coordination of the country's finances was still in the hands of a private French institution, the *Banque de Syrie et du Liban*, is an indicator of the ad hoc character of the Merchant Republic. Under Shihab and his successor Charles Helou, the array of authorities included by the late 1960s the Central Office of Statistics, the Office of Social Development, the Board for Large Scale Projects, and the Litani River Authority.

Underpinning the professionals in Shihab's parallel bureaucracy loomed the military shadow state that increasingly vexed Sunni and Maronite political chiefs.[76] Public Security (*al-Amn al-Am*) director Tawfiq Jalbut, a Sunni officer, brought younger educated people into the Shihabist network, including a twelve-member "independent bloc" in the 1960 parliament. The head of the "military room" at the presidential palace after July 1960, Ahmad al-Hajj, handled the media and Muslim leaders. The long-standing (1959–1971) chief of staff of the army, Yusuf Shmayit, dealt with the Druze. Military intelligence (*al-shu'bat al-thaniya* or *deuxième bureau*) officers Antun Sa'ad, Gabby Lahoud, and Sami al-Khatib bought, intimidated, and manipulated the urban and rural associates ("keys") of the old political bosses in Shihab's version of traditional politics.

What was the impact of the Shihabist enterprise? On the one hand, the share of the state in national income doubled to about 23 percent through Shihab's term, based on deficit spending.[77] The number of civil servants grew from 18,000 to 26,000, and military personal from 10,000 to 15,000.[78] At the same time, the Merchant Economy recovered to annual growth rates rivaling those of the mid 1950s, increasing the indirect tax take. These factors boosted the income of portions of the middle and poorer classes in all communities. Otherwise, development investment transformed Lebanon's infrastructure by 1967. For the first time, most large villages in the Shia south, the Biqa, and the Sunni north received road connections, and 279 villages joined the electricity grid.[79]

On the other hand, the service sector remained dominant and the income skew favoring the rich persisted. According to the 1961 IRFED report, 4 percent of Lebanese took 32 percent of GDP.[80] Nonetheless, Shihab accepted the economic potency of Lebanon's free market system; he sought to make it less divisive and not to change it. During his term, industry received no serious tariff protection, and the strength of the currency was maintained, making industrial exports expensive.[81] Significantly, given the limited time available, Shihabist development of the rural peripheries on balance destabilized Lebanon's politics. Particularly in the Shia south, capital investment in agriculture and irrigation displaced sharecroppers and laborers. Education improvements enhanced the pull of "town," while constrained industrial development meant unemployment for most leaving the villages for new Shia neighborhoods in southern and eastern Beirut. Much of the Shia peasantry and youth thus drifted out of the command of the rural leading families.

Shihab and his associates dabbled in political engineering among Shia. Ali Bazzi of Bint Jubayl was a close advisor of Shihab, and "the president's men" assisted him against Kamil al-Asa'ad in the 1960 elections.[82] Kamil, heir of the most venerable lineage of Jabal Amil after his father Ahmad's death in 1961, lost his seat and never forgave Shihab. The Shihabists pulled other families like the clerical Sharaf al-Dins away from the Asa'ads, permanently weakening the Asa'ads.[83] Adil Usayran and Kazim al-Khalil, allies of Chamoun, were also isolated.

Shihab favored the new activist clerical leadership of Musa al-Sadr, who came to Lebanon from Iran in 1958 to become Mufti of Tyre at the initiative of his distant relative, the senior reformist religious scholar Abd al-Husayn Sharaf al-Din.[84] The energetic, charismatic, young Sadr, only in his thirties, plunged into social work and fund-raising, including cross-sectarian agitation against poverty with Gregoire Haddad, Greek Catholic archbishop of Beirut.[85] His proclivities dovetailed with the moderate national restructuring of the Shihabists.

Al-Sadr represented an ideal alternative to the Shia political chiefs, who displayed little interest in the social improvement of the rural population, and radical ideological parties like the Communists and the Ba'th. Military intelligence supported al-Sadr in the Beirut suburbs. Presidents Shihab and Helou backed his drive for a Shia authority to match the Supreme Islamic Council of the Sunnis (1955) and the Druze Communal Council (1962). Parliament established the Higher Shia Islamic Council in May 1967, against Sunni objections but with Christian backing.[86] The Shihabists thus shepherded a new mass Shia assertion that would develop fully with the 1978–1979 Islamic revolution in Iran, ironic considering Shihab's concern with national fusion.

A turning point for Shihab came in late 1961. After the 1960 elections, the president appointed Sa'ib Salam as prime minister, perhaps to appease him. It did not go well. Salam believed that the Sunni premier should be equal to the Maronite president, certainly in choosing ministers. He also blamed Shihab's military stalwarts Ahmad al-Hajj and Sami al-Khatib for subverting his client base.[87] In October 1961, Salam resigned when the president deserted him against the insubordinate Kamal Junblat, successively his minister of education and public works. Shihab brought back Rashid Karami, and Salam joined Chamoun, Edde, and Kamil al-Asa'ad in the opposition. Then, on December 30, 1961, the SSNP and junior officers attempted a coup against Shihab.[88] The party was hounded by military intelligence and hated the regime's liaison with Nasser. Its farcical plot fell apart, but it shocked Shihab and his entourage. They regarded Chamoun and Edde as complicit and instigated political trench warfare. In following years, this tarnished Shihabism.

Overall, Shihabism only tinkered with the political and economic system and could not ultimately be satisfactory to Sunni or Shia Muslims. Shihab never got to recalibrating sectarian allocations, let alone looking beyond sectarianism. He refused to found a proper political party to sustain reform and a state freed from elite patronage politics.[89] Shihab had no confidence in anything beyond the ad hoc devices of co-opting key personalities like Karami, Junblat, and Gemayel; using the security machine to sap adversaries; and creating new bureaucracy to circumvent the old one. His vindictiveness after 1961 meant fighting fire with fire—sordid new client structures and protection rackets to bring down those of recalcitrant politicians. There is little doubt that military intelligence tipped Chamoun and Edde out of their seats in the 1964 parliamentary elections.[90] An embittered Sa'ib Salam survived in Beirut, his domination of the resources of the Maqasid foundation— more than ever the central Sunni communal institution—compensating for loss of his street enforcers or "keys."[91] Beirut's Sunni middle class stood with him, resentful of state bias toward Tripoli and the Shia. Salam also turned to Saudi support against the Egyptian embassy, the regime, and his Nasserite rival Uthman al-Dana.

Given how he came to office in 1958, Shihab could not circumvent the constitution to stay beyond 1964. The May 1964 parliamentary elections provided the votes for a new Shihabist president; Shihab promoted Charles Helou, a respected journalist and businessman. Helou was from a mountain family that had contributed a Maronite patriarch, Yuhanna al-Hilu, in the days of Bashir II Shihab. Helou founded the newspaper *Le Jour* in 1936 and organized the "third force" in 1958. However, he had no personal following.

Helou was clean, but by the mid-1960s, Shihabism reeked. Military intelligence and its agents infiltrated Beirut's criminal underworld, with possible connection to the May 1966 murder of Kamil Mrouwe, publisher-editor of the newspapers *al-Hayat* and *The Daily Star*. Mrouwe was a fierce critic of Egyptian and Nasserite influences. In October 1966, Lebanon's largest bank, Intra, owned by the Palestinian-born Orthodox Christian Yusuf Baydas, collapsed with suspicion of a regime role. Intra rose meteorically from its founding in 1951, controlled Middle East Airlines, Beirut port, and Casino du Liban. It aroused much Lebanese jealousy. Lebanon's new central bank stood aside from a crippling run on Intra deposits. The state then took over Intra assets in a holding company of the same name. A procession of smaller banks followed Intra into insolvency, and Lebanon's commercial sector faltered. Baydas fled to Brazil pursued by legal charges, which highlighted the precarious position of even wealthy Palestinians in Lebanon.

Shihab's wife later cited him as saying that he had built a state but failed to make a nation.[92] The situation was not so simple. Neither Shihab nor anyone else could make the Lebanese a conventional "nation," implying fundamental agreement on the meaning and orientation of their homeland. As for the regime, Shihab's enterprise remained in its early stages, and in the mid-1960s, the Shihabist state looked shaky in its tussle with a majority of the elite. In late 1965, its ally, Kamal Junblat, linked with the militant left, principally the Communists, because of regime shortcomings in social and sectarian affairs; the glass ceiling restricting the Druze leader to being a "local *za'im*" was becoming intolerable to him.[93] By promoting Junblat, Pierre Gemayel, and Musa al-Sadr as levers for reshaping the Merchant Republic, Shihab courted Druze, Maronites, and Shia separately. Nonetheless, this did not really compromise state integrity. The real blow for Shihab and Helou was the June 1967 "Six Day" Arab-Israeli War.

Toward Catastrophe, 1967–1975

What if the June 1967 war, with its humiliation of the Arab states and activation of the Palestinians in Lebanon, had not happened? Muslim grumblings about Maronite advantage, Shia grievances about deprivation, and social cleavages were not enough to bring the catastrophe that befell Lebanon in the mid 1970s.[94] Shihabism had for the moment lost its way, but it had narrowed infrastructural gaps, if not income disparities. Without the new Palestinian pressures in Lebanon after 1967, Shihab would probably have returned as president in 1970. If he had done so, he may well have managed to implement something like the 1989 Ta'if recalibration of Lebanese sectarian politics by the mid-1970s, avoiding fifteen years of chaos.

Without Palestinian military mobilization, Kamal Junblat could not have held destruction of the system over the heads of the Maronites, nor would Sunni bosses have pressed "the Arab cause" to the point of paralyzing the regime. As for the Shia, Musa al-Sadr would not have disappeared in wartime circumstances in 1978 and may have deflected the effects of the 1978–1979 Islamic Revolution in Iran. More broadly, Lebanon would have been spared much of its disastrous late twentieth-century evolution, perhaps the worst of the conceivable alternative realities. The Arab regimes—Ba'thist Syria and Nasser's Egypt—that so cavalierly proceeded into the June 1967 crisis have much to answer for.

Lebanon of course had issues that would have brought trouble if not dealt with. In a pessimistic 1973 analysis, Halim Barakat dissected the country as a poorly integrated "social mosaic."[95] He noted a persistent lack of consensus between Christians and Muslims about Lebanon's destiny and basic resistance to social assimilation. He was, however, wrong in representing the period from 1860 to the 1920s as characterized by "outright conflict" among communities, and his public opinion data from 1968–1969 already reflected tension arising from Palestinian militarization.[96] Whatever the falling out of individuals or the misdemeanors of the Shihabist machine, by the mid-1960s, the Maronite and Sunni elites had an unprecedented understanding of each other and operated together with increased facility after the scare of 1958. Shihab's cultivation of al-Sadr also offered a new Maronite-Shia track. A phase of sharpened communal sentiment was probably inevitable as the new Shia urban population pressed for a better deal and a greater role. Given the prominence of moderate reformers like

Shihab and al-Sadr, and without the shock of June 1967, the pressure of such sentiment could actually have assisted a more honest Lebanese partnership.

Clearly, political chiefs were not inclined to shift away from client placement in a corrupt bureaucracy or to tax for social needs. Nonetheless, Lebanon's free enterprise economy, mildly adjusted to assist industry and produce more tax revenue under a return of Fuad Shihab as president in 1970, could have financed better salaries in a cleaned-up administration and promoted upskilling of the poor. Whatever their defects, Lebanon's pluralist politics and civil society provided better prospects than authoritarian Arab states for cajoling resource provision.

Without the overwhelming impact of Palestinian militarization, there would have been time and opportunities to ameliorate domestic imbalances. Possibly Lebanon's ruling class would not have moved without urban rioting or mass Shia disobedience, which could have spilled into a 1958 style insurrection. Even with outside meddling, the latter would have been more limited than what actually began in 1975.

Without the 1967 war, the Lebanese state could have contained the Palestinians in Lebanon much longer. In parallel, the 1949 armistice with Israel would have persisted little disturbed, with the Lebanese government protesting to other Arabs its inability to confront Israel. Of course the squalid refugee camps on the fringes of Tyre, Sidon, Beirut, and Tripoli constituted a menace. Their residents had doubled from 100,000 or so in 1949, and quiescent waiting for Arab armies to liberate Palestine was cracking.[97] In the mid-1960s, Palestinian militant groups conducted military training in Lebanon after the Arab League founded the Palestine Liberation Organization (PLO) in 1964. Lebanese military intelligence monitored the camps, but a poor, stateless population with no Lebanese civil rights could not sit in stasis forever. In Beirut, increased friction with the Lebanese state was expected, especially considering the interplay of the camps with neighboring Shia suburbs in the "belt of misery"—poverty-stricken environs of the capital—that reached from Karantina and Burj Hammoud in the east, separating Christian Ashrafiya from Mount Lebanon, to Shiyyah and Burj al-Barajneh in the south. The predominance of secular rather than religious radicalism in the 1960s eased interaction of Palestinian Sunnis and Lebanese Shia. At the same time, given that the Palestinians in Lebanon were equivalent to about 8 percent of Lebanon's own people and overwhelmingly Sunni Muslim, no chance existed that Christians or Shia would accept their integration. More Palestinian problems for the Lebanese security machine, including attempts to provoke Israel, seemed likely from the mid-1960s. These would have been subdued compared with the repercussions of the 1967 war.

Overall, the outcome of the June 1967 war and its transformation of Middle Eastern geopolitics were decisive to subsequent events in Lebanon, leading to the catastrophic breakdown of the mid-1970s. Israel's seizure of all remaining territory of British mandatory Palestine, meaning the West Bank from Jordan and Gaza from Egypt, and the collapsed credibility of Arab regimes determined the Palestinian refugees in Jordan, Syria, and Lebanon on direct resistance, in contrast to 1949–1967. The stain of shame at first left the front-line Arab states of the Levant little choice but to facilitate the Palestinian will. From being on the margin of a largely dormant conflict that only sporadically concerned it between 1949 and 1967, Lebanon became uniquely exposed. First, the country offered the best access for Palestinian fighters to Israel, by both land and sea. In contrast, Israel had the buffers of the Golan Heights and the West Bank in facing Syria and Jordan. Second, Lebanon's multicommunal regime and open political system made it impossible to curb Palestinian military activity without splitting and paralyzing the regime. In contrast, once Hafiz al-Asad took full control in Damascus in late 1970 and King Hussein decided to deploy his army, the Syrian and Jordanian autocracies could rigorously regulate the Palestinians on their territories. Reconciling repression with Arab credentials simply required unloading Palestinian guerillas on Lebanon, which fell apart under the strain.

Lebanon did not face instant repercussions from the June 1967 war. Initially, the mobilizing Palestinian resistance organizations, most prominently Fatah under Yasir Arafat, attempted an uprising on the occupied West Bank, taken down by the Israelis by the end of 1967. They then established bases around new refugee camps in the Jordan valley for raids against the Israelis from Jordan. Meanwhile, Lebanon mainly continued normal life through the late 1960s. With commerce in a brief downturn after the Intra affair, President Helou took the opportunity to assist manufacturing by decreeing export subsidies and tax breaks.[98] Industry thereby expanded in the outskirts of Beirut, mainly textiles and consumer goods using cheap labor. Agriculture, however, continued to require less labor, and industry could only make up about one-fifth of rural job losses through the 1960s.[99] As a result, the service sector increased its economic predominance between 1967 and 1970.

Construction boomed as services, commerce, tourism, and the property market entered a brief new golden period in the late 1960s; the built-up area of Beirut doubled between 1968 and 1972.[100] Syrian companies and unskilled Syrian workers dominated construction. Syrians also took up seasonal work in agriculture as Lebanese left the land. They received lower remuneration than Lebanese, and employers did not have to pay into the new social security fund for them. The number of transient Syrian workers, mainly single males, rose from 50,000 in 1961 to 145,000 in 1964 and 279,000 in 1970, when they were one-third of the total workforce in Lebanon.[101] Given that 39 percent of the Lebanese workforce was unskilled in 1970, the Syrians competed with a mass of poor, uneducated Lebanese, but there was little overt friction.[102] Otherwise, the

Lebanese economy benefited from the flight of wealthy Syrians and their capital from the Ba'thist regime through the 1960s.[103]

The new Palestinian military activity began to affect Lebanon with the Karameh battle in Jordan in late March 1968. Guerillas and the Jordanian army stood firm against the Israelis, which spurred enthusiasm and recruitment in Lebanon among Palestinians and Lebanese Muslims. After a huge funeral for a Lebanese volunteer, Prime Minister Abdullah Yafi endorsed Palestinian military use of Lebanon.[104] This shocked Kata'ib leader Pierre Gemayel, notwithstanding his praise for the martyr. Gemayel had already joined Chamoun and Edde in a broad opposition, *al-hilf al-thulathi* (the tripartite alliance), for the mid-1968 parliamentary elections. Beirut Sunni leader Sa'ib Salam and the Maronite *hilf* fought the Shihabist machine to a draw in the division of the new chamber; Helou, estranged from Shihab, stood aloof.[105]

While Maronite chiefs expressed disquiet and their Sunni counterparts welcomed Lebanon's embroilment in the Arab-Israeli conflict, the Palestinians inaugurated action against Israel on the Lebanese border. Several hundred fighters from Fatah and the Syrian sponsored Sa'iqa group infiltrated from Syria into the Arqub area on the southwestern slopes of Mount Hermon, adjoining Israel and the Golan Heights.[106] The first Palestinian cross-border raid occurred in June 1968, followed in October by the first Lebanese army clash with infiltrators and the first Israeli retaliation in southern Lebanon. On December 30, 1968, Israeli commandos destroyed thirteen Middle East Airlines aircraft at Beirut airport after Palestinians from Lebanon belonging to the Marxist Popular Front for the Liberation of Palestine (PFLP) attacked an El Al plane at Athens. Lebanon was thereafter an Arab-Israeli arena.

Could Lebanon regulate the Palestinian-armed groups and maintain some say in its future? By mid-1969, the Arqub hosted up to 600 guerillas out of 4,000 in southern Lebanon.[107] When the Lebanese army tried to assert its supremacy by force in April and May, the proscribed militants of the Lebanese Left turned protest into clashes with internal security in Beirut and other towns. In October 1969, the army moved to stop Palestinian expansion west from the Arqub, laying siege to Fatah fighters in Bint Jubayl. This brought Syrian closure of the border, caused Prime Minister Karami to suspend his official activities, and precipitated street violence in Beirut, Tripoli, and Sidon. President Helou and army commander Emile Bustani were forced into a humiliating settlement with the PLO, the coordinating body of the Palestinian groups, headed by Fatah's Arafat since February 1969. On November 3, General Bustani signed the Cairo agreement with Arafat, under Nasser's supervision, by which Lebanon accepted PLO military freedom in the Arqub and the refugee camps, agreed to facilitate Palestinian access to the border with Israel, and received perfunctory affirmation of Lebanese sovereignty.[108] The Lebanese, particularly Maronites, could see that even the military stiffening and Arab orientation of the Shihabist state counted for nothing in upholding Lebanon's integrity.

Into 1970, the PLO used the Cairo agreement to build the Palestinian-armed presence in the Beirut camps, particularly Tel al-Za'atar to the east and Burj al-Barajneh to the south. PLO coordination of Palestinians in Karantina and Dbaye from Tel al-Za'atar and linkage with Shia leftists in nearby Naba'a and Burj Hammoud threatened access from Christian eastern Beirut to the mountain. Palestinian armed manifestations around Tel al-Za'atar impinged on Christian neighborhoods, triggering clashes in March 1970, including the brief abduction of Pierre Gemayel's son Bashir.[109] Most Maronites could not fathom what any of this had to do with confronting Israel. In May, PLO firing into Israel brought fierce Israeli bombardment across southern Lebanon. Many Shia now left their villages for Beirut as refugees.[110] Musa al-Sadr and Kamil al-Asa'ad held rallies slating the impotence of the Lebanese state. Both the Shia plight and the new flow of angry people into Beirut deepened Christian apprehension.

Between mid-1970 and mid-1971, developments tilted Lebanon toward unviability, though the implications took time to become apparent. Kamal Junblat, who in April 1969 set his PSP at the head of a National Movement of leftist parties demanding Palestinian freedom of action, took his opportunity as interior minister in the government preceding the August 1970 presidential election to legalize his partners—the Nasserites, Ba'thists, Communists, and the SSNP.[111] The SSNP had shifted in the late 1960s from hard right to hard left.[112] Only the PSP had real public weight, courtesy of Junblat, but all had noteworthy paramilitaries trained by the PLO.

In the run-up to the presidential election, Shihab withdrew his candidacy because he suspected Lebanon would be ungovernable. Gemayel, Chamoun, and Edde cancelled out one another, leaving the Shihabist Ilyas Sarkis and the anti-Shihabist Sulayman Faranjiya. Backed by Salam, al-Asa'ad, and the Maronite *hilf*, Sulayman embodied the Merchant Republic. He had inherited paramountcy in the Faranjiya family of Zgharta when his brother Hamid was crippled by a stroke in October 1957.[113] Also in 1957, he fled an arrest warrant after a deadly church shoot-out between the Faranjiya and Duwayhi clans, taking sanctuary in the home of a young Syrian air force officer, Hafiz al-Asad. Junblat gave Faranjiya his one-vote presidential victory in 1970; for Junblat, nothing remained of the Shihabist project except the hated military intelligence.[114] Faranjiya painted himself as liberator of the high bourgeoisie from the Shihabist state, friend of Syria who would indulge the Left and the Palestinians, and upholder of Maronite privilege and Lebanese sovereignty—an impossible mix.

A regional shift immediately followed when King Hussein of Jordan went to war with Palestinian forces encamped on his territory, threatening his rule.

In September 1970 and July 1971, the Jordanian monarch reduced and then expelled the PLO. Through 1971, thousands of guerillas and their families transited into Lebanon, with demographic and political implications alarming to Christians.[115] Equally significant, the reckless Syrian military intervention against King Hussein ordered by Ba'thist strongman Salah Jadid during the September 1970 fighting led defense minister Hafiz al-Asad to seize the Syrian presidency. Asad provided Syria with its first stable regime in two decades, and Damascus could give Lebanon more consistent attention. Up to 1973, Asad's priority was preparation, together with Egypt's Anwar Sadat, for launching the October 1973 war against Israel, but from 1973 to 1975, Syrian support encouraged the PLO to defy the Lebanese state. The new Syrian regime also showed interest in Syrian workers in Lebanon, from 1971 onward demanding reciprocal social security provision—a demand evaded by the Lebanese.[116]

The tumultuous month of September 1970 also saw the sudden death of President Gamal Abdel Nasser of Egypt after he arranged a truce between King Hussein and the PLO. Palestinian uncertainty about Nasser's successor, Anwar Sadat, and the battered condition of the PLO in 1971 temporarily lowered the temperature in Lebanon.[117] For the longer term, the PLO in Lebanon was massively reinforced, but it needed a quiet period to reorganize, re-arm the fugitives from King Husayn, and test the Faranjiya regime. Arafat arrived in Beirut from Jordan but adopted a low profile. He also had to contend with disputes between Fatah and other factions within the PLO.

How did the new Lebanese president handle his breathing space? First, Faranjiya purged military intelligence. While understandable in view of Shihabist behavior, this crippled the state in facing Palestinian, Syrian, Israeli, and local radical activities. Second, Faranjiya shied away from backing Prime Minister Sa'ib Salam against Kamal Junblat, deserting the leading Sunni of Beirut. Salam refused Junblat a cabinet post; Junblat hounded him, claiming he had links with the CIA.[118] Faranjiya thus reran Shihab's alienation of Salam. Third, although Faranjiya endorsed a technocrat government in November 1970, he would not allow ministers to address social grievances. After 1970, property speculation surged with rising Arab oil revenues. Many Lebanese, especially Muslims, simply experienced higher inflation on stagnant real incomes. An overheated, socially unbalanced economy stirred boisterous street protests, helping Junblat and the Palestinians to overawe the Sunni leadership.

The April 1972 parliamentary elections registered a last hurrah for independent Lebanon. These were "the best organized and most honest" contests ever.[119] Three radical leftists broke into the parliamentary club.[120] A Nasserite, Najah Wakim, defeated Prime Minister Salam's candidate for an Orthodox Christian seat in Beirut, taking Sunni votes. All three—a Sunni, an Orthodox, and a Shia in Tripoli, Beirut, and Tyre respectively—disrupted the lists of political bosses.

The elections produced an unprecedented thirty-nine new members, 40 percent of the chamber.

Calm between Israel and the Palestinians prevailed for a few more months, punctured in September 1972 with the massacre of Israeli athletes at the Munich Olympic games. Israel held Arafat's Fatah responsible and conducted a ground incursion and air raids in the largest assault on Lebanon yet seen. To Arab acclaim, the Lebanese army resisted the Israelis, but to Maronite bosses this was just another alarm bell. By early 1973, Arafat had tightened his grip on the PLO and dampened Palestinian factionalism. The PLO had integrated thousands of fighters from Jordan into an inflated military structure. One sign of new PLO strength was Arafat's success in January in having the Palestinian National Council establish a special authority under his headship to exert military command over all the groups.[121]

In April 1973, in more retaliation for the Munich affair, Israel landed commandos in Beirut who killed three senior PLO personalities. The landing was unopposed, and Prime Minister Salam demanded Faranjiya sack army chief Iskander Ghanim. The president refused and Salam resigned. To avoid appointing Rashid Karami, Faranjiya replaced Salam with Amin al-Hafiz, a second-rank Sunni. The Sunni establishment interpreted this as disenfranchising Sunni leaders and devaluing the premiership; it further compromised Maronite-Sunni trust as a new crisis regarding the Palestinian presence unfolded.[122]

With the PLO now rivaling the army in its number of troops and a creeping Palestinian takeover of parts of Beirut, President Faranjiya and General Ghanim inclined to last-ditch action to assert state sovereignty. When the Popular Democratic Front for the Liberation of Palestine (PDFLP) kidnapped Lebanese soldiers on May 1–2, 1973, the army launched its largest operation against the Palestinians. The army clashed with Arafat's Fatah, the PLO shelled the airport, and Faranjiya had the air force bomb the Palestinian camps. Syria and Egypt were alarmed that the events might upset their plans for war with Israel.[123] To bring his old friend to heel, Syria's Hafiz al-Asad imposed an economic boycott on Lebanon and permitted hundreds of Palestinian guerillas to cross from Syria into the Biqa and Wadi al-Taym. Within a week, in mid-May, Faranjiya suspended the offensive and made an accord with the PLO in Beirut's Melkart Hotel reiterating the 1969 Cairo agreement. The Egyptians pressured the Palestinians to accept restrictions and not to attack Israel from Lebanon.[124] In reality, the PLO did not retreat from the territories it occupied, including an enlarged buffer zone around its headquarters in the Sunni Fakhani district of western Beirut.[125] Fatah reinforcements from Syria stayed. The army had failed, and President Faranjiya advised Gemayel and Chamoun that Christians should look to their own resources.[126]

From mid-1973, Gemayel's Kata'ib and Chamoun's smaller National Liberal Party strove to close enough of the military gap with the Palestinians and the

Lebanese Left for credible deterrence. In particular, they acquired heavier weaponry—mortars and artillery—probably through a combination of Lebanese army, CIA, Jordanian, and black market channels.[127] The parties in Junblat's National Movement kept pace with them, while the Lebanese army was thereafter neutralized by regime paralysis and fears of dissolution along sectarian lines. Without the army, PLO capabilities overshadowed everyone. International diplomatic activity after the October 1973 Arab-Israeli War only intensified uneasiness. Greater Arab and international respectability for the PLO, culminating in Arafat's reception at the United Nations in November 1974, irritated Lebanese Christians; for them, it assisted the PLO in cementing its "state within the state." Simultaneously, international concentration on arrangements between Israel and Arab states excited Muslim and PLO suspicions of a sell-out of the Palestinians.

Between April and June 1974, raids into northern Israel by radical PLO factions brought Israeli bombing across Jabal Amil. More Shia villagers decamped to Beirut, where a bust in construction through 1974 meant even fewer jobs, and price inflation for staple foods reached 100 percent.[128] Already on March 17, Musa al-Sadr held a rally of 75,000 Shia in Baalbek at which he inaugurated his "movement of the deprived," soon to become the paramilitary Amal organization.[129] Continuing Shia displacement also furnished more recruits in Beirut for the Left and the PLO. Combined with Junblat's rhetoric against Maronite privilege and plain ambition to enroll Palestinian weight behind his call for a new Lebanese system, this could only further alarm Maronites. In July 1974, clashes between the Kata'ib and the Popular Front for the Liberation of Palestine General Command (PFLP-GC) around Tel al-Za'atar ended with joint Kata'ib/ PLO/army patrols. For everyone the state was becoming irrelevant.[130]

Within the political elite, convergence and divergence crisscrossed chaotically into late 1974 and early 1975. President Faranjiya gravitated to the Maronite "right" on sovereignty, but indulged the National Movement Left when he appointed Junblat's friend Rashid al-Sulh prime minister in November 1974. In appointing Rashid al-Sulh, Faranjiya brought the two stronger Sunni leaders, Karami and Salam, together against him. In late 1974, they combined with Raymond Edde, alienated from Gemayel over his brother's displacement from parliament in the 1972 elections, in an alignment (*tahaluf*) against the regime. Karami and Salam joined Musa al-Sadr and Junblat's National Movement in demanding a revised National Pact with more power for the Islamic sector. However, the non-Christian convergence was superficial. In early 1975, Karami hinted he might support a crackdown on the PLO if Gemayel accepted change in the Maronite-Sunni balance.[131] Al-Sadr did not trust either the Sunni elite or Junblat; he maintained his own channels to the Maronites. Junblat's ambition and volatility precluded smooth relations with Sunni or Shia leaders.

Popular sectarian feeling was subdued in early 1975 compared with 1958.[132] Cross-communal social and professional organizations, trade unions, and parties were at a peak, and the Kata'ib and Christian leaders had never been so open to the Arab world. For his part, Yasir Arafat wanted to keep Fatah, the largest PLO faction, out of Lebanese affairs and had decent relations with Gemayel and other Maronites. Yet the push of Junblat, the hard left, and radical PLO factions toward revolution aroused Christian fear. The magnitude of the Palestinian "state within the state" and what they saw as PLO disregard of Lebanon disturbed Maronites. Given the fragmentation of the regime and Sunni sympathy with the Palestinians, there was no control mechanism in case of shocks that might happen at any moment. Arafat's personal preferences hardly counted; Maronite leaders wanted Fatah downsized, and Junblat and the radicals wanted it embroiled.

Two events tipped Lebanon from occasional clashes into continuous hostilities between the Maronite paramilitaries and the Leftist/Palestinian combine. These hostilities sidelined the regime and state. On February 28, 1975, a gunman mortally wounded Nasserite leader Ma'ruf Sa'ad during a demonstration of Sidon fishermen against a fishing concession to a large company chaired by Camille Chamoun. Lebanese soldiers exchanged fire with Nasserites and Palestinians. Sunni leaders demanded Rashid al-Sulh's resignation as prime minister and the end of Maronite headship of the army. On this occasion, Junblat tried to calm matters, to protect his influence through Rashid al-Sulh. On April 13, the shooting of several Kata'ib personnel at an Ayn al-Rumana church precipitated the Kata'ib's killing of twenty-seven Palestinians on a bus transiting Ayn al-Rumana. Fighting ensued across suburban Beirut, with three hundred dead in three days. At the same time, Junblat's National Movement declared a boycott of any government containing the Kata'ib. This was a declaration of war.

Cultural Breakout

It is ironic that even as it approached war and state breakdown in the mid-1970s, Lebanon achieved a reduction in educational and literacy disparities and underwent literary explorations that made it a cultural trendsetter in the Arab world. In its small territory, Lebanon experienced enhanced integration of core and periphery, of village and city, as migration brought the "mountain" to Beirut and more rural and Muslim youth passed through more public schools. The problem was that different "mountains" came to different parts of Beirut, and political breakdown was to privilege communal self-consciousness over a real but fragile Lebanese identity. Even as a mounting stream of Shia arrived in the "belt of misery" from the late 1950s onward, a more measured and long-standing drift of Maronite villagers continued into eastern outliers of the capital, to inflate a Christian lower middle class that itself felt precariously poised in Lebanese society. At the same time, Lebanese cultural expression shifted from a literature and stage performance that in the 1950s emphasized a depoliticized rural ideal suitable for the regime and tourism to increasingly tense, tortured, cynical literary outputs after 1967. The latter were predominantly urban, realist, and sympathetic to the left and the Palestinians. Female novelists emerged to vent frustration with male domination of public and private life.

Lebanon had the highest literacy levels in the Arab world in the 1970s. UNESCO data indicate that 36.7 percent of the adult population was illiterate in 1970, down to 31.4 percent in 1975.[133] Comparative figures for Syria were 58.9 percent lowering to 52.3 percent, and for Jordan, 44.9 percent lowering to 37.7 percent. The gap between men and women for Lebanon remained as shocking as in other Arab countries; in 1975, male illiteracy in Lebanon was 20.1 percent compared with 42.7 percent for females. Nonetheless, Lebanon had the highest literacy for both sexes. Among the communities, the yawning gaps of 1932 data (83 percent of Shia illiterate, 66 percent of Sunnis, and 48 percent of Maronites) no longer applied in the 1970s.[134] For 1974, one estimate indicated that 32.8 percent of Muslims were illiterate or partially literate, compared with 27.8 percent of Christians.[135] Independent Lebanon had done a reasonable job of producing communal convergence in basic education.

The major achievement through the 1950s and 1960s was provision of public schools, particularly in the areas added to Mount Lebanon in 1920, to give Muslims modest compensation for the Christian edge in private education. Interestingly, although the Shihabist 1960s witnessed the most activity, the margin over the Chamounist 1950s was not great. For example, the state established thirty new schools in southern Lebanon in 1950–1959 compared to forty-eight in 1960–1969.[136] In the 1970s, the private (largely Christian, but including the Sunni Maqasid) and public (most pupils Muslim, but with many rural Christians) school networks were of similar scale. Public school growth was overwhelmingly primary; 1972 statistics indicated that 80 percent of the Lebanese workforce had either no education or none beyond primary level, although this workforce substantially comprised the less educated previous generation.[137]

In contrast to the general Arab trend, linguistic diversity continued in Lebanese schools, with prominent roles for French and English alongside Arabic. The private schools retained their qualitative superiority, including for foreign language instruction. The Muslim bourgeoisie still valued a top Maronite institution like Collège de la Sagesse, teaching in French and a century old in 1975.

There were also the Protestant schools of western Beirut, Collège Protestant Français and International College.

University education in Lebanon expanded considerably from the 1950s.[138] The state entered higher education with the founding of the Lebanese University in 1951. In its first decade, this was a modest institution in part focusing on teacher training, but it acquired new facilities in the Shihabist period and emerged as a serious national institution in the 1970s with 10,000 students. In 1960, a Sunni charity with backing from Alexandria University in Egypt established the Beirut Arab University, which grew rapidly to 14,000 students by 1970. In 1961, Pierre Gemayel led a Christian sectarian campaign against equivalence of Arab University degrees to those of other universities for entry to the professions, particularly law. The Beirut lawyers' guild declared a strike, while for Gemayel, UAR backing of the Arab University represented "Nasserite targeting of the freedom of Lebanese Christians, and of their political existence and culture."[139] In the end, the government conceded Arab University equivalence to the Lebanese University. Also in 1961, the Maronite Order of Monks founded L'Université Saint-Esprit at Kaslik, near Jounieh. This became a small high-quality institution with a fine library, a cultural showpiece for the Maronite church.

The original private universities, the Anglophone American University of Beirut (AUB) and the Francophone Université Saint-Joseph (USJ) maintained their preeminence. Each developed a full range of faculties, with both noted for medicine and USJ for law; each grew to about five thousand students by 1975. The small Haigazian University College of the Armenians (founded in 1955) and Beirut Women's College (founded in 1925), which became the coeducational Beirut University College in 1974, may be considered associates of the AUB in the 1970s. They were both Anglophone Protestant establishments.

USJ retained a largely Lebanese Christian student body, whereas by the 1970s at least half of the students at the AUB were Muslim, with many Palestinians and other Arabs. While USJ continued to provide personnel for upper echelons of the regime and administration, AUB students developed radical politics in the hothouse liberal atmosphere of Ra's Beirut. The noted Arabist thinker Constantine Zurayk, an Orthodox Christian from Damascus who became AUB vice president in the 1950s, patronized Arab nationalist students from the 1930s. The Palestinian Orthodox Christian medical graduate George Habash and like-minded Arab students established the Arab Nationalist Movement in 1951. This was socialist and opposed to Arab particularism, which made Habash's later Palestinian nationalist role as founder in 1967 of the PFLP incongruous. In 1954, the AUB administration disbanded the student council after a campus riot against the Baghdad Pact.[140] Students struck in reaction to the December 1968

Israeli raid on the Beirut airport, and thereafter the Palestinian cause convulsed the campuses of the AUB and the Lebanese and Arab Universities. In January 1971, students abandoned classes to protest Jordanian assaults on the PLO.[141] While hard left remedies for the plight of the downtrodden entranced well-heeled AUB students, the male youth of the real Maronite, Muslim, and Palestinian underclass headed toward internecine strife that would shred bourgeois leftist dreams.

Lebanon's change of gear in the late 1960s from a broadly optimistic trajectory, with bumps along the way, to increasing exposure of fragility and uncertainty is reflected in the country's literature and arts. In the 1940s and 1950s, an array of largely Christian male poets propagated the line of Michel Chiha and Khalil Gibran—building a national image centered on a special mountain society disconnected from the Arab hinterland.[142] Contributors included Ilyas Abu Shabaka, Sa'id Aql, and Michel Trad. From 1959, the image transferred to the Baalbek stage performances of Fayruz, Lebanon's great female singer, and the Rahbanis, Fayruz's husband and his brother. For Lebanese, Fayruz and the Baalbek festivities retain a powerful, even desperate magnetism both despite and because of Lebanon's late twentieth-century catastrophe.

Through the 1960s, the literary scene became more intricate. Poets involved in the *Shi'r* magazine, such as Yusuf al-Khal and the Syrian-turned-Lebanese Ali Ahmad Sa'id (Adonis), promoted revolution and greater Syria but sided with Chamoun in 1958 and pushed Western-style avant-garde against Arab conservatism.[143] In 1958, the female Shia novelist Layla Ba'albaki gave the first Lebanese exposé of male repression and denigration of women in *Ana Ahya* (*"I Live"*), and in 1964 was subjected to trial for pornography over her short story "Spaceship of Tenderness to the Moon."[144] After 1967, Fayruz and the Rahbanis joined the Palestinian fashion and devoted more stage attention to realities of urban Lebanon.

For female and male writers alike, the early 1970s presented darkening horizons and a failure of political and social imagination.[145] Tawfiq Awwad dismissed politicians and gave a cynical appraisal of the intersection of ideology and reality in his 1972 novel *Tawahin Beirut* (*"Death in Beirut"*).

> Within a few days the movement had lost its first purity. It was polluted by all kinds of dregs that brought their mud with them. Every wind that blew brought vapours from places where fanaticism and extremism were manufactured. . . . The traditional street bosses and those who dealt in influence had infiltrated the ranks of the students.[146]

On the stage, Fayruz's son Ziyad Rahbani at once satirized and flaunted social revolution in a vigorous Lebanese "national" colloquial Arabic in 1974 in his first play *Nazl al-Surur* (*"Inn of Happiness"*). Also in 1974, a female Syrian author resident in Beirut, Ghada Samman, condemned a vicious, depraved city on the road to destruction in her novel *Beirut 75*. At the end, her demented surviving character switches signs at the entrance to Beirut:

> I burst out laughing as I read the sign saying "Hospital for the Mentally Ill," with Beirut looming up behind it in dawn's light like an infernal wild beast preparing to pounce.[147]

6

Broken Lebanon, 1975–2011

Lebanon ceased to be an independent state in 1975. Thirty-six years later, it has still not recovered the independence and relative coherence it enjoyed in the mid-twentieth century. The failure of the multicommunal regime, and the intrusion of Palestinians, Israelis, Syrians and others amid a welter of blood, had contradictory implications. On one hand, the debilitation and uncertainty that the war period of 1975–1990 bequeathed the following decades fostered a desperate attachment of ordinary people to land, home, and country—to their images of their Lebanon. Yet the breaking apart of the regime and the humiliation of the Lebanese state also threw people back on communal identities. This chapter traces the slide into sectarian insecurity, changing local and external alliances, and the new wave of external interventions.

Part of the magnified communalism came from the assertion of the Twelver Shia, by the 1960s Lebanon's largest single community. In the bourgeois Christian and Sunni Muslim imagining of Lebanon, the Shia were an afterthought. Through the 1970s, with the communal leadership of Musa al-Sadr as a catalyst, many Shia moved from favoring the socialist left and the Palestinians to embracing a Shia-centered Lebanese pluralism that challenged Maronite-led communal coexistence and the Maronite/Sunni partnership.[1]

Starting in the 1980s, competing Shia agendas advanced the Shia Islam of Lebanon as the most authentic spearhead for Lebanese multicommunalism.[2] The Amal movement projected the Shia pride and Lebanon-focused Arabism of Musa al-Sadr. Hezbollah, child of Iran's Islamic revolution, made resistance to Israel and Western intrusion the criterion of loyalty to Lebanon and aspired to a Khomeinist Islamic state. The senior Lebanese Shia religious scholar of the time, Muhammad Husayn Fadlallah, asserted a pious Lebanon, whether Muslim or Christian, under Shia preeminence.[3] Fadlallah and his followers stressed commitment to modernity; Fadlallah advocated women's rights and "scientific" Islam.[4] Nonetheless, their pluralism remained religion-centered. For years after 1990, their preferred Christian interlocutor was the Maronite church.

Throughout the chaos and spikes of violence between 1975 and 1990 and in response to Syrian overlordship and the Shia challenge after 1990, the other communities also changed. As the Maronites lost their grip on Lebanon, the Christian sects sheltered behind mainly Maronite politicians and the Maronite patriarch as their senior spiritual personality. By the 1990s, there was a recognizable Christian collective with a common sense of frustration and disempowerment. In parallel, Sunnis discovered the virtues of a multicommunal Lebanese state through its absence during the war years. By the mid-1980s, their powerlessness vis-à-vis Palestinian guerillas, the warlords of the mountain communities, and the Syrian army that entered Lebanon in 1976 made reassertion in a new Lebanese republic the Sunni priority. Most Sunnis became committed Lebanese as never before, and their external ties increasingly deemphasized radical Arabs in favor of conservative Arabs and the West. As for the Druze, the war years restored a strategic salience lost since the mid-nineteenth century, but they also heightened a sense of vulnerability, first to the Maronites and later to the Shia. In the 1990s, most Druze favored Sunni strength under Prime Minister Rafiq al-Hariri, not on the basis of prewar Arabism, but simply for survival.

With the assassination of Hariri and the enforced Syrian withdrawal from Lebanon in early 2005, Shia and Sunni Muslim leaders faced each other in a new divide. By this stage Hezbollah, with its credentials from combating Israel, its weaponry surpassing that of the Lebanese army, and its alignment with the Iranian and Syrian regimes, dominated the Shia community. Most Sunnis came to regard the weaponry and the alignment as threats and Hezbollah as involved in the murder of their senior leader. Christians divided between those who preferred the Maronite/Sunni partnership that ran prewar Lebanon and those targeted when Hariri and the Syrians operated together in the 1990s. The latter moved toward an understanding with Hezbollah. In contrast, most Druze preferred to stay with the Sunnis even when their leader, Walid Junblat, swung to Hezbollah and the Syrian regime after 2008.

There was a stalemate over national identity. A Shia-led pious Lebanon could never be sold to Sunnis and Druze, who were together at least equivalent to Shia in numbers. And in the end, most Maronites and other Christians could never be comfortable with either Shia- or Sunni-led identities. The Shia had come far since the 1970s in claiming a fair share in Lebanon's story; however, by 2011, with Hezbollah faltering as Syrians rose against their regime, they had reached the limits of their claim. Overarching nationhood had to find neutral ground.

In this context, Lebanon's cultural activity after 1975 expressed common adversity but did not contribute to nationhood. Wartime and postwar novelists had only a small audience for their social realism.[5] The highbrow and lowbrow culture that developed out of the war years into Lebanon's tenuous "second republic" reflected a numbed, shattered people, largely bereft of positive momentum. Novelist Elias

Khoury captured wartime dislocation of time, space, and social existence in his abstract *Gates of the City* (1981).[6] Most postwar writing focused on unhappy Lebanese circumstances, whether dysfunctional families, survival in a chaotic Beirut, resistance to Israel in the Shia south, or the anguish of exile. Satellite television and stage shows indulged both biting criticism of the postwar order and escapism.

Lebanese cultural navel-gazing did not mean solid national identity.[7] Under Syrian hegemony after 1990, the state returned with a vengeance as a mechanism of sectarian shares. The nation still did not amount to more than an inchoate notion of distinctiveness. Communal sensibility held the high ground. Hezbollah regularly roused Shia crowds for "Jerusalem Day" parades. In 1997, Catholic Christians produced a massive turnout to greet Pope John Paul VI, and the furious Sunni response to the Hariri murder spoke for itself.

In *The Story of Zahra* (1980), Hanan al-Shaykh portrays her Shia leading lady, Zahra, as circulating in a communal ghetto: the southern suburbs of Beirut, the rural south, and the Shia Diaspora in Africa.[8] Al-Shaykh also emphasizes the diversity of her community, with its jumbled secular and religious elements. In *I Sweep the Sun off Rooftops* (1998), Almaza's tin jug in the short story "The Marriage Fair" represents a sense of proportion in life:

> She devoted all her energy to growing bamboo and weaving it into baskets, only pausing occasionally as she worked to glance at her face in the tin jug that she always had with her. It fulfilled many functions: among other things, she used it for performing the ablutions required by religion, milking the animals and watering the potted plants.[9]

In the early twenty-first century, as Hezbollah tightened its grip, such a sense of proportion seemed a thing of the past for Lebanon's Shia.

War, 1975–1990

The paroxysm of violence in Beirut between April 13 and 16, 1975, embroiling the Christian Kata'ib with the Lebanese Left and Palestinian militants, proceeded wherever Christian suburbs faced Palestinian camps or the mainly Shia poorer quarters. The coalescence of Kamal Junblat's National Movement, Prime Minister Rashid al-Sulh, and the Palestinian leadership to excoriate the Kata'ib escalated the conflict. Al-Sulh and the Left disregarded the pull of the Kata'ib on a majority of Maronites.[10] Sa'ib Salam was the only Sunni *za'im* who might have given conciliation a chance, but he was alienated from President Faranjiya. Al-Sulh resigned in mid-May when his cabinet collapsed. In early July, Faranjiya had no alternative but to accept a government under Rashid

Karami, the president's rival in northern Lebanon. Events in Beirut fanned tension between the prime minister's home city—mainly Sunni Tripoli—and neighboring Maronite Zgharta, the president's hometown.

Karami's cabinet occasioned a two-month calm by incorporating the whole political spectrum, but its continuation depended on doing nothing. Maronite groups mobilized, while the Left demanded termination of Christian political advantage. In early September, hostility between Tripoli and Zgharta brought sectarian abductions. In mid-September, the Kata'ib tried to provoke Lebanese army intervention by bombarding Muslim bazaars in central Beirut, to which the other side responded in kind. Thereafter, there was no stopping disintegration of the Lebanese capital into militia and Palestinian fiefdoms. In October, the Kata'ib moved into the hotel district of western Beirut to cover command of the port, provoking fierce resistance.

From April 1975 onward, the fifteen-year chain reaction of violence caused at least 100,000 deaths, pushed more than 800,000 people to leave Lebanon, and displaced another half million people within the country. Sociologist Salim Nasr notes that the estimated population of 2.6 million in 1975 became only 2.7 million in 1990.[11] He also observed a marked decline in fertility for Shia, the most rapidly growing community from the 1950s to the 1970s.[12]

State and regime persisted, but they did so without authority. The country became a shell filled by warlords and foreign powers. At one point or another, the cockpit of the Levant involved not just Palestinians, Syrians, and Israelis but every significant Arab state, revolutionary Shia Iran, the Soviet Union, and the United States. Émigré remittances and the Palestinian "state within the state" sustained the economy and currency up to the early 1980s. In 1982, emigrant remittances peaked at $2 billion, and the local PLO budget virtually equaled that of the Lebanese state.[13] Thereafter, remittances declined, and detectable PLO infusions ceased.

Outburst, 1975–1977

Unlike the Lebanese Left and more militant Palestinians, neither Syrian President Hafiz al-Asad nor PLO Chairman Yasir Arafat devalued the Kata'ib, and both wanted a compromise in Beirut. Asad and Arafat, however, had clashing perspectives regarding the Palestinian position in Lebanon. Asad wanted a stable and obedient western flank to buttress Syria's role in the Arab World and face Israel, particularly when Israel and Egypt were arranging deals in Sinai under U.S. patronage. Arafat wanted to reinforce Palestinian autonomy in Lebanon to protect the PLO's new Arab and international status as recognized representative of the Palestinian people. Like Asad, Arafat was nervous about Egypt's momentum, but that did not make him amenable to becoming a satellite of Syria. Within the

PLO, Arafat stood between aides, such as Abu Jihad and Hani al-Hassan, concerned with safeguarding the Palestinian presence, and Abu Salih, who supported the revolutionary drive of the Lebanese Left.[14]

Asad's December 1975 invitation to Kata'ib leader Pierre Gemayel to talks in Damascus perturbed Palestinians and the Lebanese Left. An assassination squad killed four Kata'ib militiamen, presumably to derail any Kata'ib/Syrian rapprochement.[15] Kata'ib personnel went on a rampage, murdering approximately two hundred Muslims on the basis of identity cards. This event was the infamous "Black Saturday."[16] The Murabitun, a new Fatah-patronized Sunni militia, and Leftists responded in Beirut's hotel district by driving back the Kata'ib and the latter attacked Muslims in eastern Beirut and near Zahle. In Damascus, Gemayel divined Syrian determination to impose a settlement, and the Kata'ib therefore looked to bolster the Maronite territorial position.

In early January 1976, the Kata'ib and the National Liberal Party (NLP) militia of Camille Chamoun assaulted the Palestinian/Leftist outliers in eastern Beirut— principally Tel al-Za'atar, Karantina, and the mainly Shia suburb of Naba'a. These interrupted the continuity of the Christian suburbs. By January 19, the Maronite paramilitaries captured the Palestinian enclaves of Karantina and Dbaye, clearing the coast from Beirut to the Christian port city of Jounieh. They expelled the Palestinian, Kurdish, Syrian, and Shia inhabitants of Karantina and Maslakh, killing more than one thousand people.[17] Fatah now fully joined the campaign of the Left and the Palestinian militant factions, which enabled Junblat to unleash a National Movement/PLO assault to eject Christians from Damur, Chamoun's stronghold on the coast south of Beirut airport. The Left and the Palestinians massacred several hundred people as revenge for Karantina. This secured PLO communications between Beirut and southern Lebanon.

On each side, maximum coalescence occurred by February 1976. President Faranjiya, Pierre Gemayel, Camille Chamoun, and the head of the Maronite monastic orders, Charbel Qassis, established the Lebanese Front. Among top Maronites, only Raymond Edde opposed the war. He earned the nickname "Muhammad," ironic considering Sunni hostility toward his father in the 1930s.[18] Faranjiya joined because he rejected derogation of the Maronite presidency. In the north, the president's armed retainers under his son, Tony, fought the Sunni militiamen of Tripoli. For the Left, the Muslims, and the Palestinians, the high tide of collaboration came after the fall of Karantina, when PLO factions from Fatah to the Marxist PFLP and the Syrian-sponsored Sa'iqa operated together while the Syrian regime endorsed Junblat's Damur operation.[19] In late December 1975, Syria dispatched Palestinians of the Syrian-based Palestine Liberation Army (PLA) and Sa'iqa to the Biqa to bottle-up the Kata'ib in Zahle.[20] Asad authorized escalated intervention of disguised Syrians, and Syrian commanded Palestinians in mid-January.

Even without Syria, the Leftist/Muslim/Palestinian alliance had a numerical superiority of two to one, another reason for the Maronites to solidify their territory. The Kata'ib, NLP, and smaller Christian groups could muster 12,000 fighters in early 1976, equal to the Leftists and Murabitun, whereas the PLO, with its 30,000 guerillas, backed the latter.[21] Of course, much of the PLO remained in the south to face Israel.

While Arafat became embroiled on one side, Syria's Hafiz al-Asad avoided such entanglement. Syria conceived its pressure on the Kata'ib in early 1976 as nudging the parties into a Syrian-patronized settlement. In mid-1975, a Syrian committee (*lajna*) headed by Foreign Minister Abd al-Halim Khaddam, with air force chief Naji Jamil and army commander Hikmat Shihabi, handled the "Lebanese file."[22] Khaddam shuttled to Beirut and, with Asad, received visiting Lebanese. In early February 1976, Asad took advantage of Leftist/Palestinian strength to invite President Faranjiya and Prime Minister Karami to Damascus. The outcome was Faranjiya's "Constitutional Document," which adjusted the National Pact mildly in favor of Muslims.[23] Faranjiya accepted a shift from the six to five ratio of parliamentary seats to Christian/Muslim equality. Also, the parliament would elect the Sunni prime minister, who would sign decrees and laws together with the president. Otherwise, the Maronite/Sunni monopoly of the pinnacles of the state remained as did Maronite command of the army. Asad aimed to convince Christians to trust Syria and thereby avert an isolationist Little Lebanon drifting toward Israel.

Kamal Junblat and the Left parted company with Syria over Asad's deal with Faranjiya. The Druze *za'im* would remain shut out of top state jobs, whereas Maronite privilege persisted. In such conditions, elevated Sunni privilege cut no ice with the Druze leader; instead, he favored a "military solution" regardless of Syria. At this stage, Junblat's interests coincided with those of Arafat; facing the prospect of Syrian hegemony, Arafat decided to assert PLO freedom in Lebanon.

Starting in early 1976, Fatah incited Lieutenant Ahmad Khatib to split Muslim troops away from the Lebanese army to form a "Lebanese Arab Army."[24] Bitterness among Muslim officers about the failure of the Constitutional Document to address army reform inclined many to insurrection. Rather than discuss grievances, Faranjiya branded the dissidents as deserters, and in March 1976 the army fragmented.[25] Many Sunnis joined Khatib, and Shia stood aloof. Christian officers liaised with Maronite militias and, in the case of Sa'ad Haddad, with Israelis. The high command in eastern Beirut continued communication with most units, but it lost control. This liberated the PLO from Lebanese official constraint, and Fatah received weaponry through Khatib.[26] Junblat seized the opportunity of Fatah support and the army's decomposition. He demanded Faranjiya's resignation and on March 18 opened an offensive to destroy the Lebanese regime. The National Movement and the PLO seized much of the Matn district above Beirut, threatening the Maronite position in Lebanon.[27]

Hafiz al-Asad could not accept such unilateralism. Leftist and Palestinian trashing of Lebanon's National Pact and humiliation of the Christians would cripple Syria's influence in Lebanon. The militants would bring Syria's Arab rivals to the gates of Damascus, while the Maronites would bring Israel. Syria's vital interests were tied to Faranjiya's survival and an orderly transition to a new Lebanese president in September 1976. When meeting Asad on March 27, however, Kamal Junblat would not acknowledge his concerns.[28]

For Maronites, the positives of Syrian intervention to discipline the Left and the PLO temporarily outweighed the negatives of a Syrian military presence. Armed with a formal request from President Faranjiya, Asad sent Syrian troops into the Biqa in mid-April 1976. He received the assent of the United States, which had come to view Syria as a stabilizing force. The Americans extracted Israeli acquiescence at the price of "red lines": no Syrian soldiers south of Sidon, no use of air power, and no transfer of surface-to-air missiles into Lebanon.[29] Syrian occupation of the Biqa, with reinforcement of Syrian-aligned Palestinians in Beirut, derailed Junblat's offensive against the Maronites and permitted the election in May 1976 of the Shihabist, Ilyas Sarkis, as Lebanese president.[30] It did not, however, subordinate Junblat and Arafat. In June, therefore, the Syrian army invaded the coastal regions, but it met with a reverse at PLO hands near Sidon. On July 20, the Syrian president condemned PLO involvement in Lebanese affairs in a three-hour speech: "The Palestinians fighting in Mount Lebanon are definitely not fighting for Palestine."[31]

Pierre Gemayel and Camille Chamoun had no illusions about the new turn in Maronite relations with Damascus or the implications of Syrian entry to Lebanon. They hastened to exploit the "breathing space." The Christian militias intensified their siege of the Tel al-Za'atar Palestinian camp, which fell on August 12. In September, Gemayel's ambitious younger son Bashir brought the paramilitaries of the Kata'ib, the NLP, the Tanzim, and the Guardians of the Cedars under a joint command headed by himself and termed the Lebanese Forces (LF).

Simultaneously with the fall of Tel al-Za'atar, around 100,000 Shia left Naba'a in eastern Beirut for the mainly Shia southern suburbs. They included Muhammad Husayn Fadlallah and other religious scholars. Most of the displaced were destitute, and their needs stimulated Shia solidarity and self-reliance, which focused on the urban insularity of the Dahiya (literally, "suburb"). Between 1975 and the mid-1980s, the population of the southern suburbs increased from less than 100,000 to about 350,000 as Shia arrived from eastern Beirut and southern Lebanon. Suddenly the Dahiya, before the 1970s partly Maronite and rural, was half of Shia Lebanon.[32] It became a jumble of impoverished and middle-class residents, many oscillating back and forth from Jabal Amil and the Biqa.

The Tel al-Za'atar siege, during and after which three thousand Palestinians died, shocked Arabs. The Syrian regime faced censure for facilitating Maronite operations. Asad therefore had to produce swift results in his duel with Arafat. Four days after Sarkis was installed as the new Lebanese president on September 23, Syrian forces assaulted PLO- and National Movement-held areas. Into early October, they overwhelmed their opponents above Beirut and Sidon. By this stage, much of Lebanon's Islamic sector was in Asad's pocket. The Sunni elite abandoned the Left with alacrity; Shia leader Musa al-Sadr, tiring of Palestinian impositions, turned his back on the PLO; and the pro-Syrian Ba'th and SSNP deserted Junblat.

At a special Arab summit in Riyadh on October 15, 1976, Asad recouped his pan-Arab credentials. He pleased the Saudis by agreeing to an Arab deterrent force in Beirut. A few thousand Arabs arrived to join the 40,000 Syrian troops in Lebanon, but within a few months their governments lost interest. Syria was left to its own devices but now with Arab approval. The Syrian army deployed throughout Beirut, including Christian suburbs. Arafat and the PLO adapted; they sustained their institutions and weapons in western Beirut alongside the Syrians and, courtesy of the Israeli "red lines," entrenched in southern Lebanon. There were more rounds to come between Asad and Arafat in Lebanon, but into 1977 some calm settled over the country, with the advantage in Syrian hands.

President Sarkis played his part as a pliant Maronite cooperating with pliant Muslims under Syria. He appointed a banker friend, Salim al-Huss, as prime minister. In December 1976, the pair created a government of technocrats.[33] Otherwise, Asad had unfinished business with Kamal Junblat. On March 16, 1977, an unknown assailant shot the Druze *za'im* dead in his car on the road to Mukhtara. Few doubted Syrian responsibility, but some Druze vented their fury on Maronite villagers, killing about 170. This recalled 1860 and indicated the damage done to Lebanon from 1975 to 1976.

Off and On, 1977–1982

Through 1977, dynamics among Palestinians and Maronites pointed toward renewed upheaval. The PLO returned its attention to Israel, which it had neglected since 1975. It repaired relations with Syria, especially when Egyptian President Anwar Sadat's November 1977 visit to Jerusalem indicated Egypt was cold-shouldering Arafat and Asad. In contrast, Maronites became disenchanted with Syria. At street level, Syrian troops interfered with smuggling, and pictures of Asad posted in Christian neighborhoods irritated residents.[34] At the elite level, new super-militia boss, Bashir Gemayel, conceived enticing Israel to overturn the Syrian hold, thus permitting him to bid for the presidency. In the meantime, President Sarkis drifted away from Asad and toward Bashir.

On March 11, 1978, Fatah sought to upset Israeli-Egyptian peace negotiations with a sea raid from Lebanon against central Israel. The incident had no effect on Sadat, but it had serious consequences for Lebanon. Guerillas hijacked a bus on the Haifa-Tel Aviv highway, and carnage ensued when Israeli commandos stormed the vehicle. Israel's Likud government responded by invading Lebanon up to the Litani River, damaging the PLO but leaving its infrastructure north of the Litani unscathed.[35] Approximately two thousand civilians died. United Nations Security Council resolution 425 required Israel's withdrawal and prevention of Palestinian provocations. The UN established its Interim Force in Lebanon (UNIFIL) to oversee implementation. The Israelis restricted UNIFIL deployment by sponsoring a proxy militia under Lebanese army major, Sa'ad Haddad, along the border. The PLO returned and Israeli-Palestinian clashes resumed. By July 1981, the PLO had sufficient artillery and rockets to launch a significant bombardment into northern Israel.

For most Maronites, Israel's Litani operation demonstrated Israeli power; for Bashir Gemayel and Camille Chamoun the moment had come to escape Syria. Ex-president Sulayman Faranjiya, however, regarded Israel as the origin of Lebanon's Palestinian burden and reacted angrily to Bashir's opening to "the Zionist enemy."[36] The tension led to clashes between the Kata'ib and Faranjiya's Marada militia in the north. On June 13, 1978, a Kata'ib squad infiltrated Ihdin, the summer resort of Zgharta, and killed Faranjiya's son Tony and other family members. Given the friendship between the Faranjiyas and Asads, this amounted to direct provocation of Damascus.

Syrian forces moved into the northern Maronite districts, including Bsharri, home of many Kata'ib personnel. Fierce fighting erupted between Syrian troops and Bashir Gemayel's LF in the Ashrafiya quarter of Beirut, and the Syrians shelled the Christian heartland adjoining Beirut. International pressure, Maronite resistance, and Israeli warnings persuaded the Syrians to suspend "punishment" in October 1978. President Sarkis protested Syria's bombardment by offering his resignation, knowing Asad had no alternative to him.[37] The Christian part of the Lebanese army went into effective alignment with the LF.

Between late 1978 and 1981, Lebanon experienced another lull between storms, and various de facto authorities coexisted uneasily (see figure 6.1). Apart from Syria's military presence in much of the country and Israeli influence in the southern border zone, two entities featured: the Palestinian "substitute homeland" (al-watan al-badil), as Lebanese described it, and Maronite Little Lebanon. A front, termed the "contact line" (khatt al-tamass), ran through the devastated middle of Beirut, a no-man's land populated by snipers and separating the increasingly distinct domains of mainly Muslim "West Beirut" (al-gharbiya) and Christian "East Beirut" (al-sharqiya).

From its nerve center in West Beirut, the PLO developed its political and military wings into a proto-state with a private conventional army. Deference to Syria diminished as Asad became distracted by the Muslim Brotherhood challenge at

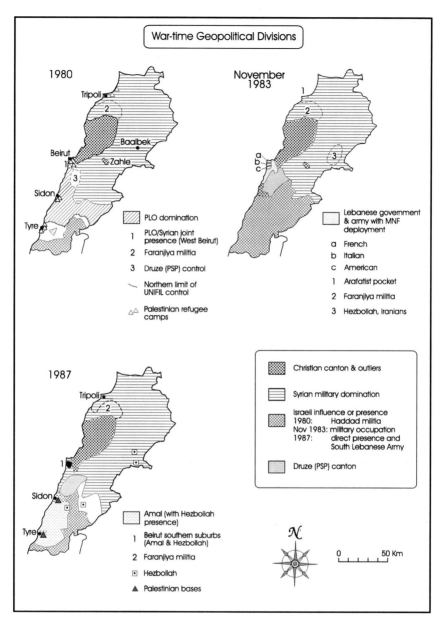

Figure 6.1 Wartime Geopolitical Divisions.

home after 1979. Well-financed media, academic, and social organs in Beirut, as well as its territorial base in southern Lebanon, elevated the PLO's profile in the Arab World. Nonetheless, the PLO was a foreign entity in Lebanon, and after Israel's offensive in March 1978, Lebanese Muslims became weary of its usurpation of the state and destructive interaction with Israel.

With Kamal Junblat's death, Arafat lost his principal Lebanese prop as the National Movement disintegrated into competing gangs. The population held the PLO responsible for ensuing disorder. Kamal's 28-year-old son, Walid, proved an effective Druze chief, surprising those who viewed him as a playboy, and he adopted a lower key relationship with the PLO than had his father. He devoted himself to his community and his father's Progressive Socialist Party (PSP), taking care to propitiate Syria's Asad. Meanwhile, the PLO "state within the state" sidelined Lebanon's Sunni politicians; whatever the sentiment for Palestine, the "alternative homeland" made Lebanese Sunnis mere auxiliaries, and they resented it.

Arafat's main problem among Lebanese Muslims, however, was divergence of interests with the Shia, who paid dearly for Fatah's March 1978 adventure. The Amal militia of charismatic Shia leader, Musa al-Sadr, mostly sat out the 1975–1976 fighting and therefore attracted fewer Shia than the Left and Palestinian organizations. This changed with the Israeli incursion to the Litani, when tens of thousands fled their villages. Sectarian security now took precedence over Lebanese/Palestinian brotherhood.[38] Through 1978, Amal became the biggest Lebanese Muslim armed group, although it had little coordination across the numerous villages from which it recruited fighters.[39]

Musa al-Sadr, whose family background and secular and religious achievements for his community earned him the title of Imam, dabbled in various associations. He hosted opponents of the Shah's regime in Iran; one, Mustafa Chamran, oversaw Amal's military elaboration. The Imam's excellent relations with Hafiz al-Asad meant that his Iranian guests traveled on Syrian diplomatic passports.[40] His independence and potential to undercut the PLO made him problematic for the Palestinians and Syria's Arab competitors. In August 1978, he disappeared on a visit to Libya. The shock rippled through Lebanese Shia simultaneously with the impact of the revolution in Iran. Amal clashed intermittently with the PLO, the Left, and the Murabitun from 1979 onward.[41] Husayn al-Husayni, al-Sadr's low-key successor as head of Amal, castigated the PLO when he resigned in June 1980. The more flamboyant Nabih Berri took over and rejected naturalization of Palestinians in Lebanon.[42]

In East Beirut, the primary development was Bashir Gemayel's assumption of Christian leadership, displacing his father and Camille Chamoun. When Chamoun's son, Dani, refused to integrate the NLP "Tigers" into the LF, Bashir had the Kata'ib attack and dismantle them on July 7, 1980. Several hundred civilians and fighters died in Maronite bloodletting. Thereafter, Bashir's LF became the most powerful Lebanese militia. The Kata'ib also flirted with Christian separatism, but Bashir knew that the Maronites could not revisit 1920; the international community would never accept a Maronite communal state. Bashir's sights settled on command of Greater Lebanon, with Israel as his instrument to chase out the PLO and Syria.

In early 1981, Bashir moved to attach the mainly Christian town of Zahle, which abutted the Syrian military deployment in the Biqa, to East Beirut by a road across Mount Sannin. The Syrians were at the same time trying to subject Zahle and Bashir's move probably had both aggressive and reactive dimensions.[43] Also, by 1981, the LF had solid relations with the Israelis that involved arms transfers and mutual visits, and a tussle with Syria would test the connection.[44] In April, the Syrians blockaded Zahle and lifted troops to Mount Sannin by helicopter. For Israelis, the Syrian use of air power violated their 1976 "red lines," and they shot down two Syrian helicopters.[45] Asad then introduced surface-to-air missile batteries to the Biqa, and a major Israeli/Syrian confrontation loomed. American and Soviet diplomacy defused the situation, but Asad would not withdraw the missiles. Israel now had unfinished business.

Reelection of the Likud in Israel in June 1981, with the energetic Ariel Sharon as defense minister in Prime Minister Menachem Begin's new government, prefigured a settling of scores with the PLO and Syria. Sharon had the like-minded Rafael Eitan as chief of the general staff. For Sharon, several factors prescribed early action: Egypt's exit from the equation; the danger and opportunity presented by Syria's weapons accumulation and domestic troubles; the PLO's inflation; and the beckoning Bashir Gemayel. In late 1981, Sharon had a "grand plan" to strike north to Beirut, evict the PLO and Syria, and overawe the September 1982 Lebanese presidential election.[46] Given that Israeli intentions were hardly a secret, the PLO avoided supplying a *casus belli* well into 1982. On June 3, however, the Iraq-based Abu Nidal Palestinian group attempted to murder the Israeli ambassador to Britain in London. Conceivably, Saddam Hussein of Iraq, at war with Syria's Iranian friends, sought to spark an Israeli invasion of Lebanon to embarrass Asad.[47] Regardless, Sharon and Eitan had their opening: they persuaded Begin and Israel commenced operations on June 6.

Israel then Syria, 1982–1986

Ariel Sharon's project to remake the Levant was a gamble. Uprooting Arafat, Fatah, and the PLO was the easy part. Both the Israeli public and the Reagan administration subscribed to a blow against the PLO—the publicly declared forty-kilometer advance—that could morph into an advance on West Beirut. For the Americans, breaking the PLO in Lebanon would enable a Jordanian-Israeli solution on the occupied West Bank. Among the Lebanese, few would mourn a comedown for the PLO.

Israel committed tens of thousands of troops to thrusts up the coast, into the Jizzin and Barouk hills, and into the southern Biqa (figure 6.2 depicts supporting artillery).[48] The coastal push, with a landing north of Sidon, reached Beirut in a few days. Sharon's problem was that he did not have an initial mandate to assault

Figure 6.2 Israeli artillery in action during the Israeli invasion of Lebanon, June 1982.
Associated Press/Yuval.

the Syrians, thus crippling them in the Biqa before Asad's Soviet backers woke
up. He took a couple of days to embroil the Syrian army in fighting the Israelis in
the hills, which freed him to send the air force to smash the missile sites in the
Biqa, drawing the Syrians into air battles in which they lost scores of aircraft to
none of the Israelis. On the ground, however, the Israelis could not make up the
delay, and Soviet pressure through the UN Security Council halted them short
of Zahle and Shtura. Syria's nerve centers in Lebanon were untouched. Earlier, in
February 1982, Asad had destroyed the Muslim Brotherhood within Syria in a
ferocious three-week showdown in Hama costing up to 20,000 lives. In strategic
terms, Ba'thist Syria thus persevered in good order even as Israel surrounded and
laid siege to the PLO in West Beirut in mid-June 1982. Asad could bounce back.

By early August, Israeli bombardment, civilian casualties running into the
thousands, and cutting of water and electricity induced the PLO to bow not just
to Israel and U.S. mediator Philip Habib but to the exhausted Lebanese residents.
An American-led multinational force supervised the shipping-out of Arafat and
his fighters in late August, and then immediately departed. Syrian units stationed
in West Beirut left as well.

Sharon's vision of a more convenient Lebanon depended on Bashir Gemayel.
Bashir avoided involvement with the Israelis against West Beirut.[49] In contacts
with the Sunni and Shia elites, he distanced himself from Israel while taking
advantage of American backing and Israel's demonstration of power. These

factors gave Bashir a parliamentary majority, and on August 23, the chamber voted him Lebanon's president. Sharon could not have hoped for more despite Bashir stressing his autonomy to Menachem Begin.[50] Israel could not have an instant peace treaty, but Bashir indicated that it would come.

Israel's supremacy in Lebanese affairs proved brief. Disaster struck on September 14 when Bashir Gemayel was assassinated in a blast that blew apart Kata'ib headquarters. A member of the Syrian-aligned SSNP confessed, and Syrian inspiration seemed more than likely. Bashir's suppleness only made him more dangerous to Asad; as president, he might be able to stabilize a new Lebanese regime that would align with the United States, Israel, Egypt, and Jordan and compel Syrian withdrawal from the Biqa.

Israel's reaction to the assassination compounded the disaster. The Israeli army moved into West Beirut, a vacuum after Bashir's death, and allowed Christian militiamen linked to LF intelligence chief Elie Hubayqa to enter the unprotected Palestinian refugee camps of Sabra and Shatila. The militiamen predictably vented their rage; during two days they massacred at least 800 civilians, mostly Palestinians but also Shia Lebanese. Given Israel's supervision of its militia ally's presence in West Beirut, global opinion blamed it for the latter's behavior. International pressure forced Israel out of the Lebanese capital, to the Shuf hills. Controversy within Israel reduced Sharon's project to whatever might justify costs—even simply trading the occupied third of Lebanon for security guarantees seemed reasonable. Israel's Kahan report on the massacre, issued in February 1983, compelled the resignation of Defense Minister Sharon.

Bashir Gemayel's older brother, Amin, filled his place as Lebanese president, receiving parliamentary assent on September 21. Amin preferred American patronage to that of Israel. An enlarged multinational force (MNF), dominated by the Americans and with French and Italian supplements, landed in West Beirut in October 1982. At first conceived as a security umbrella for Palestinians, the MNF covered U.S. promotion of Amin Gemayel's regime, including the reemerging Lebanese army. However, the Reagan administration did not push Amin to propose reforms to conciliate Shia politicians, particularly Amal's leader Nabih Berri, nor to discourage Maronite militia penetration of the Shuf, the Druze heartland.[51] The new president spurned Amal and looked to traditionalist personalities, primarily Sunnis, who had little relevance after seven years of upheaval. By 1983, only a new deal for Shia and the young Druze leader Walid Junblat might have truncated Shia radicalism and held off Damascus.

In fact, it was probably impossible to reconstruct the regime at this time. Syria would have obstructed any scheme not under its patronage; Amal's demand for abolition of political sectarianism exceeded the realistic; and only Bashir Gemayel could have delivered Maronite restraint after Arafat's expulsion from Beirut. In late 1982, Rafiq al-Hariri, an ambitious Lebanese Sunni of lower bourgeois background from Sidon who had made his fortune in construction in Saudi Arabia, appeared as Saudi mediator between Amin Gemayel and Syria.[52] He got nowhere because Amin was focused on American promotion of a Lebanese/Israeli security pact to obtain Israeli withdrawal.

On May 17, 1983, Lebanon's parliament approved a laboriously negotiated accord that was more than an armistice and less than a peace treaty, but it remained without presidential signature. It had no prospect of implementation; the Israelis handed the initiative to Hafiz al-Asad by making their retreat conditional on that of Syria. For Asad, the May 17 agreement rallied the opponents of the Lebanese regime. In Beirut, Shia parliamentary speaker Kamil al-Asa'ad committed political suicide by backing its ratification; this symbolized the fall of the old Shia leading families.

Asad's ace in hand was his possession of the Beirut-Damascus highway from the Biqa to the Dahr al-Baydar pass and hence the coastal side of Mount Lebanon, offering linkage to the Druze of the Shuf and domination of Beirut. From 1982 to 1985, he received a flood of weaponry and advisors from Soviet Russia, which interpreted the MNF, the American refurbishment of the Lebanese army, and the "Reagan plan" for an Israeli/Palestinian/Jordanian settlement as an attempted strategic coup. The Russians even helped Syria install surface-to-air missiles in Mount Lebanon above the Americans in Beirut.[53] By late 1983, Amal and its leader, Nabih Berri, disappointed with the Americans, drifted into Asad's corner. Amal was at its peak of Shia popularity. On September 4, 1983, the situation broke decisively in Syria's favor when the demoralized Israelis pulled back from the Druze Shuf to the Awali River north of Sidon.

Through late 1982 and 1983, LF partisans from East Beirut had taken advantage of Israeli occupation to enter Christian villages in the Druze hills. The Israelis soon tired of them and winked while Walid Junblat's PSP prepared to reassert Druze supremacy. For an Israel on the defensive, the Druze became more important. Israel was indifferent to American promotion of Amin Gemayel; for the Likud, Amin and the United States disdained Israel while profiting from its overthrow of the PLO. The Israelis therefore evacuated the Shuf with no arrangement to transfer it to the Lebanese army. The Syrians opened supply lines to Junblat, whose militiamen filled the vacuum. By mid-September, the PSP expelled the LF from the Shuf and part of the Matn. In the process, the Druze and Syrians shelled East Beirut, the army, and American marines at the airport. Amid killings, approximately 150,000 Christians fled the Shuf and Upper Matn. A September 25, 1983, cease-fire froze events; Junblat had still to reach the coast, Amal still hesitated to rebel in West Beirut, and the MNF remained in place (see figure 6.1).

There was no doubt, however, about the trajectory. Aside from the Christian debacle, a new Shia phenomenon proved handy for Syria and ominous for

Israel.[54] After 1979, a number of younger Shia religious scholars trained in Najaf or Qum found the new Iranian model of a Shia Islamic regime under a spiritual guide alluring. The June 1982 Israeli invasion gave the Iranians the opportunity to dispatch Revolutionary Guards to Baalbek, ostensibly to "defend" Lebanon but really to subvert the Shia in favor of religious radicals. Only weeks later, Husayn Mussawi split with Amal's Berri over Berri's openness to the United States. He formed Islamic Amal. The environment was propitious; Shia in southern Lebanon initially welcomed Israeli ejection of the PLO but by 1983 Israel's stay aroused suspicion.

Syrian and Iranian intelligence agencies channeled Shia Islamist rejection of Israel and the West into changing the correlation of forces, providing coordination that the Islamists as yet lacked. On April 18, 1983, a Shia suicide attack demolished the U.S. embassy in Beirut, killing sixty-three. On October 16, Israel gratified its enemies: an Israeli convoy entered Nabatiya on the Shia holy day of Ashura during a parade commemorating the martyrdom of the Imam Husayn. The incident sparked rioting and demonstrated astonishing insensitivity. On October 23, Shia suicide truck bombers devastated the American and French MNF compounds, killing 247 U.S. servicemen and 58 French paratroopers. On November 4, the Islamists leveled the Israeli military headquarters in Tyre, killing 28 Israelis.

Thereafter, Israel made waves of arrests and isolated the south. On February 16, 1984, the Israelis killed the religious scholar Ragheb Harb, a leader of the Islamist trend, in his home village of Jibshit. The result was mounting insurrection. The Islamists coalesced as Hezbollah, or the Party of God, which announced itself in a February 1985 manifesto, marking the first anniversary of the death of Ragheb Harb. The party dedicated itself to resistance, the elimination of Israel, and a Shia Islamic state.[55]

As for Asad, once the Americans and Israelis were rolled back, the project for Lebanon remained that of 1976—moderate reform of political sectarianism under Syrian auspices—but with tighter supervision. One thing Asad could do without was any PLO reappearance. Arafat did not oblige: expelled from Beirut by Israel, and then from Damascus by Asad, he fortified himself in Tripoli in September 1983. The Syrians promoted a split in the PLO and used Lebanese Alawites, Palestinian and SSNP clients, and their own artillery in a destructive little campaign to chase the PLO chief out of northern Lebanon.[56] France extracted Arafat, who sailed away to Tunisia in mid-November 1983, leaving behind a battered Sunni Tripoli and lieutenants in the Beirut and Sidon Palestinian camps determined to thwart Syria.

Almost at the same moment, Asad suffered a heart attack, leaving Syria rudderless for three months. Amal thus mounted its February 6, 1984, coup against Amin Gemayel's regime, seizing West Beirut in tandem with the Druze PSP and the Shia Islamists, without Syrian inspiration. The Lebanese army, whose shell-ing provoked Amal's rebellion, split once more with the Shia sixth brigade detaching itself from the army command. The PSP appropriated the coast south of the airport. President Gemayel now had no authority beyond the Christian heartland, whereas the MNF found itself purposeless amid unfriendly militias. United States marines withdrew to the offshore fleet, which soon departed. For Washington, Syria again became the stabilizer, although 155-millimeter American howitzers transferred to the army command in East Beirut assisted the Christians to defy Damascus until 1990. Compared with the decisive U.S. role in 1958, the MNF story was a miserable affair. For his part, the recuperating Syrian leader had his victory courtesy of Nabih Berri and Walid Junblat. No one was yet master of a new Lebanon.

On February 29, 1984, after veiled Syrian threats of bombardment of Zahle and Bikfaya, Amin Gemayel went to Damascus to disown the May 17 agreement.[57] During the talks, Hafiz al-Asad reportedly requested "full coop-eration" with Syria and attention to Shia aspirations.[58] Gemayel agreed to a Syr-ian-sponsored inter-Lebanese conference.[59] Lebanon's sectarian chiefs duly met in Lausanne, Switzerland, in late March where, to the delight of the Amal Shia, ex-president Faranjiya scuttled the opposition's demand to diminish the Maronite presidency in Sunni favor.[60] In late April, Abd al-Halim Khaddam's efforts pro-duced a united government, thus bringing Syria's allies into the official apparatus. Rashid Karami of Tripoli returned as prime minister; a policy statement her-alded unspecified constitutional reform; and there was an uneasy truce between East and West Beirut, which were once more split from one another.

Syria's hold began slipping almost from the moment of Amin Gemayel's sub-mission as discord in the Islamic sector encouraged Christian obduracy. Amin sacked army chief Ibrahim Tannous at the insistence of Berri and Junblat and appointed an obscure brigade commander, Michel Aoun. Amin appeared open to Syrian preferences, and the Damascus media purred about "Kata'ib modera-tion."[61] However, the president stalled on political reform because of "Christian opposition"; in March 1985, after a Kata'ib delegation visited Damascus for the first time since 1978, this "opposition" manifested itself in the takeover of the LF by anti-Syrian elements led by Samir Geagea of Bsharri.

In West Beirut, Amal could not secure the urban area through 1984 in the face of its allies and PLO resurgence in the Palestinian camps. In the year after Amal's coup, a group affiliated with Hezbollah and directed from Iran kidnapped five Americans, including CIA station head William Buckley and the journalist Terry Anderson. The Islamic sector broke apart after Israel retreated from the Awali River to a "security zone" on the Israel/Lebanon border between January and June 1985. Shia resistance and the souring Israeli public mood made Israeli control of all southern Lebanon untenable. Amal and Hezbollah jostled to command "liberated" Jabal Amil, and the PLO resuscitated its refugee camp bases near Sidon and Tyre as well as in Beirut. Amal found control of the Shuf coast by Junblat's PSP irksome because it compromised Amal's access to southern Lebanon. For their part, Druze feared Shia assertion, and the Shia influx into West Beirut after February 1984 alarmed Sunni residents.

Because of shared interests against the PLO, Syria regarded Amal as its chief agent in the Islamic sector, and Amal needed Syrian weapons. Asad also backed the PSP and Hezbollah to limit Amal. The result was a mess. In late May 1985, Amal and the army's sixth brigade besieged the Palestinians in the Beirut camps, inaugurating an intermittent "war of the camps" that lasted until 1988 and spread to Sidon and Tyre. After several weeks of hostilities around Sabra and Shatila, causing a thousand deaths, exhaustion brought a pause.

Almost the moment that the clashes died down, Syria and Amal faced Hezbollah hijacking of an American TWA airliner to Beirut on June 14, 1985. Asad and Berri could parade "good offices" to the West, but the affair embarrassed them. For Amal, it foreshadowed a showdown with Hezbollah. For Asad, Syria's weakening leverage made a Lebanese resolution more urgent.

The national unity government remained deadlocked, but in late 1985, Khaddam, appointed Syrian vice president in 1984 and still Syria's coordinator for Lebanon, detected an opportunity with the Maronite militia. In April 1985, LF chief Geagea failed to hold Christian villages east of Sidon after Israel withdrew south. Fifty thousand more Christians fled their homes to East Beirut. Geagea lost his post to LF intelligence commander Elie Hubayqa, who believed Christians must settle with Syria. He visited Damascus in September, and Khaddam evolved a scheme for a reform accord among Lebanon's three major militias (the LF, Amal, and Junblat's PSP), which would be imposed on the president.

Berri, Hubayqa, and Junblat signed the Tripartite Agreement in Damascus on December 28, 1985. It expressed Ba'thist Syria's ambition to command its neighbor.[62] Provisions for "privileged relations" between Lebanon and Syria included "complete coordination" of foreign policies, perpetuation of the Syrian military presence, joint committees to prepare "integrated" education, and prevention of any media "distortion." The text also stipulated reorganization of the Lebanese army after "confinement to barracks." Political reform repeated longstanding concepts: Christian/non-Christian equality in parliament and reduction of presidential powers in favor of the prime minister and cabinet.

Despite Syria's achievements since 1982, such a diktat proved a bridge too far. Walid Junblat never doubted the Maronites would disgorge it.[63] President Gemayel, ex-president Chamoun, and army chief Aoun united against the terms, and the church perceived a cultural threat.[64] On January 12, 1986, endorsed by the Maronite hierarchy, Samir Geagea forcibly reassumed the LF leadership. Hubayqa and his aides were expelled from East Beirut, and the Tripartite

Figure 6.3 Aftermath of a car bomb blast, East Beirut, July 28, 1986. Associated Press.

Agreement collapsed. For the moment, Lebanon confounded the Syrian regime (figure 6.3 depicts the retribution).

Militia Lebanon

The late 1980s represented the high tide of the Lebanese militias, with the PLO reduced to an irritant, Israel on the defensive in its occupied "security zone," and Syria checked. On the other hand, although the Lebanese state was at its nadir after January 1986, when Syria imposed a boycott of President Gemayel by ministers from the "Islamic and nationalist" camp, the end of Gemayel's presidency in September 1988 loomed over the militias as a marker of uncertainty. First, despite militias assuming state functions and expanded social roles, post-1984 currency collapse, pauperization, and accelerated emigration were signs of their fundamental incapacity. Second, the decline of the Soviet Union in the late 1980s heralded American efforts to stabilize the Levant to buttress its Middle Eastern supremacy, and Damascus was positioned to exploit Lebanon's 1988 presidential election for bargaining with Washington.

From 1975 to 1985, militias consolidated from opportunist vigilante groups into cantonal machines (see figure 6.1 for the geopolitics of the late 1980s). They displaced the state from tax and customs collection, diverted revenues through command of government agencies, and profited from smuggling, drug trafficking, and other illicit operations.

The Christian LF became the most sophisticated apparatus, with a salaried paramilitary of 10,000 by the mid-1980s and an annual budget estimated at $300 million.[65] The LF's limitation was that it coexisted in East Beirut with President Gemayel and the rump of the army under Aoun, comprising four brigades with 15,000 men. East Beirut's multiheaded leadership represented vulnerability: Aoun, Gemayel, and Geagea had no love for one another. The deaths of the grand old men—Pierre Gemayel in 1984 and Camille Chamoun in 1987— removed stabilizing elements. Starting in 1984, Amin Gemayel's Orthodox Christian advisors, former foreign minister Elie Salem and *al-Nahar* publisher Ghassan Tuwayni, shuttled among senior Maronites and explored solutions for Lebanon with Khaddam, Saudi envoy Hariri, and the Americans.[66] Regarding military supplies, East Beirut shifted from Israel to Saddam Hussein.

In the Druze Shuf, Walid Junblat's PSP ran the tightest cantonal operation. Approximately two-thirds of the scale of the LF, the PSP established a port at Khalde and controlled the Jiyeh power station and a cement factory.[67] After the exodus of most Christians, the region relived its old Druze exclusivity. Only Deir al-Qamar, home of the Chamouns, persisted as a Christian outpost. The PSP founded a "mountain administration" that absorbed public officials, who were still state-salaried. The Shuf was the purest militia canton because the PSP had no local competition. Although technically in conflict with East Beirut, the Druze leadership depended on the larger Christian entity to hold off a reunified Syrian commanded Lebanon.

In the Shia areas—Beirut's southern suburbs, Jabal Amil in southern Lebanon, and the northern Biqa—Amal and the newer Hezbollah jostled for precedence. Amal, by 1985 similar to the LF in manpower, controlled state agencies, principally the Council of the South, through its representatives in the government. It also pulled on the loyalty of newly rich Shia in West Africa and the United States—for example, its leader, Nabih Berri, was born in Sierra Leone, gained a law degree from the Lebanese University in 1963, and worked for General Motors in Detroit between 1976 and 1978. The movement's weakness was its incoherent organization, with myriad village bosses. Hezbollah, with a more disciplined cadre trading on religion, made inroads into Amal's popular base. While Amal fought the Palestinians on behalf of the Syrian regime, Hezbollah resisted the Israeli occupier with the support of revolutionary Iran, a comparison advantaging Hezbollah. Iran pumped weapons and subsidies of more than $100 million per annum into the Party of God, enabling it to branch into health, education, and social welfare for poorer Shia.[68] Hezbollah even collaborated with Palestinians against its Shia rival.

Syria's army occupied the Biqa, the north, and heights above Beirut—half of Lebanon—and took Zahle and Tripoli by "security plans" in 1985. Small militias under Syria included the SSNP in the Matn and Kura, the Marada in Zghorta, the Alawite Arab Democratic Party in Tripoli, and Hubayqa's retinue in Zahle, with the Lebanese Ba'th, Amal, Hezbollah, and Iranian Revolutionary Guards around Baalbek. Syrian troops overawed the population at checkpoints, while Syrian military intelligence monitored politics from the Biqa Armenian town of Anjar. Syrian officers took their cut from commerce. Akkar merchants, for example, shared profits with a Syrian protection racket in Shtura.[69]

Asad preferred to avoid entanglement in West Beirut. After the PSP and Amal disposed of the Sunni Murabitun, a PLO affiliate, in 1984, the Syrians favored a balance of militias in "Islamic and nationalist" Beirut. In February 1987, however, the PSP and the Communists forced Syria's hand when they thrashed Amal in a bid for primacy in West Beirut's bourgeois quarters. Fearful that Amal's discomfort would open the gate for Arafat, the Syrians had eight thousand soldiers descend on West Beirut through the Druze country. As a reprimand to Junblat, the Syrian army squeezed access to his port.[70]

Stiffened by Israeli troops, Israel aligned its militia proxy, the South Lebanese Army (SLA), along the Israel/Lebanon border. This successor to Major Haddad's border militia had another Lebanese officer, retired General Antoine Lahad, at its head and grew to more than two thousand Christian, Shia, and Druze personnel. Israel subsidized salaries, and militia conducted the usual smuggling and racketeering. Lahad also held the Christian town of Jizzin. The SLA sparred with Hezbollah, though Lebanon's domestic turmoil spared it and Israel real bother until the early 1990s.

What of Lebanon's economy and people in the militia jungle? The years from Israel's invasion of 1982 through the factional fighting of 1983–1985 were devastating. Before 1982, although the GDP halved in 1975–1976 and the black market bloated, the state could still mainly cover expenses through income; currency and salaries maintained their value; and quiet periods from 1977 kept the hope of recovery alive.[71] Inflation was modest, approximately 17 percent per annum. From 1982 to 1985, infrastructural damage exceeded anything yet seen; the end of the PLO mini-state removed Palestinian financial input; and new hostilities in central Lebanon from September 1983 paralyzed industry and commerce. With the country again fragmented, militias finally deprived the state of most tax and customs revenue. From 1984 on, the state could only sustain the civil service by deficit financing, and the banks began speculative buying of dollars. Both subverted the currency.[72] From 1983 to 1987, the Lebanese lira slid from 4 to 477 to the U.S. dollar, and inflation soared to more than 100 percent per annum.[73]

In militia Lebanon of the mid- to late 1980s, Christian, Druze, and Shia ghettos localized life for many people. Christian East Beirut and the Druze Shuf became cantons with hardened boundaries. Rather like the Shia evacuation of Naba'a in 1976 and the Christian flight from the Shuf in 1983, most West Beirut

Christians relocated to East Beirut or left the country in the mid-1980s because of the chaos of the "Islamic and nationalist" sector. Bourgeois Muslims who could emigrate did so. The proportion of Lebanon's Christians in the East Beirut canton increased from less than one-half before 1975 to two-thirds by 1988. As communities separated, shopping decentralized from Beirut, in particular to Jounieh and Ba'aqlin, new "capitals" for Christians and Druze.

Curiously, currency collapse went together with recovery in real GDP from 1985 to 1987.[74] This reflected less military disruption, stabilization of cantons with trade across the lines, exports from East Beirut, and expanded greenhouse agriculture.[75] Cantons, however, could not offer a decent future for the Lebanese people. In East Beirut, many Maronites faced penury, and the diminished standing of the LF militia after the Shuf debacle put the LF in a precarious position. The 40 percent of East Beirut's inhabitants who came from elsewhere longed to return home. More broadly, many Lebanese looked to General Michel Aoun's army brigades as a focus of state legitimacy that might herald a new Lebanon. These brigades came out of the mid-1980s with military credibility and included Shia and Sunnis. As Gemayel's presidency approached its close, Aoun sensed the chance to exploit weariness with militias and stir romantic nationalism in a bid for power.

Militias and cantons fostered an indifference to law that was to characterize postwar Lebanon. Militia personnel moved into Lebanon's post-militia regime. Independent Lebanon before 1975 was loose and laissez-faire, but it had a legal framework that barely functioned after 1990. By the late 1980s, the "black economy," aggregated illegal activities such as arms and drug trades, militia ports, smuggling, and protection money, underpinned GDP. Looking back in 1990, the daily *al-Nahar* estimated Lebanese profits on these activities at a minimum of $14.5 billion for the period from 1975 to 1990.[76] In the militia heyday after 1985, these profits approached two billion dollars per annum. The "black economy" criss-crossed zones of control: the opium and hashish trade from the Biqa, which exploded in the late 1980s, drew together the Syrian army, Hezbollah, Christian Zahle, Syrian aligned militias, and East Beirut. Regarding the physical environment, uncontrolled real estate development and quarrying wrecked Lebanon's landscape, and in 1987 Italians made scandalous arrangements for dumping thousands of barrels of toxic wastes in and near East Beirut.[77]

End Game, 1987–1990

Meanwhile, the Syrian regime struggled with Lebanese politics. Amal imperfectly contained the Palestinians in the Beirut and Sidon camps into 1988. In June 1987, a bomb on a helicopter killed Prime Minister Rashid Karami. The prime minister was involved in moves to resuscitate the cabinet and abrogate the

1969 Cairo agreement, which possibly bothered the LF and PLO.[78] Syria disapproved of senior Muslims contacting President Gemayel to make Salim al-Huss premier; Khaddam rebuked al-Huss at Karami's funeral.[79] In April 1988, Amal attacked Hezbollah around Nabatiya. In May, Hezbollah retaliated in Beirut's suburbs. Asad invited Hezbollah commanders to Latakia and told them that they were "the Islamic struggle in Lebanon that I have remembered in my speeches."[80] Syria then mobilized dissident Palestinians to rout Arafatists in Shatila and Burj al-Barajneh.

The United States gave Asad hope in 1988.[81] On a visit to Damascus in late February, Secretary of State George Schultz seemed receptive. Syria sought a repackaged Tripartite Agreement and would repress religious militants and extract foreign hostages in exchange for American endorsement. For Asad, the essential element was the special relationship of Syria and Lebanon, while Khaddam added a timed ending of political sectarianism.[82]

In the approach to the September presidential election, Damascus reacted icily to army commander Michel Aoun's candidacy.[83] According to Khaddam, Aoun had no acceptable "program."[84] In early September, the Americans approved the Syrian favorite, the Akkar deputy Mikhail Dahir. The Maronite leadership—army command, militia, presidency, and patriarchate—condemned this as an "imposition." The electoral process collapsed, and minutes before leaving office at midnight on September 22, 1988, a reluctant Amin Gemayel decreed a military cabinet under Aoun as prime minister.

Lebanon thus acquired two governments, with Salim al-Huss in West Beirut defending the custom of a Sunni premier. Aoun tried in vain to placate Syria. The general had a nationalist vision to revive Lebanon, and as a lower bourgeois Maronite from a Christian/Shia Beirut suburb, he had no time for the Maronite elite. As an army man, he also had no time for militias. Given that Syria forbade Muslims to join his military cabinet, Aoun felt exposed. He first needed to subordinate the LF to earn credentials to tackle other militias. However, he refused to discuss political reform given that West Beirut was subject to Syria.

For Damascus, Aoun was a new Bashir Gemayel, now from a state institution. He was unpredictable and had a cross-sectarian credibility that Bashir had lacked. Even worse, there was Saddam Hussein's intrusion. The Iraqi dictator wanted to punish his Syrian rival for backing Iran in the Iran-Iraq war from 1980 to 1988. Saddam shipped heavy weaponry to both the LF and Aoun's brigades from August 1988.[85] This provoked Asad and risked the Maronites blowing apart between their two armed forces.

The stage was set for the climax of Lebanon's war years. Aoun received a boost in January 1989 from a six-state Arab committee set up under Kuwait to contest Syria's monopoly in Lebanon. On February 14, Aoun struck the LF, which after two days bowed to the military cabinet confiscating its main port, the Beirut "fifth basin." Luckily for Aoun, Geagea, at least for the moment, preferred not to endanger East Beirut in a real fight. Flush with success, Aoun ordered the closure of illegal ports beyond East Beirut, principally those of the PSP and Amal, and on March 6 imposed a blockade. Bombardments commenced a week later. Aoun blamed Syria for frustrating "legitimate authority," declared a "war of liberation," and targeted Syrian military installations from Beirut to the Biqa.

Six months of static artillery duels and blockades followed, costing 850 lives, mainly civilian. The LF stayed aloof from Aoun's adventure but could be expected to fight any general Syrian attack. In the latter case, East Beirut, with 25,000 troops, 300 artillery pieces, and forbidding terrain, could hold off Syria; stalemate thus prevailed. In May 1989, Asad faced down Saddam at an Arab summit in Casablanca.[86] The Syrian leader refused to withdraw from Lebanon; after Saddam walked out, the summit communiqué stressed Lebanese constitutional reform and replaced the six-state forum with a tripartite committee for Lebanon comprising Saudi Arabia, Morocco, and Algeria. In July, Syria imposed a gunboat blockade on Jounieh. On July 31, the new Arab committee gratified Aoun by demanding Syria respect Lebanese sovereignty.[87] Syria responded on August 14 with its only frontal assault, which flopped. A UN Security Council resolution called for a cease-fire, and hostilities subsided.

For the United States, the next step was retooling Arab diplomatic involvement for stabilization of Lebanon under Syria. With the Cold War fading, Washington regarded Syrian hegemony in Lebanon as suiting American hegemony in the Middle East. The George H. W. Bush administration scorned Aoun's amateurish military circle. On September 6, the Americans seized on a remark by Aoun about the efficacy of Hezbollah style kidnappings and pulled out their embassy staff.[88] U.S. officials told the Arab committee that they were not interested in Syria leaving Lebanon.[89] To Arab leaders, Asad downplayed his connection with Iran and warned of a "security vacuum" if Syria left Lebanon.[90]

Steered by the Americans and Saudi Arabia, the Arab tripartite committee manufactured a National Unity Charter for Lebanon, which was unveiled on September 17, 1989, for approval by surviving deputies of the 1972 Lebanese parliament. The Saudis brought sixty-two deputies from Lebanon to Ta'if in Saudi Arabia; the East Beirut contingent was delighted to get away from Aoun. After three weeks, all but four, including the thirty-one Christians, signed the October 22, 1989, Ta'if accord for constitutional adjustment and an indefinite Syrian military presence.[91] It was the 1985 Tripartite Agreement sanitized, without crudities about Lebanese/Syrian "integration." Executive authority would shift from the Maronite president to the council of ministers, half Christian and half Muslim and Druze, chaired by the Sunni prime minister, although the president would retain prerogatives. Parliament would become more independent, with a longer term for the Shia speaker. Membership of parliament would divide equally between Christians and non-Christians, with Sunnis and Shia also equal, thus giving Maronites the largest communal allocation. The sectarian quotas would end in some hazy future. Muslims gained, but it was not bad for Christians. Sunnis, with a stronger prime minister, gained more than Shia, reflecting Saudi influence. There would be Lebanese/Syrian "coordination and cooperation," including Syrian military interventions to help the government. The agreement reconciled the Christian and Muslim elite to Syria under a Syrian protectorate.

On November 5, 1989, the Americans and Saudis reassembled the deputies in Syrian-dominated northern Lebanon to elect Rene Mu'awwad of Zgharta as president. Mu'awwad explored reconciliation with Aoun and on November 22 was assassinated in West Beirut in a car bombing.[92] Syria then cooperated with the Americans to bring deputies to Shtura in the Biqa to elect Ilyas al-Hirawi, a Zahle deputy favored in Damascus. On November 26, Hirawi announced a government under Salim al-Huss, which replaced Aoun as army commander with Emile Lahoud, who had repudiated Aoun some months before. However, the new authorities could do no more while Aoun remained entrenched in East Beirut.

The LF was the key to weakening Aoun. Americans and Christians in the new government hoped to bring the LF into the regime; Syrians hoped the LF and Aoun might cancel each other. Tension rose in East Beirut as diplomatic isolation tightened and Hirawi authorities cut pay to officials. Already Aoun's followers had forced Maronite Patriarch Nasrallah Sfeir to flee to the north after he accepted Ta'if. The LF was enticed by Hirawi and American diplomats, although the Syrians remained suspicious. Regardless, the militia had scores to settle with Aoun. On January 30, when Aoun declared their absorption into the army, the LF unleashed an onslaught on army bases. Amazingly, Aoun had made no preparations for such a fight and had to claw his way back from severe materiel and territorial losses. The army's helicopter fleet was destroyed on the first day.

From February to June 1990, the Maronite community tore itself apart. The army became exhausted trying to recover ground in displays of firepower that matched anything hitherto seen in Lebanon. In eighteen days, the death toll passed six hundred, for once mainly combatants.[93] More than 300,000 people, one-third of the population, fled East Beirut by April.[94] Reduced to half his military capability, Aoun turned to Syria's militia proxies for supplies. Asad and Khaddam had Hirawi write to LF commander Samir Geagea requiring that he accept Ta'if unreservedly, which he did by mid-year.[95] Aoun would not submit, and Syria ordered its allies to end relations with him.

Even in mid-1990, it was dubious that Syria could overturn Aoun. Washington wavered on the brink, and Israel still banned Syrian airpower. Saddam Hussein doomed East Beirut when he occupied Kuwait in August 1990. The United States needed broad Arab backing to release Kuwait and smash Saddam's challenge in the Persian Gulf. Asad offered himself as a partner in the U.S.-led coalition; hosted Secretary of State James Baker on September 13; visited Tehran at Baker's request to make sure of Iranian neutrality; and obtained U.S. approval to settle matters in Beirut. Christian deputies headed the pack in favor of a military solution, and Asad was delighted with Kata'ib leader George Sa'adeh.[96] In contrast, Walid Junblat, who could see the coming end of his canton, was summoned to Damascus and reprimanded after hosting an anti-Hirawi demonstration. On October 9, Ta'if authorities made the written appeal for Syrian military intervention required by the Americas. Washington had Israel stand aside, freeing Syria to use aircraft.

On October 13, 1990, the Syrian army invaded the Matn with air strikes on the Ba'abda presidential palace. Within three hours, the Syrians occupied Ba'abda. Aoun took sanctuary in the French embassy and later departed into exile. The great irony was that the Syrian regime's sworn enemies made Hafiz al-Asad master of Lebanon. The LF militia assault on Aoun cracked open the Maronite redoubt, and Saddam Hussein gifted the political conditions for the coup de grâce. As for the general, a Lebanese businessman on a boat leaving Jounieh for Cyprus declared: "*Shu harb al-tahrir? . . . Harrarna min mumtalikatna* [What war of liberation? . . . He liberated us from our properties]."[97]

One loose end remained for Syria: the Shia "war of brothers" that sputtered alongside the Maronite volcano. By early 1990, this focused on the Tuffah area, north of Nabatiya, which Hezbollah wanted as a base. Amal felt so threatened that it agreed to a Palestinian buffer force. A Hezbollah attack in July 1990 panicked 70,000 Shia into flight.[98] Syria's triumph in Beirut facilitated a settlement in November 1990 that compelled Amal and Hezbollah to retreat and emphasized Syria's advantage over its Iranian ally.

Syrian Hegemony, 1990–2005

In 1990, the Syrian regime reversed 1920. In place of a French high commissioner overseeing Syria from Beirut, the Syrian president commanded Lebanon from Damascus. The Asad regime had always wanted predominance on the seaward flank of its capital; Lebanon and Syria were two states for one people. In exasperation in the mid 1970s, Khaddam let slip that if Greater Lebanon could not function, the answer was not shrinkage to Mount Lebanon but Syrian absorption of everything.[99] In the 1990s, however, Hafiz al-Asad knew that the pretence of two states was de rigueur. After all, his mandate in Lebanon came from the United States, sole superpower after the Cold War, and the Americans had just reversed Iraq's absorption of Kuwait. In the last decade of the twentieth century, the United States valued cooperative autocrats in the Arab world even as it pressed democracy elsewhere. Presidents George H. W. Bush and Bill Clinton indulged the Syrian regime in its manipulation of Lebanon. For his part, unlike his son Bashar in 2003–2005, Hafiz al-Asad tested the superpower short of outright defiance.

Syrian hegemony perpetuated the communal sensitivities of the war years. Having devastated themselves, the Maronites retired into indignant impotence. The Maronite mountain had to be watched, but it ceased to be an obstacle for Damascus. Nonetheless, Christians remained more than one-third of the Lebanese population, and alienation of most of them was problematic for Syria. Otherwise, Syria balanced Sunnis and Shia, who had drifted apart after Shia factions moved into largely Sunni West Beirut in February 1984. In the 1990s, Prime Minister Rafiq al-Hariri's concentration of investment on central Beirut, and the Sunni premier's ties with Saudi Arabia, grated on Shia. Syria had Hariri's government and Hezbollah limit each other between 1992 and 1998, constraining both Saudi and Iranian influence. Syria also encouraged the Maronite president, the Shia parliamentary speaker, and senior ministers to constrict Prime Minister Hariri. Such divide and rule fed sectarian rancor.

Otherwise, warfare intensified after 1990 in southern Lebanon, where Hezbollah organized Shia military activities against the Israelis and their proxy SLA in the Israeli occupied "security zone." Israel ignored the opportunity to withdraw in 1989–1990, while the Syrians were preoccupied and Hezbollah fought Amal. Hezbollah could therefore reinflate, courtesy of Israel's presence, and displace Amal as the leading Shia faction. Throughout the 1990s, space expanded for Iranian penetration of the Shia, and despite its ambivalence about Iranian influence, Iran's Syrian ally could not resist taking advantage of Hezbollah and Iran to put pressure on Israel.

Genies let out of the bottle after 1967—sharpened Lebanese sectarianism, Syrian intervention, and Israel's collision with the Shia—plagued Lebanon into the twenty-first century.

High Hegemony, 1990–2000

Syria was in a hurry to cement its hold at the end of 1990, with regime institutions, security, and bilateral relations being the priorities. Economic affairs did not at first register despite Lebanon's prostrate condition: Syria allies had their pickings; the lower orders were destitute but not starving; and the population was too dazed to protest.

Hafiz al-Asad picked Umar Karami, brother of the assassinated Rashid, to head a National Unity Government, which was formed in December 1990 and staffed by the old elite, warlords, and Syria's loyalists. It included the Kata'ib and LF, but the latter quickly felt marginalized, and Geagea resigned in March 1991.

The Syrians supervised disbandment and disarmament of militias by mid-1991, with Hezbollah exempted because of its role against Israeli occupation. Hezbollah had to release surviving Western hostages. Army commander Emile Lahoud oversaw reintegration of the Lebanese army, with sectarian mixing in new brigades and overhaul of the officer corps. The army received aid from both Syria and the United States.

The Treaty of Brotherhood, Cooperation, and Coordination, which was signed on May 22, 1991, concretized Lebanese/Syrian "privileged relations."[100] It established a "higher council," with committees for "prime ministerial coordination," foreign affairs, defense and security, and economic and social affairs. The Syrians only dropped the word "integration" because of American objection.[101] On September 1, a Defense and Security Pact committed Lebanon to "the highest level of military coordination" and "banning any activity or organization in all military, security, political, and information fields that might . . . cause threats to the other country."[102] Syria sidestepped the Ta'if recommendation that Syrian forces redeploy in late 1992 out of Beirut to the coastal mountains. The Lebanese defense minister indicated that the army could not take over despite the capability shown in its July 1991 operation in Sidon to push Palestinian guerillas back into the Ayn al-Hilwe camp.

Lebanon's August 26, 1991, Amnesty Law expressed shared interests of the ex-warlords and Syria. The "law" endorsed impunity for criminality. It declared amnesty for war crimes committed from April 1975 to March 1991, only excepting assassinations of political and religious leaders. It sent out the message that the Lebanese state had no concern for ordinary citizens, who had best forget massacres and disappearances. The exception of high-profile assassinations gave the Syrians and the Lebanese regime the potential weapon of show trials, using cases for which the Syrian regime was not itself the prime suspect. Otherwise, no one expected activation of judicial files.

By 1992, the economy could wait no longer. Destruction in East Beirut, where most industry and commerce operated in the late 1980s, reduced Lebanon's per capita GDP in 1990 to less than 40 percent of that in 1987.[103] Rebooting the country was beyond the Karami government; in early 1992 the currency collapsed. On May 6, 1992, rioters marched on the prime minister's residence. Karami resigned, and a caretaker government managed Syria's immediate concern: the first postwar elections for the new 128-seat chamber of deputies set for August/September 1992. Governorates as five or six large constituencies, which was agreed at Ta'if, gave way to a gerrymander mixing large and small electorates to suit Syria's candidates. A voter boycott backed by Michel Aoun reduced turnout to less than 25 percent, but this only assisted Syrian and regime command of the parliament.

Thereafter, Syria swallowed its doubts about the billionaire Lebanese/Saudi Rafiq al-Hariri. A prime minister "capable of bringing foreign aid and loans to help stabilize Ta'if," in the words of Syrian Vice President Khaddam, was the only option.[104] Hariri had a vision to revive his country as regional commercial hub and alone had the dynamism, Arab and global contacts, and personal resources to drive such a vision. By natural progression, this new Lebanon would one day escape the Syrian regime. In the meantime, Hariri bowed to a division of functions. He would deal with reconstruction and finances, but accept Syrian primacy in defense and security and tolerate a financial rake-off for Syrian personalities and their Lebanese subordinates. Starting in 1993, Hariri and his partners in the Solidere Company pushed ahead with the rebuilding of central Beirut, the centerpiece of infrastructural investments in and around Beirut, to supply the physical base for Lebanon's commercial resurrection.

Hariri stabilized the currency, lowered inflation, and provided annual per capita GDP growth of 7 to 8 percent from 1993 to 1995.[105] By the early 2000s, the restored center of Beirut was considered a great planning and architectural achievement for the prime minister and his team. However, the price was massive expansion of public debt, from 39 percent of GDP in 1993 to more than 100 percent in 1998, subsequently ballooning to 159 percent in 2005.[106] Despite GDP growth, the 1995 GDP was still only 60 percent of that in 1974, and after 1995, growth faltered into the new century, in part because of the pressure of public borrowing on interest rates.[107] The economy really only boomed in property, the banking sector, and a narrow range of services. The poor stood still as the rich and the new rich prospered: in 2002, 60 percent of bank deposits were in the hands of 2.4 percent of depositors.[108] Most seriously, young people with professional and technical expertise had better prospects abroad, and about 100,000 individuals emigrated throughout the 1990s.[109]

The rebuilding of downtown Beirut, as well as the new highways and other infrastructure, required the return of Syrian labor. After declining to insignificance in the 1980s, Syrian worker numbers recovered to 200,000 in 1992, reflecting peace-time openings for cheap labor even in stagnant conditions, and climbed to about half a million by 1995 as Hariri's reconstruction gathered momentum.[110] Similarly to 1970, this represented about one-third of the total labor force. The numbers then halved by 2000 because of recession. The Syrian regime no longer had any interest in job or social security for Syrians; it shared the Lebanese free market approach.[111] Reconstruction and other possibilities in Lebanon—from shop assisting to baking, metalworking, and taxi driving—relieved Syrian unemployment and generated up to $1 billion in annual worker incomes remitted to Syria. Fearful of dismissal, Syrians accepted depressed wages.[112] In the late 1990s, with the economy tightening, they also faced new resentment from poorer Lebanese. While businessmen profited from the Syrians, ordinary Lebanese faced wage cuts and job losses. The average Lebanese "salary" was $400 per month.[113] I was in a minibus in the poor

Shia quarter of Hay al-Sulam in late 2001 when the Shia driver spotted Syrian workers and exploded: "they have destroyed Lebanon" (*kharrabu lubnan*).

Hariri had trouble with both the Shia and Maronite "streets." This arose from the liberal capitalist orientation of reconstruction, which was unavoidable in its initial stages. Both Shia and Maronites suspected colonization of Beirut by Saudi and other Sunni Arab oil money. Shia loss of the finance ministry in the first Hariri government and rumors of shanty clearance in the southern suburbs in favor of a ring road brought Hezbollah protests. Shia *alim* Muhammad Husayn Fadlallah (see figure 6.4) accused Hariri's cabinet of converting Lebanon into "a joint stock company of the rich."[114] Fearful of Shia militants, Hariri spent $15 million on fortifying the government palace and in 1996 opened the Elissar project for redevelopment in the southern suburbs to Amal and Hezbollah patronage.[115]

The Syrian regime used its Lebanese counterpart for disciplinary purposes. On September 13, 1993, Damascus endorsed the authorities when the army shot dead nine demonstrators at a Hezbollah rally. In early 1994, the government banned the LF and arrested Samir Geagea, who was thereafter tried and convicted on murder charges for the 1987 assassination of Prime Minister

Figure 6.4 Shia *alim* Muhammad Husayn Fadlallah, Beirut, 1991. Associated Press.

Rashid Karami. Geagea spent the next eleven years in the basement of the defense ministry, only being released after Syria's 2005 withdrawal from Lebanon. No other ex-warlord faced such treatment; for Syria, the LF was an old foe, and its leader declined to serve the new order. In December 1996, the authorities detained Aoun supporters and Tripoli Sunnis after an assault on a Syrian mini-bus. Many detainees ended up in the Syrian military intelligence center in Beirut (the Beau Rivage Hotel), where torture was routine.[116]

Extraordinary corruption in postwar Lebanon frustrated Hariri. Lebanese and Syrian officials and personalities diverted several billion dollars every year out of loan money, government expenditure, private investment, and assorted illegal enterprises, probably equivalent to one quarter of GDP.[117] For example, at least $500 million of $2 billion, spent uselessly on trying to reduce Lebanon's electricity generation deficit in the 1990s, disappeared as kickbacks.[118]

The Syrian leadership manipulated the appetites of Lebanon's Maronite president and Shia parliamentary speaker to constrain the prime minister. Asad rewarded Amal leader Nabih Berri with the speakership in 1992 and cultivated President Hirawi. Berri and Hirawi defended their "shares" of the bureaucracy, wrecking Hariri's plans for administrative reform. Politicians recognized that "the present republic is fragmented and that what links its pieces is the Syrian thread."[119] In the other direction, Hariri's personal relations in Syria were more with prominent Sunnis—Khaddam and chief of staff Hikmat Shihabi—than with the Alawite Asads. Hariri developed a friendship of sorts with Ghazi Kana'an, the veteran Alawite head of Syrian military intelligence in Lebanon, lubricated by money, but Asad's son and heir apparent Bashar favored Lebanese army commander Lahoud.

In July 1993 and April 1996, Israel helped entrench Syria in Beirut and strengthened Hezbollah when it unleashed large-scale bombardments of southern Lebanon (operations "accountability" and "grapes of wrath") in response to Hezbollah rockets. On both occasions, hundreds of thousands of Shia fled north, and the Americans turned to Asad to help with cease-fires. In April 1996, Israel reaped opprobrium when artillery shells killed 102 civilians at a UN post during an exchange of fire with Hezbollah. The Israelis settled for an arrangement by which Hezbollah would refrain from firing into the Galilee as long as Israel did not retaliate against Shia villages for attacks in the "security zone." Hezbollah's prestige soared, especially when it wiped out an Israeli commando unit near Tyre in September 1997. Under a clever new young secretary-general, Hasan Nasrallah, after 1992, when the Israelis killed his predecessor Abbas Musawi, the Party of God entered the Lebanese parliament and invested heavily in social services. For example, al-Mustafa schools, under Hezbollah's Foundation for Islamic Religious Education, enrolled 8,091 students in 2001.[120] Nasrallah sought a deepened social base, and Iran built up the party's arsenal.

Into the late 1990s, Syrian hegemony coexisted with Lebanese pluralism in the media, professional organizations, the union movement, and the universities. In July 1995, the regime broke a general strike and in November 1996 limited television and radio licenses. Syria toyed with the constitution and parliamentary elections and in 1998 selected army commander Lahoud as president, a shift toward a Syrian-style security regime.

President Hirawi's six-year term ended in 1995; Asad plainly felt that Lahoud was not yet ready, and Khaddam opposed a military president.[121] Ghazi Kana'an chose the September 1995 engagement party of Umar Karami's son to announce that parliament would override the constitution and vote Hirawi in for three more years.[122] Damascus had a similar no-nonsense approach to the July/August 1996 parliamentary elections. Hariri and Berri got substantial blocs for the sake of stability; the Christian opposition was enticed and then decimated; Syrian nominees swept Mount Lebanon, the north, and the Biqa; and Hezbollah got cut back to placate the Americans. *Al-Nahar's* Sarkis Na'um awarded Damascus an Oscar, and his newspaper noted the 1996 results put the infamous 1947 elections in the shade for "intimidation, forgery, and abuses."[123]

In late 1998, the guard changed. Asad was nervous about Maronite hostility, as articulated by Patriarch Nasrallah Sfeir, so a Maronite president with more weight than the ineffectual Hirawi would suit. Also, Lebanon's economy was sufficiently revived to allow experimenting with a prime minister other than Hariri. Change reflected the rising star of Bashar al-Asad, who took charge of Syria's Lebanon file. Following orders, Lebanon's parliament elected Emile Lahoud president on October 15, 1998. Deputies with channels to Bashar maneuvered for a new prime minister; Hariri withdrew from contention, and Salim al-Huss returned.[124]

Lahoud and al-Huss curried public favor with corruption allegations against Hariri's group. In June 1999, sources close to Lahoud abused Hariri, accusing him of running the state as a "private company" and colluding with Israel to curb Hezbollah.[125] In parallel, Lahoud and his Syrian backers intended the Lebanese presidency to anchor a "security regime" through which intelligence chiefs would emasculate civilian politics. Although no fan of Lahoud, Syria's local proconsul, Ghazi Kana'an, saw virtue in a bumped-up Lebanese/Syrian security apparatus monitoring all parties.

Lahoud's behavior and Bashar's intrusion provoked Hariri and Druze leader Walid Junblat, hitherto firm Syrian allies. In December 1998, Junblat sarcastically asked al-Huss if his austerity would include "military, security, and intelligence agencies," and joined Hariri in opposition.[126] A "security regime" was foreign to Lebanon's freewheeling pluralism, so different from Ba'thist Syria, and the Huss cabinet failed to arrest the economic deterioration heralded by slowing growth before Hariri left office.

Syrian Ba'thist hegemony hardened, but difficulties loomed. In Syria, Hafiz al-Asad's increasing frailty raised the prospect of less-adept Syrian management. In Israel, Ehud Barak and Labor came to government after May 1999 elections, displacing the Likud, which Syria had found usefully status quo-oriented since 1996. Barak declared that Israel would abandon the occupied "security zone" within one year. This was to liquidate a liability and to push Syria and Lebanon toward general peace. Israel's departure would remove a primary justification for Syria's military presence in Lebanon. Syrian officials hoped Israel was not serious, believing "Israel will not withdraw . . . in a unilateral manner, because it will create a vacuum."[127] Hezbollah had no such fear and relished its approaching triumph.

In March 2000, at a summit in Geneva with U.S. President Bill Clinton, a sick Hafiz al-Asad rejected ideas for an Israeli/Syrian breakthrough regarding the Golan Heights. Israel was left with no option but to implement Barak's promise to leave southern Lebanon.[128] Israeli forces pulled out of the "security zone" between May 21 and 23. Hezbollah spread through the area, and the Lebanese army stayed out. One thousand SLA personnel fled to Israel, and another 1,500 surrendered. On June 16, UN Secretary-General Kofi Annan confirmed that Israel had retired behind the "blue line," the UN-defined international boundary. Meanwhile, Hafiz al-Asad died on June 10, and his son Bashar ascended to the Syrian presidency. Lebanon faced the new millennium with a new Syrian master, and, according to the international community, with no Israeli troops on its territory for the first time since 1982.

Careless Hegemony, 2000–2005

Lebanon's July/August 2000 parliamentary elections took place in an atmosphere of new possibilities and hope of an economic rebound. For the public, money talked, and Hariri was again man of the hour. For Sunnis, the dour Salim al-Huss did not register as a credible leader, and they wanted an assertive prime minister back. Lahoud and Kana'an crafted an electoral law to hobble Hariri's bloc by splitting Beirut, but Hariri swept the board in the capital, and al-Huss lost his seat. On the one hand, Hariri never questioned Syrian hegemony even when sorely tried. Furthermore, Hariri's ally Junblat owed his own electoral success to Syrian-promoted fragmentation of Mount Lebanon, in defiance of the Ta'if accord. Therefore, Hariri and Junblat still played within the Syrian game. On the other hand, discontent existed that was not just Christian.

Hafiz al-Asad always observed appropriate courtesies in relations with Lebanese politicians and preferred aloofness in dealings with the Lebanese. Bashar al-Asad would soon exhibit less care about the niceties and had already chosen favorites. Up to 2004, Lebanese politics under Damascus comprised three elements—Syria's clients, Syria's allies, and Syria's opponents. Clients and allies were the totality of the regime, and virtually the totality of parliament, although there were gains for allies at the expense of clients in 2000.

President Lahoud, the intelligence agency chiefs, and ministers and deputies close to Syria's Alawite leadership represented the core clients after 1998. A trusted military man with Arab nationalist credentials who headed an enhanced security machine, Lahoud clawed back presidential authority, but everyone knew this derived from the Asads. Therefore, contrary to Syrian hopes, Lahoud did not dent Maronite alienation. Other clients included the SSNP, the Syrian Ba'th, and the Faranjiya faction. Despite autonomous pretensions, Parliamentary Speaker Berri and his Amal bloc were also clients.

Allies differed from clients in having serious external relations beyond Syria. The large Hariri bloc remained an ally despite its Arab and Western connections and Lahoud's hostility. Hariri carried with him the majority of the Sunni community, Druze leader Junblat, and moderate Christian deputies.

Although the Syrian regime still depended on Hariri for a profitable Lebanon, it needed Hezbollah as a lever on Israel and the Americans and to constrain Hariri. Hezbollah was the Lebanese face of revolutionary Iran, Syria's partner. It received financial and training support through Iranian revolutionary guards. The Syrian regime gave Iran access to the Levant, and Iran inflated Syria's weight in the Arab and international arenas. After Israel's retreat in 2000, Syria and Iran backed Hezbollah's conversion of southern Lebanon and part of southern Beirut into fortified enclaves. Hezbollah was not a foreign body like the PLO. In the early 2000s, it had an elite professional force of two thousand to three thousand, which was better armed and trained than the much larger Lebanese army.[129] They were all Shia.

Syria and Hezbollah were not to be cheated of legitimacy for the latter's private army by Israel's withdrawal. In April 2000, through Amal leader Berri, they asserted continued Israeli occupation of eight square miles of Lebanon, the so-called Shebaa farms (see figure 6.5). The UN initially insisted that this sliver of the rocky flank of Mount Hermon was not Lebanese but rather part of the Syrian Golan captured by Israel in 1967. The Lebanese government adopted the Shebaa farms claim, with Syrian oral approval, but Damascus held back the critical written endorsement. Hezbollah thereby had Lebanese legitimation of indefinite resistance, the Lebanese army kept out of the way, and little danger existed of the UN spoiling this happy outcome by persuading Israel to satisfy the new Lebanese demand.

Hezbollah benefited from its leader's personal rapport with the new Syrian president. Bashar al-Asad was infatuated with Hezbollah's exploits. Equipped with a flood of missiles from its Syrian and Iranian patrons, Hezbollah regarded itself as a Middle Eastern power. According to Nasrallah, "the party has outgrown the country and the [Shia] community."[130] In fact, it was stuck within the Shia third of Lebanon's people and had no alternative program for Lebanon's prosperity. Hezbollah's leaders and activists were from religious families and the artisanry, and these were economically conservative. Basically Hezbollah shared Hariri's commercial orientation but, like Bashar and his circle, loathed Hariri's external connections.

By definition, opponents of Syrian hegemony had no place in the political system. Nonetheless, they represented the predominant mood among Christians and an undertone among others. With their leaders either exiled (Aoun and Amin Gemayel) or in detention (Geagea), Syria's opponents and Christians in general lacked leadership from the early 1990s. The Maronite church stepped into the breach; Patriarch Sfeir backed the Ta'if accord, but he and the bishops denounced Syrian steerage of Lebanon.[131]

In late 2000, Druze leader Junblat edged toward opposition. Throughout the 1990s, Junblat worked as Minister for the Displaced to patronize a slow Christian return to the Shuf. By the late 1990s, only about one-fifth were back, and Christians complained about the money that went to pay off Druze squatters.[132] During and after the 2000 elections, Junblat courted the Maronites by slamming Syrian electoral interference. Given that his share in parliament since 1992 had rested on a Syrian endorsed gerrymander, this incurred special "Syrian anger."[133] In November, Junblat noted that the new Hariri government's policy statement did not mention Syrian military redeployment. Syrian officials indicated that he was *persona non grata* in Damascus. For the Syrians, Junblat compromised their portrayal of opposition as merely Maronite recidivism.

In March 2001, Secretary of State Colin Powell signaled unchanged U.S. approval of Syrian hegemony when he declined to meet Patriarch Sfeir in Washington. The Lebanese/Syrian security machine struck almost immediately. Syrian troops entered the Shuf, and the family of Junblat's associate Akram Shuhayyib received a mail bomb. In August 2001, after Sfeir visited Junblat amid excited crowds, Lahoud's agents arrested activists and Bashar dispatched reinforcements. Syrian defense minister Mustafa Tlas stressed that Damascus "stands beside President Lahoud and brotherly Lebanese army commander Michel Suleiman" in facing "suspicious movements."[134] Neither Lahoud nor Bashar consulted Hariri. Junblat sought cover from Hariri's Syrian friends, hosting Vice President Khaddam in Mukhtara in May 2002. For Khaddam, Lahoud's treatment of Lebanon "as a barracks" was simply crass.[135]

Hariri came under increasing siege. In 2002 and 2003, Lahoud frustrated the prime minister's privatization plans. Hariri also had problems with Hezbollah, which resented his reservations about its clashes with Israel in the Shebaa farms.[136] In November 2002, the prime minister obtained aid and debt restructuring worth $7 billion, helped by his friend French President Jacques

Chirac, but the financial relief simply enabled his adversaries to stall reform. In December, Bashar eliminated autonomy within Syrian military intelligence in Lebanon, replacing Ghazi Kana'an as overall chief with Rustum Ghazale, a crony of Bashar's brother-in-law Asef Shawkat. Like Khaddam, Kana'an was outside the new elite around Bashar after 2000.

The Anglo-American occupation of Iraq in March/April 2003 opened a new phase for Lebanon. Again departing from his father's practice, Bashar al-Asad improved relations with Saddam Hussein after 2000. Bashar's regime assisted Saddam to smuggle oil and break UN sanctions and profited by more than $1 billion annually. In 2003, Syria rode the wave of hostility to the United States. Bashar allowed "volunteers" through Syria to fight the Americans, sheltered Iraqi Ba'thists, and criticized the George W. Bush administration in intemperate language. At the October 2003 Islamic summit in Malaysia, Bashar described the U.S. government as a "group of extremists" who used the September 11, 2001, attacks on the United States "to assault humanitarian values and principles."[137]

Lebanon was well locked down for the crisis to Syria's east. Confidence in Lahoud's security apparatus enabled a reduction of Syrian troops from 30,000 in 2000 to 16,000 in early 2003, probably the basic level for holding Syria's flank and keeping Hariri and Hezbollah in line. With the patriarch snubbed in Washington, a Syrian military draw down in Christian areas, and French and Vatican disapproval of the Anglo-American takeover of Iraq, Maronite opposition to Syria faltered. In December 2003, Bashar al-Asad summoned the Lebanese prime minister to a conclave in Damascus.[138] The Kuwaiti daily *al-Ra'i al-Am* described Hariri's humiliation:

> Syrian officials and officers comprehensively attacked Hariri, accusing him of secretly meeting a high-ranking American official in Lebanon and working against Syria.... A close former aide of Hariri says that the prime minister felt ill and went to hospital before returning to Lebanon.[139]

Contemptuous of American staying power, Bashar took little heed of the shifting mood toward Syria in Washington. In December 2003, President Bush signed the "Syrian Accountability and Lebanese Sovereignty Restoration Act," which was passed by Congress. Just as U.S. President Bush senior had opened the gate to Syrian hegemony in Lebanon in 1990, rewarding Syrian cooperation against Saddam Hussein, so President Bush junior revoked approval of this hegemony in response to Syrian facilitation of attacks on U.S. forces in Iraq.

Bashar's inclination to impose extension of Lebanese President Lahoud's constitutional six year term, due to end in November 2004, brought matters to a head. For Bashar, Lahoud had the advantages of proven reliability and fusion of civilian and security authority. In the end, no Maronite alternative compared. In mid-2004, Hariri and Junblat rejected extension, the former exasperated by Lahoud's sabotage and the latter provoked by the security machine. The affair reconciled Washington and Paris, which were at odds over Iraq, and rekindled Maronite opposition to Syria. Bashar's monopolization of Lebanon infuriated President Chirac; at the French leader's initiative, France and the United States pondered UN Security Council action against Syria.

Bashar summoned Hariri on August 27, 2004, and ordered him to have the Lebanese government and parliament put aside Lebanon's constitution in favor of three more years for Lahoud. According to Hariri, the Syrian president threatened to "break Lebanon over his [Hariri's] head."[140] The shaken prime minister arrived back in his mountain chalet above Beirut declaring: "to them [the Syrians] we are all ants."[141] Fear secured Lahoud his extension, lowering opposition in parliament from fifty to twenty-nine members.[142] Faced with defiance of their appeals for a new Lebanese president, the United States and France co-sponsored the UN Security Council (UNSC) resolution 1559 of September 2, 2004. The resolution required the termination of Syria's twenty-eight-year military presence in Lebanon; the disbanding of private armies, principally the military wing of Hezbollah; and a normal Lebanese presidential election free of foreign pressure. Syria, Hezbollah, and President Lahoud scorned the resolution.

Hariri relinquished the premiership on October 20, 2004, after a murder attempt on Druze politician Marwan Hamade, who had resigned as a minister to protest the Lahoud coup.[143] Under Umar Karami, the government became an appendage of the security apparatus. In November, Bashar sent Hezbollah's Nasrallah to persuade Junblat to behave himself, but the Druze leader escalated his rhetoric. In late January 2005, Junblat referred to "a very dangerous Syrian/Lebanese mafia" in a speech at l'Université Saint-Joseph.[144]

Hariri initially played a backstage role in constructing an opposition coalition including his Mustaqbal (Future) Movement, Junblat's PSP, the Qurnat Shehwan bloc of Christian politicians, and the Free Patriotic Movement of Michel Aoun (still in exile). He planned to overturn the Syrian-backed government during the internationally monitored May 2005 elections and recover Lebanese independence.[145] He told the Iranian ambassador to France that his problem "was not Hezbollah but the Syrian presence and its operations."[146] Nasrallah, solidly aligned with Syria and Iran, would not have been impressed.

Syria tried to sidestep UNSC resolution 1559 through rediscovery of the 1989 Ta'if call for redeployment to the Biqa, but a February 2, 2005, opposition conclave in Beirut demanded total withdrawal of Syrian troops and intelligence agents from Lebanon. This clearly had Hariri's imprint. After a February 10 mission to Damascus, UN envoy Terje Roed-Larsen warned Hariri that he feared for his safety.[147] Bashar reportedly told Roed-Larsen: "Hariri is playing dirty roles against Syria."[148] Four days later, Rafiq al-Hariri and twenty-two others died in a truck bomb explosion that demolished most of a street. Fury swept Lebanon's Sunni Muslims. Hariri's friend Abd al-Halim Khaddam was the only prominent Syrian who dared attend the funeral, at which thousands chanted: "There is no God but God, and Asad is the enemy of God."[149] February 14, 2005, would prove a landmark date; the killers probably never imagined that the event would be other than a momentary sensation, such as had been previous political murders. No one would have predicted that within two months there would be no Syrian troops in Lebanon or that Lebanon's affairs would become intertwined with international justice.

A Tale of Two Camps, 2005–2011

After the Hariri murder, large crowds assembled on Mondays in central Beirut to pillory the Lebanese and Syrian regimes. They were heavily bourgeois and Christian, and Bashar al-Asad sneered at them.[150] The electric atmosphere, however, was too much for Prime Minister Karami, who resigned on February 28. A caretaker cabinet took over to organize the May/June parliamentary elections. Reacting, Hezbollah brought out its crowd in an overwhelmingly Shia demonstration of about half a million on March 8, 2005, a date that branded the Hezbollah-led coalition. The party expressed its solidarity with the Syrian regime, provoking the anti-Bashar camp. On March 14, approximately one million Sunnis, Christians, and Druze came to downtown Beirut, along with Shia who were prepared to defy the Party of God. General Aoun's Christian supporters stood together with the Hariris and Junblats. The March 14 gathering marked the first month after the murder and appealed for justice, independence, and Syria's departure from Lebanon.

The United States and France headed the chorus of international outrage. The UN Security Council commissioned a preliminary investigation of the Hariri murder. The March 27 report accused Syria of creating the atmosphere of intimidation preceding the crime, charged the Syrian/Lebanese security machine with negligence and covering up evidence, and recommended a full international inquiry.[151] UNSC resolution 1595 of April 7, 2005, authorized such an inquiry to identify the murderers. In the special circumstances of early 2005—U.S. and French fury over the Lahoud extension and massive Lebanese agitation—the international community became committed for the first time to the pursuit of political murder. The scale of the reaction briefly unnerved the Syrian leadership. Bashar gave way on Syria's presence in Lebanon, and by April 26, all Syrian soldiers and identifiable intelligence operatives had left the country.

The March 14 "independence" front soon split, however, with Michel Aoun and his Maronite supporters resentful of the new Sunni/Druze preeminence in the Lebanese opposition to the Syrian regime. Aoun returned from exile in May 2005 in a truculent mood, not improved by a miserly offer of parliamentary seats on the March 14 candidate allocations, the March 14 rejection of having him as president, and Junblat's tactical alignment with Hezbollah against Aounist candidates. In the May/June parliamentary elections, the first postwar poll free of Syrian interference, March 14 minus Aoun gained 72 of 128 seats; Aoun and friends won the Maronite heartland with 21 seats; and the Hezbollah/Amal combination swept the mainly Shia districts, taking 35 seats. It was a broadly accurate reflection of popular weight and sectarian differentiation. The March 14 rump—the "new majority"—led the new government under Rafiq al-Hariri's colleague Fuad Siniora as prime minister. The March 8 camp, including President Lahoud's Christian nominees, agreed to a bloc of cabinet posts one short of the one-third necessary to veto major decisions. Aoun declined to join the government and made it clear that he would not supply the votes necessary to tip Lahoud out of office.

For March 14, the remainder of 2005, dominated by the UN inquiry and more political murders, was a perilous high tide. The UN International Independent Investigating Commission (UNIIIC) began work in Beirut in June under Berlin prosecutor Detlev Mehlis. More murders and attempted murders of Lebanese critics of Syria emphasized that Lebanon's future depended on international resolve. Murder targets included Defense Minister Elias al-Murr, son-in-law of President Lahoud, who revealed his falling-out with Syria's departed supremo in Lebanon, Rustum Ghazale.[152] In the first UNIIIC report in late October, Mehlis noted "converging evidence" that the Syrian/Lebanese security machine was behind the Hariri assassination.[153] On November 10, Bashar al-Asad termed Lebanon's governing majority a "factory" for conspiracies against Syria, and on December 12, the same day Mehlis submitted his second report, a bomb blast killed Jibran Tuwayni, al-Nahar publisher, and the leading Christian activist in the March 14 parliamentary bloc.[154] The second UNIIIC report, again the unanimous view of all seven international prosecutors in the team, defined unnamed Syrian officials as "suspects."[155] The UN Security Council proposed a tribunal of international and Lebanese judges, sitting outside Lebanon, to indict and try those identified as responsible for the Hariri murder and multiplying associated crimes. Advised that he could no longer operate in Beirut because of death threats, Detlev Mehlis withdrew as UNIIIC head in January 2006 and was replaced by Belgian prosecutor Serge Brammertz.[156]

Although Syria and Hezbollah remained on the defensive in early 2006, the advantage shifted. In February, Michel Aoun met Hezbollah chief Hasan Nasrallah, and Aoun's Free Patriotic Movement (FPM) joined the March 8 front, handing Syria's allies cross-communal credibility. Perversely, the prospect of an international tribunal relaxed UNIIIC pressure on the Syrians. Brammertz backed away from indictments assessed by Mehlis as almost viable and concentrated on reviewing evidence.[157] Syria and Hezbollah could see space for a counter-strike just when a Lebanese "national dialogue" forced a consensus endorsing justice for Hariri and subjected Hezbollah to hitherto unheard-of questioning of its private army. Brammertz's June 2006 report focused on Syria and suggested a "multi-layered" murder conspiracy.[158] It was time for Hezbollah to turn the tables on March 14, to reiterate the primacy of resistance to Israel and deflate the threat of the Hariri case.

On July 12, 2006, Hezbollah raided across the Israel/Lebanon border in the Galilee, far from the disputed Shebaa farms, kidnapping two Israeli soldiers and killing three. Hezbollah claimed this was to compel release of Lebanese and Palestinian prisoners, and Nasrallah later asserted he had not anticipated a large-scale Israeli response. The latter was disingenuous because a challenge to Israel on its own territory of such a scale was certain to bring a conflagration. In the event, the destruction may have gone beyond Hezbollah's calculation of a small war for its convenience, but that is beside the point. The hostilities that Hezbollah triggered lasted five weeks, during which Israel used aerial bombardment and ground assault to degrade Hezbollah, causing devastation and approximately one thousand deaths in the Shia areas of Lebanon. Hezbollah suffered painful casualties among its small professional force but fired missiles into Israel until the cease-fire. It fought well and hid its losses, and its publicity organs trumpeted the "divine victory."

After the August 14, 2006, cease-fire, the struggle within Lebanon between the March 14 and March 8 camps intensified. Under the March 14 banner, most non-Shia Lebanese resented Hezbollah's war decision in disregard of the Lebanese government. The balance was ambiguous. The government, with its March 14 majority, survived. UNSC resolution 1701 fingered Hezbollah for initiating the fighting and reiterated the demand for an end to private armies. The party had to accept a boosted UNIFIL and Lebanese army deployment to the border with Israel (see figure 6.5). Most Lebanese Shia remained loyal to Hezbollah, although it would be perilous for the party again to plunge them into the maelstrom. Hezbollah received new weaponry from Syria; the army did not dare challenge the party; and Iran bankrolled both civilian reconstruction and a new line of missile bunkers north of the Litani River.

On November 10, 2006, the draft UN protocol for a mixed international/Lebanese murder tribunal arrived in Beirut for approval by the Lebanese government and parliament. Rafiq al-Hariri's son Sa'ad, the March 14 leader, placed a copy on his father's grave. Hezbollah, Amal, and other pro-Syrian ministers resigned to derail official endorsement, but the government used its two-thirds quorum to pass the tribunal protocol. Hezbollah and its allies declared the government illegitimate and began street agitation. Prime Minister Siniora's rump cabinet endured from November 2006 until May 2008. The murder machine reappeared with assassinations of three more March 14 parliamentarians. Siniora's vindication came in June 2007; ignoring Bashar al-Asad's threats of violence in Lebanon, the UN Security Council bypassed the paralyzed Lebanese parliament and unilaterally established the Special Tribunal for Lebanon (STL).[159]

An uprising of Sunni Islamists in the Nahr al-Barid Palestinian refugee camp near Tripoli, involving Syrian military intelligence, promptly followed.[160] The Lebanese army overcame the rebels by September, but their leader slipped back to Syria. Even with Palestinian population growth limited by emigration, the

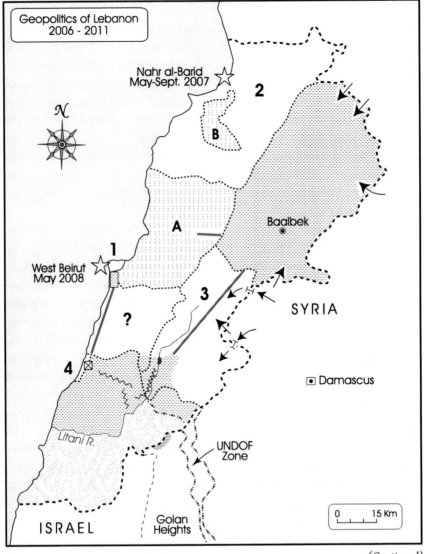

Geopolitics of Lebanon
2006 - 2011

Nahr al-Barid
May-Sept. 2007

West Beirut
May 2008

Baalbek

SYRIA

Damascus

Litani R.

UNDOF
Zone

ISRAEL

Golan
Heights

0   15 Km

(Continued)

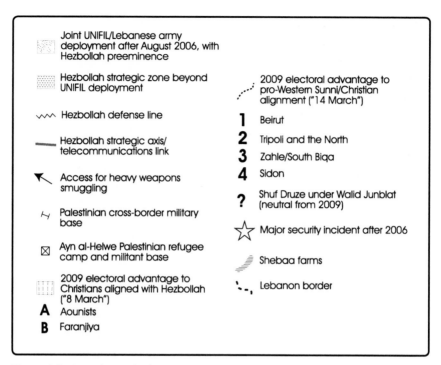

Joint UNIFIL/Lebanese army deployment after August 2006, with Hezbollah preeminence

Hezbollah strategic zone beyond UNIFIL deployment

⋁⋁⋁ Hezbollah defense line

━━ Hezbollah strategic axis/ telecommunications link

❮ Access for heavy weapons smuggling

⊢ Palestinian cross-border military base

⊠ Ayn al-Helwe Palestinian refugee camp and militant base

2009 electoral advantage to Christians aligned with Hezbollah ("8 March")
A Aounists
B Faranjiya

2009 electoral advantage to pro-Western Sunni/Christian alignment ("14 March")

1 Beirut
2 Tripoli and the North
3 Zahle/South Biqa
4 Sidon

? Shuf Druze under Walid Junblat (neutral from 2009)

☆ Major security incident after 2006

Shebaa farms

Lebanon border

Figure 6.5 Geopolitics of Lebanon, 2006–2011.

larger refugee camps remained lawless islands beyond the Lebanese state. The facilities of Syrian-aligned Palestinian groups, such as the PFLP-GC, infringed Lebanese sovereignty on the Lebanese/Syrian border, providing staging posts for armed infiltration (figure 6.5).[161]

Emile Lahoud departed office in November 2007, leaving a six-month presidential vacuum. Blocked on civilian options, March 14 proposed army commander Michel Suleiman for president. March 8 accepted his candidacy but refused his election unless they obtained the veto third in a new government. Hezbollah and Syria viewed Suleiman as a weak person whom they could push around. Murder took a new twist with terrorization of Lebanon's military and investigative apparatus. On December 12, 2007, and January 25, 2008, car bombs killed, respectively, General François al-Hajj, an independent-minded officer likely to become army chief, and Captain Wissam Eid, head of communications investigations in the Hariri case. In parallel, a new president of France, Nicolas Sarkozy, sought a "realist" deal with Bashar, who could also look forward to a more accommodating U.S. president in early 2009.

In May 2008, the Siniora government confronted Hezbollah and tested Western backing by dismissing the Hezbollah aligned Shia officer in charge of airport security and launching a probe of the party's communications network. Hezbollah announced a threat to the "resistance" by those servicing Israel, and on 8–9 May, the party and Syria's armed clients invaded mainly Sunni quarters of West Beirut.[162] Hezbollah's "operation smashing the balance" [*amaliyat kasr al-tawazun*] demonstrated that the party would assault problematic Lebanese. Receiving no Western support, the government reversed its decisions. The Arab League then brokered a settlement in Doha. Suleiman became president, praising the "resistance," and March 8 achieved the blocking third in a new Siniora cabinet.[163]

Thereafter, March 14 retained its parliamentary majority in the mid-2009 elections, but new Prime Minister Sa'ad al-Hariri became politically crippled when Druze leader Walid Junblat took his bloc out of March 14 in early 2010. Junblat, a bitter critic of the Syrian regime in 2005–2006, was convinced by 2009 that Syria and Iran had the upper hand and that the policy of the new U.S. president, Barack Obama—to "engage" Bashar al-Asad—meant that the West would betray its Lebanese friends. He reversed his positions and reconciled with Bashar and Hasan Nasrallah. Sa'ad al-Hariri had no choice as prime minister of a "national unity government" but to go to Damascus in December 2009 to meet the Syrian president, whom he regarded as complicit in his father's murder.

The STL came into existence in The Hague in March 2009. The special tribunal's Canadian prosecutor, Daniel Bellemare, pursued telecommunications evidence that implicated Hezbollah in the Hariri murder. After 13 incidents, 58 deaths, and at least 335 injured, the post-Cold War world's most dramatic political murder series ended with the Eid killing in early 2008. This coincided with the assassination in Damascus of Hezbollah intelligence chief Imad Mughniya, possibly the link between Hezbollah and the Syrian leadership in the chain of responsibility.

In July 2010, Hezbollah leader Nasrallah said he expected STL charges against members of his organization. Hezbollah denounced the tribunal as an Israeli-American plot and, together with the Syrian regime, required that the Lebanese government disown it. Sa'ad al-Hariri refused, and on January 13, 2011, the March 8 camp left the government, forcing the prime minister to resign. Six months later, on June 13, Najib Mikati, the Sunni prime ministerial nominee of Hezbollah, Aoun, and Junblat, formed a government subordinate to Hezbollah.

By mid-2011, however, Hezbollah and the Syrian regime faced a crisis that overshadowed their Lebanese coup. On June 29, the STL officially delivered murder indictments against Hezbollah members. Concurrently, the savagery of the Syrian regime against a popular uprising in its own country that began in March 2011 provoked repudiation of Bashar al-Asad by most Syrians. Hezbollah, party of the oppressed, backed repression in Syria. Within Lebanon, Prime Minister Mikati could not defy his own community by following Hezbollah against either the Syrian uprising or the STL.

Overall, the lack of social responsibility of the Lebanese high bourgeoisie alongside Hezbollah weapons hindered the progress of the Lebanese state into the new century. Modest gains for public education and social services in the 1960s were lost during wartime disruption. Neither received priority after 1990. This was the period of Shia growth and concentration in the southern suburbs of Beirut, and Shia were left to themselves. The state similarly absented itself from the Sunni north. Christians could fall back on an older private education system, but many could not afford it.

As for the judiciary, Lebanon developed decent civil and criminal courts on the French model, a legacy of the mandate and the mid-twentieth century, but terrorization and dilapidation after 1975 meant they lost credibility. Only international justice in the shape of the STL offers hope for renewed judicial authority in Lebanon.

Like its public institutions, Lebanon's economy after 2005 was makeshift. Hezbollah's July 2006 military adventure resulted in damages of around $3.6 billion, but through 2006, $5 billion of émigré remittances flowed into the country.[164] This gave Lebanon the second highest remittances-to-GDP ratio in the world, at 22.3 percent.[165] Lebanon's Diaspora, its robust banks, and the flow of money from the Arab oil states and Iran into the rival camps guaranteed that the country could bump along. The conservative proclivities of the banks, which avoided exotic financial derivatives, and surging Gulf Arab tourism, supporting everything from malls to prostitution, floated Lebanon through the 2008–2009 global recession.

In environmental terms, the country remained a shambles, with shocking air and water pollution and landscape degradation. No one took seriously Beirut's vulnerability to a major earthquake. Because of public debt, the social facilities phase of reconstruction never arrived. Tripoli and the north endure "extreme poverty."[166] Employment discrimination against Palestinians has continued, and many Syrian workers fled the country after the Hariri murder, returning after the Syrian military departure. The most callously treated in recent years have been the 200,000 migrant domestic workers from South and South East Asia. A September 2010 Human Rights Watch report detailed abuse and slave labor conditions.[167]

Each of the Lebanese political blocs that emerged in 2005–2006 was cross-sectarian. Differences related to external associations of each camp and clamping down on assassins. March 14 looked to the West and conservative Arabs, emphasized freedoms, and wanted private armies disbanded but offered no social development policy. March 8 looked to the Syrian ruling clique and Iran and acquiesced in Hezbollah's agenda: supremacy of "resistance" to Israel over all else and denigration of international justice. There was no economic policy difference between the camps after 2005.[168] March 8 has a "new rich" flavor, especially Hezbollah's backers in the Shia Diaspora, whereas March 14 draws on the secularized bourgeoisie of Beirut, including Shia. Both mass retinues encompass all classes. March 14 has reached into the poorest part of Lebanon—the Sunni north—but without doing the north any good.

Cross-sectarian dimensions could not disguise Sunni/Shia sensitivity. Sunnis clustered in March 14 behind Prime Ministers Fuad Siniora (2005–2009) and Sa'ad al-Hariri (2009–2011); locked into siege thinking, most Shia supported Hezbollah or Amal, primarily the former. Sunni humiliation in May 2008 took Beirut beyond the worst days of Sunni hostility to the Shia assertion of the 1980s. Salafists and other Islamists gained Sunni support as March 14 seemed ineffectual. Most scorned Shia. The Christian 35 percent of Lebanon had the casting political vote, but it was split between the Kata'ib, the LF, and Patriarch Sfeir, who went with March 14, and the Aounists, who joined March 8, embracing their former Syrian enemy. Sour Christian defeatism negated Christian defense of pluralism. What could be said—whatever Maronite irritation there was about Sunni advantage after 1990—was that Christians and Sunnis agreed on arms and the state. An April 2006 opinion survey indicated that more than 80 percent of Christians and Sunnis, but only 40 percent of Shia, endorsed a state monopoly of force.[169]

Could most Shia and most other Lebanese accommodate one another? Hezbollah's absolutism was not promising, nor was the absence within the March 14 camp of any imaginative vision of a new Lebanon. Such a vision implied restructured politics, perhaps a legislature mixing communal and non-communal representation added to rotation of executive positions. It was intolerable that Shia, Druze, and non-Maronite Christians—half the population—could never be president or prime minister.

Sunni and Christian disdain and Shia sensitivity stiffened Hezbollah's militarized autonomy. The party's melding of Iranian support with communal revenues gave it financial viability. Its education activities, health clinics, care of families of martyrs, and reconstruction aid after the 2006 warfare targeted groups neglected by the state. Facing international murder indictments in late 2011, Hezbollah has an indulgent Shia public. Party leader Nasrallah, deputy leader Na'im Qasim, a former chemistry teacher, and Hezbollah's al-Manar satellite television station parade victimhood. The question is whether Shia will stay with Hezbollah through the party's confrontation with international justice, its partisanship in Syria, and revelations of financial irregularities.[170]

Five years after Hezbollah's 2006 warfare with Israel, Lebanese Shia cannot endure repetition; the party's remote control of government has excited hostility in the rest of Lebanon; and Shia competitors endure. Fadlallah's charitable institutions live on after his death in 2010.[171] Leaders of Amal, the party's atrophied partner, detest Hezbollah. Old leading clans, together with leftists persecuted by both Hezbollah and Amal, nurse their bitterness. Even so, Hezbollah has Shia insecurity and the Iranian theocracy to help it survive any collapse of the Asad regime, its Arab patron. More broadly, transformation in Syria would convulse the affairs of all Lebanon's little worlds.

Conclusion

In 1689 and 1700, the renowned Sunni Muslim poet and Sufi sheikh of Damascus, Abd al-Ghani al-Nabulusi, traveled in the vicinity of Mount Lebanon. On each occasion he wrote an account of his journey. He wrote glowingly of the gardens, rivers, orchards, and towns. He even provides us with an early Muslim reference to "Lebanon" when writing in verse about his crossing of the Litani River on the way from the Biqa to Sidon in the Spring of 1700: "Greetings to the valley in the expanse of Lebanon (*salaam ala al-wadi bi sahat lubnan*)."[1] It is not clear what the term meant to him, except that it encompassed the Litani.

Unsurprisingly, al-Nabulusi was at home with the Sunni Muslim elite of the coastal towns, where he had intellectual discussions, admired the stone architecture of Beirut and Tripoli, and toured the mosques and saints' tombs. The mountains, however, at times seemed beyond his comfort zone. Spending a night at Deir al-Qamar in the Shuf, old seat of the Druze lords, he mainly complained of the vicious insect life. As for the Druze of the mountain, in his 1689 Biqa travelogue he recounts the tale of "a group of Druze" who killed a wild boar and ate it after washing the carcass in the water of a certain well.[2] The well then dried up and no water ever reappeared. The Maronites of the high peaks behind Tripoli seem to have left al-Nabulusi cold—literally. Al-Nabulusi and his party spent a miserable spring night in 1700 in the village of Aynata on the Biqa side of the main pass from Tripoli:

> We endured there a night of biting cold (*layla barida ka annaha al-zamharir*). And there is no wonder about that because the people are Christians and the mountain above is covered with a great deal of snow.[3]

Al-Nabulusi projects the sectarian consciousness of his milieu and an interweaving of familiarity and difference for a Damascene visiting the coast and Mount Lebanon. These features continue from the seventeenth century and earlier through to the twenty-first century. They have come to be expressed, respectively, in the multicommunalism of modern Lebanon and the tight but fraught relations between the new countries of Lebanon and Syria from 1920 onward.

Beginning with the Maronite Catholics in the early nineteenth century, long-standing sectarian identities went through a metamorphosis that produced the demand for representation of sects as political collectives. Maronites developed what might be termed "sectarian nationalism" with territorial claims first to Mount Lebanon and later to additional territories. They adapted these claims to the existence and reactions of other local communities in the concept of multicommunalism under Maronite leadership. The Maronite church also provided the prototype of institutional sectarianism through the nineteenth century: mobilization of peasantry for political purposes, organized communal lobbying, and a general institutional embodiment of the sectarian collective. Its role climaxed in the involvement of Patriarch al-Huwayyik in the creation of Greater Lebanon in 1920. The other communities, mainly after being involuntarily brought together in Greater Lebanon by France and the Maronite elite, evolved their own Lebanese institutions through the twentieth century. The increasing cohesion and assertiveness of the Twelver Shia, from establishment of the Ja'afari courts in the 1920s to Musa al-Sadr and the Higher Shia Islamic Council in the 1960s to Hezbollah's communal hegemony after 2000, provides the most comparable illustration. The Druze already had the strongest informal coherence of any Lebanese community, under their ad hoc lordly leadership, while Sunnis had command of urban Islamic institutions from the Ottoman period.

Obviously political and institutional sectarianism transformed and magnified the sense of being a Maronite or Orthodox Christian, a Sunni or Shia Muslim, or a Druze in Mount Lebanon and Greater Lebanon from 1840 onward. Equally, as anywhere else, Lebanese have and had multiple shifting identities, with the balance varying from person to person. Family, sect, state, nation, religion, and whatever understandings of each all contribute to the mix. Further, loyalty to a religion-derived community does not necessarily mean religiosity; there are numerous agnostic and even atheist Maronites, Sunnis, and Shia. Nonetheless, for most Lebanese, religion and community do run together to a greater or lesser extent. Whatever the identity mix, it is difficult to deny the potency of a sectarian community in Lebanese affairs and among the Lebanese people since late Ottoman times. Also, communal identities, without political effect but with political potential, and with only rudimentary institutional expression, predated political sectarianism by many centuries. These identities were Lebanon's chief cultural features from medieval times and became the framework of the modern country.

Family alignments have, of course, divided and criss-crossed communities. Among Maronites, the feud between the Faranjiyas and the Gemayels was a subplot of the war years after the 1978 killing of Tony Faranjiya in a militia raid. Competition among leading families for the prime minister's chair has destabilized Lebanese Sunnis since 1943. The Shihabs have Maronite and Sunni branches, and Orthodox Christian Tuwaynis have Druze Hamade descent. The vendettas among Shia clans in the Biqa persist. All the same, people need a social anchor bigger than family, and in Lebanon, sect—even if represented by a segment of the sect—to a substantial degree became that anchor.

Is there anything decisive that distinguishes the story of Mount Lebanon and its surrounds from the rest of the Levant and in particular from interior Syria? It is certainly true that the local communal identities, clan jostling, and feudal-style arrangements of the Mamluk and Ottoman periods were more general characteristics of Bilad al-Sham, or geographical Syria. As an Ottoman device for indirect rule and tax gathering, the informal mountain emirate of the Ma'ns and Shihabs had a number of counterparts in interior Syria and Palestine.[4]

Yet Mount Lebanon did have distinguishing peculiarities. First, its cohabitation by three entrenched non-Sunni sectarian communities, two with high profile external associations—the Maronites with western Europe and the Twelver Shia with Iran—had no counterpart. Second, no other local autonomy in the Ottoman Levant—for example those of Zahir al-Umar in northern Palestine or the Azms as governors of Damascus—matched the quarter millennium longevity of the Ma'ns and their Shihab relatives, from the 1590s to the 1840s. The Ma'n/Shihab story culminated in what came close to a real principality of Mount Lebanon under Bashar II Shihab in the early nineteenth century. Third, the growing strength of the Maronite Catholics assisted by European cultural and economic penetration—a unique combination of circumstances—clearly played a role in this longevity and its outcome. In sum, Mount Lebanon stood out in geographical Syria before it became a special administration and the nucleus of a new country after 1860.

Whatever the special attributes of Mount Lebanon and its coast through the centuries, its people and communities all had and continue to have fundamental associations with the rest of the Levant. The Maronites originated in northern Syria, near Homs, and a significant number of Maronites live in modern Syria. Apart from modern political experience and institutional development, Lebanese Sunni Muslims are intimately interconnected with the Sunni Muslim majority of interior Syria through family ties and common Arabist sentiment. Much the same applies for Orthodox Christians, whose patriarch resides in Damascus. The Twelver Shia may be more exclusively concentrated in Lebanon than any other community, but they originally had a wider spread encompassing northern Palestine and southern Syria, and they have a great shrine in Damascus—the tomb of Sitt Zeinab, sister of the Imam Husayn and once a prisoner of the Umayyad Caliph Yazid. The modern Shia political leadership also has had the closest relations with Syria's ruling Asad family, members of the Twelver Shia-derived Alawite sect. The modern states of Lebanon and Syria share language, dialect, culture, and sectarian variety. Up to World War I, they shared a history of common Islamic overlords as well as the medieval crusader challenge, and between the world wars they were both under French hegemony as a "mandate" of the League of Nations.

Finally diverging, modern Lebanon and Syria followed different political and economic paths after they became independent states in the 1940s. Lebanon maintained upper bourgeois parliamentary politics, the freewheeling liberal economics of the "merchant republic," and the sectarian pluralism and public freedoms of "confessional democracy" until external pressures acting on internal imbalances brought the breakdown of the state in the 1970s. The country preserved its pluralist and liberal commercial commitments through the subsequent chaos into the twenty-first century. In contrast, Syria proceeded through military coups and increasing state steerage of the economy to the dictatorship of the Arab nationalist and semi-socialist Ba'th party in the 1960s. Thereafter, the Syrian people entered four decades of Orwellian stability and secret police supervision under Hafiz and Bashar al-Asad. As for sectarianism, the Lebanese operated it while Ba'thist Syria denied it, even though a portion of the Alawite minority commanded the Syrian state. Such dissimilar modern experiences through three generations began to make the inhabitants of the initially artificial new territorial states different peoples.

In 2011, the difference is being tested; Lebanese are bemused and divided as they watch masses of ordinary Syrians courageously attempt to discard dictatorship and aspire to their own pluralism. Many Lebanese Maronites and Shia fear the unknown of a new Syria, while the assertion of the Syrian majority stirs Lebanese Sunnis. In close proximity to the drama in Syria, Lebanon's secular and spiritual leaders present a dispiriting spectacle, mostly either paralyzed and waiting to see where to drift with events or fellow travelers with the blood-soaked Syrian ruling clique. The year 2011 marked one of the low points of the 1,400 years covered in this book.

The late twentieth-century rise to prominence of Lebanon's Shia community threw into relief the relative neglect of Shia in historical accounts of Mount Lebanon and its neighborhood. A flood of literature has ensued on the past and present of the Shia that has not merely filled the gap, but after twenty years raises the question of inattention to the rest of Lebanon. Fashions will doubtless shift, but there has also been a broader questioning of representations of the long run of the past that privilege trends among Druze and Maronites.

The Maronites of Mount Lebanon are at the core of the "Lebanist" historiography that accompanied the emergence of a Maronite-dominated Lebanese polity in the early twentieth century. In this narrative, the Druze lords of the Shuf, particularly Fakhr al-Din Ma'n, were the handmaidens of Maronite supremacy. Fakhr al-Din purportedly envisaged "an independent greater Lebanon," he was a closet Maronite, and his domain was a crucial precedent for the modern state.[5] For "Lebanists," the Druze and Maronite elite hierarchy and the rise of the Maronite church and peasants were the central dynamic of the eighteenth and early nineteenth centuries.[6]

"Lebanists" divine the singularity of Mount Lebanon in the Levant from the accounts of Maronite, Sunni, and Druze chroniclers: Ibn al-Qila'i, Salih bin Yahya, al-Khalidi al-Safadi, Istifan Duwayhi, Haydar al-Shihabi, and Tannus al-Shidyaq. Two points must be made, regardless of either "Lebanists" or errors and agendas in the chronicles. First, these chronicles are crucial sources for the detailed history of Mount Lebanon in medieval and early modern times. Second, good arguments can be made for according Druze and Maronites privileged places in the history of the territory that has become modern Lebanon. The Druze lords provided the historical foundations of the political order that prevailed in Mount Lebanon after about 1700. The Maronites—church, secular leaders, and commoners— provided the demographic, cultural, and political impetus toward the emergence of modern Lebanon between about 1800 and 1943.[7]

Revisionist accounts of Ottoman Mount Lebanon variously downgrade any idea of the mountain being exceptional in Ottoman Syria, upgrade the Shia, and identify European involvement as decisive in precipitating the political sectarianism of the modern state. The verdict on an exceptional Mount Lebanon must be ambiguous. The administrative arrangements were technically standard, but their actual operation and the Christian and Druze context were both unusual. As for the Shia, the Hamade chiefs of northern Mount Lebanon and the Harfush clan of the Biqa certainly rivaled the Druze Ma'ns in sixteenth and seventeenth-century Ottoman dispositions.[8] In the north, Maronite church factions long looked to the patronage of Shia lords. Jabal Amil always made the Shia a vital part of the mountain story. Regarding communal political ambitions, the revisionist narrative rejects any communal political coloring for the Ma'n/Shihab informal principality. In this interpretation, political agendas based on sectarian identity arose in the mid-nineteenth century principally out of colonialist intrusion.[9] There was no serious indigenous evolution toward communal political claims, specifically those of the Maronites; political sectarianism resulted from European interaction with the Ottomans and local society, disconnected from preceding sectarian identity.

Recent scholarship has settled several matters. There was no principality of the Ma'ns and Shihabs as a "Lebanon in waiting" from the sixteenth century; no "Lebanese" or communal political claims can be identified before 1800; and the Shia and Jabal Amil have a legitimate claim to their portion of the central ground of Lebanese history alongside the Maronites, Druze, and Mount Lebanon—as also do the Sunnis of the coastal towns.

Nonetheless we should not be dogmatic. The 1519 entry in the Arslani *Sijill* refers explicitly to a "principality of Mount Lebanon" (*imarat jabal lubnan*) under Druze lords in late Mamluk times.[10] Thereafter, Fakhr al-Din Ma'n's exertions between 1590 and 1633 did have an impact that, perhaps fortuitously, turned out to be lasting. He brought communal chiefs into tentative interaction, and he inaugurated a line of mountain lords that could have dissolved at almost any point but instead produced a real de facto mountain polity two hundred years later. Along the way, a battle at Ayn Dara high above Beirut in 1711 affected the balance of the mountain elite to make something like the Maronite dominated polity of Bashir II Shihab more likely. This is far removed from claiming an "inter-confessional system of rule under the Druze emirs."[11]

Otherwise, the Druze/Maronite coexistence that eased Christian expansion through much of Mount Lebanon in the seventeenth and eighteenth centuries brought demographic and social shifts that made development of communal identity into communal politics increasingly possible. Tentative demographic evidence indicates an astonishing shift in communal proportions between about 1550 and the 1860s, principally in favor of the Maronites. Added to the personal factor of the socially disruptive behavior of Bashir II Shihab, there was a route to Maronite political sectarianism substantially by indigenous evolution. European colonialist intrusion was not necessarily decisive.

From the late eighteenth century to the mid-twentieth century, from the Shihab peak to modern Lebanon's independence, the Maronite story was the center of gravity of Lebanon's story. The Druze became dwarfed and the Shia went into eclipse until the 1960s. The main new element, when the Maronites overreached themselves in the creation of Greater Lebanon in 1920, was the necessity of Christian partnership with the Sunni Muslims of Beirut, Tripoli, and Sidon. The latter were the initially unwilling new second community of the new country when the French added the coast, the Biqa, and the fringing ranges to Mount Lebanon.

What about sectarianism in Lebanon's continuing story? Sectarianism is stubborn in Lebanon. Many, especially in an insouciant bourgeoisie looking again to make Beirut a world city, manage to turn it aside and emphasize other orientations in their work and social affairs. Many others, however, still look to sect as a group reference point, a focus of collective pride and patronage networks, and a protective umbrella in times of insecurity. In the late twentieth and early twenty-first centuries, a new sectarian saga unfolded as the Shia resurfaced and emphasis shifted from Christian/Muslim to Shia/Sunni sensitivity. By this stage, "confessional democracy" and sectarian personal status had been organizing principles of the modern state for the entire eight decades of its existence.

Many Lebanese say they want a nonsectarian political system. Some simply calculate the advantage of this for their favored sectarian parties; their motives may be questioned. A June 2006 draft law for partial proportional voting proposed by middle class and intellectual proponents of democracy and electoral reform caused a flurry of debate aborted by Hezbollah's fight with Israel. The proposal did not regain traction. The only real hope for revitalizing Lebanese democracy lies in the new environment that would come with a democratic revolution in Syria.

After 2005, Lebanon divided between those prioritizing a fortress defying Israel and America and those prioritizing a revamped peaceable merchant republic, with members of all sects on both sides.[12] Nonetheless, even in this seemingly nonsectarian argument, the hegemonic Shia party was on one side and the mass of Sunnis were on the other. The same applied to the controversy over the Special Tribunal for Lebanon. Maronites split according to which side they interpreted as more or less subversive of Christian Lebanon.

In short, it was too easy to declare communal identities irrelevant and to elevate the ersatz Lebanon of such 2009–2010 culinary stunts as the world's largest kibbeh (Lebanese meat pie), tabouleh (parsley-based salad), or hummus (crushed chick peas). It was plain that most Sunnis of Tripoli, Shia of the Dahiya, Christians of the Kisrawan, and Druze of the Shuf remained hesitant to melt together. There were different imaginings of the character and external ties of a common Lebanon—imaginings varying within sects but also, and more broadly, between their majority orientations. It was unrealistic to expect smooth coalescence in a country that was still more the communal conglomerate of the long run of its history than a real nation state.

The long run also resonated in other respects despite the immensely different context of the past century and a half compared with all previous history in terms of population growth, technological advance, and compression of time and space. The weight and sophistication of human infrastructure in a densely packed modern Lebanon of more than four million people that can be traversed by road in a couple of hours differs stunningly from medieval Mount Lebanon, with its primitive communications, small and largely illiterate population, isolated communities, and nightly shutdown. Roads were tracks, and an army would take two days to cross the Biqa from Damascus. A mere couple of hundred thousand inhabitants obviously gave a sense of uncluttered space that has been lost. Nonetheless, local leadership challenges amid the close interest of greater powers have hardly changed at all. In 759, Christians in Mount Lebanon launched a tax revolt against the Abbasids in coordination with a Byzantine landing at Tripoli, bringing a fierce response—just as Syria and Soviet Russia reacted to American linkage with President Amin Gemayel in 1983. In 1110 and 1277, Druze lords provoked the Franks and Mamluks respectively, attracting deadly punishment—as did Kamal Junblat with Syria in 1976–1977.

The celebrated modern Lebanese writer Elias Khoury reminds readers of the deep groove of the long run in his novel, *The Gates of the City*.

> The storyteller said: That things are just what they are, things, and this happened a thousand years ago and will happen again in a thousand years. And the storyteller was laughing. . . .[13]

ABBREVIATIONS

AUB	American University of Beirut
CIA	Central Intelligence Agency
CUP	Committee for Union and Progress
GDP	Gross Domestic Product
IRFED	Institut de Recherche et de Formation en vue de Développement
LF	Lebanese Forces
MNF	Multinational force
NATO	North Atlantic Treaty Organization
NLP	National Liberal Party
PDFLP	Popular Democratic Front for the Liberation of Palestine
PFLP	Popular Front for the Liberation of Palestine
PFLP-GC	Popular Front for the Liberation of Palestine General Command
PLA	Palestine Liberation Army
PLO	Palestine Liberation Organization
PSP	Progressive Socialist Party
SLA	South Lebanese Army
SSNP	Syrian Social Nationalist Party
STL	Special Tribunal for Lebanon
TWA	Trans World Airlines
UAR	United Arab Republic
UN	United Nations
UNESCO	United Nations Educational, Scientific and Cultural Organization
UNIFIL	United Nations Interim Force in Lebanon
UNIIIC	United Nations International Independent Investigating Commission
UNSC	United Nations Security Council
USJ	L'Université Saint-Joseph

NOTES

Introduction

1. Ghada Samman, *The Square Moon: Supernatural Tales*, trans. Issa Boullata (Fayetteville: University of Arkansas Press, 1998), 65.

2. Al-Muqaddasi, *The Best Divisions for Knowledge of the Regions*, trans. Basil Collins (Reading: Garnet Publishing, 1994), 150; al-Mas'udi, *Kitab al-Tanbih wa al-Ashraf* (Beirut: Khayyat, 1965), 153–54. Both wrote in the tenth century.

3. Akram Khater, *Inventing Home: Emigration, Gender, and the Middle Class in Lebanon, 1870–1920* (Berkeley and Los Angeles: University of California Press, 2001), 48–71, 108–45.

4. For discussion of the global evidence, consult Malcolm Hughes and Henry Diaz, eds., *The Medieval Warm Period* (Dordrecht: Kluwer Academic Publishers, 1994). See also C. Loehle, "A 2000-year global temperature reconstruction based on non-treering proxies," *Energy and Environment* 18 (2007), 1049–58.

5. For analysis of "Consequences of the Little Ice Age Climatic Fluctuation," see Jean Groves, *Little Ice Ages Ancient and Modern*, 2nd ed. (London: Routledge, 2004), 2: chap. 18.

6. Richard Bulliet, *The Camel and the Wheel* (Cambridge: Harvard University Press, 1975), 9. The Damascene Sufi poet Abd al-Ghani al-Nabulusi was impressed with the arched stone bridges over the Beirut and Ibrahim rivers when traveling from Beirut to Tripoli in 1700. See Abd al-Ghani al-Nabulusi, "Al-Tuhfa al-Nabulusiya fi al-Rihla al-Tarabulusiya," in *Die Reise des 'Abd al-Gani an-Nabulusi durch den Libanon*, ed. Heribert Busse (Beirut: Orient-Institut der DMG, 2003), 43–46. The English traveler Henry Maundrell noted the same bridges when proceeding south by mule in 1697. He also commented on the precarious condition of the Litani bridge north of Tyre. See Henry Maundrell, "A Journey from Aleppo to Jerusalem at Easter AD 1697," in *A General Collection of the Best and Most Interesting Voyages and Travels*, 17 vols., ed. John Pinkerton (London: 1811), 10: 329, 323–24.

7. Bulliet, *The Camel and the Wheel*, 109–10, 227–28.

8. Istifan Duwayhi, *Tarikh al-Azmina, 1090–1699*, ed. Ferdinan Tawtal (Beirut: Al-Matba'at al-Kathulikiya, 1951), 22.

9. John Gulick, *Tripoli: A Modern Arab City* (Cambridge: Harvard University Press, 1967), 16.

10. Edward Lear to Lady Waldegrave, Damascus, 27 May 1858, in *Edward Lear's Diaries: The Private Journals of a Landscape Painter*, accessed September 30, 2010, http://www.nonsenselit.org/diaries/letters/letter-to-lady-waldegrave-from-damascus-27-May-1858/.

11. Isma'il Haqqi, ed., *Lubnan: Mabahith Ilmiya wa Ijtima'iya*, ed. Fuad Bustani from the 1918 original, 2 vols. (Beirut: Manshurat al-Jami'at al-Lubnaniya, Qism al-Dirasat al-Tarikhiya, 1970), 2: 459.

12. Studies include Joseph Chamie, "Differentials in Fertility: Lebanon, 1971," *Population Studies* 31 no. 2 (1977), 365–82; Muhammad Faour, "The Demography of Lebanon: A Reappraisal," *Middle Eastern Studies* 27 no. 4 (1991), 631–41; Faour, "Religion, Demography, and Politics

in Lebanon," *Middle Eastern Studies* 43 no. 6 (2007), 909–21; Mark Farha, "Demographic Dilemmas," in *Lebanon: Liberation, Conflict, and Crisis*, ed. Barry Rubin (New York: Palgrave Macmillan, 2009), 83–97; and William Harris, *Faces of Lebanon: Sects, Wars, and Global Extensions* (Princeton: Markus Wiener Publishers, 1996), 82–86.

13. *Al-Hayat*, January 1, 1999.

14. For a penetrating discussion of the Druze, see Fuad Khuri, *Being a Druze* (London: Druze Heritage Foundation, 2004).

15. Judith Harik, "*Shaykh al-'Aql* and the Druze of Mount Lebanon: Conflict and Accommodation," *Middle Eastern Studies* 30 no. 3 (1994), 469.

16. Yvette Talhamy, "The *Fatwas* and the Nusayri/Alawis of Syria," *Middle Eastern Studies* 46 no. 2 (April 2010), 189–90.

17. Benjamin of Tudela, *The Itinerary of Benjamin of Tudela: Travels in the Middle Ages*, trans. Marcus Adler (Malibu, California: Pangloss Press, 1983), 77–79.

18. *Encyclopaedia Judaica*, 16 vols. (Jerusalem: Keter Publishing House, 1971), 4: 402.

19. Ibid., 4: 402–03.

20. Hanna Ziadeh, *Sectarianism and Inter-Communal Nation-Building in Lebanon* (London: Hurst & Company, 2006) gives a critical appreciation of major crises and developments in the sectarian political system from the 1840s on.

21. Sami Baroudi, "Sectarianism and Business Associations in Postwar Lebanon," *Arab Studies Quarterly* 22 no. 4 (Fall, 2000), 81–107.

22. Ahmad bin Muhammad al-Khalidi al-Safadi, *Lubnan fi Ahd al-Amir Fakhr al-Din al-Ma'ni al-Thani*, ed. Asad Rustum and Fuad al-Bustani (Beirut: Al-Maktabat al-Bulusiya, 1985), 23: "When the sheikhs and lords saw these forces advancing on the Shuf they became convinced that their lives were at risk and compelled Emir Yunis to send his mother to the army commander, putting the fate of the Shuf country in her hands."

23. Khater, *Inventing Home*, particularly chapter 6, "A Woman's Boundaries," 146–78.

24. Ibid., 147–59, 161–62.

25. Hanan al-Shaykh, *The Story of Zahra*, trans. Peter Ford (London: Quartet Books, 1986).

26. Samir Kassir, *Beirut* (Berkeley and Los Angeles: University of California Press, 2010), 316–17.

27. Max Weiss, *In the Shadow of Sectarianism: Law, Shi'ism, and the Making of Modern Lebanon* (Cambridge: Harvard University Press, 2010), 172–82.

28. Lara Deeb, *An Enchanted Modern: Gender and Public Piety in Shi'i Lebanon* (Princeton: Princeton University Press, 2006).

29. Ibid., 207.

30. For data on gender differentiation in modern Lebanese legal codes, consult Maya Mikdashi, "A Legal Guide to Being a Lebanese Woman (Part 1)," *Jadaliyya*, Dec. 3, 2010, http://www.jadaliyya.com/pages/index/376/a-legal-guide-to-being-a-lebanese-woman-(part-1); also see Zeina Zaatari, *Women's Rights in the Middle East and North Africa: Lebanon Country Report*, accessed May 29, 2010, http://www.freedomhouse.org/template.cfm?page=176.

31. Malek Abisaab, "'Unruly' Factory Women in Lebanon: Contesting French Colonialism and the National State," *Journal of Women's History* 16 no. 3 (Fall, 2004), 55–82.

32. Zaatari, *Women's Rights*.

33. Emily Nasrallah, *Flight Against Time*, trans. Issa Boullata (Charlottetown, Prince Edward Island: Ragweed Press, 1987), 127.

34. Augustus Richard Norton, *Amal and the Shi'a: Struggle for the Soul of Lebanon* (Austin: University of Texas Press, 1988), 23; Rodger Shanahan, *The Shi'a of Lebanon: Clans, Parties and Clerics* (London: I. B. Tauris, 2005), 32–33.

35. Author's discussions with Argentine and Chilean Foreign Ministry officials, Buenos Aires and Santiago, June/July 2002.

Chapter 1

1. A. Palmer, trans. *The Maronite Chronicle, The Seventh Century in the West-Syrian Chronicles* (Liverpool: Liverpool University Press, 1993), 29–35.

2. Ibid., 30.

3. Muhammad al-Basha and Riyadh Ghannam, eds. *Al-Sijill al-Arslani* (Beirut: Nawfal, 1999), 13–14.

4. Al-Ya'qubi, *Tarikh al-Ya'qubi* (Beirut: Dar Beirut, 1980), 2: 480.

5. Several modern scholars have surveyed the sources to give useful portrayals in Arabic of medieval Mount Lebanon. Kamal Salibi in *Muntalaq Tarikh Lubnan* (Beirut: Caravan, 1979) and Elias al-Qittar in *Lubnan fil-Qurun al-Wusta* (Beirut: Murex, 2004) provide broad contours. Umar Tadmuri supplies further detail in *Lubnan min al-Fath al-Islami hatta Suqut al-Dawla al-Umawiya* (Tripoli, Lebanon: Jarrus Bris, 1990) and *Lubnan min Qiyam al-Dawla al-Abbasiya hatta Suqut al-Dawla al-Ikhshidiya* (Tripoli, Lebanon: Jarrus Bris, 1992). Ibrahim Beydoun's essay "Lubnan fi al-Ahdayn al-Umawi wa al-Abbasi," in *Lubnan fi Tarikhihi wa Turathihi*, ed. Adil Isma'il, 2 vols. (Beirut: Merkaz al-Hariri al-Thaqafi, 1993), 1: 153–79, is also worthwhile. Sami Makarim's *Lubnan fi Ahd al-Umara al-Tanukhiyin* (Beirut: Dar Sader, 2000) gives a fascinating account of the Arslan clan, the first leaders of the Druze community. For the mountain communities during the Frankish period, Salibi's Arabic and English works, including his articles in the journal *Arabica*, remain indispensable.

6. Historians disagree on the condition of the empire in the late sixth century. See John Haldon, "Economy and Administration," in *The Cambridge Companion to Age of Justinian*, ed. Michael Maas (New York: Cambridge University Press, 2005), 54–55, and Chris Wickham, *The Inheritance of Rome: A History of Europe from 400 to 1000* (London: Penguin, 2009), 94, 217, 353. Haldon refers to "strategic overextension of the empire, combined with a declining population and the systemic fiscal problems." Wickham assesses Justinian's western campaigns as within the empire's capacity, downplays the plague, and cites "the archaeology of Syria" as not supporting "population collapse."

7. Ata Elias et al., "Active Thrusting Offshore Mount Lebanon: Source of the Tsunamigenic AD 551 Beirut-Tripoli Earthquake," *Geology* 35 no. 8 (Aug. 2007): 755–58.

8. Theophanes, *The Chronicle of Theophanes Confessor: Byzantine and Near Eastern History AD 284–813*, trans. Cyril Mango and Roger Scott (Oxford: Clarendon Press, 1997), 332.

9. A. H. M. Jones, *The Later Roman Empire, 284–602*, 3 vols. (Oxford: Blackwell, 1964), 2: 939.

10. Maurice Sartre, *The Middle East Under Rome* (Cambridge: Belknap Press, 2005), 208.

11. Al-Tabari, *The History of al-Tabari*, ed. Ehsan Yar Shater, 40 vols. (Albany: State University of New York Press, 1979–2007): Vol. XII, *The Battle of Qadisiyyah and the Conquest of Syria and Palestine*, trans. Yohanan Friedman (1992), 132.

12. Al-Baladhuri, *The Origins of the Islamic State*, trans. Philip Hitti (Beirut: Khayyat, 1966), 179, 198.

13. Matti Moosa, *The Maronites in History* (Syracuse: Syracuse University Press, 1986), 100.

14. Al-Mas'udi, *Kitab al-Tanbih wa al-Ashraf*, 53–155.

15. Hugh Kennedy, *The Great Arab Conquests* (London: Phoenix, 2007).

16. Al-Baladhuri, *The Origins of the Islamic State*, 180, 194.

17. Ibid., 180.

18. See comment in Kennedy, *The Great Arab Conquests*, 96.

19. Al-Baladhuri, *The Origins of the Islamic State*, 180, 195.

20. Umar Tadmuri, *Lubnan min al-Fath al-Islami hatta Suqut al-Dawla al-Umawiya*, 178.

21. Muhammad Jabir Al Safa, *Tarikh Jabal Amil* (Beirut: Dar al-Nahar, 2004), 33.

22. See, for example, Al-Malik al-Muayyad Imad al-Din Isma'il Abu al-Fida, *Kitab al-Mukhtasar fi Akhbar al-Bashr* (Beirut, Dar al-Fikr, 1956–1961), Part I: 131.

23. Al-Baladhuri, *The Origins of the Islamic State*, 198.

24. Al-Mas'udi, *Kitab al-Tanbih wa al-Ashraf*, 153–54. "This monastery and the monks' dwellings around it were ruined by persistent Arab in-fighting and the injustice of the ruler."

25. Palmer, *The Maronite Chronicle*, 30.

26. Jibra'il Ibn al-Qila'i, *Zajaliyat*, ed. Butros al-Jumayyil (Beirut: Dar Lahad Khatar, 1982); Istifan Duwayhi, *Tarikh al-Ta'ifa al-Maruniya* (Beirut: Al-Matba'at al-Kathulikiya, 1890). See commentaries in Moosa, *The Maronites in History*, and in Kamal Salibi, *Maronite Historians of Modern Lebanon* (New York: AMS Press, 1959).

27. Moosa, *The Maronites in History*, 100, 135, 207–16.

28. Ibid., 141–45; Tadmuri, *Lubnan min al-Fath al-Islami hatta Suqut al-Dawla al-Umawiya*, 120–24.

29. Theophanes, *The Chronicle of Theophanes Confessor*, 496.

30. A. Palmer, trans., *Dionysius Reconstituted, The Seventh Century in the West-Syrian Chronicles*, 195.

31. Matti Moosa, "The Relation of the Maronites of Lebanon to the Mardaites and Al-Jarajima," *Speculum* 44 no. 4 (Oct. 1969), 607–08.

32. Al-Mas'udi, *Kitab al-Tanbih wa al-Ashraf*, 153

33. Theophanes, *The Chronicle of Theophanes Confessor*, 496.

34. Ibid., 506.

35. Ibid. Regarding the estimate of 12,000 evacuees, also see *Dionysius Reconstituted*, 200.

36. Al-Baladhuri, *The Origins of the Islamic State*, 247.

37. *Al-Sijill al-Arslani*, 55, 63, 73.

38. Moosa, *The Maronites in History*, 103–04.

39. Ibid., 101.

40. Kamal Salibi, *Muntalaq Tarikh Lubnan*, 35–36.

41. John Haldon, "Seventh Century Continuities: The Ajnad and the 'Thematic Myth,'" in Averil Cameron, ed., *The Byzantine and Early Islamic Near East: States, Resources and Armies* (Princeton: Darwin Press, 1995), 402, 411–12.

42. Al-Baladhuri, *The Origins of the Islamic State*, 181.

43. Elias al-Qittar, *Lubnan fi al-Qurun al-Wusta*, 58.

44. Maurice Chehab, "The Umayyad Palace at Anjar," *Ars Orientalis* 5 (1963): 21.

45. Theophanes, *The Chronicle of Theophanes Confessor*, 580.

46. Ibid., 594–96. According to Theophanes, the Orthodox patriarch of Antioch was accused of espionage on behalf of the emperor.

47. *Al-Sijill al-Arslani*, 13–14.

48. Ibid., 45.

49. Theophanes, *The Chronicle of Theophanes Confessor*, 597; Al-Baladhuri, *The Origins of the Islamic State*, 250–51. Also see commentaries in al-Qittar, *Lubnan fi al-Qurun al-Wusta*, 74–77: Salibi, *Muntalaq Tarikh Lubnan*, 55–57; Tadmuri, *Lubnan min Qiyam al-Dawla al-Abbasiya hatta Suqut al-Dawla al-Ikhshidiya*, 306.

50. Salibi, *Muntalaq Tarikh Lubnan*, 57.

51. Ibrahim Beydoun, "Lubnan fi al-Ahdayn al-Umawi wa al-Abbasi," 169.

52. Al-Baladhuri, *The Origins of the Islamic State*, 251.

53. Al-Muqaddasi, *The Best Divisions for the Knowledge of the Regions*, 150. Writing in the late tenth century, al-Muqaddasi recorded Shia majorities or pluralities in the Upper Jordan Valley flanking Jabal Amil, Tiberias (administrative center of the *jund* of al-Urdun), Nablus, and Amman.

54. Ibrahim Beydoun "Lubnan fi al-Ahdayn al-Umawi wa al-Abbasi," 170–71; Al-Qittar, *Lubnan fi al-Qurun al-Wusta*, 95–98.

55. Al-Tabari gives a biographical entry: "Al-Awza'i lived in Beirut. . . . He was one of the muftis and transmitters of tradition of that locality in his time and one of the excellent [people there]." Al-Tabari, *The History of al-Tabari–Vol. XXXIX, Biographies of the Prophet's Companions and their Successors*, trans. Ella Landau-Tasseron (1998), 255.

56. Al-Qittar, *Lubnan fi al-Qurun al-Wusta*, 96.

57. Al-Tabari, *The History of al-Tabari–Vol. XXX, The Abbasid Caliphate in Equilibrium*, trans. C. E. Bosworth (1989), 56.

58. Al-Qittar, *Lubnan fi al-Qurun al-Wusta*, 59–61.

59. Tadmuri, *Lubnan min al-Fath al-Islami hatta suqut al-Dawla al-Umawiya*, 251.

60. Tadmuri, *Lubnan min Qiyam al-Dawla al-Abbasiya hatta Suqut al-Dawla al-Ikhshidiya*, 308–09.

61. Ibid., 165–89.

62. Hugh Kennedy, *When Baghdad Ruled the Muslim World—The Rise and Fall of Islam's Greatest Dynasty* (Cambridge: Da Capo Press, 2005), 256.

63. Oliver Kahl, "Qusta Ibn Luqa on Sleeplessness," *Journal of Semitic Studies* XLIII: 2 (Autumn 1998): 311–26.

64. Sami Makarim, *Lubnan fi Ahd al-Umara al-Tanukhiyin* (Beirut: Dar Sader, 2000), 42; Tannus al-Shidyaq, *Kitab Akhbar al-Ayan fi Jabal Lubnan*, 2 vols. (Beirut: Lebanese University Publications, 1970), 2: 496.

65. *Al-Sijill al-Arslani*, 52; al-Shidyaq, *Kitab Akhbar al-Ayan*, 2: 496.

66. Makarim, *Lubnan fi Ahd al-Umara al-Tanukhiyin*, 43; al-Shidyaq, *Kitab Akhbar al-Ayan*, 2: 497.

67. Al-Qittar, *Lubnan fi al-Qurun al-Wusta*, 80–81; Al-Ya'qubi, *Tarikh al-Ya'qubi*, 2: 480. Al-Ya'qubi observed that the "Amila" were among the followers of Mubarqa'a.

68. Al-Tabari, *The History of al-Tabari*–Vol. XXXIII, *Storm and Stress along the Northern Frontier of the Abbasid Caliphate*, trans. C. E. Bosworth (1991), 203–05.

69. *Al-Sijill al-Arslani*, 55–56.

70. Al-Qittar, *Lubnan fi al-Qurun al-Wusta*, 81.

71. Al-Tabari comments that they "moved on Baalbek and killed most of its inhabitants." Al-Tabari, *The History of al-Tabari*–Vol. XXXVIII, *The Return of the Caliphate to Baghdad*, trans. Franz Rosenthal (1985), 122.

72. *Al-Sijill al-Arslani*, 71–72.

73. John Pryor and Elizabeth Jeffreys, *The Age of the Dromon: The Byzantine Navy ca 500–1204* (Leiden: Brill, 2006), 62–64.

74. For a good short account, see Heinz Halm, *Shi'ism*, 2nd ed. (New York: Columbia University Press, 2004).

75. Al-Mas'udi, *Kitab al-Tanbih wa al-Ashraf*, 153, refers to Maronites in Shayzar and Ma'arat Na'aman in the Orontes Valley in the mid-tenth century. Salibi, *Muntalaq Tarikh Lubnan*, 64, notes that there is no significant trace of these Maronites after the collapse of Byzantine Antioch in the late eleventh century. Of course, some or all may have moved during the advances of the Seljuk Turks, 1071–1085.

76. Anonymous author, "Campaign Organization and Tactics," in George Dennis, *Three Byzantine Military Treatises: Text, Translation, and Notes* (Washington, DC: Dumbarton Oaks, 2008), 303.

77. *Al-Sijill al-Arslani*, 55–56.

78. Izz al-Din Abu al-Hasan Ali Ibn al-Athir, *Al-Kamil fi al-Tarikh*, ed. Carl Tornberg. 13 vols. (Beirut: Dar Sader, 1965–1967), 8: 596.

79. Makarim, *Lubnan fi Ahd al-Umara al-Tanukhiyin*, 51.

80. Tzimiskes received the voluntary submission of Sidon, and local leaders in Beirut delivered the Fatimid garrison commander to the emperor. See "The Crusade of John Tzimisces in the Light of New Arabic Evidence," in Paul Walker, *Fatimid History and Ismaili Doctrine* (Aldershot: Ashgate/Variorum, 2008), VI: 321–22.

81. Makarim, *Lubnan fi Ahd al-Umara al-Tanukhiyin*, 52.

82. Ibid., 53.

83. Halm, *Shi'ism*, 178–79.

84. Ahmad bin Ali bin al-Maghribi Ibn al-Hariri, *Muntakhab al-Zaman fi Tarikh al-Khulafa wa al-Ulama wa al-Ayan*, ed. Abdo Khalifa (Beirut: Dar Ishtar, 1995), 258–59. Also see Ibn al-Hariri's close contemporary, the Damascus historian Shams al-Din Muhammad Ibn Tulun in *al-Lama'at al-Barqiya fi Nuqat al-Tarikhiya*, ed. Muhammad Khayr Ramadan Yusuf (Beirut: Dar Ibn Hazm, 1994), 93—"Al-Hakim sent him to al-Sham, and he went off to Wadi al-Taym, and Jabal Baniyas, and bought the people there."

85. Makarim, *Lubnan fi Ahd al-Umara al-Tanukhiyin*, 55–56.

86. Walker, *Fatimid History and Ismaili Doctrine*, III: 38.

87. Makarim, *Lubnan fi Ahd al-Umara al-Tanukhiyin*, 58.

88. Warren Treadgold, *A History of the Byzantine State and Society* (Stanford: Stanford University Press, 1997), 569–79. Treadgold's estimate is that the empire's population increased from about seven million in 780 to about twelve million in 1025. State revenue grew by 50 percent from 959 to 1025. Antalya became the major entrepot for trade with the Muslims, linking westward through Byzantine waters to Naples, Amalfi, and Venice.

89. Al-Muqaddasi, *The Best Divisions for the Knowledge of the Regions*, 139, 151.

90. Ibid., 151.

91. Umar Tadmuri, *Tarikh Tarabulus al-Siyasi wa al-Hadari abr al-Usur*, 2 vols. (Tripoli: Dar al-Balad, 1978–1981), 1: 230. Tadmuri comments: "Tripoli took the fruits of the Fatimid-Byzantine truce. . . . Many Frankish and Muslim merchants coming from Byzantium, Spain, Sicily, and Western Europe frequented its port."

92. Salibi, *Muntalaq Tarikh Lubnan*, 65.
93. Tadmuri, *Tarikh Tarabulus*, 1: 229.
94. Ibid., 233.
95. Ibid., 251–52.
96. Ibid., 252.
97. Muqaddasi, *The Best Divisions for the Knowledge of the Regions*, 137.
98. Al-Qittar, *Lubnan fi al-Qurun al-Wusta*, 134.
99. Tadmuri, *Tarikh Tarabulus*, 1: 232; al-Qittar, *Lubnan fi al-Qurun al-Wusta*, 134.
100. Impressively surveyed in Tadmuri's *Tarikh Tarabulus*, 1: 239–333.
101. Ibid., 253.
102. Ibid., 250.
103. Ibid., 264.
104. Ronnie Ellenblum, *Crusader Castles and Modern Histories* (Cambridge: Cambridge University Press, 2007), 112.
105. *Al-Sijill al-Arslani*, 101.
106. Bernard Hamilton, *The Leper King and His Heirs: Baldwin IV and the Crusader Kingdom of Jerusalem* (Cambridge: Cambridge University Press, 2000), 47; P. M. Holt, *The Age of the Crusades: The Near East from the Eleventh Century to 1517* (London: Longman, 1986), 33; Joshua Prawer, *Crusader Institutions* (Oxford: Clarendon, 1980), 380–81.
107. Pierre Zalloua et al., "Y-Chromosomal Diversity in Lebanon Is Structured by Recent Historical Events," *The American Journal of Human Genetics* 82 no, 4 (April 2008): 873–82.
108. Usama Ibn Munqidh, *The Book of Contemplation*, trans. Paul Cobb (London: Penguin Classics, 2008), 91, on "The Value of One Good Man: The Case of Yunan of Tripoli."
109. William of Tyre, *A History of Deeds Done Beyond the Sea*, 2: 214.
110. Ibn Jubayr, *The Travels of Ibn Jubayr*, trans. R. J. C. Broadhurst (London: Jonathan Cape, 1952), 319.
111. Donald Richards, "A Text of Imad al-Din on 12th Century Frankish-Muslim Relations," *Arabica* 25 (1978): 203.
112. See Joshua Prawer, *The Latin Kingdom of Jerusalem* (London: Weidenfeld and Nicolson, 1972), 393, for the estimate of weaver numbers.
113. Prawer, *Crusader Institutions*, 182.
114. Benjamin of Tudela, *The Itinerary of Benjamin of Tudela*, 79.
115. Ibn Jubayr accompanied one such caravan from Damascus to Tyre and Acre in 1185. See Ibn Jubayr, *The Travels of Ibn Jubayr*, 313–18.
116. Haqqi, *Lubnan*, 2: 562.
117. Ibid.
118. Duwayhi, *Tarikh al-Azmina*, 22. Haqqi, *Lubnan*, 2: 563, citing Duwayhi.
119. Jean Richard, *The Crusades c. 1071–c. 1291* (Cambridge: Cambridge University press, 1999), 323, 328.
120. Tadmuri, *Tarikh Tarabulus*, 1: 446.
121. Richard, *The Crusades c. 1071–c. 1291*, 462.
122. For a good eyewitness account, see Abu al-Fida, *Kitab al-Mukhtasar fi Akhbar al-Bashr*, Part 7: 29–30.
123. William of Tyre, *A History of Deeds Done Beyond the Sea*, 1: 330.
124. William of Tyre, *A History of Deeds Done Beyond the Sea*, 2: 458.
125. William of Tyre, *A History of Deeds Done Beyond the Sea*, 1: 330.
126. Ibn al-Athir, *al-Kamil fi al-Tarikh*, 10: 120.
127. Duwayhi, *Tarikh al-Azmina*, 15.
128. Ibn al-Qila'i, *Zajaliyat*, 92–93 (discussed in Salibi, *Maronite Historians of Medieval Lebanon*, 48–51). Salibi assesses the stories as factually based and observes that the reference to the plainly Christian lord of Jubayl dates them to the crusades.
129. "Affrontement ou Confrontation? Les Contacts entre Deux Mondes au Pays de Tripoli aux Temps des Croisades," XII: 15, in Jean Richard, *Francs et Orientaux dans le Monde des Croisades* (Aldershot: Ashgate/Valiorum, 2003).
130. See below, p. 64, for discussion of the claims of Henri Lammens.

131. Duwayhi, *Tarikh al-Azmina*, 38. Salibi (*Maronite Historians of Medieval Lebanon*, 47) doubts Duwayhi's 1131 dating, noting that the pope sent an envoy in 1139.

132. William of Tyre, *A History of Deeds Done Beyond the Sea*, 2: 82–83.

133. Ibid., 458–49.

134. Moosa, *The Maronites in History*, 135–36, 219–20.

135. Salibi, *Maronite Historians of Medieval Lebanon*, 63–64; Ibn al-Qila'i, *Zajaliyat*, 99.

136. Taqi al-Din Ahmad Ibn Ali al-Maqrizi, *Al-Suluk li Ma'rifat Duwal al-Muluk*, ed. Muhammad al-Qadir Atar, 8 vols. (Beirut: Dar al-Kutub, 1997), 2: 49.

137. "Vassaux, tributaires ou alliés? Les chefferies montagnardes et les Ismaîliens dans l'orbite des États des Croisés," XI: 147, in Jean Richard, *Francs et Orientaux dans le Monde des Croisades* (Aldershot: Ashgate/Valiorum, 2003). For example, Ibn al-Qila'i refers to a Maronite muqaddam Bakhus as the "assistant" (*adad*) of the child lord of Jubayl around 1230. Ibn al-Qila'i, *Zajaliyat*, 99.

138. Makarim, *Lubnan fi Ahd al-Umara al-Tanukhiyin*, 69.

139. *Al-Sijill al-Arslani*, 105.

140. Salih Bin Yahya, *Tarikh Bayrut wa Akhbar al-Umara al-Buhturiyin min Bani al-Gharb*, ed. Louis Cheykho (Beirut: Al-Matba'at al-Kathulikiya, 1927) 46–47.

141. Al-Shidyaq, *Kitab Akhbar al-Ayan*, 1: 217.

142. Kamal Salibi, "The Buhturids of the Gharb: Medieval Lords of Beirut and of Southern Lebanon," *Arabica* VIII (1961): 79.

143. Bin Yahya, *Tarikh Bayrut*, 43. Also see Makarim, *Lubnan fi Ahd al-Umara al-Tanukhiyin*, 69.

144. Bin Yahya, *Tarikh Beirut*, 47.

145. Makarim, *Lubnan fi Ahd al-Umara al-Tanukhiyin*, 69–75.

146. Al-Shidyaq, *Kitab Akhbar al-Ayan*, 1: 235; Salibi, "The Buhturids of the Gharb," 79–81.

147. Makarim, *Lubnan fi Ahd al-Umara al-Tanukhiyin*, 261–62.

148. Al-Shidyaq, *Kitab Akhbar al-Ayan*, 1: 235.

149. Ibid., 174.

150. Ahmad Hatit, "Lubnan fi Ahd al-Faranja" in *Lubnan fi Tarikhihi wa Turathihi*, ed. Adil Isma'il, 2 vols. (Beirut: Merkaz al-Hariri al-Thaqafi, 1993), 1: 192; Richard, "Vassaux, tributaires ou alliés?," 145.

151. Al-Shidyaq, *Kitab Akhbar al-Ayan*, 1: 37.

152. Ibid., 235–36.

153. Benjamin of Tudela, *The Itinerary of Benjamin of Tudela*, 78.

154. William of Tyre, *A History of Deeds Done Beyond the Sea*, 2: 391.

155. This is indicated by the existence of a small Frankish lordship of the Shuf, in addition to the absence of comparable incidents. See "Vassaux, tributaires ou alliés? Les chefferies montagnardes et les Ismailiens dans l'orbite des États des Croisés," XI: 145, in Jean Richard, *Francs et Orientaux dans le Monde des Croisades* (Aldershot: Ashgate/Variorum, 2003).

156. Salibi, "The Buhturids of the Gharb," 83.

157. See the account in William of Tyre, *A History of Deeds done beyond the Sea*, 2: 475–79.

158. Makarim, *Lubnan fi Ahd al-Umara al-Tanukhiyin*, 81.

159. Ibid., 84; Salibi, "The Buhturids of the Gharb," 84.

160. In *al-Sijill al-Arslani*, 110, note 13, editors al-Basha and Ghanim claim that Najm al-Din Muhammad died while "fighting with the Kisrawanis," without supplying any source.

161. Richard, "Vassaux, tributaires ou alliés?," 147.

162. Bin Yahya, *Tarikh Bayrut*, 60.

163. Salibi gives a summary, based on Bin Yahya, in "The Buhturids of the Gharb," 86–87.

164. *Al-Sijill al-Arslani*, 109; Bin Yahya, *Tarikh Bayrut*, 81.

165. *Al-Sijill al-Arslani*, 115.

166. Makarim, *Lubnan fi Ahd al-Umara al-Tanukhiyin*, 93–94.

167. Salibi, "The Buhturids of the Gharb," 88.

168. Makarim, *Lubnan fi Ahd al-Umara al-Tanukhiyin*, 98–100.

169. Ibid., 103–07; Salibi, "The Buhturids of the Gharb," 88–89.

170. Al-Shidyaq, *Kitab Akhbar al-Ayan*, 1: 39–40.

171. Al-Muqaddasi, *The Best Divisions for the Knowledge of the Regions*, 150.

172. Ja'afar al-Muhajir, *Jabal Amil taht al-Ihtilal al-Salibi* (Beirut: Dar al-Haqq, 2001), 36–37.

173. Ibid., 39, 55.
174. Muhammad Makhzum, "Jabal Amil fi al-Ahdayn al-Salibi wa al-Mamluki," in *Safahat min Tarikh Jabal Amil*, ed. South Lebanon Cultural Council (Beirut: Dar al-Farabi, 1979), 37–39.
175. William of Tyre, *A History of Deeds Done Beyond the Sea*, 2: 294.
176. Ibn al-Qalanisi, *The Damascus Chronicle of the Crusades*, trans. H. A. R. Gibb (London: Luzac & Co., 1932), 331.
177. Ibn Jubayr, *The Travels of Ibn Jubayr*, trans. R. J. C. Broadhurst (London: Jonathan Cape, 1952), 316–17.
178. Al-Muhajir, *Jabal Amil taht al-Ihtilal al-Salibi*, 38, 42.
179. Ibid., 74–77.
180. Richard, *The Crusades c. 1071–c. 1291*, 298.
181. Ibn al-Hariri, *Muntakhab al-Zaman fi Tarikh al-Khulafa wa al-Ulama wa al-Ayan*, 327–28.
182. Ibn al-Athir, *Al-Kamil fi al-Tarikh*, 12: 482.
183. Al Safa, *Tarikh Jabal Amil*, 36.
184. See the analysis by Henri Lammens, "Les Nosairis dans Le Liban," *Revue de l'Orient Chrétien*, VII (1902): 452–77.
185. Halm, *Shi'ism*, 159.
186. See the interpretation in Isa al-Ma'luf, *Dawani al-Qutuf fi Tarikh Bani al-Ma'luf*, 2 vols. (1907–1908; reprint, Damascus, Dar Hawran, 2003), 1: 203.
187. Abu al-Fida, *Kitab al-Mukhtasar fi Akhbar al-Bashar*, Part 7: 63.
188. Lammens, "Les Nosairis dans le Liban," 469–70.

Chapter 2

1. *Al-Sijill al-Arslani*, 119.
2. "The Mamluks and Naval Power," VI: 7–12, in David Ayalon, *Studies on the Mamluks of Egypt* (London: Variorum Reprints, 1977).
3. Ahmad bin Muhammad al-Khalidi al-Safadi, *Lubnan fi Ahd al-Amir Fakhr al-Din al-Ma'ni al-Thani*, ed. Asad Rustum and Fuad al-Bustani (Beirut: al-Maktabat al-Bulusiya, 1985).
4. Badr al-Din al-Ayni, *Iqd al-Juman fi Tarikh Ahl al-Zaman—Asr Salatin al-Mamalik*, ed. Muhammad Amin. 4 vols. (Cairo: Al-Hayat al-Misriya al-Ama lil Kitab, 1987–1992), 3: 127.
5. Ibid.
6. Ibid., 128.
7. Salibi, *Maronite Historians of Medieval Lebanon*, 69–71. For the Arabic text, see al-Qila'i, *Zajaliyat*, 102–05.
8. Al-Ayni, *Iqd al-Juman fi Tarikh Ahl al-Zaman*, 3: 128–29.
9. Makarim, *Lubnan fi Ahd al-Umara al-Tanukhiyin*, 111, 114.
10. Tadmuri, *Tarikh Tarabulus*, 2: 17.
11. Bin Yahya, *Tarikh Bayrut*, 84. Both Nahid al-Din and Ala al-Din became "emirs of forty."
12. Al-Maqrizi, *Al-Suluk li Ma'rifat Duwal al-Muluk*, 2: 331.
13. Al-Ayni, *Iqd al-Juman fi Tarikh Ahl al-Zaman*, 4: 81.
14. Bin Yahya, *Tarikh Bayrut*, 32; Al-Maqrizi, *Al-Suluk li Ma'rifat Duwal al-Muluk*, 2: 384–85.
15. Ibid, 2: 389; al-Ayni, *Iqd al-Juman fi Tarikh Ahl al-Zaman*, 4: 385; Bin Yahya, *Tarikh Bayrut*, 32.
16. Al-Maqrizi, *Al-Suluk li Ma'rifat Duwal al-Muluk*, 2: 389.
17. Makarim, *Lubnan fi Ahd al-Umara al-Tanukhiyin*, 119.
18. Kamal Salibi, "The Maronites of Lebanon under Frankish and Mamluk Rule (1099–1516)," *Arabica*, IV (1957): 13.
19. Abu al-Fida, *Kitab al-Mukhtasar fi Akhbar al-Bashr*, Part 7: 63.
20. Bin Yahya, *Tarikh Bayrut*, 33; Tadmuri, *Tarikh Tarabulus*, 102.
21. Makarim, *Lubnan fi Ahd al-Umara al-Tanukhiyin*, 123–24. Bin Yahya (*Tarikh Bayrut*, 101) records that "Nasr al-Din received a reprimand from the authorities when they heard that he was stopping Kisrawanis given safety guarantees [to leave their homes] when they passed through the Beirut district."
22. Al-Ma'luf, *Dawani al-Qutuf*, 1: 204, locates the Assafs in the Kura before they moved into the Kisrawan.

23. Makarim, *Lubnan fi Ahd al-Umara al-Tanukhiyin*, 118–19. According to Bin Yahya (*Tarikh Bayrut*, 33), the Turcomans were charged with "oversight of the sea and the land tracks from the outskirts of Beirut to the province of Tripoli."

24. Makarim, *Lubnan fi Ahd al-Umara al-Tanukhiyin*, 137.

25. Stefan Winter, *The Shiites of Lebanon under Ottoman Rule* (Leiden: Cambridge University Press, 2010), 63, 70.

26. A. N. Poliak, "The Demographic Evolution of the Middle East: Population Trends since 1348," *Palestine and the Middle East* 10, no. 5 (May 1938): 201–05.

27. Michael Dols, *The Black Death in the Middle East* (Princeton: Princeton University Press, 1977), 218–21.

28. For good summaries of the Nasiri *rawk*, see Robert Irwin, *The Middle East in the Middle Ages—The Early Mamluk Sultanate, 1250–1382* (Carbondale and Ewardsville: Southern Illinois University Press, 1986), 109–12; P. M. Holt, *The Age of the Crusades—The Near East from the Eleventh Century to 1517* (London: Longman, 1986), 116–17.

29. Makarim, *Lubnan fi Ahd al-Umara al-Tanukhiyin*, 128; Salibi, "The Buhturids of the Gharb," 90.

30. For explanation of these ranks, see David Ayalon, "Studies on the Structure of the Mamluk Army—II," *Bulletin of the School of Oriental and African Studies, University of London* 15 no. 3 (1953): 469–70.

31. Makarim, *Lubnan fi Ahd al-Umara al-Tanukhiyin*, 140, 145.

32. Ibid., 145.

33. Ibid., 144.

34. Ibid., 157.

35. Ibid., 158–60; Salibi, *Muntalaq Tarikh Lubnan*, 146. Bin Yahya (*Tarikh Bayrut*, 168) reports the chief secretary as arguing that the Buhturids had merited their *iqta* from the days of the Ayyubids and that they remained an asset to the state.

36. Makarim, *Lubnan fi Ahd al-Umara al-Tanukhiyin*, 174. Bin Yahya (*Tarikh Bayrut*, 182) quotes the *na'ib* as telling Sayf al-Din: "You are secretly with the Franks against the Muslims." The use of the term *mubatin* (concealed tendency) may have been a slur against Sayf al-Din's Druzism.

37. Makarim, *Lubnan fi Ahd al-Umara al-Tanukhiyin*, 176.

38. Ibid., 180–83; Salibi, "The Buhturids of the Gharb," 95–96. Salibi is almost certainly mistaken in accusing the Buhturids of destroying the "Bani al-Jaysh."

39. *Al-Sijill al-Arslani*, 124–26.

40. Makarim, *Lubnan fi Ahd al-Umara al-Tanukhiyin*, 186.

41. Salibi ("The Buhturids of the Gharb," 96) proposes the former, and Makarim (*Lubnan fi Ahd al-Umara al-Tanukhiyin*, 188) the latter.

42. Makarim, *Lubnan fi Ahd al-Umara al-Tanukhiyin*, 169–70. Bin Yahya (*Tarikh Bayrut*, 177–78) notes that the *na'ib* of Damascus "did not find [Shihab al-Din] in agreement" about the value of the timber. He continues: "I am told from that time the people of the Shuf took care to cut down the plum trees, to prevent their growth, and to uproot them lest the state bother them. . . ."

43. *Al-Sijill al-Arslani*, 126–27.

44. Makarim, *Lubnan fi Ahd al-Umara al-Tanukhiyin*, 202–03.

45. Ibid., 205–07.

46. Salibi, *Muntalaq Tarikh Lubnan*, 152–53.

47. Hamza Ibn Ahmad Ibn Sibat, *Tarikh al-Duruz fi Akhir Ahd al-Mamalik* (originally *Sidq al-Akhbar*), ed. Naila Kaedbay (Beirut: Dar al-Awda, 1989), 72–73. Ibn Sibat gives a fulsome description of the influence and prestige of *al-Amir al-Sayyid*, including his hostility to alcohol and his network of disciples conducting moral and religious teaching sessions. He instructed his followers "to give [the people] a clear vision of the delights of paradise and to make them fear the fire and its fury."

48. Makarim, *Lubnan fi Ahd al-Umara al-Tanukhiyin*, 232–33.

49. Ibid., 225–27.

50. Ibn Sibat, *Tarikh al-Duruz*, 45. Ibn Sibat portrays Jamal al-Din Hajji as a strong-willed character with a fierce temper who also helped the weak at considerable cost.

51. Salibi, *Muntalaq Tarikh Lubnan*, 153; Makarim, *Lubnan fi Ahd al-Umara al-Tanukhiyin*, 256.

52. Salibi, *Muntalaq Tarikh Lubnan*, 154.

53. Makarim (*Lubnan fi Ahd al-Umara al-Tanukhiyin*, 264) noted Bin Yahya's recollection of his father making the Hajj to Mecca with three Ma'ns in 1388. Al-Shidyaq (*Kitab Akhbar al-Ayan*, 1: 237) observed: "In 1470 Emir Ali al-Shihabi fled the prison of his [paternal] uncle Amir Bakr to Ba'aqlin and his [maternal] uncle Amir Yusuf [Ma'n] received him smiling." The next year, however, Yusuf returned Ali "forcibly."

54. Al-Shidyaq, *Kitab Akhbar al-Ayan*, 1: 237.

55. Ibid.

56. Tadmuri, *Tarikh Tarabulus*, 2: 206–09. Al-Maqrizi, *Al-Suluk li Ma'rifat Duwal al-Muluk* 4: 103–04, gives a lively account of the episode.

57. Tadmuri, *Tarikh Tarabulus*, 2: 215–23.

58. Ibid., 223–34.

59. Ibid., 44–47.

60. Ibid., 411.

61. Irwin, *The Middle East in the Middle Ages*, 145.

62. Tadmuri, *Tarikh Tarabulus*, 2: 244.

63. Ibid., 245.

64. Ibid., 482.

65. Ibid., 427–97.

66. Duwayhi, *Tarikh al-Azmina*, 166.

67. This is the view of Kamal Salibi in "The *Muqaddams* of Bsharri: Maronite Chieftains of the Northern Lebanon, 1382–1621," *Arabica*, XV (1968): 65.

68. Salibi (*Muntalaq Tarikh Lubnan*, 154) claimed the former, and Moosa (*The Maronites in History*, 237) the latter.

69. Al-Maqrizi, *Al-Suluk li Ma'rifat Duwal al-Muluk*, 3: 282–83.

70. Tadmuri, *Tarikh Tarabulus*, 2: 152–53; Duwayhi, *Tarikh al-Azmina*, 185–86. Duwayhi ignored the Frankish raid on Tripoli, attributing the incident to Mamluk spite after the raid on Alexandria.

71. Duwayhi, *Tarikh al-Azmina*, 190.

72. Salibi (*Maronite Historians of Medieval Lebanon*, 148) assesses the story as possibly but not certainly accurate.

73. Ibid., 148–49. Salibi discusses continuing prosperity into the 1470s.

74. Duwayhi, *Tarikh al-Azmina*, 205; Moosa, *The Maronites in History*, 229.

75. Salibi, "The *Muqaddams* of Bsharri," 68 (citing Duwayhi, *Tarikh al-Azmina*, 205–06). Duwayhi reports: "When the news spread about the [papal] confirmation of the patriarch, there was joy and a great uproar [*rahja azima*] in the city."

76. Moosa, *The Maronites in History*, 231.

77. Ibid., 236.

78. Salibi, *Maronite Historians of Medieval Lebanon*, 153–59; Moosa, *The Maronites in History*, 247.

79. Duwayhi, *Tarikh al-Azmina*, 207.

80. Salibi, *Maronite Historians of Medieval Lebanon*, 150–51. This includes a translation of Duwayhi's account (*Tarikh al-Azmina*, 218–19).

81. Duwayhi (*Tarikh al-Azmina*, 214) reports that Ibn al-Qila'i left Lebanon in 1471 for study in Rome, via Jerusalem.

82. Moosa, *The Maronites in History*, 240–41.

83. Bin Yahya, *Tarikh Bayrut*, 100.

84. Albert Hourani, "From Jabal Amil to Persia," in *Distant Relations: Iran and Lebanon in the Last 500 Years*, ed. H. E. Chehabi (London: I. B. Tauris, 2006), 53.

85. Ibid.

86. For discussion of Al-Karki and of perspectives on Arab Shia migration to Safavid Iran, see Rula Abisaab, "History and Self-Image: The 'Amili Ulema in Syria and Iran (Fourteenth to Sixteenth Centuries)," in *Distant Relations: Iran and Lebanon in the last 500 years*, ed. H. E. Chehabi (London: I. B. Tauris, 2006), 62–95; Devin Stewart, "Notes on the Migration of 'Amili Scholars to Safavid Iran," *Journal of Near Eastern Studies*, 55 no. 2 (April 1996): 81–103; Andrew Newman, "The Myth of the Clerical Migration to Safawid Iran: Arab Shiite Opposition to Ali al-Karaki and Safawid Shiism," *Die Welt des Islams*, New Series, 33 no. 1 (April 1993): 66–112.

87. Abisaab, "History and Self-Image," 69.
88. Ibid., 70.
89. Al Safa, *Tarikh Jabal Amil*, 36.
90. Ibid., 42.
91. Ibid., 38, 40–41.
92. Shams al-Din Muhammad bin Ali Ibn Tulun, *Al-Lama'at al-Barqiya fi al-Nukat al-Tarikhiya*, ed. Muhammad Khayr Ramadan Yusuf (Beirut: Dar Ibn Hazm, 1994), 107.
93. Muhsin al-Amin, *Khitat Jabal Amil* (Beirut: Al-Dar al-Alimiya, 1984), 78.
94. Ibn Sibat, *Tarikh al-Duruz*, 100.
95. Ibid. Also see Salibi, *Muntalaq Tarikh Lubnan*, 153.
96. Ibn Sibat, *Tarikh al-Duruz*, 100–01.
97. Ibn Tulun (*Al-Lama'at al-Barqiya*, 84) observes that Kark Nuah was "a large village . . . and its people famous for refusal," meaning that they were Shia. He terms a prominent local expert on hadith "a vicious refuser" (*rafidi khabith*).
98. Salibi, *Maronite Historians of Medieval Lebanon*, 128.
99. Abdul-Rahman Abu Husayn, *Provincial Leaderships in Syria, 1575–1650* (Beirut: American University of Beirut, 1985), 130.
100. Salibi, "The *Muqaddams* of Bsharri," 76–77.
101. Ibn Tulun, *Al-Lama'at al-Barqiya*, 97.
102. Abdul-Rahman Abu-Husayn, "Problems in the Ottoman Administration in Syria During the 16th and 17th Centuries: The Case of the Sanjak of Sidon-Beirut," *International Journal of Middle East Studies*, 24 (1992): 667, 674.
103. Duwayhi, *Tarikh al-Azmina*, 258, refers to a Shaykh Hamade killed in a fracas with the Maronites near Bsharri in 1547 as "the head of the Hamades who moved with his brothers from the land of the Persians to Qamhaz [above Jubayl] when Tabriz was conquered [presumably the first Ottoman capture of the city in 1514]." Winter (*The Shiites of Mount Lebanon*, 69–70) disputes Duwayhi, noting a late fifteenth-century local report about an "Ibn Hamada" receiving a financial indemnity in 1471. He proposes that the Hamades were of local origin, as strongly asserted by the family itself.
104. Isam Khalife, *Nawahi Lubnan fi al-Qarn al-Sadis Ashr: Al-Taqsimat al-Idariya—al-Demografiya—al-Adyan wa al-Madhahib* (Beirut: I. K. Khalife, 2004).
105. Ibid., 59.
106. Ibid., 229–30.
107. Ibid., 124–27.
108. Ibid., 128–31.
109. Ibid., 174–77, 206.
110. Ibid., 223.
111. Ibid, 154.
112. Ibid., 158.
113. Kamal Salibi, "Northern Lebanon Under the Dominance of Ghazir (1517–1591)," *Arabica*, XIV (1967): 149–50, 153, 156–57.
114. Makarim, *Lubnan fi Ahd al-Umara al-Tanukhiyin*, 258; Ibn Sibat, *Tarikh al-Duruz*, 45–46.
115. Salibi, "Northern Lebanon Under the Dominance of Ghazir," 158–61.
116. Ibid., 153.
117. Ibid., 162 (from Duwayhi, *Tarikh al-Azmina*, 257).
118. Al-Ma'luf, *Dawani al-Qutuf*, 1: 205.
119. Salibi, "The Muqaddams of Bsharri," 75–76.
120. Ibid., 80.
121. Abu-Husayn, *Provincial Leaderships in Syria*, 16–17.
122. Makarim, *Lubnan fi Ahd al-Umara al-Tanukhiyin*, 275; Abu-Husayn, "Problems in the Ottoman Administration in Syria," 668.
123. Makarim, *Lubnan fi Ahd al-Umara al-Tanukhiyin*, 276–77.
124. Abu-Husayn, "Problems in the Ottoman Administration in Syria," 668.
125. Abdul-Rahman Abu-Husayn, *The View from Istanbul: Ottoman Lebanon and the Druze Emirate* (London: I. B. Tauris, 2004), 24–25. Translated Ottoman *Muhimme Defteri* (MD) 5, no. 565, 1564–65. Also see Abul-Husayn, "Problems in the Ottoman Administration in Syria," 668–69.

126. Abu-Husayn, *The View from Istanbul*, 24–35.
127. Ibid., 30–31. Translated MD 46, no. 518, 1581–82.
128. Ibid.
129. Ibid., 31. Translated MD 49, no. 110, 1583.
130. Duwayhi, *Tarikh al-Azmina*, 284; Abdul-Rahman Abu-Husayn, "The Ottoman Invasion of the Shuf in 1585: A Reconsideration," *Al-Abhath*, 33 (1985): 13–21.
131. Makarim, *Lubnan fi Ahd al-Umara al-Tanukhiyin*, 284.
132. Ibid., 285–86, suggesting the latter and citing the work of the nineteenth-century German orientalist scholar Heinrich-Ferdinand Füstenfeld.
133. Abu-Husayn, "Problems in the Ottoman Administration in Syria," 670.
134. Salibi, "The Sayfas and the Eyalat of Tripoli, 1579–1640," *Arabica*, XX (1973): 31–32.
135. Abu-Husayn, *Provincial Leaderships in Syria*, 80–81.
136. Ibid., 22–23, 83; Salibi, The Sayfas and the Eyalat of Tripoli," 32.
137. Duwayhi, *Tarikh al-Azmina*, 295, reports that the Hamades killed the four muqaddams of Jaj and replaced them in the headship (*mashyakha*) of Jubayl.
138. Moosa, *The Maronites in History*, 265.
139. Duwayhi, *Tarikh al-Azmina*, 263.
140. Ibid., 256.
141. Moosa, *The Maronites in History*, 242–43.
142. Ibid., 245–55, on the Eliano mission.
143. Duwayhi (*Tarikh al-Azmina*, 285) notes: "A year before his death when the Maronite students in Rome multiplied, the pope [Gregory XIII] ordered their transfer from the school for novices in religion and established a special college for them."
144. Moosa, *The Maronites in History*, 256–68, on the Dandini mission and Patriarch Yusuf Ruzzi.
145. Giralamo Dandini, "A Voyage to Mont Libanus wherein is an account of the customs, and manners & etc., of the Turks. Also a description of Candia, Nicosia, Tripoli, Alexandretta & etc.," in *A General Collection of the best and most interesting Voyages and Travels*, 17 vols., ed. John Pinkerton (London: 1811), 10: 300.
146. Ibid., 289.
147. Ibid.
148. Winter, *The Shiites of Lebanon*, 23–24. For detail on Zayn al-Din and the relevant biographical sources, also see Abisaab, "History and Self-Image: The 'Amili Ulema in Syria and Iran," 71–73; Stewart, "Notes on the Migration of 'Amili Scholars to Safavid Iran," 90–93, 100–02.
149. Stewart, "Notes on the Migration of 'Amili Scholars to Safavid Iran," 93–94, quoting Ibn al-Awdi in the biographical source *al-Durr al-Manthur min al-Ma'thur wa Ghayr al-Ma'thur*, 2 vols., ed. Ahmad al-Husayni (Qum, 1978), 2: 156.
150. Winter, *The Shiites of Lebanon*, 24.
151. Abisaab, "History and Self-Image: The 'Amili Ulema in Syria and Iran," 82–86.
152. Ibid., 88–93.
153. Stewart, "Notes on the Migration of 'Amili Scholars to Safavid Iran," 97, 100–02.
154. Kamal Salibi, *A House of Many Mansions: The History of Lebanon Reconsidered* (Berkeley and Los Angeles: University of California Press, 1988), 127.
155. Bulos Qara'li, *Ali Pasha Junblat Wali Halab, 1605–1611* (Beirut, Manshurat Dar al-Makshuf, 1939), 14–15.
156. Abul-Husayn, *The View from Istanbul*, 20.
157. George Sandys, *A relation of a journey begun an. Dom. 1610: Containing a description of the Turkish Empire, of Egypt, of the Holy Land, of the remote parts of Italy, and islands adjoining*, 3rd edition (London, 1632), 212.
158. Deidre Pettet, "A Veritable Bedouin: The Chevalier d'Arvieux in the Camp of the Emir Turabey," in *Distant Lands and Diverse Cultures: The French Experience in Asia, 1600–1700*, ed. Glen Ames and Ronald Love (Westport: Greenwood Press, 2003), 25.
159. Sandys, *A relation of a journey begun an. Dom. 1610*, 210.
160. Ibid., 211–12.
161. Abdul-Rahim Abu-Husayn, *Provincial Leaderships in Syria 1575–1650* (Beirut: American University of Beirut Press, 1985).
162. Ibid., 84.

163. See Makarim, *Lubnan fi Ahd al-Umara al-Tanukhiyin*, 290–93, for discussion and dismissal of the Khazen story. Makarim assesses that Fakhr al-Din and his brother stayed with their Buhturid maternal uncle for protection from the Alam al-Din clan.

164. Al-Shidyaq, *Kitab Akhbar al-Ayan*, 1: 67.

165. Colin Imber, *The Ottoman Empire, 1300–1650: The Structure of Power* (Basingstoke: Palgrave Macmillan, 2002), 74.

166. Abu-Husayn, *Provincial Leaderships in Syria*, 85–87; al-Shidyaq, *Kitab Akhbar al-Ayan*, 1: 239–40.

167. Al-Shidyaq, *Kitab Akhbar al-Ayan*, 1: 141.

168. Al-Khalidi al-Safadi, *Lubnan fi Ahd al-Amir Fakhr al-Din al-Ma'ni al-Thani*, 32.

169. Abu-Husayn, *Provincial Leaderships in Syria*, 88–93.

170. Hafez Chehab, "Reconstructing the Medici Portrait of Fakhr al-Din al-Ma'ni," *Muqarnas*, 11 (1994): 117.

171. Makarim, *Lubnan fi Ahd al-Umara al-Tanukhiyin*, 295.

172. Abu-Husayn, *Provincial Leaderships in Syria*, 103; Al Safa, *Tarikh Jabal Amil*, 49; al-Shidyaq, *Kitab Akhbar al-Ayan*, 1: 243.

173. Al-Khalidi al-Safadi, *Lubnan fi Ahd al-Amir Fakhr al-Din al-Ma'ni al-Thani*, 33, 53. The references to the Khazens are in alternative manuscripts of Al-Khalidi al-Safadi's work.

174. Ibid., 62–63; al-Shidyaq, *Kitab Akhbar al-Ayan*, 1: 254–55.

175. Abu-Husayn (*Provincial Leaderships in Syria*, 107) confuses 1617 with 1618.

176. Ibid., 107, 109.

177. Ibid., 43–52, for discussion of Fakhr al-Din's erosion of the Sayfas, 1618–1623.

178. Al-Khalidi al-Safadi, *Lubnan fi Ahd al-Amir Fakhr al-Din al-Ma'ni al-Thani*, 77 (reference to an alternative manuscript).

179. Winter (*The Shiites of Lebanon*, 39) rejects Duwayhi's claim that Fakhr al-Din formally received the governorship.

180. Abu-Husayn, *Provincial Leaderships in Syria*, 145–48, for discussion of the final stage of the conflict between Fakhr al-Din and Yunus al-Harfush.

181. Duwayhi, *Tarikh al-Azmina*, 323.

182. Abu-Husayn, *Provincial Leaderships in Syria*, 64–65.

183. Duwayhi, *Tarikh al-Azmina*, 326.

184. Ibid., 324, 326.

185. Ibid., 326.

186. Ibid., 324.

187. Ibid., 325.

188. Ibid.

189. Abu-Husayn, *Provincial Leaderships in Syria*, 125.

190. Al-Shidyaq, *Kitab Akhbar al-Ayan*, 1; 289.

191. Ibid.

Chapter 3

1. The mid-sixteenth century estimate is based on numbers for component districts taken from Isam Khalife, *Nawahi Lubnan fi al-Qarn al-Sadis Ashr*. The 1783 estimate is from Constantin-François Volney, *Travels through Egypt and Syria, in the years 1783, 1784 & 1785. Containing the present natural and political state of those countries; their productions, arts, manufactures & commerce; with observations on the manners, customs and government of the Turks & Arabs*, 2 vols. Translated from the French (New York: J. Tiebout, 1798), 2: 14, 46.

2. Winter, *The Shiites of Lebanon*, 56–57, 78–80. Using a combination of Ottoman chancery materials and contemporary court records, Winter offers a wide-ranging portrayal of both Shia prominence in early Ottoman Mount Lebanon and the later erosion of the Shia position in the north and Jabal Amil.

3. Ibid., 39–40.

4. Ibid., 101–04.

5. Ibid., 156, 168.

6. Ibid., 123.

7. In other words, I question the priority given to European interference in Usama Makdisi's *The Culture of Sectarianism* (Berkeley and Los Angeles: University of California Press, 2000).
8. Salibi, *A House of Many Mansions*, 127–28.
9. Abu-Husayn, *The View from Istanbul*, 38–39.
10. For the final years of the Sayfas, see Abu-Husayn, *Provincial Leaderships in Syria*, 56–60, and Salibi, "The Sayfas and the Eyalat of Tripoli," 50–52.
11. Duwayhi, *Tarikh al-Azmina*, 334.
12. Ibid., 337.
13. Al Safa, *Tarikh Jabal Amil*, 83.
14. Duwayhi, *Tarikh al-Azmina*, 337.
15. Abu-Husayn, *The View from Istanbul*, 21–22
16. Abdul-Rahim Abu-Husayn, "The Unknown Career of Ahmad Ma'n (1667–1697)," *Archivum Ottomanicum* 17 (1999): 242.
17. Richard van Leeuwen, *Notables and Clergy in Mount Lebanon: The Khazin Sheikhs & the Maronite Church (1736–1840)* (Leiden, E. J. Brill, 1994), 82, 84–85.
18. Ibid., 105–06.
19. Ibid., 82–83, 102.
20. For the Junblats between 1640 and 1712, see al-Shidyaq, *Kitab Akhbar al-Ayan*, 1: 141.
21. Ibid., 44 and 46.
22. Duwayhi, *Tarikh al-Azmina*, 347; al-Shidyaq, *Kitab Akhbar al-Ayan*, 1: 44. Duwayhi gives the date as 1650, whereas al-Shidyaq says it was 1651.
23. Duwayhi, *Tarikh al-Azmina*, 347.
24. Ibid., 350.
25. For the 1660 events, see Duwayhi, *Tarikh al-Azmina*, 357–59; al-Shidyaq, *Kitab Akhbar al-Ayan*, 1: 44–45. The latter appears to derive substantially from the former, with some additional detail.
26. Duwayhi, *Tarikh al-Azmina*, 360.
27. Ibid., 363.
28. Abu-Husayn, *The View from Istanbul*, 22–23.
29. Duwayhi, *Tarikh al-Azmina*, 359.
30. Khalife, *Nawahi Lubnan*, 150–54.
31. Al Safa, *Tarikh Jabal Amil*, 113.
32. Ibid.
33. Abu-Husayn, *Provincial Leaderships in Syria*, 152.
34. Duwayhi, *Tarikh al-Azmina*, 366.
35. Al-Shidyaq, *Kitab Akhbar al-Ayan*, 1: 46.
36. Van Leeuwen, *Notables and Clergy in Mount Lebanon*, 74.
37. Duwayhi, *Tarikh al-Azmina*, 340–41.
38. Ibid., 356.
39. See al-Shidyaq, *Kitab Akhbar al-Ayan*, 1: 194, for a summary of the affairs of the Hamades in the 1670s. Also see the detail in Duwayhi, *Tarikh al-Azmina*, 368–72.
40. Al-Shidyaq, *Kitab Akhbar al-Ayan*, 1: 194–95; Duwayhi, *Tarikh al-Azmina*, 376.
41. Al-Shidyaq, *Kitab Akhbar al-Ayan*, 1: 195; Duwayhi, *Tarikh al-Azmina*, 377.
42. Duwayhi, *Tarikh al-Azmina*, 378.
43. Abu-Husayn, "The Unknown Career of Ahmad Ma'n," 242–43.
44. Al-Shidyaq, *Kitab Akhbar al-Ayan*, 1: 195; Duwayhi, *Tarikh al-Azmina*, 378–80.
45. Duwayhi, *Tarikh al-Azmina*, 380–81.
46. Al-Shidyaq, *Kitab Akhbar al-Ayan*, 1: 300, provides detail additional to Duwayhi's account, presumably from his Shihab sources.
47. Abu-Husayn, *The View from Istanbul*, 39–62.
48. Duwayhi, *Tarikh al-Azmina*, 381.
49. Caroline Finkel, *Osman's Dream: The Story of the Ottoman Empire, 1300–1923* (London: John Murray, 2006), 315–18.
50. Also see Abbas Abu Salih, "Al-Sira ala al-Sulta fi al-Imara al-Shihabiya," in *Lubnan fi al-Qarn al-Thamin'ashr: al-Mu'tamar al-Awal lil-Jami'ya al-Lubnaniya lil-Dirasat al-Uthmaniya*, ed. Butros Labaki (Beirut: Dar al-Muntakhab al-Arabi, 1996), 134–35.

51. Duwayhi, *Tarikh al-Azmina*, 382.
52. Abu-Husayn, *The View from Istanbul*, 65, cites a January 1707 order from Istanbul to the governor of Sidon (Translated MD 115, no. 798): "Upon the death of one of the sons of Ma'n—[the ibn] Ma'n who held tax farms by concession in the *eyalat* of Sidon-Beirut—the one who was appointed in his place [Emir Bashir ibn Shihab] agreed to pay the money owed by the deceased. . . ."
53. Duwayhi, *Tarikh al-Azmina*, 383–84.
54. Ibid., 383.
55. Haydar Ahmad al-Shihabi, *Lubnan fi Ahd al-Umara al-Shihabiyin*, ed. Asad Rustum and Fuad al-Bustani, 3 vols. (Beirut: al-Makataba al-Bulusiya, 1984), 1: 6.
56. Estelle (French consul in Sidon) to Pontchartrain (State Secretary for Foreign Affairs, Paris), May 1704 and March 1705, in Munir Isma'il and Adil Isma'il, *Tarikh Lubnan al-Hadith: al-Watha'iq al-Diblumasiya—al-Qism al-Awal, al-Juz al-Awal* (Beirut: Dar al-Nashr lil Siyasa wa al-Tarikh, 1990), 58–60.
57. Al-Shihabi, *Lubnan fi Ahd al-Umara al-Shihabiyin*, 1: 7.
58. Ibid., 8.
59. Abu Husayn, *The View from Istanbul*, 67–72.
60. Al-Shihabi, *Lubnan fi Ahd al-Umara al-Shihabiyin*, 1: 9.
61. Ibid., 9–11. Also see Abu Salih, "Al-Sira ala al-Sulta fi al-Imara al-Shihabiya," 138–39.
62. For the battle of Ayn Dara and its immediate aftermath, see al-Shihabi, *Lubnan fi Ahd al-Umara al-Shihabiyin*, 1: 12–14; al-Shidyaq, *Kitab Akhbar al-Ayan*, 2: 314–16; and Abu Salih, "Al-Sira ala al-Sulta fi al-Imara al-Shihabiya," 140–42.
63. Winter, *The Shiites of Lebanon*, 148. Winter cites French consular reports.
64. "Emir Haydar roused his followers and assembled them on the night of Friday the eighteenth of the sacred month of Muharram of the aforementioned year [1122]"—al-Shihabi, *Lubnan fi Ahd al-Umara al-Shihabiyin*, 1: 13. The date corresponds to March 19, 1710.
65. Khuri, *Being a Druze*, 32.
66. For stress on the demographic impact of Ayn Dara, see Munir Isma'il, "Al-Tahawulat al-Siyasiya fi Mujtama al-Imara al-Shihabiya," in *Lubnan fi al-Qarn al-Thamin'ashr: al-Mu'tamar al-Awal al-Lubnaniya lil-Dirasat al-Uthmaniya*, ed. Butros Labaki (Beirut: Dar al-Muntakhab al-Arabi, 1996), 91. Isma'il, however, does not provide statistical evidence.
67. I differ here with Winter, *The Shiites of Lebanon*, 40. This book instead endorses the view of Salibi in *The Modern History of Lebanon*, 8.
68. Ilya Harik, *Politics and Change in a Traditional Society—Lebanon 1711–1845* (Princeton: Princeton University Press, 1968), 53.
69. Van Leeuwen, *Notables and Clergy in Mount Lebanon*, 74.
70. Kamal Salibi, "The Secret of the House of Ma'n," *International Journal of Middle Eastern Studies* 4 (1973): 272–87.
71. For accounts of the Shihabi system in English, see Harik, *Politics and Change in a Traditional Society*, 37–73; Kamal Salibi, *The Modern History of Lebanon* (New York: Caravan Books, 1977), 3–17; Van Leeuwen, *Notables & Clergy in Mount Lebanon*, 51–62.
72. Kamal Salibi, "The Lebanese Emirate, 1667–1841," *Al-Abhath*, XX (1967): 7, 14–15, presents the argument that the Druze always regarded the emirate "as alien," and the paramount emirs as nothing more than "Ottoman *multazims*."
73. Harik, *Politics and Change in a Traditional Society*, 48–64.
74. Samir Khalaf, *Civil and Uncivil Violence in Lebanon: A History of the Internationalization of Communal Conflict* (New York: Columbia University Press, 2002), 65–67; Axel Havemann, "The Impact of Peasant Resistance on Nineteenth-Century Mount Lebanon" in Farhad Kazemi and John Waterbury eds. *Peasants & Politics in the Modern Middle East* (Miami: Florida International University Press, 1991), 86–87.
75. Al-Shihabi, *Lubnan fi Ahd al-Umara al-Shihabiyin*, 1: 29.
76. Ibid., 28.
77. Ibid., 40–41.
78. Salibi, *The Modern History of Lebanon*, 9.
79. Al-Shihabi, *Lubnan fi Ahd al-Umara al-Shihabiyin*, 1: 37.
80. Harik, *Politics and Change in a Traditional Society*, 46–47; Salibi, "The Lebanese Emirate," 13.

81. Al-Shihabi, *Lubnan fi Ahd al-Umara al-Shihabiyin*, 1: 43.

82. Ibid., 49–51.

83. In the 1770s, the qirsh was worth about 44 percent of a Spanish dollar, down from parity in 1688. This value is established from a 1770s rate of 10 qirsh to the pound sterling—see Sevket Pamuk, "Money in the Ottoman Empire," in *An Economic and Social History of the Ottoman Empire*, ed. Halil Inalcik and Donald Quataert (Cambridge: Cambridge University Press), 968—integrated with a rate of 4.4 dollars to the pound. It is estimated that the purchasing power of a Spanish dollar in 1774 equaled that of $US 27.9 in 2010—see "Purchasing power of money in the United States from 1774 to Present," accessed October 2, 2010, http//www.measuringworth.com/ppowerus.

84. Al-Shihabi, *Lubnan fi Ahd al-Umara al-Shihabiyin*, 60–62.

85. Harik, *Politics and Change in a Traditional Society*, 31–32; Van Leeuven, *Notables & Clergy in Mount Lebanon*, 74.

86. Al-Shihabi, *Lubnan fi Ahd al-Umara al-Shihabiyin*, 1: 62.

87. Winter, *The Shi'ites of Lebanon*, 158–59, citing Isa Hamade's protection of Patriarch Ya'qub Awwad between 1714 and 1717.

88. Ibid., 160–61.

89. Majed Halawi, *A Lebanon Defied—Musa al-Sadr and the Shi'a Community* (Boulder: Westview Press, 1992), 32–33.

90. Al-Safa, *Tarikh Jabal Amil*, 118.

91. According to Al-Shihabi, *Lubnan fi Ahd al-Umara al-Shihabiyin*, 1: 85, Mansur Shihab "much loved Zahir al-Umar. And he rejoiced greatly at the coming of [Muhammad] Abu al-Dhahab into these lands [Palestine and Syria]."

92. Ibid., 89. Zahir al-Umar complained to Ali Bey that Muhammad Abu al-Dhahab "took the country [Damascus] without a fight. Then he abandoned it without any cause or excuse."

93. Al-Safa, *Tarikh Jabal Amil*, 122–24; Al-Shihabi, *Lubnan fi Ahd al-Umara al-Shihabiyin*, 1: 89. Al-Safa emphasizes the Shia role.

94. Al-Safa, *Tarikh Jabal Amil*, 131.

95. Al-Shihabi, *Lubnan fi Ahd al-Umara al-Shihabiyin*, 1: 91.

96. Ibid., 92–94, on the events around Sidon and Beirut.

97. Ibid., 94.

98. Ibid., 97–101, on the siege of al-Jazzar in Beirut.

99. Ibid., 103.

100. Ibid., 115.

101. Al-Safa, *Tarikh Jabal Amil*, 137.

102. Ibid., 138.

103. Ibid., 138; Halawi, *A Lebanon Defied*, 34–35.

104. Al-Shihabi, *Lubnan fi Ahd al-Umara al-Shihabiyin*, 1: 123.

105. Ibid., 127–32, on the events of 1780.

106. Ibid., 135–40, on the affair of Isma'il Shihab.

107. Ibid., 141.

108. Ibid., 142–60, on the 1788 battles between the forces of Emir Yusuf and al-Jazzar, the installing of Bashir II Shihab as Hakim in 1789, and the demise of Yusuf in 1790.

109. According to al-Shidyaq, *Kitab Akhbar al-Ayan*, 2: 355, al-Jazzar had second thoughts and countermanded his order, but the hanging went ahead anyway. In al-Shidyaq's rendering, Ghandur al-Khuri "died of fright."

110. Richard van Leeuwen, "Monastic Estates and Agricultural Transformation in Mount Lebanon in the 18th century," *International Journal of Middle East Studies*, 23: 4 (1991): 601–617.

111. For elaboration on the growth of Zahle and Deir al-Qamar between 1750 and the 1840s, consult Fruma Zachs, *The Making of a Syrian Identity—Intellectuals and Merchants in Nineteenth Century Beirut* (Leiden: Brill, 2005), 18–27.

112. Ibid., 19.

113. In 1833, Bashir II sent five hundred fighters from Zahle and Biskinta to help the Egyptians suppress the Alawites north of Mount Lebanon (al-Shidyaq, *Kitab Akhbar al-Ayan*, 2: 453).

114. Harik, *Politics and Change in a Traditional Society*, 250.
115. Volney, *Travels through Egypt and Syria*, 2: 107, 114, 128.
116. Ibid., 114.
117. Khalid Ziyade, "Takawun al-A'ilat fi Tarabulus," in *Lubnan fi al-Qarn al-Thamin'ashr: al-Mu'tamar al-Awal lil-Jami'ya al-Lubnaniya lil-Dirasat al-Uthmaniya*, ed. Butros Labaki (Beirut: Dar al-Muntakhab al-Arabi, 1996), 306.
118. Ambrosio Bembo, *The Travels and Journal of Ambrosio Bembo*, ed. Anthony Welch, trans. Clara Bargellini (Berkely and Los Angeles: University of California Press, 2007), 43.
119. Ibid.
120. Ziyade, "Takawun al-A'ilat fi Tarabulus," 305–08.
121. See, for example, al-Nabulusi, "Al-Tuhfa al-Nabulusiya fi al-Rihla al-Tarabulusiya," 48–49, 72, 86.
122. Ziyade, "Takawun al-A'ilat fi Tarabulus," 313.
123. See the account in Faruq Hablas, "Al-Intifadat al-Sha'biya fi Tarabulus," in *Lubnan fi al-Qarn al-Thamin'ashr: al-Mu'tamar al-Awal lil-Jami'ya al-Lubnaniya lil-Dirasat al-Uthmaniya*, ed. Butros Labaki (Beirut: Dar al-Muntakhab al-Arabi, 1996), 286–301.
124. Ibid., 291. The French consul, in a report to Paris, estimated the crowd at five thousand.
125. Qasim al-Samad, "Muqata'jiya al-Dinniya wa Mawqifhum min al-Sira ala al-Imara al-Shihabiya," in *Lubnan fi al-Qarn al-Thamin'ashr: al-Mu'tamar al-Awal lil-Jami'ya al-Lubnaniya lil-Dirasat al-Uthmaniya*, ed. Butros Labaki (Beirut: Dar al-Muntakhab al-Arabi, 1996), 162.
126. Ibid., 165.
127. Ibid, 176.
128. Ibid., 168.
129. Volney, *Travels through Egypt and Syria*, 2: 114, 128.
130. Ibid., 114.
131. See the account in Husayn Sulayman, "Thulathi al-Quwa al-Mahaliya Yantazi Saida min al-Saytara al-Uthmaniya," in *Lubnan fi al-Qarn al-Thamin'ashr: al-Mu'tamar al-Awal lil-Jami'ya al-Lubnaniya lil-Dirasat al-Uthmaniya*, ed. Butros Labaki (Beirut: Dar al-Muntakhab al-Arabi, 1996), 321–44.
132. Rafic Chikhani, "Communautés Libanaises vues par des Voyageurs Français au XVIII Siècle," in *Lubnan fi al-Qarn al-Thamin'ashr: al-Mu'tamar al-Awal lil-Jami'ya al-Lubnaniya lil-Dirasat al-Uthmaniya*, ed. Butros Labaki (Beirut: Dar al-Muntakhab al-Arabi, 1996), 254.
133. Volney, *Travels through Egypt and Syria*, 2: 14, 46.
134. Van Leeuwen, *Notables & Clergy in Mount Lebanon*, 190. In 1764, a papal envoy proposed thirteen estates go to the *Baladi* wing and five to the *Halabis*.
135. Ibid., 180.
136. Joseph Abu Nahra, "Intiqal al-Milkiya min al-Lama'iyin ila al-Aklirus fi al-Matn," in *Lubnan fi al-Qarn al-Thamin'ashr: al-Mu'tamar al-Awal lil-Jami'ya al-Lubnaniya lil-Dirasat al-Uthmaniya*, ed. Butros Labaki (Beirut: Dar al-Muntakhab al-Arabi, 1996), 190–94.
137. Van Leeuwen, *Notables & Clergy in Mount Lebanon*, 107.
138. Ibid., 130–33.
139. Ibid., 135–37.
140. Ibid., 143.
141. Haqqi, *Lubnan*, 2: 567; Harik, *Politics and Change in a Traditional Society*, 160–61.
142. Volney, *Travels through Egypt and Syria*, 2: 117.
143. Haqqi, *Lubnan*, 2: 566.
144. Harik, *Politics and Change in a Traditional Society*, 161–62.
145. For detail, see Haqqi, *Lubnan*, 2: 567.
146. Harik, *Politics and Change in a Traditional Society*, 162.
147. Ibid., 164–65.
148. Al-Shihabi, *Lubnan fi Ahd al-Umara al-Shihabiyin*, 1: 192.
149. Al-Shidyaq, *Kitab Akhbar al-Ayan*, 2: 361.
150. Harik, *Politics and Change in a Traditional Society*, 178–79.
151. Al-Shidyaq, *Kitab Akhbar al-Ayan*, 2: 365.

152. Harik, *Politics and Change in a Traditional Society*, 180; al-Shidyaq, *Kitab Akhbar al-Ayan*, 2: 368.

153. Al-Shidyaq, *Kitab Akhbar al-Ayan*, 1: 170.

154. Al-Shidyaq, *Kitab Akhbar al-Ayan*, 2: 365.

155. See summary of these events in Harik, *Politics and Change in a Traditional Society*, 180–81.

156. Al-Shidyaq, *Kitab Akhbar al-Ayan*, 2: 369–70 comments: "Captain [Sir Sidney] Smith spoke to al-Jazzar about the emir and didn't get a response. He sailed to Alexandria exasperated with al-Jazzar and wrote to the grand vizier requesting him to leave Emir Bashir Shihab as Hakim and to deter al-Jazzar from harming him."

157. Ibid., 370.

158. Ibid., 375.

159. Ibid., 378.

160. Ibid., 378–80.

161. Ibid., 381.

162. For detailed analysis of Baz, his role, and his demise see Harik, *Politics and Change in a Traditional Society*, 186–99.

163. Al-Shihabi, *Lubnan fi Ahd al-Umara al-Shihabiyin*, 2: 512–13; al-Shidyaq, *Kitab Akhbar al-Ayan*, 2: 385–86.

164. Ibrahim al-Awra, *Tarikh Wilayat Sulayman Pasha al-Adil, 1804–1819*, ed. Antun Qiqanu (Beirut: Dar al-Hadkhat, 1989), 94.

165. Al-Shihabi, *Lubnan fi Ahd al-Umara al-Shihabiyin*, 2: 513–14; al-Shidyaq, *Kitab Akhbar al-Ayan*, 2: 387–88.

166. Harik, *Politics and Change in a Traditional Society*, 205–06.

167. Al-Awra, *Tarikh Wilayat Sulayman Pasha*, 59–60; Al Safa, *Tarikh Jabal Amil*, 140–42.

168. Al-Awra, *Tarikh Wilayat Sulayman Pasha*, 139.

169. Al Safa, *Tarikh Jabal Amil*, 142–43.

170. Van Leeuwen, *Notables & Clergy in Mount Lebanon*, 67–68.

171. For details of the *ammiya* events, consult Harik, *Politics and Change in a Traditional Society*, 208–22. According to al-Shidyaq (*Kitab Akhbar al-Ayan*, 2: 400–01): "The Emir imposed a sum on the merchants and demanded from the Christians that they pay the land tax [*al-amwal al-amiriya*] ahead of time.... The Christians of the Matn were indignant and refused to pay.... They wrote to the people of the Kisrawan asking them also to refuse. They all assembled in Antelias and appointed two representatives for each village as proposed by Bishop Yusuf Istfan, head and founder of the Ayn Waraqa college. And they swore that they would only pay the emir the land and head taxes once.... They wrote to the governor informing him that they were meeting because of the tyranny of Emir Bashir in requiring them to pay and not others [i.e. the Druze]." Also see al-Shihabi, *Lubnan fi Ahd al-Umara al-Shihabiyin*, 3: 659.

172. Al-Shihabi, *Lubnan fi Ahd al-Umara al-Shihabiyin*, 3: 685

173. Harik, *Politics and Change in a Traditional Society*, 136–39.

174. For the Ottoman orders against Abdullah Pasha and Emir Bashir, see al-Shihabi, *Lubnan fi Ahd al-Umara al-Shihabiyin*, 3: 720–21.

175. See the account of "The Mukhtarah Affair" in Harik, *Politics and Change in a Traditional Society*, 225–27.

176. Ibid., 238–39.

177. Salibi, *A House of Many Mansions*, 108.

178. Van Leeuwen, *Notables & Clergy in Mount Lebanon*, 70.

179. For populations of Beirut and Tripoli in the early nineteenth century, see Charles Issawi, *The Fertile Crescent 1800–1914: A Documentary Economic History* (New York: Oxford University Press, 1988), 28, and Leila Fawaz, *Merchants and Migrants in Nineteenth Century Beirut* (Cambridge: Harvard Univerity Press, 1983), 30–31.

180. Van Leeuwen, *Notables & Clergy in Mount Lebanon*, 69–70.

181. Caesar Farah, *The Politics of Interventionism in Ottoman Lebanon, 1830–1861* (London: I. B. Tauris, 2000), 19–21.

182. Al Safa, *Tarikh Jabal Amil*, 147.

183. Ibid.

184. Ibid., 147–48. Al Safa relates the story of the self-sacrifice of a Musa Qlayt from the village of Yatar, who impersonated Husayn's brother Muhammad Ali so he could escape capture by the Egyptians. Qlayt and Husayn Ibn Shabib were hung in Damascus. Muhammad Ali Ibn Shabib lived another forty years.

185. Harik, *Politics and Change in a Traditional Society*, 241–42. From Patriarch Hubaysh's papers, Harik cites an 1832 case of church pressure on a Maronite resident of a mixed village in the Matn concerning his relations with Druze.

186. In a curious anomaly, Tannus al-Shidyaq, the foremost contemporary chronicler, gives 1835 as the year of the insurrection. For accounts of the events, see Kamal Salibi, *The Modern History of Lebanon* (New York: Caravan, 1977), 34–36; Farah, *The Politics of Interventionism*, 22–23, 34–36; al-Shidyaq, *Kitab Akhbar al-Ayan*, 2: 454–57.

187. Harik, *Politics and Change in a Traditional Society*, 237.

188. Al-Shidyaq (*Kitab Akhbar al-Ayan*, 2: 457–58) relates: "When [Muhammad Ali] heard [about European intentions] he ordered the drafting of Muslim youth in his country. The army conscripted them, and also the Lebanese Christian students in the medical school there on the assumption that they were Muslims. When the news circulated in Syria that Muhammad Ali was conscripting Christians with the Muslims, the Lebanese Christians became afraid and agitated, believing that he would do the same with their youth. Meanwhile there was information of the advance of Egyptian regiments to Baalbek and Tripoli, and the arrival in Beirut of a ship carrying military uniforms. Rumor spread that these uniforms were for Lebanese Christian youth."

189. Harik, *Politics and Change in a Traditional Society*, 243.

190. Salibi, *The Modern History of Lebanon*, 38–39; Farah, *The Politics of Interventionism*, 35–36.

191. Al-Shidyaq, *Kitab Akhbar al-Ayan*, 2: 458.

192. Ibid., 459.

193. Wood was a Catholic and worked hard on the Maronite clergy and *muqata'ji*s, and also with some Druze chiefs. Farah, *The Politics of Interventionism*, 33, 35.

194. Ibid., 37–38; Harik, *Politics and Change in a Traditional Society*, 246–47.

195. Farah, *The Politics of Interventionism*, 36.

196. Salibi, *The Modern History of Lebanon*, 34.

197. Farah, *The Politics of Interventionism*, 69. Farah notes that Bashir III made threats to confiscate the property of Druze chiefs and even "to subordinate them to the Maronite patriarch."

198. Salibi, *The Modern History of Lebanon*, 47.

199. Farah, *The Politics of Interventionism*, 68–70.

200. For reviews of the October/November 1841 Maronite/Druze fighting, see Charles Churchill, *The Druze and the Maronites under the Turkish Rule from 1840 to 1860* (London: Bernard Quaritch, 1862), 44–52; Farah, *The Politics of Interventionism*, 101–15; Harik, *Politics and Change in a Traditional Society*, 261–66; Salibi, *The Modern History of Lebanon*, 49–52.

201. Churchill, *The Druze and the Maronites*, 50–51.

Chapter 4

1. Haqqi, *Lubnan*, 2: 626, gives the sectarian breakdown from the 1860–1867 Ottoman census of adult males. The proportions in the full census of 1911 (Haqqi, *Lubnan*, 2: 643) were 58 percent Maronite and 79 percent Christian—virtually unchanged five decades later and despite substantial Christian emigration.

2. Albert Hourani, *Arabic Thought in the Liberal Age, 1798–1959* (Cambridge: Cambridge University Press, 1983), 274–77; Salibi, *The Modern History of Lebanon*, 144–47.

3. Ibid., 143–46.

4. Jens Hanssen, *Fin de Siècle Beirut—The Making of an Ottoman Provincial Capital* (Oxford: Oxford University Press, 2005); see chapter 6 "Provincial Classrooms," 163–89.

5. Hourani, *Arabic Thought in the Liberal Age*, 284.

6. Salibi, *The Modern History of Lebanon*, 118; Hourani, *Arabic Thought in the Liberal Age*, 275. Both cite M. Jouplain (pseudonym of Bulus Nujaym) in his 1908 tract *La Question du Liban*.

7. Farah, *The Politics of Interventionism*, 153–249, gives detailed analysis of Ömer's year in Mount Lebanon. Also see Salibi, *The Modern History of Lebanon*, 53–62. Tannus al-Shidyaq was a contemporary reporter of these developments and presents his interpretation in *Kitab Akhbar al-Ayan*, 2: 490–94.

8. In *Kitab Akhbar al-Ayan*, 2:491, al-Shidyaq indicates that the Druze lords had good reason for irritation—"Ömer Pasha took the Christians as allies to make them content with the conduct of the state. He brought some of them into his service as soldiers, and made Abu Samra and Shantiri their commanders. He stopped the Druze from bothering the Christians. . . ." Abu Samra Ghanim and Yusuf Shantiri had led attacks on the Druze in 1841.

9. Ibid., 493, notes that by late 1842, Druze chiefs were prepared to contemplate a return of Shihab rule with a council of four *muqata'ji mudabbirs*, two Druze, and two Maronite. At that stage, Ottoman army commander Mustafa Pasha wrote to the Maronites "warning them of the misdemeanors and dirty tricks of the Druze."

10. Farah, *The Politics of Interventionism*, 212, 214–15.

11. Ibid., 325.

12. Ibid., 360, 362–65.

13. Churchill, *The Druze and the Maronites*, 89, provides a contemporary view: "He [Sa'id] had early secured the patronage, and even the official protection of the British government, which imagined it saw, in the effective maintenance of his power and ascendancy, a means of establishing through the Druze sect a political influence, to counterbalance that possessed by France over the Maronites."

14. Farah, *The Politics of Interventionism*, 392–93.

15. Salibi, *The Modern History of Lebanon*, 64.

16. Farah, *The Politics of Interventionism*, 259, 263.

17. Ibid., 264; Salibi, *The Modern History of Lebanon*, 65.

18. For detailed treatment, see Farah, *The Politics of Interventionism*, 342–58.

19. Ibid., 377.

20. Ibid., 376–402.

21. Ibid., 438–39, 458–62; Harik, *Politics and Change in a Traditional Society*, 272–73; Salibi, *The Modern History of Lebanon*, 71–73.

22. Farah, *The Politics of Interventionism*, 485–87.

23. Salibi, *The Modern History of Lebanon*, 76–77.

24. Caesar Farah, *Papers on Lebanon 13: The Road to Intervention – Fiscal Politics in Ottoman Lebanon* (Oxford: Centre for Lebanese Studies, 1992).

25. Leila Fawaz, *Merchants and Migrants in Nineteenth Century Beirut*, 31, 49, 128.

26. Ibid., 34.

27. Salibi, *The Modern History of Lebanon*, 133–34.

28. Ibid., 135–36.

29. Ibid., 138.

30. Fawaz, *Merchants and Migrants*, 89–98.

31. Ibid., 96.

32. Al Safa, *Tarikh Jabal Amil*, 150–51.

33. Farah, *The Road to Intervention*, 35–36; Halawi, *A Lebanon Defied*, 36–37.

34. Farah, *The Politics of Interventionism*, 491.

35. Ibid., 501.

36. See Churchill, *The Druze and the Maronites*, 122–25, for an informative, albeit opiniated, contemporary account. Churchill describes the activities of Bashir Ahmad as follows: "Ere long the Maronite aristocracy found the kaimmakam invading their rights, assailing their privileges, and assuming the exercise of his own direct functions in matters which had for ages been referred to them alone. . . . The natural consequence of such proceedings was a feeling of excitement and discontent throughout the Maronite districts. . . . The Haazin sheiks, rulers of the populous district of the Kesrouan, had committed the unpardonable offence of seeking the support of the British government to the representation of their grievances at the Porte."

37. Farah, *The Politics of Interventionism*, 509–12; Salibi, *The Modern History of Lebanon*, 82.

38. Ibid., 84.
39. Farah, *The Politics of Interventionism*, 533.
40. Ibid., 534.
41. Ibid., 542.
42. Salibi (*The Modern History of Lebanon*, 88–91) emphasizes parallel Maronite and Druze preparations. Farah (*The Politics of Interventionism*, 545–48, 557–59) records Christian belligerence and provocation.
43. Churchill, *The Druzes and the Maronites*, 148, notes: "The Druzes, in general, had formed a very erroneous and exaggerated idea of the power which the Christians might bring to bear upon them in the present crisis, and were greatly alarmed at their own position."
44. Ibid., 138.
45. Farah, *The Politics of Interventionism*, 563.
46. For modern academic accounts of the 1860 events, see Leila Fawaz, *An Occasion for War: Civil Conflict in Lebanon and Damascus in 1860* (London: I. B. Tauris, 1994), 47–77; Karam Rizk, *Les Événements de 1860 et le Premier Mutasarrifiya: Tenants et Aboutissants du Grand-Liban* (Kaslik: Bibliothèque de l'Université Saint-Esprit, 1992), 121–71; Farah, *The Politics of Interventionism*, 554–87; Salibi, *The Modern History of Lebanon*, 98–105.
47. Salibi, *The Modern History of Lebanon*, 101.
48. Fawaz, *An Occasion for War*, 35–36.
49. Farah (*The Politics of Interventionism*, 557) refers to the Orthodox bishop of Sidon responding positively to a battle call from Bishop Aoun and instructing his community in Hasbaya and Rashaya to prepare for war.
50. Ibid., 568–69. Fawaz, *An Occasion for War*, 64, using several sources, estimates 1,800 deaths in these massacres.
51. Farah, *The Politics of Interventionism*, 581. Fawaz, *An Occasion for War*, 72, cites a witness's guess of two thousand corpses.
52. Michael Johnson, *Class and Client in Beirut: The Sunni Muslim Community and the Lebanese State 1840–1985* (London and Atlantic Highlands: Ithaca Press, 1986), 19. Churchill, *The Druzes and the Maronites*, 196, observes: "On the 22nd of June [1860] a Mahommedan was assassinated close to the walls of [Beirut]. Immediately the shout arose that a Christian had committed the deed. . . . An armed rabble paraded the streets crying aloud for revenge. . . . At this critical juncture a Turkish line-of-battle ship anchored in the port with troops under the command of Ismail Pasha (General Kmety) who were instantly disembarked."
53. Farah, *The Politics of Interventionism*, 175. This is the lowest estimate.
54. Ibid., 677–78; Rizk, *Les Événements de 1860 et le Premier Mutasarrifiya*, 201.
55. The best detailed accounts in English of Mount Lebanon and Beirut in the new era are Engin Akarli, *The Long Peace: Ottoman Lebanon, 1861–1920* (London: I. B. Tauris, 1993); John Spagnolo, *France and Ottoman Lebanon, 1861–1914* (London: Ithaca, 1977); Jens Hanssen, *Fin de Siècle Beirut*; and Akram Khater, *Inventing Home*.
56. Farah, *The Politics of Interventionism*, 625–26.
57. Akarli, *The Long Peace*, 154–55, 157.
58. Ibid., 161; Spagnolo, *France and Ottoman Lebanon*, 92–93; Rizk, *Les Événements de 1860 et le Premier Mutasarrifiya*, 230–32.
59. Akarli, *The Long Peace*, 132–40.
60. For detail, see Butrus Abu Manneh, "The Establishing and Dismantling of the Province of Syria," in *Problems of the Middle East in Historical Perspective: Essays in Honour of Albert Hourani*, ed. John Spagnolo (Reading: Ithaca Press, 1992), 7–26.
61. Khater, *Inventing Home*, 51, 54.
62. Spagnolo, *France and Ottoman Lebanon*, 118–19. Spagnolo cites French ambassador to Istanbul Prosper Bourée as observing that even "a small harmless Maronite Montenegro" would reduce French ability to block Russia.
63. Ibid., 130–31.
64. Akarli, *The Long Peace*, 152.
65. Spagnolo, *France and Ottoman Lebanon*, 68–70.

66. Akarli, *The Long Peace*, 37–38; Rizk, *Les Événements de 1860 et le Premier Mutasarrifiya*, 220–22, 233–47.
67. Spagnolo, *France and Ottoman Lebanon*, 113–14.
68. Ibid., 128.
69. Akarli, *The Long Peace*, 87.
70. Spagnolo, *France and Ottoman Lebanon*, 156.
71. Ibid., 162–66; Akarli, *The Long Peace*, 43.
72. Spagnolo, *France and Ottoman Lebanon*, 232, notes the March 1907 electoral victory of "liberal" candidate Jirjus Zuayn over the incumbent Sheikh Hubaysh by 85 to 35 headman votes.
73. Akarli, *The Long Peace*, 169–70.
74. Ibid., 113.
75. Ibid., 114.
76. Haqqi, *Lubnan*, 2: 602–03.
77. Khater, *Inventing Home*, 22.
78. Haqqi, *Lubnan*, 2: 478.
79. Khater, *Inventing Home*, 31.
80. Ibid., 32–33.
81. Ibid., 35–37.
82. Haqqi, *Lubnan*, 2: 643, gives the number and defines the exclusions (females and males under fifteen years old). Considering the large family sizes cited in Khater, *Inventing Home*, 60 (French consul-general Bourée's 1847 estimate of 6.2 children for a Maronite family and 4.6 for Druze), it would seem reasonable to add at least one-third to the male population for those under age fifteen. It is interesting that the Ottoman *Salname-yi Jabal Lubnan 1309 (H)* repeats the figure of 99,834 for 1891/92, with no updating, an anachronism that would explain the discrepancy with foreign estimates of the population reported in J. M. Wagstaff, "A Note on Some Nineteenth Century Population Statistics for Lebanon," *Bulletin (British Society for Middle Eastern Studies)* 13 no. 1 (1986): 27–35.
83. Haqqi, *Lubnan*, 2: 626.
84. Khalife, *Nawahi Lubnan*—data for districts and localities within the *mutasarrifiya* as defined by the map attached to Haqqi, *Lubnan*; Volney, *Travels through Egypt and Syria*, 2: 14, 46. Khater, *Inventing Home*, 59, mistakenly gives Volney's estimate for the southern districts (the Druze country) as being for the whole mountain.
85. Haqqi, *Lubnan*, 2: 644, gives full tabulation of the 1911 results by sect and sex. Also see Akarli, *The Long Peace*, 105–06, for English rendition.
86. Issawi, *The Fertile Crescent*, 20, for the total emigrant estimate; Khater, *Inventing Home*, 209, for estimates of returnees.
87. Ibid., 57.
88. Ibid., 36–47, 59; Carolyn Gates, *The Merchant Republic of Lebanon: Rise of an Open Economy* (London: I. B. Tauris, 1998), 14. For the silk industry, Gates cites Butros Labaki, *Introduction à l'histoire économique du Liban: soie et commerce extérieur en fin de période ottomane, 1840–1914* (Beirut: Publications de l'Université Libanaise, 1984).
89. For groundbreaking exploration of the impact of the returnees, see Khater, *Inventing Home*, 108–45 (Chapter 5, "Back to the Mountain").
90. Haqqi, *Lubnan*, 2: 472–73.
91. Khater, *Inventing Home*, 143.
92. Spagnolo, *France and Ottoman Lebanon*, 276–78.
93. Akarli, *The Long Peace*, 79, 99–100; Spagnolo, *France and Ottoman Lebanon*, 285–286.
94. Fawaz, *Merchants and Migrants*, 128–29; Hanssen, *Fin de Siècle Beirut*, 141.
95. Sectarian fractions from tables in Fawaz, *Merchants and Migrants*, 51, 127–32.
96. *Salname-yi Vilayet-i Beyrut 1318 (H)*.
97. Hanssen, *Fin de Siècle Beirut*, 86–87, 111.
98. Johnson, *Class and Client*, 18–22.
99. Samir Khalaf, *Persistance and Change in Nineteenth Century Lebanon* (Beirut: American University of Beirut, 1979), 108.

100. Fawaz, *Merchants and Migrants*, 105.
101. Hanssen, *Fin de Siècle Beirut*, 39.
102. Ibid., 87–92, 96–99.
103. Ibid., 163–89; Salibi, *The Modern History of Lebanon*, 136–40.
104. Adel Ismail, *Documents Diplomatiques et Consulaires relatifs à l'Histoire du Liban, Les Sources Françaises, t. 16, Consulat de France à Beyrouth* (Beirut: Editions des oeuvres politiques et historiques, 2001), 313–14 (report of French consul-general to Ministry of Foreign Affairs, March 31, 1896).
105. Salibi, *The Modern History of Lebanon*, 144; Hanssen, *Fin de Siècle Beirut*, 169.
106. Kassir, *Beirut*, 198.
107. Ibid., 197.
108. Ibid., 170; Johnson, *Class and Client*, 14.
109. Hanssen, *Fin de Siècle Beirut*, 182–83.
110. Tamara Chalabi, *The Shi'is of Jabal 'Amil and the New Lebanon—Community and Nation-State, 1918–1943* (New York & Basingstoke: Palgrave-Macmillan, 2006), 18–20.
111. Al Safa, *Tarikh Jabal Amil*, 208.
112. Chalabi, *The Shi'is of Jabal 'Amil*, 40–41.
113. Issawi, *The Fertile Crescent*, 28.
114. Hanssen, *Fin de Siècle Beirut*, 36, 174.
115. Gulick, *Tripoli: A Modern Arab City*, 177–83.
116. Hanssen, *Fin de Siècle Beirut*, 78–79.
117. Al Safa, *Tarikh Jabal Amil*, 212–17. Al Safa was plainly uncomfortable with the role of Kamil al-Asa'ad. He emphasizes the latter's Arab nationalist credentials and that al-Asa'ad did not intend the outcome that occurred.
118. L. Schatkowski Schilcher, "The Famine of 1915–1918 in Ottoman Syria," in J. Spagnolo ed., *Problems of the Modern Middle East in Historical Perspective: Essays in Honour of Albert Hourani* (Reading: Ithaca, 1992), 234–38.
119. Ibid., 229; Isam Khalife, *Lubnan 1914–1918 min khilal Arshif Wizarat al-Kharijiya al-Faransiya* (Beirut: Isam Khalife, 2005), 39. Both Schilcher and Khalife estimated up to 200,000 deaths in the mountain. Mount Lebanon's prewar population was around 400,000.
120. Salibi, *The Modern History of Lebanon*, 116–17; Akarli, *The Long Peace*, 259.
121. Khalife, *Lubnan 1914–1918*, 38, cites a French intelligence officer's estimate of 110,000 deaths in the Kisrawan, Jubayl, Batrun, and the Matn up to December 1916. This alone represents more than one-fifth of the total loss in the Levant for 1915–1918.
122. Akarli, *The Long Peace*, 174.
123. Denise Ammoun, *Histoire du Liban Contemporain 1860–1943* (Paris: Fayard, 1997), 236–37.
124. Meir Zamir, *The Formation of Modern Lebanon* (Ithaca: Cornell University Press, 1985), 61.
125. Ibid., 70–72.
126. Ibid., 73.
127. Chalabi, *The Shi'is of Jabal 'Amil*, 90; Ammoun, *Histoire 1860–1943*, 226–27, quotes the Aministrative Council's interpretation of Beaufort's map as: "To the north, the Nahr al-Kabir, to the south the Nahr al-Kasmiye, to the east the mountain of the Anti-Lebanon, to the limits of the districts of Baalbek, the Biqa, Hasbaya and Rashaya, and to the west the sea."
128. Asher Kaufman, *Reviving Phoenicia: The Search for Identity in Lebanon* (London: I. B. Tauris, 2004), 22.
129. Ibid., 159–68; Kais Firro, *Inventing Lebanon: Nationalism and the State under the Mandate* (London: I.B. Tauris, 2003), 30–37.
130. Elise Salem, *Constructing Lebanon: A Century of Literary Narratives* (Gainesville: University Press of Florida, 2003), 19–34.
131. Zamir, *The Formation of Modern Lebanon*, 92.
132. The pressure is apparent in the account of Al Safa in *Tarikh Jabal Amil*, 226: "And when the writ of the rebels grew intolerable and indignation mounted among the educated people of the land, Kamil Bek al-Asa'ad sent out invitations to the *ulama*, chiefs, and intellectuals to attend a meeting of the Shia of Jabal Amil at the head of the Hujayr stream. . . ."
133. Ibid., 227.

134. Zamir, *The Formation of Modern Lebanon*, 89–91.

135. Ibid., 93.

136. Ibid., 110–12.

137. Akarli, *The Long Peace*, 106 for the 1913–1914 statistics; Zamir, *The Formation of Modern Lebanon*, 98, for the 1921 census.

138. Ibid., 113–14, 196–98.

139. Ibid., 198.

140. Ibid., 150–51, 182–83.

141. Weiss, *In the Shadow of Sectarianism*, Chapter 4 (126–56), explores Ja'afari court defense of communal property (*waqf* and cemeteries). Chapter 5 (157–85) considers court social intervention in the domain of personal status law (marriage, divorce, inheritance, dowries, maintenance, child custody).

142. Ibid., 58, cites the 1921 French census as counting 3,274 Shia in Beirut (about 4 percent of the city's population).

143. Ibid., 231, 234–35.

144. Arnold Hottinger, "Zu'ama in Historical Perspective" in L. Binder ed. *Politics in Lebanon* (New York: John Wiley and Sons, 1966), 95.

145. See Zamir, *The Formation of Modern Lebanon*, 174, on the opposed positions of Adil and Fuad Arslan toward the 1925 Syrian revolt.

146. Firro, *Inventing Lebanon*, 77; Zamir, *The Formation of Modern Lebanon*, 142–43.

147. Firro, *Inventing Lebanon*, 112, citing the 1932 report of the mandatory authorities to the League of Nations.

148. For more detail on the early Maqasid and Salim Salam's role, see Johnson, *Class and Client in Beirut*, 46–47, 67–69.

149. Meir Zamir, *Lebanon's Quest: The Road to Statehood, 1926–1939* (London: I. B. Tauris, 1997), 58.

150. Stephen Longrigg, *Syria and Lebanon under the French Mandate* (Oxford: Oxford University Press, 1958), 135–37.

151. For discussion of the constitution, see Ziadeh, *Sectarianism and Inter-Communal Nation Building*, 91, 94–97; Zamir, *Lebanon's Quest*, 29–30; Salibi, *Modern History of Lebanon*, 167–68.

152. Zamir, *Lebanon's Quest*, 49–54, for Ponsot's outlook and the 1927 amendments.

153. Firro, *Inventing Lebanon*, 117–18.

154. Zamir, *Lebanon's Quest*, 31–33.

155. Firro notes the implications for Tripoli in *Inventing Lebanon*, 84.

156. Zamir, *Lebanon's Quest*, 70–72.

157. Saqr Yusuf Saqr, *A'ilat Hakamat Lubnan* (Beirut: Al-Merkaz al-Arabi lil-Ma'lumat, 2008), 200.

158. Zamir, *Lebanon's Quest*, 76–82.

159. Ibid., 120–22.

160. Ibid., 122–23.

161. Firro, *Inventing Lebanon*, 116; Zamir, *Lebanon's Quest*, 123.

162. For the best discussion of various versions of the census results, with and without emigrants, consult Firro, *Inventing Lebanon*, 118–22.

163. Gates, *The Merchant Republic*, 16, 22. Gates cites estimated merchant war profits in Lebanon and Syria at seven million Turkish pounds in 1914, increasing to eighteen million in 1918.

164. Ibid., 20, noting a 64 percent devaluation of the Syro-Lebanese pound, pegged to the French franc, against the US dollar from 1920 to 1939.

165. Firro, *Inventing Lebanon*, 121, gives the emigrant statistics. Gates, *The Merchant Republic*, 22, quotes remittance transfers of thirty million French francs per annum between 1920 and 1926.

166. Firro, *Inventing Lebanon*, 84, 101.

167. Ibid., 105–06.

168. Zamir, *Lebanon's Quest*, 67.

169. Ibid., 41, for the Beirut data.

170. Longrigg, *Syria and Lebanon*, 225–26.

171. Camille Chamoun, *Crise au Moyen-Orient* (Paris: Gallimard, 1963), 86–87. Also see Ammoun, *Histoire 1860–1943*, 359.

172. Zamir, *Lebanon's Quest*, 163–67; Longrigg, *Syria and Lebanon*, 206–07.
173. Zamir, *Lebanon's Quest*, 112; Firro, *Inventing Lebanon*, 57–58, 134–35.
174. Zamir, *Lebanon's Quest*, 110.
175. Ibid., 176–77.
176. Raghid el-Solh, *Lebanon and Arabism: National Identity and State Formation*, (London, I. B. Tauris, 2004), 30–31.
177. Ammoun, *Histoire 1860–1943*, 377–78, presents extracts from the Franco-Lebanese treaty.
178. Zamir, *Lebanon's Quest*, 214.
179. Ibid., 229.
180. Johnson, *Class and Client*, 19, cites press reports of four dead and fifty injured in Beirut.
181. Philip Khoury, *Syria and the French Mandate: The Politics of Arab Nationalism, 1920–1945* (Princeton: Princeton University Press, 1987), 579.
182. Zamir, *Lebanon's Quest*, 211.
183. Johnson, *Class and Client*, 25–26.
184. Firro, *Inventing Lebanon*, 168–75.
185. Weiss, *In the Shadow of Sectarianism*, 188–97.
186. Firro, *Inventing Lebanon*, 170.
187. Chalabi, *The Shi'is of Jabal 'Amil*, 131.
188. Firro, *Inventing Lebanon*, 170, citing the Shia mufti of Sidon, Hasan Sadiq.
189. See analysis in Carolyn Gates, *Papers on Lebanon 12: The Historical Role of Political Economy in the Development of Modern Lebanon* (Oxford: Centre for Lebanese Studies, 1989), 28–29.
190. Gates, *The Merchant Republic*, 25–27.
191. Toufic Gaspard, *A Political Economy of Lebanon, 1948–2002* (Leiden: Brill, 2004). Gaspard suggests and develops the "Singapore" argument.
192. Firro, *Inventing Lebanon*, 183–86.
193. See Churchill's own account in Winston Churchill, *The Second World War, Volume III: The Grand Alliance* (London: Penguin Books, 2005), 287–97. Churchill emphasizes the landing of one hundred German aircraft in Syria May 9–31, 1941, ferrying material to the rebel "Golden Square" officers in Iraq.

Chapter 5

1. The concept of Lebanon as a Phoenician-style commercial entity and the term "merchant republic" originated in Michel Chiha's writings. Kamal Salibi, for example, in "Lebanon under Fuad Chehab, 1958–1964," *Middle Eastern Studies* 2 no. 3 (1966): 214, and Caroline Gates in *The Merchant Republic* both adopted it.
2. Kassir, *Beirut*, 369.
3. Gates, *The Merchant Republic*, 145–46.
4. El-Solh, *Lebanon and Arabism*, 159–61; Eyal Zisser, *Lebanon: The Challenge of Independence* (London: I. B. Tauris, 2000), 34–35.
5. Charles de Gaulle, *The Complete War Memoirs of Charles de Gaulle*, trans. Jonathan Griffin and Richard Howard (New York: Carroll and Graf Publishers, 1998), 341.
6. Salibi, *The Modern History of Lebanon*, 187.
7. Firro, *Inventing Lebanon*, 202.
8. Farid el-Khazen, *Papers on Lebanon 12: The Communal Pact of National Identities—The Making and Politics of the 1943 National Pact* (Oxford: Centre for Lebanese Studies, 1991), 59.
9. Zisser, *Lebanon: The Challenge of Independence*, 70.
10. Denise Ammoun, *Histoire du Liban Contemporain 1943–1990* (Paris: Fayard, 2004), 60–61, records al-Sulh's success in obtaining Syrian acquiescence in the October 1944 Alexandra protocol affirming Lebanon's independence and sovereignty within its existing frontiers.
11. Ibid., 73–74.
12. De Gaulle, *The Complete War Memoirs*, 882.
13. Niqula Nassif, *Jumhuriyat Fuad Shihab* (Beirut: Dar al-Nahar, 2008), 73; Oren Barak, *The Lebanese Army: A National Institution in a Divided Society* (Albany: State University of New York Press, 2009), 26.
14. For an interpretation of the role of Far'un, see Johnson, *Class and Client*, 120–21.

15. According to Ammoun, *Histoire 1943–1990*, 14, al-Solh told his daughter Alia: "It is not high treason, it is a point of view. In November France was still an option and many Christians did not accept this independence that lost them French protection."

16. Ibid., 66. Ammoun captures the disingenuous stance of al-Khuri: "The government of Riyadh al-Sulh was the daily prey of attacks launched by the party of independence [in the context of the Arab League terms] led by Abd al-Hamid Karami and Henri Far'un. Conscious of the difficulties of the situation and the impossibility of al-Sulh continuing, the president counseled him to resign."

17. Zisser, *Lebanon: The Challenge of Independence*, 115, 194.

18. Ibid., 129–33.

19. Johnson, *Class and Client*, 85–86.

20. Bishara al-Khuri, *Haqa'iq Lubnaniya*, 3 vols. (Beirut: Awraq Lubnaniya, 1961), 3: 100.

21. Caroline Attié, *Struggle in the Levant: Lebanon in the 1950s* (London: I. B. Tauris, 2004), 40–41.

22. Gates, *The Merchant Republic*, 112.

23. Zisser, *Lebanon: The Challenge of Independence*, 154–55.

24. Al-Khuri, *Haqa'iq*, 3: 207: "We were very worried about Shukri al-Quwatli, who was dear to us all, and close to us as a person and a head of state. . . . [Al-Za'im] accused Riyadh al-Sulh of inciting some Lebanese newspapers to attack the new situation and of working feverishly to blacken the name of the lord of the coup [*sahib al-inqilab*] among the Arab states. . . . Nationalist newspapers in Lebanon didn't need any inspiration to attack the reckless coup."

25. Zisser, *Lebanon: The Challenge of Independence*, 181–89, gives a good survey of the SSNP affair in 1949.

26. Al-Khuri, *Haqa'iq*, 3: 229: "The government decided to dissolve the Syrian National Party, which was working against the existence of Lebanon."

27. Ibid., 287, "The Lebanese government learned about [the boycott] from Damascus Radio on 15 March, and the Damascus government ordered that travellers and goods be stopped from crossing the border to Lebanon."

28. Gates, *The Merchant Republic*, 90–92.

29. Ibid., 146.

30. Zisser, *Lebanon: The Challenge of Independence*, 222–24.

31. Ibid., 227–28.

32. Ibid., 213–14.

33. Ibid., 230, gives translated extracts.

34. Ibid., 231. According to Ammoun, *Histoire 1943–1990*, 117, Chiha had earlier advised al-Khuri against his 1948 presidential extension.

35. Zisser, *Lebanon: The Challenge of Independence*, 237.

36. Igor Timoviev, *Kamal Junblat: Al-Rajul wa al-Ustura* (translated from the Russian by Khayri al-Damin) (Beirut: Dar al-Nahar, 2001), 222.

37. Clyde Hess and Herbert Bodman, "Confessionalism and Feudality in Lebanese Politics," *The Middle East Journal* 8 no. 1 (1954): 18.

38. Attié, *Struggle in the Levant*, 51.

39. Hess and Bodman, "Confessionalism and Feudality," 19.

40. Ibid., 21.

41. Isa al-Ma'luf, *Dawani al-Qutuf fi Tarikh Bani al-Ma'luf*, 2 vols. (1907–1908; reprint, Damascus, Dar Hawran, 2003), 2: 508.

42. As a result Chamoun has not fared well at the hands of analysts. See, for example, Wade Goria, *Sovereignty and Leadership in Lebanon, 1943–1976* (London: Ithaca, 1985): 36–44.

43. Gates, *The Merchant Republic*, 146.

44. Attié, *Struggle in the Levant*, 53.

45. Abdul-Amir Badrud-Din, *The Bank of Lebanon: Central Banking in a Financial Centre and Entrepot* (London: Frances Pinter, 1984), 26.

46. Gates, *The Merchant Republic*, 132–33.

47. Attié, *Struggle in the Levant*, 53.

48. Ibid., 55–56.

49. Ibid., 130–31.

50. Ammoun, *Histoire 1943–1990*, 200.

51. Erika Alin, *The United States and the 1958 Lebanon Crisis: American Intervention in the Middle East* (Lanham, Maryland: University Press of America, 1994), 22–23.

52. Attié, *Struggle in the Levant*,

53. Ibid., 163.

54. Ibid., 136, 142–43; Alin, *The United States and the 1958 Lebanon Crisis*, 57–58.

55. Timoviev, *Kamal Junblat*, 261, notes that the loss of Junblat's seat was decisive for him: "What would Ghandi have done if he had lived in Lebanon, ruled by highway robbers who don't accept any argument except force. . . . Junblat wrote later that he came at that point to an absolute conclusion about the necessity of rebellion against the regime."

56. Ammoun, *Histoire 1943–1990*, 257.

57. Attié, *Struggle in the Levant*, 48.

58. Alin, *The United States and the 1958 Lebanon Crisis*, 77–97, gives detail on deliberations in Washington.

59. Attié, *Struggle in the Levant*, 50.

60. Alin, *The United States and the 1958 Lebanon Crisis*, 119–23.

61. Nassif, *Jumhuriyat Fuad Shihab*, 40.

62. Ibid., 282–83.

63. Ibid., 297. Shihab commented to his aide-de-camp, Hanna Bu Milhem, that he wished to ensure "the Kisrawan would not become a graveyard for Christians because of isolation from the rest of the areas."

64. Ibid., 294, 377.

65. Ibid., 371. Naqqash titled his lecture "Shihabism: A New Method," and described Shihab's election in epochal terms: "It wasn't the man who went out to meet history, but history that went out to find the man." Naqqash preferred to emphasize the brighter side of "Shihabism."

66. Ammoun, *Histoire 1943–1990*, 306; Johnson, *Class and Client*, 86.

67. Nassif, *Jumhuriyat Fuad Shihab*, 325. In May 1958, Karami had spoken of Tripoli seceding and joining the UAR if his allies in Beirut did not adhere to insurrection against Chamoun. However, on becoming prime minister in September he declared that Lebanon joining the UAR was "impossible because all Lebanese are agreed on safeguarding Lebanon's independence and preserving it absolutely."

68. Ibid., 273–74; Ammoun, *Histoire 1943–1990*, 302.

69. Nassif, *Jumhuriyat Fuad Shihab*, 329.

70. Salibi, "Lebanon under Fuad Chehab," 224, gives a contemporary interpretation.

71. Johnson, *Class and Client*, 141.

72. Nassif, *Jumhuriyat Fuad Shihab*, 271.

73. Ralph Crow, "Religious Sectarianism in the Lebanese Political System," *The Journal of Politics* 24 (1962): 510. For these numbers, Crow draws on Halim Fayyad, "The Effects of Sectarianism in Lebanese Administration" (MA diss., American University of Beirut, 1956), 71.

74. Ibid.

75. Badrud-Din, *The Bank of Lebanon*, 40–58.

76. See Nassif, *Jumhiriyat Fuad Shihab*, 242–46, for detail on senior security officials.

77. Michael Hudson, *The Precarious Republic: Political Modernization in Lebanon* (New York: Random House, 1968), 308.

78. Michael Hudson, "Democracy and Social Mobilization in Lebanese Politics," in *Analyzing the Third World: Essays from Comparative Politics*, ed. Norman Provizer (Cambridge: Schenkman Publishing Company, 1978), 286.

79. Amoun, *Histoire 1943–1990*, 324.

80. Ibid., 341.

81. Johnson, *Class and Client*, 146.

82. Nassif, *Jumhuriyat Fuad Shihab*, 317.

83. Ibid., 316.

84. For assessments of Musa al-Sadr and his communal context, see Fouad Ajami, *The Vanished Imam: Musa Al Sadr and the Shia of Lebanon* (Ithaca: Cornell University Press, 1992), and Halawi, *A Lebanon Defied*.

85. Halawi, *A Lebanon Defied*, 136–37.
86. Ibid., 140–41.
87. Nassif, *Jumhuriyat Fuad Shihab*, 313–15.
88. For a fascinating detailed account, see Adel Beshara, *Lebanon: The Politics of Frustration—The Failed Coup of 1961* (Abingdon, Oxon: RoutledgeCurzon, 2005).
89. Nassif, *Jumhiryat Fuad Shihab*, 288–90; Johnson, *Class and Client*, 148–49.
90. Ammoun, *Histoire 1943–1990*, 379, cites military intelligence officer Gabby Lahoud: "In 1964, Shihab did not [formally] agree to scuttle Chamoun, but we were determined to achieve this objective."
91. Johnson, *Class and Client*, 152.
92. Nassif, *Jumhuriyat Fuad Shihab*, 53.
93. Timoviev, *Kamal Junblat*, 219–21, indicates that under President Helou, Junblat became increasingly disillusioned with regime stagnation. He made an informal front with mainly proscribed leftists in late summer 1965 and backed union and social protests, for example apple-grower fury over rigged prices.
94. Farid el-Khazen's *The Breakdown of the State in Lebanon, 1967–1976* (Cambridge: Harvard University Press, 2000) provides a strong presentation of this perspective.
95. Halim Barakat, "Social and Political Integration in Lebanon: A Case of Social Mosaic," *The Middle East Journal* 27: 3 (1973): 301–18.
96. Ibid., 303, 306–07.
97. Samir Kassir, *La Guerre du Liban: De la dissension nationale au conflit régional* (Paris: Karthala, 1994), 74, gives a Lebanese Interior Ministry figure of 223,000 for the Palestinian population in Lebanon in 1968.
98. Johnson, *Class and Client*, 146.
99. Ibid., 147.
100. John Chalcraft, *The Invisible Cage: Syrian Migrant Workers in Lebanon* (Stanford: Stanford University Press, 2009), 78–79. Chalcraft provides the definitive study of Syrian labor migration to Lebanon, a widely misunderstood dimension of Lebanese/Syrian affairs.
101. Ibid., 55.
102. Ibid., 82, 84–88.
103. Ibid., 70–71.
104. Goria, *Sovereignty and Leadership*, 92.
105. According to Ammoun, *Histoire 1943–1990*, 379, the falling out began when Helou demonstrated his autonomy by helping Raymond Edde return to parliament in a 1965 Jubayl by-election.
106. El-Khazen, *The Breakdown of the State*, 137.
107. Yezid Sayigh, *Armed Struggle and the Search for a State: The Palestinian National Movement 1949–1993* (Oxford: Oxford University Press, 1997), 190, reports 500 to 600 in the Arqub—200 from Fatah, 200 from al-Sa'iqa, and around 150 from other groups. El-Khazen, *The Breakdown of the State*, 142, cites Lebanese Public Security (*al-Amn al-Am*) for the overall 4,000, including in the refugee camps adjoining Sidon and Tyre.
108. Ibid., 160–62; Sayigh, *Armed Struggle*, 192; Ammoun, *Histoire 1943–1990*, 445–46.
109. El-Khazen, *The Breakdown of the State*, 189.
110. Ibid., 190.
111. Timoviev, *Kamal Junblat*, 348.
112. Adel Beshara, *The Politics of Frustration*, 160–61.
113. See detail in Michael Johnson, *All Honourable Men: The Social Origins of War in Lebanon* (London: I. B. Tauris, 2001), 115–17; Goria, *Sovereignty and Leadership*, 123–24.
114. Timoviev, *Kamal Junblat*, 336, 349–50. According to Timoviev, the Soviet Union preferred Faranjiya because of his good relations with Syria and his stand against military intelligence. Moscow suspected CIA penetration of the latter.
115. Ibid., 357. From his West Beirut sources, Timoviev concluded: "Sa'ib Salam and the other Sunni bosses were happy with the new wave of refugees, believing that it would help change the demographic distribution in the country to [Sunni] Muslim favor." This was despite the negative implications for their grip on their community.
116. Chalcraft, *The Invisible Cage*, 107, 118.

117. El-Khazen, *The Breakdown of the State*, 193–94.

118. Goria, *Sovereignty and Leadership*, 135.

119. Ammoun, *Histoire 1943–1990*, 490.

120. El-Khazen, *The Breakdown of the State*, 198; David Gordon, *Lebanon: The Fragmented Nation* (London: Croom Helm, 1980), 75.

121. Sayigh, *Armed Struggle*, 312.

122. Goria, *Sovereignty and Leadership*, 157.

123. Ibid., 314.

124. El-Khazen, *The Breakdown of the State*, 209–10.

125. Sayigh, *Armed Struggle*, 316.

126. Ibid., 358.

127. Ibid., 317, 361; El-Khazen, *The Breakdown of the State*, 225.

128. Johnson, *Class and Client*, 165.

129. Augustus Richard Norton's *Amal and the Shi'a: Struggle for the Soul of Lebanon* (Austin: University of Texas Press, 1987) remains the best study of Amal.

130. El-Khazen, *The Breakdown of the State*, 223.

131. Goria, *Sovereignty and Leadership*, 179–80.

132. El-Khazen, *The Breakdown of the State*, 238–39.

133. For the illiteracy data cited in this paragraph, see UNESCO Institute for Statistics, *Adult Illiteracy for Population Aged 15 Years and Over, by Country and by Gender 1970-2015*, July 2002 assessment.

134. El-Khazen, *The Breakdown of the State*, 65, citing Boutros Labaki, *Education et Mobilité Sociale Dans la Société Multicommunautaire du Liban* (Frankfurt: Deutsches Institut Für Internationale Pädagogische Forschung, 1988).

135. Ibid., citing Yves Schemeil, "Sociologie du Système Politique Libanais" (PhD diss., Université de Grenoble, 1976).

136. Ibid., 68.

137. Chalcraft, *The Invisible Cage*, 81, citing data from Lebanon's Central Administration of Statistics.

138. For information on student numbers, sectarian distributions, and university faculties in the 1970s, see Gordon, *Lebanon: The Fragmented Nation*, 184–87.

139. Nassif, *Jumhuriyat Fuad Shihab*, 311.

140. Betty Anderson, "Voices of Protest: Arab Nationalism and the Palestinian Revolution at the American University of Beirut," *Comparative Studies of South Asia, Africa, and the Middle East* 28 no. 3 (2008): 396.

141. Ibid., 401.

142. Salem, *Constructing Lebanon*, 48–57.

143. Ibid., 65–70.

144. Ibid. For an English rendering of the story, see Roseanne Saad Khalaf, ed. *Hikayat: Short Stories by Lebanese Women* (London: Telegram Books, 2006), 25–32.

145. Salem, *Constructing Lebanon*, 80–96.

146. Tawfiq Awwad, *Death in Beirut*, trans. Leslie McLoughlin (London: Heinemann, 1976), 110.

147. Ghada Samman, *Beirut 75*, trans. Nancy Roberts (Fayetteville: University of Arkansas Press, 1995), 115.

Chapter 6

1. Shaery-Eisenlohr, *Shi'ite Lebanon*, 22–23, interprets these outlooks.

2. Ibid., 71.

3. Ibid., 148–50, summarizes Fadlallah's position.

4. Ibid., 76, 137–38, 154–55. On Fadlallah and women's rights also see Hanin Ghaddar, "Fadlallah and the Shia, beyond Hezbollah, or how Fadlallah changed my father," *NOW Lebanon*, July 10, 2010, accessed July 7, 2011, http://www.nowlebanon.com/NewsArchiveDetails.aspx?ID=184682.

5. Salem, *Constructing Lebanon*, 245.

6. Elias Khoury, *The Gates of the City*, trans. Paula Haydar (Minneapolis: University of Minnesota Press, 1993).

7. For a more optimistic perspective on Lebanese nationhood, see Theodore Hanf, *Coexistence in Wartime Lebanon: Decline of a State and Rise of a Nation*, trans. from German by John Richardson (London: I. B. Tauris, 1993).

8. Hanan al-Shaykh, *The Story of Zahra*, trans. Peter Ford (London: Quartet Books, 1986).

9. Hanan al-Shaykh, *I Sweep the Sun off Rooftops*, trans. Catherine Cobham (London: Bloomsbury, 1998), 31.

10. Goria in *Sovereignty and Leadership*, 227, estimates majority support in all the large Christian communities for Kata'ib/NLP positions, even the Orthodox and Armenians (the Tashnak, the largest Armenian party, aligned with the Kata'ib), and around 75 percent overall. He points to solid Greek Catholic support in Zahle for the Kata'ib and NLP.

11. Salim Nasr, "The New Social Map," in *Lebanon in Limbo: Postwar Society and State in an Uncertain Regional Environment*, ed. Theodor Hanf and Nawaf Salam (Baden-Baden: Nomos Verlagsgesellschaft, 2003), 144–45. Estimates of deaths range from 3 to 5 percent of the 1975 population, with Nasr suggesting 120,000 and Samir Makdisi in *The Lesson of Lebanon: The Economies of War and Development* (London: I. B. Tauris, 2004), 35, citing 144,000 from a war casualty analysis in *al-Nahar*, March 5, 1992.

12. Nasr, "The New Social Map," 144–45.

13. Makdisi, *The Lesson of Lebanon*, 41, 52.

14. Kassir, *La Guerre du Liban*, 141.

15. El Khazen, *The Breakdown of the State*, 323–24.

16. Kassir, *La Guerre du Liban*, 134.

17. Ibid., 157. Goria, *Sovereignty and Leadership*, 216, suggests 1,500.

18. Gordon, *Lebanon*, 242.

19. Kassir, *La Guerre du Liban*, 157; el Khazen, *The Breakdown of the State*, 325.

20. Author's interview with former Syrian Vice-President and Foreign Minister Abd al-Halim Khaddam, Paris, December 12, 2009.

21. El Khazen, *The Breakdown of the State*, 299–305, 325.

22. Author's interview with Abd al-Halim Khaddam, December 12, 2009.

23. See analysis in el-Khazen, *Papers on Lebanon 12: The Communal Pact of National Identities*, 64. Also Goria, *Sovereignty and Leadership*, 218–19.

24. Kassir, *La Guerre du Liban*, 163, also cites repercussions within the army after its limited involvement on the Maronite side at Tel al-Za'atar and Damur.

25. Ibid., 168.

26. Sayigh, *Armed Struggle*, 379.

27. Kassir, *La Guerre du Liban*, 174.

28. Ibid., and Goria, *Sovereignty and Leadership*, 226–28.

29. Yair Evron, *War and Intervention in Lebanon: The Israeli-Syrian Deterrence Dialogue* (London: Croom Helm, 1987), 46–47.

30. Kassir, *La Guerre du Liban*, 179–80, notes U.S. support for Sarkis against Raymond Edde, the candidate of those opposed to Syrian dictation of the election, principally Sa'ib Salam and the National Movement.

31. Itamar Rabinovich, *The War for Lebanon, 1970–1983* (Ithaca: Cornell University Press, 1984), 183–218. Translation of Asad's speech from Radio Damascus by FBIS, Daily Report, July 20, 1976.

32. Deeb, *An Enchanted Modern*, 47, gives a rough population estimate of 30,000 in 1970 for Shiyah, then the main urban component of the Dahiya. Deeb indicates that the Shia population had more than doubled since the 1930s, presumably reflecting the accelerated rural to urban migration of the 1960s.

33. Kassir, *La Guerre du Liban*, 257–59.

34. Johnson, *Class and Client*, 195.

35. See Avner Yaniv, *Dilemmas of Security: Politics, Strategy, and the Israeli Experience in Lebanon* (New York: Oxford University Press, 1987), 72–75. Yaniv assesses Israel's Litani operation as "close to a fiasco."

36. Author's interview with Sulayman Faranjiya, Zgharta, April 12, 1984.

37. Kassir, *La Guerre du Liban*, 352.

38. Norton, *Amal and the Shi'a*, 51.

39. Ibid., 61.
40. Manal Lotfi cites Abd al-Halim Khaddam in "Musa al-Sadr: The Untold Story," *Asharq alaw-sat English Edition,* May 31, 2008, accessed December 4, 2011, http://www.asharq-e.com/news.asp?section=3&id=12930.
41. Kassir, *La Guerre du Liban,* 401; Sayigh, *Armed Struggle,* 496.
42. Ibid., 499.
43. William Harris, "The View from Zahle: Security and Economic Conditions in the Central Beqa'a, 1983–85," *Middle East Journal,* 39 no. 3 (1985): 270–86.
44. Kirsten Schulze, *Israel's Covert Diplomacy in Lebanon* (Basingstoke: Macmillan Press, 1998), 104–08.
45. Ze'ev Schiff report in *Ha'aretz* daily newspaper, Tel Aviv, April 29, 1981: "Two Syrian heli-copters downed north of Zahle. Security sources—in recent days the Syrians have crossed 'the red line.'"
46. Ze'ev Schiff and Ehud Ya'ari, *Israel's Lebanon War* (London: Allen & Unwin, 1985), 42.
47. Ibid., 100.
48. Ibid., chapters 7, 8, and 9. Also see Evron, *War and Intervention,* 132–38.
49. Schulze, *Israel's Covert Diplomacy,* 130–33.
50. Schiff and Ya'ari, *Israel's Lebanon War,* 234–36.
51. A detailed survey of 1982–1983 U.S./Lebanese contacts by the then Lebanese foreign minister makes it plain that senior American officials were interested virtually exclusively in producing a Lebanese/Israeli agreement—Elie Salem, *Violence & Diplomacy in Lebanon* (London: I. B. Tauris, 1995).
52. Author's interview with Abd al-Halim Khaddam, December 12, 2009. Khaddam noted that Hariri visited him in Damascus for this purpose in late 1982, and that this inaugurated their personal connection.
53. Syrian soldiers told the author and David Hirst of *The Guardian* of the presence of Russian advisors in the Upper Matn, November 1983.
54. For Khaddam, the rise of Hezbollah was the rise of resistance to Israel, and "met with the interests of Syria and Iran"—Author's interview with Abd al-Halim Khaddam, December 12, 2009.
55. "Our Objectives in Lebanon," in *Nass al-risala al-maftuha alati wajahha hizballah ila al-mustada'fin fi lubnan wa al-alim,* February 16, 1985, 15.
56. With *The Guardian* correspondent David Hirst, the author visited Arafat in Tripoli in November 1983.
57. In discussion with the author, Lebanese foreign ministry officials reported Syrian hints of military action by "allies" against the two towns, Beirut, February 29, 1984.
58. Information from the Lebanese delegation to a correspondent for the Israeli newspaper *Ha'aretz*—*Ha'aretz,* March 4, 1984.
59. See a first-hand account in Salem, *Violence & Diplomacy,* 151–53.
60. Author's interviews with Amal command member Ghassan Siblani, Beirut, April 4, 1984, and Sulayman Faranjiya, April 12, 1984.
61. *Al-Thawra* (Syrian armed forces daily), Damascus, November 10, 1984.
62. Arabic text in Lebanese Center for Documentation and Research (CEDRE), *Al-Alaqat al-Lubnaniya al-Suriya 1943–1985: Waqa'i, Bibliografiya, Watha'iq,* ed. Sam Menassa, 2 vols. (Beirut, Bayt al-Mustaqbal, 1986), 2: 342–53.
63. Author's conversation with Walid Junblat, Mukhtara, December 1985.
64. A senior officer interpreted the outlook of the army command to the author, Beirut, April 1986.
65. Elizabeth Picard, "The Political Economy of Civil War in Lebanon," in *War, Institutions, and Social Change in the Middle East,* ed. Steven Heydemann (Berkeley and Los Angeles: University of California Press, 2000), 312.
66. Elie Salem's *Violence & Diplomacy* gives a nuanced and entertaining record.
67. Picard, "The Political Economy of Civil War in Lebanon," 314.
68. Georges Corm in *Le Liban Contemporain: Histoire et Société* (Paris: Éditions la Découverte, 2003), 209, notes: "The budget of the Iranian embassy in Lebanon allocated, from 1982/1983 on, more than $100 million annually to pay militiamen recruited by Hezbollah."

69. People from Qubbayat discussed the arrangement with the author, Beirut, 1987.

70. The United Nations Truce Supervision Organization (UNTSO) Beirut Observer Group noted almost complete cessation of traffic at the PSP Khalde port, March-May 1987—information to the author from an UNTSO officer. The author observed a Syrian military presence near the port installations in November 1987.

71. Nasser Saidi, *Papers on Lebanon 5: Economic Consequences of the War in Lebanon* (Oxford: Centre for Lebanese Studies, 1986), 5. Also see GDP statistics in Makdisi, *The Lessons of Lebanon*, 83 (table 2.2).

72. Ibid., 56; Gaspard, *A Political Economy of Lebanon*, 200–03.

73. Makdisi, *The Lessons of Lebanon*, 59, 87 (table 2.8).

74. Ibid., 83 (table 2.2) for the GDP data.

75. Gaspard, *A Political Economy of Lebanon*, 207.

76. *Al-Nahar*, October 13, 1990. The report assessed annual returns over the whole war period for drugs, arms trafficking, and protection at $600 million, $150 million, and $200 million respectively.

77. *Al-Wasat* weekly, London, February 13, 1995.

78. Author's interview with Salim al-Huss, Beirut, July 1987. According to al-Huss, Karami reached an understanding with Dani Chamoun on the cabinet being an institution autonomous of the presidency.

79. *Al-Afkar* weekly, Beirut, June 8, 1987. Also reported to the author by a U.S. diplomat, Beirut, June 1987.

80. Hezbollah spokesman Ibrahim Amin quoting Asad—*al-Safir*, 28 May, 1987.

81. See Salem, *Violence and Diplomacy*, 250–70, for the detail on the last months of Amin Gemayel's presidency.

82. Ibid., 226–27.

83. *Al-Safir*, 5 and August 11, 1988.

84. Author's interview with Abd al-Halim Khaddam, December 12, 2009.

85. *Al-Majalla* weekly, London, September 7, 1988, reported the first big Iraqi consignment for the LF arriving in August 1988.

86. *Al-Safir*, May 26, 1989, quotes Asad's three-hour presentation to the conference.

87. *Al-Nahar*, August 1, 1989, on the 31 July Arab committee report.

88. Sarkis Na'um in *al-Nahar*, September 7, 1989; Jim Hoagland in *International Herald Tribune*, 9–10 September 1989, citing "reliable sources" regarding prior discussion about evacuating the staff.

89. Emile Khoury in *al-Nahar*, September 16, 1989, quoting political sources close to Damascus.

90. Ibid.

91. For an English translation of the agreement and associated August 1990 amendments to the Lebanese constitution see Lebanese Center for Policy Studies, "Documents: The Constitution of Lebanon after the Amendments of August 21, 1990, and Sections of the Ta'if Agreement not included in the Constitution," *Beirut Review*, 1 no. 1 (Spring 1991): 119–72. For critical commentary, see Maila, Joseph, *The Document of National Understanding: A Commentary* (Oxford: Centre for Lebanese Studies, 1992), and Institute for Human Rights in Lebanon, *Muqarrarat al-Ta'if wa Huquq al-Insan* (Beirut: Institute for Human Rights in Lebanon, 1990).

92. Abbot Bulos Na'aman described the subject matter of the Mu'awwad-Aoun contacts to the author, East Beirut, January 1990. Na'aman was involved in these contacts.

93. Data from Radio Monte Carlo Arabic, February 18, 1990.

94. Muwaffaq al-Madani in *al-Safir*, April 9, 1990, estimated that 250,000 fled to West Beirut and 70,000 to Damascus.

95. *Al-Safir*, April 14, 1990, after a "secret" Asad/al-Hirawi summit.

96. *Al-Safir*, July 28, 1990, reported that Asad was so pleased with Sa'adeh at a late July audience that he asked him "not to stay away from us too long."

97. The author was among the audience, February 1990.

98. *Al-Safir*, July 27, 1990. The report also referred to demonstrations in southern Lebanon against "the Iranian invasion."

99. Kassir, *La Guerre du Liban*, 159, citing remarks by Khaddam to the Kuwaiti newspaper *al-Ra'i al-Am* in a January 7, 1976 interview.

100. For full text, see William Harris, "Lebanon," in *Middle East Contemporary Survey, Vol. XV, 1991*, ed. Ami Ayalon (Boulder: Westview, 1993), 570–72.

101. Sarkis Na'um in *al-Nahar*, May 21, 1991.

102. For full text, see William Harris, "Lebanon," 572–73.

103. *Lebanon GDP per capita* (purchasing power parity), accessed August 21, 2010, http://www.indexmundi.com/lebanon/gdp_per_capita_(ppp).html.

104. Fuad Da'bul in *al-Anwar* daily, Beirut, March 23, 1992.

105. *Lebanon GDP per capita*.

106. *Lebanese Ministry of Finance—General Debt Overview*, accessed August 21, 2010, http://www.finance.gov.lb/Public+Finances/Public+Debt+Overview/.

107. Makdisi, *The Lesson of Lebanon*, 119.

108. Ibid., 150.

109. Ibid., 143.

110. Chalcraft, *The Invisible Cage*, 145–48, considers the wildly different estimates and the difficulty of establishing even rough numbers.

111. Ibid., 143–44.

112. Ibid., 163–69.

113. Ibid., 188–92.

114. *Al-Anwar*, November 28, 1992.

115. See *Al-Anwar*, November 8, 1992, for the expenditure on the government palace.

116. For discussion of the behavior of Syrian military intelligence in Lebanon, including abuses of human rights, see *Human Rights Watch*, "Syria/Lebanon: An Alliance Beyond the Law," May 11, 1997, accessed August 24, 2010, http://www.hrw.org/en/reports/1997/05/11/syrialebanon-alliance-beyond-law.

117. See a careful, detailed argument in Gary Gambill, "Syria after Lebanon: Hooked on Lebanon," *The Middle East Quarterly* 12 no. 3 (Fall 2005): 35–42. Gambill considers kickbacks from government spending, drug trading, money laundering, and smuggling, among other activities. He notes the unpublished UN (2001) corruption assessment report on Lebanon, which estimated a loss of $1.5 billion per annum (10 percent of GDP) in bribes and kickbacks.

118. Ibid., 38.

119. Ghassan Charbel in *al-Wasat*, February 3, 1997.

120. Shaery-Eisenlohr, *Shi'ite Lebanon*, 64–65.

121. Author's interview with Abd al-Halim Khaddam, December 12, 2009.

122. *Al-Hayat*, October 2, 1998. "Kana'an then raised his hand, saying that the vote would take place by a raising of hands and would not be secret.... Karami stood and his color changed.... The party broke up early. Presidential hopefuls departed with their wives, one complaining of tiredness, another saying he had a headache."

123. Sarkis Na'um in *al-Nahar*, 22 August, and *al-Nahar*, August 19, 1996.

124. *Al-Hayat*, November 30, 1998.

125. *Mideast Mirror*, June 16, 1999.

126. *Al-Hayat*, December 17, 1998.

127. *Al-Hayat*, February 10, 2000.

128. *Ha'aretz*, March 28, 2000, reported: "The assessment in the IDF is that the failure of the Geneva summit greatly increases the prospect of a unilateral withdrawal from southern Lebanon." Also see Dan Margalit in *Ha'aretz*, March 30, 2000.

129. See, for example, International Institute of Strategic Studies (IISS), *The Military Balance, 2003–2004* (London: IISS, 2003), 114–15. The IISS estimated Hezbollah's core force as 300 to 500 regulars with 2,000 other trained fighters in support. It listed the active personnel of the Lebanese armed services as numbering 72,000, including 22,600 conscripts.

130. Ibrahim Bayram report in *al-Wasat*, October 23, 2000.

131. See *Al-Nahar*, September 21, 2000, for the text of the council of Maronite bishops communiqué assailing the Syrian regime's "total hegemony."

132. In March 1997, Patriarch Sfeir claimed that only 20 percent had returned—*al-Hayat*, March 27, 1997. In a squabble between Junblat and Hariri in July 1998, Hariri remarked that Junblat's

"war language" made refugees reluctant to return and that "the refugee fund is not a channel for camp followers, protégés, and villains. . . . How can Junblat ask the fund to compensate 1,250 families in a village with 280 houses?"—*al-Hayat*, July 6, 1998.

133. Walid Shuqayr in *al-Hayat*, August 26, 2000.

134. Tlas gave Bashar's address at an officers' graduation ceremony—*al-Hayat*, August 20, 2001.

135. Author's interview with Abd al-Halim Khaddam, December 12, 2009.

136. In June 2002, Hezbollah supporters roughed up a Hariri aide at a bridge inauguration function. See *al-Hayat*, 27 June 2002 ("Crisis between Hariri and Hezbollah with the beginning of work on the Awza'i bridge project").

137. *Al-Hayat*, October 17, 2003.

138. Nicholas Blanford, *Killing Mr Lebanon: The Assassination of Rafik Hariri and its Impact on the Middle East* (London: I. B. Tauris, 2006), 92–93.

139. Samih Nazih in *al-Ra'i al-Am* daily, Kuwait, October 15, 2005.

140. UN Security Council. S/2005/203, *Report of the Fact-finding Mission to Lebanon inquiring into the causes, circumstances and consequences of the assassination of former Prime Minister Rafik Hariri*, March 24, 2005, page 5, accessed September 19, 2011, http://www.undemocracy.com/S-2005-203.

141. Nicholas Blanford, Richard Beeston, and James Bone in *The Times*, London, March 18, 2005.

142. See cases of intimidation of parliamentary deputies cited in *al-Nahar*, 31 August and September 1, 2004. For numerical attrition, see *al-Nahar*, 1 and September 3, 2004.

143. Consult David Hirst, *Beware of Small States: Lebanon, Battleground of the Middle East* (New York: Nation Books, 2010), 303–04. Hirst, based in Beirut and a long-time, highly respected Middle East correspondent of *The Guardian*, reports that the Syrian leadership told Hariri "to step down as prime minister."

144. *Al-Nahar*, January 27, 2005.

145. Randa Taki al-Din in *al-Hayat*, February 18, 2005, and *al-Hayat*, February 21, 2005.

146. *Al-Hayat*, February 21, 2005.

147. *The Times*, March 18, 2005.

148. *Al-Qabas* daily, Kuwait, October 29, 2005, on Roed-Larsen's testimony to the UN murder inquiry—which was held back from publication in the October 20, 2005 UN International Independent Investigating Commission (UNIIIC) report.

149. *Al-Nahar*, February 17, 2005.

150. Michael Young, *The Ghosts of Martyr's Square: An Eyewitness Account of Lebanon's Life Struggle* (New York: Simon & Schuster, 2010), 50.

151. UN Security Council Report. S/2005/203, *supra* note 140.

152. Elias al-Murr interview with Lebanese Broadcasting Corporation (LBC) television, September 27, 2005.

153. UNIIIC, *Unedited Report of the International Independent Investigating Commission Established Pursuant to Security Council Resolution 1595 (2005)*, paragraph 203, Detlev Mehlis (commissioner), Beirut, October 19, 2005, accessed September 19, 2011, www.washingtonpost.com/wp-srv/world/syria/mehlis.report.doc,

154. For Bashar's 10 November speech at Damascus University, see *al-Hayat*, November 11, 2005. The Syrian president labeled Lebanese Prime Minister Fuad Siniora "the hired slave of a hired slave," the latter being Rafiq al-Hariri's son Sa'ad.

155. UNIIIC, S/2005/775/12 Dec 2005 *Second Report*, paragraph 26.

156. Detlev Mehlis in discussion with the author on the circumstances of his decision not to continue beyond his initial six-month contract, May 2009.

157. Detlev Mehlis was of the view that UNIIIC had sufficient evidence by early 2006 to indict at least one senior Syrian and one Lebanese—comment to the author, May 2009.

158. UNIIIC, S/2006/355/10 June 2006 *Fourth Report*, paragraphs 58 and 104.

159. See United Nations, *Official U.N. transcript of the meeting of U.N. Secretary-General Ban Ki-moon with Bashar al-Asad. Damascus, April 24, 2007*, 3–4. According to the UN note-taker, Bashar warned: "Instability would intensify if the Special Tribunal were established. This was particularly the case if the Tribunal were established under Chapter 7 of the Charter.

This could easily ignite a conflict which would result in civil war [in Lebanon] and provoke divisions between Sunni and Shi'a from the Mediterranean to the Caspian Sea. . . . If the tribunal was achieved via Chapter 7 it would have grave consequences that could not be contained in Lebanon. . . . The present government in Lebanon was not legal and the Syrian people hated the March 14 Movement."

160. In *al-Hayat*, May 21, 2007, the respected journalist Muhammad Shuqayr, with information from Palestinian informants in northern Lebanon, named Syrian intelligence officers who were coordinating the Fath al-Islam jihadist group in Tripoli and Nahr al-Barid. *Al-Sharq al-Awsat* daily, London, June 9, 2007, reported from Jordanian judicial sources that Fath al-Islam leader Shakir al-Abssi ran a training camp in Syria "to house and equip suicide bombers and elements involved in al-Qaeda before their dispatch to battle in Iraq," this before he moved from Syria to Lebanon in 2005. *Al-Nahar*, 22 and August 23, 2007, interviewed former prisoners in Syrian jails on Syrian intelligence mobilization of imprisoned Sunni jihadists ("Have Syrian jails become a 'land of support' for jihad in Iraq and Lebanon?").

161. United Nations, *Report of the Lebanon Independent Border Assessment Team (LIBAT) to the U.N. Security Council, June 22, 2007*, accessed September 25, 2010, http://www.clhrf.com/unresagreements/1701.report22.6.07.pdf. LIBAT, a UN group of border police experts, concluded: "The presence of armed Palestinian camps in the border zone constitutes a major obstacle to the notion of border security" (paragraph 168). Regarding one such camp on the Rus ridge, LIBAT noted: "The Palestinian area extends from Lebanese territory into Syria, with the official borderline running through the area. . . . The completely uncontrolled area creates very good conditions for illegal and unhindered cross border activities recently documented by information . . . from the Lebanese Government" (paragraph 142).

162. *Al-Nahar*, May 5, 2008, quoted Hezbollah parliamentary deputy Hasan Fadlallah as warning that anyone questioning Hezbollah's communications—part of "the weaponry of the resistance"—was "serving the Israeli enemy."

163. "Suleiman: The Resistance is a Source of Strength for Lebanon," *al-Hayat*, July 8, 2008.

164. Nimrod Raphaeli, "Lebanese Economy between Violence and Political Stalemate," in *Lebanon: Liberation, Conflict, and Crisis*, ed. Barry Rubin (New York: Palgrave Macmillan, 2009), 115, 120.

165. Ibid., 120.

166. Heba Laithy, Khalid Abu-Ismail, and Kamal Hamdan, *International Poverty Centre Country Study 13: Poverty, Growth and Income Distribution in Lebanon* (Brasilia: International Poverty Centre, U.N. Development Programme, 2008), accessed September 23, 2010, http://www.ipc-undp.org/pub/IPCCountryStudy13.pdf.

167. *Human Rights Watch*, "Without Protection: How the Lebanese Justice System fails Migrant Domestic Workers," September 16, 2010, accessed September 23, 2010, http://www.hrw.org/en/reports/2010/09/16/without-protection?.

168. For a Hezbollah view, see Tim Cavanaugh interview with parliamentary deputy Muhammad Fneish, "Meet Hizbollah: The Party of God's MP Talks About Islam, Iraq, and the War on Terror," *Reason Magazine*, March 11, 2004: "The vision that the government does everything for the people is the wrong vision. The government should be taking a limited role in social services." Accessed September 23, 2010, http://reason.com/archives/2004/03/11/meet-hizbollah.

169. Statistics Lebanon Ltd. sampled four hundred residents throughout Lebanon, 19–April 24, 2006. The relevant question was: "Do you think the Lebanese army should be the only armed forces in Lebanon?" Full report in *al-Nahar*, May 18, 2006.

170. For an example of financial irregularities, see Robert Worth, "Billion—Dollar Pyramid Scheme Rivets Lebanon," *New York Times*, September 15, 2009, on $1 billion of losses to Shia caused by Hezbollah-associated Saleh Ezzedine.

171. Shaery-Eisenlohr, *Shi'ite Lebanon*, 60–65 and 74–76, gives partial statistics for numbers of students—all Shia—in Fadlallah (14,300), Hezbollah (12,091), and Amal (9,176) private schools in the early 2000s. Fadlallah's investment of alms income in education created what remains a formidable apparatus.

Conclusion

1. Al-Nabulusi, "Al-Tuhfa al-Nabulusiya fi al-Rihla al-Tarabulusiya," 3.
2. Abd al-Ghani al-Nabulusi, "Hullat al-Dhahab al-Ibriz fi Rihlat Ba'albak wa al-Biqa al-Aziz," in *Zwei Beschreibungen des Libanon: Abdalgani an-Nabulusis Reise durch die Biqa und al-Utaifis Reise Nach Tripolis*, ed. Stefan Wild (Beirut: Orient-Institut, 1979), 109.
3. Al-Nabulusi, "Al Tuhfa al-Nabulusiya fi al-Rihla al-Tarabulusiya," 97.
4. See comment in Salibi, *A House of Many Mansions*, 128, and van Leeuwen, *Notables and Clergy in Mount Lebanon*, 38.
5. Philip Hitti, *History of the Arabs from the earliest times to the present* (London: Macmillan, 1968), 729–31.
6. Harik, *Politics and Change in a Traditional Society*.
7. Salibi, *A House of Many Mansions*.
8. Winter, *The Shiites of Lebanon*.
9. Makdisi, *The Culture of Sectarianism*.
10. *Al-Sijill al-Arslani*, 131.
11. Winter, *The Shiites of Lebanon*, 34, justifiably dismisses such interpretations.
12. For elaboration, see Nadim Shehadi, "Riviera vs Citadel: The battle for Lebanon," *OpenDemocracy*, July 13, 2007, accessed July 22, 2011, http://www.opendemocracy.net/conflict-middle_east_politics/Riviera_citadel_3841.jsp.
13. Khoury, *The Gates of the City*, 90.

BIBLIOGRAPHY

Primary Sources—Arabic

Abu al-Fida, Al-Malik al-Muayyad Imad al-Din Isma'il. *Kitab al-Mukhtasar fi Akhbar al-Bashr*. Beirut: Dar al-Fikr, 1956–61.

Al-Awra, Ibrahim. *Tarikh Wilayat Sulayman Pasha al-Adil, 1804–1819*. Edited by Antun Qiqanu. Beirut: Dar al-Hadkhat, 1989.

Al-Ayni, Badr al-Din. *Iqd al-Juman fi Tarikh Ahl al-Zaman—Asr Salatin al-Mamalik*. Edited by Muhammad Amin. 4 vols. Cairo: Al-Hayat al-Misriya al-Ama l'il Kitab, 1987–92.

Al-Basha, Muhammad Khalil, and Riyadh Husayn Ghannam, eds. *Al-Sijill al-Arslani*. Beirut: Nawfal, 1999.

Bin Yahya, Salih. *Tarikh Bayrut wa Akhbar al-Umara al-Buhturiyin min Bani al-Gharb*. Edited by Louis Cheykho. Beirut: Al-Matba'at al-Kathulikiya, 1927.

Duwayhi, Istifan. *Tarikh al-Azmina, 1090–1699*. Edited by Ferdinan Tawtal. Beirut: Al-Matba'at al-Kathulikiya, 1951.

Haqqi, Isma'il, ed. *Lubnan: Mabahith Ilmiya wa Ijtima'iya*. Edited by Fuad Bustani from the 1918 original. 2 vols. Beirut: Manshurat al-Jami'at al-Lubnaniya, Qism al-Dirasat al-Tarikhiya, 1969–70.

Hezbollah. *Nass al-risala al-maftuha alati wajahha hizballah ila al-mustada'fin fi lubnan wa al-alam*. Beirut, February 16, 1985.

Ibn al-Athir, Izz al-Din Abu al-Hasan Ali. *Al-Kamil fi al-Tarikh*. Edited by Carl Tornberg. 13 vols. Beirut: Dar al-Sader, 1965–67.

Ibn al-Hariri, Ahmad bin Ali bin al-Maghrabi. *Muntakhab al-Zaman fi Tarikh al-Khulafa wa al-Ulama wa al-Ayan*. Edited by Abdo Khalifa. Beirut: Dar Ashtar, 1995.

Ibn al-Qila'i, Jibra'il. *Zajaliyat*. Edited by Butros al-Jumayyil. Beirut: Dar Lahad Khatar, 1982.

Ibn Sibat, Hamza Ibn Ahmad. *Tarikh al-Duruz fi Akhir Ahd al-Mamalik*. Ibn Sibat's *Sidq al-Akhbar*. Edited by Naila Kaedbay. Beirut: Dar al-Awda, 1989.

Ibn Tulun, Shams al-Din Muhammad bin Ali. *Al-Lama'at al-Barqiya fi al-Nukat al-Tarikhiya*. Edited by Muhammad Khayr Ramadan Yusuf. Beirut: Dar Ibn Hazm, 1994.

Al-Khalidi al-Safadi, Ahmad bin Muhammad. *Lubnan fi Ahd al-Amir Fakhr al-Din al-Ma'ni al-Thani*. Edited by Asad Rustum and Fuad Bustani. Beirut: Al-Maktabat al-Bulusiya, 1985.

Al-Khuri, Bishara. *Haqa'iq Lubnaniya*. 3 vols. Beirut: Awraq Lubnaniya, 1961.

Lebanese Center for Documentation and Research (CEDRE). *Al-Alaqat al-Lubnaniya al-Suriya 1943–1985: Waqa'i, Bibliografiya, Watha'iq*. 2 vols. Edited by Sam Menassa. Beirut: Bayt al-Mustaqbal, 1986.

Al-Maqrizi, Ahmad Ibn Ali. *Al-Suluk li Ma'rifat Duwal al-Muluk*. Edited by Muhammad al-Qadir Atar. 8 vols. Beirut: Dar al-Kutub al-Ilmiya, 1997.

Al-Mas'udi. *Kitab al-Tanbih wa al-Ashraf.* Beirut: Khayyat, 1965.

Al-Nabulusi, Abd al-Ghani. "Al-Tuhfa al-Nabulusiya fi al-Rihla al-Tarabulusiya." In *Die Reise des 'Abd al-Gani an-Nabulusi durch den Libanon.* Edited by Heribert Busse. Beirut: Orient-Institut der DMG, 2003.

———. "Hullat al-Dhahab al-Ibriz fi Rihlat Ba'albak wa al-Biqa al-Aziz." In *Zwei Beschreibungen des Lebanon: Abdalgani an-Nabulusis Reise durch die Biqa und al-Utaifis Reise Nach Tripolis.* Edited by Stefan Wild. Beirut: Orient-Institut, 1979.

Al-Shidyaq, Tannus. *Kitab Akhbar al-Ayan fi Jabal Lubnan.* Edited by Fuad Bustani. 2 vols. Beirut: Lebanese University Publications, 1970.

Al-Shihabi, Haydar Ahmad. *Lubnan fi Ahd al-Umara al-Shihabiyin.* Edited by Asad Rustum and Fuad Bustani. 3 vols. Beirut: al-Makataba al-Bulusiya, 1984.

Al-Ya'qubi. *Tarikh al-Ya'qubi.* Beirut: Dar Beirut, 1980.

Primary Sources—Other Languages

Anonymous. "Campaign Organization and Tactics." In *Three Byzantine Military Treatises: Text, Translation, and Notes.* Translated by George Dennis, 9–141. Washington, DC: Dumbarton Oaks, 2008.

Al-Baladhuri. *The Origins of the Islamic State.* Translated by Philip Hitti. Beirut: Khayyat, 1966.

Bembo, Ambrosio, *The Travels and Journal of Ambrosio Bembo.* Edited by Anthony Welch. Translated by Clara Bargellini. Berkeley and Los Angeles: University of California Press, 2007.

Benjamin of Tudela. *The Itinerary of Benjamin of Tudela: Travels in the Middle Ages.* Translated by Marcus Adler. Malibu: Pangloss Press, 1983.

Churchill, Charles. *The Druze and the Maronites under the Turkish Rule from 1840 to 1860.* London: Bernard Quaritch, 1862.

Dandini, Giralamo. "A Voyage to Mont Libanus wherein is an account of the customs, and manners & etc., of the Turks. Also a description of Candia, Nicosia, Tripoli, Alexandretta & etc." Vol. 10 of *A General Collection of the Best and Most Interesting Voyages and Travels.* Edited by John Pinkerton. London, 1811.

De Gaulle, Charles. *The Complete War Memoirs of Charles de Gaulle.* Translated by Jonathan Griffin and Richard Howard. New York: Carroll and Graf Publishers, 1998.

Ibn Jubayr. *The Travels of Ibn Jubayr.* Translated by R. J. C. Broadhurst. London: Jonathan Cape, 1952.

Ibn al-Qalanisi. *The Damascus Chronicle of the Crusades.* Translated by H. A. R. Gibb. London: Luzac & Co., 1932.

Ismail, Adel. *Documents Diplomatiques et Consulaires relatifs à l'Histoire du Liban, Les Sources Françaises, t. 16, Consulat de France à Beyrouth.* Beirut: Editions des oeuvres politiques et historiques, 2001.

Lebanese Center for Policy Studies. "Documents: The Constitution of Lebanon after the Amendments of August 21, 1990, and Sections of the Ta'if Agreement not included in the Constitution." *Beirut Review* 1 no. 1 (Spring 1991): 119–72.

Maundrell, Henry. "A Journey from Aleppo to Jerusalem at Easter A.D. 1697." Vol. 10 of *A General Collection of the Best and Most Interesting Voyages and Travels.* Edited by John Pinkerton. London, 1811.

Munqidh, Usama Ibn. *The Book of Contemplation.* Translated by Paul Cobb. London: Penguin Classics, 2008.

Al-Muqaddasi. *The Best Divisions for the Knowledge of the Regions.* Translated by Basil Collins. Reading: Garnet Publishing, 1994.

Palmer, Andrew, trans. "Dionysius Reconstituted." In *The Seventh Century in the West-Syrian Chronicles,* 111–221. Liverpool: Liverpool University Press, 1993.

Palmer, Andrew, trans. "The Maronite Chronicle." In *The Seventh Century in the West-Syrian Chronicles,* 29–35. Liverpool: Liverpool University Press, 1993.

Salname-yi Jabal Lubnan. 1309 (H)/1891–1892. (Note: This is the Ottoman year book for the Islamic year 1309. "H" stands for "hijra," Muhammad's move from Mecca to Medina that marked the beginning of the Islamic calendar.)

Salname-yi Vilayet-i Beyrut. 1318 (H)/1900–1901. (Note: This is the Ottoman year book for the Islamic year 1318. "H" stands for "hijra," Muhammad's move from Mecca to Medina that marked the beginning of the Islamic calendar.)

Sandys, George. *A Relation of a Journey Begun an. Dom. 1610: Containing a Description of the Turkish Empire, of Egypt, of the Holy Land, of the Remote Parts of Italy, and Islands Adjoining.* 3rd ed. London, 1632.

Al-Tabari. *The History of al-Tabari.* Edited by Ehsan Yar Shater. 40 vols. Albany: State University of New York Press, 1979–2007.

Theophanes. *The Chronicle of Theophanes Confessor: Byzantine and Near Eastern History AD 284–813.* Translated by Cyril Mango and Roger Scott. Oxford: Clarendon Press, 1997.

UNESCO Institute for Statistics. *Adult Illiteracy for Population Aged 15 Years and Over, by Country and by Gender 1970–2015.* July 2002 Assessment.

United Nations. Official U.N. transcript of the meeting of U.N. Secretary-General Ban Ki-moon with Bashar al-Asad. Damascus, April 24, 2007.

Volney, Constantin-François. *Travels through Egypt and Syria, in the years 1783, 1784 & 1785. Containing the present natural and political state of those countries; their productions, arts, manufactures & commerce; with observations on the manners, customs and government of the Turks & Arabs.* Trans. from the French. 2 vols. New York: J. Tiebout, 1798.

William of Tyre. *A History of Deeds Done Beyond the Sea.* Translated by Emily Babcock and A. C. Krey. 2 vols. New York: Columbia University Press, 1943.

Newspapers, Magazines, News Monitoring Services

Al-Afkar weekly. Beirut

Al-Anwar daily. Beirut.

Al-Hayat daily. London.

Al-Majalla weekly. London.

Al-Nahar daily. Beirut

Al-Qabas daily. Kuwait.

Al-Ra'i al-Am daily. Kuwait.

Al-Safir daily. Beirut.

Al-Sharq al-Awsat daily. London.

Al-Thawra daily. Damascus.

Al-Wasat weekly. London.

Foreign Broadcast Information Service (FBIS), *Daily Report: Near East and South Asia.* Monitoring published in English translation, U.S. Government.

Ha'aretz daily. Tel Aviv.

MidEast Mirror daily. London.

Naharnet Arabic News Service. Beirut.

New York Times daily. New York.

The Times daily. London.

Interviews

Author's records of interviews and discussions with Lebanese and Syrian personalities, as detailed in chapter notes.

Secondary Sources

Abisaab, Malek. "'Unruly' Factory Women in Lebanon: Contesting French Colonialism and the National State." *Journal of Women's History* 16 no. 3 (Fall 2004): 55–82.

Abisaab, Rula. "History and Self-Image: The 'Amili Ulema in Syria and Iran (Fourteenth to Sixteenth Centuries)." In *Distant Relations: Iran and Lebanon in the Last 500 years.* Edited by H. E. Chehabi, 62–95. London: I. B. Tauris, 2006.

Abu-Husayn, Abdul-Rahim. "The Ottoman Invasion of the Shuf in 1585: A Reconsideration."
    Al-Abhath 33 (1985): 13–21.
——. *Provincial Leaderships in Syria, 1575–1650*. Beirut: American University of Beirut, 1985.
——. "Problems in the Ottoman Administration in Syria During the 16th and 17th Centuries:
    The Case of the Sanjak of Sidon-Beirut." *International Journal of Middle East Studies* 24
    (1992): 665–75.
——. "The Unknown Career of Ahmad Ma'n (1667–1697)." *Archivum Ottomanicum*, 17 (1999):
    241–47.
——. *The View from Istanbul: Ottoman Lebanon and the Druze Emirate*. London: I. B. Tauris,
    2004.
Abu Nahra, Joseph. "Intiqal al-Milkiya min al-Lama'iyin ila al-Aklirus fi al-Matn." In *Lubnan fi
    al-Qarn al-Thamin'ashr: al-Mu'tamar al-Awal lil-Jami'ya al-Lubnaniya lil-Dirasat al-Uthmaniya.*
    Edited by Butros Labaki, 179–200. Beirut: Dar al-Muntakhab al-Arabi, 1996.
Abu Salih, Abbas. "Al-Sira ala al-Sulta fi al-Imara al-Shihabiya." In *Lubnan fi al-Qarn al-Thamin'ashr:
    al-Mu'tamar al-Awal lil-Jami'ya al-Lubnaniya lil-Dirasat al-Uthmaniya.* Edited by Butros
    Labaki, 128–58. Beirut: Dar al-Muntakhab al-Arabi, 1996.
Ajami, Fouad. *The Vanished Imam: Musa Al Sadr and the Shia of Lebanon*. Ithaca: Cornell University
    Press, 1992.
Akarli, Engin. *The Long Peace: Ottoman Lebanon, 1861–1920*. London: I. B. Tauris, 1993.
Alin, Erika. *The United States and the 1958 Lebanon Crisis: American Intervention in the Middle East.*
    Lanham, MD: University Press of America, 1994.
Al Safa, Muhammad Jabir. *Tarikh Jabal Amil*. Beirut: Dar al-Nahar, 2004.
Al-Amin, Muhsin. *Khitat Jabal Amil*. Beirut: Al-Dar al-Alimiya, 1984.
Ammoun, Denise. *Histoire du Liban Contemporain 1860–1943*. Paris: Fayard, 1997.
——. *Histoire du Liban Contemporain 1943–1990*. Paris: Fayard, 2004.
Anderson, Betty. "Voices of Protest: Arab Nationalism and the Palestinian Revolution at the
    American University of Beirut." *Comparative Studies of South Asia, Africa, and the Middle East*
    28 no. 3 (2008): 390–403.
Attié, Caroline. *Struggle in the Levant: Lebanon in the 1950s*. London: I. B. Tauris, 2004.
Awwad, Tawfiq. *Death in Beirut*. Translated by Leslie McLoughlin. London: Heinemann, 1976.
Ayalon, David. "Studies on the Structure of the Mamluk Army—II." *Bulletin of the School of Oriental
    and African Studies, University of London* 15 no. 3 (1953): 448–76.
——. *Studies on the Mamluks of Egypt*. London: Variorum Reprints, 1977.
Badrud-Din, Abdul-Amir. *The Bank of Lebanon: Central Banking in a Financial Centre and Entrepot.*
    London: Frances Pinter, 1984.
Barak, Oren. *The Lebanese Army: A National Institution in a Divided Society*. Albany: State University
    of New York Press, 2009.
Baroudi, Sami. "Sectarianism and Business Associations in Postwar Lebanon." *Arab Studies
    Quarterly* 22 no. 4 (Fall 2000): 81–107.
Beshara, Adel. *Lebanon: The Politics of Frustration—The Failed Coup of 1961*. Abingdon, Oxon:
    Routledge Curzon, 2005.
Beydoun, Ibrahim. "Lubnan fi al-Ahdayn al-Umawi wa al-Abbasi." Vol. 1 of *Lubnan fi Tarikhihi wa
    Turathihi*. Edited by Adil Isma'il. Beirut: Merkaz al-Hariri al-Thaqafi, 1993.
Blanford, Nicholas. *Killing Mr. Lebanon: The Assassination of Rafik Hariri and its Impact on the
    Middle East*. London: I. B. Tauris, 2006.
Bulliet, Richard. *The Camel and the Wheel*. Cambridge: Harvard University Press, 1975.
Chalabi, Tamara. *The Shi'is of Jabal 'Amil and the New Lebanon—Community and Nation-State,
    1918–1943*. New York and Basingstoke: Palgrave-Macmillan, 2006.
Chalcraft, John. *The Invisible Cage: Syrian Migrant Workers in Lebanon*. Stanford: Stanford University
    Press, 2009.
Chamie, Joseph. "Differentials in Fertility: Lebanon, 1971." *Population Studies* 31 no. 2 (1977):
    365–82.
Chamoun, Camille. *Crise au Moyen-Orient*. Paris: Gallimard, 1963.

Chehab, Hafez. "Reconstructing the Medici Portrait of Fakhr al-Din al-Ma'ni." *Muqarnas* 11 (1994): 117–24.

Chehab, Maurice. "The Umayyad Palace at Anjar." *Ars Orientalis* 5 (1963): 17–25.

Chikhani, Rafic. "Communautés Libanaises vues par des Voyageurs Français au XVIII Siècle." In *Lubnan fi al-Qarn al-Thamin'ashr: al-Mu'tamar al-Awal lil-Jami'ya al-Lubnaniya lil-Dirasat al-Uthmaniya*. Edited by Butros Labaki, 246–65. Beirut: Dar al-Muntakhab al-Arabi, 1996.

Churchill, Winston. *The Second World War, Volume III: The Grand Alliance*. London: Penguin Books, 2005.

Corm, Georges. *Le Liban Contemporain: Histoire et Société*. Paris: Éditions la Découverte, 2003.

Crow, Ralph. "Religious Sectarianism in the Lebanese Political System." *The Journal of Politics* 24 no. 3 (1962): 489–520.

Deeb, Lara. *An Enchanted Modern: Gender and Public Piety in Shi'i Lebanon*. Princeton: Princeton University Press, 2006.

Dols, Michael. *The Black Death in the Middle East*. Princeton: Princeton University Press, 1977.

Elias, Ata, Paul Tapponnier, Satish C. Singh, Geoffrey C. P. King, Anne Briais, Mathieu Daëron, Helene Carton, Alexander Sursock, Eric Jacques, Rachid Jomaa, and Yann Klinger. "Active Thrusting Offshore Mount Lebanon: Source of the Tsunamigenic A.D. 551 Beirut-Tripoli Earthquake." *Geology* 35 no. 8 (August 2007): 755–58.

Ellenblum, Ronnie. *Crusader Castles and Modern Histories*. Cambridge: Cambridge University Press, 2007.

Encyclopaedia Judaica. 16 vols. Jerusalem: Keter Publishing House, 1971.

Evron, Yair. *War and Intervention in Lebanon: The Israeli-Syrian Deterrence Dialogue*. London: Croom Helm, 1987.

Faour, Muhammad. "The Demography of Lebanon: A Reappraisal." *Middle Eastern Studies* 27 no. 4 (1991): 631–41.

———. "Religion, Demography, and Politics in Lebanon." *Middle Eastern Studies* 43 no. 6 (2007): 909–21.

Farah, Caesar. *Papers on Lebanon 13: The Road to Intervention—Fiscal Politics in Ottoman Lebanon*. Oxford: Centre for Lebanese Studies, 1992.

———. *The Politics of Interventionism in Ottoman Lebanon, 1830–1861*. London: I. B. Tauris, 2000.

Farha, Mark. "Demographic Dilemmas." In *Lebanon: Liberation, Conflict, and Crisis*. Edited by Barry Rubin, 83–97. New York: Palgrave Macmillan, 2009.

Fawaz, Leila. *Merchants and Migrants in Nineteenth Century Beirut*. Cambridge: Harvard University Press, 1983.

———. *An Occasion for War: Civil Conflict in Lebanon and Damascus in 1860*. London: I. B. Tauris, 1994.

Finkel, Caroline. *Osman's Dream: The Story of the Ottoman Empire, 1300–1923*. London: John Murray, 2006.

Firro, Kais. *Inventing Lebanon: Nationalism and the State under the Mandate*. London: I. B. Tauris, 2003.

Gambill, Gary. "Syria after Lebanon: Hooked on Lebanon." *The Middle East Quarterly*, 12 no. 3 (Fall 2005): 35–42.

Gaspard, Toufic, *A Political Economy of Lebanon, 1948–2002*. Leiden: Brill, 2004.

Gates, Carolyn. *Papers on Lebanon 10: The Historical Role of Political Economy in the Development of Modern Lebanon*. Oxford: Centre for Lebanese Studies, 1989.

———. *The Merchant Republic of Lebanon: Rise of an Open Economy*. London: I. B. Tauris, 1998.

Gordon, David. *Lebanon: The Fragmented Nation*. London: Croom Helm, 1980.

Goria, Wade. *Sovereignty and Leadership in Lebanon, 1943–1976*. London: Ithaca, 1985.

Groves, Jean. *Little Ice Ages Ancient and Modern*, 2nd ed. London: Routledge, 2004.

Gulick, John. *Tripoli: A Modern Arab City*. Cambridge: Harvard University Press, 1967.

Hablas, Faruq. "Al-Intifadat al-Sha'biya fi Tarabulus." In *Lubnan fi al-Qarn al-Thamin'ashr: al-Mu'tamar al-Awal lil-Jami'ya al-Lubnaniya lil-Dirasat al-Uthmaniya*. Edited by Butros Labaki, 286–301. Beirut: Dar al-Muntakhab al-Arabi, 1996.

Halawi, Majed. *A Lebanon Defied—Musa al-Sadr and the Shi'a Community*. Boulder: Westview Press, 1992.

Haldon, John. "Seventh Century Continuities: The Ajnad and the 'Thematic Myth.'" In *The Byzantine and Early Islamic Near East, III: States, Resources and Armies*. Edited by Averil Cameron, 379–424. Princeton: Darwin Press, 1995.

———. "Economy and Administration: How Did the Empire Work?" In *The Cambridge Companion to the Age of Justinian*. Edited by Michael Maas, 28–59. New York: Cambridge University Press, 2005.

Halm, Heinz. *Shi'ism*, 2nd ed. New York: Columbia University Press, 2004.

Hamilton, Bernard. *The Leper King and His Heirs: Baldwin IV and the Crusader Kingdom of Jerusalem*. Cambridge: Cambridge University Press, 2000.

Hanf, Theodore. *Coexistence in Wartime Lebanon: Decline of a State and Rise of a Nation*. Translated by John Richardson. London: I. B. Tauris, 1993.

Hanssen, Jens. *Fin de Siècle Beirut—The Making of an Ottoman Provincial Capital*. Oxford: Oxford University Press, 2005.

Harik, Ilya. *Politics and Change in a Traditional Society—Lebanon 1711–1845*. Princeton: Princeton University Press, 1968.

Harik, Judith. "Shaykh al-'Aql and the Druze of Mount Lebanon: Conflict and Accommodation." *Middle Eastern Studies* 30 no. 3 (1994): 461–85.

Harris, William. "The View from Zahle: Security and Economic Conditions in the Central Beqa'a, 1983–85." *Middle East Journal* 39 no. 3 (1985): 270–86.

———. "Lebanon." *Middle East Contemporary Survey*, vol. XV, 1991. Edited by Ami Ayalon, 540–76. Boulder: Westview, 1993.

———. *Faces of Lebanon: Sects, Wars, and Global Extensions*. Princeton: Markus Wiener Publishers, 1996.

Hatit, Ahmad. "Lubnan fi Ahd al-Faranja." Vol. 1 of *Lubnan fi Tarikhihi wa Turathihi*. Edited by Adil Isma'il, 181–208. Beirut: Merkaz al-Hariri al-Thaqafi, 1993.

Havemann, Axel. "The Impact of Peasant Resistance on Nineteenth Century Mount Lebanon." In *Peasants & Politics in the Modern Middle East*. Edited by Farhad Kazemi and John Waterbury, 85–100. Miami: Florida International University Press, 1991.

Hess, Clyde, and Herbert Bodman. "Confessionalism and Feudality in Lebanese Politics." *Middle East Journal* 8 no. 1 (1954): 10–26.

Hirst, David. *Beware of Small States: Lebanon, Battleground of the Middle East*. New York: Nation Books, 2010.

Hitti, Philip. *History of the Arabs from the Earliest Times to the Present*. London: Macmillan, 1968.

Holt, P. M. *The Age of the Crusades: The Near East from the Eleventh Century to 1517*. London: Longman, 1986.

Hottinger, Arnold. "Zu'ama in Historical Perspective." In *Politics in Lebanon*. Edited by L. Binder, 86–105. New York: John Wiley and Sons, 1966.

Hourani, Albert. *Arabic Thought in the Liberal Age, 1798–1959*. Cambridge: Cambridge University Press, 1983.

———. "From Jabal Amil to Persia." In *Distant Relations: Iran and Lebanon in the Last 500 Years*. Edited by H. E. Chehabi, 51–61. London: I. B. Tauris, 2006.

Hudson, Michael. *The Precarious Republic: Political Modernization in Lebanon*. New York: Random House, 1968.

———. "Democracy and Social Mobilization in Lebanese Politics." In *Analyzing the Third World: Essays from Comparative Politics*. Edited by Norman Provizer, 271–92. Cambridge: Schenkman Publishing Company, 1978.

Hughes, Malcolm, and Henry Diaz, eds. *The Medieval Warm Period*. Dordrecht: Kluwer Academic Publishers, 1994.

Imber, Colin. *The Ottoman Empire, 1300–1650: The Structure of Power*. Basingstoke: Palgrave Macmillan, 2002.

Institute for Human Rights in Lebanon. *Muqarrarat al-Ta'if wa Huquq al-Insan*. Beirut: Institute for Human Rights in Lebanon, 1990.

International Institute of Strategic Studies (IISS), *The Military Balance, 2003–2004*. London: IISS, 2003.

Irwin, Robert. *The Middle East in the Middle Ages—The Early Mamluk Sultanate, 1250–1382*. Carbondale and Ewardsville: Southern Illinois University Press, 1986.

Isma'il, Munir. "Al-Tahawulat al-Siyasiya fi Mujtama al-Imara al-Shihabiya." In *Lubnan fi al-Qarn al-Thamin'ashr: al-Mu'tamar al-Awal al-Lubnaniya lil-Dirasat al-Uthmaniya*. Edited by Butros Labaki, 83–101. Beirut: Dar al-Muntakhab al-Arabi, 1996.

Isma'il, Munir, and Adil Isma'il. *Tarikh Lubnan al-Hadith: al-Watha'iq al-Diblumasiya—al-Qism al-Awal, al-Juz al-Awal*. Beirut: Dar al-Nashr lil Siyasa wa al-Tarikh, 1990.

Issawi, Charles. *The Fertile Crescent 1800–1914: A Documentary Economic History*. New York: Oxford University Press, 1988.

Johnson, Michael. *Class and Client in Beirut: The Sunni Muslim Community and the Lebanese State 1840–1985*. London and Atlantic Highlands: Ithaca Press, 1986.

———. *All Honourable Men: The Social Origins of War in Lebanon*. London: I. B. Tauris, 2001.

Jones, A. H. M. *The Later Roman Empire, 284–602*. Oxford: Blackwell, 1964.

Kahl, Oliver. "Qusta Ibn Luqa on Sleeplessness." *Journal of Semitic Studies* XLIII no. 2 (Autumn 1998): 311–26.

Kassir, Samir. *La Guerre du Liban: De la dissension nationale au conflit régional*. Paris: Karthala, 1994.

———. *Beirut*. Berkeley and Los Angeles: University of California Press, 2010.

Kaufman, Asher. *Reviving Phoenicia: The Search for Identity in Lebanon*. London: I. B. Tauris, 2004.

Kennedy, Hugh. *When Baghdad Ruled the Muslim World—The Rise and Fall of Islam's Greatest Dynasty*. Cambridge: Da Capo Press, 2005.

———. *The Great Arab Conquests*. London: Phoenix, 2007.

Khalaf, Roseanne Saad, ed. *Hikayat: Short Stories by Lebanese Women*. London: Telegram Books, 2006.

Khalaf, Samir. *Persistence and Change in Nineteenth Century Lebanon*. Beirut: American University of Beirut, 1979.

———. *Civil and Uncivil Violence in Lebanon: A History of the Internationalization of Communal Conflict*. New York: Columbia University Press, 2002.

Khalife, Isam. *Nawahi Lubnan fi al-Qarn al-Sadis Ashr: Al-Taqsimat al-Idariya—al-Demografiya— al-Adyan wa al-Madhahib*. Beirut: I. K. Khalife, 2004.

———. *Lubnan 1914–1918 min khilal Arshif Wizarat al-Kharijiya al-Faransiya*. Beirut: Isam Khalife, 2005.

Khater, Akram. *Inventing Home: Emigration, Gender, and the Middle Class in Lebanon, 1970–1920*. Berkeley and Los Angeles: University of California Press, 2001.

El-Khazen, Farid. *Papers on Lebanon 12: The Communal Pact of National Identities—The Making and Politics of the 1943 National Pact*. Oxford: Centre for Lebanese Studies, 1991.

———. *The Breakdown of the State in Lebanon, 1967–1976*. Cambridge: Harvard University Press, 2000.

Khoury, Elias. *The Gates of the City*. Translated by Paula Haydar. Minneapolis: University of Minnesota Press, 1993.

Khoury, Philip. *Syria and the French Mandate: The Politics of Arab Nationalism, 1920–1945*. Princeton: Princeton University Press, 1987.

Khuri, Fuad. *Being a Druze*. London: Druze Heritage Foundation, 2004.

Lammens, Henri. "Les Nosairis dans Le Liban." *Revue de l'Orient Chrétien* VII (1902): 452–77.

Loehle, C. "A 2000-year global temperature reconstruction based on non-treering proxies." *Energy and Environment* 18 (2007): 1049–58.

Longrigg, Stephen. *Syria and Lebanon under the French Mandate*. Oxford: Oxford University Press, 1958.

Maila, Joseph. *The Document of National Understanding: A Commentary*. Oxford: Centre for Lebanese Studies, 1992.

Makarim, Sami. *Lubnan fi Ahd al-Umara al-Tanukhiyin*. Beirut: Dar Sader, 2000.

Makdisi, Samir. *The Lesson of Lebanon: The Economies of War and Development*. London: I. B. Tauris, 2004.

Makdisi, Usama. *The Culture of Sectarianism: Community, History, and Violence in Nineteenth-Century Ottoman Lebanon*. Berkeley and Los Angeles: University of California Press, 2000.

Makhzum, Muhammad. "Jabal Amil fi al-Ahdayn al-Salibi wa al-Mamluki." In *Safahat min Tarikh Jabal Amil*. Edited by South Lebanon Cultural Council, 33–53. Beirut: Dar al-Farabi, 1979.

al-Ma'luf, Isa. *Dawani al-Qutuf fi Tarikh Bani al-Ma'luf*. 1907–1908. 2 vols. Damascus: Dar Hawran, 2003 (reprint).

Manneh, Butrus Abu. "The Establishing and Dismantling of the Province of Syria." In *Problems of the Middle East in Historical Perspective: Essays in Honour of Albert Hourani*. Edited by John Spagnolo, 7–26. Reading: Ithaca Press, 1992.

Moosa, Matti. "The Relation of the Maronites of Lebanon to the Mardaites and Al-Jarajima." *Speculum* 44 no. 4 (October 1969): 597–608.

———. *The Maronites in History*. Syracuse: Syracuse University Press, 1986.

Al-Muhajir, Ja'afar. *Jabal Amil taht al-Ihtilal al-Salibi*. Beirut: Dar al-Haqq, 2001.

Nasr, Salim. "The New Social Map." In *Lebanon in Limbo: Postwar Society and State in an Uncertain Regional Environment*. Edited by Theodor Hanf and Nawaf Salam, 143–58. Baden-Baden: Nomos Verlagsgesellschaft, 2003.

Nasrallah, Emily. *Flight Against Time*. Translated by Issa Boullata. Charlottetown, Prince Edward Island: Ragweed Press, 1987.

Nassif, Niqula. *Jumhuriyat Fuad Shihab*. Beirut: Dar al-Nahar, 2008.

Newman, Andrew. "The Myth of the Clerical Migration to Safawid Iran: Arab Shiite Opposition to Ali al-Karaki and Safawid Shiism." *Die Welt des Islams, New Series* 33 no. 1 (April 1993): 66–112.

Norton, Augustus Richard. *Amal and the Shi'a: Struggle for the Soul of Lebanon*. Austin: University of Texas Press, 1988.

Pamuk, Sevket, "Money in the Ottoman Empire." In *An Economic and Social History of the Ottoman Empire 1300–1914*. Edited by Halil Inalcık and Donald Quataert, 947–80. Cambridge: Cambridge University Press, 1994.

Pettet, Deidre. "A Veritable Bedouin: The Chevalier d'Arvieux in the Camp of the Emir Turabey." In *Distant Lands and Diverse Cultures: The French Experience in Asia, 1600–1700*. Edited by Glen Ames and Ronald Love, 21–46. Westport, CT: Greenwood Press, 2003.

Picard, Elizabeth. "The Political Economy of Civil War in Lebanon." In *War, Institutions, and Social Change in the Middle East*. Edited by Steven Heydemann, 292–323. Berkeley and Los Angeles: University of California Press, 2000.

Pitcher, Donald. *An Historical Geography of the Ottoman Empire from Earliest Times to the End of the Sixteenth Century*. Leiden: E. J. Brill, 1972.

Poliak, A. N. "The Demographic Evolution of the Middle East: Population Trends since 1348." *Palestine and the Middle East* 10 no. 5 (May 1938): 201–05.

Prawer, Joshua. *The Latin Kingdom of Jerusalem*. London: Weidenfeld & Nicolson, 1972.

———. *Crusader Institutions*. Oxford: Clarendon, 1980.

Pryor, John, and Elizabeth Jeffreys. *The Age of the Dromon: The Byzantine Navy ca 500–1204*. Leiden: Brill, 2006.

Qara'li, Bulos, *Ali Pasha Junblat Wali Halab, 1605–1611*. Beirut: Manshurat Dar al-Makshuf, 1939.

Al-Qittar, Elias. *Lubnan fi al-Qurun al-Wusta*. Ba'abda: Murex, 2004.

Rabinovich, Itamar. *The War for Lebanon, 1970–1983*. Ithaca: Cornell University Press, 1984.

Raphaeli, Nimrod. "Lebanese Economy between Violence and Political Stalemate." In *Lebanon: Liberation, Conflict, and Crisis*. Edited by Barry Rubin, 109–30. New York: Palgrave Macmillan, 2009.

Richard, Jean. *The Crusades c. 1071–c. 1291*. Cambridge: Cambridge University Press, 1999.

———. *Francs et Orientaux dans le Monde des Croisades*. Aldershot: Ashgate/Valiorum, 2003.

Richards, Donald. "A Text of Imad al-Din on 12th Century Frankish-Muslim Relations." *Arabica* 25 (1978): 202–04.

Rizk, Karam. *Les Événements de 1860 et le Premier Mutasarrifiya: Tenants et Aboutissants du Grand-Liban*. Kaslik: Bibliothèque de l'Université Saint-Esprit, 1992.

Russell, Josiah. "The Population of the Crusader States." In *A History of the Crusades, Vol. V: The Impact of the Crusades on the Near East*. Edited by Norman Zacour and Harry Hazard, 295–315. Madison: University of Wisconsin Press, 1985.

Saidi, Nasser. *Papers on Lebanon 5: Economic Consequences of the War in Lebanon.* Oxford: Centre for Lebanese Studies, 1986.

Salem, Elie. *Violence & Diplomacy in Lebanon.* London: I. B. Tauris, 1995.

Salem, Elise. *Constructing Lebanon: A Century of Literary Narratives.* Gainesville: University Press of Florida, 2003.

Salibi, Kamal. "The Maronites of Lebanon under Frankish and Mamluk Rule (1099–1516)." *Arabica* IV (1957): 288–303.

———. *Maronite Historians of Modern Lebanon.* New York: AMS Press, 1959.

———. "The Buhturids of the Gharb: Medieval Lords of Beirut and of Southern Lebanon." *Arabica* VIII (1961): 75–97.

———. "The Lebanese Emirate, 1667–1841." *Al-Abhath* XX (1967): 1–16.

———. "Northern Lebanon Under the Dominance of Ghazir (1517–1591)." *Arabica* XIV (1967): 144–66.

———. "The Muqaddams of Bsharri: Maronite Chieftains of the Northern Lebanon, 1382–1621." *Arabica* XV (1968): 63–86.

———. "The Sayfas and the Eyalat of Tripoli, 1579–1640." *Arabica* XX (1973): 25–52.

———. "The Secret of the House of Ma'n." *International Journal of Middle Eastern Studies* 4 (1973): 272–87.

———. *The Modern History of Lebanon.* New York: Caravan Books, 1977.

———. *Muntalaq Tarikh Lubnan.* Beirut: Caravan, 1979.

———. *A House of Many Mansions: The History of Lebanon Reconsidered.* Berkeley and Los Angeles: University of California Press, 1988.

Al-Samad, Qasim. "Muqata'jiya al-Dinniya wa Mawqifhum min al-Sira ala al-Imara al-Shihabiya." In *Lubnan fi al-Qarn al-Thamin'ashr: al-Mu'tamar al-Awal lil-Jami'ya al-Lubnaniya lil-Dirasat al-Uthmaniya.* Edited by Butros Labaki, 161–78. Beirut: Dar al-Muntakhab al-Arabi, 1996.

Samman, Ghada. *The Square Moon: Supernatural Tales.* Translated by Issa Boullata. Fayetteville: University of Arkansas Press, 1998.

Saqr, Yusuf. *A'ilat Hakamat Lubnan.* Beirut: Al-Merkaz al-Arabi lil-Ma'lumat, 2008.

Sartre, Maurice. *The Middle East Under Rome.* Cambridge: Belknap Press, 2005.

Sayigh, Yezid. *Armed Struggle and the Search for a State: The Palestinian National Movement 1949–1993.* Oxford: Oxford University Press, 1997.

Schiff, Ze'ev and Ehud Ya'ari. *Israel's Lebanon War.* London: Allen & Unwin, 1985.

Schilcher, L. Schatkowski. "The Famine of 1915–1918 in Ottoman Syria." In *Problems of the Modern Middle East in Historical Perspective: Essays in Honour of Albert Hourani.* Edited by J. Spagnolo, 229–58. Reading: Ithaca, 1992.

Schulze, Kirsten. *Israel's Covert Diplomacy in Lebanon.* Basingstoke: Macmillan Press, 1998.

Shaery-Eisenlohr, Roschanack. *Shi'ite Lebanon: Transnational Religion and the Making of National Identities.* New York: Columbia University Press, 2008.

Shanahan, Rodger. *The Shi'a of Lebanon: Clans, Parties and Clerics.* London: I. B. Tauris, 2005.

Al-Shaykh, Hanan. *The Story of Zahra.* Translated by Peter Ford. London: Quartet Books, 1986.

———. *I Sweep the Sun off Rooftops.* Translated by Catherine Cobham. London: Bloomsbury, 1998.

El-Solh, Raghid. *Lebanon and Arabism: National Identity and State Formation.* London: I. B. Tauris, 2004.

Spagnolo, John. *France and Ottoman Lebanon, 1861–1914.* London: Ithaca, 1977.

Stewart, Devin. "Notes on the Migration of 'Amili Scholars to Safavid Iran." *Journal of Near Eastern Studies* 55 no. 2 (April 1996): 81–103.

Sulayman, Husayn. "Thulathi al-Quwa al-Mahaliya Yantazi Saida min al-Saytara al-Uthmaniya." In *Lubnan fi al-Qarn al-Thamin'ashr: al-Mu'tamar al-Awal lil-Jami'ya al-Lubnaniya lil-Dirasat al-Uthmaniya.* Edited by Butros Labaki, 321–44. Beirut: Dar al-Muntakhab al-Arabi, 1996.

Tadmuri, Umar. *Tarikh Tarabulus al-Siyasi wa al-Hadari abr al-Usur.* 2 vols. Tripoli: Dar al-Balad, 1978–81.

———. *Lubnan min al-Fath al-Islami hatta Suqut al-Dawla al-Umawiya.* Tripoli, Lebanon: Jarrus Bris, 1990.

———. *Lubnan min Qiyam al-Dawla al-Abbasiya hatta Suqut al-Dawla al-Ikhshidiya.* Tripoli, Lebanon: Jarrus Bris, 1992.

Talhamy, Yvette. "The Fatwas and the Nusayri/Alawis of Syria." *Middle Eastern Studies* 46 no. 2 (April 2010): 175–94.

Timoviev, Igor. *Kamal Junblat: Al-Rajul wa al-Ustura.* Translated from Russian into Arabic by Khayri al-Damin. Beirut: Dar al-Nahar, 2001.

Treadgold, Warren. *A History of the Byzantine State and Society.* Stanford: Stanford University Press, 1997.

Vallaud, Pierre, ed. *Atlas du Liban: Géographie, Histoire, Économie et Société.* Beirut: Presses de L'Université Saint-Joseph, 2006.

Van Leeuwen, Richard. "Monastic Estates and Agricultural Transformation in Mount Lebanon in the 18th Century." *International Journal of Middle East Studies* 23 no. 4 (1991): 601–617.

———. *Notables and Clergy in Mount Lebanon: The Khazin Sheikhs & the Maronite Church (1736–1840).* Leiden: E. J. Brill, 1994.

Wagstaff, J. M. "A Note on Some Nineteenth Century Population Statistics for Lebanon." *Bulletin (British Society for Middle Eastern Studies)* 13 no. 1 (1986): 27–35.

Walker, Paul. *Fatimid History and Ismaili Doctrine.* Aldershot: Ashgate/Variorum, 2008.

Weiss, Max. *In the Shadow of Sectarianism: Law, Shi'ism, and the Making of Modern Lebanon.* Cambridge: Harvard University Press, 2010.

Wickham, Chris. *The Inheritance of Rome: A History of Europe from 400 to 1000.* London: Penguin, 2010.

Winter, Stefan. *The Shi'ites of Lebanon Under Ottoman Rule, 1516–1788.* Cambridge: Cambridge University Press, 2010.

Yaniv, Avner. *Dilemmas of Security: Politics, Strategy, and the Israeli Experience in Lebanon.* New York: Oxford University Press, 1987.

Young, Michael. *The Ghosts of Martyr's Square: An Eyewitness Account of Lebanon's Life Struggle.* New York: Simon & Schuster, 2010.

Zachs, Fruma. *The Making of a Syrian Identity—Intellectuals and Merchants in Nineteenth Century Beirut.* Leiden: Brill, 2005.

Zalloua, Pierre, Yali Xue, Jade Khalife, Nadine Makhoul, Labib Debiane, Daniel E. Platt, Ajay K. Royyuru, Rene J. Herrera, David F. Soria Hernanz, Jason Blue-Smith, R. Spencer Wells, David Comas, Jaume Bertranpetit, Chris Tyler-Smith, and The Genographic Consortium. "Y-Chromosomal Diversity in Lebanon Is Structured by Recent Historical Events." *The American Journal of Human Genetics* 82 no. 4 (April 2008): 873–82.

Zamir, Meir. *The Formation of Modern Lebanon.* Ithaca: Cornell University Press, 1985.

———. *Lebanon's Quest: The Road to Statehood, 1926–1939.* London: I. B. Tauris, 1997.

Ziadeh, Hanna. *Sectarianism and Inter-communal Nation-Building in Lebanon.* London: Hurst & Company, 2006.

Zisser, Eyal. *Lebanon: The Challenge of Independence.* London: I. B. Tauris, 2000.

Ziyade, Khalid. "Takawun al-A'ilat fi Tarabulus." In *Lubnan fi al-Qarn al-Thamin'ashr: al-Mu'tamar al-Awal lil-Jami'ya al-Lubnaniya lil-Dirasat al-Uthmaniya.* Edited by Butros Labaki, 305–20. Beirut: Dar al-Muntakhab al-Arabi, 1996.

Internet Sources

Fneish, Muhammad. Interview with Tim Cavanaugh. "The Party of God's MP talks about Islam, Iraq, and the war on terror: A Reason interview," *Reason Magazine.* March 11, 2004. Accessed September 23, 2010. http://reason.com/archives/2004/03/11/meet-hizbollah.

Ghaddar, Hanin. "Fadlallah and the Shia, beyond Hezbollah, or How Fadlallah Changed My Father," *NOW Lebanon.* July 10, 2010. Accessed July 7, 2011. http://www.nowlebanon.com/NewsArchiveDetails.aspx?ID=184682.

Human Rights Watch. *Syria/Lebanon: An Alliance beyond the Law.* May 11, 1997. Accessed August 24, 2010. http://www.hrw.org/en/reports/1997/05/11/syrialebanon-alliance-beyond-law.

Human Rights Watch. *Without Protection: How the Lebanese Justice System Fails Migrant Domestic Workers.* September 16, 2010. Accessed September 23, 2010. http://www.hrw.org/en/reports/2010/09/16/without-protection?.

Laithy, Heba, Khalid Abu-Ismail, and Kamal Hamdan. *International Poverty Centre Country Study 13: Poverty, Growth and Income Distribution in Lebanon.* Brasilia: International Poverty Centre. January 2008. Accessed September 23, 2010. http://www.ipc-undp.org/pub/IPC CountryStudy13.pdf.

Lear, Edward. *Letter to Lady Waldegrave from Damascus, May 27, 1858.* Accessed September 30, 2010. http://www.nonsenselit.org/diaries/letters/letter-to-lady-waldegrave-from-damascus-27-May-1858/.

Lotfy, Manal. "Musa al-Sadr: The Untold Story." *Asharq alawsat English Edition.* May 31, 2008. Accessed January 3, 2012. http://www.asharq-e.com/news.asp?section=3&id=12930.

Lebanese Ministry of Finance—General Debt Overview. Accessed August 21, 2010. http://www.finance.gov.lb/Public+Finances/Public+Debt+Overview/.

Lebanon GDP per capita (purchasing power parity). Accessed August 21, 2010. http://www.indexmundi.com/lebanon/gdp_per_capita_(ppp).html.

Mikdashi, Maya, "A Legal Guide to Being a Lebanese Woman (Part 1)," *Jadaliyya,* December 3, 2010. Accessed December 28, 2011, http://www.jadaliyya.com/pages/index/376/a-legal-guide-to-being-a-lebanese-woman-(part-1).

Shehadi, Nadim. "Riviera vs Citadel: The Battle for Lebanon," *Open Democracy,* July 13, 2007. Accessed July 22, 2011. http://www.opendemocracy.net/conflict-middle_east_politics/Riviera_citadel_3841.jsp.

United Nations. *Report of the Lebanon Independent Border Assessment Team (LIBAT) to the U.N. Security Council. June 22, 2007.* Accessed Sept 25, 2010. http://www.clhrf.com/unresagreements/1701.report22.6.07.pdf.

United Nations Security Council. S/2005/203, *Report of the Fact-finding Mission to Lebanon inquiring into the causes, circumstances and consequences of the assassination of former Prime Minister Rafik Hariri,* March 24, 2005. Accessed September 19, 2011. http://www.undemocracy.com/S-2005-203.

UNIIIC. *Unedited Report of the U.N. International Independent Investigating Commission Established Pursuit to Security Council Resolution 1595 (2005).* Detlev Mehlis (commissioner), Beirut, October 19, 2005. Accessed September 19, 2011 www.washingtonpost.com/wp-srv/world/syria/mehlis.report.doc.

UNIIIC. S/2005/662/20 Oct 2005 *Report of the U.N. International Independent Investigating Commission Established Pursuant to Security Council Resolution 1595 (2005),* Detlev Mehlis (commissioner), Beirut. Accessed January 3, 2012. http://undemocracy.com/S-2005-662.

UNIIIC. S/2005/775/12 Dec 2005 *Second Report of the U.N. International Independent Investigating Commission established pursuant to Security Council resolutions 1595 (2005) and 1636 (2005).* Detlev Mehlis (commissioner), Beirut. Accessed January 3, 2012. http://undemocracy.com/S-2005-775.

UNIIIC. S/2006/355/10 Jun 2006 *Fourth Report of the U.N. International Independent Investigating Commission established pursuant to Security Council resolutions 1595 (2005), 1636(2005) and 1644 (2005).* Serge Brammertz (commissioner), Beirut. Accessed January 3, 2012. http://undemocracy.com/S-2006-355.

Zaatari, Zeina. *Women's Rights in the Middle East and North Africa: Lebanon Country Report.* Accessed May 29, 2010. http://www.freedomhouse.org/template.cfm?page=176.

INDEX

Personalities from the Buhtur, Ma'n, and Shihab clans are listed under those names
Page numbers in **bold** refer to illustrations.